BUILDING INTEGRATED ECONOMIES IN WEST AFRICA

Lessons in Managing Growth, Inclusiveness, and Volatility

Editor
Alexei P. Kireyev

INTERNATIONAL MONETARY FUND

Cover design: Joseph Procopio with IMF Multimedia Services Division.

Cataloging-in-Publication Data
Joint Bank-Fund Library

Names: Kireyev, Alexei. | International Monetary Fund.
Title: Building integrated economies in West Africa : lessons in managing growth, inclusiveness, and volatility / Alexei P. Kireyev, editor.
Description: Washington, DC : International Monetary Fund, 2016.
Identifiers: ISBN 978-1-51351-183-2
Subjects: LCSH: Union économique et monétaire ouest africaine. | Monetary unions -- Africa, West. | Monetary policy -- Africa, West.
Classification: LCC HG3986.5.B84 2016

Please send orders to:
International Monetary Fund, Publication Services
P.O. Box 92780, Washington, DC 20090, U.S.A.
Tel.: (202) 623-7430 Fax: (202) 623-7201
E-mail: publications@imf.org
Internet: www.elibrary.imf.org
www.imfbookstore.org

Contents

Foreword

West African countries have made great strides in building monetary unity in the region. Its institutional core, the West African Economic and Monetary Union (WAEMU), has been central to the region's successful adoption of a common currency, establishment of a common market, and the formation of institutions tasked with coordinating economic policies. And the eight individual WAEMU member countries—Benin, Burkina Faso, Côte d'Ivoire, Guinea-Bissau, Mali, Niger, Senegal, Togo—are to be commended for their dedicated efforts in preserving macroeconomic stability, low inflation, fiscal integrity, debt sustainability, and a fixed exchange rate.

At the same time, WAEMU policymakers face major challenges: achieving high and inclusive growth, reducing poverty, managing commodity price volatility, and addressing domestic and external shocks. They have to balance pressing development needs against the imperative to maintain economic stability and contain government deficits. Regional growth remains uneven, and making decisive progress in reducing poverty does not come easily. Currently, international competitiveness of local products is not sufficient, regional trade is low, and the private sector needs more vibrancy to bolster growth and job creation.

This book takes stock of key developments in the WAEMU in recent years and sketches the agenda for reforms that could foster further growth, inclusiveness, and integration. Drawing on a wide range of work that captures the depth and breadth of the IMF's analysis of the region, it covers such key issues as growth and inclusiveness, fiscal policy and coordination, single monetary policy, financial sector development and regional capital markets, along with trade and competitiveness. Furthermore, given the considerable interest in monetary unions in general, this book's authors aim to outline the costs and benefits for policymakers in other countries contemplating joining an existing currency union or establishing a new one.

The IMF is committed to being a partner to help WAEMU countries manage the challenges, and we have stepped up efforts to support them through continued policy dialogue, increased capacity building, more analytical work, and additional financing.

This book is one facet of that continued commitment. It draws on international experience and contributions from regional policymakers, IMF and World Bank staff, and academics. The findings and policy discussions collected within focus on both the WAEMU as a whole as well as the individual circumstances of its member countries.

We hope this book will serve as a resource for policymakers in the region and for those more generally interested in monetary unions and low-income countries.

Christine Lagarde
Managing Director

Acknowledgments

This book provides a comprehensive analysis of the key macroeconomic and financial sector issues in the West African Economic and Monetary Union (WAEMU). It combines coverage of the various analytical topics with a discussion of the institutional setup of the economic and monetary union, and provides background information on the institutional and economic setting. An understanding of all of these areas is important for the formulation and successful implementation of sound policies.

This book completes the series of books on regional integrations in developing countries published recently by the IMF. Included among them are *The CFA Franc Zone: Common Currency, Uncommon Challenges* (C. Tsangarides and A-M. Gulde, editors, 2008); *Oil Wealth in Central Africa: Policies for Inclusive Growth* (B. Akitoby and S. Coorey, editors, IMF, 2012); *The Eastern Caribbean Economic and Currency Union: Macroeconomic and Financial Systems* (A. Schipke, A. Cebotari, and N. Thacker, editors, IMF, 2013); and *The Quest for Regional Integration in the East African Community* (P. Drummond, S. Kal Wajid, and O. Williams, editors, 2014).

The authors would like to express special thanks to Antoinette Sayeh, Roger Nord, and Ali Mansoor for guidance and encouragement. This book would not have been possible without the support of many economists and research assistants, cutting across a large number of IMF departments and the experts of the BCEAO, the WAEMU Commission, and the WAEMU Securities Agency. The authors would also like to express their appreciation for the useful comments and suggestions received from the authorities in the region during annual regional consultations with WAEMU institutions. The authors are also indebted to Bruno Cabrillac (Bank of France) and colleagues from the World Bank for their comments.

Yanmin Ye and Jessica Witten have provided research assistance and formatted the many figures and tables in record time. The authors would also like to thank Linda Kean and Patricia Loo for useful input. Most important, the authors would like to thank Lorraine Coffey for an outstanding job in copy editing the manuscript and Joseph V. Procopio of the IMF Communications Department, who managed the book's editorial production from beginning to end.

Contributors

Calixte Ahokpossi is an economist in the Strategy, Policy, and Review Department of the International Monetary Fund. He holds a Ph.D. in Economics from Boston University. His research interest includes fiscal and monetary policy, financial sector development, industrial organization, and international macroeconomics.

Karim Barhoumi is an economist in the African Department at the IMF. He holds a Ph.D. in applied econometrics from Marseille University in France. Prior to joining IMF, he worked as an economist at the French central bank and at the IMF Center of Economics and Finance in Kuwait. He has published in several international journals in the area of applied macroeconomics and short forecasting (*Economic Modeling*, *Oxford Bulletin of Economic and Statistics*, *Journal of Policy Modeling*).

Olivier Basdevant is a senior economist at the IMF. He holds a Ph.D. in economics from the Sorbonne University in Paris. Prior to joining the IMF he advised ministries of finance (Russia, Lithuania), as well as central banks (Estonia, New Zealand), on enhancing their economic forecasting tools. His publications have focused on economic modeling and forecasting, fiscal rules, strategies for fiscal adjustment, inflation targeting, and inclusive growth.

François Boutin-Dufresne is a strategist in economics and global markets. Prior to joining Pavilion Global Markets, he worked at the IMF, the Caisse de Dépôt et Placement du Québec, and the Government of Canada. In addition to his professional duties, François was also part-time professor at the University of Ottawa and the Université de Montréal. Over the past years, he has published several articles on global economics and finance for various audiences, including a book with the chief economist of the World Bank, *Trajectories of the World Economy.* In his career, he worked on a broad set of issues ranging from development economics and finance to global financial markets to developing and emerging markets both in the public and private sector.

Qiang Cui is an economist at the IMF. He has worked on economic research and policy in Africa, Asia, Europe, and the Carribean region. Previously, he also worked on economic policy and regional infrastructure issues at the World Bank and on public policy and private sector consulting in China and in the United States. He has published on macroeconomic and fiscal policy issues in *Comparative Economic Studies*, *European Investment Bank Staff Papers*, *World Development*, and several IMF and World Bank publications. He holds degrees of B.Sc. from East China Normal University and of MPA/ID from Harvard University.

Sébastien Dessus is a program leader at the World Bank, in charge of macroeconomic, governance, and poverty programs for Sahelian countries. He previously served as lead economist for Ghana, Sierra Leone, Liberia, and Guinea, as senior economist for Lebanon and West Bank and Gaza, and for the office of the World Bank Chief Economist. Prior to joining the World Bank, he served as a senior economist at the OECD Development Center. Sébastien Dessus holds a Ph.D. in economics from Paris 1 Panthéon-Sorbonne University, and has published extensively in academic journals and books on issues related to growth, trade, environment, poverty, political economy, and general equilibrium modeling.

Jose L. Diaz-Sanchez is an economist at the Office of the World Bank Chief Economist. He has also held assignments at the World Bank's Independent Evaluation Group, the International Monetary Fund, and the Central Bank of Peru. He obtained his Ph.D. in economics from Paris 1

Panthéon-Sorbonne University (Paris School of Economics). Dr. Diaz-Sanchez has researched and published on macroeconomics topics such as housing macrolinkages, public finance, internal and external imbalances, and international finance.

Christine Dieterich is Deputy Division Chief in the IMF's African Department and mission chief for Benin. Prior to joining the IMF, she worked in the German Ministry of Finance on international relations. Her main area of expertise is fiscal policy, in particular, tax policy and international macroeconomics.

Mame Astou Diouf is an economist in the Surveillance Policy Division of the IMF's Strategy, Policy, and Review Department. She has worked extensively on the design of Fund surveillance policies. Prior to joining the IMF, she worked at the World Bank and in the telecommunications sector in Senegal. Dr. Diouf has a Ph.D. in economics from the Université de Montréal (Canada) and a master's degree from Toulouse School of Economics (France) in econometrics, economics and statistics, and finance.

William Gbohoui is completing a Ph.D. in macroeconomics and public economics at the University of Montreal (Canada), where he also taught macroeconomics and econometrics. His research interests lie on quantitative macroeconomic theory, empirical macroeconomics, fiscal policy, and international trade. His ongoing research develops dynamic stochastic general equilibrium models to assess the implications of public policies. He also holds an M.Sc. in statistics and economics from ENSEA (Abidjan) and a B.Sc. in statistics from ENEAM (University d'Abomey-Calavi, Benin). Previously, he was a program officer at the Ministry of Labor in Benin. He also worked for the International Monetary Fund and the African Development Bank.

Samuel Guérineau is an associate professor, Université d'Auvergne (UDA) since 2003, researcher at the Centre d'Etudes et de Recherches sur le Développement International (CERDI), thesis supervisor since 2010, and director of studies of the School of Economics-UDA since 2012. He has been a consultant for the World Bank, UNDP, AFD, French treasury, French Ministry of Foreign Affairs, and BCEAO. His research is focused on macroeconomic policies in developing economies, mainly financial development, monetary, fiscal and exchange rate policies, and economic integration. His work has been published in French and English-speaking peer-reviewed journals. He has been an editor of a book dedicated to economic integration in the WAEMU and CEMAC.

Ermal Hitaj is an economist in the African Department at the IMF. He holds a Ph.D. in Economics from the University of Maryland–College Park. He previously worked as an economist at the Central Bank of Albania. Ermal's work has focused on fiscal rules, remittances, public finance, and the political economy of development.

John Hooley is an economist in the African Department at the IMF. Prior to joining the Fund he was a senior economist at the Bank of England where he had held a number of roles across monetary policy, financial stability, and emerging markets. His publications to date have focused on cross-border capital flows and international shock transmission. John holds degrees in economics from the London School of Economics and Cambridge University.

Patrick Imam is a senior economist at the IMF. Since joining the Fund, he has worked on IMF programs and surveillance cases in the Middle East and Central Asia Department, the African Department, the IMF Institute, and more recently in the Monetary and Capital Markets Department. His publications have focused on issues related to financial stability, macroprudential policies, and financial sector development. Prior to joining the Fund, he worked as an Investment Banker at Credit Suisse First Boston in London. He has a Ph.D. in economics from Cambridge University.

Kareem Ismail is an economist at the Strategy, Policy, and Review Department of the International Monetary Fund. He holds a Ph.D. in economics from Johns Hopkins University. His research interest is mainly on fiscal, external, and financial implications from commodity price fluctuations on natural resource intensive economies.

Christian Josz is the Iraq Deputy Division Chief at the IMF. He has led missions to Chad, Mali, and the WAEMU and was senior economist on Senegal and Madagascar, assignments which gave him in-depth exposure to financial programming in the context of the use of IMF financial resources. Prior to joining the Fund, he was advisor at the Cabinet of the Minister of Economy of Belgium, financial analyst in a multinational company, and senior economist at the Belgian central bank with postings at the Belgian delegation to the OECD and the Office of the Belgian Executive Director at the IMF. He holds a master's degree in business and engineering from the Université Libre de Bruxelles and a Master's in Business Administration from the University of Toronto.

Sudipto Karmakar is an economist in the Financial Intermediation Division of the Economic Research Department at Banco de Portugal since 2013. He holds a B.Sc. in economics from Presidency College, Kolkata, an M.Sc. in economics from the University of Calcutta, and a Ph.D. in economics from Boston University. He conducts theoretical and empirical research on issues related to macroprudential regulation and real-financial sector linkages.

Alexei Kireyev is a senior economist at the IMF and former IMF representative to the WTO. He has led advance IMF missions to member countries, provided advice on macroeconomic policies to countries with IMF-supported programs, and reviewed IMF policy advice, financing, and technical assistance. Before his IMF career, he was an economic advisor to the president, economist at the World Bank, and professor of international economics at universities in Russia and the United States. His degrees include a master's degree in economics from George Washington University and a Ph.D. (Doctor of Sciences) in economics from Moscow State Institute of International Relations. Dr. Kireyev has researched and published extensively on international economics and trade, applied macroeconomics, principles of economics, and the economic problems of low-income countries. His most recent publications include a two-volume book on *International Microeconomics* and *International Macroeconomics*.

Stefan Klos is a research analyst in the African Department of the IMF, concentrating mainly on Article IV research and program work for Mali, Guinea-Bissau, and WAEMU. Prior to his time at the fund, Stefan received a bachelor's degree in mathematics and economics from Northeastern University in Boston. Topics of interest include governance, inequality, and their effects on economic performance.

Christina Kolerus is an economist at the Strategy, Policy, and Review Department at the IMF. Holding a Ph.D. from Mannheim University, she has worked in the Fiscal Affairs Department and African Department, in particular on WAEMU countries. Prior to joining the Fund, she was a consultant and visiting scholar at the OECD and ECB. Her published research includes areas such as fiscal policy, labor markets, and political economy.

Mesmin Koulet-Vickot is a senior economist at the International Monetary Fund (IMF). He graduated in economics from the University of Clermont-Ferrand (CERDI, France). Prior to joining the IMF, he worked at the Central Bank (BEAC) in the Research Department and as assistant to the deputy governor. His research interest includes monetary policy, financial sector development, and international macroeconomics.

Mario Mansour is Deputy Chief, Tax Policy Division, in the Fiscal Affairs Department of the IMF. Prior to joining the Fund in 2004, he worked at a Canadian consultancy as a lead economist on tax reform projects in the Middle East and the Eastern Caribbean regions (2000–03), and at the Canadian Department of Finance as a tax policy analyst (1992–2000). He has advised on tax policy issues in over 25 countries. His research work includes evaluation of investment tax incentives, modeling effective tax rates on capital income, microsimulation of revenue and distributional impacts of tax reform, estimation and analysis of tax expenditures, and more recently tax policy issues in Africa and the Middle East regions.

Monique Newiak is an economist in the African Department of the International Monetary Fund. She participated in several country and regional missions in Western Africa, including during the WAEMU 2015 regional consultation but also Article IV and IMF-program missions, including to Ghana, Senegal, The Gambia, and Guinea-Bissau. Before joining the African Department, she worked in the External Sector Unit of the IMF's Strategy, Policy, and Review Department. Monique Newiak holds a Ph.D. from Ludwig-Maximilans-University in Munich, and master's degrees in business administration and economics. Her research has focused on development economics, international economics, and the economics of gender.

Yasin Onder is an economist in the Research Department at the Central Bank of Turkey. He holds a Ph.D. in economics from the University of Georgetown. Yasin's research has focused on sovereign default, bailouts, and financial stability.

Alexander Raabe is a research analyst at the IMF. He particiapted in a program negotiation mission to Ghana covering the real sector and contributed to publications in the area of fiscal and investment policy as well as financial integration. Prior to joining the IMF, he obtained a master's degree in international economics from Johns Hopkins University's School of Advanced International Studies and a bachelor's degree in economics and corporate management from a leading business school in Germany. Mr. Raabe also worked at UNDP Malaysia, UNCTAD, and in the European and German foreign service in Thailand, Malaysia, and Mexico.

Grégoire Rota-Graziosi is full professor, Université d'Auvergne (UdA), researcher at the Centre d'Etudes et de Recherches sur le Développement International (CERDI), and senior fellow at the Fondation pour les Etudes et Recherches sur le Développement International (FERDI). He is also scientific editor of the *Revue d'Economie du Développement*. From 2010 to 2015 he was a senior economist in tax policy, Fiscal Affairs Department, at the IMF. He has led multiple technical assistance missions in French-speaking countries and particularly in WAEMU member countries. These missions reviewed countries' general tax systems (direct and indirect taxation) and tax regimes of the natural resource sector. He published in several academic journals (*American Economic Review, Journal of Public Economics,* and *Revue d'Economie du Développement*) on tax competition, decentralization, and political economy.

Douglas Shapiro is a former research analyst at the International Monetary Fund. During his three years at the IMF he worked on the Guinea-Bissau, Gambia, Mali, Senegal, Niger, and WAEMU country teams. He dreams of a world where everyone has economic opportunity.

Sergio Sola is an economist in the Middle East and Central Asia Department of the IMF. He holds a Ph.D. in international economics from the Graduate Institute of International Studies in Geneva. His research focus is on fiscal and monetary policy, financial markets, and applied macroeconometrics.

Aristomene Varoudakis is an economic adviser at the Office of the World Bank Chief Economist. He has previously served as a lead economist and country manager at the World Bank's Europe and Central Asia and Middle East and North Africa Departments and as an adviser at the World Bank's Independent Evaluation Group. Prior to joining the World Bank, he served as a senior economist in the OECD Economics Department and the OECD Development Center. He is professor of economics, on leave from the University of Strasbourg, France, where he taught at the Institut d'Etudes Politiques and the Department of Economics. His research interests include macroeconomics and growth, development economics, public finance, international finance, and exchange rates. His work has been published in academic journals and collected volumes. He is the author or coauthor of four books.

Aleksandra Zdzienicka is an economist in the Strategy, Policy, and Review Department of the IMF. She holds a Ph.D. in international economics and finance from the University of Lyon and an M.Sc. in engineering studies from the Silesian University of Technology. Aleksandra previously worked as an economist at Centre d'Etudes Prospectives et d'Information Internationales in Paris and a consultant at the Economic Department of the Organization for Economic Co-operation and Development. She has published in international journals in the area of macroeconomics, international finance, and macroeconomics.

Abbreviations

AML/CFT	anti-money laundering/countering the financing of terrorism
ATM	automated teller machine
BCEAO	Banque Centrale des Etats de l'Afrique de l'Ouest (Central Bank of West African States)
BOAD	Banque Ouest Africaine de Développement (West African Development Bank)
BRVM	Bourse Régionale des Valeurs Mobiliéres (Regional Stock Exchange)
CEMAC	Communauté Économique et Monétaire de l'Afrique Centrale (Central African Economic and Monetary Community)
CET	Common External Tariff
CFA	Communauté Financière Africaine (African Financial Community)
CIT	Corporate income tax
COMESA	Common Market for Eastern and Southern Africa
CPI	Consumer price index
CREPMF	Conseil Régional de l'Epargne Publique et des Marchés Financiers (Regional Council of Public Savings and Financial Markets)
DC/BR	Central Deposit and Settlement Organization
EAC	East African Community
ECB	European Central Bank
ECCU	Eastern Caribbean Currency Union
ECM	Error correction model
EPA	Economic Partnership Agreement
EU	European Union
FDI	Foreign direct investment
GATT	General Agreement on Tariffs and Trade
GCR	Global Competitiveness Report
GDP	Gross domestic product
GSP	Generalized System of Preferences
HDI	Human Development Index
HIPC	Heavily Indebted Poor Countries
HS	Harmonized System
IC	Investment code
ICRG	International Country Risk Guide
IFS	International Financial Statistics
IHPC	Harmonized Consumer Price Index
IMF	International Monetary Fund
INS	Information Notice System
LIC	Low-income countries
MDRI	Multilateral Debt Relief Initiative
MFI	Microfinance institution
MFN	Most favored nation
MLD	Mean log deviation
MPC	Monetary Policy Committee
MTT	Multilateral tax treaty

NEER	Nominal effective exchange rate
NPL	Nonperforming loan
OECD	Organization for Economic Cooperation and Development
PE	Permanent establishment
PPP	Purchasing power parity
PRSP	Poverty reduction strategy paper
REER	Real effective exchange rate
REP	Regional Economic Plan
ROW	rest of the world
SADC	Southern African Development Community
SME	Small and medium-sized enterprise
SSA	Sub-Saharan Africa
TFP	Total factor productivity
ULC	Unit labor cost
UN COMTRADE	United Nations Commodity Trade Statistics database
VAR	Vector autoregression
VAT	Value-added tax
WAEMU	West African Economic and Monetary Union
WAMU	West African Monetary Union
WCY	World Customs Organization
WEF	World Economic Forum
WEO	World Economic Outlook
WGI	World Governance Indicators
WTO	World Trade Organization

Lessons from the WAEMU: Findings and Recommendations

ALEXEI KIREYEV

The West African Economic and Monetary Union (WAEMU) is one of four currency unions in the world. The WAEMU consists of eight low-income countries—Benin, Burkina Faso, Côte d'Ivoire, Guinea-Bissau, Mali, Niger, Senegal, and Togo. It coordinates its member countries' macroeconomic policies, and addresses a number of important common challenges they face. The Central Bank of West African States (BCEAO),[1] the central bank of the WAEMU, issues the common currency, the Communauté Financière Africaine (CFA) franc,[2] pegged to the euro; conducts a single regional monetary policy; pools foreign exchange reserves of members; and supervises the banking system of the WAEMU.

The WAEMU has reached an important milestone in its development and needs to advance to the next level, which would bring most of its countries closer to the status of emerging economies. Against the background of the long and varied history of this unique monetary union, this book examines how the WAEMU can achieve its development and stability objectives, improve the livelihood of its people and inclusiveness of economic growth, while preserving financial stability, enhancing competitiveness, and maintaining the fixed exchange rate.

The WAEMU and its member countries face distinct challenges in meeting these goals:

1. Increasing trend growth, while making it more inclusive and poverty-reducing.
2. Creating sufficient fiscal space for growth-enhancing projects, while preserving macroeconomic stability and avoiding unsustainable debt buildup.
3. Improving the efficiency of regional monetary policy so that it can contribute more actively to achieving the goals of price stability and credibility of the currency peg, and to the overall economic development of the union.
4. Enhancing financial inclusiveness, stability, and depth so that the financial sector can play its role in mobilizing savings and converting them into productive investments.
5. Accelerating regional integration, deriving more benefit from regional trade and financial integration, while using the benefits of the economy of scale to increase international competitiveness.

These five challenges are the organizing principle for this book.

OVERVIEW AND POLICY SETTING

The WAEMU, simultaneously a customs and a currency union, is heading toward a single market with increasingly common standards and is probably one of the most advanced integration groups among developing countries. Improved competitiveness, economic convergence, common market, policy coordination, and law harmonization are the statutory objective of the Union. The

[1] Banque Centrale des Etats de l'Afrique de l'Ouest.

[2] The International Organization for Standardization currency code for the West Africal CFA franc is XOF.

monetary union, while not well equipped to deal with idiosyncratic economic shocks, has been a significant factor of resilience for countries having endured severe social and political crises. Achievements have been substantial but much remains to be done. The Union is working on improving compliance with the convergence criteria, that is, the common integration goals set by WAEMU members, which were revised in 2015 and should be met by 2019. The WAEMU is moving toward harmonizing budget laws and procedures in member countries, including budget and accounting laws, and laws governing public accounting and the chart of accounts, although progress has been slow. Multilateral surveillance focuses on members' compliance with convergence criteria and their compatibility with the Union's monetary policy. The Union has achieved progress in pursuing a common market and has established a common external tariff, which was expanded and revised in 2015 to include all Economic Community of West African States (ECOWAS) countries. However, nontariff restrictions on regional trade still persist and not all impediments to the declared free movement of people and capital in the region have been eliminated. Finally, the WAEMU conducts a single monetary policy, with the goal of preserving price stability, although its effectiveness remains constrained by shallow financial markets.

The macroeconomic performance of the WAEMU has been uneven and has not yet led to decisive breakthroughs in poverty reduction or improvement in overall quality of living. Though historically low, growth in the WAEMU has increased recently, driven by structural reforms and economic recovery in the region's largest countries. With the currency pegged to the euro, inflation in the region had traditionally been low. However, high fiscal deficits have been exerting increasing pressures on the external position. The combined fiscal deficit of the WAEMU has widened recently, largely reflecting rising levels of public investment in infrastructure in several countries. Because of the high import content of this investment, the rising fiscal deficits have exerted pressure on the current account deficit, the gross reserves of the BCEAO, and the net foreign assets of commercial banks. Fiscal consolidation is needed in coming years, consistent with the recently reaffirmed WAEMU convergence criteria. To maintain much-needed infrastructure investment, including public investment, steps to increase tax revenue and control current expenditure will be essential. Should the planned fiscal consolidation in member countries fail to materialize, the BCEAO may need to consider a tighter stance. Prudential standards in the WAEMU are weaker than in comparable countries. About a quarter of banks do not meet these prudential standards. Ongoing efforts to strengthen bank supervision and raise prudential standards go in the right direction but will take time and need to be accelerated. Steps to upgrade the regulatory framework and build buffers in the financial system should be accelerated before downside risks materialize.

The WAEMU has all the necessary institutional instruments to implement sound and coordinated macroeconomic policies. Fiscal-monetary policy coordination is an important precondition for macroeconomic stability in a currency union. There is room for improvement of such coordination in the WAEMU. A coherent framework is needed for the WAEMU Commission and the BCEAO. This could help align and mutually reinforce their so-far largely autonomous efforts at coordinating fiscal and implementing monetary policies. There is ample theoretical evidence that mutual adaptation of fiscal and monetary policy on a continuous timeline can lead to successfully reaching policy objectives. In normal times, ministries of finance should continue to target long-term debt sustainability, while the BCEAO should focus on inflation. This can be achieved through mutual adaptation of fiscal deficit levels and policy rates. During stress times, the fiscal policies of finance ministries should still target debt sustainability, while the BCEAO's monetary policies should still target inflation. However, in the short term, the BCEAO should be willing to tolerate temporarily high inflation as a strategy for increasing the likelihood of meeting the inflation target in the long term. Ministries of finance can focus on stabilizing output and employment while preserving a sustainable debt path.

GROWTH AND INCLUSIVENESS

The WAEMU remains vulnerable to exogenous shocks. It should increase its resilience to these shocks and reduce its macroeconomic volatility. The WAEMU's economic performance has improved only modestly, while idiosyncratic shocks have been frequent. Although further growth diagnostics would be needed to better understand the cause of these shocks, some unambiguous recommendations emerge at this point. Political stability is clearly a must. At the same time, continuous broad-based reforms are needed to foster investment, trade and structural competitiveness, and financial development. Improvements in health, education, and institutional quality also are essential for economic development. In addition, there is a need for more efficient shock-smoothing mechanisms such as larger fiscal buffers, greater financial market development and, eventually, a centralized insurance scheme.

The WAEMU's insufficient product diversification is one reason for the region's low resilience to shocks. Diversification should be strengthened through further structural transformation. The structure of economies in the WAEMU has changed very slowly over the past decades, as has been the case for many other low-income countries. The majority of the region's population is still employed in low-productivity agriculture and the secondary sector is underdeveloped. Further structural transformation and diversification of output and exports could yield significant growth dividends as resources are reallocated from low-productivity sectors, such as agriculture, to higher productivity sectors, such as manufacturing. This process should be assisted by policies that focus on addressing weaknesses that hinder entry into new lines of economic activity. These weaknesses include deficiencies in infrastructure, education and training, financial services, trade networks, functioning factor markets, and supportive regulatory environments. The regional economic plan hopes to target key areas such as improvements to governance, access to energy, and the development of regional infrastructure and human resources. But structural transformation can also occur "within sectors" and create productivity gains through, for example, implementation of quality improvements to existing products and services. To promote strong, inclusive growth, agriculture should be a particular focus of "within sector" productivity improvements in the WAEMU, as well as in other low-income countries where the primary sector employs a relatively high share of the workforce and has a low productivity level. Agriculture is particularly important in the context of rapid population growth, since other sectors are unlikely to be capable of creating sufficient jobs to absorb the large projected increases in the workforce.

For growth in the WAEMU to be durable and sustained, it should be inclusive, with benefits shared widely across income and gender groups, and between rural and urban areas. Growth performance depends on its distributional characteristics. While inclusivity is good for poverty reduction, growth is even more important. Although growth episodes in the world have sometimes been accompanied by increased inequalities, the fundamental question is one of equality: Are the benefits of growth shared equally across different income groups and do all income groups and both genders have an equal opportunity to contribute their fair share to growth? While poverty has fallen in the last two decades in most WAEMU countries, poverty reduction has slowed in recent years. Although available indicators sometimes give conflicting signals on distributional shifts, two case studies—one on Senegal and one on Mali—suggest that people in the middle of the income distribution usually receive the most benefit of growth, and mainly in urban areas. Further progress in poverty reduction and inclusiveness would require sustained high growth and exploration of growth opportunities in the sectors with high earning potential for the poor. Better-targeted social policies and more attention to regional distribution of spending would also help reduce poverty and improve inclusiveness.

To achieve sustainable high growth, substantial additional financial resources should be mobilized from both regional and international sources. The regional financial market has grown substantially in the past decade but still remains relatively shallow and falls short of supplying sufficient long-term financing for growth-enhancing public and private investment projects. Although the institutional structure for financing mobilization is broadly in place, a number of factors increase financing costs and hinder market efficiency. These include the undiversified issuer and narrow investor bases, banks' preference for short-term securities, the limited set of maturities offered by sovereigns, underdeveloped secondary markets for bills and bonds, organizational issues, and limited access to information. The yield curve in the region has been generally upward sloping as interest rates at issuance were higher for securities with longer maturities. Interest rates have been largely driven by country ratings, market liquidity conditions, and bidder appetite at the time of issuance. The principal component analysis suggests that the issuance volumes offered also affected the level of interest rates, with seasonality, issuance procedures, and the frequency and predictability of issues each playing a role. Further reforms could help the region reap the full benefits of a more dynamic securities market to finance growth-enhancing projects.

FISCAL POLICY AND COORDINATION

Fiscal policy will remain the primary policy tool available to individual WAEMU countries and should be strengthened by the application of well-designed fiscal rules. However, high fiscal deficits are exerting increasing pressures on the external position often reflecting the high import content of domestic investment. These rising fiscal deficits continue to exert pressure on the current account deficit, the gross reserves of the BCEAO, the common central bank, and the net foreign assets of commercial banks. Fiscal consolidation during the coming years is needed, consistent with the recently reaffirmed WAEMU convergence criteria. In this context, well-designed fiscal rules could be helpful in achieving the consolidation objective and disciplining individual countries' performance. In practice, the existing convergence criteria and other fiscal rules applied in the WAEMU have proven to be of limited effectiveness.

Economic convergence and the recently revised convergence criteria provide an important tool for safeguarding macroeconomic stability in the monetary union and preserving the single currency and the fixed exchange rate regime. The recent revision of convergence criteria is a step in the right direction, with its reduction in the number of convergence criteria and focus on fiscal sustainability of the revised surveillance framework. However, scope should be provided to exceed the budget deficit convergence criterion for temporary periods in the event of adverse economic shocks, subject to well-defined rules. The 70 percent of debt-to-GDP ratio should be viewed as an upper limit and not an optimal level toward which to converge, and debt management should be driven by regular debt sustainability analyses rather than by the debt criterion. Steps are needed to increase countries' ownership of the new criteria by encouraging them to transpose regional rules into national laws and strengthen monitoring and oversight, including through the establishment of fiscal councils at the national level.

Markets have an important role to play in enforcing macroeconomic discipline and their further development should be a significant part of the agenda of WAEMU governments. Achieving fiscal discipline in a monetary union without a central fiscal authority, while crucial for the union's stability, is challenging institutionally and practically. While sovereign interest rates are broadly responsive to governments' fiscal behavior, further development of the regional financial market is needed for an improvement of the effectiveness of market discipline in the WAEMU. In addition, fiscal aspects of the WAEMU's regional surveillance framework should be reconsidered to improve both design and enforceability. Fiscal risks should be better mitigated. In particular, as countries start to broaden their financing options for large investment projects, policymakers' attention should turn to fiscal risks, including those related to contingent liabilities and off-balance-sheet items, which may not be fully apparent in "headline" fiscal indicators.

Transparent disclosure and management of fiscal risks would help reach this objective. This should be carried out by strengthening incentives to ensure that risks are identified, estimated, and carefully managed; promoting earlier, smoother policy responses; increasing confidence among stakeholders in the quality of fiscal management; reducing uncertainty for investors and taxpayers; and improving access to international capital markets.

The procyclical nature of public investment is a significant impediment to stable and high growth in the WAEMU and needs to be reconsidered. Countries facing difficulties seem compelled to drastically cut back investment in bad times. Countercyclical fiscal policy rules could help preserve investment levels in the WAEMU, where such rules can become important anchors of medium-term fiscal policy over the cycle. This would help preserve fiscal discipline at the aggregate level. Some flexibility in fiscal convergence criteria could help mitigate the strong pro-cyclicality of public investment. A countercyclical fiscal rule would allow for some positive correlation, with smaller deficits (larger surpluses) in booms and larger deficits (smaller surpluses) in contractions. At the same time, because shocks affecting WAEMU countries are highly asymmetric, there is room for establishing fiscal federalism arrangements or for adopting a form of risk sharing (or group insurance) to mitigate the incidence of these shocks. Risk-sharing mechanisms would aim to allocate larger financial resources to the union members exposed to negative shocks.

Creating the fiscal space needed to finance growth-enhancing projects will remain a major challenge for all WAEMU countries. This should be addressed on both the country and the regional level. To create more fiscal space for priority spending, including infrastructure investment, it will be important to look at how much current spending could be constrained, for example, by reducing subsidies and transfers. It will also be essential to minimize the risk that a gradual increase in some countries' central government wage bill as a share of GDP undermines the capacity to undertake progrowth policies in the Union. The reversal of any such trend (currently projected for some countries) will require firm regional resolve. Additional efforts in these areas will be instrumental to closing the gap between the WAEMU and high-growth countries. In the context of supporting growth, tax policies should also aim at enhancing efficiency, in addition to creating fiscal space. To improve the quality of spending, greater emphasis needs to be placed on adequate safeguards for a well-functioning public investment system. Such safeguards could include strategic guidance for public investment and preliminary screening for consistency with the strategic goals of government; formal project appraisal; independent review of appraisals; transparent project selection and well-structured budgeting; timely project implementation; active adjustment for changes in project circumstances; facility operation; and ex-post project evaluations against approved projects. Additional efforts are needed to raise revenue and improve fiscal institutions to enhance the composition and quality of spending. Also, investments need to be fully integrated in medium-term budget frameworks and significant maintenance costs must be taken into account.

Better tax coordination and tax policy harmonization could help improve revenue collection and enhance the fiscal space. The WAEMU's tax coordination process is one of the most advanced in the world but remains in many areas ineffective. The framework has, to some extent, succeeded in converging tax systems, particularly statutory tax rates, and may have contributed to improving revenue mobilization. Important lessons can be drawn from the WAEMU experience, especially whether it's best to take a top-down approach to coordination or a softer approach of sharing best practices and limiting certain types of harmful tax competition. Sound budget institutions are essential to implementing tax and broader fiscal policies effectively and efficiently. Such institutions—defined as the structures and formal and informal rules and procedures that govern budget planning, approval, and implementation—help ensure government accountability and prevent leakage of public funds. They also increase efficiency of scarce public resources and improve the chance of maintaining fiscal stability and meeting social development needs.

REGIONAL MONETARY POLICY

Regional monetary policy has substantial scope for becoming a more active contributor to regional development and financial stability, but remains constrained by shallow financial markets. The institutional and other characteristics jointly needed for an independent monetary policy under a fixed exchange rate regime are present. The BCEAO can control regional interest rates, which diverge substantially from the euro area rates, as capital mobility is limited. Moreover, the BCEAO has substantial weight in the banking system and therefore can exercise sufficient influence on monetary conditions in the area. The BCEAO has the needed instruments (interest rates and reserve requirements) for achieving the goals of its monetary policy. In the absence of the exchange rate channel, all other channels of monetary policy transmission (through the volume of credit, interest rates, asset prices, and expectations) can in principle be more active. However, shallow financial markets and interest rate rigidities impede the transmission of monetary policy signals and the link from the BCEAO's policy actions to market interest rates. Inflation remains low and can affect both only marginally. To improve monetary policy implementation, the BCEAO should also continue developing deep and functioning interbank, secondary debt, stock, and other financial markets. Improving the transmission of BCEAO policy actions to inflation by reducing price and interest rate rigidities, in particular by introducing more flexibility of deposit rates, is also important. The overall monetary stance remains appropriate. However, if the planned fiscal consolidation in member countries fails to materialize, the BCEAO will need to monitor the risks and consider a tighter stance.

Regional monetary policy could have a stronger impact on liquidity conditions and inflation in the region and on individual WAEMU countries if the transmission mechanism were improved. The transmission to individual WAEMU countries of the BCEAO's single monetary policy has remained, on average, limited and asymmetric. This is despite some recent progress in regional financial development. The impact of a single monetary policy can be limited for the region as a whole, but may be significant for individual countries with more developed financial markets and/or different product market structures and institutions. The hypothesis of an asymmetric transmission of single monetary policy actions to individual countries can be tested empirically, in particular, the impact of the policy interest rate changes on each WAEMU country's deposit and lending rates and inflation. BCEAO policy rate changes have little impact on deposit rates. The main channel of transmission of a single monetary policy to individual countries is through the link between BCEAO's single policy rate and the lending rates in individual countries; this link is relatively strong in Benin, Burkina Faso, Guinea-Bissau, Mali, Senegal, and Togo. It is very weak in Cote d'Ivoire and Niger. The link to core inflation can be established only in the same countries. However, the link to overall inflation, which is the ultimate goal of monetary policy, can be reliably traced only in Benin, Senegal, and Togo. In this context, further developing financial markets, increasing financial intermediation, and fostering competition in the banking sector are crucial to improving the effectiveness of a single monetary policy for individual WAEMU countries.

Elevated levels of central bank liquidity provision to commercial banks poses potential risks to stability. Commercial bank borrowing from the central bank represents around 10 percent of total liabilities in WAEMU countries compared with less than 1 percent in most other African countries. The underlying causes of elevated liquidity provision are likely to be at the regional level, widening fiscal and external imbalances. To the extent that these drivers, in turn, result from weaknesses in fiscal, monetary, or supervisory coordination between national and supranational bodies, the WAEMU experience may also provide lessons for other monetary unions. High levels of central bank borrowing by the banking sector can pose risks to fiscal and financial stability, financial development, and monetary policy effectiveness.

Therefore, even in the absence of a change in the inflation outlook, the BCEAO should monitor closely the evolution of such risks and consider whether any preemptive policy action might be appropriate. Possible measures might include reducing fiscal deficits of individual countries in the Union, which would reduce commercial banks' demand for central bank funding to finance them; discouraging carry trade activity by commercial banks; mitigating market distortions through changes in prudential regulation; relaxing regulatory barriers to entry for financial institutions other than domestic banks; and issuing a greater share of public debt externally.

The implementation of the BCEAO's monetary policy with a view to achieving the price stability objective requires a better understanding of the degree of sensitivity of the inflation rate to changes in the economic and financial environment. The results show that monetary and financial variables have an influence on inflation. Their impact on the evolution of prices is evident over the short and long terms. In particular, the impact of the BCEAO marginal lending rate and money market rate on inflation is significant, whatever the time horizon. Domestic credit is just as significant as the BCEAO's key rates and the money supply. The impact of domestic credit on inflation appears to be stronger than that of interest rates. Furthermore, the output gap, which has been negative, has had an overall moderating effect on inflation over the recent period. The impact observed over the long term is related to the fact that the transmission of interest rate fluctuations to inflation depends heavily on the manner and speed with which they are reflected in borrowing rates and in demand among economic agents. In addition, the fiscal deficit (or public spending), as well as imported inflation, have considerable effects on the dynamics of inflation in the WAEMU. The impact of imported inflation is stronger than that of the marginal lending rate.

FINANCIAL DEVELOPMENT AND STABILITY

The level of financial development in the WAEMU remains insufficient to support financial inclusion and broad-based growth. The financial system in the WAEMU is dominated by the banking sector, but is evolving rapidly with the emergence of new transnational banking groups and microfinance institutions. The regional securities and equity market is a marginal source of funding, except for governments. The interbank market remains shallow. The banking system in the region is highly heterogeneous. While most banks are adequately capitalized and profitable, pockets of vulnerability, including public banks, have been identified. Compliance with prudential norms remains low for a number of ratios, suggesting a degree of regulatory forbearance, and some of these norms are not in line with international standards. Stress tests and financial soundness indicators show that concentration of lending and asset quality pose significant risks. The rising sovereign-bank linkage requires close monitoring. Compliance with key prudential ratios remains insufficient and needs to improve. Recent capacity building efforts at the WAEMU Banking Commission are welcome but need to be reinforced by strengthening and effectively implementing risk-based supervisory tools and processes, including those related to supervision of anti-money laundering/countering the financing of terrorism (AML/CFT) measures. A stronger corrective action framework should be put in place to reduce regulatory forbearance and better enforce compliance with prudential norms. This should include taking timely and effective corrective measures against weak and/or noncompliant banks. The move to Basel II/III standards will be an opportunity to bring prudential rules closer to international norms. As this process is taking time, authorities should meanwhile tighten certain rules, such as that governing risk concentration and the provisioning of nonperforming loans. Authorities should also increase banks' capital adequacy levels, including by raising operating banks' minimum share capital to 10 billion CFA franc. The authorities should also closely monitor banks' exposure to foreign exchange risks and strengthen prudential limits to address them. Moving to consolidated supervision and application of International Financial Reporting Standards should also be a high priority.

Financial inclusion is an important component of inclusive growth and needs to be improved in the WAEMU. WAEMU countries lag behind peer countries in several dimensions of financial inclusion: access to finance is low, especially for the most vulnerable parts of the population, and the financial sector appears to only modestly contribute to the population's ability to deal with shocks. Private sector credit-to-GDP ratios, however, appear broadly in line with WAEMU countries' fundamentals. Public policies, such as investments in infrastructure and the social sectors, could help close these gaps. From the firms' perspectives, policies to reduce participation costs in the financial sector and to lower collateral requirements could increase firms' access to financing, and thus significantly boost GDP. Further development of well-regulated and supervised microfinance institutions could also help improve financial inclusion. Trust is an essential ingredient for financial sector development. To build this trust, it is essential that first-time depositors in microfinance institutions have a positive experience with depositing their hard-earned savings in these institutions. This seems to require a consolidation of the many small and unprofitable microfinance institutions that have proliferated and operated out of the authorities' control.

Preserving financial stability will be critical for the proper functioning of the financial system and growth as the regions open up to more foreign investment and capital flows. The WAEMU authorities should enforce existing prudential regulations and raise standards to international best practice. Ongoing efforts to strengthen bank supervision and raise prudential standards are going in the right direction but will take time and need to be accelerated. In the interim, it is important to proceed expeditiously with plans to raise banks' capital requirements. Steps to upgrade the regulatory framework and build buffers in the financial system should be accelerated before downside risks materialize. It is also urgent to subject bank holding companies incorporated in the WAEMU to appropriate banking regulation and consolidated supervision. Deposit insurance and financial stability funds should be made operational as a matter of priority. A single and independent administrative resolution authority should be established to ensure prompt and effective resolution of banks with negative capital. The emergence of regional banking groups requires the development of supervision on a consolidated basis and strengthening of cooperation with banking supervisors in countries where these groups operate. The increasing exposure of banks to sovereigns is also a risk that needs to be recognized, including through a nonzero weight on government paper in capital adequacy calculations. Microprudential regulation should be revised to bring certain prudential standards closer to international best practice, for example on risk concentration, classification of claims, and provisioning, while taking into account the regional context. The move to Basel II will help address many of these issues.

The WAEMU's financial crisis prevention mechanism is a critical instrument in the maintenance of macroeconomic stability, and its framework needs strengthening. Crisis prevention requires greater transparency, including through the regular and timely compilation and publication of financial soundness indicators for all member countries. Regular stress tests would be a welcome step toward the introduction of an early warning system. There is also substantial scope for improving the bank resolution framework, which would reduce the budgetary cost of government intervention. Swift action is necessary, including giving broader powers to the supervisor and close collaboration with other supervisors in the case of cross-border groups. To improve transparency and market discipline, authorities should improve the quality of financial data as well as compile and publish financial soundness indicators on a regular and timely basis. They should also continue developing macroprudential policy and analyses, with regular stress tests and early-warning indicators. The deposit insurance and financial stability funds are key components of a financial stability and resolution toolkit and should be made operational without any further delay. Bank resolution is a protracted process in the WAEMU, due to the division of power among a number of institutions at the regional and national levels. The authorities should reconsider this architecture and put in place a single and independent administrative resolution authority to allow for a less complicated and faster resolution, in line with international standards and best practices.

Mobile banking offers opportunities to jump-start financial inclusion in the WAEMU. Mobile phone penetration in the WAEMU is the same as it is in Kenya and Tanzania. However, while mobile banking has taken off in these countries, it has not done so in the WAEMU. Transaction costs, issues of network interoperability, and legal and regulatory barriers may represent substantial constraints to the mobile market development in the WAEMU. To increase mobile banking in the WAEMU, several safeguards will have to be put into place including minimum market entry requirements, financial integrity controls, funds safeguards, and payment stability.

Fast-developing regional banking groups create new opportunities but also new risks for financial sector stability and development in the WAEMU. Pan-African banking groups hold about 50 percent of the assets of the WAEMU banking system. Some originated in neighboring countries and brought along expertise in providing financial services to underserved customers such as women, people with primary or less education, and people living in rural areas. A few of these pan-African banking groups originated in the WAEMU and hold more assets abroad than they hold in the WAEMU. To reap the full benefits of these pan-African groups, the authorities need to subject resident holding companies of banking groups to bank regulation and supervision, consolidated supervision, and stress tests. They also need to build on their experience in supervisory colleges of pan-African banking groups with a non-resident parent to set up supervisory colleges for pan-African groups with a WAEMU parent.

COMPETITIVENESS AND INTEGRATION

With very few exportable products, external competitiveness largely depends on upgrading capacity in a few key sectors. The WAEMU's external competiveness remains low. The current account deficit is relatively high and driven by continued investment efforts. In the medium term, it would gradually decline and be matched by sufficient financial inflows subject to the implementation of government's consolidation plans, and helped by a favorable oil price outlook. The real effective exchange rate of the CFA franc appears to be broadly in line with fundamentals based on different methodologies that give a qualitatively similar assessment. However, international reserve coverage should increase to provide stronger buffers against immediate short-term risks. Structural nonprice competitiveness and investment efficiency are also insufficient, and improvements will be essential to ensure that planned large investment programs translate into growth and export gains as well as increased private inflows into the region.

WAEMU countries should start exploiting the full potential of regional trade as an engine for growth. Regional trade is dominated by a few countries and flows. The basic structure of trade interconnectedness in the WAEMU remains broadly unchanged, although regional trade became, on average, tighter with increased bilateral flows and more focus by individual countries on regional trade. The power structure in the region has shifted as Côte d'Ivoire emerged as the only key trading partner and Senegal remained mainly an intermediary. There is a large core and a small periphery in regional trade. All WAEMU countries participating in regional trade experience a network effect. This explicitly takes into account the fact that a country is connected to other countries in the region and assesses the value of these connections. The difference between the nominal GDP and the network value of a country can be positive, neutral, or negative, depending on the value of its connections to other countries in the region. Côte d'Ivoire, Senegal, and Mali can be the main origin of shocks for the rest of the WAEMU economies, including the core and the periphery. They can also be the main origin of shocks to each other, as they belong to the same cluster. Côte d'Ivoire and Senegal are simultaneously playing the gatekeeping role and can be factors for either propagation or absorption of shocks originating elsewhere in the network.

To preserve the gains of regional integration, WAEMU countries should refrain from deviating from the common external tariff of the ECOWAS. The macroeconomic effects of a replacement of the WAEMU common external tariff with the ECOWAS common external tariff on WAEMU member states could be substantial. The new tariff would have an impact on trade levels, government revenue, and growth. The change in the tariff would increase WAEMU imports from other ECOWAS countries but reduce imports from the rest of the world. The impact on government revenue would vary widely by country, ranging from a loss in most countries of up to 2½ percent of current revenue to an increase in a few countries of up to 3 percent. Finally, an increase in relative import prices induced by an increase in the average tariff rate could yield a negative effect on GDP. The WAEMU Commission's intention to safeguard the common market through a uniform application of the ECOWAS common external tariff across WAEMU member countries and nonapplication of additional protection to 3 percent of tariff lines is welcome.

The WAEMU region can do more to attract foreign investment. Even government debt, the least risky investment instrument, attracts very little attention from nonresident investors, unlike in neighboring Ghana and Nigeria. Possible reasons for this situation include unattractive nominal interest rates in the region, the relatively small size of the market, the lack of a secondary market, cumbersome exchange controls and regulations, fragmentation of the regional market, insufficient communication on the issuances and the language issue, insufficient political stability, and poor investment climate. To make the regional market more attractive to foreign investors, sound macroeconomic policies and a solid financial sector are prerequisites. Beyond this, communication with nonresidents should be improved with WAEMU Securities Agency playing a key role in this area; the development of WAEMU financial markets, including the secondary market for government securities, should be accelerated; the size of the market should be increased by eliminating segmentation of the sovereign bond market; and finally, taxation needs to be harmonized and double taxation avoided.

The WAEMU's experience shows that economic integration may have a significant impact on poverty reduction. Until now, the capacity of trade and financial and deep integration to foster growth has been rather disappointing. This result has been partly due to weak implementation of regional rules. However, the WAEMU has benefitted from a good growth-to-poverty reduction conversion. The WAEMU's experience suggests two lessons to improve the poverty reduction impact of economic integration. First, community policies should be targeted in sectors where regional policies' comparative advantage is the strongest. It is therefore a political priority to strengthen regional public goods supply, particularly for regional transportation and energy networks, but also for regional financial information networks. Second, particular attention must be given to the distributive effects of economic integration. The effect of integration policies on living and poverty standards within the WAEMU is different across sectors. A number of regional policies spontaneously contribute to gap reduction between member countries. These include agricultural market integration, epidemic reduction programs, and financial service access development. Inversely, trade integration, transportation network development, and skilled labor mobility can lead to a concentration of benefits in the countries initially the richest. Increased momentum for intracommunity transfers must accompany a strengthened integration in order to compensate its distributive effects.

PART 1

Overview and Policy Setting

PREFACE

The West African Economic and Monetary Union (WAEMU) is part of the Communauté Financière Africaine (CFA) franc zone, an arrangement between France and a number of countries in Africa, which dates back to the early hours of World War II. While the geography of the CFA zone has evolved from the mid-1940s, the zone includes two African monetary unions: the WAEMU, comprised of Benin, Burkina Faso, Côte d'Ivoire, Guinea-Bissau, Mali, Niger, Senegal, and Togo; and the Central African Economic and Monetary Community (CEMAC), comprised of Cameroon, Central African Republic, Chad, Republic of Congo, Equatorial Guinea, and Gabon. The CFA zone also includes Comoros.

The West African Monetary Union (WAMU) was created in 1962. It first became a formal monetary union of independent states (the WAMU) in 1962. It was then broadened to a monetary *and* economic union when the WAEMU Treaty was signed in 1994 in Dakar, Senegal, by the heads of state and governments of Benin, Burkina Faso, Côte d'Ivoire, Mali, Niger, Senegal, and Togo. In 1997, Guinea-Bissau became the Union's eighth (and only non-Francophone) member country. The WAEMU Treaty has four main strands: harmonization of the legal and regulatory framework, establishment of a common market, multilateral surveillance of macroeconomic policies, and coordination of national sectoral policies in major economic areas. The CFA franc has been devalued only once, in 1994, when a 50 percent adjustment in the nominal rate reversed domestic and external disequilibria that had built up since the mid-1980s.

The WAEMU, as part of the CFA franc zone, functions under the following operating principles: (1) a fixed parity of the CFA against the euro adjustable if required by economic reasons and after consultations with the French government and by a unanimous decision of all members; (2) convertibility of the CFA franc into the euro without fluctuation margins at the rate 655.957 CFAF = € 1; (3) guarantee of convertibility by the French Treasury through the establishment by the Central Bank of West African States (BCEAO) of an operating account with the French Treasury on the name of BCEAO with market-related yield or charges; (4) free capital mobility inside the WAEMU, between the WAEMU and CEMAC, and with France; (5) pooling of exchange reserves in the WAEMU. In practice, there is no longer free capital mobility between WAEMU and CEMAC or between these two unions and France.

To preserve these principles and promote financial discipline, additional operating rules are included in the arrangements between France and the WAEMU: (1) the BCEAO should maintain at least 50 percent of its foreign assets in its operating account with the French treasury; (2) the BCEAO should maintain the cover in foreign currency of at least 20 percent of its reserve money (the 20 percent coverage of base money is a warning signal, not formally an obligation); (3) direct credit by the BCEAO to governments is not allowed; (4) the guarantee of convertibility of the CFA by the French Treasury does not oblige the European Central Bank to support the fixed parity of the CFA to the euro. Neither the ECB nor the Bank of France (hence the Eurosystem) are involved in this arrangement. There is an explicit waiver in the Maastricht Treaty.

While the BCEAO has unlimited recourse to advances from the French Treasury, these should be used in exceptional circumstances. When the liquid funds available on the operational account are projected to be insufficient to meet future settlements, the BCEAO must replenish the operational account by drawing from the liquid funds in foreign currencies, requesting that foreign currencies held by public or private institutions of member countries be transferred to the BCEAO in exchange for CFA francs, and calling upon member countries to make use of their drawing rights at the IMF. As a counterpart to the guarantee, France is represented on the board of the BCEAO and the Monetary Policy Committee. France has also two representatives in the Banking Commission. Cooperation between France and franc zone countries takes the form of biannual meetings of finance ministers of franc zone countries.

The WAEMU is a customs union and currency union. Chapter 1, Institutional Arrangements and Regional Integration, reviews the institutional arrangements. Improved competitiveness, economic convergence, common market, policy coordination, and law harmonization for better functioning of the common market are the statutory objectives of the Union, led by the Conference of Heads of State and Government, which is the Union's highest governing body. Achievements have been substantial but much remains to be done. Several countries remain noncompliant with the convergence criteria, which were revised in 2015 and should be met by 2019. The WAEMU is moving toward harmonizing budget laws and procedures in member countries—including budget and accounting laws and laws governing public accounting, budget transparency, and the chart of accounts—although progress has been slow. Multilateral surveillance focuses on members' compliance with convergence criteria and their compatibility with the Union's monetary policy. The Union has achieved progress in pursuing a common market and has established a common external tariff, which was expanded and revised in 2015 to include all Economic Community of West African States (ECOWAS) members. However, nontariff restrictions on regional trade still persist and not all impediments to the declared free movement of people and capital in the region have been eliminated. Finally, the WAEMU conducts a single monetary policy, the main goal of which is to preserve price stability. However, its effectiveness remains constrained by shallow financial markets.

Economic performance of the WAEMU has been uneven. Chapter 2, Macroeconomic Setting and Current Challenges, argues that economic growth in the WAEMU has been historically low but has increased recently, driven by structural reforms and economic recovery in the region's largest countries. With the currency pegged to the euro, inflation in the regions had been traditionally low. However, high fiscal deficits have been exerting increasing pressures on the external position. The evolution of the combined fiscal deficit of the WAEMU largely reflects the rising levels of public investment in infrastructure in several countries. Because of the high import content of this investment, rising fiscal deficits have exerted pressure on the current account deficit, the gross reserves of the BCEAO, and the net foreign assets of commercial banks. Fiscal consolidation during the coming years is needed, consistent with the recently revised WAEMU convergence criteria. To maintain much-needed infrastructure investment, including public investment, steps to increase tax revenue and control current expenditure will be essential. Should the planned fiscal consolidation in member countries fail to materialize, the BCEAO may need to consider a tighter stance. The prudential standards in the WAEMU are weaker than they are in comparable countries. About a quarter of banks do not meet these prudential standards. Ongoing efforts to strengthen bank supervision and raise prudential standards go in the right direction but will take time and need to be accelerated. Steps to upgrade the regulatory framework and build buffers in the financial system should be accelerated before downside risks materialize.

WAEMU countries implement independent fiscal policies but have a single monetary policy, which makes a strong theoretical and practical argument for fiscal-monetary policy coordination. Chapter 3, Macroeconomic Policy Coordination, discusses the coordination challenges facing the WAEMU and suggests a framework for such coordination. National ministries of finance are in charge of the formulation and implementation of fiscal policies. The WAEMU Commission coordinates fiscal policies among member states, whereas the BCEAO, the regional central bank, conducts the single monetary policy. As in any monetary union, this institutional setup raises an important practical question of coordination between heterogeneous fiscal policies and a homogeneous monetary policy. Fiscal-monetary policy coordination is a stated goal of the WAEMU but in practice it has been limited, leading to undesirable side effects. A coherent framework is needed for the WAEMU Commission and the BCEAO, which could help align and mutually reinforce their so-far largely autonomous efforts in the implementation of their fiscal and monetary policies. There is ample theoretical evidence that mutual adaptation of fiscal and monetary policy on a continuous timeline would lead to superior outcomes in terms of reaching policy objectives. In normal times, ministries of finance should continue to target long-term debt sustainability while the monetary policy of the BCEAO should focus on inflation. This can be achieved through mutual adaptation of levels of fiscal deficit and policy rates. During stress times, the fiscal policies of finance ministries should still target debt sustainability, while the BCEAO's monetary policies should target inflation. However, in the short term, the BCEAO should be willing to tolerate temporarily high inflation as a strategy for increasing the likelihood of meeting the inflation target in the long term. Ministries of finances can focus on stabilizing output and employment while preserving a sustainable debt path.

CHAPTER 1

Institutional Arrangements and Regional Integration

ALEXEI KIREYEV

The West African Economic and Monetary Union (WAEMU) is a currency and a customs union. Improved competitiveness, economic convergence, common market, policy coordination, and law harmonization are the statutory objectives of the Union, which is led by the Conference of Heads of State and Government, its highest governing body. Achievements have been substantial, but much remains to be done. Several countries remain noncompliant with the convergence criteria, which were revised in 2015 and should be met by 2019. The WAEMU is moving toward harmonizing budget laws and procedures in member countries—including budget and accounting laws, laws governing public accounting, and the chart of accounts—although progress has been slow. Multilateral surveillance focuses on members' compliance with convergence criteria and their compatibility with the Union's monetary policy. The Union has achieved progress in pursuing a common market and has established a common external tariff, which was expanded and revised in 2015 to include all Economic Community of West African States (ECOWAS) countries. However, nontariff restrictions on regional trade still persist and not all impediments to the declared free movement of people and capital in the region have been eliminated. Finally, the WAEMU has common institutions responsible for the monetary policy and banking supervision for the region as a whole.

INSTITUTIONAL SETUP

The WAEMU was created by a treaty signed at Dakar, Senegal, in 1994, by the heads of state and governments of Benin, Burkina Faso, Côte d'Ivoire, Mali, Niger, Senegal, and Togo. In 1997, Guinea-Bissau became the organization's eighth (and only non-Francophone) member country. The WAEMU is a customs union and a currency union. Its objectives include greater economic competitiveness through open markets, in addition to the rationalization and harmonization of the legal environment; convergence of macroeconomic policies and indicators; creation of a common market; coordination of sectoral policies; and harmonization of fiscal policies. Key institutional arrangements are spelled out in the WAEMU Treaty.

The Union pursues the following objectives:

- Increasing the competitiveness of the member countries' economic and financial activities in the context of an open, competitive market and a rational, harmonized legal environment
- Ensuring the convergence of member countries' economic performance and policies through the institution of a multilateral surveillance procedure
- Creating a common market among member states, based on the free movement of persons, goods, services, and capital; the right of establishment of independent or employed professionals; a common external tariff; and a common trade policy
- Coordinating national sector policies through the implementation of joint actions and, eventually, common policies, particularly in the areas of human resources, regional planning

and development, transportation and telecommunications, the environment, agriculture, energy, industry, and mines

- Harmonizing member countries' laws—with an emphasis on tax laws—to the extent necessary for the orderly functioning of the common market

Historically, the WAEMU has started as a monetary institution. The West African Monetary Union (WAMU) was established in 1962 and reformed twice, in 1973 and 2010, to streamline its institutional architecture. The WAMU is organized around the following principles: a common currency, the Communauté Financière Africaine (CFA) franc; the free circulation of banknotes and coins and freedom of transfers among members of the Union; pooling of foreign currency reserve; the harmonization of monetary, banking, and foreign currency legislation (Figure 1.1).

WAMU bodies include the Conference of Heads of State and Government, which is the supreme authority of the Union; the Council of Ministers, which is its executive body; the Banking Commission, responsible for the organization and supervision of credit institutions; and the Regional Council for Public Saving and Financial Markets, responsible for the organization and supervision of public offerings and for the licensing and supervision of participants in regional financial market. The Institutions of the WAMU are: the Central Bank of West African States (BCEAO), the common central bank, and the West African Development Bank (BOAD), whose mission is to promote the balanced development of the WAMU member states and contribute to their economic integration.

The 1994 WAEMU Treaty supplemented the monetary integration based in the WAMU Treaty with deeper economic integration. The WAEMU retained the same policy-making bodies and is managed by the same authorities as the WAMU. However, WAEMU has its own specific institutions, which are: the WAEMU Commission, which represents the overall interests of the

Figure 1.1. Members of WAEMU

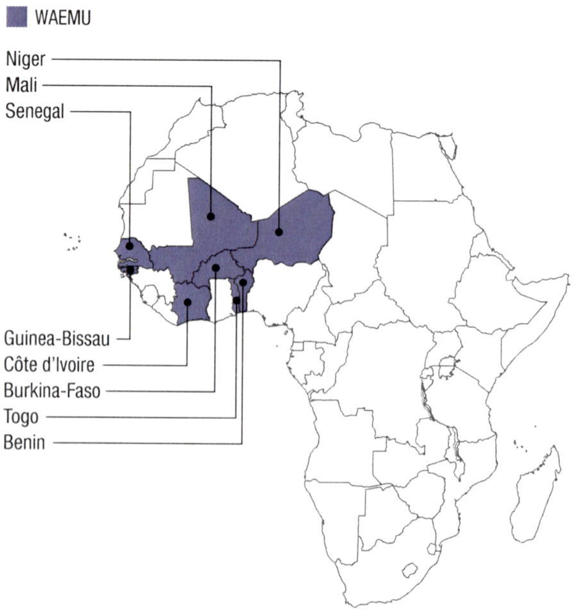

Note: WAEMU = West African Economic and Monetary Union.

community and its role consists in making policy proposals; Council of Ministers; the WAEMU Parliament; and the Court of Justice and the Court of Auditors, the WAEMU judicial review authority.

The primary objective of the WAEMU Treaty is economic integration, beyond the already existent monetary integration. In that context, the WAEMU Treaty seeks to broaden the scope of the community, notably through: creating a common, harmonized legal and fiscal environment; harmonization of fiscal policies; strengthening of the economic competitiveness of member states in the context of a market-based economy; and coordination of economic and sectoral policies.

This parallel functioning of the WAMU and WAEMU has a twofold objective. First, from a legal and political standpoint, the aim is to strengthen the principle of the supranational nature of community institutions, decisions, and instruments. The instruments enacted by the bodies of the Union to meet the objectives of this treaty, and in accordance with the rules and procedures contained therein, are implemented in all member states regardless of any previous or subsequent national legislation to the contrary. Second, the intent is to develop a common market over time. To that end, the WAEMU has provided for multilateral surveillance mechanisms and penalties with a view to harmonize economic policies. On the whole, both treaties are mutually reinforcing and are expected to be merged over time, in keeping with Article 112 of the WAEMU Treaty, which states that the Conference of Heads of State and Government shall adopt a treaty merging the WAMU Treaty with this WAEMU Treaty at the appropriate time (Box 1.1).

The budget for the Union is voted before the beginning of the fiscal year by a two-thirds majority of the Council. The budget includes all revenue of the Union and all expenditures of the institutions with the exception of the specialized autonomous institutions, the BCEAO, the BOAD, and the institutions involved in implementing common policies, and should be balanced. The resources of the Union are derived, among other things, from a fraction of the proceeds of the common external tariff and indirect taxes received throughout the Union. Additional taxes may also be introduced by the Union as needed. The Union may receive loans, subsidies, and external assistance compatible with its objectives. The resources of the Union are subject to the principle of financial solidarity and individual countries cannot claim equivalence between its financial contributions and the advantages it receives from the Union. The budget is executed by the WAEMU Commission.

CONVERGENCE CRITERIA

WAEMU members conduct economic policies to ensure sustainable convergence of their economic performance and establish the bases for sustainable growth. The Council adopts the rules required for the convergence of national economic policies and their harmonization with the regional monetary policy; establishes the rules, the terms of their application, and the timetable for their implementation; and determines the reference values for the quantitative criteria on which compliance with convergence rules is based. The Council reviews policies that relate to the economic objectives of member countries—particularly to the objectives for sustained growth and revenue collection, revenue allocation, sustainable current balance of payments, and improved international competitiveness. Common policies also take account of the need for consistency between fiscal policies and monetary policy objectives, particularly the objective of price stability.

On January 19, 2015, the Conference of Heads of State and Government of the WAEMU adopted a new set of convergence criteria to be met by 2019. First-order criteria now include a ceiling on overall fiscal balance, a ceiling on average consumer price inflation, and a ceiling on

BOX 1.1. WAEMU Governing Bodies

The WAEMU's governing structure makes it possible to centralize monetary transactions while taking into account the economic and political interests of each member country.

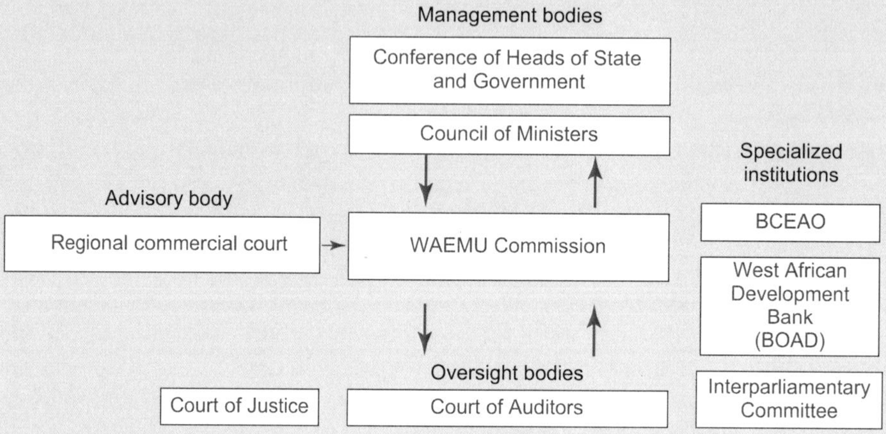

Source: Banque de France (2015).

- **The Conference of Heads of State and Government** is the highest governing body of the WAEMU. This body defines the general framework for the policies of the Union and meets at least once year.
- **The Council of Ministers** implements the general framework defined by the Conference of Heads of State and Government and meets at least twice a year. The Council of Ministers is primarily convened in the form of the Council of the ministers in charge of economy, finance, and planning, but for the purpose of adopting decisions in other areas the Council convenes ministers responsible for these areas. The Council may delegate to the WAEMU Commission the enactment of regulations implementing the instruments it adopts.
- **The WAEMU Commission** promotes the orderly functioning and developments of the Union, executes the Union budget, collects information useful to the accomplishment of its mandate, prepares an annual general report and an action plan, and publishes the Official Bulletin of the Union. Commissioners are appointed by the Conference of Heads of State and Government based on expertise and personal integrity. They serve a renewable four-year term. Commission members perform their duties with full independence and in the general interests of the Union. They refrain from soliciting or accepting instructions from any government or organization. The decisions of the Commission are adopted by simple majority of its members.
- **The Parliament** provides democratic oversight of the bodies at the Union. The Parliament takes part in the Union's decision-making processes and integration efforts in the areas covered by the WAEMU Treaty. The Parliament meets in two ordinary sessions per year. At the initiative of the Parliament or at its request, the Council president, the president and members of the Commission, the BCEAO governor, and the president of the BOAD may be heard by the Parliament. The president of the Commission submits a general report on the functioning and evolution of the Union to the Parliament each year for review. The Parliament may be dissolved by the Conference of Heads of State and Government of the WAEMU.
- **The Court of Justice and the Court of Auditors** are the judicial oversight bodies of the Union.
- **The BCEAO** and **the BOAD** serve as the specialized autonomous institutions of the Union. Without prejudice to the objectives attributed to them by the WAEMU Treaty, the BCEAO and the BOAD function independently toward the fulfillment of the objectives of the treaty. The governor of the BCEAO is entitled to participate in Commission meetings on an advisory basis, and may designate a representative for that purpose. The BCEAO governor may request that items be included on the Commission's agenda or suggest to the Council of Ministers to invite the Commission to undertake an initiating within its mandate.

TABLE 1.1

WAEMU: Compliance with New Convergence Criteria
(Number of Countries Noncompliant with Criteria)

	2011	2012	2013	2014	2015	2016	2017	2018	2019	2020
	Actual				Est.	Projected				
First-order criteria										
Overall balance/GDP (≥ −3 percent)	4	2	3	4	5	5	5	3	2	2
Average consumer price inflation (≤ 3 percent)	5	3	0	0	0	0	0	0	0	0
Total debt/GDP (≤ 70 percent)	0	0	0	0	0	0	0	0	0	0
Second-order criteria										
Wages and salaries/tax revenue (≤ 35 percent)	5	6	5	5	6	5	5	5	5	5
Tax revenue/GDP (≥ 20 percent)	8	8	8	8	8	8	8	8	8	7

Sources: WAEMU; BCEAO; and staff estimates and projections.

total debt-to-GDP ratio. Second-order criteria include wages and salaries-to-tax revenue ratio and tax revenue-to-GDP ratio. The nonaccumulation of arrears, the limit on the current account deficit, and the floor on investment-expenditure-to-revenue ratio were eliminated from the list of criteria.

While progress has been achieved, compliance with convergence criteria remains uneven, particularly with the second-order criteria (Table 1.1).

Under the convergence rules, any excessive deficit should be eliminated, and budget policies must respect a common discipline of supporting multiyear efforts toward fiscal consolidation and improving the structure of public revenue and expenditures.

As part of convergence, WAEMU countries are working towards harmonization of their fiscal policies. The aim is to reduce existing excessive disparities in the structure and amount of their respective tax structures. The Union is moving toward harmonizing budget laws and procedures, including budget and accounting laws and laws governing public accounting and the chart of accounts.

MULTILATERAL SURVEILLANCE

Convergence in the WAEMU is monitored by members through the multilateral surveillance mechanism. For the purposes of multilateral surveillance, the WAEMU Commission issues decisions specifying the types of information required for surveillance, and members on a regular basis transmit it to the Commission, including statistical data and information relating to economic policy measures. The Commission prepares and publishes a semiannual execution report about its multilateral surveillance procedures. The report discusses the convergence of economic policies and their compatibility with the Union's monetary policy.

The WAEMU Treaty specifies measures, which can be taken in principle, to promote compliance with regional convergence criteria. If a member country fails to satisfy the convergence requirements, the Commission can propose corrective measures, which should be adopted by the Council by two-thirds majority of its members. The member country, which fails to meet the convergence requirements, is required to prepare and implement a program of corrective measures.

The Council may enhance these procedures by implementing a range of explicit positive or negative measures. Positive measures include the publication of a communiqué from the Commission, the Union's support in the search for financing required to execute the program of corrective measures, and priority access to the resources of the Union.

Negative measures (sanctions) may be applied if a member country has not prepared a corrective program, if such a program is not compliant with the Union economic policy, or if the program was not executed. In this case, the Commission may transmit a report to the Council, accompanied by recommendations on possible negative measures. The decisions of the Council on possible negative measures are made by a majority of two-thirds of its members.

Negative measures that may be applied in principle include the following: the Council's publication of a communiqué with the information on the situation of the country; the publicly announced withdrawal of positive measures previously granted; the recommendation that the BOAD review its intervention policy with respect to the member country concerned; and the suspension of Union assistance. The Conference of Heads of State and Government may supplement the range of measures with additional measures deemed necessary to increase the effectiveness of the Union's multilateral surveillance. In practice, negative measures have not been used.

COMMON MARKET

In line with the WAEMU Treaty, the Union pursues the objective of instituting a common market. The steps in this direction include:

- Elimination in trade between member countries of customs duties, quantitative restrictions on imports and exports, taxes having an equivalent effect
- Establishment of a common external tariff
- Institution of common rules of competition applicable to public and private enterprises and public aid
- Implementation of the principles of free movement of persons, establishments, and the provision of services and the lack of restrictions on capital flows required for the development of a regional financial market
- Harmonization and mutual recognition of technical standards, as well as procedures for standardization and certification of compliance.

To accomplish the free movement of merchandise, member countries refrain from introducing new import or export duties between themselves or any taxes having an equivalent effect, or increasing the taxes or duties applied in commercial relations between themselves. They also refrain from introducing new quantitative restrictions on imports and exports between themselves or measures having an equivalent effect, or from making quotas, standards, or any other provisions of equivalent effect more restrictive. In accordance with World Trade Organization rules, the Union ensures that the overall impact of customs duties and other trade regulations applied to third countries is no more restrictive than was the impact of provisions in effect prior to the creation of the Union.

Member countries retain the authority to maintain and issue prohibitions or restrictions on import, export, and transit justified on grounds of public morality; public policy; public security; protection of the health or life of persons or animals; preservation of the environment; protection of national artistic, historical, or archaeological heritage; and the protection of industrial or commercial property. However, member countries must notify the Commission of all trade restrictions. The Commission reviews such restrictions each year with a view of their harmonization and gradual elimination.

Regarding commercial policy, the Council has adopted measures concerning the harmonization of member countries' laws, regulations, and administrative provisions required for the functioning of the customs union; regulations concerning the common external tariff; regulations establishing the trade policy regime with third countries; and provisions applicable to products of local origin and artisanal products.

Member countries may take protective measures in case of serious difficulties in some sectors of their economies. These measures are treated in the WAEMU as an exception to the general rules of the customs union and common trade policy. They may remain in force for a maximum period of six months but are potentially renewable.

Regional competition is promoted in the WAEMU. Its treaty explicitly prohibits alliances, or concerted practices to restrain or distort competition within the Union; all practices equivalent to abuse of a dominant position in the common market; and public assistance that distorts competition by favoring certain firms or products. The Commission, under the supervision of the Court of Justice, is responsible for enforcing these competition rules.

Nationals of member countries—subject to limitations based on the grounds of public order, public safety, and public health—have the right of free movement and residency throughout the territory of the Union. This includes the right to travel to and remain in the territory of all member countries and the right to reside there. The nationals of a member country enjoy also the "right of establishment" throughout the territory of the Union. Companies and legal entities established in accordance with the laws of a member country are treated as nationals of member countries. Restrictions on the movement within the Union of capital belonging to persons residing in the member countries are prohibited.

MONETARY INSTITUTIONS

Regional monetary policy is conducted by the BCEAO, a public institution formed between the member countries of the WAMU. The BCEAO's headquarters is in Dakar, Senegal, with national directorates located in each member country. The main bodies of the BCEAO are the governor, the Monetary Policy Committee, the Board of Directors, the Audit Committee, and National Credit Councils in each member country.

The main objective of the BCEAO's monetary policy is to ensure price stability. The inflation target is defined by its Monetary Policy Committee. The BCEAO also provides support to economic policies of WAEMU countries with the view to achieve healthy and sustainable growth. The BCEAO has the following basic tasks: defining and implementing monetary policy in the WAEMU, ensuring stability of the banking and financial systems of the WAEMU, promoting the smooth operation and supervision of the payment system, implementing the exchange policy on the conditions established by the Council of Ministers, and managing official foreign reserves of the WAEMU. The BCEAO also contributes to improving the environment of monetary policy, diversifying and strengthening the WAEMU's financial system, and improving the technical capacity of the banking and financial sector.

The BCEAO has the exclusive right to issue bank notes, coins, and other legal tenders in WAMU member states. The BCEAO may carry out operations with gold, means of payment, and securities denominated in foreign currencies. It can lend or borrow money in the currency of its issuance from foreign banks, monetary institutions, and foreign and international organizations. It may also conduct open-market operations; buy and sell outright; spot, forward, repo operations; and lend and borrow with eligible participants. The BCEAO requires credit institutions to hold minimum reserves and oversees the operation and safety of the regional payment systems.

The BCEAO keeps accounts of the WAMU countries' treasuries at no cost. It also assists in the implementation of external financial operations of member governments. At the request of the government of a member country, the WAMU may manage that country's external and domestic public debt. At the government's request, it may also assist in negotiating external borrowing and in studying conditions for the issuance and redemption of domestic borrowing. In addition, the BCEAO assists governments in their relations with financial and monetary institutions in negotiations of international financial agreements and may be responsible for the implementation of these agreements.

The BCEAO regulates member countries' shares in the IMF, performs operations and transactions in the special drawing rights allocated to them, and cooperates with other central banks. The BCEAO may join any regional institution and any international agreement concerning monetary and financial matters.

The BCEAO's Monetary Policy Committee is responsible for the definition of monetary policy in the WAMU and its instruments. The committee includes the BCEAO's governor; the vice governor; one member nominated by each of the member states' governments; one member appointed by France (as the state providing the guarantee of convertibility of the common currency); and four representatives from WAMU member countries, who are personally appointed by the Council of Ministers. The Council draws from a list of potential appointees based on their professional experience in the areas of monetary, financial, economic, or legal policies. Member of the Monetary Policy Committee serve five-year terms that are renewable once.

The Monetary Policy Committee is chaired by the BCEAO governor. The president of the WAEMU Commission may attend meetings of the Monetary Policy Committee. Decisions of the Monetary Policy Committee are made by a simple majority of votes cast by the members.

The WAEMU Banking Commission is in charge of the supervision of banks and other financial institutions in the region. It approves the establishment of banks and financial institutions, monitors their activities and compliance with prudential regulations, and can take administrative and disciplinary measures in case of noncompliance. The Banking Commission is chaired by the governor of the BCEAO and includes one representative from each member country and eight members appointed by the Council in their personal capacity

National Credit Councils have been established in each WAEMU country to coordinate regional monetary policy with national economic priorities. The councils are chaired by the country's Minister of Finance and include a BCEAO representative, one or more members of the BCEAO's Monetary Policy Committee, nationals of the member of the country concerned, four members appointed by the country's government, two members appointed by consumer associations representing the interests of customers of banks and financial institutions, two members designated by universities and centers, and four individuals appointed in a personal capacity because of their expertise in the areas of economic, monetary, financial, legal policies or accounting. Each credit council prepares an annual report on the evolution of the monetary situation and credit as well as the banking and financial system in its country.

REFERENCES

Banque de France. 2015. Note di Information Relative á Zone Franc. www.Bangue-France.fr.

BCEAO Statute, http://www.bceao.int.

WAEMU Treaty, http://www.uemoa.int.

CHAPTER 2

Macroeconomic Setting and Current Challenges

MONIQUE NEWIAK AND CHRISTIAN JOSZ

Economic growth in the West African Economic and Monetary Union (WAEMU) has been historically low but has increased recently, driven by structural reforms and economic recovery in the region's largest countries. With the currency pegged to the euro, inflation in the region had traditionally been low. However, high fiscal deficits have been exerting increasing pressures on the external position. The combined fiscal deficit of the WAEMU has widened recently, largely reflecting rising levels of public investment in infrastructure in several countries. Because of the high import content of this investment, rising fiscal deficits have exerted pressure on the current account deficit, the gross reserves of the Central Bank of West African States (BCEAO), and the net foreign assets of commercial banks. Fiscal consolidation is needed in coming years, consistent with the recently reaffirmed WAEMU convergence criteria. To maintain much-needed infrastructure investment, including public investment, steps to increase tax revenue and control current expenditure will be essential. Should the planned fiscal consolidation in member countries fail to materialize, the BCEAO may need to consider a tighter stance. Prudential standards in the WAEMU are weaker than they are in comparable countries. About a quarter of banks do not meet these prudential standards. Ongoing efforts to strengthen bank supervision and raise prudential standards go in the right direction but will take time and need to be accelerated. Steps to upgrade the regulatory framework and build buffers in the financial system should be accelerated before downside risks materialize.

MACROECONOMIC SETTING

Since 2012, the WAEMU region has experienced strong average growth despite adverse challenges including security issues in some member states. The rebound that started in 2012 as Côte d'Ivoire began its postcrisis recovery is still firming up, helped by rising public investment mainly in infrastructure, as well as private investment. Rising public infrastructure investment also stimulated economic activity. The impact of Ebola on growth, although very important in Guinea, Liberia, and Sierra Leone, was small in WAEMU countries. Consumer prices and underlying inflation have been historically low, and, with the exception of several spikes related to food and fuel prices, approached zero in 2014 (Table 2.1).

The consolidated fiscal deficit of the region remains relatively high. The overall budget deficit (including grants) reached 4.6 percent of GDP in 2014, compared with an average of 2.9 percent of GDP during the past decade, owing to rising public investment to address the infrastructure gap, especially in Burkina Faso, Côte d'Ivoire, Mali, and Niger. With tax revenue remaining broadly unchanged at 16 percent of GDP, countries increasingly tapped the regional financial market. In 2014, average Treasury bill rates increased by about ½ percentage point since the beginning of 2014, going from 4.8 to 5.6 percent. Total public debt declined slightly to 38.1 percent of GDP. Fiscal policy and the situation of public finances are the reflection of planned shifts made by governments toward public investment to support growth. The overall budget deficit increase was due to rising public investment to address the infrastructure gap, as transitioning

TABLE 2.1

WAEMU: Long-Term Economic Trends

2014	Population (Millions)	Per Capita GDP (U.S. dollars)	Exports (Percent of GDP)	Current Account (Percent of GDP)	Government Revenues/GDP (Percent)	Financial Depth (M2/GDP)	Main Export Product
WAEMU	86.7	588.5	32.1	−4.3	17.2	26.9	
Benin	8.4	623.9	10.8	−6.4	16.8	29.3	Cotton
Burkina Faso	13.2	448.9	11.9	−10.3	12.5	19.6	Cotton
Côte d'Ivoire	18.2	951.0	51.3	3.0	18.2	25.0	Cocoa
Guinea-Bissau	1.6	188.5	22.9	−12.2	19.5	34.3	Banana
Mali	13.5	486.9	30.6	−4.9	17.1	28.5	Gold
Niger	14.0	283.0	15.7	−8.3	13.1	14.9	Uranium
Senegal	11.7	820.5	25.8	−10.1	20.0	36.3	Fish
Togo	6.2	350.7	40.5	−6.0	16.9	33.2	Cement

Sources: IMF, International Financial Statistics and World Economic Outlook database; and UN COMTRADE.

from the primacy of current expenditures to productive investment outlays has been a long overdue endeavor in most of the WAEMU countries. The current momentum, therefore, goes in the right direction; and, coming from very low levels of investment, the rise of the deficit can be seen as temporary.

Monetary policy has been supportive of growth. By keeping a low refinancing rate of 2.5 percent since September 2013, the central bank has helped banks invest part of their high level of liquidity in sovereign bonds on the regional market. Credit to the economy has continued to grow at robust rates and credit to governments at even higher rates. Recently, refinancing operations by the BCEAO have risen sharply and commercial banks' liquidity position with the central bank has turned from a net creditor to a net debtor position. Commercial banks' borrowing from the central bank has reached 9 percent of banks' liabilities, and governments' borrowing from commercial banks has risen to about 20 percent of commercial banks' assets. The positive interest rate differential between central bank refinancing and Treasury bills and bonds, and the zero capital requirements for WAEMU government paper, may also have provided an incentive to borrow from the central bank and invest in government paper. The rise of sovereign issuance is a positive development in the region, to be further enhanced as the secondary bond market develops. Governments in the region have regularly and correctly managed the debt stemming from these sovereign issuances and WAEMU authorities do not see major risks in this area. In the meantime, transactions turnover in the interbank market has shrunk.

The external current account deficit has remained well above its historical average. The deterioration of the current account deficit in recent years has been due to an increasing savings-investment gap in both the public and private sectors. The expansion of the private savings-investment gap is mainly driven by a sharp increase in private consumption in Côte d'Ivoire. After some temporary decline, the international reserves of the BCEAO rose slightly in 2014, owing notably to stricter implementation of the obligation to repatriate export receipts, although this was broadly offset by the decline in the net foreign asset positions of commercial banks.

The external position remains sustainable but vulnerabilities have increased. The exchange rate appears broadly in line with fundamentals, but external buffers have not been stable. The BCEAO's gross international reserves coverage stood at about five months of imports at the end of 2014; commercial banks' net foreign exchange position has declined and turned negative. The level of gross international reserves is below optimal, based on standard metrics (5–12 months of imports). However, gross international reserves are still significantly higher than the floor that acts as a warning signal under the zone's monetary arrangement with France (84 percent of narrow money compared with 20 percent).

OUTLOOK AND RISKS

In the medium term, regional growth should remain strong and fiscal and current account deficits should gradually decline if governments implement their fiscal consolidation plans (Figure 2.1). Growth is projected to exceed 6 percent owing to continued buoyant public and private sector investment and be supported by the weakening of the euro (to which the CFA franc is pegged) and improvement in the terms of trade compared to the IMF's 2014 Article IV assessment, owing notably to the decline in international oil prices. Meanwhile, inflation is expected to average around 2 percent over the medium term. The overall fiscal deficit should gradually decrease below 3 percent of GDP by 2019 if governments implement their fiscal consolidation plans. Total public debt is projected to stabilize at moderate levels (about 40 percent of GDP). Owing to the decrease in oil prices and fiscal consolidation, the current account deficit (including grants) should gradually improve to about 6 percent of GDP by 2020, with reserve coverage staying above four months of imports. Moreover, the fall in oil prices and the weakening of the CFAF may also lead to a strengthening of the external current account. Overall, these are positive developments that bode well for the future of the region.

The outlook for the WAEMU is subject to downside risks. A further decrease in non-oil commodity prices as a result of a slowdown of growth in advanced and emerging market countries would aggregate the negative impact on the external accounts of the recent fall in commodity prices of commodity exporters such as Burkina Faso, Mali, and Niger. Tighter external financing conditions due to the normalization of monetary policy in the United States have increased financing costs in many sub-Saharan Africa frontier markets, including Côte d'Ivoire and Senegal. A further tightening can exacerbate these tensions. The absence of fiscal consolidation and slow structural reform implementation, including reforms to increase public investment efficiency, would reduce growth and worsen the external and fiscal positions of the region. The decline in Ebola infections in the three most affected countries is welcome; a flare-up would pose renewed risks for the region.

FINANCIAL SECTOR DEVELOPMENT

Prudential standards in the WAEMU remain low by international standards and their observance is incomplete. The average capital-adequacy ratio of banks is about half that observed in comparable Sub-Saharan African countries, and is lower than the minimum requirement of 8 percent in half of the countries. In addition, the enforcement of prudential standards is loose. Indeed, about 10 percent of banks have negative capital. About one-fourth of banks do not meet the minimum capital requirement. About one-fourth of banks do not comply with the connected lending limit. About half of banks do not respect the relatively high single large-exposure limit, owing partly to the lack of economic diversification. Asset quality is also an issue, as illustrated by the high level of nonperforming loans under less demanding provisioning rules. The substantially negative net foreign assets in banks also cause prudential concerns, as they may signal that banks are exposed to an increasingly high level of foreign exchange risk. Finally, fast-developing regional banking groups, which account for almost 70 percent of WAEMU's banking sector assets, raise new opportunities but also pose risks, as bank holding companies in WAEMU are not subject to banking regulation or consolidated supervision (Figure 2.2).

WAEMU authorities should enforce existing prudential regulations and raise standards to international best practice. The ongoing efforts to strengthen bank supervision and raise prudential standards go in the right direction but will take time and need to be accelerated. In the interim, it will be important to proceed expeditiously with plans to raise banks' capital

Figure 2.1. WAEMU Medium-term Outlook, 2015–2020

Growth should remain strong in the medium term . . .

1. Real GDP Growth, 2015–2020
(Annual, percent)

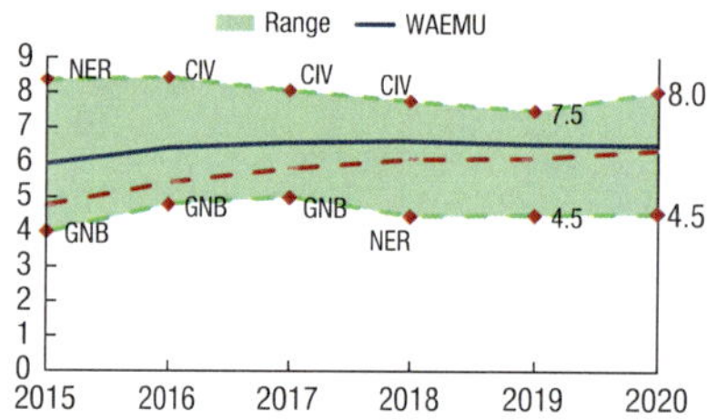

. . . and inflation low.

2. Inflation and Terms of Trade
(Annual changes, percent)

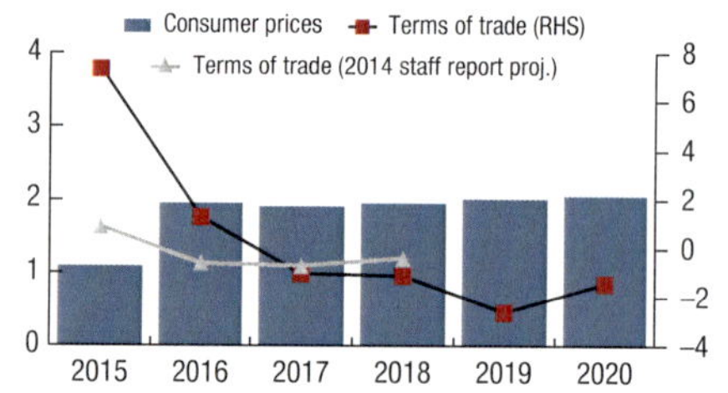

In line with governments' plans to consolidate the fiscal deficit below 3 percent by 2019, . . .

3. Overall Fiscal Balance and Components, 2015-2020
(Percent of GDP)

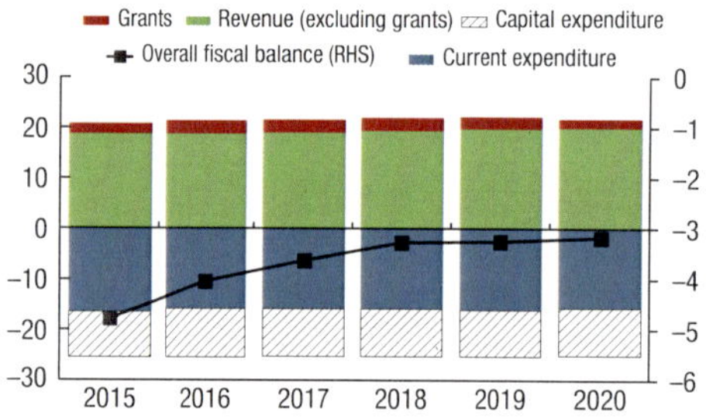

. . . the region's savings-investment gap would decrease, while public and private investments would remain high.

4. National Savings and Investment
(Percent of GDP)

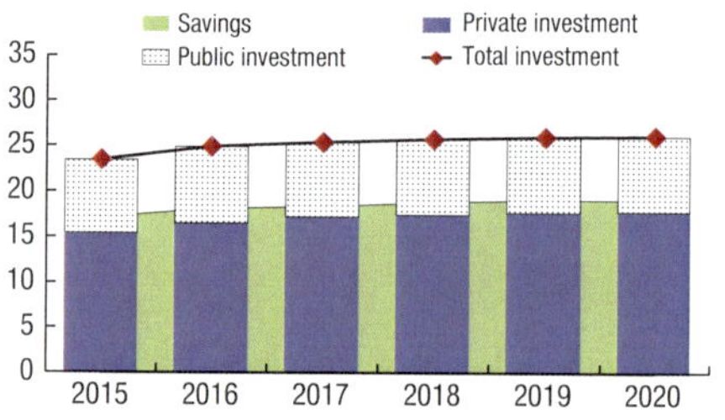

Financial and capital accounts would on average finance the current account deficit, . . .

5. Financing Sources
(Percent of GDP)

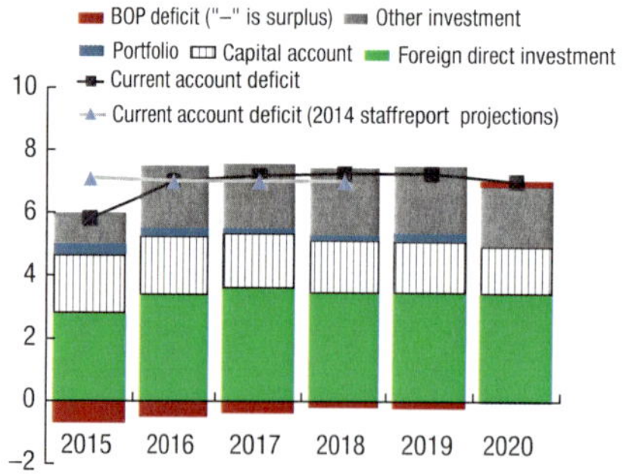

. . . stabilizing their GIR coverage in the medium-term, provided fiscal consolidation is implemented as planned.

6. Gross International Reserves
(Months of next years extra-regional imports)

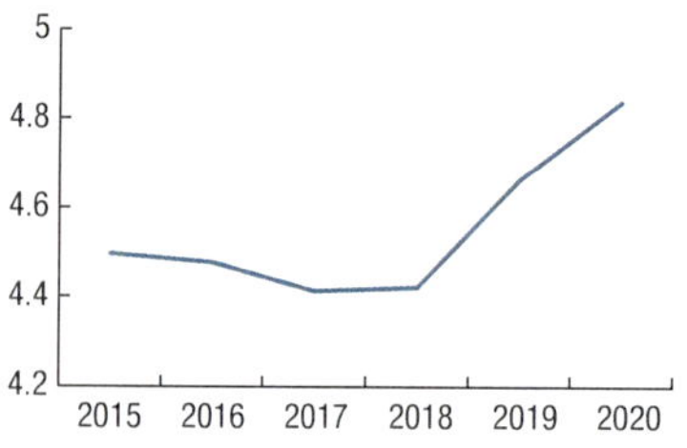

Sources: Central Bank of Western African States; IMF African Department database; IMF, *World Economic Outlook*; and IMF staff estimates and projections.

Note: Three-letter International Organization for Standardization abbreviations used for country names. RHS = right-hand side; WAEMU = West African Economic and Monetary Union.

Figure 2.2. WAEMU: Financial Stability and Development

Nonperforming loans have been increasing in some countries . . .

1. Nonperforming Loans, 2012–2014
(Percent of total loans)

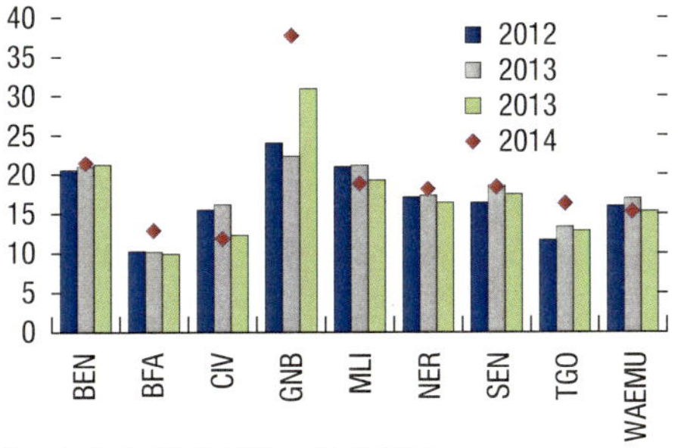

Source: Central Bank of West African States.
Note: Three-letter International Organization for Standardization abbreviations used for country names.
WAEMU = West African Economic and Monetary Union.

. . . and the capital adequacy ratio has declined on average in the region.

2. Capital Adequacy Ratios, 2013–2014
(Percent)

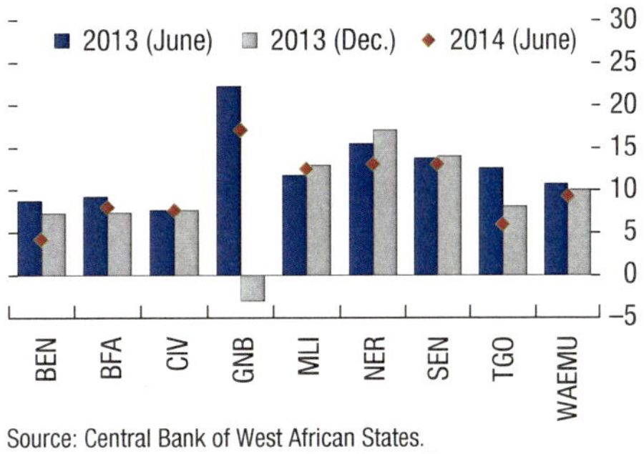

Source: Central Bank of West African States.
Note: Three-letter International Organization for Standardization abbreviations used for country names.
WAEMU = West African Economic and Monetary Union.

Prudential indicators do not compare favorably with those of other African peers . . .

3. Financial Soundness Indicators in the WAEMU and Sub-Saharan Africa *(Percent)*

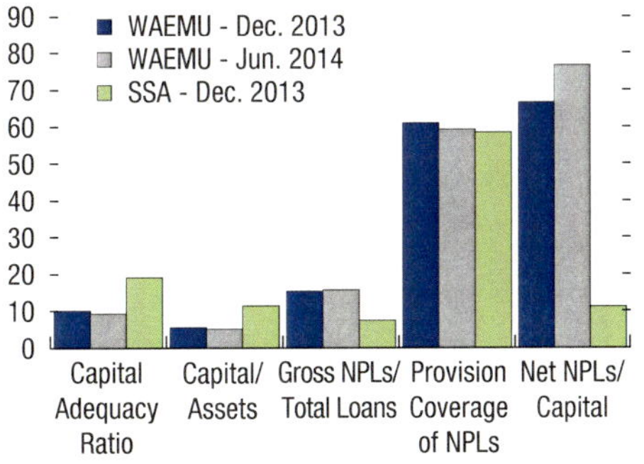

Note: WAEMU indicators based on data received from the authorities, SSA indicators based on the simple average of FSIs compiled by the IMF for reporting SSA countries (Burundi, Cameroon, Congo, Gabon, Ghana, Kenya, Lesotho, Mauritius, Mozambique, Namibia, Nigeria, Rwanda, Senegal, Seychelles, Sierra Leone, South Africa, Swaziland, Tanzania, Uganda, Zambia). Comparison should be cautiously considered since different countries may be adopting different capital adequacy and loan classification and provisioning standards. FSIs = financial stability indicators; NPL = nonperforming loans; SSA = sub-Saharan Africa.

. . . and compliance to prudential norms is weak and has not improved on average.

4. Compliance to Prudential Ratios, 2012–2014
(Percent of banks complying)

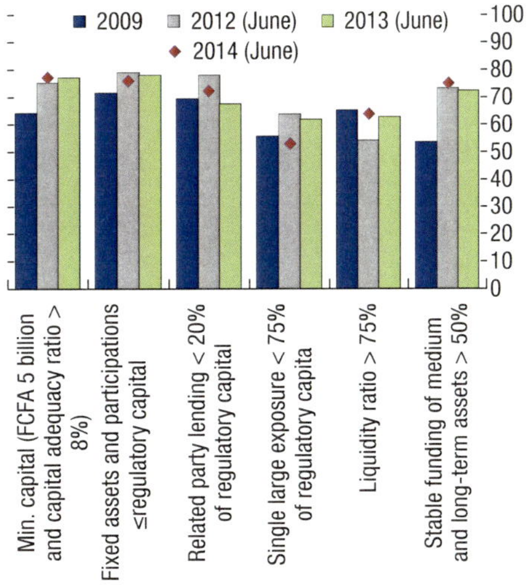

Source: Central Bank of West African States.

Access to financial services has increased but at a slower pace than in benchmark countries, . . .

5. Depositors with Commercial Banks
(Per thousands of adults)

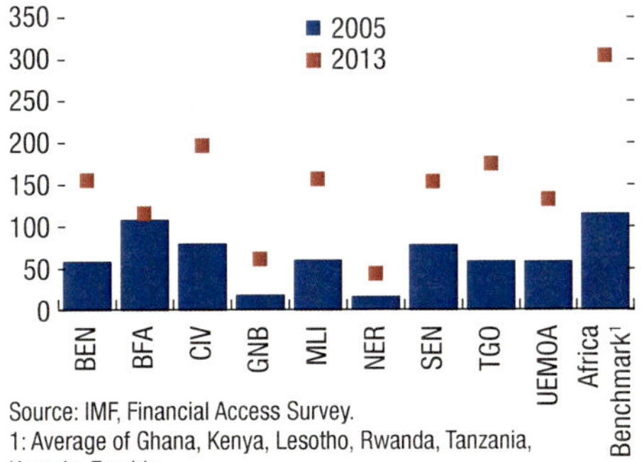

Source: IMF, Financial Access Survey.
1: Average of Ghana, Kenya, Lesotho, Rwanda, Tanzania, Uganda, Zambia.
Note: Three-letter International Organization for Standardization abbreviations used for country names. WAEMU = West African Economic and Monetary Union.

. . . while credit growth has been strong and in line with African peers.

6. Outstanding Loans from Commercial Banks
(Percent of GDP)

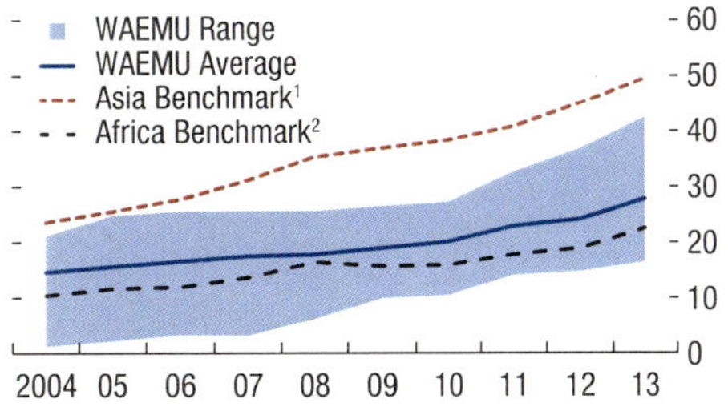

Source: IMF, Financial Access Survey.
1: Bangladesh, Cambodia, India, Laos, Nepal, Vietnam.
2: Ghana, Kenya, Lesotho, Rwanda, Tanzania, Uganda, Zambia.

requirements. As the current macroeconomic environment is rather favorable, the steps to upgrade the regulatory framework and build buffers in the financial system should be accelerated before downside risks materialize. It is also important and urgent to subject bank holding companies incorporated in the WAEMU to appropriate banking regulation and consolidated supervision. Deposit insurance and financial stability funds should be made operational as a matter of priority. A single and independent administrative resolution authority should be established to ensure prompt and effective resolution of banks with negative capital.

Authorities are taking steps to upgrade the regulatory framework to international standards and strengthen prudential supervision. The BCEAO has initiated a process aimed at implementing Basel II/III standards and better aligning regulations with Basel principles, including those on consolidated supervision. The WAEMU Banking Commission has put considerable effort into building operational capacity and enhancing banking supervision in the last few years. A deposit insurance fund and a financial stability fund have been established and are expected to start operations soon.

Financial sector development remains one of the main objectives on the WAEMU authorities' agenda and actions on several fronts are underway. First, the authorities are cognizant that the deepening of the financial sector will help improve the transmission channels of the monetary policy. The BCEAO, in coordination with national authorities, has launched a vast reform program in that regard. This includes the inception of new institutions such as credit bureaus to improve information and boost lending activities, and the development of electronic systems to enhance the interbank market.

Most governments in the region are implementing financial sector development strategies with the view to boost credit to the economy. Key pillars of these strategies include: attracting new banks to address the shallowness of the banking sector and associated weaknesses such as low competition, high borrowing costs, and high concentration of credit; enhancing financial inclusion by lifting bottlenecks and increasing access to banking services; and developing microfinance and mobile banking.

Sovereign bond issuance is also an important instrument for the development of the regional financial market. A specific agency—WAEMU Securities Agency—has been created with the main task of coordinating bond issuance among countries to keep yields under control. Alongside this agency, authorities are stepping up efforts to reap the full benefits of sovereign issuance on the regional market, including licensing primary dealers in government securities to activate the secondary market for government paper.

The administrative and disciplinary measures taken have translated into an improvement in banks' financial situations. WAEMU authorities are also putting a particular emphasis on the supervision of pan-African banks. As for the whole banking sector, the BCEAO management has liaised with the supervisory bodies of parent banks to coordinate their efforts and harmonize practices for the supervision of pan-African banks.

STRUCTURAL TRANSFORMATION AND DIVERSIFICATION

Production and export diversification of the region remain low, even by African standards. The structure of the economies has changed little in the past quarter century. The majority of the region's population is employed in low-productivity agriculture and the secondary sector is underdeveloped. Further structural transformation and diversification of output and exports could yield significant growth dividends. Weaknesses include gaps in infrastructure, education and training, finance, trade networks, functioning factor markets, and supportive regulatory environments. While the evidence is more mixed concerning the success of industry-focused measures, the WAEMU's agricultural sector warrants special attention, given its large potential for productivity and quality improvements and its high share of employment. The authorities' regional economic plan, though being only about half covered through committed financing so far, targets key areas such as improvements to governance, access to energy, and the development of regional infrastructure and human resources.

Embarking on a structural transformation agenda and diversifying the economies of the region are at the forefront of the WAEMU authorities' demand in terms of development programs. The strong growth momentum in the region, paired with macroeconomic stability and a set of favorable global conditions, should be put to profit by member countries to lay the ground for higher potential growth. WAEMU authorities are committed to endeavor in that direction as evidenced by efforts on many fronts.

Most countries in the region have designed development plans with the ambition of transitioning to emerging market economies in the coming decades. This is a clear indication of a paradigm shift from fiscal stance-centered plans to ambitious economic transformation plans. Closing the infrastructure gap is one of the first steps of this agenda. In this regard, efforts at the country level are being supplemented by regional programs in the areas of energy and roads. Several corridors have been identified and the project preparation is very advanced for some of them, including the highway between Abidjan-Lagos. Implementation of the second phase of the Regional Economic Program also includes the provision of regional infrastructure and access to energy.

Improving the business climate in other areas, such as enhancing the judicial system, reducing red tape, and accelerating the process of setting up a business, is also being taken on at both the country and regional levels. The WAEMU Commission is also creating the infrastructure to harmonize and disseminate best practices in reforms evaluated in the World Bank's Doing Business assessment among countries. The WAEMU implements a common industrial policy to supplement national initiatives, with an emphasis on the development of small and medium-sized enterprises. The objective is to create a single market for small and medium-sized enterprises and establish linkages with bigger companies, especially to subcontract public procurements across countries.

WAEMU countries are exporters of agricultural commodities, and intrasector structural transformation is a major agenda item for the region's policymakers. To this end, adding value to agricultural products through processing is a step in countries' development plans and a part of the Union's common industrial policy as well. Likewise, governments' efforts to attract foreign investment are aimed at enhancing the share of the manufacturing sector in domestic output. This intrasector structural transformation should help transfer resources from the low-productivity agriculture sector toward the manufacturing and service sectors and help broaden employment opportunities for educated youths.

REGIONAL INTEGRATION

Promoting regional integration is also a priority for WAEMU authorities, as a way to create a large market of 230 million consumers within the Economic Community of Western African States (ECOWAS). The ECOWAS Common External Tariff became effective in January 2015. Liberalizing trade within the whole region would provide a greater playing field for the private sector to thrive and reap the growth dividends. The implementation of the ECOWAS Common External Tariff offers opportunities for boosting regional trade but also entails risks for regional integration. However, it increases tariff protection for WAEMU countries with the introduction of a new 35 percent tariff band for specific goods, and the possibility to deviate from the common external tariff for 3 percent of countries' tariff lines for several years, with negligible impact on tax revenue.

Overall, amid the global slowdown and manifold challenges, the WAEMU region has maintained a strong growth momentum. Buoyant public investment, especially in infrastructure that has been held back for too long, stood as one of the key drivers of this performance. Going forward, the opportunity for the region to seize the moment and entrench growth lies in WAEMU authorities' unwavering commitment to and policies aimed at fostering the structural transformation of their economies. This is the most sustainable way to diversify economies and create the conditions for long-term macroeconomic stability.

CHAPTER 3

Macroeconomic Policy Coordination

ALEXEI KIREYEV

There is a strong theoretical and practical argument for fiscal-monetary policy coordination in the West African Economic and Monetary Union (WAEMU). WAEMU countries conduct independent fiscal policies but implement a single regional monetary policy. National ministries of finance are in charge of the formulation and implementation of fiscal policies; the WAEMU Commission coordinates fiscal policies among member states, whereas the Central Bank of West African States (BCEAO), the regional central bank, conducts the single monetary policy. As in any monetary union, this institutional setup raises an important practical question of coordination between heterogeneous fiscal policies and a homogeneous monetary policy. Fiscal-monetary policy coordination is a stated goal of the WAEMU but in practice it has been limited, leading to undesirable side effects. A coherent framework is needed for the WAEMU Commission and the BCEAO, which could help align and mutually reinforce their so-far largely autonomous efforts in the implementation of their fiscal and monetary policies. There is ample theoretical evidence that mutual adaptation of fiscal and monetary policy on a continuous timeline would lead to superior outcomes in terms of reaching policy objectives. In normal times, ministries of finance should continue to target long-term debt sustainability while the BCEAO should focus on inflation. This can be achieved through mutual adaptation of levels of fiscal deficit and policy rates. During stress times, the fiscal policies of finance ministries should still target debt sustainability, while the BCEAO's monetary policies should target inflation. However, in the short term, the BCEAO should be willing to tolerate temporarily high inflation as a strategy for increasing the likelihood of meeting the inflation target in the long term. Ministries of finances (MoFs) can focus on stabilizing output and employment at the expense of a temporary deviation from a sustainable debt path.

INSTITUTIONAL SETUP

Fiscal policy refers to the government's use of taxation and spending to regulate the aggregate level of economic activity. The use of fiscal policy consists of changes in the level or composition of taxation or government spending, and hence in the government's financial position relative to the rest of the economy (Hilbers 2005). Key policy variables include government deficits and debt, as well as tax and expenditure types and levels, fiscal deficits, and public debt.

Monetary policy refers to the central bank's control of the availability of credit in the economy to achieve the broad objectives of economic policy. Control can be exerted by operating on such aggregates as the level and structure of interest rates, the money supply, and other conditions affecting credit. The most important objective of most central banks is price stability, but there can be others such as promoting economic development and growth, stabilizing the exchange rate, safeguarding the balance of external payments, and maintaining financial stability. Key variables in this policy area include interest rates, money and credit supply, and the exchange rate.

While fiscal and monetary policies are implemented by different institutions, national ministries of finance and central banks, these policies are closely interlinked. A change in fiscal policy impacts the effectiveness of monetary policy and thereby affects the overall macroeconomic policy stance. The opposite is also true, as any changes in monetary policy have an impact on fiscal policies and therefore on the overall effectiveness of macroeconomic policies. That is why it is crucial to pursue a consistent fiscal-monetary policy mix to avoid tensions and achieve optimal impact. Credibility of the overall policy mix depends on credibility of each of the policies. This policy mix is a key component of the IMF's macroeconomic policy advice.

The goal of this section is to suggest a framework of fiscal-monetary policy coordination in the context of the WAEMU. WAEMU countries conduct independent fiscal policies but have a single monetary policy. The WAEMU Commission is charged with the coordination of tax policies and monitoring fiscal convergence criteria, whereas the BCEAO, the regional central bank, conducts the single monetary policy. As in any monetary union, this raises an important practical question of coordination between heterogeneous fiscal policies and a homogeneous monetary policy.

Since WAEMU countries have a common monetary policy and different fiscal policies, coordination is developing at two levels: ensuring convergence of countries in fiscal policies and coordination between fiscal policies and the common monetary policy. After the adjustment of the parity of the CFA franc in 1994, WAEMU countries adopted the Covenant on Convergence, Growth and Solidarity between Member States, which formally expanded monetary integration to the economic sphere and introduced formal provisions for coordination of economic policies.

Provisions for coordination between fiscal and monetary policies are included in the founding documents of the WAEMU and in the recently revised BCEAO statute (Box 3.1). The WAEMU Treaty recognizes economic policies of member countries as an area of common interest, which should be coordinated (Article 63). Special attention should be paid to the consistency of fiscal policies with the objectives of the monetary policy, in particular price stability (Article 64). Specifically, the treaty calls for harmonization of the domestic legislation of member countries,

BOX 3.1. Statutory Provisions for Policy Coordination

WAEMU Treaty

Article 4. Without prejudice to the objectives defined in the Treaty, the Union pursues the following objectives: . . . harmonize, to the extent necessary for the proper functioning of the common market, the laws of the member states and in particular the system of taxation.

Article 63. Member States shall consider their economic policies as a matter of common concern and shall coordinate them within the Council. . . .

Article 64. On a proposal from the Commission, the Council decides on major guidelines on the economic policies of the Member States and the Union by way of providing recommendations. . . . These guidelines also take into account the requirement for compatibility of budgetary policies with the objectives of monetary policy, in particular that of price stability.

WAEMU Commission

The Commissioner of the Department of Economic Policy and Internal Taxation supervises, directs and coordinates joint EU policies in the following areas: harmonization of legal and accounting framework of public finances; the harmonization of domestic tax systems, direct and indirect taxes economic analyzes and forecasting. . . .

BCEAO Statute

Article 18. The claims of the Central Bank collateralized with securities issued or guaranteed by the treasuries, local authorities or all other public bodies in the Member States can not exceed a percentage of national tax revenues in the penultimate fiscal year, as set by the Monetary Policy Committee.

Article 61. The Governor of the Central Bank can make statements at the Council of Ministers on general economic policies of Member States, particularly on their fiscal issues and debt.

including their tax regimes (Article 4). The WAEMU Commission supervises, directs, and coordinates common policies on the harmonization of legal and accounting frameworks of public finances, as well as of domestic direct and indirect taxes. According to the BCEAO statute, the BCEAO governor has the right to raise at the Council of Ministers the economic policies of member countries, including their budget and debt policies (Article 61). The BCEAO statute also puts a ceiling on the amount of budget financing that can be backed by rediscounting government paper at the central bank (Article 18). While legal provisions for coordination are present, in practice such coordination has been limited.

The institutional setup of the WAEMU is generally adequate for effective fiscal-monetary policy coordination. As orientation for the medium term, governments approve *multiyear programs of economic development*, in line with their medium-term development plans and poverty reduction strategy papers (PRSPs). For comparability proposes, these programs are presented in a consistent manner across all WAEMU countries and include projections of key macroeconomic variables, including levels of fiscal deficits and a discussion of options for financing and debt policies for the medium term. National authorities submit these multiyear programs to the WAEMU Commission for assessment of consistency with the convergence criteria agreed to at the regional levels. The WAEMU Commission in its regular *Multilateral Surveillance Report* analyzes the multiyear programs for their structures, realism of underlying assumptions, and consistency with reaching the convergence criteria. If countries diverge from the convergence criteria, the WAEMU commission provides recommendations on the needed adjustments. To increase peer pressure on countries to comply, the report is submitted for consideration to the Council of WAEMU Ministers and is published on the WAEMU Commission Web site. The Council of Ministers, on which each country is represented by two ministers including the minister of finance, directs the overall macroeconomic policies of the union. The BCEAO is represented at its meetings by the governor, in an advisory capacity.

Regional arrangements have also been established for short-term coordination of fiscal and monetary policy. The Monetary Policy Committee, charged with the formulation and daily implementation of monetary policies, includes representatives of each WAEMU government. In addition, in each WAEMU country there is a National Credit Council (Conseil National du Crédit), an advisory body to the minister of finance, which consists of the representatives of the government (including the ministry of finance), the private sector, and the national branch of the BCEAO. It is chaired by the minister of finance. The council reviews national financial conditions and can provide advice to the minister of finance on all issues related to money and credit. Finally, the BCEAO has established a surveillance committee to monitor the issuance of government paper.

FISCAL-MONETARY POLICY MIX

Fiscal and monetary policies have different but complementary policy objectives (Figure 3.1). At the institutional level, fiscal and monetary policies are designed and implemented by different bodies. In the context of the WAEMU, eight national ministries of finance are changed with the design and implementation of fiscal policies in their respective countries, whereas the BCEAO is responsible for the design and implementation of a single monetary policy in the interest of all eight countries of the region. The BCEAO is an intergovernmental institution, formally independent of national governments and their ministries of finance.

The objectives of fiscal and monetary policies are different but complementary (Blinter 1982; Canzoneri, Cumby, and Diba 2010).

- The main objective of fiscal policy, and actually often its formal long-term anchor, is a sustainable level of public debt, as well as macroeconomic stability and economic growth.

Figure 3.1. Complementary Policy Objectives

	Fiscal policy	Monetary policy
Institutions	National MoF/WAEMU Commission	BCEAO
Objectives	Real growth, sustainable public debt, employment	Price stability, financial sector stability
Instruments	Taxes: types, levels, exemptions; Expenditure: composition, structure	Interest rates, open market operations, reserve requirements
Timeframe	Long-term	Short-term
Constraints	Monetary dominance, implementation lags, low market access, tax policy rigidities, legal constraints	Fiscal dominance, mutually excluding goals (price and exchange rate stability), insufficient credibility, lack of transparency

Common policy objectives
Macroeconomic stability
Aggregate demand

Source: Authors' presentation.
Note: BCEAO = Central Bank of West African States; MoF = ministry of finance; WAEMU = West African Economic and Monetary Union.

Generally, the objectives of fiscal policy are not enshrined in law. In the WAEMU context, constitutions of individual countries only mention that budget law will set the level of revenues and expenditures every year. The budget framework law usually establishes the structure, amendment, and voting requirements for the budget law, but does not specify any objective for either fiscal policy. National development strategies in individual countries in most cases backed by an IMF-supported program contain similar wording but include the important dimension of inclusiveness as part of the objectives for fiscal policy. WAEMU regional convergence criteria are the only documents that set specific fiscal policy objectives.

- The main objective of monetary policy is normally low and stable inflation, often supplemented by the additional objectives of maintaining an overall economic stability and achieving higher growth. The BCEAO defines price stability as an annual average inflation rate of 2 percent plus or minus 1 percentage point and set over a 24-month horizon. It mentions a number of secondary objectives such as support of sound and sustainable growth, and support of integration in the WAEMU.

Fiscal and monetary authorities use different types of instruments.

- Fiscal policy instruments operate by setting tax rates and expenditure priorities. Tax and spending instruments are generally used to counter cyclical fluctuation and are often targeted to support growth and employment, rather than to reduce inflation. Fiscal deficits are generally expansionary and lead to increased aggregate demand, interest rates, and inflation. Fiscal surpluses are contractionary and lead to lower aggregate demand, interest rates, and inflation.
- The instruments of monetary policy include policy interest rate, money supply, and reserve requirements. Central banks lower interest rates in recession and raise them to counter inflationary pressures. Lower interest rates increase aggregate demand, are expansionary, and

generally lead to real depreciation and higher inflation. Higher interest rates are contractionary, lower the aggregate demand, may cause real appreciation, and reduce inflation.

Monetary and fiscal policies operate on a different time scale.

- Fiscal policies are set in annual budgets, which at times are integral parts of medium-term fiscal frameworks. Tax types, rates, and bases, and other characteristics of the tax regime are set in the tax and customs codes and other laws. As these laws require parliamentary approval, tax regimes cannot be adjusted quickly. Financing also often depends on foreign donors, which commit their resources in advance and cannot revise their contributions in the course of the fiscal year. Therefore, long periods are generally required to alter the fiscal stance, and fiscal policy itself is better suited to addressing long-term fundamental challenges such as growth or unemployment.
- Monetary policy can be adjusted to change economic conditions relatively fast, at least within a given year. Central banks' monetary policy committees or similar bodies usually meet at least quarterly and the central bank can act independently of the legislature. Therefore, the monetary policy stance can be adjusted relatively quickly as a short-term reaction to spikes in inflation, exchange rate volatility, or credit conditions in the economy.

Both fiscal and monetary policies face important constraints, in particular under a fixed exchange rate arrangement with limited capital mobility.

- In this institutional setup, fiscal policy efficiency is constrained, as a fiscal expansion in the form of higher fiscal deficits can initially lead to an increase of aggregate demand and, therefore, to higher output and employment. But it also leads to an increase in money demand in the form of higher credit to the government from the banking system, which with unchanged money supply, should lead to an increase in interest rates. Higher interest rates would hold back economic activities and offset the initial positive impact of fiscal expansion, at least in part. In addition, fiscal policy is hindered by long implementation lags, often low efficiency of public investment, and little flexibility with spending composition.
- Monetary policy efficiency under a fixed exchange rate and limited capital mobility is also highly constrained, as changes in the policy interest rate can operate only in a short run. In this institutional setup, any monetary loosening would initially increase the GDP as credit became more affordable, but with time would lead to higher inflation and real exchange rate appreciation, even if the nominal rate were pegged. This would reduce export demand and therefore offset part of the GDP gains. Moreover, monetary policy is often handicapped by fiscal dominance, the need to play under political pressure the role of the lender of last resort for problem banks. In addition, monetary policy may be charged with mutually excluding goals, such as simultaneous price and exchange rate stability, and suffer from insufficient credibility and lack of transparency.

At the same time, fiscal and monetary policies are highly complementary. Both policies ultimately pursue a common goal of macroeconomic stability and can influence in a significant way aggregate demand. In an appropriate policy mix, each policy would play a supportive role to the other, with the view of achieving this common goal. On the other hand, the absence of coordination leads to suboptimal outcomes. It can result in either fiscal dominance, if fiscal policies play the central role, or monetary dominance, if this role belongs to monetary policies. Would it be better for the economy if fiscal or monetary authorities took decisions on their policies independently? Or would it be better if they cooperated and consulted each other before making policy decisions?

Owing to the specificity of the instructional setup of the WAEMU, fiscal and monetary policies are interlinked in a special way. In this setup, monetary policy can have a short-term impact on output because of temporary price and wage rigidities and can lead to several fiscal effects (Dahan 1998). The opposite is also true: fiscal policies have important monetary effects (Figure 3.2).

Central bank independence by itself cannot safeguard monetary policy objectives from the impact of fiscal policy. Even when the central bank has independence, and hence is not constrained by the financing needs of the government, the need to offset the impact of expansionary fiscal policy on aggregate demand and inflation could prompt it to tighten monetary policy by

Figure 3.2. Mutual Effect of Macroeconomic Policies

Fiscal effects of monetary policy	Monetary effects of fiscal policy
• *Tax revenue effect.* Higher interest rates may dampen economic activities, reduce demand for credit, and lead to slower GDP growth. As a result, the taxable base would be reduced, which would negatively affect tax revenue collection and could increase the fiscal deficit. The size of the revenue effect would depend on the elasticity of tax collection with respect to GDP and short-term rigidities of prices and wages in the economy. If automatic stabilizers were built into the design of the tax system, the negative revenue effect could be even larger than the drop in nominal growth.	• *Deficit monetization effect.* In an extreme case, the budget deficit is financed by central bank credit, which leads to a direct increase in reserve money and a negative impact on inflation, policy credibility, and over all macrostability. Even if such direct financing is not allowed, the central bank can be forced by the need to support weak banks and inject liquidity in to the banking system, often with the view to give the means to commercial bank to lend to the government. This quasi-monetization operation still expands broad money and may have negative implications for inflation, the primary objective of monetary policy.
• *Interest payment effect.* Higher policy interest rates may lead to an increase in the interest payments on domestic government debt. If the transmission mechanism of the monetary policy functions well, an increase in policy rates would affect the whole term structure of interest rates, including the rates government has to pay on its Treasury bills and bonds. As interest payments are included above the line in budgets as government expenditure, additional debt service costs would increase the fiscal deficit.	• *Crowding-out effect.* If a government finances its deficit by issuing government paper in the market, large borrowings by the government can displace the private sector from the financial market. With limited credit resources available, such crowding out would mean that the remaining financial resources could become scarce and too expensive for the private sector, which would harm economic development. Credit availability for the private sector in the economy is an important objective of monetary policy, which may be thus undermined.
• *Deficit financing effect.* A cut in policy interest rates would make bank credit less expensive for both the government and the private sector. If the resulting decline in market borrowing rates is asymmetric, banks may revise their lending strategies and direct their credit to the more profitable private sector customers, where they can charge higher rates. If the budget relies in large part on domestic bank financing, this may pose problems for the financing of the deficit.	• *External sustainability effect.* Governments may finance their deficits externally, which is also an area of concern for the central bank. Excessive external financing may heighten balance-of-payments risks; lead to unsustainable current account deficits and exploding levels of external debt; and undermine exchange rate stability and other external risks, all of which are in the purview of the central bank.
• *Asset price effect.* Higher interest rates due to tight monetary policies reduce prices of almost all assets, including government paper. The market value of government debt (both domestic and foreign) would unambiguously drop in the short run, which could help press down inflation, nominal growth, and tax revenue.	• *Price effect.* Unsustainably high fiscal deficits could force governments to resort to increases in indirect taxes, which would have an immediate impact on inflation. Moreover, such an increase in taxes could drive the wage-price increase spiral and set firm expectations of higher inflation in the future, which are hard to reverse. This would invalidate the efforts of the central bank to control inflation, as financial behavior of economic agents often depends directly on their perception of fiscal sustainability.

raising interest rates or reducing credit. The resulting high interest rates could depress economic activity and attract short-term and easily reversible capital flows, thereby adding to inflation and appreciation pressures on the currency, and eventually damaging macroeconomic and financial stability.

FRAMEWORK FOR THE WAEMU

In the WAEMU, fiscal and monetary policies are designed and implemented by institutionally independent bodies. Eight ministries of finance are responsible for fiscal policies in each of the WAEMU countries, whereas the BCEAO conducts a single monetary policy in the interest of the region as a whole. The visualization of the WAEMU's financial flows allows identifying the role of individual finance ministries and the BCEAO in the regional system (Figure 3.3). With the nodes proportional to fiscal revenue of individual countries, Côte d'Ivoire is squarely placed in the middle with the largest and presumably most influential finance ministry in the region, followed by Senegal and Burkina Faso. The same countries are linked by the most substantial financial flows. The BCEAO node is proportional to its balance sheet, which is comparable in magnitude to budget revenue of individual countries. The BCEAO is linked to individual countries, as the regional banking system supported by BCEAO liquidity injections provides financing to fiscal deficits. These links are not particularly large relative to other financial flows in the region, which places the BCEAO at a substantial distance from individual countries.

Budget financing and public debts are the two main areas of interaction between fiscal and monetary policies in the WAEMU. Fiscal deficits are set by individual WAEMU governments, often in cooperation with the IMF. The flow of government borrowing translates into changes in the stock of public debt and has immediate implications for public debt levels and sustainability. However, the conditions of government borrowing (for example, interest rate and collateral requirements) and the overall availability of credit resources to the government depend directly

Figure 3.3. WAEMU: Network Interdependence for Policy Coordination

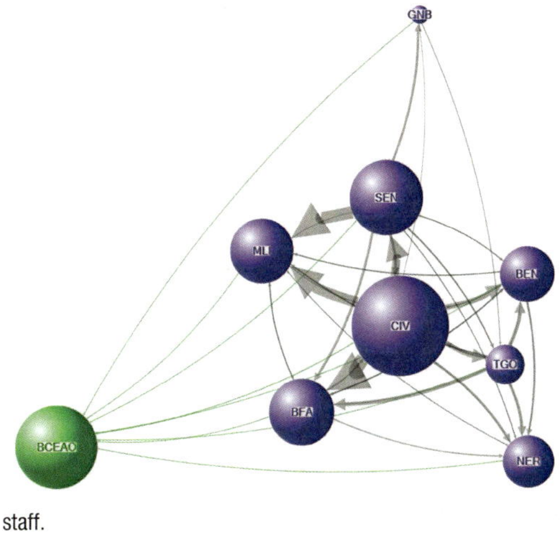

Source: IMF staff.
Note: Three-letter International Organization for Standardization abbreviations used for country names. BCEAO = Central Bank of West African States. Based on the Fruchterman-Reingold (1991) force-directed layout algorithm to determine the attractive forces among countries. The larger the flow, the stronger is the attractive force between the countries it links, assuming the strength of the repulsive force of 10 with 100 iterations per layout.

Figure 3.4. Key Areas of Policy Coordination in the WAEMU

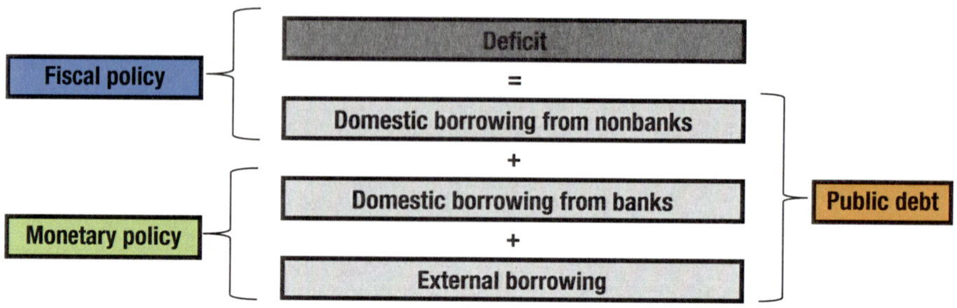

Source: IMF staff.

on the BCEAO's monetary policy (Figure 3.4). To help avoid crowding out of the private sector by excessive government borrowing, and to constrain marginal expenditure decisions, most IMF programs with individual WAEMU countries include explicit ceilings on net domestic credit to governments in addition to the fiscal deficit.

The overall conditions of the fiscal deficit and public debt in the WAEMU are broadly conducive for policy coordination. Fiscal deficits and debt accumulation in the WAEMU are projected to stay on broadly sustainable paths subject to the implementation of good policies as planned by the authorities (Figure 3.5). After a slight increase in the overall fiscal deficit driven by government financing of a large hydrocarbon project in Niger, fiscal consolidation is set to continue in all WAEMU countries, with the exception of Burkina Faso, which intends to scale up investment spending. In the medium term, the rhythm of fiscal consolidation should be slightly slower than projected earlier with the need to finance new development programs and infrastructural projects in most countries. However, fiscal balances are projected to stay within the 3–4 percent of GDP range in the medium term in all WAEMU countries. Total public debt also is projected to remain sustainable, irrespective of a substantial scaling up planned in individual countries. The nominal level of total external and domestic public debt is projected to stay below 40 percent of GDP on average for the WAEMU. Only in Guinea-Bissau, Togo, and Senegal is the level of debt hovering at about 50 percent of GDP, which is the level some of the governments in the region target themselves. In all cases, the overall public debt is well below the WAEMU convergence criteria of 70 percent of GDP, which is considered a ceiling, rather than the targeted level.

Four kinds of interactions between fiscal-monetary policies are possible in the context of the WAEMU. These are illustrated by the option matrix in Figure 3.6. The matrix lays out possible fiscal-monetary policy interaction options for the eight finance ministries and the BCEAO. The two fundamental options are to coordinate policies (Yes) or not to coordinate them (No).

Case I. MoFs and the BCEAO set policy objectives independently

Each WAEMU country prepares its budget without consultation with other members or with the BCEAO. This is possible, as each country has its own economic structure and therefore main revenue streams, mainly related to key commodities (for example, cocoa in Côte d'Ivoire, uranium in Niger, and gold in Mali). Also, WAEMU countries face asymmetric exogenous shocks (droughts or Ebola may affect different countries), and have different policy priorities (geopolitical risks, domestic security situation) with fiscal policy the only instrument to address them. The BCEAO sets interest rates and defines the monetary stance that reflects the priorities of the

Figure 3.5. Fiscal Balances and Public Debt in the WAEMU

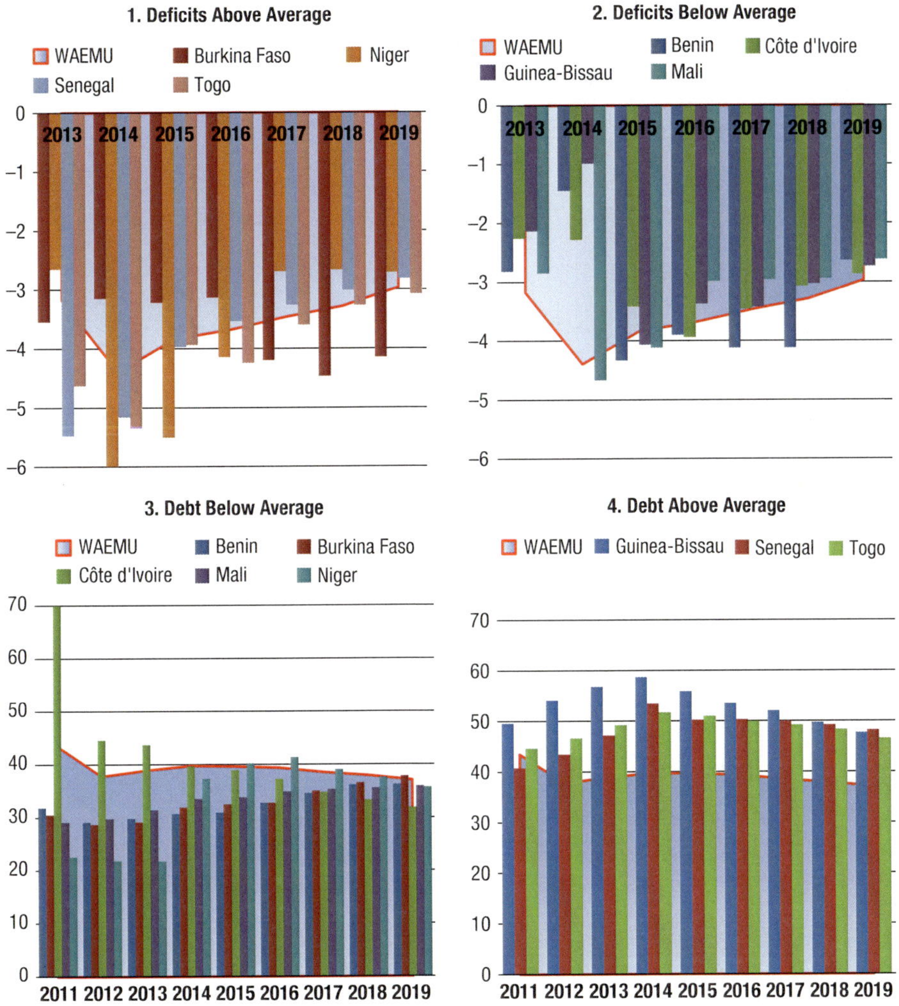

region as a whole, but without consulting with the ministries of finance (MoFs) of individual countries.

Case II. The BCEAO sets monetary stance independently from MoFs' financing needs

This is the case of monetary dominance. The BCEAO sets the policy rate at a level consistent with the money supply needed to achieve the inflation target for the region as a whole. As countries' transmission mechanisms differ, inflation in individual countries may deviate from the targeted level. The BCEAO determines its money supply, mainly the domestic component of reserve money. The resulting policy rate may be too high for national MoFs, which will incur additional debt-servicing costs on interest payments and therefore will have to adjust by expanding their deficits beyond the levels needed for debt sustainability. Alternatively, credit availability may not be sufficient to accommodate both the needs of governments and the private sector.

Figure 3.6. WAEMU: Options for Fiscal-Monetary Policy Coordination

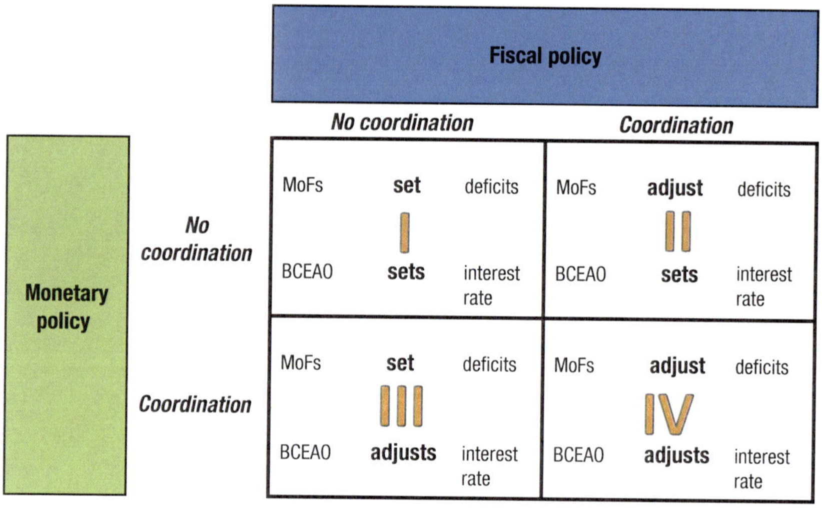

Source: IMF staff presentation.
Note: BCEAO = Central Bank of West African States; MoF = ministry of finance.

Case III. MoFs set fiscal deficits independently from the BCEAO's monetary stance, which has to adjust its policy

This is the case of a complete fiscal dominance. Each country sets its own deficit based on national priorities; national MoFs do not coordinate the levels of deficits. Once national budgets are approved, the BCEAO is informed of the decisions taken at national levels and has to accept the aggregated fiscal deficit at the regional level. Because the governments' financing requirements are given, the BCEAO is forced to adjust its monetary policy by providing direct financing for fiscal deficits, for example in the form of now discontinued statutory advances, or finance them indirectly. In the latter case, through refinancing operation the BCEAO has to provide liquidity to commercial banks in the amounts needed to finance the aggregated fiscal deficit, while leaving sufficient credit resources for the private sector. In this case, the BCEAO cannot control domestic credit and the goal of price stability may be jeopardized. Alternatively, if the overall fiscal deficit at the WAEMU level is too large, the private sector may be crowded out.

Case IV. MoFs coordinate among themselves and with the BCEAO

National MoFs set their deficit targets consistent with short-term national priorities and long-term debt sustainability criteria. They inform each other of the selected paths for the fiscal deficits at an early stage of the annual budget preparation process. The mechanism of regional consultations and exchange of information is used for this purpose. The MoFs consult with the BCEAO on potential monetary effects of their fiscal policies. In turn, the BCEAO preselects the level of the policy rate needed to preserve the inflation target for the region and consults with the MoFs regarding potential fiscal effects of its suggested monetary policy stance. Through this iterative process and mutual adjustments, the appropriate fiscal-monetary policy mix is set for the medium term.

STATUS OF COORDINATION

What is the current status of fiscal-monetary policy coordination in the WAEMU according to these metrics? There is no single answer. There is a certain degree of regional policy coordination in the region. The Council of Ministers, represented in most cases by ministers of finance, is a decision-making body of the WAEMU, and the BCEAO is a specialized autonomous body of the WAEMU. Also, national MoFs share their borrowing plans with the BCEAO on a regular basis and coordinate their debt issuances through the recently established WAEMU Securities Agency. This rules out Case 1 (no coordination). Under a fixed-exchange-rate arrangement, Case 2 (monetary dominance) also should be ruled out. Fiscal policy is clearly the main tool for achieving any national and regional goals, and monetary policy in such an institutional setup can play at best a support role. Case 4 requires a functioning instructional consultative infrastructure and procedures. While the WAEMU commission is charged with fiscal harmonization of tax policies and monitoring convergence criteria, it has no direct authority for fiscal policy coordination. The WAEMU Commission's ability to influence national governments' decisions on the level of fiscal deficit and the sources of their financing is very limited. Also, fiscal coordination is perceived in a very restricted sense, mainly as harmonization of tax levels and providing encouragement to countries to implement WAEMU directives. Ideally, developed financial markets, in particular a secondary market for government securities, are needed, so that price signals could be transmitted between fiscal and monetary policies, with both MoFs and the BCEAO adjusting their stances in an iterative manner. There is clearly not the case in the WAEMU where key financial markets are at an early stage of development.

Therefore, it is possible to argue that national MoFs set fiscal policies with little coordination among each other and with the BCEAO (Case 3). Several facts in recent history could lead one to this conclusion:

1. The overall level of fiscal deficit for the region is largely viewed not as a regional policy variable but rather as a simple aggregation of fiscal deficits adopted by individual countries.
2. Based on financing needs expressed by individual countries, regional monetary policy has to be accommodative in providing the required financing for fiscal deficits from the regional market and ensuring its affordability to governments in terms of its costs.
3. The BCEAO and the WAEMU Commission have limited influence on governments in which there is a need to modify fiscal policy stance based on broader regional considerations.
4. The capacity of the regional financial market to absorb government debt is not sufficiently taken into account in setting the levels of fiscal deficits.
5. Monetary policy considerations (for example, the need to eliminate persistent structural liquidity surpluses in the region), are not taken into account in setting fiscal policies of individual countries.

Current coordination efforts are limited. One consequence of this lack of coordination is the necessity to have binding rules on monetary financing of governments. Direct financing by BCEAO is formally forbidden, while there are some exceptions, refinancing banks on sovereign collateral is limited to 35 percent of fiscal revenue. These rules are a key item of the monetary union. The BCEAO monitors the overall fiscal and debt stance of the region and makes its views known to the national governments through the appropriate WAEMU mechanisms, aggregates fiscal and debt data, and provides indicative ceilings on the resources available to each country in the regional market. The WAEMU commission monitors tax harmonization and implementation of the respective WAEMU directives and convergence criteria. The WAEMU Securities Agency coordinates issuances of government paper on the regional market by individual treasuries, mainly to avoid bunching.

Therefore, there is a strong theoretical and practical argument for fiscal-monetary policy coordination in the WAEMU. There is ample theoretical evidence that Case 4, with mutual adaptation of fiscal and monetary policy on a continuous timeline, would lead to superior outcomes in terms of reaching policy objectives (Gali and Monacelli 2008); (Fragetta and Kirsanova 2010); (Hallett, Libich, and Stehlk 2011); (Daly and Smida 2013). In normal times, MoFs should continue to target-long term debt sustainability while the BCEAO should focus on inflation. This can be achieved through mutual adaptation of the levels of fiscal deficit and the policy rates so as to meet both targets. Ideally, the signals for policy adjustments should be provided by market prices rather than by explicit operational coordination arrangements. But for that, financial market development should be better developed to transmit better policy signals from fiscal and monetary authorities to economic agents, which is not the case in the WAEMU. During times of stress, the fiscal policies of finance ministries should still target debt sustainability, while the BCEAO's monetary policies should target inflation. However, in the short term, the BCEAO should be willing to tolerate temporarily high inflation as a strategy for increasing the likelihood of meeting the inflation target in the long term. Ministries of finances can focus on stabilizing output and employment at the expense of a temporary deviation from a sustainable debt path.

REFERENCES

Blinter, A. 1982. "Issues in the Coordination of Monetary and Fiscal Policy." NBER Working Paper No. 982.

Canzoneri, M., R. Cumby, and B. Diba. 2010. "The Interaction Between Monetary and Fiscal Policy." In *Handbook of Monetary Economics, Volume 3*, edited by B. M. Friedman and M. Woodford, 935-99. San Diego: Elsevier.

Dahan, M. 1988. "The Fiscal Effects of Monetary Policy." May 1998. IMF Working Paper 98/66. International Monetary Fund, Washington.

Daly, H., and M. Smida. 2013. "Coordination of Monetary and Fiscal Policies: Theoretical Overview." Munich Personal RePEc Archive (MPRA) Paper No. 48066.

Fragetta, M., and T. Kirsanova. 2010. "Strategic Monetary and Fiscal Policy Interactions: An Empirical Investigation." *European Economic Review* 54 (7): 855–79.

Fruchterman, T., and J. Reingold, E. M. 1991. "Graph Drawing by Force-Directed Placement." *Software: Practice and Experience* 21(11): 1129–64.

Gali, J., and T. Monacelli. 2008. "Optimal Monetary Policy and Fiscal Policy in a Currency Union." *Journal of International Economics* 76: 116–32.

Hallett, A., J. Libich, and P. Stehlk. 2011. "Welfare Improving Coordination of Fiscal and Monetary Policy." *AUCO Czech Economic Review* 5: 7–26.

Hilbers, P. 2005. "Interaction of Monetary and Fiscal Policies: Why Central Bankers Worry About Government Budgets." IMF Seminar on Current Development in Monetary and Financial Law. International Monetary Fund, Washington.

PART 2

Growth and Inclusiveness

PREFACE

Economic performance in most West African Economic and Monetary Union (WAEMU) countries has strengthened over the past two decades. Most WAEMU countries have weathered well the impact of the global financial crisis, the earlier oil and food price shocks, and later security shocks in the region. Improvements in economic fundamentals, together with focused policy responses to the crises, limited global financial integration, and the relatively fast economic recovery in the largest countries helped to cushion the impact of external shocks at the regional level.

However, despite improvements in fundamentals, the long-term growth in WAEMU countries has been lower than that in sub-Saharan Africa's top-performing countries. Despite higher growth since the mid-1990s, the average per capita income level in the WAEMU remains still broadly at its 1980 level. The divergence with faster-growing sub-Saharan countries became more pronounced in the past two decades, the period dubbed "the great African takeoff."

Why has growth in the WAEMU been lower than growth in the rest of Africa and what can be done about it? This part of the book seeks to answer this pertinent question.

In the last two decades per capita growth has increased only moderately on average in the WAEMU, while it has more than doubled in faster-growing sub-Saharan countries. Chapter 4, Quest for Higher Growth, suggests that the reasons for the growth divergence between the WAEMU and the fastest-growing countries in Africa are complex, and no single factor or simple story emerges. The divergence can be explained by political instability in some WAEMU countries, weak business and legal environments, infrastructural deficiencies, and weak institutional and public investment management capacity relative to other countries in sub-Saharan Africa. These factors may have affected both the level of investment and even more its efficiency, and prevented most WAEMU countries from achieving sustainably high growth. On average, high-growth sub-Saharan African countries fared somewhat better on a range of determinants of per capita growth, pointing to the need for further broad-based reforms in the WAEMU.

One of the reasons for growth underperformance is that the region has been negatively affected by macroeconomic shocks. Chapter 5, Shocks to Growth, explores this reason in more detail. Such shocks can be symmetric, affecting similarly all countries of the Union simultaneously, or asymmetric, affecting just some of the countries in the WAEMU. Asymmetric shocks prevail in the region and their smoothing is limited. Therefore, coordinated fiscal policy has an important role to play in addressing both symmetric and asymmetric shocks. Further integration and strengthening of market-based smoothing mechanisms (for example, developing and improving access to the financial system) would also likely reduce the occurrence and economic impact of asymmetric shocks. A symmetric shock can, in principle, be addressed by a common monetary policy or a coordinated fiscal policy response. For asymmetric shocks, a national fiscal policy response, supported by structural reforms, remains the main available instrument.

Slow structural transformation and export diversification may be yet another reason for the relatively slow growth in the WAEMU. Chapter 6, Structural Transformation and Diversification, takes stock of the WAEMU's progress in this important area. It concludes that slow structural transformation and diversification may explain the relative growth underperformance, as the majority of the population is employed in low-productivity agriculture, which is prone to climatic shocks, while the manufacturing sector remains underdeveloped. Further structural transformation of output and diversification of exports could yield significant growth dividends. Achieving transformation and diversification will be challenging in the context of a rapid projected increase in the workforce over coming decades, much of which would need to be absorbed by the agricultural sector. Policies should focus on easing the constraints to structural transformation in key areas such as education and the business climate, as well as devising a clear strategy for tackling the challenges posed by rapid population growth.

Insufficient inclusiveness across income and gender groups has been an additional constraint to growth in the WAEMU. Chapter 7, Growth Inclusiveness and Equality, demonstrates that growth performance depends heavily on its distributional characteristics. The fundamental question is equality, that is, whether the benefits of growth are shared equally across different income groups and whether all income groups and both genders have an equal opportunity to contribute their fair share to growth. While poverty has fallen in the last two decades in most WAEMU countries, poverty reduction has slowed in recent years. Although available indicators sometimes give conflicting signals on distributional shifts, two case studies—one on Senegal and one on Mali—suggest that people in the middle of the income distribution usually received the most benefit of growth, and mainly in urban areas. Further progress in poverty reduction and inclusiveness would require sustained high growth and exploration of growth opportunities in the sectors with high earning potential for the poor. Better-targeted social policies and more attention to the regional distribution of spending would also help reduce poverty and improve inclusiveness.

To increase growth, WAEMU countries need to mobilize financial resources, including in the regional financial market. Chapter 8, Financing Growth, looks in detail at the regional financial market as an important source for resource mobilization. This market has grown substantially in the past decade but still remains relatively shallow and falls short of supplying sufficient long-term financing for growth-enhancing public and private investment projects. Although the institutional structure for financing mobilization is broadly in place, the undiversified issuer and narrow investor bases, banks' preferences for short-term securities, the limited set of maturities offered by sovereigns, the underdeveloped secondary market for bills and bonds, organizational issues, and limited access to information increase financing costs and hinder market efficiency. Interest rates have been largely driven by country ratings, market liquidity conditions, and bidders' appetites at the time of issuances. The volumes of issuance also mattered for the level of interest rates, with seasonality, issuance procedures, and the frequency and predictability of issues also playing their roles. Further reforms could help the region reap the full benefits of a more dynamic securities market to finance growth-enhancing projects.

CHAPTER 4

Quest for Higher Growth

DOUGLAS SHAPIRO AND ALEKSANDRA ZDZIENICKA

Growth takeoff in Africa has been one of the salient facts of the global economy in the last two decades. However, while per capita GDP has more than doubled in faster-growing sub-Saharan economies during this period, it has increased only moderately on average in the West African Economic and Monetary Union (WAEMU). This divergence can be explained by political instability, challenging business and legal environments, a substantial infrastructure gap, and weak institutional and public investment management capacity in the WAEMU relative to other countries in sub-Saharan Africa. These factors may have affected both the level of investment and, even more, its efficiency—and prevented most WAEMU countries from achieving sustainable high growth.

UNEVEN GROWTH PERFORMANCE

While economic performance has significantly improved in faster-growing sub-Saharan African countries over the last two decades, it has changed only modestly, on average, in the WAEMU (Figure 4.1). Economic growth has increased significantly in a fairly large set of sub-Saharan African countries since the mid-1990s. While natural resources have played a role in a number of countries, a few non-resource-rich sub-Saharan African countries (Cape Verde, Ethiopia, Ghana, Mozambique, Rwanda, Tanzania, Uganda) have also recorded sustained and robust growth, with a doubling of per-capita income during this period. Robust and sustained growth episodes are identified as periods of at least five consecutive years in which per-capita growth has been at least 3 percent (Berg, Ostry, and Zettlemeyer 2008; IMF 2008).

Despite relatively similar initial conditions, average performance in the WAEMU has been much more modest than that in sub-Saharan Africa, with a 20 percent increase in per-capita income since 1995. Growth underperformance in the WAEMU therefore seems to be "more than a commodity story" (IMF 2013a). There are, however, substantial differences across WAEMU countries, with Burkina Faso recording a performance similar to that of Uganda or Tanzania, and others registering a decrease in per-capita GDP (Côte d'Ivoire, Niger, Guinea-Bissau).

This growth divergence between the WAEMU and the sample of fast-growing, non-resource-rich sub-Saharan African countries can be explained using several approaches. First, the differences between the two groups with regard to external and domestic indicators through a benchmarking exercise can be identified. Second, some elements of a growth diagnostic suggested in Haussman, Rodrik, and Velasco (2006) for WAEMU countries can be used. Finally, a growth regression can be used to provide a quantitative assessment of the main factors at play.

FACTORS AFFECTING GROWTH

External volatility, which can affect growth, does not seem to have been higher in the WAEMU than in the rest of the world (Figure 4.2). Average shock synchronization with the rest of the world—a broad measure of country or region-specific shocks—has been broadly similar. Fluctuations of external demand seem to have had a lower impact on growth in the WAEMU than in the benchmark countries. On average, a 1 percentage point change in real GDP growth

Figure 4.1. Growth Performance

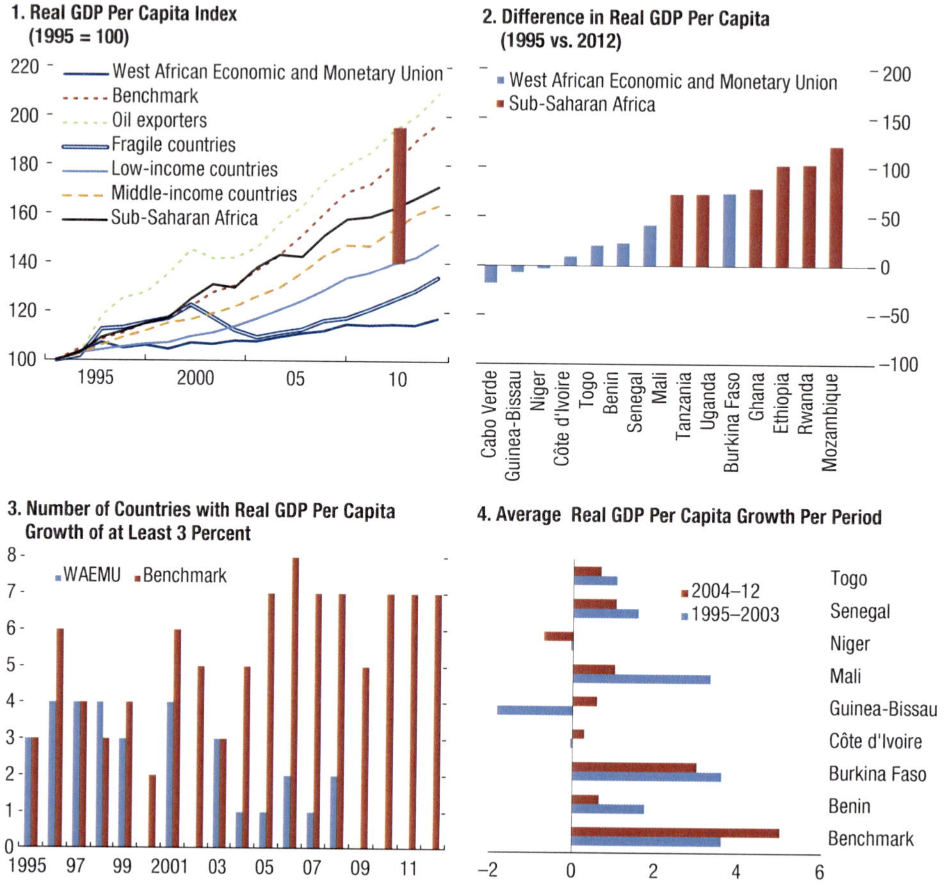

Source: IMF staff computation.

in 95 percent of trading partners led to a 0.1 percentage point change in WAEMU growth and a 0.2 percentage point change in the benchmark growth one year later. Our estimates also suggest that WAEMU countries' growth reacts more slowly to external changes and tracks less closely compared with advanced economies' growth. Terms of trade have had a more favorable trend in the WAEMU, but their volatility seems to have been slightly higher than in the benchmark sample. A similar analysis for individual WAEMU countries supports these conclusions.

WAEMU countries, however, have received less foreign direct investment and foreign aid than have benchmark countries (Figure 4.2). The difference amounts to an (unweighted) average of about 2 percent of GDP over the entire period. There are, however, significant differences across countries. For instance, Niger, Mali, and Togo have received relatively large foreign direct investment inflows, while Guinea-Bissau, Burkina Faso, and to the lesser extent Benin and Niger, received relatively large aid inflows.

A better inflation performance, but also higher external debt and lower and/or less efficient public investment, were recorded in the WAEMU during the last two decades (Figure 4.3). Inflation has been on average lower and much less volatile in the WAEMU, a likely consequence of its exchange rate and monetary regime. Current account deficits have been broadly comparable across the two groups of countries. External debt, however, was on average higher in WAEMU

Figure 4.2. External Environment

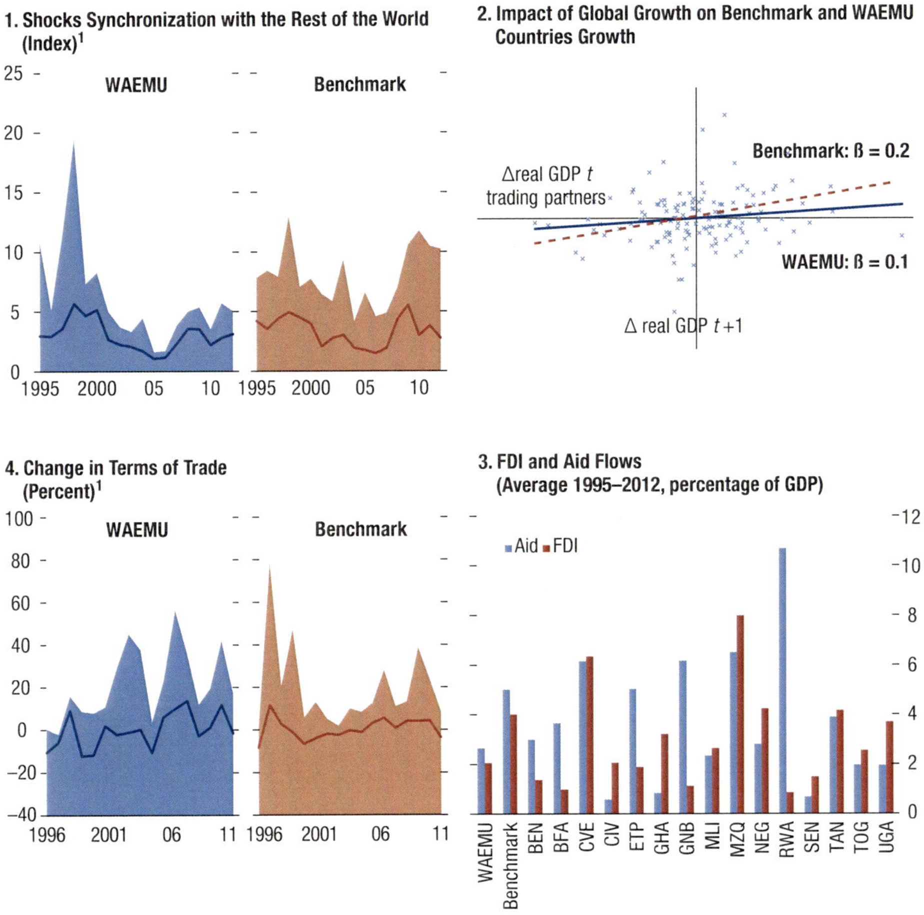

Source: IMF staff computations.
Note: Three-letter International Organization for Standardization abbreviations used for country names.
WAEMU = West African Economic and Monetary Union.
[1] Shaded area corresponds to maximum and minimum values for WAEMU or benchmark countries, lines to unweighted regional average.

countries until recently. Public investment has been higher in benchmark countries on average (particularly so in Cape Verde, Mozambique, and Ethiopia). Differences in public investment ratios, however, have been limited between Burkina Faso, Mali, Benin, Togo, and Senegal and the other benchmark countries, suggesting that public investment efficiency may be lower in the WAEMU.

Lower total factor productivity growth explains a large part of the WAEMU's underperformance (Figure 4.4). Average total factor productivity growth has been negative in Guinea-Bissau, Côte d'Ivoire, Senegal, and Togo and low in Niger, Benin, and Mali. Burkina Faso has been the only WAEMU country with a significant increase in total factor productivity over the last 20 years. This low total factor productivity growth might reflect a number of structural factors, such as limited structural transformation and innovation, weak governance and regulatory frameworks, and, more generally, a more unfavorable business climate in WAEMU countries. Although

Figure 4.3. Macroeconomic Environment

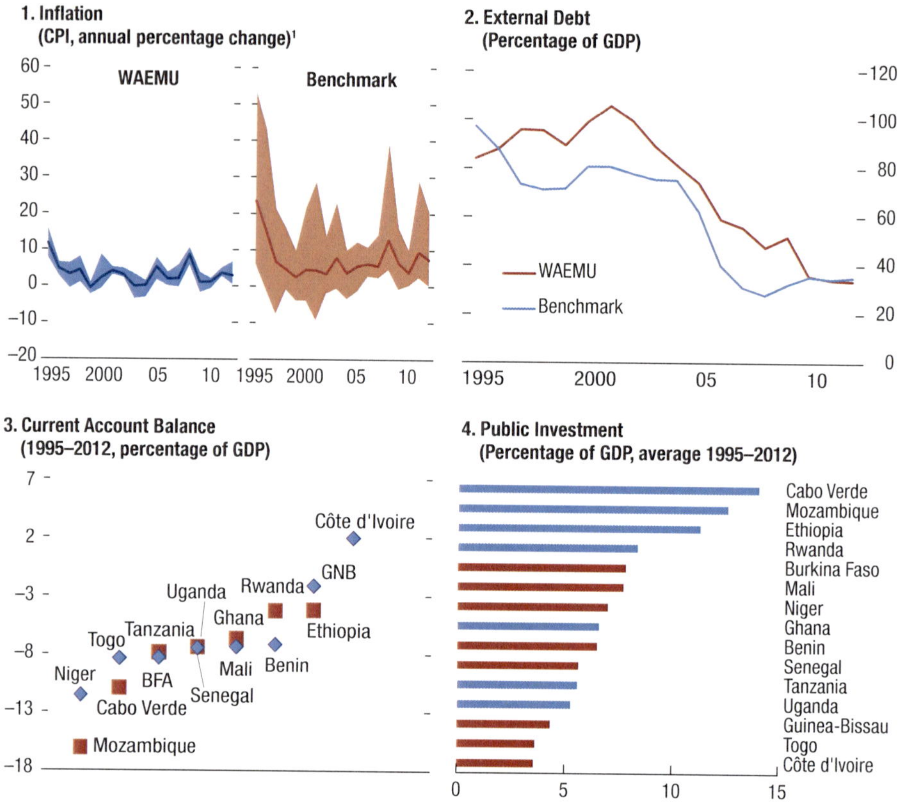

Sources: Barro and Lee (2012); PWT; WITS; and IMF staff calculations.
Note: BFA = Burkina Faso; GNB = Guinea-Bissau; WAEMU = West African Economic and Monetary Union.
[1] Shaded area corresponds to maximum and minimum values for WAEMU or benchmark countries, lines to unweighted regional average.

weak structural competitiveness has been an important impediment for growth in the WAEMU, price competitiveness does not seem to have been an important issue. Since the 1994 devaluation of the CFA franc, the real effective exchange rate has been broadly in line with the region's economic fundamentals. Some of the benchmark economies have actually recorded larger real effective exchange rate appreciations. Slower capital accumulation was also a factor behind the WAEMU's lower growth performance.

Despite increasing openness, the structure of trade and structural competitiveness remain important obstacles to growth in the WAEMU. The two groups of countries have similar degrees of openness (Figure 4.4). One possible reason that this trade openness has not contributed to higher growth in the WAEMU is that structural transformation has been much more limited there on average. In particular, the share of industry and services in GDP has not increased significantly in the WAEMU. The share of industry has actually decreased (except in Côte d'Ivoire), a marked difference from benchmark countries. The share of services in GDP has increased less on average in the WAEMU than it has in the benchmark countries. Also, although export composition has changed in some countries, such as Mali, Togo, and Burkina-Faso, most WAEMU countries continue to export mainly nontransformed commodities. Structural com-

Figure 4.4. Structural Environment

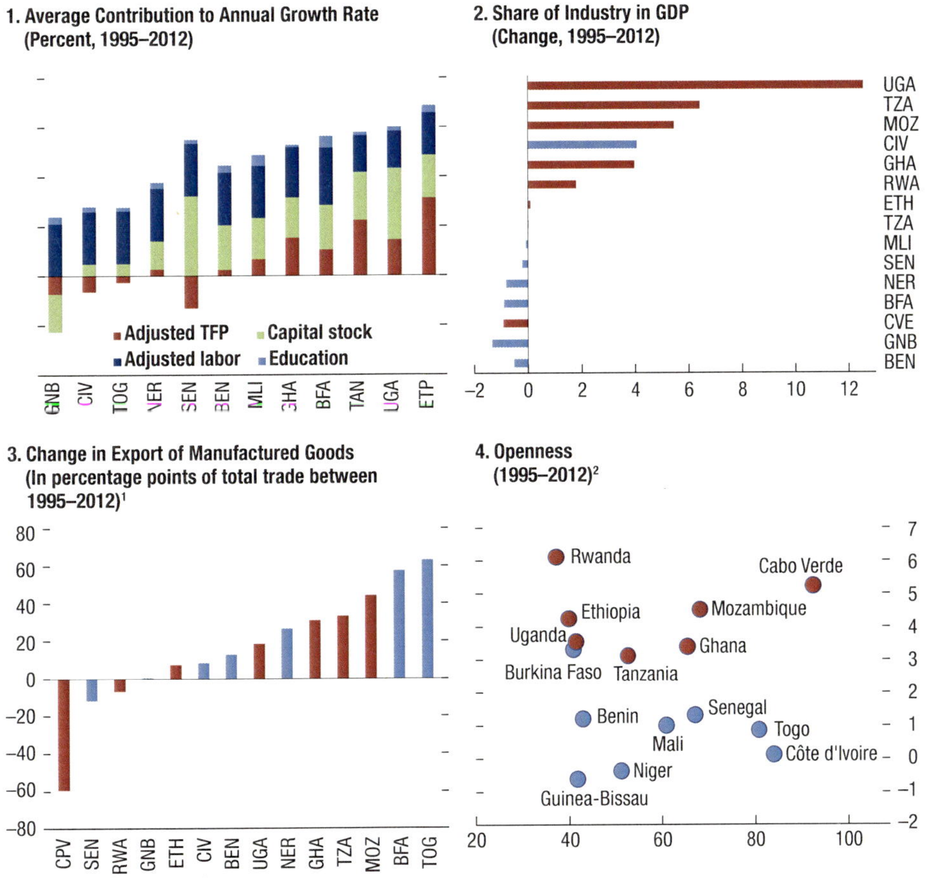

Sources: Barro and Lee (2012); PWT; WITS; and IMF staff calculations.
Note: Three-letter International Organization for Standardization abbreviations used for country names; TFP = total factor productivity.
[1]Chemicals, manufactured goods, commodities; Mali is excluded due to data availability.
[2]Measured as sum of exports and imports over GDP.

petitiveness (measured here by business climate indicators) has also remained low, which may have hampered structural transformation in the WAEMU and the full growth benefits of higher trade integration with the rest of the world.

Institutional quality seems to contribute to the WAEMU underperformance (Figure 4.5). Institutional quality remains an important issue in most sub-Saharan African countries, particularly in the WAEMU. WAEMU countries score significantly lower than do sub-Saharan African countries, on average, on quality of governance and property rights, transparency, accountability, and corruption. WAEMU countries' weaker institutions and governance frameworks, in turn, affect business climate and private investment, both domestic and foreign (Rodrik 1999).

Political instability has played an important role in a number of WAEMU countries. Although on average the number of social conflicts has been similar in both groups of countries, their severity and frequency has been more important in the WAEMU. The economic impact of social unrest has also been larger as illustrated by a slower postconflict recovery in WAEMU countries.

Figure 4.5. Institutional Environment

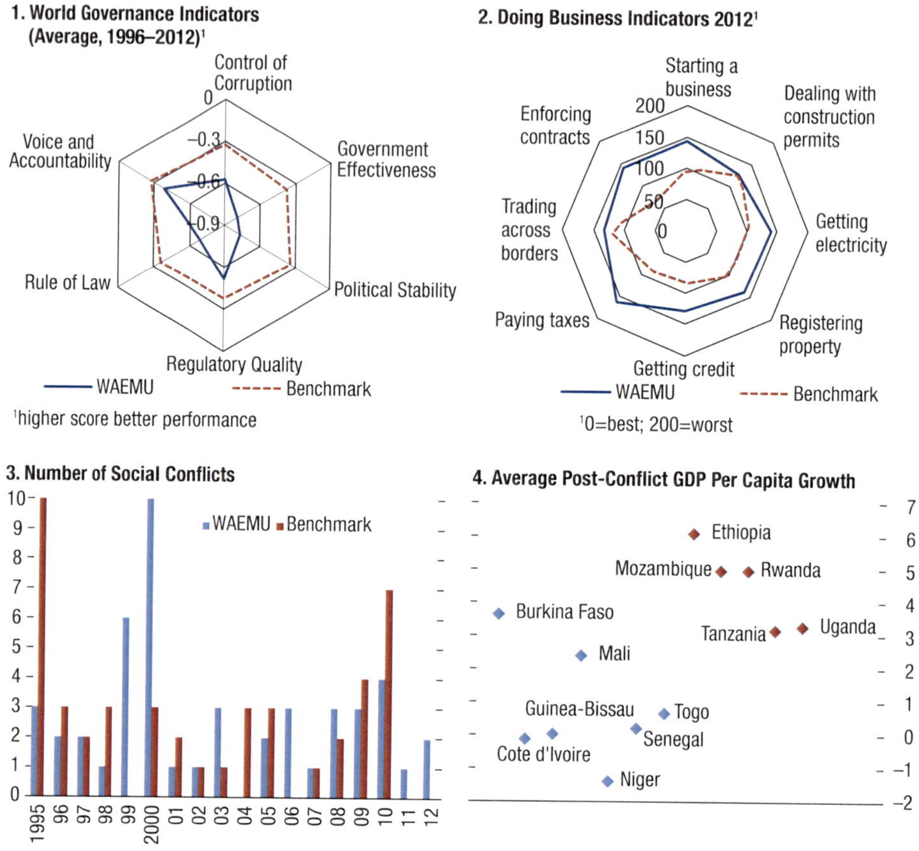

Sources: CNTS; WGI, Doing Business Indicators; and IMF staff computations.
Note: Social conflicts include assassinations, riots, guerrilla warfare, major government crises, purges.

GROWTH DIAGNOSTICS

Differences in private investment explain to some extent lower growth in the WAEMU. As mentioned above, capital accumulation has been slower in the WAEMU. Average domestic private investment and its growth have been lower there (Figure 4.6). Some differences, however, exist across countries. For instance, the level of private investment has been higher in Mali and Senegal, and has increased significantly in Niger in the recent period. In the growth diagnostics framework, two sets of factors can explain low private investment, high cost of finance, and low return on economic activity.

The cost of financing seems to play only a limited role in explaining WAEMU underperformance. Although WAEMU countries have attracted less foreign investment and aggregate domestic savings appear slightly lower, costs and access to capital seem to be broadly similar to those in the benchmark countries. In particular, the development and efficiency of the banking sector appear to be broadly comparable while returns on capital are sometimes lower in the WAEMU (Figure 4.6).

Low return on investment appears to be the biggest obstacle to WAEMU growth in this framework. While social returns to investment seem broadly similar between both groups of

Figure 4.6. Private Investment Environment

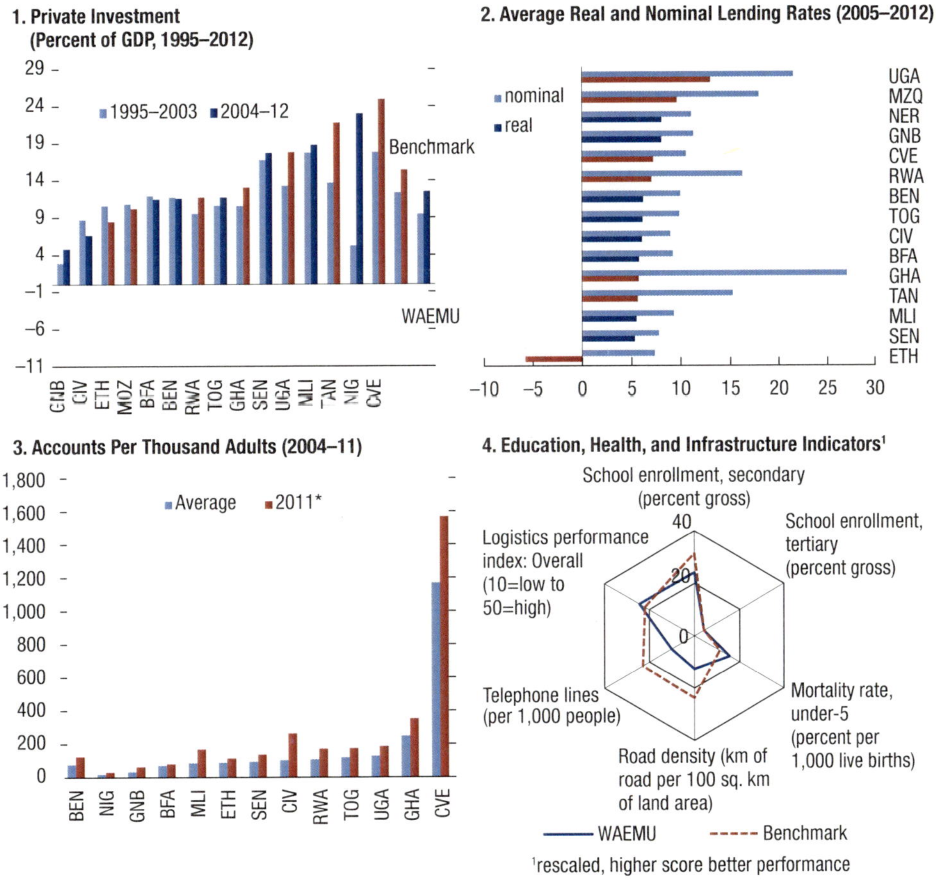

Sources: Central Bank of West African States (BCEAO); FinStats; World Development Indicators (WDI); and IMF staff computations.
Note: Three-letter International Organization for Standardization abbreviations used for country names.
WAEMU = West African Economic and Monetary Union.

countries, high microeconomic risks prevent them from being easily transferred to the individual level. In particular, relatively weaker institutional and legal environments, higher political instability, complicated tax procedures (Figure 4.5) and, sometimes more important infrastructure gaps (Figure 4.6) are the main constraints to increasing the efficiency of private investment and entrepreneurship. An inadequate business environment also prevents the development of new ideas (for example, nontraditional products and higher productivity activities) and these market failures undermine competitiveness and slow structural transformation in the region.

QUANTITATIVE ASSESSMENT

The quantitative assessment points to the role of institutional and macroeconomic factors in explaining growth underperformance in WAEMU countries (Table 4.1). The level of external indebtedness, public investment, and political instability are the main factors explaining the growth differential between WAEMU and benchmark countries. In particular, social conflicts

TABLE 4.1

Growth Regression

	External	Macro	Structural	Institutional		All
Terms of trade growth	−0.005					
	(−0.28)					
Openness	0.04					
	(−0.59)					
Shock synchronization	0.094					
	(−0.39)					
Inflation		0.088				
		(−0.71)				
Current account (% of GDP)		0.121				
		(−0.65)				
External debt (% of GDP)		−0.033**				−0.016***
		(−3.37)				(−4.00)
Public investment (% of GDP)		0.814*				0.425**
		(−2.25)				(−2.59)
Services (% of GDP)			−0.702			
			(−1.12)			
Industry (% of GDP)			−0.147			
			(−1.62)			
Social conflicts				−0.823**	−0.580*	−0.612***
				(−3.94)	(−1.84)	(−2.94)
Governance					−0.912	
					(−0.74)	
N	131	136	136	136	111	135
R^2	0.36	0.35	0.28	0.26	0.24	0.44

Source: IMF staff computation.

Note: Estimations for eight WAEMU countries over the period 1995–2012; Variables are taken in relative terms compared to the benchmark; Governance indicator is computed using a principal component analysis and WGI; Country and time fixed effects included but not reported; *t*-statistics basic on clustered standard errors reported in parenthesis. ***,**,* denote significance at 1%, 5%, and 10%, respectively.

seem to have had a large impact on the growth gap between both groups as an occurrence of a new conflict in the WAEMU increases this differential by about 0.6–0.8 percentage point. The impact of public investment also seems substantial, with a 1 percentage point increase in the public investment-to-GDP ratio in WAEMU countries reducing the growth gap by about 0.5–0.7 percentage point. External indebtedness appears to play a statistically significant, but less important, role. Empirical results also suggest that the quality of institutions and governance, the efficiency of the legal environment, and transparency have an impact on growth by affecting political stability.

These results show that the effect of political instability is significantly reduced when governance variables are controlled for. In addition, the empirical analysis (results available upon request) based on Probit regressions suggests that an improvement in institutional quality significantly decreases the probability of the occurrence of a social conflict. This result is consistent with previous findings in the literature, suggesting that the level of governance plays a significant role in reducing the probability that social conflicts will occur (Bernal-Verdugo, Furceri, and Guillaume 2013) and in accelerating post-conflict recovery (David, Rodrigues Bastos, and Mills 2011).

REFERENCES

Berg, A., J. D. Ostry, and J. Zettelmeyer. 2008. "What Makes Growth Sustained?", IMF Working Paper 8/59, International Monetary Fund, Washington.

Bernal-Verdugo, L. E., D. Furceri, and D. M. Guillaume. 2013. "The Dynamic Effect of Social and Political Instability on Output: The Role of Reforms." IMF Working Paper 13/91, International Monetary Fund, Washington.

David, A. C., F. Rodrigues Bastos, and M. Mills. 2011. "Post-conflict Recovery: Institutions, Aid or Luck?" IMF Working Paper 11/149, International Monetary Fund, Washington.
Hausmann, R., D. Rodrik, and A.Velasco. 2006. "Getting the Diagnosis Right." *Finance and Development*, 43/1, International Monetary Fund, Washington.
International Monetary Fund (IMF). 2008. *Regional Economic Outlook*, October 2008.
———. 2013a. "Sub-Saharan Africa. Keeping the Pace." *Regional Economic Outlook*, October.
Rodrik, D., 1999. "Where Did All the Growth Go? External Shocks, Social Conflict, and Growth Collapses." *Journal of Economic Growth*, Springer, 4(4): 385–412.
World Bank. 2015. World Development Indicators. Washington.
World Bank. 2015. Worldwide Governance Indicators. Washington.

CHAPTER 5

Shocks to Growth

Aleksandra Zdzienicka and Christina Kolerus

Growth in the West African Economic and Monetary Union (WAEMU) has been negatively affected by macroeconomic shocks. Such shocks can be symmetric, affecting similarly all countries of the Union simultaneously, or asymmetric, affecting only some of the countries in the WAEMU. A symmetric shock can, in principle, be addressed by a common monetary policy or a coordinated fiscal policy response. For asymmetric shocks, a national fiscal policy response, supported by structural reforms, remains the main available instrument. An additional constraint in the WAEMU for dealing with shocks is that the exchange rate of the common currency, the CFA franc, is pegged to the euro, which limits the scope for active monetary policy. Therefore, whether or not business cycles are synchronized in the WAEMU and how this synchronization has evolved over time represent important question for policymakers. The analysis presented in this chapter suggests asymmetric shocks prevail in the region and their smoothing is limited. Therefore, coordinated fiscal policy has an important role to play in addressing both symmetric and asymmetric shocks. Further integration and strengthening of market-based smoothing mechanisms (for example, developing and improving access to the financial system) would also likely reduce the occurrence and economic impact of asymmetric shocks.

SHOCK VULNERABILITY OF GROWTH

Shocks in the WAEMU have been frequent and often asymmetric. Some of them have been of a political nature, as illustrated by the crises experienced in the past few years in Côte d'Ivoire, Guinea-Bissau, and Mali. The region is also affected by a large number of exogenous shocks of various natures. These include climate-related shocks (for example, droughts and floods), which take a heavy toll on populations and agriculture, and economic shocks (for example, terms of trade gyrations). These exogenous shocks have had a large impact on key sectors and the cost of living. More generally, business cycle synchronization within the WAEMU seems low.

Addressing these shocks, while preserving the stability of the Union, is therefore a critical issue. With a limited scope for monetary policy responses and in the absence of fiscal transfers at the regional level, national fiscal policies should, in principle, play an important role in the response to shocks, both symmetric and asymmetric. The scope for countercyclical fiscal policies is, however, constrained by the limited development of the financial sector in the WAEMU. In addition, preserving debt sustainability and the stability of the Union in the medium term require strong coordination of fiscal policies. The experience of the euro area has shown that fiscal discipline in each member of a monetary union is critical for the stability of the union, and that this discipline could be weakened by externalities, such as a noncredible no-bailout commitment.

The monetary policy framework in the WAEMU has ensured price and exchange rate stability, but reduces the ability of member countries to respond to asymmetric shocks. This framework has produced substantial benefits in terms of price and exchange rate stability and convertibility of the CFA franc. At the same time, it can make maintaining macroeconomic stability more challenging if the business cycles of the member countries are not well synchronized and stabilization mechanisms aimed at absorbing common and idiosyncratic shocks are absent or ineffective (Karras 2006).

Figure 5.1. Vulnerabilites of WAEMU Economies

Some member states rely heavily on agriculture and economies are poorly diversified...

1. Sectoral Composition of GDP, 2012
(Percent)

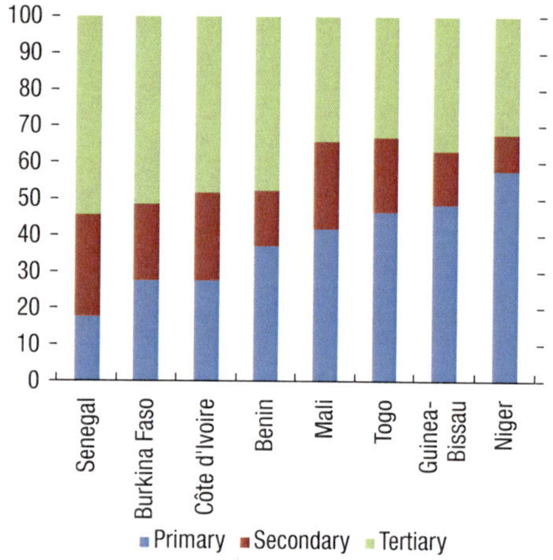

...while the financial sector remains relatively shallow.

2. Broad Money, End 2011
(As percent of GDP)

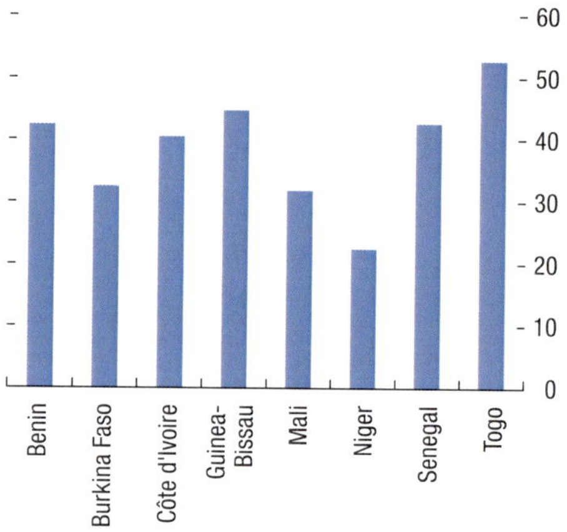

The export pattern reflects both the lack of diversification and strong heterogeneity among WAEMU countries.

3. WAEMU Export Categories, Average 2000–2010
(Percent of total exports)

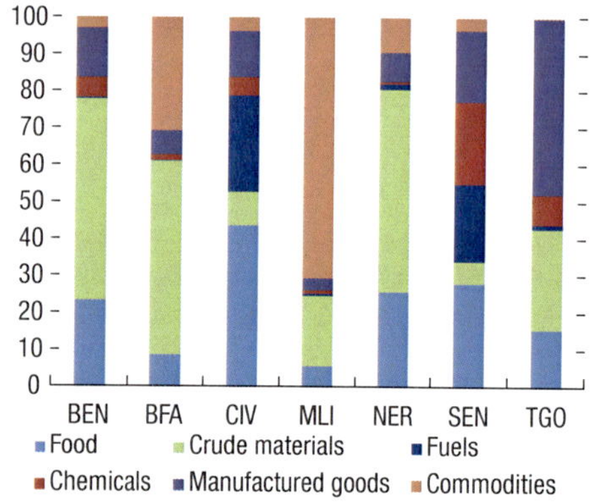

The region's economies are exposed to shocks in Europe, emerging Asia, and neighboring Africa.

4. Top Three Export Markets, Average 2000–2011
(Percent of total exports)

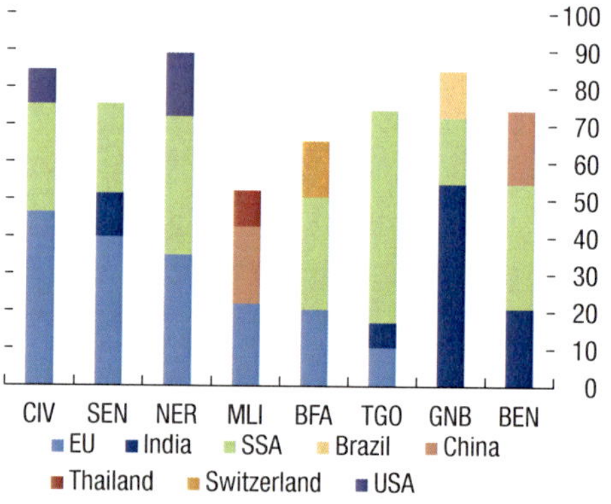

In line with heterogenous trade patterns, Intraregional Trade has remained relatively small.

5. Intraregional Trade
(1990–2011, In percentage of total trade)

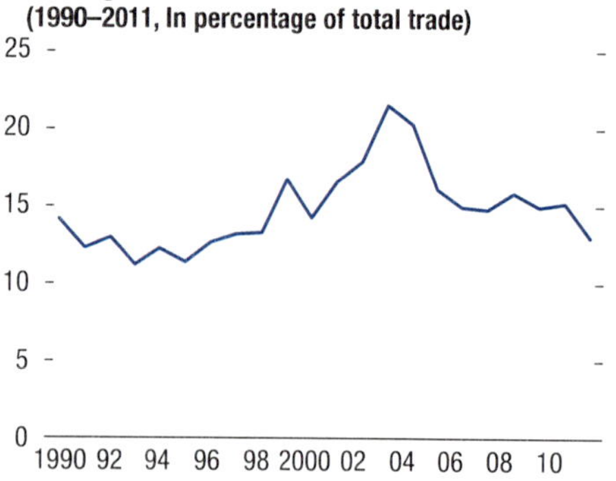

As a consequence, real GDP Growth has been volatile during the past decades reflecting large vulnerabilities.

6. WAEMU Real GDP Growth
(1980–2012, In percent)

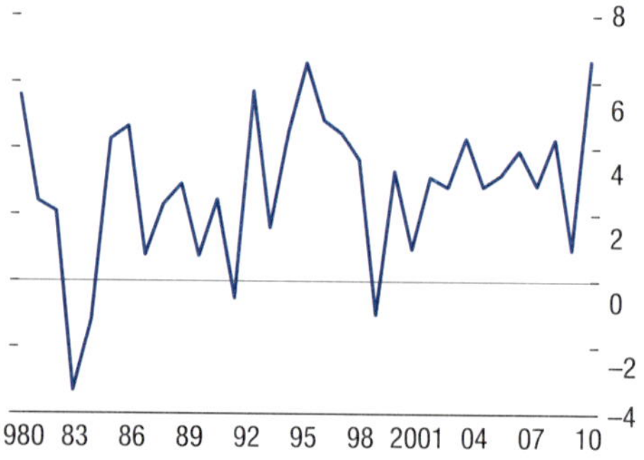

Sources: Central Bank of West African States; DTTS; WITS; and IMF staff calculations.
Notes: Three-letter International Organization for Standardization abbreviations used for country names.
WAEMU = West African Economic and Monetary Union.

TABLE 5.1

WAEMU: Business Cycle Correlation with WAEMU Aggregate[1] (1980–2012)

	1980s	1990s	2000s	Since 2007
Benin	0.37	0.12	0.47	–0.11
Burkina Faso	0.76	0.57	0.71	0.44
Guinea-Bissau	0.35	–0.13	0.26	0.03
Côte d'Ivoire	0.63	0.03	0.30	0.15
Mail	0.36	0.63	0.90	0.43
Niger	0.34	0.11	0.56	0.41
Senegal	0.12	0.14	0.39	0.05
Togo	0.22	–0.80	–0.03	0.17
Average	0.39	0.08	0.45	0.20

Source: IMF staff estimations.
[1] Each country is taken out in the computation of the WAEMU aggregate for its respective correlation.

Susceptibility to idiosyncratic shocks reflects structural characteristics and a lack of integration. The degree of business cycle synchronization depends on factors such as the similarity of economic structure, trade and financial openness, the presence and type of idiosyncratic shocks, and the efficiency of adjustment mechanisms to deal with such shocks (De Grauwe 2005). Some authors (Frankel and Rose 1998) have argued that business cycle synchronization may be endogenous and increase over time with the level of economic integration within a monetary union. WAEMU countries are characterized by heterogeneous economic structures. In addition, limited economic diversification and a range of geographical conditions make them prone to output volatility. Although they have been members of a monetary union for decades, trade, labor, and capital market integration has not progressed significantly. Output volatility remains large (Figure 5.1).

BUSINESS CYCLE AND SHOCK CONVERGENCE

Business cycle synchronization in the WAEMU has been modest (Table 5.1).[1] Over the period 1980–2012, business cycle synchronization in the WAEMU has averaged at about 0.2, ranging from about -0.2 for Togo (the less-synchronized economy) to about 0.5 for Mali and 0.6 for Burkina Faso (the most-synchronized economies). The degree of business cycle synchronization has varied over the last three decades, with a low point during the 1990s and an increase during the 2000s. Synchronization has decreased again during the most recent years, possibly reflecting political instability in a number of countries (Côte d'Ivoire, Guinea-Bissau, Mali). Business cycle correlation has tended to be higher in landlocked countries (Burkina Faso, Mali, Niger), which are more dependent on intra-WAEMU trade, and lower in countries with higher extra-zone trade links (Benin, Senegal, Togo).

The business cycles of many WAEMU countries have become more synchronized with that of the euro area (Table 5.2). This synchronization has become relatively strong in several countries in the recent period (with the notable exceptions of Côte d'Ivoire, probably due to its political crisis at the time, and Togo). This increased correlation may reflect the impact of the global crisis. Business cycle correlation with China (taken as a proxy for emerging markets) remains limited on average, except for Guinea-Bissau and Senegal.

[1] Business cycle synchronization measures for WAEMU countries are obtained by: (1) de-trending the series of real GDP using a Hodrick-Prescott filter with a smoothness parameter equal to 1 (Rand and Tarp 2002); and (2) computing the correlation between the country's cyclical component and WAEMU's cyclical component.

TABLE 5.2

WAEMU: Business Cycle Correlation with the Euro Area and China (1990–2012)

	The Euro Area			China		
	1990s	2000s	Since 2007	1990s	2000s	Since 2007
Benin	−0.53	0.39	0.40	−0.71	0.16	0.16
Burkina Faso	−0.53	0.00	0.47	−0.01	−0.07	−0.08
Guinea-Bissau	−0.01	0.34	0.58	0.01	0.01	0.33
Côte d'Ivoire	−0.95	−0.44	−0.30	0.15	−0.27	−0.09
Mali	−0.44	−0.21	0.43	−0.55	−0.04	−0.20
Niger	−0.32	0.15	0.55	−0.07	−0.02	−0.08
Senegal	0.14	0.18	0.94	0.12	0.17	0.86
Togo	0.73	−0.25	−0.37	−0.40	0.02	−0.51
WAEMU	−0.84	−0.14	0.02	−0.08	−0.09	0.00

Source: IMF staff estimations.

BOX 5.1. Structural Shock Convergence

Structural shock convergence is assessed following a two-step approach. In the first step, three types of structural shocks—supply, real demand, and nominal—are identified using a structural vector autoregressive (VAR) model[1] with the Blanchard and Quah (1989) long-term restrictions, as developed by Clarida and Gali (1994).

$$\begin{pmatrix} \Delta y_t \\ \Delta reer_t \\ \Delta p_t \end{pmatrix} = \begin{pmatrix} A_{11} & A_{12} & A_{13} \\ A_{12} & A_{22} & A_{23} \\ A_{13} & A_{23} & A_{33} \end{pmatrix} \begin{pmatrix} e_{supply,t} \\ e_{real\ dem,t} \\ e_{nominal,t} \end{pmatrix} \quad (1)$$

In particular, it is assumed that: (1) only supply shocks, such as productivity or demographic shocks, affect output (Δy_t) in the long term; (2) both supply and real demand shocks (government spending or change in fiscal policy) affect the real exchange rate ($\Delta reer_t$) in the long term; and (3) all shocks influence prices (Δp_t). These restrictions require that $A_{12} = A_{13} = A_{23} = 0$. The structural shocks are serially uncorrelated and have a covariance matrix normalized to the identity matrix. A reduced-form of the VAR model is then estimated and the time series of structural shocks are recovered.

In the second step, a dynamic space-state model using the Kalman filter technique[2] is estimated to assess how shock convergence has evolved.

$$(e_t^w - e_t^i) = \alpha_t + \beta_t\,(e_t^w - e_t^k) + \omega_t \quad (2)$$

The dependent variable in (2) represents asymmetric shocks, measured as the difference between shocks affecting WAEMU (e_t^w) and each country (e_t^i). A time-varying coefficient β_t getting closer to zero is interpreted as increasing convergence, while β_t close to one suggests that shocks affecting the rest of the world (e_t^k) affect countries in an asymmetric fashion. α_t denotes the time-varying coefficients, capturing idiosyncratic shocks not related to the external environment. The two time-varying coefficients are shown in Figure 5.2.

[1] The data are annual and taken from the IMF database; they cover the period 1970–2012.
[2] See Boone (1997), Babetski, Boone, and Maurel (2003), and Zdzienicka (2010) for details.

Supply shocks have not converged across all WAEMU countries. The methodology used to identify various kinds of shocks and their dynamics is detailed in Box 5.1. Supply shocks appear very heterogeneous among WAEMU members. In Burkina Faso, Mali, Niger, and Senegal, supply shocks have become more asymmetric (Figure 5.2). They have become more symmetric in other countries.[2]

[2] Similar analysis shows a higher symmetry of demand shocks in the WAEMU.

Figure 5.2. Dynamics in Supply Shocks Convergence in the WAEMU (1994–2012)

1. Burkina Faso, Mali, Niger, and Senegal

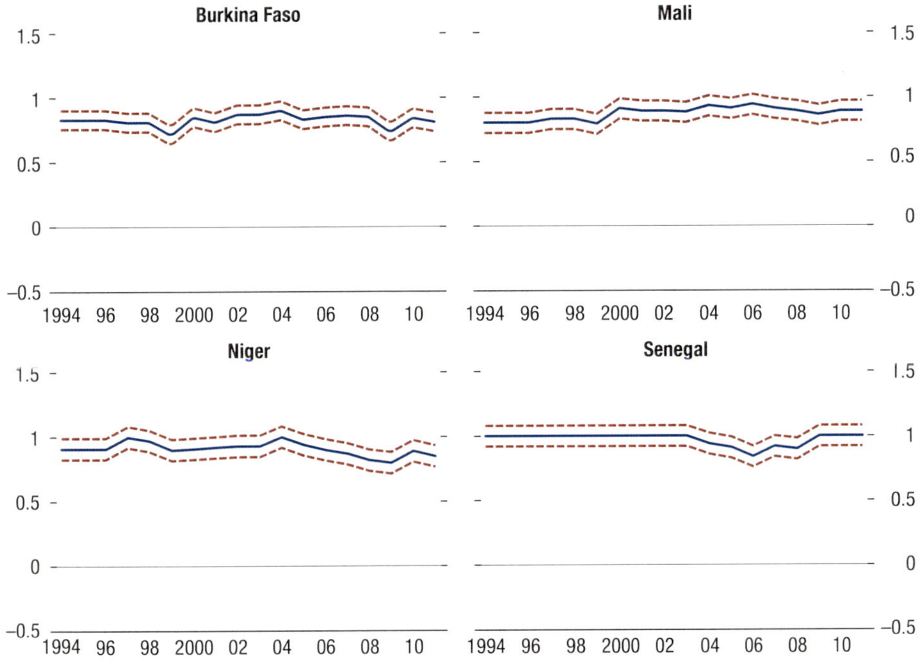

2. Benin, Côte d'Ivoire, Guinea-Bissau, and Togo

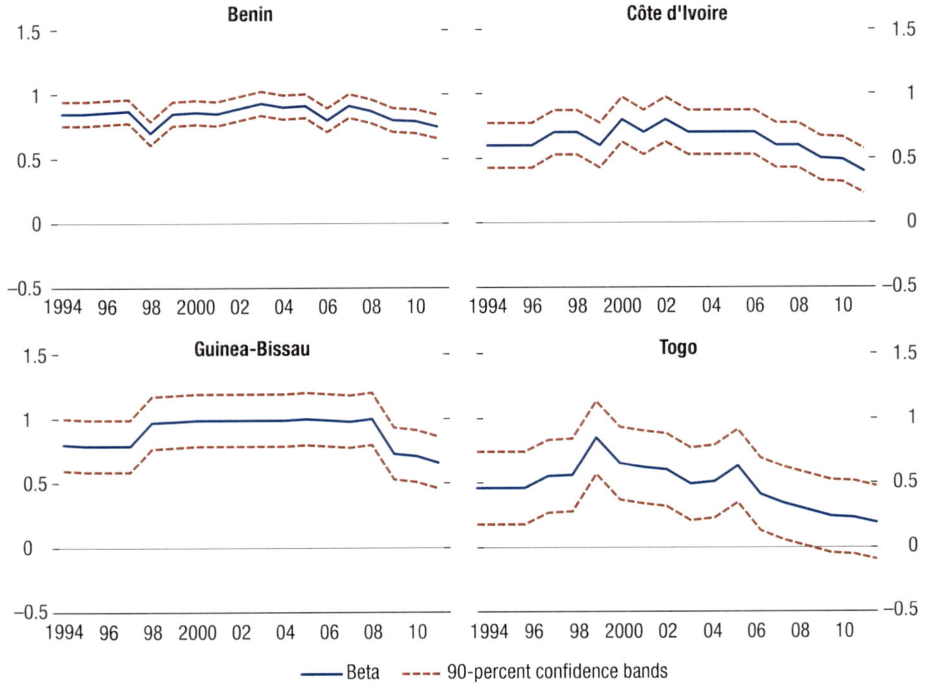

Source: IMF staff calculations.

Figure 5.3. The Effect of the Monetary Policy Rate on Credit Growth
(Percentage points)

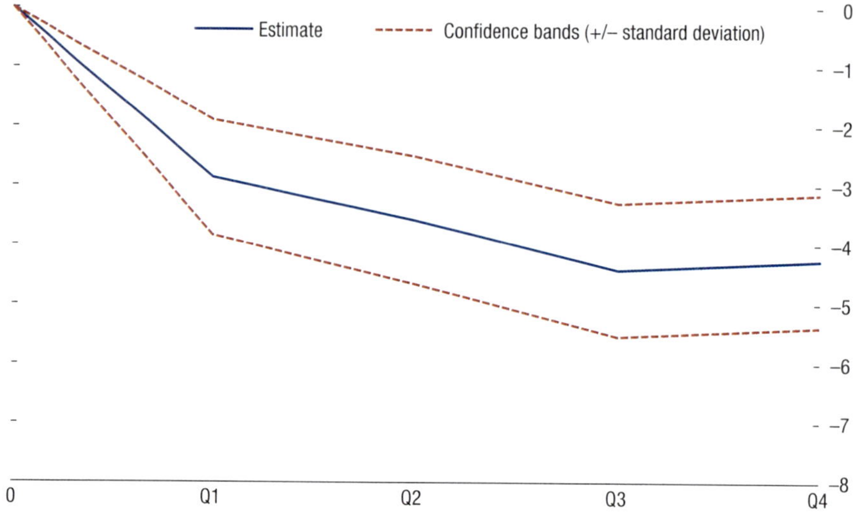

Source: IMF staff estimates.

SHOCK-SMOOTHING MECHANISMS

In principle, in the WAEMU, as in any monetary union, monetary policy should be the primary mechanism to address symmetric shocks. Although the CFA franc is pegged to the euro, there is some scope for an active monetary policy in the WAEMU because of limited capital mobility. The most important transmission channel of monetary policy in the region is the bank lending channel. While transmission is imperfect due to a shallow interbank market, there is a correlation of about 0.5 between policy rates and interbank market rates after one to four quarters. The absence of a secondary government debt market and relatively illiquid equity and real estate markets make it difficult for the asset and interest rate channels to be effective.

However, monetary policy seems to have relatively small impact on economic activity via the credit market.[3] An increase of 100 basis points in the main monetary policy rate is found to decrease private credit growth by about 3 percentage points after one quarter and 4 percentage points after one year (noncumulative) (Figure 5.3). Reserve requirements are found not to affect credit growth in the short term. When testing the effect of changes in both interest rates and reserve requirements by means of an index, the impact of monetary policy is higher.

Rather, smoothing the impact of macroeconomic shocks occurs mainly through a range of other mechanisms. Among them: (1) private insurance via international capital markets (for example, through the holding of diversified portfolios of international assets or explicit insurance); (2) saving and borrowing via international credit markets; (3) private transfers (for example, remittances) and official ones (for example, foreign aid); and (4) fiscal risk sharing across countries (for example, via intra-union transfers). A methodology to measure the effect of some of these mechanisms is presented in Box 5.2.

[3]The impact of monetary policy measures is identified by estimating panel regression equations of the changes in the monetary policy rate on private sector credit up to four quarters ahead.

BOX 5.2. Measuring the Effectiveness of Smoothing Mechanisms

The effectiveness of shock-smoothing mechanisms in the WAEMU is estimated using the approach proposed by Asdrubali, Sorensen, and Yosha (1996). The approach consists in disaggregating GDP into different national account aggregates: gross national product (GNP), net national income (NI), disposable national income (DNI), and the sum of government consumption and private consumption (G+C). Using these aggregates, GDP can be decomposed as follows:

$$GDP_i = \frac{GDP_i}{GNP_i}\frac{GNP_i}{NI_i}\frac{NI_i}{DNI_i}\frac{DNI_i}{(C+G)_i}(C+G)_i \tag{1}$$

where i denotes each WAEMU state. Each ratio measures a specific smoothing mechanism. For instance, if $\frac{GDP_i}{GNP_i}$ varies like GDP_i, then smoothing is taking place through international income transfers (which reduces GNP variations). The $\frac{GNP_i}{NI_i}$ ratio will measure smoothing through capital depreciation or unilateral transfers (foreign aid). Further smoothing may take place through net international transfers and taxes $\left(\frac{NI_i}{DNI_i}\right)$ and total saving $\left(\frac{DNI_i}{(C+G)_i}\right)$.

Full smoothing of shocks (deviations from the trend) occurs if total consumption remains unchanged when GDP varies.

To measure the contribution of each factor (channel) in smoothing shocks to GDP, we take the log and first difference of both sides of equation (1), and we multiply each term by $\Delta\log GDP_i$. The cross-sectional variance in GDP is then divided by $\Delta\log GDP_i$, to obtain the following equation:

$$1 = \beta^m + \beta^d + \beta^g + \beta^v + \beta^s + \beta^u \tag{2}$$

The β^s are then estimated running the following system of independent panel regressions:

$$\Delta\log GDP_{i,t} - \Delta\log GNP_{i,t} = \alpha_t^m + \beta^m \Delta\log GDP_{i,t} + \varepsilon_{i,t}^m \tag{3}$$

$$\Delta\log GNP_{i,t} - \Delta\log NI_{i,t} = \alpha_t^d + \beta^d \Delta\log GDP_{i,t} + \varepsilon_{i,t}^d \tag{4}$$

$$\Delta\log NI_{i,t} - \Delta\log DNI_{i,t} = \alpha_t^g + \beta^g \Delta\log GDP_{i,t} + \varepsilon_{i,t}^g \tag{5}$$

$$\Delta\log DNI_{i,t} - \Delta\log(DNI+G)_{i,t} = \alpha_t^p + \beta^p \Delta\log GDP_{i,t} + \varepsilon_{i,t}^p \tag{6.1}$$

$$\Delta\log(DNI+G)_{i,t} - \Delta\log(C+G)_{i,t} = \alpha_t^s + \beta^s \Delta\log GDP_{i,t} + \varepsilon_{i,t}^s \tag{6.2}$$

$$\Delta\log(C+G)_{i,t} = \alpha_t^u + \beta^u \Delta\log GDP_{i,t} + \varepsilon_{i,t}^u \tag{7}$$

Each β measures the incremental percentage of smoothing achieved by each channel described above[1] and β^u measures the part of the shock to GDP which is not smoothed. The β coefficients are not constrained; a negative value indicates amplification, rather than smoothing, of a shock. The α_t^u coefficients capture time fixed effects.

[1] Table 5.3 presents how the β coefficients changed over time. Capital depreciation (equation 4) and net tax and transfers (equation 5) channels are reported jointly because of data availability issues.

TABLE 5.3

WAEMU: Channels of Output Smoothing

Risk-Smoothing Channels[1]	B Coefficient[2] 1980–2010	1980–1994	1995–2010
Factor income flows	0.068**	0.170	0.205***
	[−1.91]	[0.39]	[2.84]
Capital depreciation &	0.098	0.138	−0.006
Net tax and transfers	[−1.27]	[1.30]	[−0.04]
Saving			
Public	0.004	0.261	0.151
	[0.90]	[0.51]	[1.24]
Private	0.055	0.087	−0.179
	[0.46]	[0.61]	[−0.54]
Unsmoothed	0.878***	0.884***	0.830***
	[8.56]	[7.94]	[2.83]

Source: IMF staff estimates.
[1] Indicates the risk-smoothing channels identified by equation (4)–(7) in Box 5.2.
[2] Reports the percentage of smoothing achieved by each channel; ***, **, * denotes significance at 1%, 5%, 10%, respectively.

Shock smoothing, while on the rise, remains limited in WAEMU countries (Table 5.3). A large share of shocks to GDP (about 83 percent in the period between 1995 and 2000) is not smoothed in the WAEMU, which generates substantial consumption volatility (and likely welfare losses). In particular, net taxes and transfers and public and private saving do not have a statistically significant effect on consumption smoothing. The main (statistically significant) smoothing mechanism in the recent period has been factor income (most likely remittances, which have been shown to be countercyclical). Smoothing has modestly increased over the past three decades. The limited amount of smoothing likely reflects a number of factors: (1) limited access to credit markets, which reduces the scope for countercyclical fiscal policies (with possible adverse implications for investment volatility too); (2) the fact that most aid flows tend to be procyclical; and (3) the absence of significant risk-sharing mechanisms at the level of the region.

REFERENCES

Asdrubali, P., B., Sorensen, B., and O. Yosha. 1996. "Channels of Interstate Risk Sharing: United States 1963–90." *Quarterly Journal of Economics* 111, 1081–1110.

Babetski, J., L. Boone, and M. Maurel. 2003. "Exchange Rate Regimes and Supply Shocks Asymmetry: The Case of the Accession Countries." CERGE-EI, Working Paper Series 206.

Blanchard, O. J., and D. Quah. 1989. "The Dynamic Effects of Aggregate Demand and Supply Disturbances." *American Economic Review* 79 (4).

Boone, L. 1997. "Symmetry and Asymmetry of Supply and Demand Shocks in the European Monetary Union." Paris, Centre de recherche français dans le domaine de l'économie internationale (CEPII) Working Paper, 97/.

Clarida, R., and J. Gali. 1994. "Sources of Real Exchange Rate Fluctuations: How Important Are Nominal Shocks?" Rochester, Carnegie-Rochester Conference Series on Public Policy, 41.

De Grauwe, P. 2005. *Economics of Monetary Union.* Oxford: Oxford University Press.

Frankel, J., and A. K. Rose. 1998. "The Endogeneity of the Optimum Currency Area Criteria." *Economic Journal* 108 (449): 1009–25.

Karras, G. 2006. "Is Africa an Optimum Currency Area? A Comparison of Macroeconomic Costs and Benefits." *Journal of African Economies* 16 (2): 234–58.

Rand, J., and F. Tarp. 2002. "Business Cycles in Developing Countries Are They Different?" *World Development* 30 (12): 2071–88.

Zdzienicka, A. 2010. "The Dynamics of Structural Shocks." *The IUP Journal of Monetary Economics* 8 (3): 31–59.

CHAPTER 6

Structural Transformation and Diversification

JOHN HOOLEY AND MONIQUE NEWIAK

Growth in the West African Economic and Monetary Union (WAEMU) in the past has been overall disappointing and highly volatile compared with growth in a group of comparator countries. Slow structural transformation and diversification may explain this relative underperformance, as the majority of the population is employed in low-productivity agriculture, which is prone to climatic shocks, while the manufacturing sector remains underdeveloped. Further structural transformation of output and diversification of exports could yield significant growth dividends. Achieving transformation and diversification will be challenging in the context of a rapid projected increase in the workforce over coming decades, much of which would need to be absorbed by the agricultural sector. Policies should focus on easing the constraints to structural transformation in key areas such as education and the business climate, as well as on devising a clear strategy for tackling the challenges posed by rapid population growth.

GROWTH, VOLATILITY, AND PRODUCTIVITY

Growth in the WAEMU in the past has been comparatively weak and highly volatile (Figure 6.1). Despite a lower starting level of income per capita, WAEMU countries—both on average and individually—have grown more slowly over the past two decades relative to the rest of sub-Saharan Africa. With real per capita growth averaging only 0.5 percent over the past 25 years, the WAEMU has disappointed relative to a set of peer countries in both sub-Saharan Africa and Asia, which had a similar level of per capita income to the WAEMU in 1990, but are now almost two times richer in purchasing power parity (PPP) terms.[1] This underperformance has been most pronounced since the turn of the century; although growth in the WAEMU was weaker in absolute terms in the 1990s, it is the 2000s that appears to be a lost decade of sorts. In this period, growth took off in many low-income countries, but saw only a slight acceleration in the WAEMU. Growth also remains relatively more volatile than it does in peer countries, despite having declined in recent years.

Comparatively low human capital accumulation and total factor productivity appear to have driven slow growth (Figure 6.2). A growth decomposition exercise suggests that two-thirds of growth over the past two decades can be attributed to labor accumulation, while capital accumulation accounts for almost a third. In contrast, human capital and productivity appear to have been the main drivers of the mediocre growth performance, and are the factors in which the

[1]The WAEMU had a per capita income in 1990 of $805 in purchasing power parity (PPP) terms compared with $1,401 in 2013. A sub-Saharan Africa peer group consisting of Lesotho, Kenya, Rwanda, Ghana, Tanzania, Zambia, and Uganda had an average per capita income of $765 in 1990 vs. $2,003 in 2013. And an Asian peer group of India, Laos, Bangladesh, Vietnam, and Cambodia had an average per capita income of $649 in 1990 vs. $2,887 in 2013.

Figure 6.1 WAEMU: Growth and Volatility

Output growth per capita in the WAEMU has been relatively weak over the past two decades...

1. GDP Per Capita
(Current U.S. dollars, purchasing power parity)

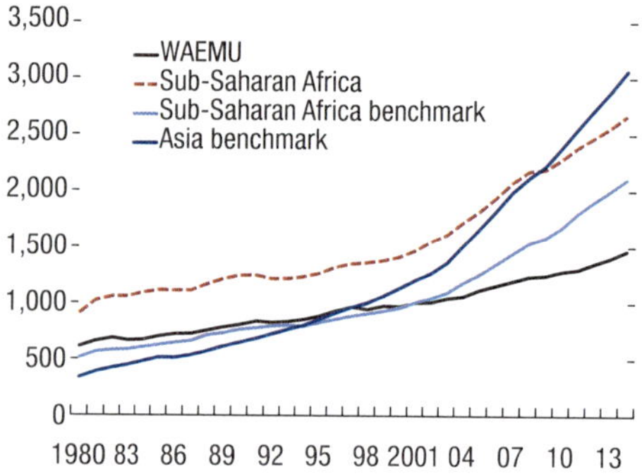

Sources: IMF; and World Bank.

...both on average and across individual member countries.

2. GDP Per Capita
(Current U.S. dollars, purchasing power parity)

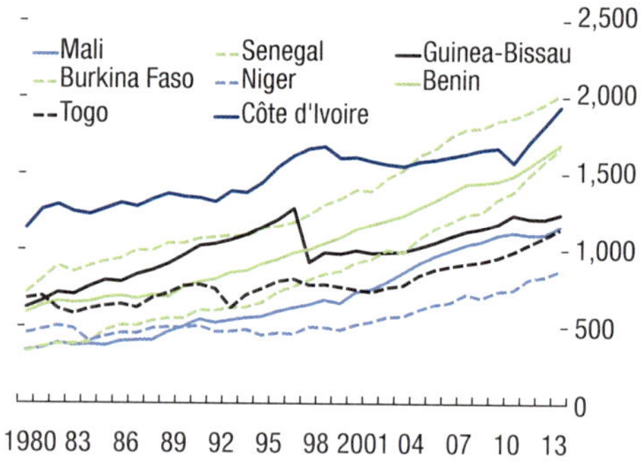

Source: IMF *World Economic Outlook*.

Growth was particularly weak in the 2000s relative to peers—a "lost decade" perhaps?

3. Real GDP Per Capita Growth 1990–2013
(In percent)

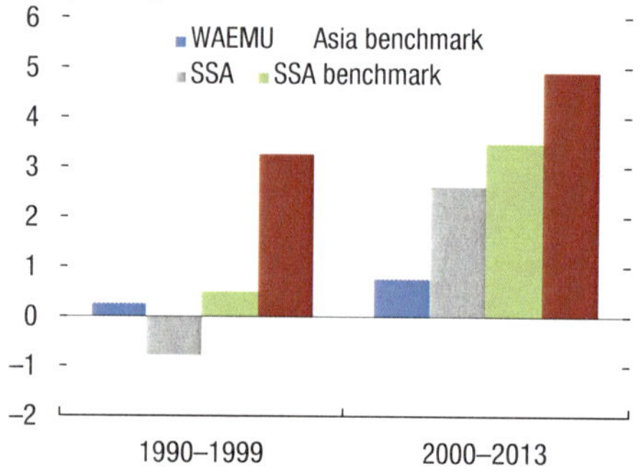

Source: IMF *World Economic Outlook*.
Note: SSA = Sub-Saharan Africa; WAEMU = West African Economic and Monetary Union.

Growth has also been volatile...

4. Real GDP Growth, 2000–2013
(Annual change, in percent)

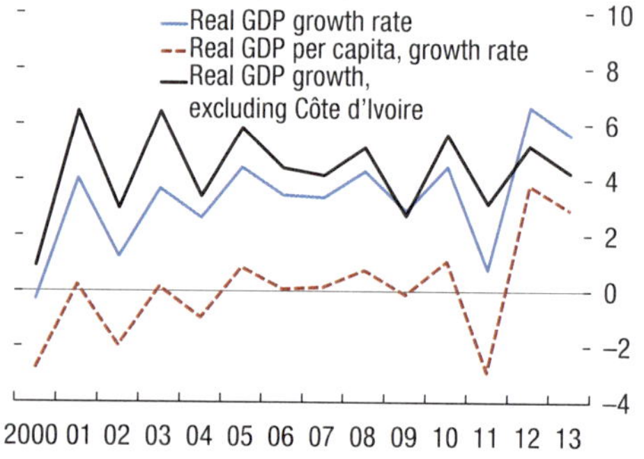

Sources: Country authorities and staff estimates.

...and more so than in peer countries.

5. Relative Volatility, 1994–2013 (Ratio of Standard Deviation to Average Growth Rate per Period)

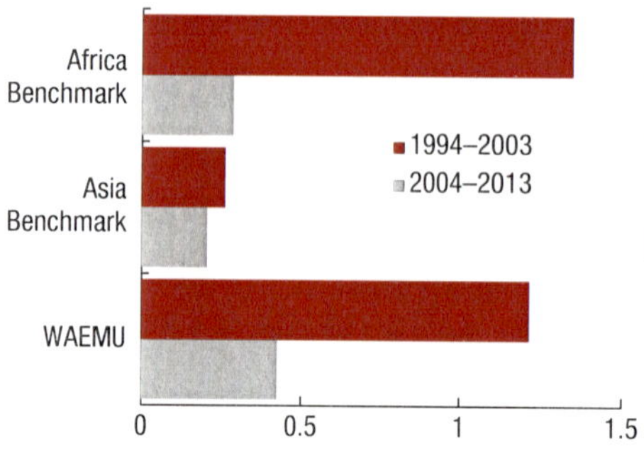

Sources: Country authorities; *World Economic Outlook*; and IMF staff estimates.

The volatility of overall GDP growth is much lower than for individual sectors, since services behave countercylically relative to agriculture and industry.

6. Sectoral Output Growth, 1970–2012

Cross-correlation matrix (1970–2012)	GDP	Agriculture	Secondary	Tertiary
GDP	1	0.23	0.34	0.71
Agriculture	0.23	1	0.38	–0.30
Secondary	0.34	0.38	1	–0.22
Tertiary	0.71	–0.30	–0.22	1

Standard deviation (1970–2012)	GDP	Agriculture	Secondary	Tertiary
	2.72	5.86	4.36	4.51

WAEMU lags most relative to other countries. Basic education rates in the WAEMU are significantly lower than they are in sub-Saharan African and Asian benchmark countries, and more unequally distributed across the population. Public investment efficiency remains relatively low (Dabla-Norris and others 2011), and a challenging business environment impedes productive private sector activity on the external stability assessment. These factor "gaps" suggest that policies

Figure 6.2. WAEMU: Productivity

Growth has been driven primarily by labor and capital accumulation over the past decade...

1. Average Contribution to Annual Growth Rate
(In percentage points, 1995–2012)

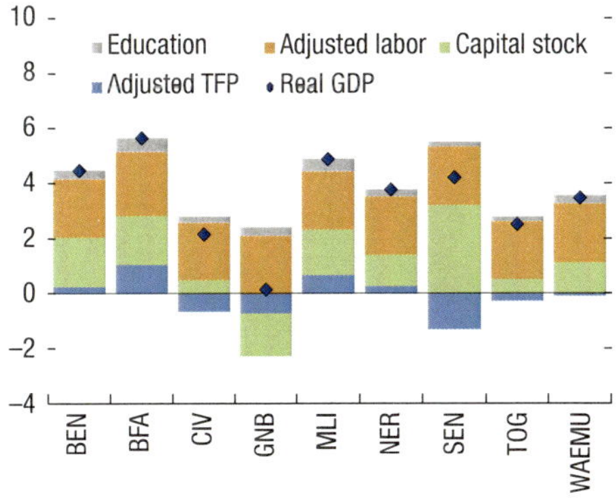

Note: Three-letter International Organization for Standardization abbreviations used for country names. TFP = total factor productivity.

...while the levels of other factor inputs are comparatively low. Policies should thus focus on...

2. Factor Inputs
(Relative to U.S. level)

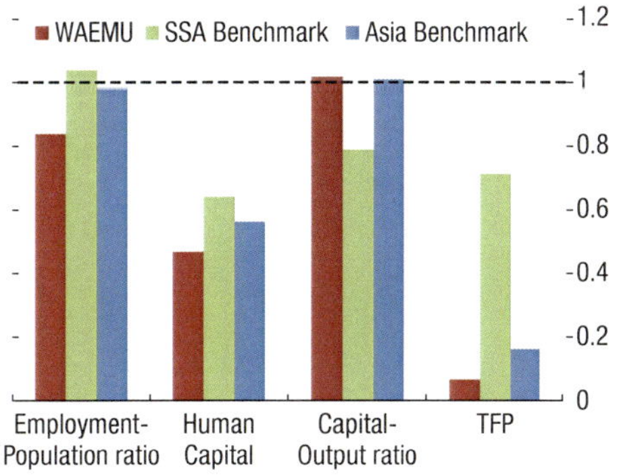

Source: Dabla-Norris and others (2013).
Note: SSA = Sub-Saharan Africa; TFP = total factor productivity; WEMU = West African Economic and Monetary Union.

...boosting human capital by increasing the quantity, quality and equality of education...

3. Adult Literacy Rates, 2012 or Latest Available
(In percent of population)

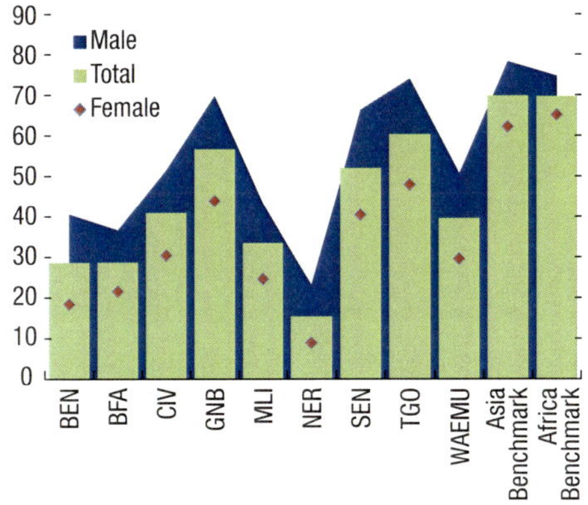

Source: UNESCO Institute for Statistics.
Note: Three-letter International Organization for Standardization abbreviations used for country names. WAEMU = West African Economic and Monetary Union.

...strengthening the labor force by, for example, boosting female participation in the workforce, ...

4. Gains from Gender Equality

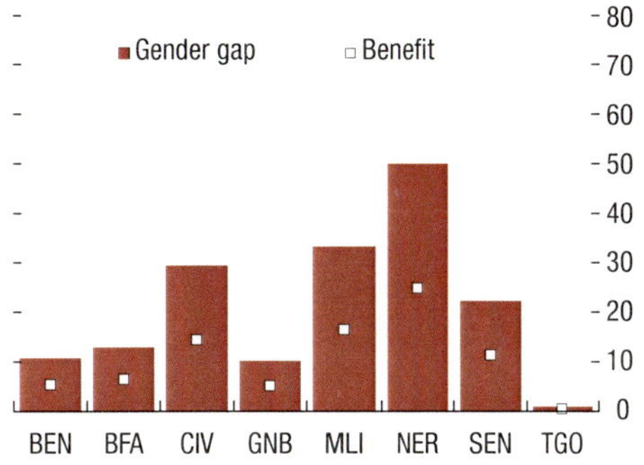

Sources: EDI; ILO KILM.
Note: Three-letter International Organization for Standardization abbreviations used for country names. (Gender gap = male minus female labor force participation; Benefit = total participation at closed gap)

(Continued)

...increasing TFP gains by increasing the efficiency of public investment...

5. Public Investment Efficiency (PIMI Score)

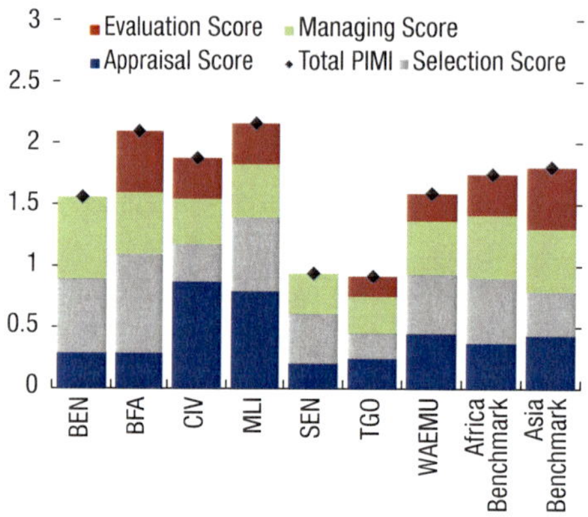

Source: Dabla-Norris and others (2011).
Note: Three-letter International Organization for Standardization abbreviations used for country names. WAEMU = West African Economic and Monetary Union.

...and strengthening the business environment.[1]

6. Ease of Doing Business 2015 (Rank among 189 Economies)

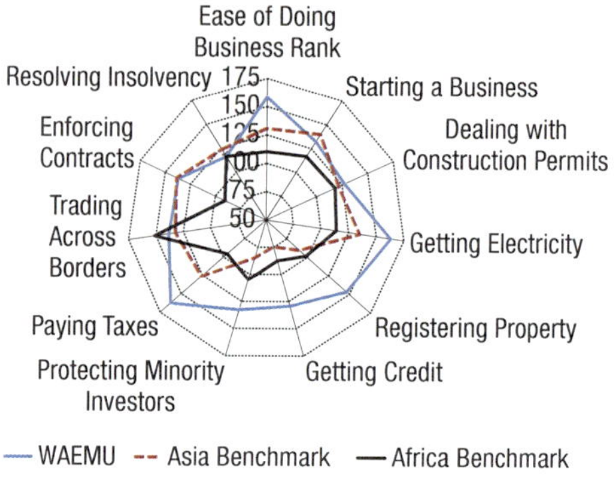

Source: World Bank, Doing Business 2015.

[1]Doing Business indicators should be interpreted with caution because of the limited number of respondents, a limited geographical coverage, and standardized assumptions on business constraints and information availability.

should target access and quality of education, public financial management reforms to improve the efficiency of public investment, and key areas of the business environment such as contract enforcement and efficient electricity provision.

OUTPUT AND EXPORT TRENDS

There has been relatively little evidence of structural change in the WAEMU over time (Figure 6.3). The sectoral composition of output has remained remarkably stable and the level of diversification low. The service sector accounts for over 50 percent of economic activity, while agriculture and industry account for around 30 percent and less than 20 percent, respectively, shares that have changed little since 1970, the first year for which data are available. The level of output diversification—based on a Theil Index measure (Box 6.1)—is also low and has remained stagnant, in contrast to faster-growing benchmark countries, which have witnessed sharp increases in diversification over time.

The WAEMU has experienced a modest deindustrialization, contrasting with a sharp industrial expansion in this sector among benchmark countries. The share of the manufacturing sector in output fell from 14 percent to 10 percent in the WAEMU but increased from 10 percent to 16 percent in the Asian peer group between 1990 and 2012. Conversely, the share of the agricultural sector has declined across low-income countries over time but has remained elevated in the WAEMU.

Export diversification has been stagnant on average (Figure 6.4). While there is some variation across WAEMU countries, on average, diversification of exports has not taken place. In contrast, African benchmark countries diversified quite strongly after 1990 and have caught up to Asian benchmark countries whose diversification levels were already comparatively high before that time. The number of export partners has increased on average, but the shares of the main export

Figure 6.3. Output Diversification

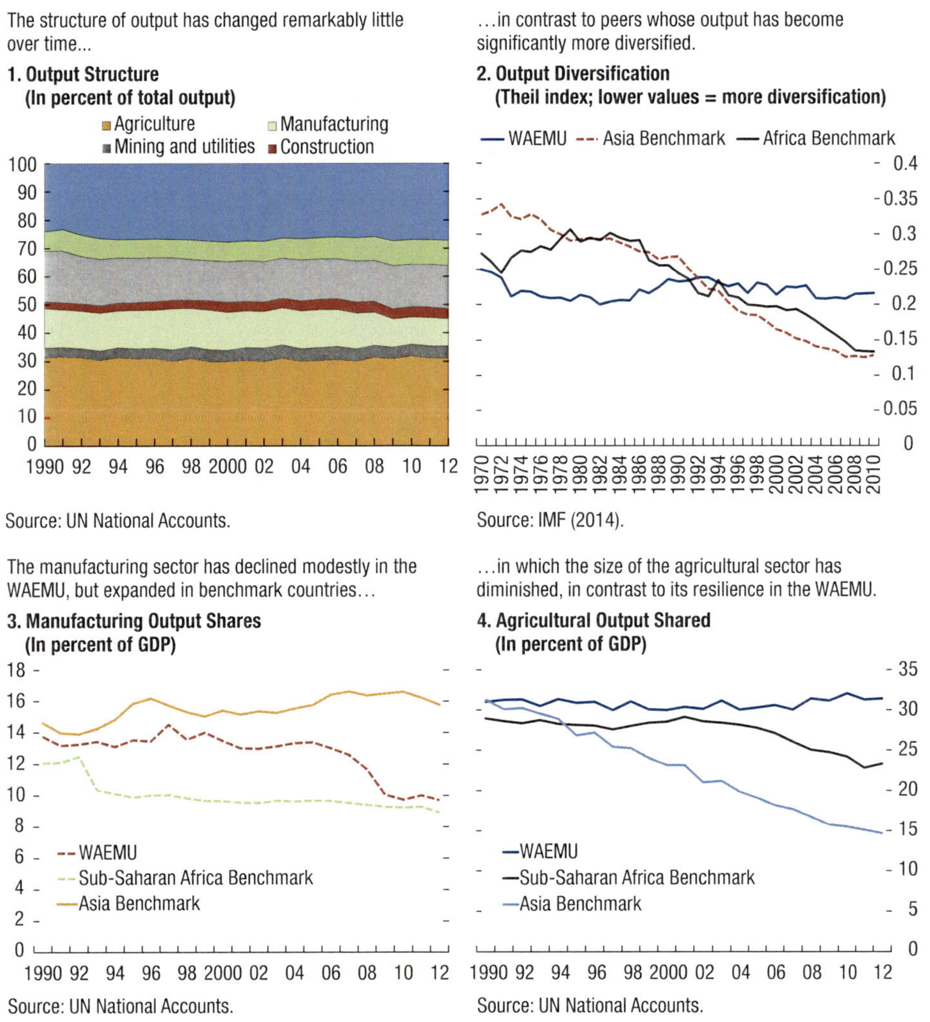

partners remain dominant on the implementation of Economic Community of West African States' common external tariff.

Relative export quality has decreased for some sectors and been stagnant in others (Figure 6.5). While not far from benchmark country levels, agricultural and manufacturing export quality has been stagnant on average. Relative commodity export quality has decreased steadily since the 1990s and appears to be far below that of benchmark countries now. The last panel in Figure 6.5 plots the export quality for each of the five largest sectors (2-digit Standard International Trade Classification) in each WAEMU country. It suggests that, while some countries have succeeded in achieving a high product quality in at least one of their top export sectors, export concentration in many countries remains high in sectors of relatively low quality.

BOX 6.1. Export Diversification and Quality

This box is based on IMF (2014) and Henn, Papageorgiou, and Spatafora (2013).

Export product diversification is captured by the Theil index which can be decomposed into a "between" and a "within" subindex:

$$\text{Theil Index} = \frac{1}{N}\sum_{i}^{N}\frac{\text{Export Value}_i}{\text{Average Exp. Value}}\cdot \ln\frac{\text{Export Value}_i}{\text{Average Exp. Value}}$$

$$= Theil_{between} + Theil_{within},$$

in which i is the product index and N the total number of products. The "between" Theil index captures the *extensive margin* of diversification, that is, the number of products, while the "within" Theil index captures the intensive margin (product shares).

Export partner diversification. The Theil index is also available across export partners. In this case, i and N in the above relationship represent the export partner index and number of export partners, respectively.

Export quality is measured by the export's unit value adjusted for differences in production costs, relative distance to the trade partner, and the development of a country through the following relationship:

$$Trade\ Price_{mxt} = \alpha_0 + \alpha_1' \ln unobservable\ quality_{mxt} + \alpha_2 \ln p.c.\ income_{mxt} + \alpha_3 \ln Distance_{mxt} + Error_{mxt},$$

in which the subscripts m, x, and t denote importer, exporter, and time period, respectively.

TRANSFORMATION AND DIVERSIFICATION BENEFITS

Structural transformation and diversification of output has the potential to boost growth and reduce volatility in the WAEMU. Through the reallocation of resources from low productivity sectors, such as agriculture, to higher productivity sectors, such as manufacturing, "between-sector" structural transformation can boost overall productivity. Structural transformation can also occur "within sectors," creating productivity gains through, for example, implementing quality improvements to existing products and services, focusing production on relatively high value-added activities, or diversifying into new high value-added products. Output diversification can not only yield growth benefits, but also reduce the volatility of growth, since new products and services are likely to be subject to different demand and supply shocks than existing ones.

Estimates suggest these benefits could be substantial (Figure 6.6).[2] A 1 percentage point reallocation of labor from agriculture to manufacturing (keeping sectoral productivity levels constant) could raise output by 1.1 percent; such is the gulf in labor productivity levels between the two sectors. Similarly, a 1 percent increase in agricultural productivity (keeping resource allocation constant) could raise aggregate output by 0.3 percent, given the concentration of labor in this sector. Increasing output diversification to the level of benchmark countries could increase average growth by 0.6 to 0.9 percent. According to the IMF (2014), similar results hold for more export diversification. Here, a 1 standard deviation increase in low-income countries' (LICs) export diversification raises the growth rate by about 0.8 percentage points, which translates into a potential ½ percentage point growth gain if export diversification were raised to levels observed

[2]The magnitude of these potential growth gains will vary across member economies, as a function of their different starting structures, productivity levels, and extent of diversification.

Figure 6.4. Export Product and Partner Diversification

Progress in export product diversification has been insignificant on average…

1. WAEMU: Export Product Diversification (Theil Index decomposition, lower values = more diversication)

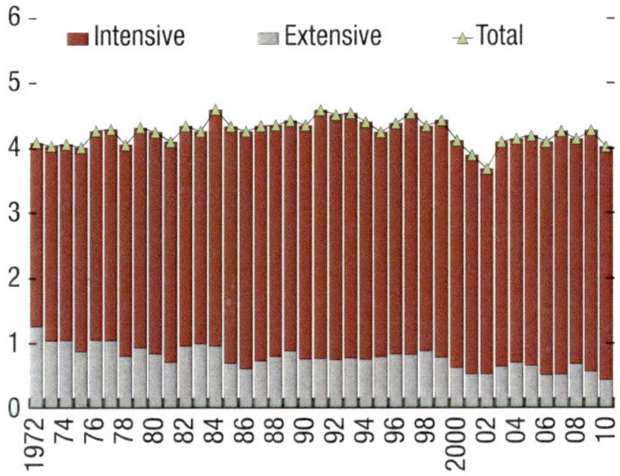

…in contrast to progress in benchmark countries.

2. Export Product Diversification (Theil Index decomposition, lower values = more diversication)

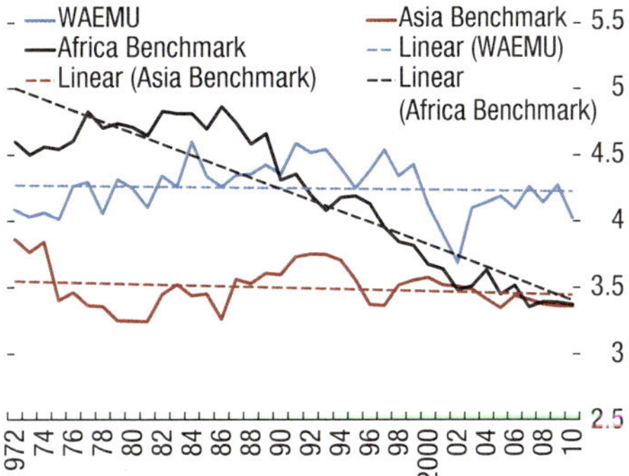

Exports tend to be concentrated in a few major products in the majority of countries.

3. Share of Three Major Exports in Total Exports, 1991–2010 (Export product measured at 2-Digit SITC level)

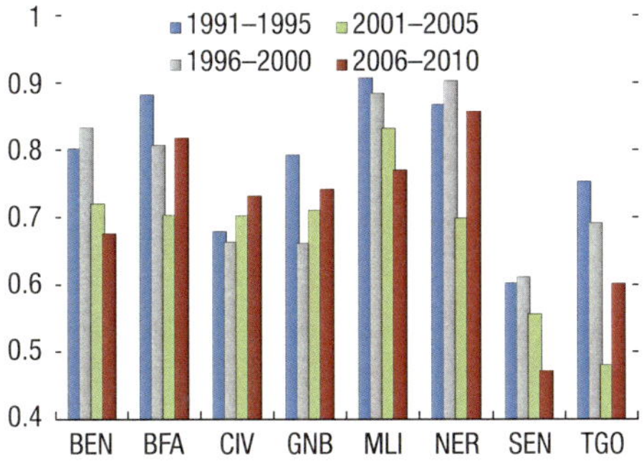

Senegal and Togo appear to be the most diversified economies in the region.

4. Export Product Diversification, 2006–2010 (Theil Index decomposition, lower values = more diversication)

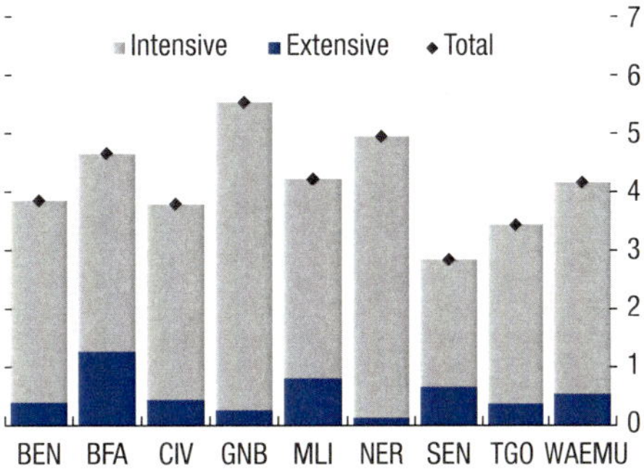

The number of export partners has increased in the WAEMU, but concentration across partners remains high…

5. WAEMU: Export Partner Diversification (Theil Index decomposition, lower values = more diversication)

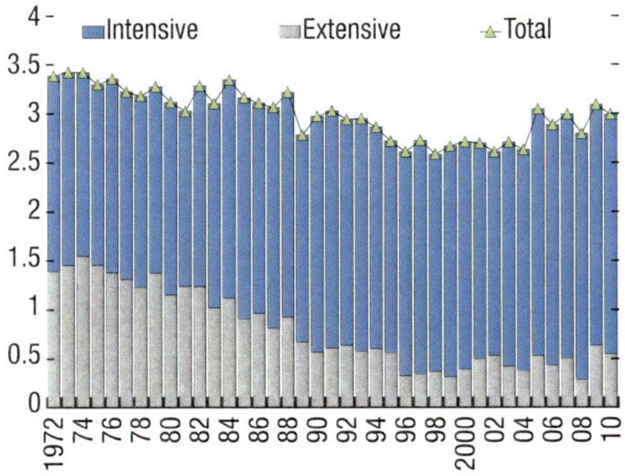

…and overall diversification remains low compared with African benchmark countries.

6. Export Partner Diversification (Theil Index decomposition, lower values = more diversication)

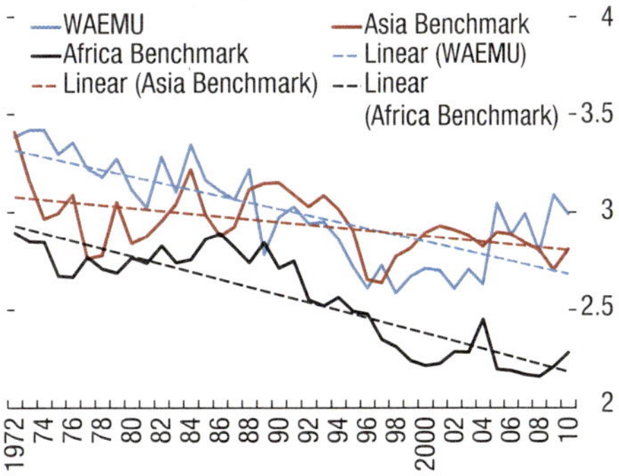

Source: IMF (2014).
Note: Three-letter International Organization for Standardization abbreviations used for country names.
WAEMU = West African Economic and Monetary Union.

Figure 6.5. Export Quality

Commodity export quality has declined relatively in the last two decades.

1. Commodity Quality
(1 = 90 Percentile of all countries)

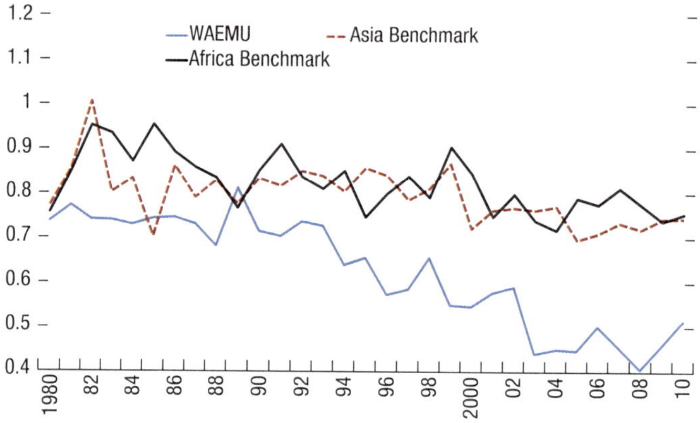

Manufacturing quality has performed well based on SSA standards, but is outperformed by other benchmarks.

2. Manufacturing Quality
(1 = 90 Percentile of all countries)

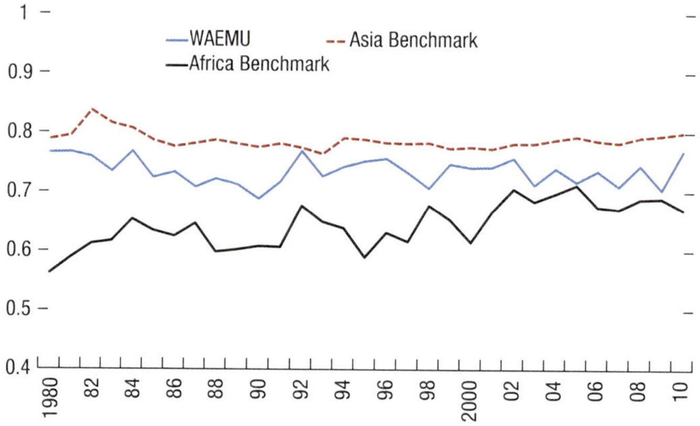

In some WAEMU countries, the largest export industries are those of relatively lower quality.

3. Export Quality for Five Largest Export Sectors
(1 = 90 Quality percentile of all countries;
size of bubbles proportional to product share)

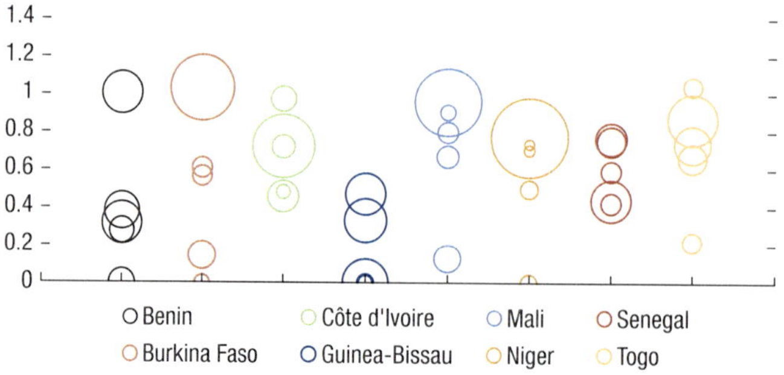

Source: IMF (2014).

Figure 6.6. Gains from Structural Transformation, Diversification, and Quality Upgrading

Even relatively modest structural transformation in the region could yield significant growth gains.

1. Potential Output Gains from Structural Transformation (In percent of real GDP)

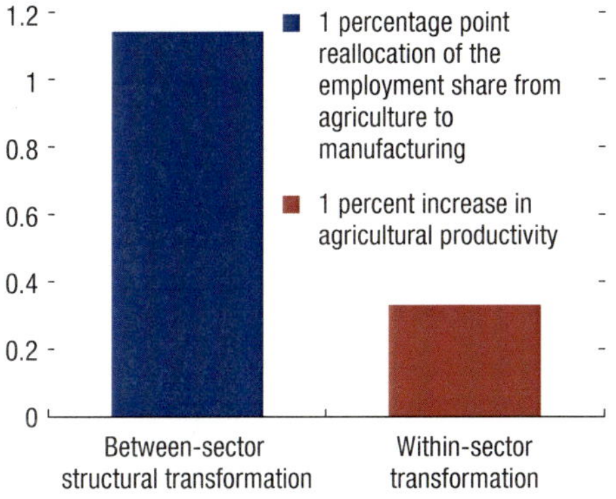

Raising the region's output diversification to benchmark levels could yield significant growth gains...

2. Potential Growth Effects from Raising Output Diversification in the WAEMU to Benchmark Levels

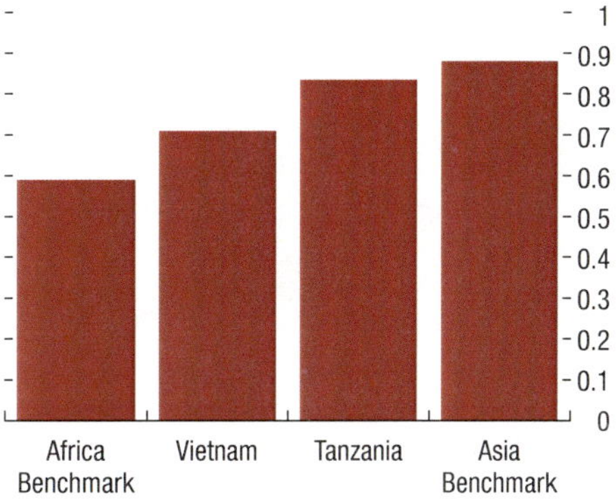

Sources: UN National Accounts; WDI; and IMF staff estimates.

...as would an increase in export diversification.

3. Growth Effects from Increased Diversification across WAEMU Countries (Increase in annual growth rate, average 2001–2010)

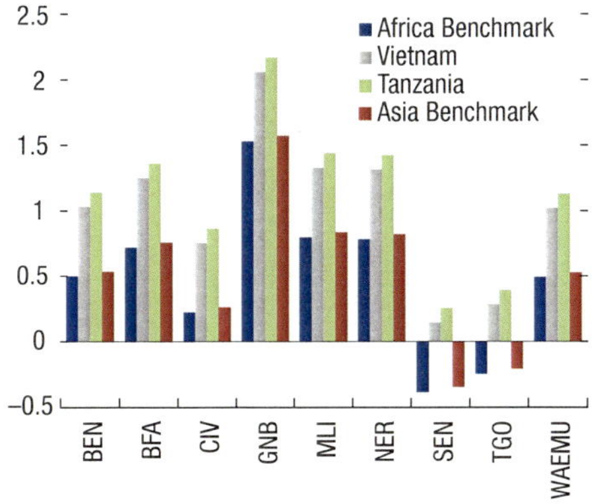

Volatility could decrease by similar magnitudes.

4. Growth Effects from Increased Diversification in the WAEMU (Increase in annual growth rate, average 2001–2010)

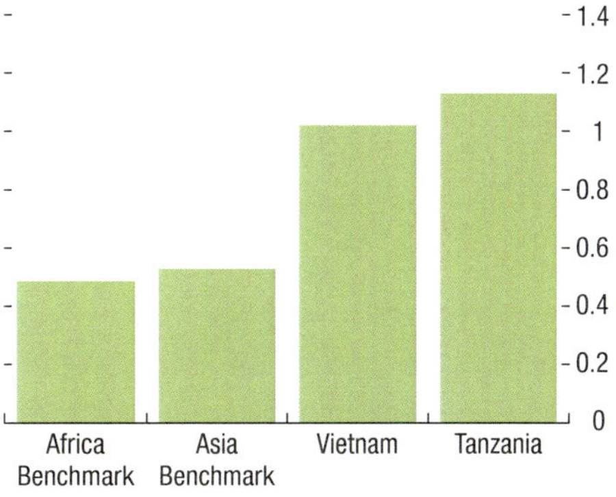

The potential growth effects from increased diversification vary across WAEMU countries.

5. Volatility Gains from Increased Diversification in the WAEMU (Decrease in average 5-year volatility, of growth)

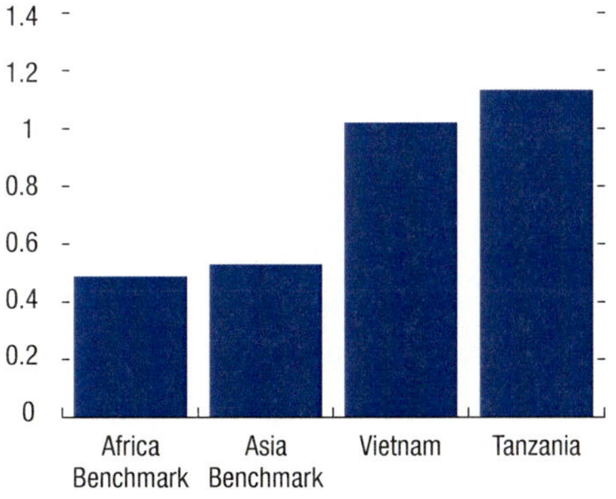

Further growth gains could be realized from upgrading manufacturing quality to benchmark levels.

6. Growth Effects from Increased Manufacturing in the WAEMU to Benchmark Levels (Increase in annual growth rate, average 2001–2010)

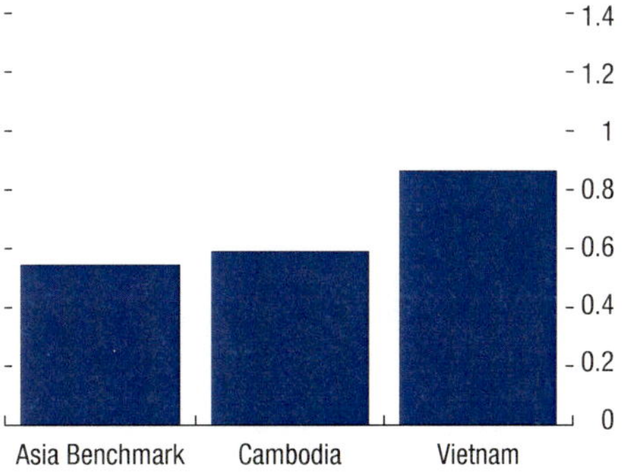

Source: IMF (2014) and own calculations.
Note: Three-letter International Organization for Standardization abbreviations used for country names.

in Asian or sub-Saharan African benchmark countries. Output growth volatility could be significantly reduced as well.

Policies to promote structural transformation and diversification should focus on addressing market failures that hinder entry into new lines of economic activity (IMF 2014). Market failures abound in the WAEMU in terms of the provision of infrastructure, accumulation of human capital, provision of finance, establishment of trade networks and functioning of factor markets, regulatory and institutional environment, and creation and management of ideas. Evidence from cross-country comparisons and individual case studies suggests that policies targeting these areas can be successful in fostering structural transformation and diversification, while the evidence is more mixed concerning the success of industry-focused and narrowly targeted measures (Box 6.2). That said, in the WAEMU, the agricultural sector does warrant special attention, given its large scope for productivity and quality improvements and its high share of employment (Box 6.3).

DEMOGRAPHIC GROWTH DIVIDEND

Structural transformation and improvements in diversification will take several years and occur against the backdrop of challenging population dynamics (Figure 6.7). Fertility rates in the WAEMU remain among the highest in the world, despite rapid declines in child mortality. As a result, the WAEMU's population structure is young; in 2010 almost half the population was below the age of 15. Over the next two decades, the population could double, from around 100 to 200 million, with a net annual increase in the labor force of around 1.3 million new workers.

A young population presents the opportunity of a "growth dividend" from a demographic transition that boosts the working-age population share (Box 6.4). If fertility rates in the WAEMU decline from their current level of 5.7 children per woman, to 3.8 children per woman

BOX 6.2. Reforms That Foster Structural Transformation

While there is no silver bullet of reform to foster structural transformation, the following general policies have emerged from successful country case studies and cross-country evidence (IMF 2014; Henn, Papageorgiou, and Spatafora 2013; Dabla-Norris and others 2013). Several of these policies may be addressed at both the national and regional levels.

- *Macroeconomic stability*—In Vietnam, Rwanda, Malaysia, and Tanzania successful diversification has coincided with stronger macroeconomic policies and a greater degree of stability.
- *Market entry*—Reduced entry barriers can motivate entrepreneurs to expand their activities. In Vietnam, collectivization was reversed, which led to the emergence of a more diverse agricultural sector. In Rwanda, a large divestment of state enterprises stimulated private sector activity, and in Tanzania, the dismantling of the state distribution system has positively affected the private sector as well. The liberalization of the electricity market has been associated with higher degrees of structural transformation as well.
- *Education*—Education has been associated with higher levels of diversification and export quality. In Vietnam, years of education increased by about 50 percent in just two decades. In Rwanda, education has been expanded through ninth grade for all students.
- *Institutions and the business environment*—Henn, Papageorgiou, and Spatafora (2013) report that a 1 standard deviation increase in institutional quality is associated with a 0.3 increase in quality upgrading. In Bangladesh, the removal of red tape has been associated with large investments in export processing zones.
- *Industrial policies*—The support of specific industries has shown mixed results. In Malaysia and Bangladesh, the targeting of specific industries has been successful, but the targeted sectors have become dominant, decreasing export diversification. In natural-resource-dominated economies, however, such targeting may help the economy to diversify.

BOX 6.3. The Role of Agriculture in Structural Transformation

The agricultural sector accounts for a significant share of output, employment, and external trade in the WAEMU and is likely to continue to do so in the medium term, even if there is an expansion of the manufacturing sector. Structural transformation within the agriculture sector, through productivity improvements to existing activities and boosting of the sector's external performance, should thus be key focuses of growth-enhancing policies.

Agriculture has the highest share of employment in the WAEMU, so inclusive growth depends on its prospects (Figure 6.3.1). Agriculture currently employs around 60 percent of the workforce in the WAEMU and is likely to remain the largest employer in the medium term. Applying the methodology in Fox and others (2013), the number of workers in agriculture could double, with the share in total employment declining only from around 60 percent to 50 percent (Figure 6.3.2).

Figure 6.3.1. Employment by Sector, 2011 or Latest Available (In percent of total employment)

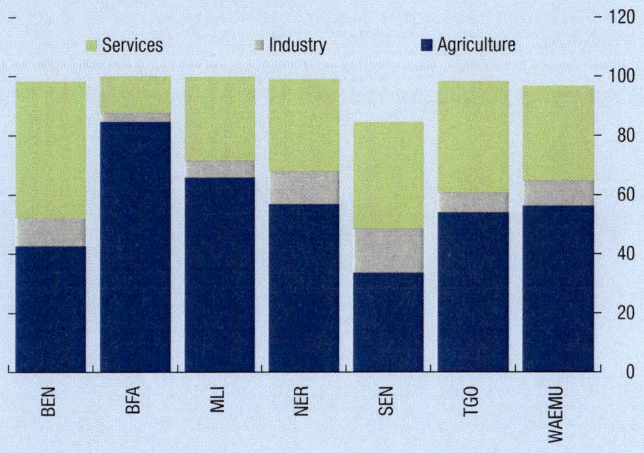

Sources: WDI 2014; ILO KILM.
Note: Three-letter International Organization for Standardization abbreviations used for country names.

Figure 6.3.2. Employment Projections by Sector (Millions, right-hand side, and percent of total, left-hand side)

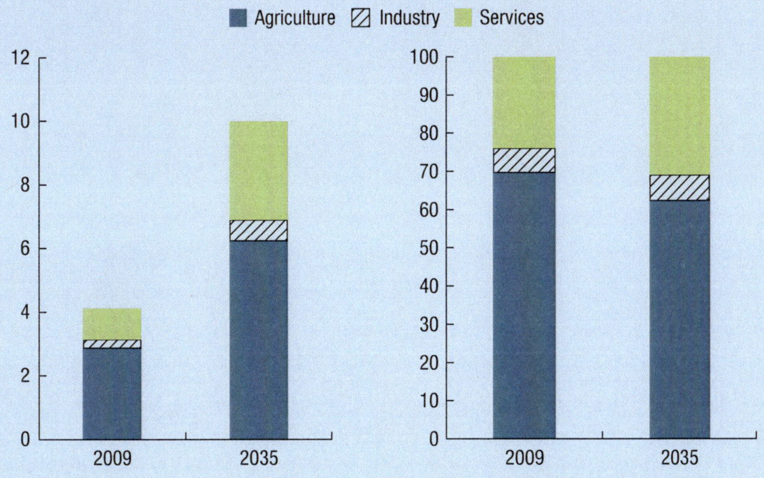

BOX 6.3. *(continued)*

Policies targeting productivity improvements within agriculture may have the most traction in the medium term. The expected continued buoyant supply of agricultural labor suggests that large-scale 'between-sector' structural change (through a large shift in the share of workers in agriculture to the manufacturing sector) may be unlikely to materialize in the medium term. Instead, productivity improvements within the agricultural sector may provide a more fruitful focus for policies. The data suggest that agricultural productivity is relatively low in the WAEMU, indicating substantial scope for progress. For example, cereal yields remain below those in benchmark countries (Figure 6.3.3), while the relative quality of agricultural exports has been on a declining trend (Figure 6.3.4).

Figure 6.3.3. Agricultural Indicators, 2011

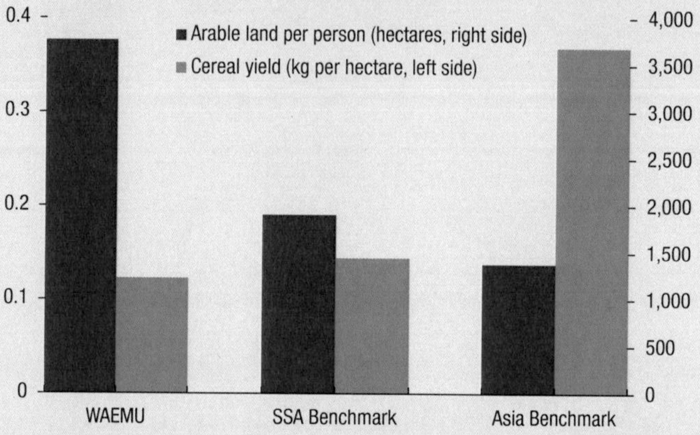

Source: Food and Agriculture Organization of the United Nations.
Note: SSA = Sub-Saharan Africa; WAEMU = West African Economic and Monetary Union.

Figure 6.3.4. Agricultural Quality (1 = 90 percentile of all countries)

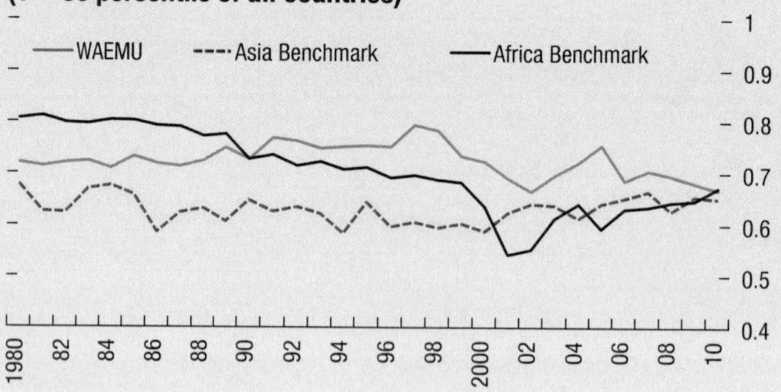

Source: IMF (2014).

Another set of policies could focus on the external competitiveness of the agricultural sector. Although agriculture is the WAEMU's largest employer and accounts for a large share of output, the agricultural trade balance is negative in some member countries, which in turn contributes to the regional external deficit. Moreover, several countries import the same agricultural products that they export. The WAEMU's trade balance could therefore be improved by policies encouraging countries to increase exports of agricultural products that they produce domestically and with which they have a comparative advantage. At the same

BOX 6.3. *(continued)*

time, such policies could encourage these countries to reduce imports of these products. The WAEMU would appear to have scope to increase the quantity of agricultural exports, as well as abundant agricultural labor. The share of uncultivated arable land is relatively high and several neighboring countries are large importers of agricultural products (Figure 6.3.5 and Figure 6.3.6).

Figure 6.3.5. Food and Agricultural Imports in Neighboring Countries, 2011

	Billions of U.S. Dollars	Percent of WAEMU GDP
Nigeria	19.5	25.0
Algeria	11.5	14.7
Ghana	2.4	3.1
Mauritania	0.4	0.5
Gambia	0.1	0.1
WAEMU	4.9	7.2

Sources: UN Comtrade database; and World Bank.

Figure 6.3.6. Agriculture and Food Trade Balance (In percent of GDP)

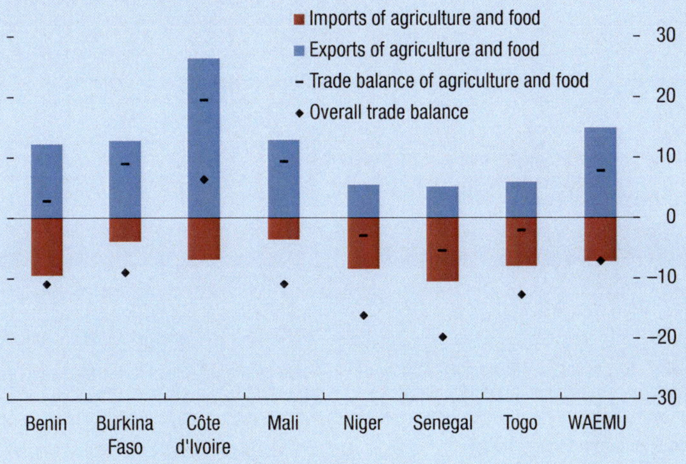

Sources: UN Comtrade database; and World Bank.

(the UN's most optimistic scenario), the share of working-age population will increase from 52 percent to 58 percent by 2035. This demographic transition would be characterized by a higher share of the population that was potentially economically productive and could create income, boost fiscal revenues, and ease the burden of fiscal expenditure on services such as health care and education. The potential impact on growth from these effects could be important. A recent paper (Drummond, Thakoor, and Yu 2014) estimated that a 1 percentage point increase in the working-age population increases real GDP growth per capita by 0.5 percentage point.

Figure 6.7. Demographics

Fertility rates in the WAEMU are among the highest in the world and have only declined modestly over recent decades…

1. Fertility Rates
(Number of children per woman)

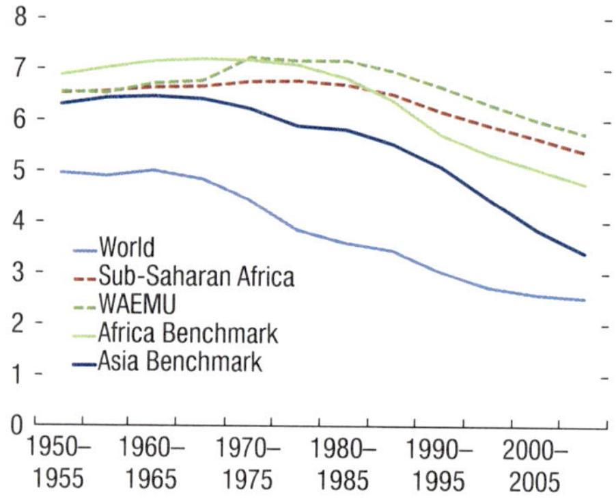

Sources: UN population projections, 2012.

…despite a rapid fall in child mortality rates…

2. Child Mortality
(Deaths under age 5 per 1,000 live births)

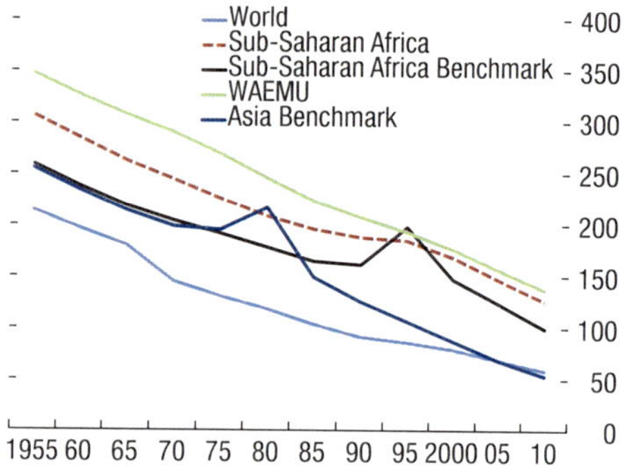

Sources: UN population projections, 2012.

This has led to a very young population, with almost half under the age of 24…

3. Population Pyramid - WAEMU
(In millions)

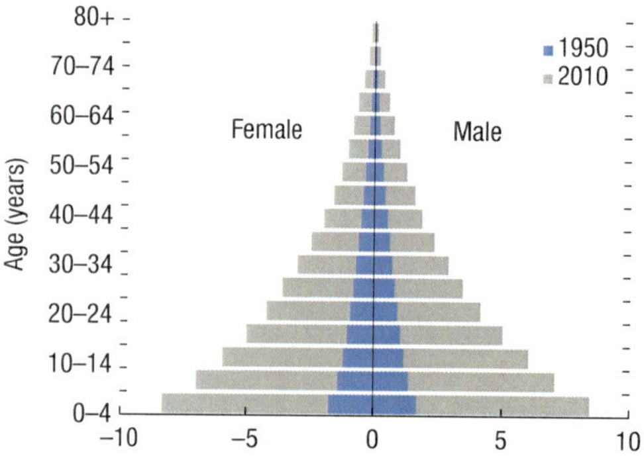

Sources: UN World Population Prospects, 2012

…and the labor force is expected to increase by around 1.3 million workers each year between now and 2035.

4. WAEMU Population Projections
(In millions)

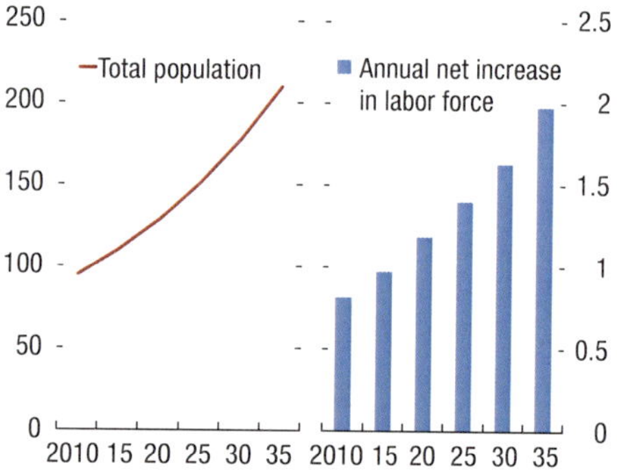

Sources: UN Population Projections, 2012

Note: Based on current labor force participation rates.

A decline in fertility rates would provide a significant boost to the working-age population and the opportunity of a demographic growth dividend.

5. Working-Age Population Share (15–64)
(Percent of total population)

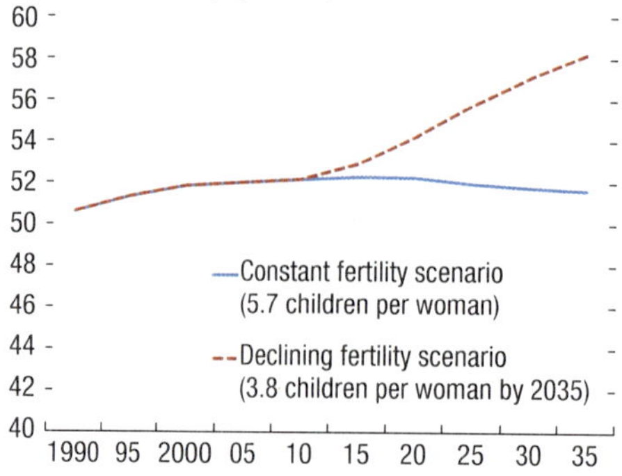

Source: UN Population Projections, 2012.

Generating a decline in the fertility rate will be challenging but one focus of policies in this area could be to increase the use of contraception among women who desire it.

6. Contraceptive Prevalance and Unmet Need
(Percent of women aged 15–49)

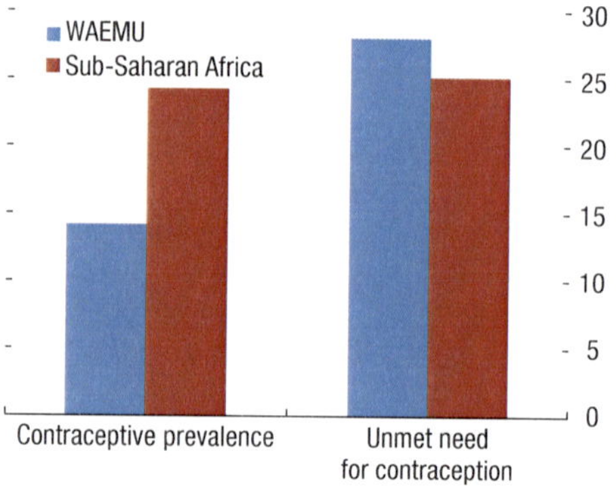

Source: WDI.

BOX 6.4. The Demographic Dividend

There are two main channels of demographic growth dividends (Mason and Lee 2006). The first is the result of a rapid growth of the working age population, followed by a decline of fertility rates. As a consequence, the economy's dependency ratios decline. The second one arises later, when parents have fewer children and accumulate savings in anticipation of aging. With a large number of young people projected to enter the labor market in the WAEMU in the next decades, the WAEMU could benefit from the first dividend if fertility rates were declining.

The demographic dividend has been substantial in several countries (see Figures 6.4.1 and 6.4.2). For the case of India, Aiyar and Mody (2011) estimate that 40 to 50 percent of per capita growth has been attributable to the demographic dividend since the 1970s. In East Asia, the demographic transition has likely contributed one-fourth to two-fifths to a GDP per capita growth rate of around 6 percent between 1965 and 1990 (Bloom, Canning, and Sevilla 2003). However, even with an increasing ratio of working-age population to population, the growth effects of the demographic dividend are not automatic. The shift in demographics needs to be complemented by investments in education to ensure the entrance of a productive workforce into the labor market at higher wages.

Figure 6.4.1. Dependency Ratio, 1961–2013 (People younger than 15 or older than 64 in percent of working-age population)

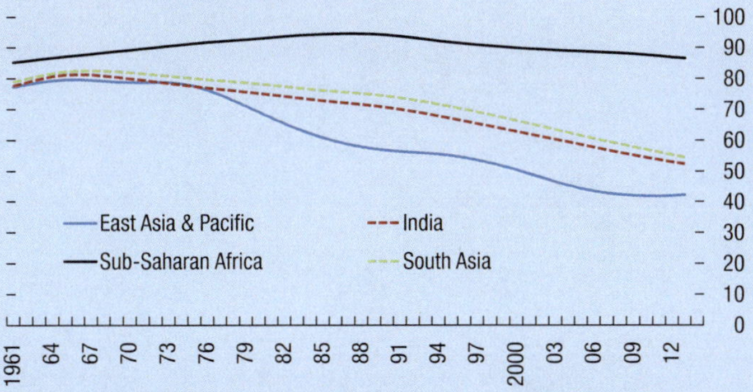

Sources: UNI World Population Prospects; WDI.

Figure 6.4.2. Dependency Ratio, 1961–2013 (People younger than 15 or older than 64 in percent of working-age population)

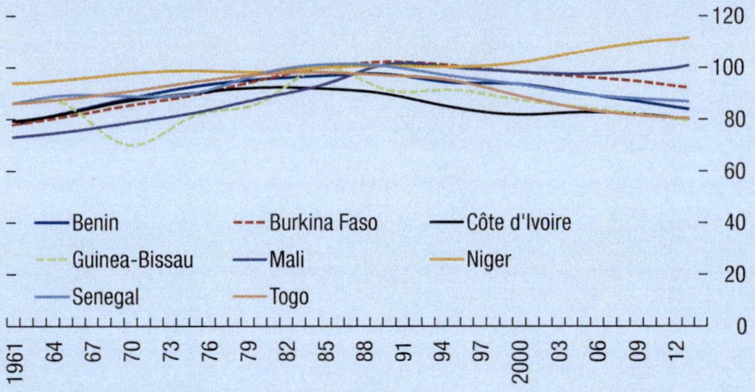

Sources: UNI World Population Prospects; WDI.

But the WAEMU could miss out on a demographic growth dividend if fertility rates do not decline or if the labor market cannot absorb new workers in productive activities. If fertility rates in the WAEMU do not decline from their current elevated levels, the working-age population share will also stay constant and the demographic transition and associated growth dividend will remain elusive in the medium term. Moreover, this scenario would not be innocuous for growth: the rapid increase in population would still pose enormous pressure on public services and infrastructure, which are inadequate even at current population levels. And even if fertility rates do decline, the increase in the working age population share may not yield growth benefits. Recent evidence (Fox and others 2013) suggests that there are speed limits with which the manufacturing and service sectors can absorb new workers, with any excess labor forced to seek informal employment in low productivity (often subsistence) agriculture (see Box 6.3), or enter unemployment. Both of these outcomes would pose risks to overall productivity growth, poverty levels, and social cohesion.

Policymakers aiming to promote structural transformation cannot ignore these demographic challenges. A large number of new workers could be a boon for structural transformation and diversification, as young workers are likely to be more flexible than existing ones to enter into new economic activities. Policies should thus focus on ensuring the demographic transition takes place by managing fertility rates (for example, through promoting increased use of contraception), by harnessing the growth benefits of any transition, and by providing the necessary education to ensure new entrants to the labor force have the skills needed to be fully employed in high value-added activities.

REFERENCES

Aiyar, Shekhar, and Ashoka Mody. 2011. "The Demographic Dividend: Evidence from the Indian States." IMF Working Paper 11/38, International Monetary Fund, Washington.

Bloom, E., D. Canning, and J. Sevilla. 2003. "The Demographic Dividend. A New Perspective on the Economic Consequences of Population Change." RAND, MR-1274, The Rand Corporation, Santa Monica.

Dabla-Norris, Era, Giang Ho, Kalpana Kochhar, Annette Kyobe, and Robert Tchaidze. 2013. "Anchoring Growth: The Importance of Productivity-Enhancing Reforms in Emerging Market and Developing Economies." IMF Staff Discussion Note 13/08, International Monetary Fund, Washington.

Dabla-Norris, Era, Jim Brumby, Annette Kyobe, Zac Mills, and Chris Papageorgiou. 2011. "Investing in Public Investment Efficiency." IMF Working Paper 11/97, International Monetary Fund, Washington.

Drummond, Paulo, Vimal Thakoor, and Shu Yu. 2014. "Africa Rising: Harnessing the Demographic Dividend." IMF Working Paper 14/143, International Monetary Fund, Washington.

Fox, Louise, Cleary Haines, Jorge Huerta Munoz, and Alun H. Thomas. 2013. "Africa's Got Work to Do: Employment Prospects in the New Century." IMF Working Paper 13/201, International Monetary Fund, Washington.

Henn, Christian, Chris Papageorgiou, and Nikola Spatafora. 2013. "Export Quality in Developing Countries." IMF Working Paper 13/108, International Monetary Fund, Washington.

International Monetary Fund (IMF). 2014. "Sustaining Long-Run Growth and Macroeconomic Stability in Low-Income Countries—The Role of Structural Transformation and Diversification." Background Notes, International Monetary Fund, Washington.

Mason, Andrew, and Ronald Lee. 2006. "Reform and Support Systems for the Elderly in Developing Countries: Capturing the Second Demographic Dividend." Prepared for the IUSSP/Asian Meta Centre "International Seminar on the Demographic Window and Health Aging: Socioeconomic Challenges and Opportunities," Center for Health Aging and Family Studies and the China Centre for Economic Research, Peking University, Beijing, May 10-11, 2004.

CHAPTER 7

Growth Inclusiveness and Equality

ALEXEI KIREYEV, STEFAN KLOS, CHRISTINA KOLERUS, AND MONIQUE NEWIAK

Growth performance depends heavily on its distributional characteristics. The fundamental question is equality, that is, whether the benefits of growth are shared equally across different income groups and whether all income groups and both genders have an equal opportunity to contribute their fair share to growth. While poverty has fallen in the last two decades in most of the West African Economic and Monetary Union (WAEMU) countries, poverty reduction has slowed in recent years. Although available indicators sometimes give conflicting signals on distributional shifts, two case studies—one on Senegal and one on Mali—suggest that people in the middle of the income distribution usually received the most benefit of growth, and mainly in urban areas. Further progress in poverty reduction and inclusiveness would require sustained high growth and exploration of growth opportunities in the sectors with high earning potential for the poor. Better targeted social policies and more attention to the regional distribution of spending would also help reduce poverty and improve inclusiveness. The WAEMU's growth could significantly benefit from the reduction in gender and income inequality.

GROWTH AND POVERTY REDUCTION

The high-growth episode in sub-Saharan Africa that started in the early 1990s has been fairly inclusive. The October 2011 *Regional Economic Outlook: Sub-Saharan Africa* found that although the pickup in growth has been accompanied by a fairly modest reduction in poverty, some progress has been achieved in terms of improving equality and social and health outcomes (IMF 2011). Meanwhile, the global financial crisis and social turmoil in different parts of the world have heightened global awareness of the potential impact of rising inequality on economic and social stability and on the sustainability of growth (Berg and Ostry 2011). The social and political dimensions make it important to look at inclusiveness of growth in individual African countries.

Senegal

The overall poverty level is relatively lower in Senegal than it is in most other sub-Saharan African countries. At the revised international poverty line, which usually differs somewhat from the national poverty line, Senegal is in the top quarter of sub-Saharan African countries for which data are available (Figure 7.1). At the $1.25 a day poverty line (in 2005 prices), Senegal in 2011 was comparable to Ethiopia and Ghana but was behind other countries in the region, such as Gabon, Cameroon, and Côte d'Ivoire.

The 2011 household survey in Senegal indicated that poverty remains high, although it declined in the most recent two decades. More than 6 million people were living on a household income below the national poverty line. In 1994–2001, GDP growth in Senegal was about 5 percent a year; the poverty rate fell significantly, from 68 percent in 1994/95 to 55 percent in 2001/02. In 2002–05, GDP growth reached 4.7 percent, allowing the poverty rate to decline further to about 48.5 percent. However, since 2005–06, repeated shocks have contributed to

Figure 7.1. Poverty Headcount Rate at International Poverty Line

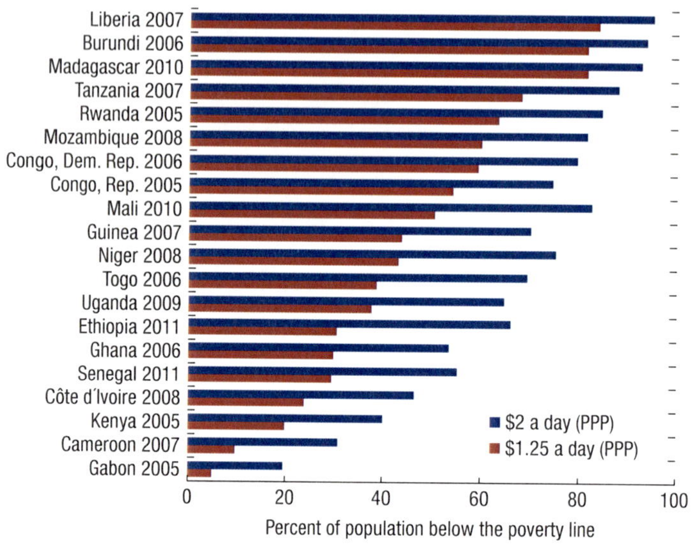

Source: World Development Indicators, World Bank.
Note: PPP = Purchasing power parity.

reducing per-capita income growth to little more than the rate of population growth. The 2011 household survey suggests that in the past five years, poverty incidence has declined by only 1.8 percentage points to 46.7 percent.

Growth is usually defined as pro-poor if it reduces poverty. Several metrics are used to measure the change in poverty: the change in the share of population living below the poverty line; monthly per-capita consumption, income, or expenditure; and the change in the poverty gap. The *poverty line* is the minimum level of income deemed adequate for meeting basic consumption needs in a given country, and it differs from country to country. For international comparison, two poverty lines are usually used: daily income of $1.25 and $2 at 2005 purchasing power parity. The *poverty gap* is the mean distance from the poverty line (counting the non-poor as having zero shortfall), expressed as a percentage of the poverty line. This measure reflects the depth of poverty and its incidence.

The recent prolonged episode of growth has led to a significant reduction in poverty. Based on several household surveys, poverty in Senegal—defined as the share of people below the national poverty line—declined from 55.2 percent in 2001 to 46.7 percent in 2011 (Table 7.1). The poverty gap declined from 17.2 to 14.5; other metrics also point to a continued trend in the reduction in poverty, although the pace of improvement declined during the second half of the decade and may not be statistically significant between 2006 and 2011.

Progress achieved in poverty reduction has been more pronounced in Senegal than it has in some regional peers. In 1994–2005, the share of population living on less than $1.25 a day declined by about 20 percentage points, and for people living on less than $2 a day, by about 19 percentage points (Figure 7.2). By the latter metric, which may be more appropriate for Senegal, given its per-capita income, Senegal's poverty dropped faster than poverty dropped in other WAEMU countries (15 percentage points) in approximately the same period. The dynamics of poverty reduction in the region have been significantly affected by an increase in poverty in Guinea-Bissau and Côte d'Ivoire during political crises in these countries.

TABLE 7.1

Senegal: Poverty Indicators, 2001–11

	2001	2005	2011
Poverty incidence	55.2	48.3	46.7
Confidence interval (95%)	52.9–57.5	46.1–50.6	44.1–49.3
Poverty gap	17.3	15.5	14.5

Source: Agence Nationale de Statistique et de la Démographie, 2012, www.ansd.sn.

Figure 7.2. Change in Poverty Rate

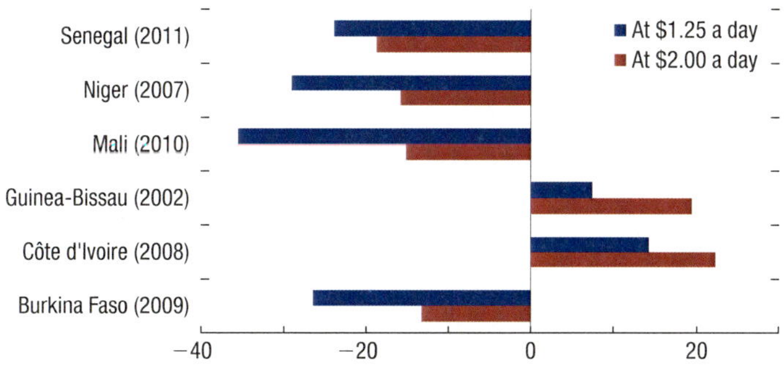

Source: PovCalNet, World Bank, 2013, http://iresearch.worldbank.org/PovCalNet.
Note: At 2005 PPP prices. In parentheses, the latest available year and corresponding headcount ratio at $1.25 a day and $2 a day, respectively. Change to 1994 for Burkina Faso, 1985 for Côte d'Ivoire, 1991 for Guinea-Bissau, 1994 for Mali, 1992 for Niger, and 1994 for Senegal.

The level of poverty also differs significantly among different regions of Senegal. In 2011, for example, the poverty incidence in the poorest regions (such as Kolda, Fatick, and Ziguinchor) was 67–73 percent, whereas it was only 26 percent in Dakar.

This outcome reflects higher growth and a higher sensitivity to growth of poverty reduction in Senegal. Unlike a number of countries in the WAEMU, particularly those affected by internal conflicts or crises (for example, Guinea-Bissau and Côte d'Ivoire in the 2000s), real per-capita GDP growth in Senegal was always positive in 1995–2011 and in some years it was quite significant (Figure 7.3, panel 1). In addition, the elasticity of poverty reduction to per-capita income growth has been significant in Senegal in regional comparisons. In 2001–11, this elasticity was about −1.3 in Senegal, above that of some other fast-growing WAEMU countries (for example, Burkina Faso) (Figure 7.3, panel 2).

Although growth seems to have been a major factor behind the reduction of poverty, this conclusion should be treated with caution. First, an increase in real GDP per capita does not necessarily imply a reduction of poverty and requires supplementary information on the distribution of this additional income among different groups of the population. If the initial distribution of income is highly unequal, the impact of growth on poverty may not be significant. In an extreme case, if all benefits of higher growth were captured by the wealthiest part of the population, the impact of growth on poverty reduction may be negative. Second, the elasticity of poverty reduction to growth in per-capita income depends on the shape of income or consumption distribution and on the position of the poverty line with respect to this distribution. Normally, the closer the poverty line is to the median of the distribution, the higher will be the elasticity of the poverty rate to real per-capita growth. Finally, more regular household surveys based on consis-

Figure 7.3. Factors Contributing to Pro-Poor Growth

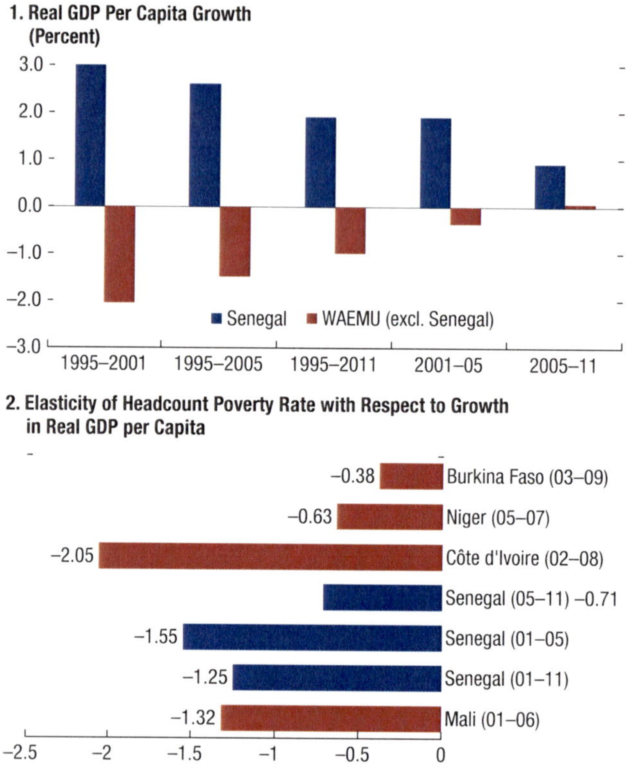

Sources: WDI; *World Economic Outlook*; and IMF staff estimates.

tent methodologies are needed to assess the evolution of growth inclusiveness through time. This impact assessment would be better served by the use of more advanced econometric techniques, which is difficult in the absence of high-frequency poverty datasets.

GROWTH INCIDENCE CURVES

Growth is usually considered inclusive if its benefits are widely shared across the population. Although there is no commonly accepted definition, inclusive growth usually refers to the goal of fostering high growth while providing productive employment and equal opportunities, so that all segments of society can share in the growth and employment, while redressing inequalities in outcomes, particularly those experienced by the poor (see IMF 2013 for an overview). For analytical purposes, growth is usually considered inclusive if it is high, sustained over time, and broad-based across sectors; creates productive employment opportunities; and includes a large part of a country's labor force. Additional dimensions of inclusive growth include gender, regional diversification, and empowerment of the poor, including through inclusive institutions. This chapter focuses only on the distributional characteristics of growth. Therefore, in this chapter growth is considered inclusive if it helps improve equality.

Several statistical metrics allow evaluation of different aspects of inclusiveness in this narrow definition. The squared poverty gap assesses inequality, as it captures differences in the severity of poverty among the poor. The Watts index is a distribution-sensitive poverty measure because it reflects the fact that an increase in income of a poor household reduces poverty more than does a comparable increase in income of a rich household. The Gini coefficient shows a deviation of income per decile from the perfect equality line. The mean log deviation index is more sensitive to changes at the lower end of the income distribution. The decile ratio is the ratio of the average consumption of income of the richest 10 percent of the population divided by the average income of the poorest 10 percent. Finally, in dynamic terms, the increase of income in the bottom deciles can be compared with the average income increase or the income increase in the highest deciles of the population. If the income of the bottom decile in the distribution tends to rise proportionately or faster than does the average income, growth would be considered inclusive. Although the squared poverty gap and the Watts index take into account the distributional characteristics of growth indirectly, all other methods measure equality directly.

Senegal

Different statistical measures suggest that, although poverty declined, overall inequality in Senegal remains broadly unchanged. In 1994–2011, the squared poverty gap shrank by more than half, suggesting that poverty among the poorest people became less severe in Senegal (Table 7.2). The Watts index also dropped substantially, suggesting a relatively faster improvement in the situation of people with the lowest incomes. At the same time, both the Gini coefficient and the mean log deviation (MLD) index declined a bit in 1994–2005 and increased again in 2005–11, suggesting no major changes in the overall level of inequality.

A simple decile ratio also suggests that the level of inequality remained broadly unchanged. The ratio of consumption in the top decile relative to the bottom decile of the population did not change much between 1994 and 2011. It stood at 12.9 in 1994, declined to about 11.8 in both 2001 and 2005 but increased again to 12.5 in 2011, suggesting the richest consume on average 12–13 times more than the poorest. The richest two deciles of the population consume about half the goods and services in the country, roughly the same amount as is consumed by the seven bottom deciles of the population (Figure 7.4), suggesting a substantial level of income disparity and inequality, although lower than the average for sub-Saharan Africa.

Growth in the level of consumption in 2006–11 was positive but low and almost equal among different deciles of the population (Figure 7.5). No significant changes occurred in inequality during this period because growth in consumption of the bottom deciles was only slightly higher than that of the top deciles. In contrast, in 2001–05 the poorest fifth of the population experienced a decline in consumption, while all middle deciles registered significant growth in consumption, although the increase of the consumption level of the richest groups was insignificant.

TABLE 7.2

Senegal: Inequality Indicators, 1994–2011[1]

	Square Poverty Gap	Watts Index	Gini Coefficient	MLD Index
1994	9.09	0.27	41.44	0.30
2001	6.18	0.19	41.25	0.29
2005	4.67	0.15	39.19	0.26
2011	3.77	0.12	40.30	0.27

Source: PovCalNet; World Bank, 2013.

[1]PPP-based calculations. The Gini index and income shares may differ from the aggregates used for the national poverty lines. The Gini index based on ESAM 2001/02, ESPS 2005/06 and ESPS 2011 household surveys was 39.2 in 2001, 38.1 in 2005, and 37.8 in 2011. All income/consumption shares by decile are based on estimated Lorenz curves. Households are ranked by income or consumption per person. Distributions are population (household-size and sampling expansion factor) weighted.

Figure 7.4. Distributional Dimensions of Poverty

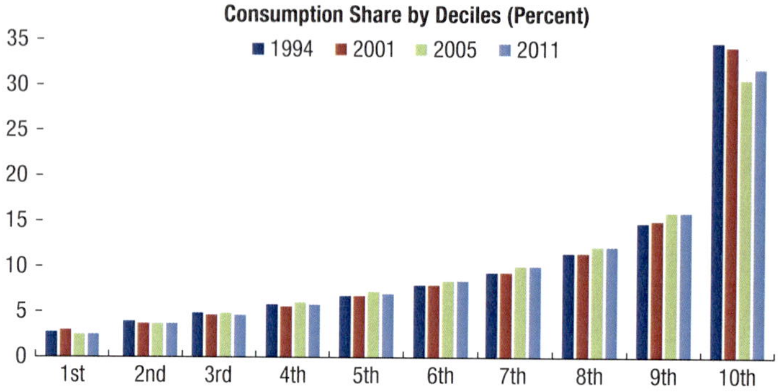

Source: PovCalNet, World Bank, 2013.
Note: Purchasing power parity-based calculations. The Gini index and income shares may differ from the aggregates used for the national poverty lines. The Gini index based on Enquête Sénégalaise Auprès des Ménages (ESAM) 2001/02, Enquête Suivi de la Pauvreté au Sénégal (ESPS) 2005/06 and Enquête Suivi de la Pauvreté au Sénégal (ESPS) 2011 household surveys was 39.2 in 2001, 38.1 in 2005, and 37.8 in 2011.
All income/consumption shares by decile are based on estimated Lorenz curves. Households are ranked by income or consumption per person. Distributions are population (household-size and sampling expansion factor) weighted.

Figure 7.5. Senegal Consumption Growth by Welfare Groups (Percent)

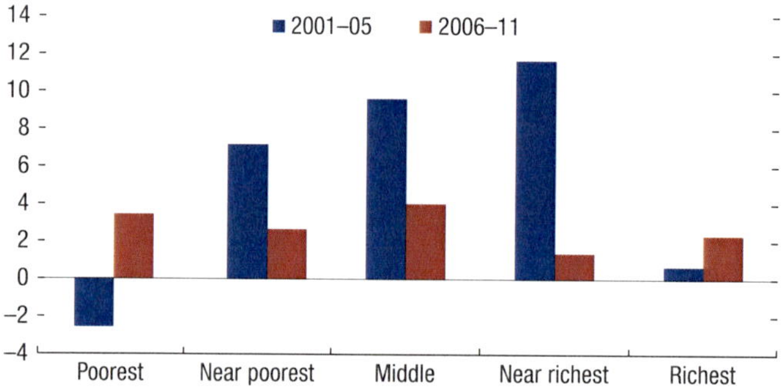

Sources: Enquête Sénégalaise Auprès des Ménages (ESAM) 2001/02; Enquête Suivi de la Pauvreté au Sénégal (ESPS) 2005/06; Enquête Suivi de la Pauvreté au Sénégal (ESPS) 2011.

A dynamic measure of inclusiveness of growth can be derived from the growth incidence curve. The estimation of growth incidence curves is a methodology that helps identify the extent to which each decile of households benefits from growth (Ravallion and Chen 2003). In plotting growth incidence curves, the vertical axis reports the growth rate of consumption expenditure, and the horizontal axis reports consumption expenditure percentiles (Foster and others 2013). The growth incidence curve assesses how consumption at each percentile changes over time. The part of the curve above zero points at the deciles that benefit from growth, and the part below zero points at the deciles that lost because of growth. The part of the curve that is above its own mean points at the deciles of the population that benefit from growth relatively more than does an average household.

The part of the curve below the mean, but still above zero, points at the deciles that also benefit from growth but less so than does an average household. A negatively sloping growth incidence curve suggests that income or spending of the poorer deciles of the population grows faster than does income or spending of the richer deciles. Because in this case the poorer groups of the population are catching up with the richer, a negatively sloping growth incidence curve can be viewed as one indication of inclusiveness of growth. Improvements in the degree of inclusiveness of growth would be signaled by the growth incidence curve changing the slope from positive to negative, and progress in poverty reduction would lead to the mean of the growth incidence curve and the curve itself moving up.

Although growth incidence curves give somewhat conflicting signals on distributional shifts in Senegal, they seem to confirm that growth benefited most those people in the middle of the income distribution. Between 2001 and 2005 (Figure 7.6), consumption increased on average, because the mean of the growth incidence curve is above zero, driven by the middle of the distribution (from the 3rd to the 8th deciles). The growth incidence curve is positively sloped, suggesting some increase in inequality during this period. Between 2005 and 2011, the mean of the growth incidence curve is above zero but the curve is broadly flat, suggesting no clear trend in changes in inequality. On average for 2001–11, a clear increase in mean consumption confirms the decline in poverty, as the middle class improved its relative position. However, for 2001–11 as a whole, the growth incidence curve has a slightly positive slope, which may point to some worsening of inclusiveness. This trend may not be statistically significant, indicating no substantial distributional changes during this period other than the improvement in the relative position of the middle class. This overall result, however, masks significant differences in growth inclusiveness between urban and rural areas.

Although available indicators sometimes give conflicting signals on distributional shifts, a statistical analysis of the distributional characteristics of growth suggests the following: (1) poverty in Senegal has fallen in the last two decades, although poverty reduction has slowed in recent years; (2) although available indicators sometimes give conflicting signals on distributional shifts, growth seems to have benefited most people in the middle of the income distribution; (3) the middle class has benefited from growth, mainly in urban areas, while both the poorest and the richest have lost ground; (4) growth in rural areas has been less inclusive than it has been in urban areas.

Mali

In Mali, fairly high growth has led to substantial poverty reduction. After a decade of relatively low per-capita growth in the 1990s, economic activity picked up and averaged 3.2 percent during 2001–10. Although GDP growth has been volatile, Mali's share of poor households has decreased substantially from 55.6 percent in 2001 to 43.6 in 2010, taking into account the national poverty line at CFAF 453 per day of household consumption. Also, in comparison with other countries, Mali's poverty reduction was remarkable. While per-capita growth was comparable in Mali and sub-Saharan Africa during 2001–10, poverty reduction was significantly stronger in the former. This is also shown by higher elasticities of poverty reduction relative to GDP growth in Mali than was the case in comparable countries (Figure 7.7).

Growth in Mali's economic activity has been largely inclusive, meaning that it has not been associated with an increase in inequality (Rauniyar and Kanbur 2010) or with a reduction in the share of the bottom quintile of the income distribution. During 2001–10, the growth incidence curve—depicting the changes in household consumption according to consumption percentiles—features a clear downward slope, implying an increase in consumption of poorer households

Figure 7.6. Growth Incidence Curve for Total Population, 2001, 2005, 2011

1. 2001 and 2005

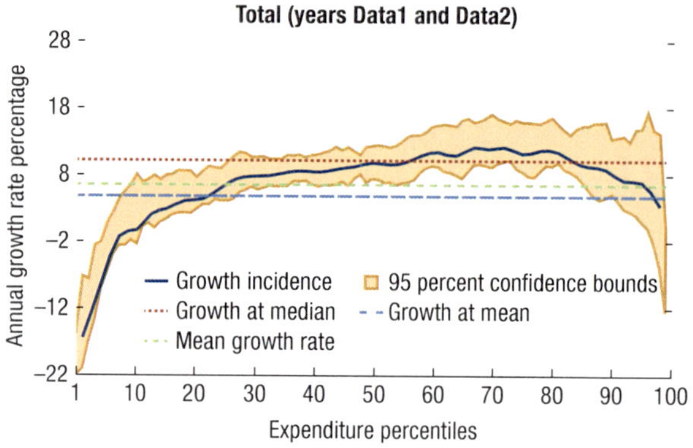

2. 2005 and 2011

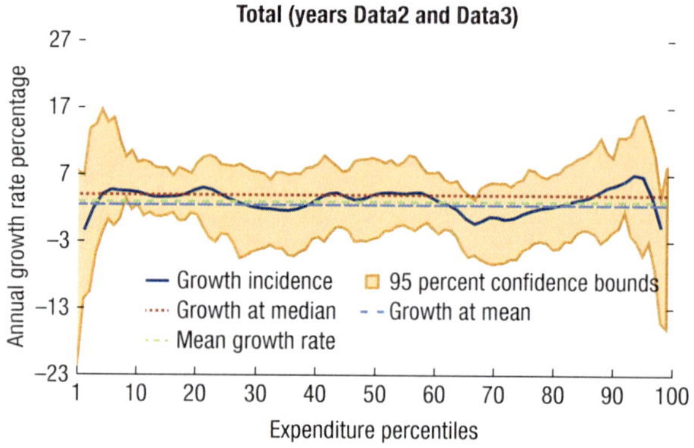

3. 2001 and 2011

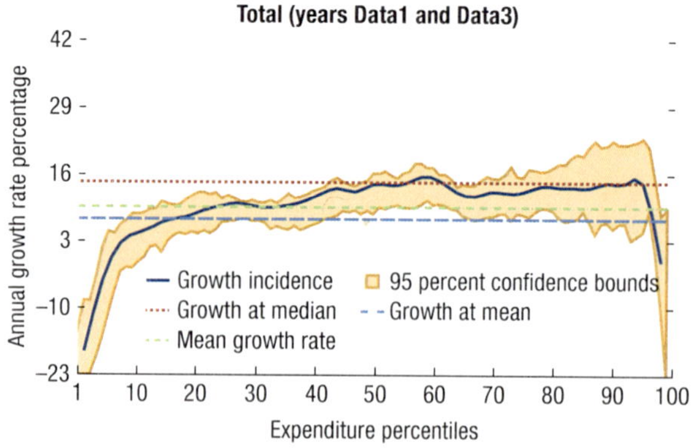

Source: World Bank, ESAM2001, ESPS2005, ESPS2011 databases processed using ADePT 5.1 platform for automated economic analysis, household-level data. The data may include outliers at both tails of the distribution.

Figure 7.7. Inclusiveness of Growth in Mali

Growth was volatile but relatively high from 2001 to 2011...

1. Real GDP Growth (In percent)

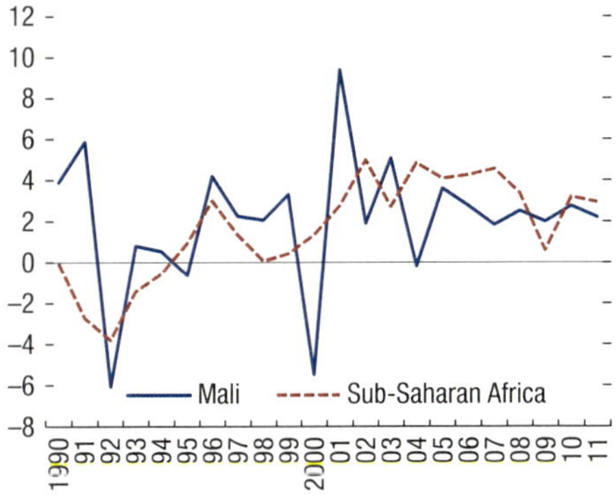

... and poverty has been reduced substantially.

2. Living Under $1.25 Per Day (Percent of population)

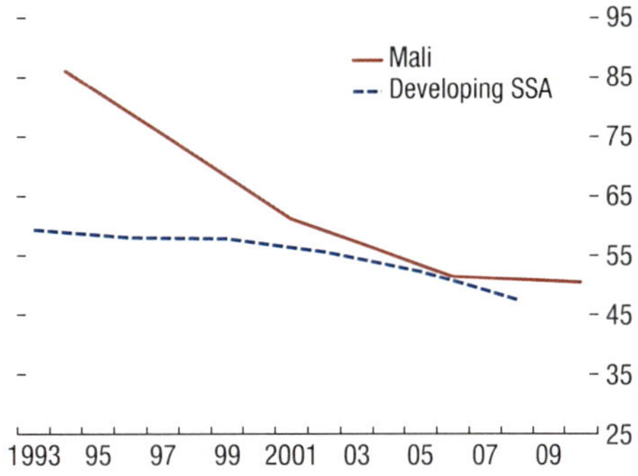

Mali's economic development was inclusive: poorer households experienced higher consumption growth...

3. Real Consumption Growth, 2001–10

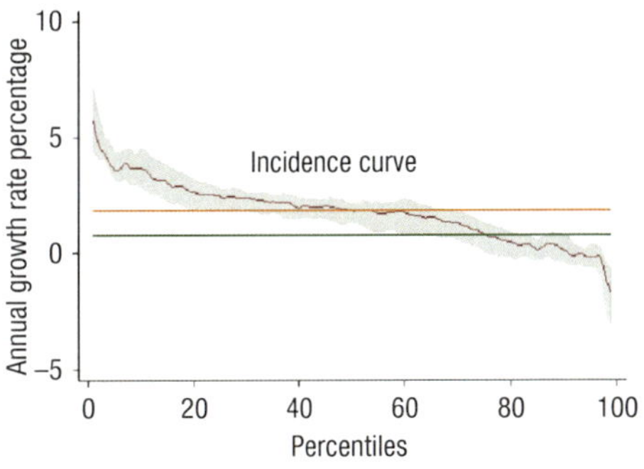

Note: The shaded area depicts the 90 percent confidence interval.

...and inequality decreased.

4. Gini Coefficient

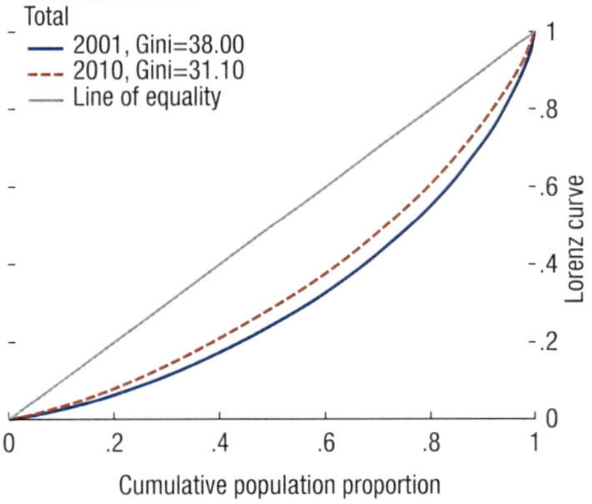

GDP per capita growth was more inclusive than in other comparable countries...

5. Elasticity of Headcount Poverty Rate with Respect to Growth in Real GDP Per Capita

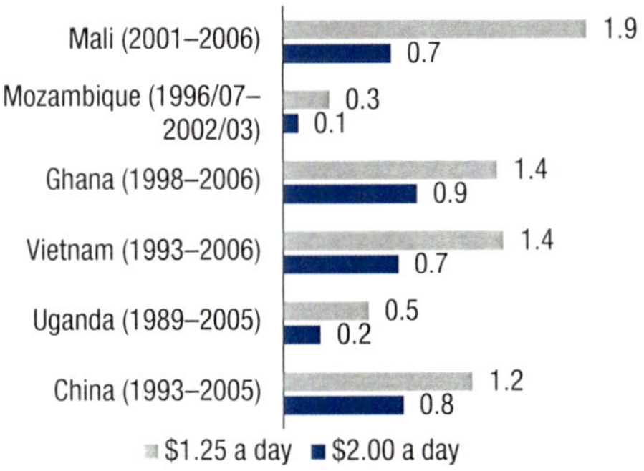

Sources: IMF staff estimates, Malian authorities; WEO; World Bank staff estimates, and World Development Indicators.

...but Mali is still one of the poorest countries.

6. Poverty Headcount Rate at International Poverty Lines[1]

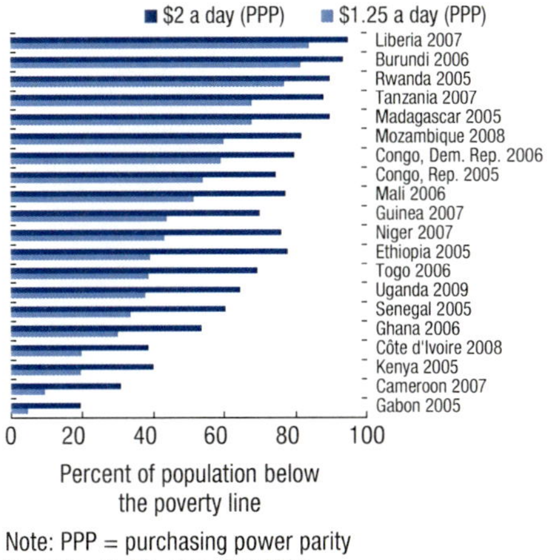

Note: PPP = purchasing power parity
[1]Latest available year after 2005

relative to richer households. Real consumption for households below the poverty line increased by 25 percent ("pro-poor growth"), while average consumption grew by 7.5 percent.

Poverty in Mali is mainly rural and concentrated among farmers. The results from a regression analysis pooling data of three household surveys (2001, 2006, and 2010) suggest that being a farmer implies a lower consumption by 33 percent (Table 7.3). In 2010 this effect was less pronounced, at 24 percent, reflecting an overall improvement of farmers' consumption relative to the rest of the population. Subsequently, urban poverty increased in the second part of the decade, mainly due to migration to Bamako (Figure 7.8). Further, a higher number of household members and an older age of the household head affect consumption negatively while civil servants are clearly better off than others. The results of Table 7.3 are broadly similar to regression analyses performed on comparable sub-Saharan countries (IMF 2011). However, the rural-urban divide seems more pronounced in Mali, and household size and age have a positive influence in other countries studied in IMF 2011, as opposed to a negative effect in Mali. The latter might be partially explained by Mali's higher population growth and more children per household than is the case in comparable countries.

Agriculture and Growth Inclusiveness

Poverty reduction in Mali was higher in the first part of the decade (2001–06) than it was during the second part (2006–10). While the magnitude of real GDP growth was broadly comparable throughout the decade, the number of households below the poverty line decreased more strongly during the first part. This is also reflected in a higher elasticity of poverty reduction to economic growth (Table 7.4). Moreover, in the first part of the decade Mali made more substantial progress toward achieving the millennium development goals than it did in the second part of the decade.

Consumption by the poorest rose and inequality decreased more strongly during 2006–10. As depicted in the growth incidence curves in Figure 7.8, the slope of the 2006–10 curve features a pronounced downward slope with steepening tails. Hence, the poorest quintile of the population benefited most, while the richest quintile lost relative to the rest of the population. The growth

TABLE 7.3

Mali: Determinants of Household Consumption

	(1)	(2)	(3)
Household size	−0.0161***	−0.0161***	−0.0161***
Age	−0.0587***	−0.0629***	−0.0632***
Sex	−0.010	−0.007	−0.004
Urban	0.284***	0.283***	0.284***
Farmer	−0.279***	−0.327***	−0.282***
Civil servant	0.299***	0.307***	0.297***
Self employed	0.020	0.024	0.019
Unemployed	−0.0714***	−0.0659***	−0.0676***
Year 2006	0.0337***	−0.003	0.012
Year 2010	0.171***	0.116***	0.191***
Farmer* 2006		0.0553***	
Farmer* 2010		0.0868***	
Urban* 2006			0.0805***
Urban* 2010			−0.0879***
Constant	12.33***	12.37***	12.34***
Observations	18454	18454	18454

Sources: Malian authorities; and IMF staff calculations.

Note: *, **, and *** indicate statistical significance at the 90, 95, and 99 percent confidence interval, respectively.

Figure 7.8. Mali: Patterns of Poverty, Poverty Reduction, and Obstacles

Poverty has declined in rural areas but increased recently in urban areas.

1. Incidence of Poverty by Region, 2001–10

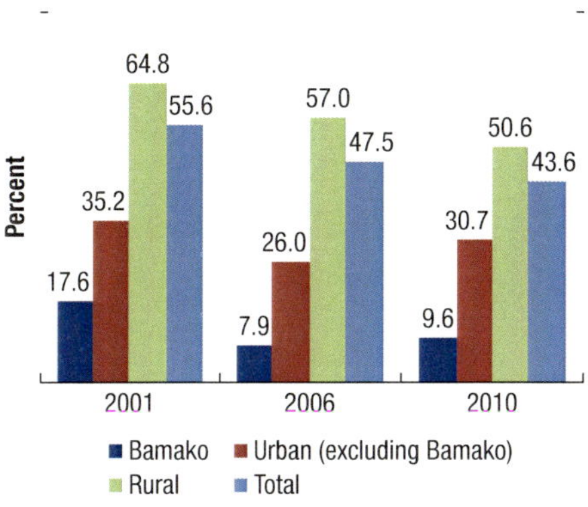

Poverty is most pronounced among agricultural workers.

2. Poverty by Type of Employment, 2010

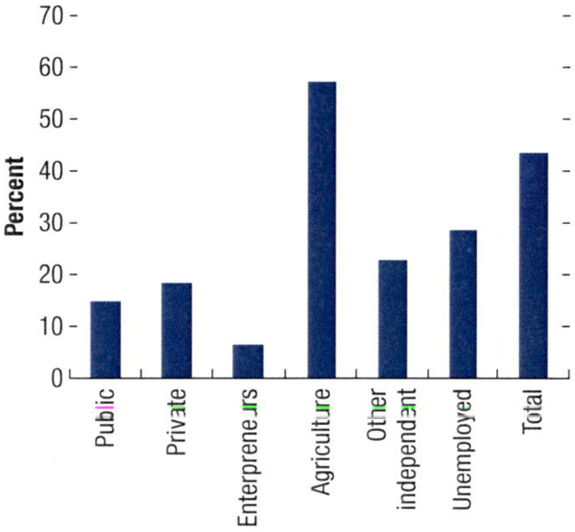

While consumption growth was slightly higher for the bottom half of the population from 2001 to 2006...

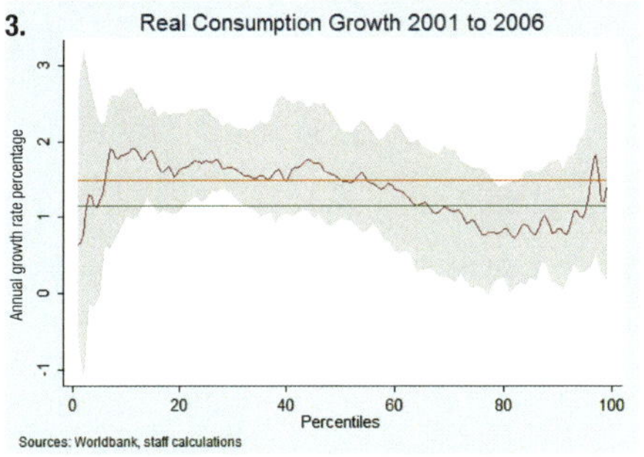

Note: The shaded area depicts the 90 percent confidence interval.

...it was mainly beneficial to the very poor from 2006 to 2010.

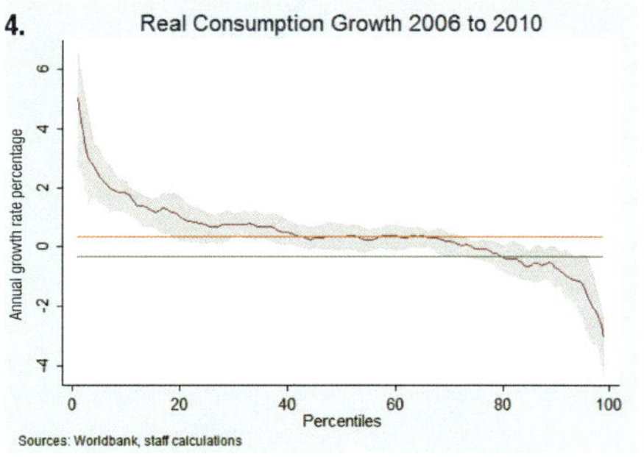

Note: The shaded area depicts the 90 percent confidence interval.

High population growth and demographics pose a huge challenge to maintaining inclusive growth...

5. Population, Average 2000–10 (Percent of Total)

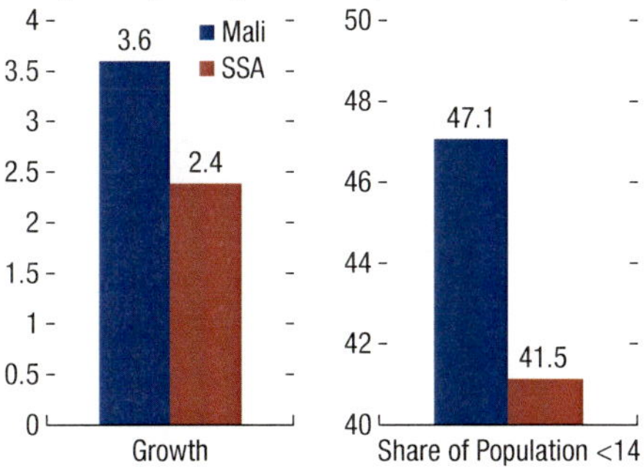

Sources: Malian authorities; World Development Indicators; and IMF staff estimates.

...as does reliance on subsistence agriculture.

6. Value Added by Economic Activity as Share of Real GDP, 2010

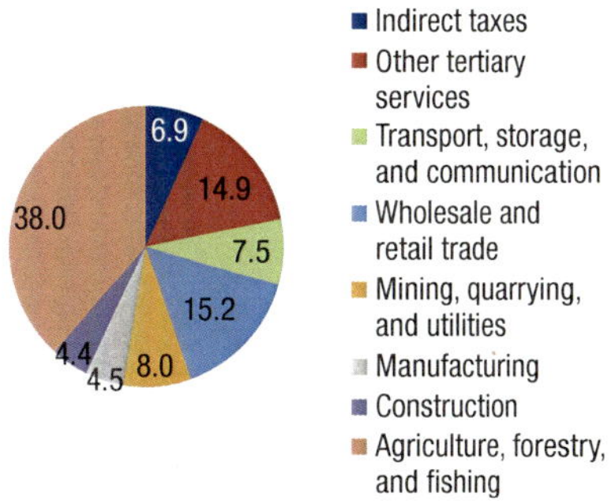

TABLE 7.4

Mali: National Accounts and Household Survey Data

	2001		2006		2010
National Accounts			(period average annual growth rates)		
Real GDP		5.1		4.9	
Real GDP per capita		2.6		2.3	
Real agricultural output		4.6		8.2	
Real industry output		5.9		−1.9	
Real services output		5.7		5.7	
Household Surveys			(in percent)		
Poverty incidence (national poverty line)	55.6		47.4		43.6
			(period average annual growth rates)		
Elasticity of poverty with regards to growth		−1.8		−1.5	
World Development Indicators					
Mortality rate under 5 (per 1,000)	217.3		199.5		191.1
School enrollment primary (percent net)	44.4		63.1		72.9

Sources: IMF; Malian authorities; World Development Indicators.
Note: School enrollment 1999 and 2009, mortality rate 2009.

incidence curve of 2001–06 still implies higher consumption growth for the bottom half of households, but it is flatter and the poorest households are not better off than the average.

During 2001–06, the economy grew at an equal pace in all three sectors. Manufacturing contracted and agricultural production boomed during 2006–10. Particularly good weather conditions helped agricultural output in 2006–10 to increase by 8 percent on average per year. Since the very poor are mostly farmers, their consumption basket expanded during this part of the decade. But as most farmers produce on a subsistence level, these gains in agricultural production could not be translated into an overall increase in production and employment elsewhere. Hence, the impressive growth in agriculture during 2006–10 allowed the very poor to improve their lives relative to the rest of the population, but the balanced growth during 2001–06 helped more households to escape poverty.

Gender inequality

Gender inequality in the WAEMU remains among the highest in the world (Figure 7.9). The United Nations gender inequality index measures gender inequality of outcomes (the gap between and male labor force participation rates and the share of women's seats in parliament) as well as inequality of opportunity (gender gaps in education and indicators of female health, such as the maternal death ratio and adolescent fertility). It shows that, when aggregating these categories, the WAEMU performs worse than most of the countries in the world. Surprisingly, female labor force participation is very low in some of the WAEMU countries even at very low levels of per-capita incomes (Mali, Niger). At these levels, countries usually observe higher labor force participation rates by women as women need to work for subsistence. Adult literacy rates, while lower in most WAEMU countries as compared to benchmark groups, remain particularly low for women. Health indicators remain poor in several WAEMU countries, especially in Mali and Niger.

At the global level, there is evidence that higher income inequality can impede growth. Lower net income inequality has been associated with faster and more sustained economic growth in both advanced and developing countries (Berg and Ostry 2011; Ostry, Berg, and Tsangarides 2014). With imperfect credit markets, income inequality prevents an efficient allocation of resources by decreasing poorer households' ability to make investments into human and physical capital (Galor and Zeira 1993; Corak 2013). Higher income and wealth inequality can also lead to socio-political instability and poor governance, thus discouraging investment (Bardhan 2005).

Figure 7.9. Gender Inequality in the WAEMU

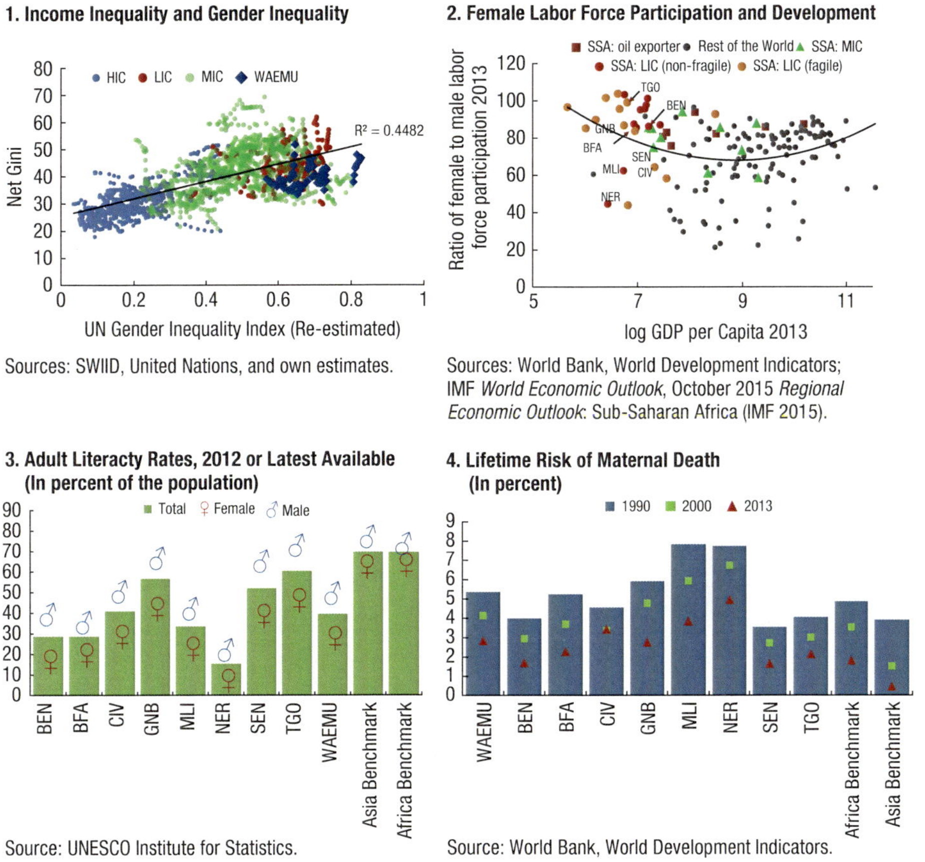

Sources (panel 1): SWIID, United Nations, and own estimates.

Sources (panel 2): World Bank, World Development Indicators; IMF *World Economic Outlook*, October 2015 *Regional Economic Outlook*: Sub-Saharan Africa (IMF 2015).

Source (panel 3): UNESCO Institute for Statistics.

Source (panel 4): World Bank, World Development Indicators.

The evidence that gender inequality is impeding economic growth is also growing. Gender inequality has been associated with worse growth and development outcomes (WEF 2014; Elborgh-Woytek and others 2013; IMF 2015; Gonzales and others 2015). Gender gaps in economic participation restrict the pool of talent on the labor market and can yield a less efficient allocation of resources, lower productivity, and hence lower GDP growth (Cuberes and Teignier 2015; Loko and Diouf 2009). Women are more likely than men to invest a large proportion of their household income in the education of their children so that higher economic participation and earnings by women translate into higher expenditure on school enrollment for children (Duflo 2003; Duflo 2012; Heintz 2006; Miller 2008; Rubalcava and others 2004; Thomas 1990). IMF (2015) highlights reductions in gender inequality as one of the most promising avenues to boost growth in the region—together with closing gaps in infrastructure and education. It shows that decreasing income and gender inequality in sub-Saharan African countries to levels observed in the ASEAN 5 (Indonesia, Malaysia, the Philippines, Thailand, Vietnam) could increase real GDP per-capita growth by about 1 percentage point on average.

In particular, the WAEMU's real GDP per-capita growth could significantly benefit from realistically implementable decreases in gender and income inequality (Figure 7.10). We follow the approach taken in IMF (2015) to decompose the differences in average real GDP per capita

Figure 7.10. Explaining the WAEMU's Growth Differential to Benchmark Countries

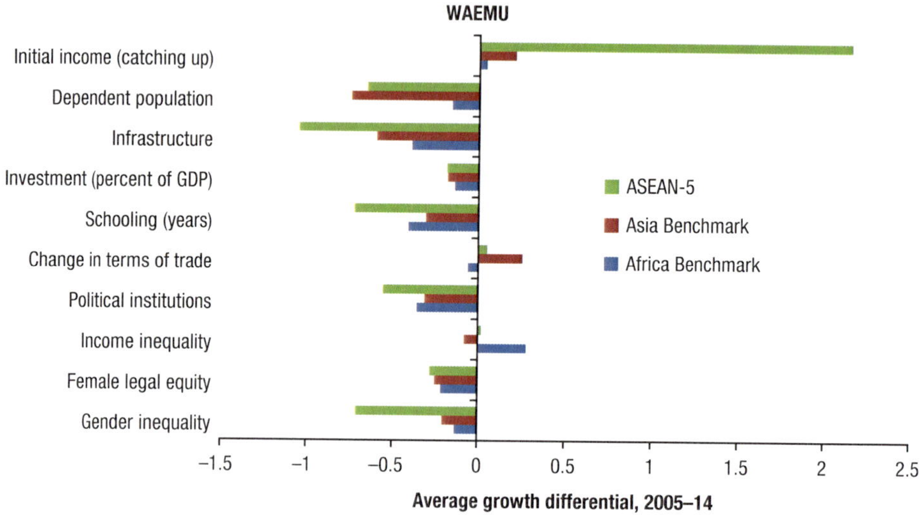

growth rates in the WAEMU and two benchmarks: a group of African benchmark countries (Ghana, Kenya, Lesotho, Rwanda, Tanzania, Uganda, Zambia) and a group of Asian benchmark countries (Bangladesh, Cambodia, India, Laos, Nepal, Vietnam), which have experienced around 2½ and 3½ percentage points higher real GDP growth compared to the WAEMU in the last two decades. The results of this approach reveal, that, in addition to large overall educational and infrastructure gaps, income and gender inequality can explain around 0.5 percentage points of the WAEMU's real GDP per capita income shortfall compared to the Asian Benchmark group. The potential effects are even larger for more ambitious targets: Decreasing gender inequality, including legal restrictions to the fast growing ASEAN-5 (Indonesia, Malaysia, Philippines, Thailand, Vietnam) could accelerate growth by one percentage point.

The magnitudes of these effects vary across WAEMU countries (Figure 7.11). While income and gender inequality have on average significantly contributed to the growth shortfall of the WAEMU relative to benchmark groups, the magnitudes of the effect vary. For instance, in Burkina Faso, income and gender inequality have been lower than in benchmark groups which has positively affected growth in Burkina Faso vis-à-vis the benchmarks. In Mali and Niger, with a high share of the population living in poverty, income inequality is relatively low. However, gender inequality is high in absolute and relative terms in Niger and Mali. In particular, in Mali, a reduction of gender inequality and an increase of legal equality between men and women alone could have resulted in a real GDP per capita boost of 0.6 percentage points of GDP, if reduced to the African benchmark level, or as much as 1.25 points of GDP if reduced to the average level of the ASEAN-5.

POLICIES TO INCREASE INCLUSIVENESS

Sustained overall economic growth is a precondition for further poverty reduction. A number of studies confirm that sustained growth is a key factor in enhancing inclusiveness. Kraay (2004) showed that in developing countries, growth of average income explains 70 percent of the

Figure 7.11. Differential Effects of Closing the Gap in Income and Gender Inequality in the WAEMU to Benchmark countries

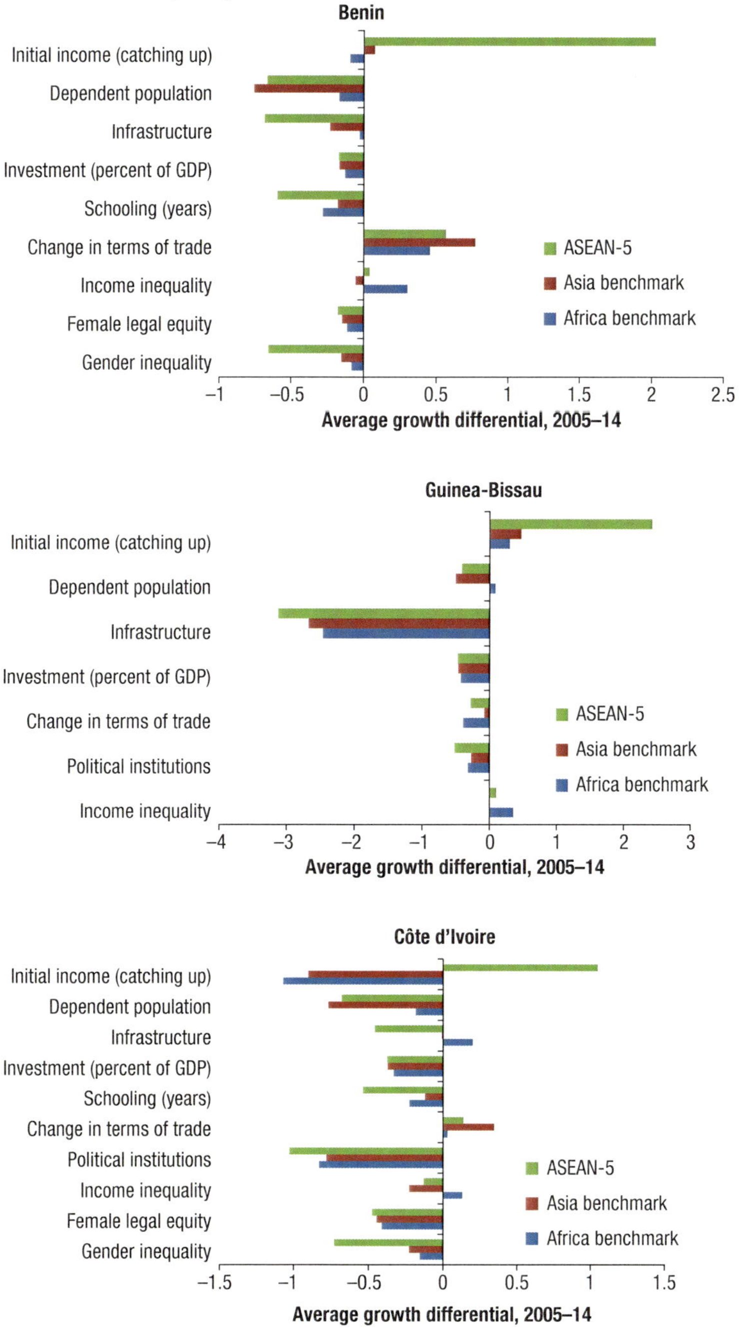

(*Continued*)

Figure 7.11. ***(continued)***

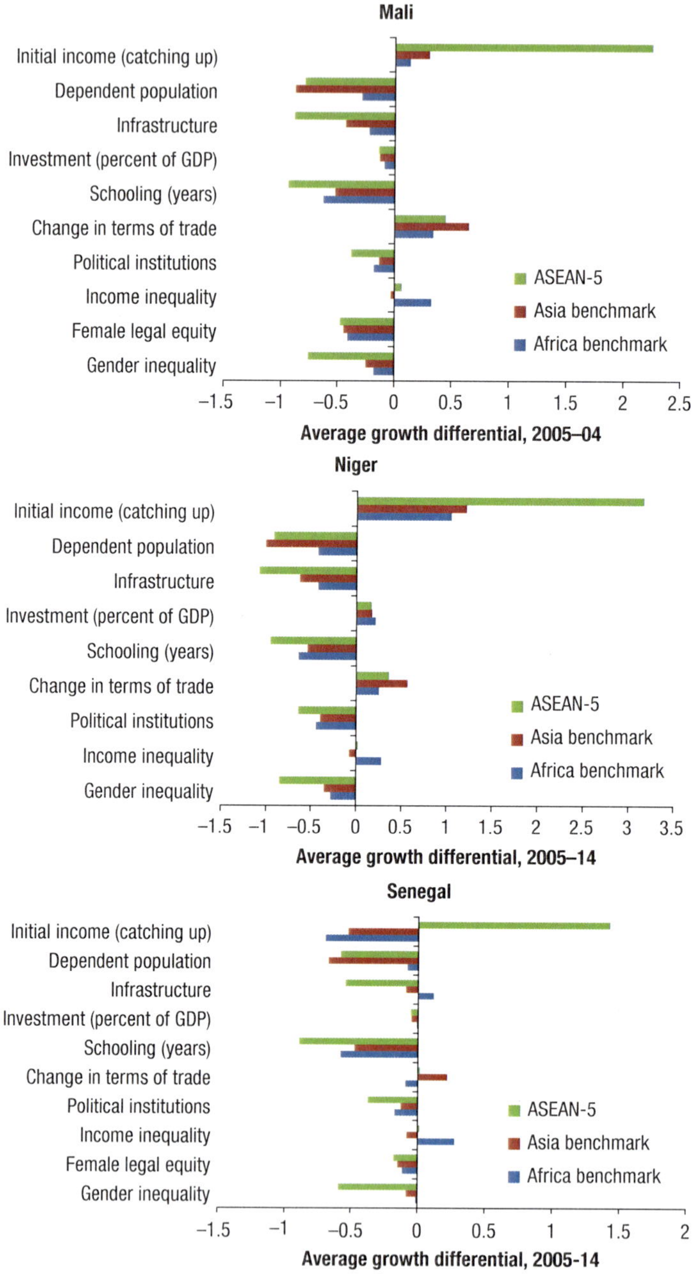

(Continued)

Figure 7.11. ***(continued)***

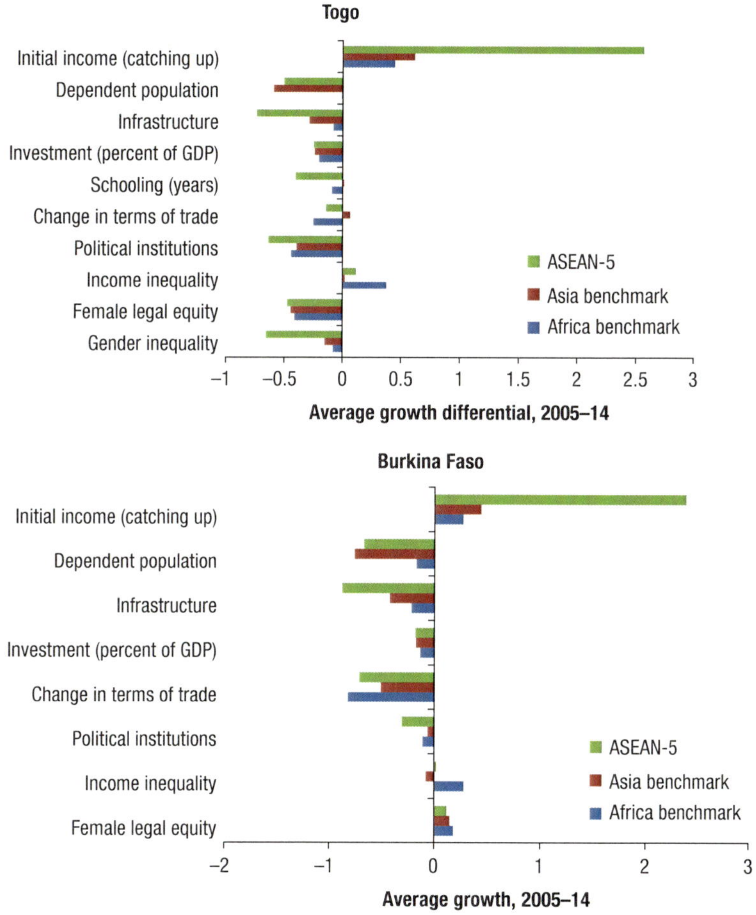

variation in poverty reduction in the short term. Berg and Ostry (2011) argue that longer growth spells are robustly associated with more equality in income distribution. Lopez and Servén (2006) suggest that for a given inequality level, the poorer the country, the more important the growth component is in explaining poverty reduction. Affandi and Peiris (2012) showed that growth is in general pro-poor, with growth leading to significant declines in poverty across economies and time periods. Specifically, a 1 percent increase in real per-capita income leads to about a 2 percent decline in the poverty-headcount ratio. Therefore, any successful pro-poor growth strategy should have at its core measures to achieve sustained and rapid economic growth. Senegal's experience is consistent with this cross-country evidence.

Special attention should be given to the distributional dimension of growth. An increase in inequality may offset and even exceed the beneficial impact on poverty reduction of the same increase in income (Affandi and Peiris 2012). According to recent estimates, about two-thirds of poverty reduction within a country comes from growth, and greater equality contributes the other third. A 1 percent increase in incomes in the most unequal countries produces a mere 0.6 percent reduction in poverty, while in the most equal countries, it yields a 4.3 percent cut

(Ravallion 2013). Because inclusiveness of growth is associated with a number of macroeconomic outcomes and policies, it is important to analyze growth and inclusiveness simultaneously. Increased inequality may dampen growth, but at the same time poorly designed measures to increase inclusiveness could undermine growth. For instance, increasing farm productivity and broadening rural job opportunities is important in addressing rural poverty. In the long term, attention to inclusiveness can bring significant benefits for growth.

Well-designed public policies are also important for promoting inclusiveness. The recommendations of the 2008 Poverty and Social Impact Analysis for Senegal remain broadly valid. Poorer households could be protected against food and fuel price increases in the short term at a lower budgetary cost and more effectively by redirecting resources to better-targeted measures. For example, poor groups could be targeted through measures such as school lunches and public works programs, and tariffs could be better targeted for small quantities of electricity to protect some of the urban poor. In the medium term, a well-targeted and conditional cash transfer system is the best option for assistance for the poorest.

Structural policies promoting employment and productivity increases, in particular in agriculture, could also help increase inclusiveness. According to the World Bank (2010), several policies have been successful in increasing the agricultural earnings of the poor in other low-income countries. These policies could be applicable in Senegal. They include improving market access and lowering transaction costs; strengthening property rights for land; creating an incentive framework that benefits all farmers; expanding the technology available to smallholder producers; and helping poorer and smaller producers handle risk. To expand nonagricultural and urban employment opportunities for poor households, other sub-Saharan African countries took steps to improve the investment climate; expand access to secondary and girls' education; design labor market regulations to create attractive employment opportunities; and increase access to infrastructure, especially roads and electricity.

Inclusive institutions have also been found to be important for growth inclusiveness. Acemoglu and Robinson (2012) argue that rich countries are rich by virtue of having inclusive institutions, that is, economic and political institutions that include the large majority of the population in the political and economic community. An initial set of inclusive economic institutions would include secure property rights, rule of law, public services, and freedom to contract. The role of the state would be to impose law and order, enforce contracts, and prevent theft and fraud.

Coherent labor market policies are also needed for increasing inclusiveness. The challenges of growth, job creation, and inclusion are closely linked, because creating productive employment opportunities throughout the economy is an important way to generate inclusive growth (IMF 2013). In Senegal, creation of employment opportunities and increasing productivity in rural areas, in particular in agriculture, would prompt higher consumption growth among poorer households. For example, the stronger per-capita consumption growth observed in Cameroon and Uganda at the poorest levels seems to relate to high agricultural employment growth (IMF 2011). By contrast, rural agricultural employment fell in Mozambique and Zambia where the poorest experienced weaker or negative per-capita consumption growth.

Deepening the financial sector through policies that give better access to the poor for financial services would increase inclusiveness. A number of studies found that financial development generally increases incomes of the poorest households (Claessens 2005), whereas unequal access to financial markets can reduce incomes by impeding investments in human and physical capital. These barriers are widespread in Senegal, where most people lack access to the formal financial system. At the same time, microfinance and other rural finance and expanding credit information sharing could significantly expand credit availability. Some promising initiatives in this area are underway in Senegal.

Improving agricultural production is key to helping the poorest of the poor. Given the current opportunities, investments in agriculture can diminish the poverty gap and promote poverty reduction. Possible measures include: building and maintaining irrigation infrastructure (less than 15 percent of potentially irrigated land is actually irrigated), modernizing family farming and subsistence agriculture to agribusinesses and food processing, making public-sector support to agriculture more efficient, and improving access to finance.

Finally, the WAEMU's real GDP per-capita growth could significantly benefit from the reduction in gender and income inequality. Decreasing income inequality and gender inequality are desirable from a political preference or human rights perspective. It is also smart economics, since the associated gains in real GPD per-capita growth are large for policy moves that are realistically implementable in shorter time horizons.

REFERENCES

Acemoglu, D., and J. Robinson. 2012. *Why Nations Fail: The Origins of Power, Prosperity, and Poverty*. New York: Crown Business.

Affandi, Y., and S. Peiris. 2012. "Building Inclusive Growth in the Philippines." IMF Country Report No. 12/50, International Monetary Fund, Washington.

Bardhan, P. K. 2005. *Scarcity, Conflicts, and Cooperation: Essays in the Political and Institutional Economics of Development*. Cambridge, Massachusetts: MIT Press.

Berg, A., and J. Ostry. 2011. "Inequality and Unsustainable Growth: Two Sides of the Same Coin?" IMF Staff Discussion Note, April 8, SDN/11/08. International Monetary Fund, Washington.

Claessens, S. 2005. "Access to Financial Services: A Review of the Issues and Public Policy Objectives." Policy Research Working Paper Series 3589, World Bank, Washington.

Corak, M. 2013. "Income Inequality, Equality of Opportunity, and Intergenerational Mobility." *Journal of Economic Perspectives* 27 (3): 79–102.

Cuberes, D., and M. Teignier. 2015. "Aggregate Effects of Gender Gaps in the Labor Market: A Quantitative Estimate." *Journal of Human Capital*, forthcoming.

Duflo, E. 2003. "Grandmothers and Granddaughters: Old-Age Pensions and Intrahousehold Allocation in South Africa." *The World Bank Economic Review* 17 (1): 1–25.

———. 2012. "Women Empowerment and Economic Development." *Journal of Economic Literature* 50 (4): 1051–79.

Elborgh-Woytek, K., M. Newiak, K. Kochhar, S. Fabrizio, K. Kpodar, P. Wingender, B. Clements, and G. Schwartz. 2013. "Women, Work, and the Economy: Macroeconomic Gains from Gender Equity." Staff Discussion Note, SDN/13/10, International Monetary Fund, Washington.

Enquête Suivi de la Pauvreté au Sénégal (ESPS-II 2010–2011). 2012. ANSD, Dakar.

Foster, J., S. Seth, M. Lokshin, and Z. Sajaia. 2013. *A Unified Approach to Measuring Poverty and Inequality: Theory and Practice*. Washington: World Bank.

Galor, O., and J. Zeira. 1993. "Income Distribution and Macroeconomics." *The Review of Economic Studies* 60 (1): 35–52.

Gonzales, C., S. Jain-Chandra, K. Kochhar, M. Newiak, and T. Zeinullayev. 2015. "Catalyst for Change: Empowering Women and Tackling Income Inequality." Staff Discussion Note, SDN 15/20, International Monetary Fund, Washington.

Heintz, J. 2006. "Globalization, Economic Policy and Employment: Poverty and Gender Implications." International Labour Organization, Geneva.

International Monetary Fund (IMF). 2011. "How Inclusive Has Africa's Recent High-Growth Episode Been?" *Regional Economic Outlook: Sub-Saharan Africa*, Washington, October.

———. 2013. "Jobs and Growth: Analytical and Operational Considerations for the Fund." International Monetary Fund, Washington. Available at www.imf.org.

———. 2015. "Inequality and Economic Outcomes in Sub-Saharan Africa." October 2015 *Regional Economic Outlook: Sub-Saharan Africa*. Forthcoming.

Kraay, A. 2004. "When Is Growth Pro-Poor? Cross-Country Evidence." IMF Working Paper No. 2004/12, International Monetary Fund, Washington.

Loko, B., and M. A. Diouf. 2009. "Revisiting the Determinants of Productivity Growth: What's New?" IMF Working Paper 09/225, International Monetary Fund, Washington.

Lopez, H., and L. Servén. 2006. "A Normal Relationship? Poverty, Growth, and Inequality." Policy Research Working Paper Series 3814, World Bank, Washington.

Miller, G. 2008, "Women's Suffrage, Political Responsiveness, and Child Survival in American History," *The Quarterly Journal of Economics* (August), 1287–326.

Ostry, J., A. Berg, and C. Tsangarides. 2014. "Redistribution, Inequality, and Growth." IMF Staff Discussion Note 14/02, International Monetary Fund, Washington.

Rauniyar, Ganesh P., and Ravi Kanbur. 2010. "Inclusive Development: Two Papers on Conceptualization, Application, and the ADB Perspective." Working Papers 57036, Cornell University, Department of Applied Economics and Management, Ithaca, Cornell University.

Ravallion, M. 2013. "How Long Will It Take to Lift One Billion People Out of Poverty?" World Bank Policy Research Working Paper 6325, World Bank, Washington.

Ravallion, M., and S. Chen. 2003. "Measuring Pro-Poor Growth." *Economics Letters* 78: 93–99.

Rubalcava, L., G. Teruel, and D. Thomas. 2004. "Spending, Saving and Public Transfers to Women," California Center of Population Research UCLA, On-Line Working Paper Series, CCPR-024-04.

Thomas, D. 1990. "Intra-Household Resource Allocation. An Inferential Approach," *The Journal of Human Resources* 25 (4): 635–64.

World Bank. 2010. *Pro-Poor Growth in the 1990s: Lessons and Insights from 14 Countries.* Washington: World Bank.

World Economic Forum (WEF). 2014. *The Global Gender Gap Report 2014.* Basel: WEF.

CHAPTER 8

Financing Growth

Mame Astou Diouf and François Boutin-Dufresne

The West African Economic and Monetary Union (WAEMU) region faces the challenge of mobilizing resources for growth financing. The regional financial market has grown substantially in the past decade but still remains relatively shallow and falls short of supplying sufficient long-term financing for growth-enhancing public and private investment projects. Although the institutional structure for financing mobilization is broadly in place, the undiversified issuer and narrow investor bases, banks' preferences for short-term securities, the limited set of maturities offered by sovereigns, underdeveloped secondary markets for bills and bonds, organizational issues, and limited access to information increase financing costs and hinder market efficiency. The yield curve in the region has been generally upward sloping, as interest rates at issuance were higher for securities with longer maturities. The interest rates have been largely driven by country ratings, market liquidity conditions, and bidders' appetites at the time of issuance. The principal component analysis in this chapter suggests that the issuance volumes offered also mattered for the level of interest rates, with seasonality, issuance procedures, and the frequency and predictability of issues also playing their roles. Further reforms could help the region reap the full benefits of a more dynamic securities market to finance growth-enhancing projects.

RESOURCE MOBILIZATION

To finance growth, several initiatives to create regional financial markets in Asia, Europe, and Africa have been pushed forward in the last decade. The global financial crisis highlighted the importance of regional financial markets' ability to provide liquidity to governments and private sector actors during periods of heightened economic and financial uncertainty. The launching of regional markets aimed to cater to governments' and the private sector's financing needs and growth ambitions, and to smooth out global economic and financial woes by sustaining adequate spending and investment levels during economic and financial volatility.

The WAEMU region, which faces challenges of mobilizing resources for growth financing, was no stranger to this trend. The WAEMU securities market was launched in 1998. Its creation followed the decision of the region's Council of Ministers in 1993 to establish a common financial market to respond in a more transparent, efficient, and harmonized manner to the financing needs of WAEMU countries and private corporations. That mandate was reinforced by the 2001 decision to gradually phase out statutory advances with a total elimination by 2010, which encouraged governments to substitute sovereign issues to the Central Bank of West African States' (BCEAO's) direct lending.

The securities market benefited from the region's economic and monetary integration, notably its shared institutions and harmonized financial regulations. When the securities market became operational in 1999—more than three decades after the WAMU[1] was set—the region was already functioning in a coordinated manner with a common central bank, regional monetary policy, and

[1]The West African Monetary Union (WAMU) was created in 1962. It became a monetary and economic union (WAEMU) in 1994.

uniform banking and financial regulations. The creation of the regional securities market completed the WAEMU's financial integration by facilitating cross-regional funding for governments while reducing transaction costs through harmonized issuance procedures. In addition to these enabling preconditions, the market benefited from the region's relatively strong macroeconomic and political stability—notwithstanding the crisis in Côte d'Ivoire and Mali—and from the strong credibility of the CFA franc/euro peg.

While the securities market succeeded in providing short-term financing to actors, it fell short of expectations regarding the financing of growth-enhancing, long-term investment projects. With the region's high investment needs, the market was initially expected to increase financial intermediation and help spur public and private investment. Moreover, the reduction of foreign aid and private capital flows to the region in the early 2000s, combined with the commodity-led swings in regional terms of trade, underscored the need for countries to find more stable sources of finance through the deepening of the regional financial market. However, to date, the WAEMU securities market has failed to catalyze large long-term financing for public and private entities, pointing to several impediments to its full development.

INSTITUTIONAL FRAMEWORK AND INSTRUMENTS

The WAEMU regional securities market is managed by four institutions (Figure 8.1): the BCEAO, the Regional Council for Public Savings and Financial Markets (CREPMF),[2] the Regional Stock Exchange (BRVM),[3] and the Central Deposit and Settlement Organization (DC/BR).[4] The BCEAO manages sovereign securities issued through auctions by WAEMU

Figure 8.1. Organigram of the WAEMU Securities Market

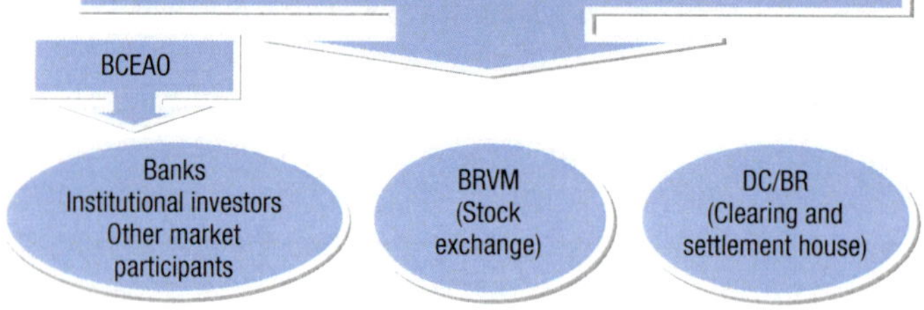

Source: Authors' presentation.
Note: BCEAO = Central Bank of West African States; BRVM = Regional Stock Exchange; CREPMF = Regional Council for Public Savings and Financial Markets; DC/BR = Central Deposit and Settlement Organization; WAEMU = West African Economic and Monetary Union.

[2] Conseil Régional de l'Epargne Publique et des Marchè Financiers (CREPMF).
[3] Bourse Régionale des valeurs mobilières (BRVM).
[4] Dépositaire Central/Banque de Règlement (DC/BR).

countries. It takes care of issuances and acts as book runner and clearinghouse for market participants. In addition, the BCEAO helps regulate the sovereign debt market, as well as commercial banks and nonbank financial institutions. The CREPMF, BRVM, and DC/BR manage the securities beyond the BCEAO's scope of action. The CREPMF is a surveillance body that manages initial public offerings and regulates market participants. It reports directly to the WAEMU Council of Ministers. The BRVM ensures the quotation and negotiation of transferable securities and supplies market information to participants. The DC/BR acts as a custodian for investors and as an overall clearing house. Commercial operators who intervene in the market include banks and asset managers (acting on their own account or on behalf of their clients), asset custodians, business developers, and incubators, all of which are regulated by the CREPMF.

The regional securities market offers the following investment instruments, which include both equity (stocks) and debt securities:

- *Stocks*—Offered by listed companies and traded on the stock exchange.
- *Treasury bills and bonds*—Issued by treasuries of WAEMU member countries. Treasury bills have maturities of 3–24 months whereas Treasury bonds are of 2–7-year maturity. The maturities of Treasury bills typically range from 3 to 12 months. On rare occasions, Treasury bills of 24-month maturity were issued.
- *Regional bills and bonds*—Issued by regional institutions such as the West African Development Bank and the Economic Community of West African States Bank for Investment and Development.
- *Kola bills and bonds*—Issued by non-WAEMU resident institutions such as the International Finance Corporation (IFC), and the French Development Agency. This segment of the market was launched in 2006 with the IFC's first local currency bond issuance in sub-Saharan Africa.
- *Corporate bills and bonds*—Issued by WAEMU resident private companies, including state-owned enterprises.
- *Other quoted securities.*

Issuance procedures for securities depend on the type of security. Although regional regulations require that government bills and bonds be auctioned on the primary market, some Treasury bonds are still issued by syndication. Treasury bill and Treasury bond auctions are carried out for each member country at the national branches of the BCEAO. This is done by an appointed issuance committee composed of three representatives of the ministry of finance and three representatives of the BCEAO national branch. Auctions are open to investors who bid prices, interest rates, and quantities, mostly through financial institutions acting as primary dealers in the process. Bids are also open to foreign investors who have an account in the region's commercial banks. National Treasury bill issuance calendars are typically published on a quarterly basis, after the region's ministers of finance and the BCEAO agree on treasuries' liquidity needs. Corporate and other types of nonsovereign bonds are issued via syndication to market participants, while stock initial public offerings are auctioned by the DC/BR. All quotations are made by the BRVM.

Three categories of securities are publicly placed in the WAEMU bond market: (1) negotiable securities, including Treasury bills, commercial paper, regional financial institution negotiable bills, and certificates of deposit; (2) public debt securities, which include securitization of statutory advances and other debt arrears of governments and public enterprises; and (3) non-negotiable bonds, including notably sovereign and corporate bonds.

A number of initiatives and reforms are under way to support development of the WAEMU bond market. As part of a strategy to attract greater and more diverse foreign capital flows, some of the region's governments have sought the service of credit rating agencies (Table 8.1). In addition, the WAEMU launched a process to harmonize the taxation of securities listed on the regional market. Government securities are tax-exempt, increasing their attractiveness to

TABLE 8.1

WAEMU: Countries' Sovereign Debt Ratings

	Bonds		T-Bills	
Country	Standard and Poor's	Fitch	Standard and Poor's	Fitch
Benin	B	B	B	B
Burkina Faso	B	—	B	—
Senegal	B+	—	B	—
Mali[1]	—	Discontinued	—	—

Source: Bloomberg, L.P., as of December 2010.
[1] Mali's rating was discontinued by Fitch as of 12/04/09.

potential investors. Conversely, other types of bonds are taxed with a progressive rate favoring long-term investment. Interest payments on bonds of 10-year maturity or higher are tax-exempt, while the tax rate for Treasury bonds of maturities between 5 and 10 years is 3 percent. The rate is 6 percent for maturities of less than 5 years. Distributions of corporate dividends are taxed at a rate of between 10 and 15 percent, and dividends of companies listed on the regional stock market for listings approved by CFEPMF are taxed at a rate of between 2 and 7 percent. Finally, the WAEMU Council of Ministers granted a tax exemption to interest payments on IFC Kola bonds for 5 years.

OPERATIONS

The WAEMU regional bond market expanded relatively rapidly in the first decade of 2000, owing to regular issuances of government securities (Figure 8.2). The total amount of publicly placed securities almost doubled during the period. This dynamism was mainly driven by regular public debt issues, reflecting the increasing resorting of governments to the bond market after the elimination of central bank financing. The predominant part of securities was issued by the region's treasuries, whereas issuances by corporate and other institutions were limited. On average, Treasury bills and bonds issued represented barely a fifth of WAEMU countries' total financing (aid flows, central bank financing, nonbank financing, and privatization revenue), showing that the market is far from being their main source of financing.

Issuances were dominated by sovereign short-term borrowing, sustained by treasuries' liquidity needs and a hefty appetite from commercial banks. Treasury bill issuances have dominated market operations. Such large issues are accommodated by banks' appetites for Treasury bills, owing to the many advantages they bear. In fact, the acquisition of Treasury bills by banks does not hinder commercial banks' capital adequacy requirements. They are of short maturity, count as "capital" holdings in banks' balance sheets, and bear a zero-risk weight in the calculation of capital adequacy ratios. Besides, Treasury bills can be traded in any of the eight WAEMU countries and can be used for refinancing at the central bank.

Treasury issues and holdings generally show a high concentration of both issuers and investors, a significant excess demand, and a predominance of securities with less than ½-year maturities (Figure 8.2 and Table 8.2). Using 2010 as example, Côte d'Ivoire alone issued about ⅔ of the total amount of traded Treasury bills, dominating the market in that year owing to the country's special circumstances. Benin, Burkina Faso, Senegal, and Mali issued less than ⅓ percent of the Treasury bills. A large part of those Treasury bills was of less than ½-year maturities, with a predominance of three- and six-month maturities. Financial institutions from Côte d'Ivoire, Senegal, Burkina Faso, and Mali bought ¾ of the securities, though the distribution of actual investors is unknown because operations are handled by financial intermediaries. For each country, investors

Figure 8.2. WAEMU: Issuance of Debt Securities, 2001–10[1]

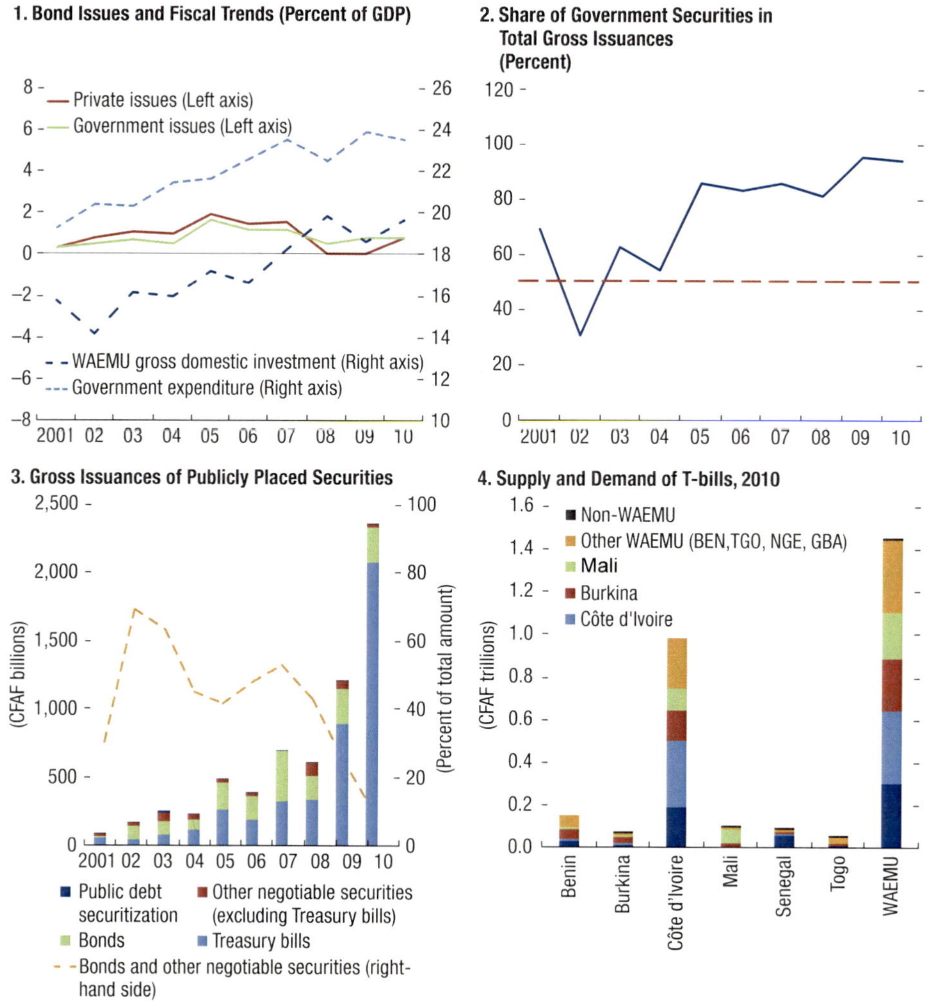

Sources: BCEAO and IMF staff calculations.
[1]Data up to December 19, 2010.

Sources: Central Bank of West African States and IMF staff calculations.
Note: Three-letter International Organization for Standardization abbreviations used for country names. WAEMU = West African Economic and Monetary Union.

registered in other WAEMU countries bought a nonnegligible part of the domestic securities, even if cross-border investment was still timid.

Similarly, long-term securities show a low diversification in issuers and maturities (Table 8.3). The governments of Côte d'Ivoire, Senegal, and Burkina Faso are the main issuers in the market, with about half of the total long-term, nonnegotiable securities issued. They are followed by the West African Development Bank, with about 20 percent of the long-term, nonnegotiable securities. The regional development bank issues bonds regularly, acting *de facto* as a benchmark issuer for nonsovereigns. During the first decade of 2000 period, 20 private corporations issued bonds, representing merely 15 percent of total bond issues. Issuing companies included public utilities, telecommunication companies, and banks. Most of the long-term securities had five- to seven-year maturities.

TABLE 8.2

WAEMU: Government Debt Issues, 2010[1]

	Amount[2]	Average Maturity[3,4]	Interest Rate at Issuance[5]		Average Coverage Rate[5]
			Average[3]	Range	
Treasury bills					
WAEMU	**1452.4**	**185.3**	**5.1**	**[4.1, 6.8]**	**194.0**
Benin	154.7	364.0	5.8	[5.5, 6.0]	166.0
Burkina Faso	70.2	91.0	4.7	[4.1, 5.5]	484.9
Côte d'Ivoire	982.3	140.0	5.7	[4.8, 6.8]	171.3
Guinea-Bissau	—	—	—	—	—
Mali	99.5	276.2	5.1	[4.9, 5.3]	218.6
Niger	—	—	—	—	—
Senegal	94.7	389.1	5.6	[5.1, 6.4]	213.3
Togo	51.0	91.0	4.7	[4.5, 4.9]	239.9
Treasury bonds					
WAEMU	**127.4**	**5.7**	**6.6**	**[6.6, 7.0]**	**—**
Benin	—	—	—	—	—
Burkina Faso	43.3	7.0	6.5	6.5	—
Côte d'Ivoire	35.6	7.0	7.0	7.0	—
Guinea-Bissau	—	—	—	—	—
Mali	—	—	—	—	—
Niger	—	—	—	—	—
Senegal	31.4	3.0	6.0	6.0	—
Togo	17.1	5.0	7.0	7.0	—

Sources: Central Bank of West African States; IMF staff calculations.
[1] Gross issuance. At November 10, 2010, for bills and at end-June 2010 for bonds.
[2] In CFAF trillions.
[3] Weighted average.
[4] Number of days for bills and number of years for bonds.
[5] In percent.

Foreign participation in the bond market remained marginal. The region's relative economic stability and pegged exchange rate was expected to foster greater participation of foreign investors in the market. On the contrary, external portfolio flows to the region were dismal in the last decade.

INTEREST RATES DETERMINANTS

The term structure of interest rates—or yield curve—for sovereign securities shows that for all countries, interest rates at issuance were higher for securities with longer maturities (Figure 8.3). The yield curves of all WAEMU countries show an upward trend, signaling investors' general preferences for shorter-term, thus less risky, securities. Investors imposed a risk premium on long-term, less liquid securities, which is actually an indicator of investors' rational market behavior. Nevertheless, the yield and term premiums imposed by investors differed from country to country as revealed by the curves' levels and shapes. For example, with a yield curve above that of other WAEMU countries, the cost of financing for Côte d'Ivoire was, on average, higher than that of other WAEMU countries. Moreover, Côte d'Ivoire and Senegal had especially steep yield curves for short maturities, signaling that investors requested for the two countries risk premiums that were proportionally higher than the increases in maturity. By contrast, the yield curve for Burkina Faso was among the lowest in the region and had an almost linear shape. All securities issued by Benin were of the same maturity (one year); this was similar for Togo (three months). The latter benefited from the lowest interest rates on the market, except for two Burkina Faso issues of equivalent maturities.

TABLE 8.3

WAEMU: Issuance of Long-Term Securities, 1999–2010[1,2]

	Amount (CFAF billions)		Number of Issuance		Maturity (years)		Interest Rate at Issuance (percent)	
	1999–2010[2]	2010[2]	1999–2010[2]	2010[2]	Average[3]	Range	Average[3]	Range
Negotiable debt securities	**209.63**	**0**	**11**	**0**	**7.0**	**[3, 7]**	**4.4**	**[3.3, 7.0]**
Sovereign	—	—	—	0	—	—	—	—
BOAD[4]	207.7	0	8	0	7	7	4.4	[3.3, 5.9]
Other nontreasury	1.93	0	3	0	3.4	[3, 4]	6.7	[5.5, 7.0]
Nonnegotiable debt securities	**1575.7**	**137.4**	**60**	**5**	**6.0**	**[3, 10]**	**6.2**	**[4.5, 7.5]**
BOAD[4]	144.4	0	10	0	6.9	[3, 10]	5.5	[4.5, 6.3]
BIDC[5]	24.1	0	1	0	7.0	7	5.6	5.6
IFC[6]	22.0	0	1	0	5.0	5	4.8	4.8
AFD[7]	20.0	0	1	0	8.0	8	5.3	5.3
Sovereign	1121.9	127.4	27	4	5.9	[3, 10]	6.3	[5.5, 7.0]
Other (corporate)	243.4	10	20	1	6.0	[5, 7]	6.6	[5.9, 7.5]

Sources: Central Bank of West African States; IMF staff calculations.
[1] Securities with maturities of more than two years.
[2] As of end-June 2010.
[3] Weighted average.
[4] West African Development Bank. It issued its first nonnegotiable bond in 1995.
[5] Economic Community of West African States (ECOWAS) Bank for Investment and Development. The bond was issued in 2006.
[6] International Finance Corporation. The bond was issued in 2006.
[7] French Development Agency. The bond was issued in 2008.

Figure 8.3. WAEMU: Determinants of T-Bills' Interest Rates, 2010[1]

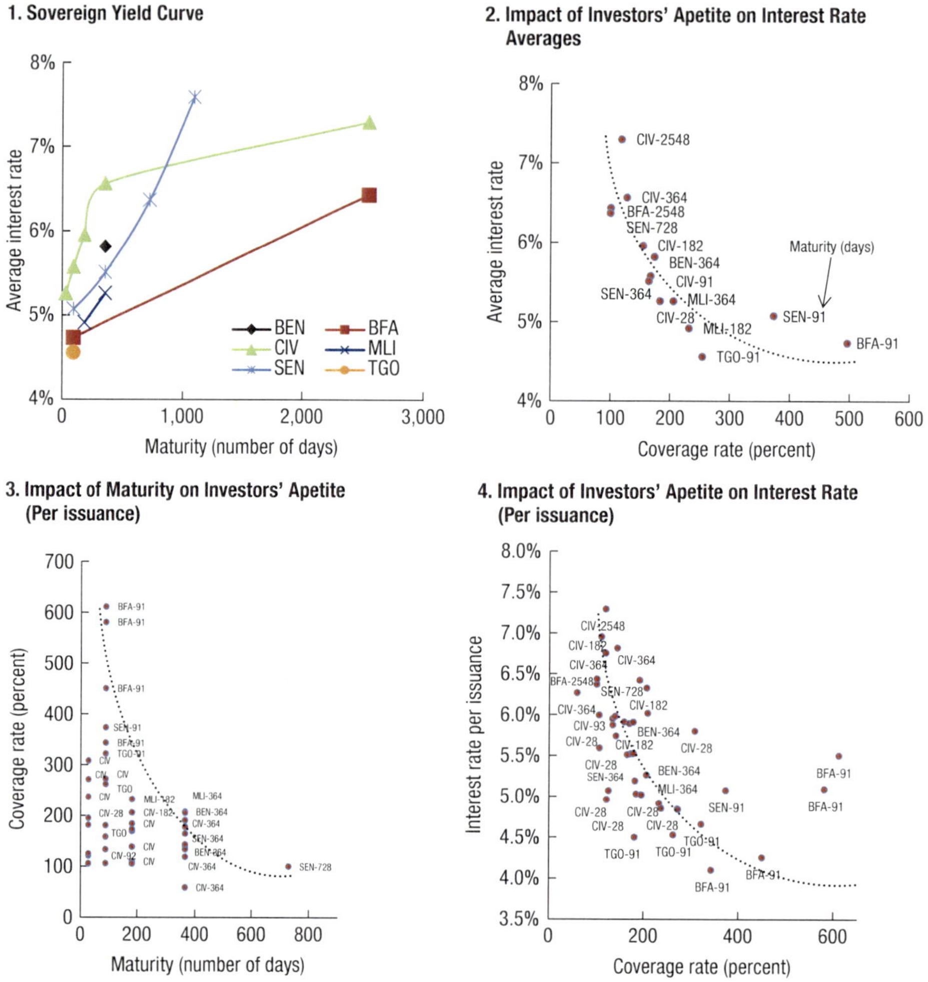

Sources: Central Bank of West African States; and IMF staff calculations.
Note: BEN = Benin; BFA = Burkina Faso; CIV = Côte d'Ivoire; GNB = Guinea-Bissau; MLI = Mali; NER = Niger; SEN = Senegal; TGO = Togo.
[1]Data up to December 19, 2010.

Country ratings had some beneficial impact on Treasury bond interest rates (Tables 8.1 and 8.2). Interest rates on Treasury bonds appear to react positively to country ratings. The interest rate on the Treasury bond issued by Burkina Faso was lower than that for Togo, which did not have a rating for its bonds at that time—even though the maturity of the Burkina Faso bond was longer than that of the Togo bond. The interest rate on the Treasury bond issued by Senegal, which has the highest Treasury bond rating in the region, was the lowest of the year, but this could also be due to its lower maturity.

However, other factors seem predominant in explaining cross-country differences in Treasury bills (Tables 8.1 and 8.2). The relationship between interest rates and Treasury bill ratings appears less straightforward than for Treasury bonds. Again, using 2010 as an example, interest rates on

Togo Treasury bills were among the lowest in the region, though the bills were not rated. Similarly, interest rates on some three-month Treasury bills issued by Burkina Faso were about 100 basis points lower than those for Senegal, notwithstanding their equivalent ratings. However, even if ratings did not matter predominantly, signals of risk levels did. For example, economic and political conditions mattered for Côte d'Ivoire: interest rates on the country's issues were at odds with interest rates for other countries' issues, with some of its 28-day Treasury bills sold at an interest rate even higher than that of Mali's one-year Treasury bill.

Further analysis reveals that interest rates on sovereign securities were affected by the market's liquidity conditions and bidders' appetites at the time of issuances (Figure 8.3). Coverage rates, maturity, and interest rates appear closely linked in a three-way relationship. Coverage rates decreased sharply as maturity increased, both at the country and aggregate levels. Three-month Treasury bills attracted typically more than twice the amount offered by countries, whereas issues at higher maturities barely covered the total amount. Hence, interest rates' positive correlations with maturity could actually be due to the negative impact of maturity on coverage rates. Securities with shorter maturities attracted more bids, hence higher coverage rates and lower interest rates. Burkina Faso registered the highest demand, with up to 600 percent of coverage for some of its 91-day Treasury bills, hence the very low interest rates compared to the other issues.

Results from principal component analysis show that issuance volumes offered at each date also mattered and provide a profile of countries' interventions (Figure 8.4). Principal component analysis using securities' coverage rates, maturity, average interest rates, and the amount sold at each issuance confirms that high interest rates are associated with low coverage rates and long maturities, but the degree of association for the former is much stronger than it is for the latter. Principal component analysis also shows that most of the large issuances in terms of volume were for securities with short maturities. Results also provide a profile of issues for each country. Issues by Mali and Côte d'Ivoire were large, albeit with short maturities compared with other countries. Issues by Burkina Faso were of smaller amounts and rather constant maturities, and benefited from both relatively high coverage rates and low interest rates. Most issues by Benin and Senegal

Figure 8.4. WAEMU: Government Issues Profiling Using Principal Component Analysis, 2010[1]

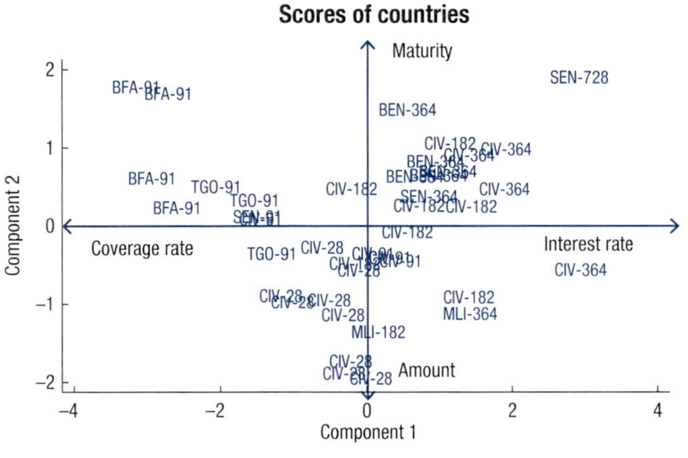

Sources: Central Bank of West African States; and IMF staff calculations.
Note: Three-letter International Organization for Standardization abbreviations used for country names. WAEMU = West African Economic and Monetary Union.
[1]Data up to December 19, 2010.

were also of relatively small amounts and long maturities but had lower coverage rates than did issues by Burkina Faso and Togo, and hence higher interest rates.

Finally, other less quantifiable factors such as seasonality, issuance procedures, and the frequency and predictability of issues could also have played a role, either indirectly through their effects on coverage rates or more directly. Some apparent inconsistencies show that other factors could have had an impact on interest rates, independent of coverage rates. Togo, for example, had a lower interest rate on some of its three-month Treasury bills than did Burkina Faso and Senegal, even though the coverage rates for those issuances were lower. Among the contributing factors are: (1) seasonal effects, that is, the issuance with the lowest interest rate of the year took place during the last quarter and the issuer, Burkina Faso, benefited from decreasing interest rates during the year despite decreasing coverage rates and constant maturity; (2) securities' modes of issuance, that is, bonds issued by auction benefit from more competition than do those issued by syndication; (3) frequency and predictability of countries' issues, that is, Burkina Faso, which had some of the lowest interest rates, issued Treasury bills with the same maturity (three months) every two to three months; and (4) countries' outstanding stocks of securities. More detailed data spanning over several years, however, would be needed to have conclusive evidence of the impact of those factors on interest rates.

CONSTRAINTS TO REGIONAL FINANCING

Among the most acute constraints are the bond market's undiversified issuers and narrow investor bases. On the first challenge, our analysis highlighted that market activity is overwhelmingly driven by government issues. Market interventions by nonsovereign issuers—including nonbank financial institutions, private companies, and regional and international institutions—remain scarce. On the second challenge, data on primary market activity show that WAEMU commercial banks are the main investors on the market. Even though some of the region's governments have sought ratings from credit rating agencies to attract more foreign capital, very few nonresident investors showed interest in purchasing securities on the market.

As a consequence, issuers stay captive of banks' preferences for short-term securities while investment opportunities are constrained to the limited set of maturities offered by sovereigns. Banks have not only a strong preference for Treasury bills because those securities bear multiple advantages, but also because of a lack of other equally attractive risk-adjusted investment alternatives. As such, the region's banking system assets are predominantly composed of short-term government securities, which accounted on average for about a fourth of the net total assets of WAEMU banks. These preferences also reflect the short-term nature of bank liabilities, which essentially consist of deposits from the public and private sectors. Such constraints benefit governments that use the Treasury bill market to finance treasury needs, thus providing an ample supply of low-risk assets to banks that are more than willing to invest in high-yielding, short-term, risk-free government paper. However, those constraints also weigh on issuers' abilities to raise long-term financing. In fact, long-term issues are still facing a lack of interest in the market, while investors are calling for a more diverse set of maturities than are typically proposed by issuers. Our analysis showed that coverage rates decrease sharply as maturity increases, suggesting that the market may not be deep enough to cover the region's long-term financing needs.

Another consequence is that the secondary market for bills and bonds remains underdeveloped. Excess liquidity in the financial system and the interest rate spread between the refinancing operations at the central bank and sovereign securities tends to encourage banks to buy and hold government securities until maturity rather than to trade them frequently as part of an active and diversified investment strategy. In addition, the lack of competing investors, such as social security bodies and pension funds, keeps the nonbank buy side for securities shallow, reducing trade opportunities in the secondary market. Also, the scarcity of long-term securities with intermediate maturities, between two and seven years, limits the spectrum of investment strategies on the market. Also, capacity constraints prevent adequate pricing of securities traded in the secondary market, thus reducing the profitability of such operations. Finally, differences in tax regimes among WAEMU member states complicate the pricing process on the secondary market.

Organizational issues and limited access to information increase financing costs and hinder the market's efficiency and integration. First, though member countries are required to submit a schedule of public debt issuance at the beginning of each year, these are not binding and often lack reliability partly owing to issues in forecasting treasury cash-flow needs. Hence, the poor coordination between Treasury bill and Treasury bond offerings among WAEMU treasuries leads to unpredictable demand for liquidity on the market. In some instances, bond issuances were even substantially undersubscribed. Second, insufficient information sharing and transparency hampers investors' abilities to analyze market information and make optimal investment choices. Debt data and governments' debt management strategies over the medium term are not readily available to the public and often lack reliability. Similarly, detailed data on issuances' outcomes for all countries and over a long period are difficult to gather. Benchmarking is also challenging owing to the irregularity and nondiversification of issues, in particular long-term ones. Third, governments tend to issue higher amounts than those announced before the bidding process, contributing to blurring the market's signaling system. All these factors reduce the market's efficiency and favor its segmentation, also triggering supplemental financing costs for issuers.

Finally, mitigating the systemic risk emanating from banks' relatively large exposure to government securities could prove challenging. Net bank holdings of government debt are substantial; its amount was roughly equivalent to the ratio of regulatory capital to risk-weighted assets of the region's banking system. Such large exposure to government paper could pose a solvency issue for some banks in times of economic crisis, and hence a systemic threat to the region's banking system.

CHALLENGES AHEAD

Substantial progress has been achieved in mobilizing resources to finance growth on the regional market. Market operations expanded considerably over the last decade, but are still predominantly dominated by sovereign debt issuances and fueled by banks' supply of liquidity. Moreover, recalling the market's initial goal of providing a more transparent and efficient source of capital for the region's governments and corporations, the WAEMU regional bond market has succeeded in providing sufficient short-term financing to governments. However, the market fell short in providing long-term financing for both member countries and the private sector. Against this backdrop, the tax exemption granted to IFC bonds could help bolster future issuances in the Kola bond segment.

Notwithstanding the recent improvements, significant progress is needed for the market to reach its full potential and support the region's growth ambitions. Among the challenges to the market's development are the undiversified issuer and narrow investor bases, regulations favoring banks' preferences for short-term securities, the lack of diversity in maturities, an undeveloped secondary market owing to a shallow buy side, organizational issues including insufficient coordination of issuances by member countries and low reliability of issuance plans (both dates and volume), insufficient information sharing, and relatively high financing costs for prospective borrowers.

Witnessing the strong activity in the primary market for Treasury bills, market authorities and participants should address the issues that delay the development of a secondary market. Because the region's banks boast very high liquidity ratios and intermediation of savings into loans to the private sector is very low, a further deepening of the financial sector would allow private corporations to raise more financing on the regional market. The empowerment of local and regional investors and the development of new instruments to collect long-term savings (for example, life insurance, complementary retirement plans, and mutual funds) could be important steps in this direction.

Authorities should also tackle impediments to the issuance of securities with longer maturities. This could be helped by broadening offerings of longer-term government bonds to help benchmark financial risk for private issuers. Moreover, regional capital and exchange rate controls could also be revisited to attract more foreign investors to the market.

The current challenges associated with the financing of growth in the region should further encourage authorities to pursue reforms both at national and regional levels. The swift implementation of pending reforms, such as the adoption of national treasury cash-flow plans, the coordination of debt issuance schedules at the regional level, and the improvement of governments' debt management capacity could help market players better reap the benefits of a vibrant regional financial market. Moreover, strengthening the pension and social security systems through comprehensive reforms could also help broaden the investor base and increase market activity, notably in the secondary market.

Taking stock of regulatory issues that hamper market development and preparing a strategy to address those issues would also be beneficial. Such a strategy should include a rethinking of the role of the BCEAO in the sovereign issuance process. In that regard, the creation of the WAEMU-Securities Agency (Agence UEMOA-Titres) with the goal of supporting WAEMU countries in the issue and management of public debt securities is a welcome step forward. Finally, the BCEAO should develop contingency plans to address the systemic risk that could arise from the banking sector's large exposure to government securities.

PART III

Fiscal Policy and Coordination

PREFACE

West African Economic and Monetary Union (WAEMU) countries conduct independent fiscal policies but coordinate some aspects of these policies within the regional institutional framework. National ministries of finance are in charge of the formulation and implementation of fiscal policies. The WAEMU Commission coordinates fiscal policies, including tax policies and observance of fiscal convergence criteria among member states. In WAEMU countries, as in any other country, "fiscal policy" generally refers to the government's use of taxation and spending to regulate the aggregate level of economic activity. The use of fiscal policy consists of changes in the level or composition of taxation or government spending, and hence, in the government's financial position relative to the rest of the economy. Key policy variables include government deficits and debt, as well as tax and expenditure types and levels, fiscal deficits, and public debt. The peculiarity of the WAEMU is that this fiscal policy is conducted within the framework of a regional monetary union in which certain provisions for fiscal policy coordination are spelled out in more detail than is the case in most other monetary unions of the world.

Fiscal policy is the main policy tool available to WAEMU countries and is critical to the stability of the monetary union. Chapter 9, Fiscal Rules and Institutions, argues that in the WAEMU, national fiscal policies are the main stabilization instrument in a region where macroeconomic volatility remains high and asymmetric shocks are frequent. Fiscal policies also need to contribute to addressing member countries' large development needs. Fiscal rules and institutions in the WAEMU can be strengthened based on international experience. The WAEMU has a set of regional fiscal rules that try to balance stability and development needs. These rules, in practice, have proven to be of limited effectiveness, either because of noncompliance (for example, the fiscal deficit convergence criterion) or because they are not binding in the short term (for example, the debt convergence criterion).

When coupled with market discipline, fiscal rules can be an effective additional tool for ensuring fiscal sustainability in the WAEMU. Chapter 10, Fiscal Discipline: Rules and Markets, suggests that fiscal rules should be supported by market discipline. While sovereign interest rates are broadly responsive to governments' fiscal behavior, further development of the regional financial market is needed to improve the effectiveness of market discipline in the WAEMU. In addition, fiscal aspects of the WAEMU's regional surveillance framework could be reconsidered to improve both design and enforceability.

Fiscal rules can help deal with the procyclical nature of public investment in the WAEMU. Chapter 11, Public Investment and Fiscal Rules, documents WAEMU governments' trend toward cutting domestically financed investment more in "bad times" than expanding them in "good times." Such policies may contribute to enhancing exogenous shocks. The procyclicality of public investment in the WAEMU leads to the fact that fiscal deficits have been largely uncorrelated with GDP growth. The procyclicality of public expenditure and the high asymmetry of shocks that affect WAEMU countries justify exploring options for greater countercyclicality of rules-based fiscal frameworks and for risk sharing. In this area, WAEMU fiscal rules can become important anchors for the medium-term fiscal policy so as to preserve fiscal discipline at the aggregate level. Some flexibility to fiscal convergence criteria, such as a countercyclical fiscal rule, could help mitigate the procyclicality of public expenditure, including of public investment. The rule would allow for some positive correlation, with smaller deficits (larger surpluses) in booms and larger deficits (smaller surpluses) in contractions. There is room for fiscal federalism or for a risk-sharing (or group insurance) arrangement to mitigate the incidence of asymmetric shocks. Risk-sharing arrangements would aim to allocate financial resources to the WAEMU members exposed to negative shocks. As WAEMU countries seem compelled to drastically cut back investment in bad times, such arrangements would also help preserve investment levels and growth.

WAEMU countries face an important common challenge of creating sufficient fiscal space to finance ambitious development and poverty-reducing programs. Chapter 12, Fiscal Space and Investment Scaling Up, looks at the options to generate such additional fiscal space. In principle, it can be created by either enhancing tax revenue or improving the efficiency of spending. While WAEMU countries are broadly in line with comparator countries in total tax collection, WAEMU's tax revenues rely heavily on trade taxes, which will inevitably be reduced with impending trade liberalization. Also, high reliance on trade taxes makes WAEMU's revenue base vulnerable to the fluctuation of international prices. Panel regression and stochastic frontier analyses suggest that there is substantial room to improve domestic tax collection in the WAEMU. The effort should be country-specific, with each government focusing on its underperforming taxes. On the expenditure side, WAEMU countries have significant scope to improve the efficiency of their spending in education and health. If all WAEMU countries achieve the highest spending efficiency of the top performer among them, the cumulative fiscal savings can add 1–3 percent of GDP to the available fiscal space of the region.

Fiscal space can also be created through better tax coordination, which is the statutory objective of the WAEMU. Better tax coordination has large potential but limited success so far. Chapter 13, Tax Coordination and Tax Competition, assesses in detail the current state of the WAEMU tax coordination framework against the main tax policy coordination objectives of the WAEMU Treaty of 1994. These objectives include reducing distortions to intracommunity trade and mobilizing domestic tax revenue. The process of tax coordination in the WAEMU is one of the most advanced in the world de jure, but remains in many areas ineffective de facto. The framework has broadly succeeded in converging tax systems, particularly statutory tax rates, and has contributed to improving revenue mobilization. From the experience of the WAEMU, important lessons can be drawn for other regions that are contemplating coordination of their tax policies. The leaders in the WAEMU underestimated the difficulties and challenges of tariff and tax coordination and did not take sufficiently into account the implementation and enforcement implications at the regional level, particularly the need for effective surveillance. The credibility of the coordination framework depends in large part on the credibility of its regional institutions. Having borrowed extensively from the European Union model of economic integration and tax coordination, the WAEMU has yet to provide its regional institutions with the necessary resources to undertake effective surveillance. The tax coordination framework may have had the unintended effect of contributing to the fragmentation of policy making at the national level by providing countries with the incentive to enact special tax regimes outside their tax laws. The coordination framework has allowed some convergence of countries' tax systems (notably statutory tax rates), which in turn may have contributed to the positive revenue performance observed in WAEMU member states. In the future, WAEMU countries could deepen harmonization through a stronger political commitment to the process and by granting sufficient authority and resources to regional institutions so that they can effectively monitor compliance.

The WAEMU is undertaking an ambitious program to develop the regional market for government securities as a means to mobilize additional financing for development. Chapter 14, Regional Sovereign Debt Market, takes stock of its development and highlights key reforms undertaken by regional authorities. In the past decade, the sovereign debt issuances have increased rapidly. However, the development of the sovereign debt market has been held back by the absence of the infrastructure for the secondary market, market fragmentation of procedures and instruments, lack of a structured issuance policy and other problems. To address these issues, the regional authorities established the WAEMU Securities Agency with the mandate to assist member countries with resource mobilization needed to finance growth at manageable cost and consistent with debt sustainability. The agency has undertaken a number of important initiatives—coordinated issuance calendar, organized securities auctions, provided market oversight and distributed market information through internationally recognized platforms, prepared market guides and provided training to market participants. These efforts allowed reinvigorating the market and making it more transparent and accessible for potential investors. The regional sovereign debt market still remains at an early stage of development. Substantial further reforms are planned for the near future.

CHAPTER 9

Fiscal Rules and Institutions

OLIVIER BASDEVANT AND ALEKSANDRA ZDZIENICKA

Fiscal policy is the main policy tool available to West African Economic and Monetary Union (WAEMU) countries, and is critical to the stability of the monetary union. In the WAEMU, the fixed exchange rate regime, limited scope for active monetary policy, low labor mobility within the region, and no significant intraregional fiscal transfers make national fiscal policies the main stabilization instrument in a region where macroeconomic volatility remains high, and asymmetric shocks are frequent. Fiscal policies also need to contribute to addressing member countries' large development needs. Fiscal rules and institutions in the WAEMU can be strengthened based on international experience. The WAEMU has a set of regional fiscal rules that try to balance stability and development needs. These rules, in practice, have proven to be of limited effectiveness, either because of noncompliance (for example, the fiscal deficit convergence criterion) or because they are not binding in the short term (for example, the debt convergence criterion).

FISCAL RULES RECONSIDERED

WAEMU convergence criteria include fiscal rules, but the two main ones are either not observed (deficit) or not binding (debt). The target of a positive basic fiscal balance—the "key convergence criterion"—has been missed in a large majority of cases over the past five years (Figure 9.1, panel 1). In addition, new economic conditions (for example, access to international markets) raise the issue of whether targeting the basic fiscal balance, which excludes foreign-financed expenditures, is still adequate. The target of a public debt ratio below 70 percent of GDP is now easily met by all WAEMU countries, thanks to debt relief (Figure 9.1, panel 2). This target was set at a time when all of these countries were heavily indebted, and restoring fiscal sustainability was the main objective. Beyond redesigning specific rules, another critical issue to reconsider is the enforcement mechanism, which has not proved fully effective.

The existence of deficit biases, which create fiscal risks, is the main rationale for fiscal rules. As Table 9.1 shows, a number of WAEMU countries have accumulated significant public debt since relief was provided through the Multilateral Debt Relief Initiative. For some countries, this public debt is the result of a deficit bias, illustrated by repeatedly missed deficit targets. While WAEMU countries have experienced significant differences, deficit biases are on average of about 1 percent of GDP (Figure 9.1, panel 3). In particular, the predicted deficits one and two years ahead at the time the budget for year T is formulated, underestimate the outturn by significant margins. Over time, this tends to produce significantly higher-than-expected debt levels. This bias is found elsewhere in the world. In fiscal strategy plans reviewed in Mauro (2011), primary fiscal deficit turned out to be higher by ½ percent of GDP on average than was initially planned. Numerical fiscal rules can be helpful to address issues related to recurrent deficit biases. Credible rules can, in principle, lead to higher welfare than can discretion (Barro and Gordon 1983; Drazen 2000), as well as to lower risk premia (Hallerberg and Wolff 2006).

Figure 9.1. WAEMU: Deficits, Growth, and Debt

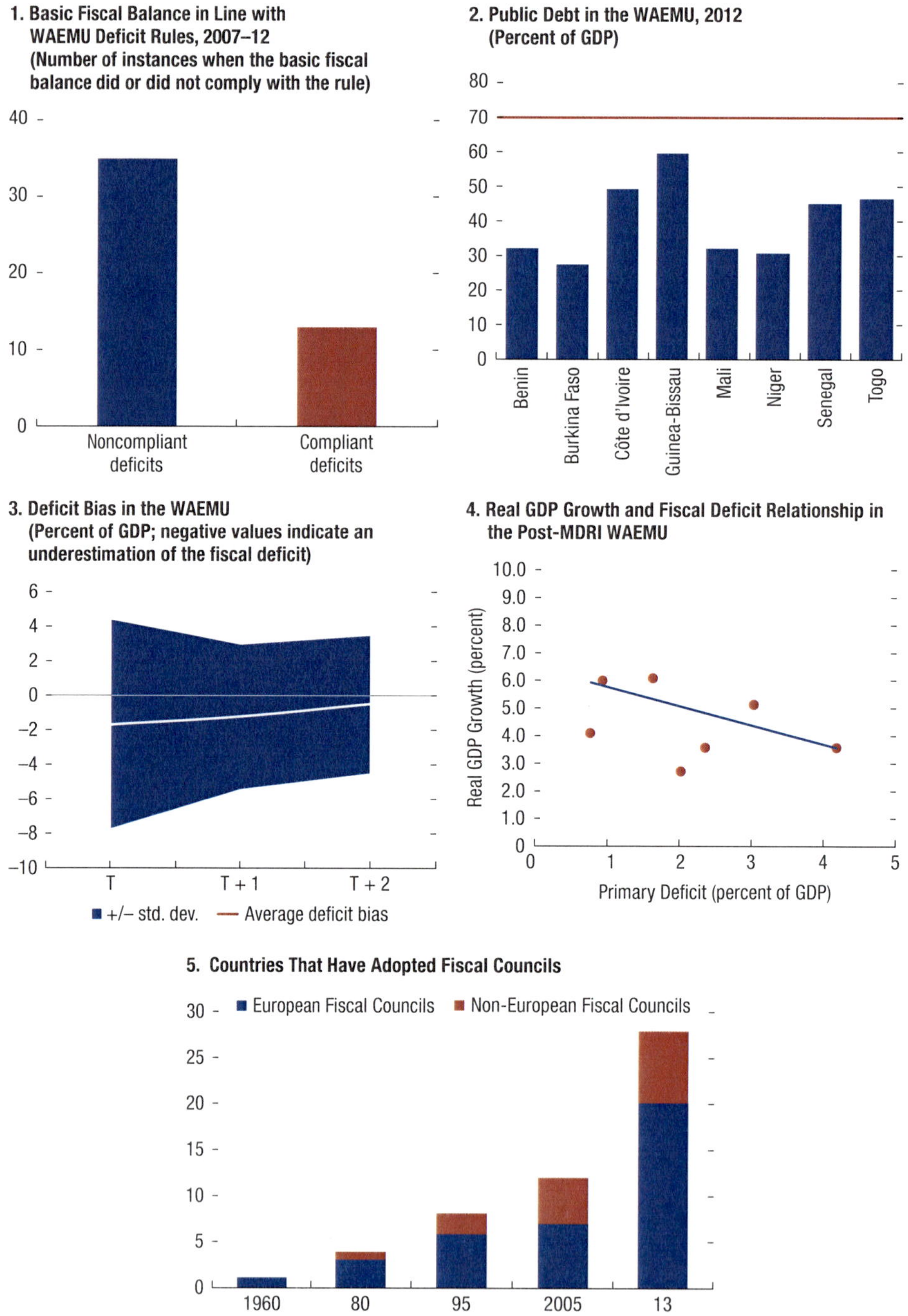

Sources: Country authorities; IMF Staff computation.
Note: MDRI = Multilateral Debt Relief Initiative; std dev. = standard deviation; WAEMU = West African Economic and Monetary Union.

TABLE 9.1

Key Debt Indicators Since MDRI

	MDRI Year	General Government Debt: MDRI Year	General Government Debt: In 2013	Average Increase since MDRI	Risk of Debt Distress[1]
		(Percent of GDP)			
Benin	2006	12.5	27.7	2.2	Low
Burkina Faso	2006	22.6	33.3	1.5	Moderate
Côte d'Ivoire	2012	45.8	42.9	–2.9	Moderate
Guinea-Bissau	2010	51.7	61.0	3.1	Moderate
Mali	2006	20.4	33.4	1.9	Moderate
Niger	2006	27.1	23.2	–0.6	Moderate
Senegal	2006	21.8	45.2	3.3	Low
Togo	2010	47.3	43.3	–1.4	Moderate

Sources: IMF Debt Sustainability Analyses; World Economic Outlook database.
Note: MDRI = Multilateral Debt Relief Initiative
[1]The risk of debt distress is carried out by the Joint IMF-World Bank Debt Sustainability Analysis for the latest available year, which differs by country.

DEFINING FISCAL RULES

Several approaches may be considered for any future revision of fiscal rules. These include:

- *Specifying the ultimate objective*—Existing convergence criteria are numerous and target multiple objectives such as fiscal sustainability, the composition of spending, and revenue mobilization. The ultimate objective should be fiscal sustainability, which is critical for the stability of the monetary union and exchange rate regime.
- *Keeping a short list of criteria that are directly related to attaining the ultimate objective*—Having too many criteria runs the risk that the authorities do not focus sufficiently on those that are critical for fiscal sustainability. From this perspective, only two or three criteria would be kept, while the others would become indicators that would continue to be monitored. One of the remaining criteria could be on the stock of public debt and another one related to flows contributing to debt accumulation (for example, a deficit rule).
- *Ensuring, as much as possible, the internal coherence of the set of remaining criteria*—If a debt criterion and a deficit criterion are kept, the link between the two should be as clear as possible. For instance, a ceiling on the deficit should not be set at a level so high that it would likely lead in the medium term to a breach of the debt ceiling by most countries. From this perspective, relying on comprehensive debt sustainability analysis would help ensure this consistency. Another way to force this consistency would be to introduce "debt brakes," which would adjust the deficit ceiling based on past deviations from targets or the distance to the debt ceiling.
- *Keeping rules simple and easy to implement and monitor*—Sophisticated rules can help address simultaneously a number of issues. For instance, a structural deficit rule may help preserve fiscal sustainability while allowing for countercyclical policy. However, defining, calculating, and monitoring a structural deficit would likely be challenging in countries with data availability and quality problems and where the existence of an economic cycle is debatable. Simple rules might be cruder, but they would have the advantage of being easy to understand and implement.
- *Allowing for some tailoring of the rules at the national level*—While general principles should be common to all countries and defined at the regional level, this does not necessarily preclude different specific rules at the national level, as long as they take into account country circumstances and are consistent with the general principles. For instance, countries with a

high share of revenue coming from natural resources may wish to adopt rules specifying how this revenue should be saved for a rainy day if prices for natural resources are high, saved for future generations (because of the exhaustibility of the resources), or invested in public infrastructure. Countries with stronger budget processes, including effective medium-term frameworks, and with easy access to financing may wish to specify the scope for countercyclical policies.

- *Not construing any ceiling as an optimal level*—Ceilings on public debt and the fiscal deficit are typically levels that countries should try to stay away from, not optimal levels to target. This means, in particular, that the deficit should be significantly lower than the ceiling when economic circumstances are favorable. In other words, fiscal rules with ceilings on debt and the deficit say little about how fiscal policy should be conducted and can be complemented by additional rules at the country level (as discussed earlier in this section).

Overall, fiscal rules should contribute to a strengthening of budget processes. The latter are critical to avoid deficit biases (Milesi-Ferretti 1997) and, therefore, to achieve fiscal sustainability. The WAEMU has a number of recent public financial management rules, which are spelled out in directives. However, countries are late in transposing these rules into their national laws (with only Senegal having finished this first step, which was expected to be completed by the end of 2011) and this raises doubts as to whether the deadlines for implementation will be met. Accelerating this process is therefore of critical importance. In particular, framing a fiscal strategy in a credible and binding medium-term fiscal framework would help ensure that deficit biases are avoided.

Addressing fiscal risks and planning for contingencies is also key to the success of fiscal rules. Delivering on a fiscal strategy requires not only a plan, but also measures to address fiscal vulnerabilities. For example, countries facing specific expenditure risks need to implement measures to mitigate these risks to ensure the success of their fiscal strategies (IMF 2010). A typical issue for WAEMU countries in this regard is the risks pertaining to the energy sector. The budgetary cost of supporting energy sectors has not only tended to be high, but it has often been higher than initially budgeted, thus complicating fiscal management and adherence to fiscal rules. This has also led to inefficient adjustment, with investment spending bearing the brunt of spending cuts. Contingency planning is therefore highly desirable to avoid such outcomes.

FISCAL RULES FLEXIBILITY

Fiscal rules do not preclude growth-friendly fiscal policies. A concern often expressed is that rules focusing on fiscal sustainability will hamper growth and development. However, the contribution of fiscal policy to growth is not through permanently higher deficits. As Figure 9.1, panel 4 shows, larger fiscal deficits in the WAEMU have not been associated with higher growth rates since implementation of the Multilateral Debt Relief Initiative. The empirical literature also suggests that fiscal multipliers tend to be small in developing countries (see Spilimbergo, Symansky, and Schindler 2009). These results suggest that growth should not be sought through sustained fiscal stimulus. There is likely a larger role for fiscal policy to foster growth through contributing to macroeconomic stability, the composition and quality of spending (for example, favoring investment over inefficient transfers such as generalized price subsidies), and more efficient tax systems that reduce distortions.

Fiscal rules are helpful to address deficit biases, but can affect to various degrees the ability to conduct countercyclical policies. Simple rules usually imply a trade-off between a focus on debt

TABLE 9.2

Performances of Simple Numerical Rules against Key Objectives

	Simple Rules Setting a Ceiling On:			
	Debt Ratio	Overall Deficit	Primary Deficit	Expenditure
Preserve a sustainable debt ratio	+++	++	+	–
Maintain sound deficit level	–	+++	++	–
Avoid large adjustments in a single year	–	+	+	+++
Limit procyclicality	–	–	–	++
Target controllable variables	–	+	+	+++
Achieve comprehensive coverage	+++	+++	+++	–

Source: IMF staff.
Note: +++ = very good, ++ = good, + = fair, – = poor.

sustainability (for example, debt or deficit rules) or on avoiding procyclical policies (for example, expenditure rules). Table 9.2 summarizes the properties of commonly used fiscal rules. As discussed above, the procyclicality of certain rules, such as ceilings on the debt ratio or the overall deficit, can be greatly reduced by staying away from the ceilings in favorable economic circumstances and thereby building buffers to be used in the event of a negative shock.

Well-defined escape clauses can play a useful role. They allow for the temporary suspension of the fiscal rule in exceptional circumstances. However, they too need to be designed carefully to avoid abuse. A typical way to address such a hurdle is to require supermajorities (for example, from parliament) to approve the temporary suspension of a rule.

ADHERENCE TO FISCAL RULES

One of the reasons for the lack of effectiveness of WAEMU fiscal rules is the insufficient incentives for compliance. The WAEMU Commission is in charge of regional surveillance, but its mission is hampered by the lack of availability and timeliness of data, and also by capacity issues (IMF 2013). Sanctions are possible but not applied. For example, under the excessive deficit procedure, a deviating country is given 30 days to develop an adjustment strategy, which can benefit from financial support from the Union. Otherwise the country would expose itself to potential sanctions.

International experience suggests that incentive mechanisms are more effective at the national level. Regional rules are desirable in a monetary union because of externalities. In the WAEMU, they are even more critical because of the need to ensure that the regional fiscal stance is consistent with the exchange rate regime. However, regional rules may not be fully owned by the national authorities. Adopting binding rules at the country level may help foster ownership and adherence. The fundamental issue is to encourage policymakers to comply with rules by increasing costs for deviations. Financial sanctions have proven ineffective; costs therefore need to be of a different nature. Typically these costs can be either legal or political (by raising public awareness of deviations and their economic implications). Thus, two avenues, which have been taken by some countries, could be explored. First, rules could be transposed into domestic laws (or even enshrined in constitutions), which would increase their binding characters for national policymakers. Second, fiscal councils could strengthen compliance by increasing public awareness of potential deviations from announced policies (as discussed in the following section).

National fiscal councils could play an important role in increasing fiscal transparency. To the extent that fiscal councils are independent, perceived as such, and credible, they can provide an effective contribution to fiscal stability and growth. They are increasingly used across countries (Figure 9.1, panel 5), and are typically in charge of an independent assessment of public finances and public information about this assessment. There are many design options, ranging from fiscal councils simply reporting to the public and parliament about compliance of budgets and their executions with rules, to more elaborate options that provide in-house fiscal projections. In resource-constrained countries like the WAEMU members, there could be fiscal councils solely dedicated to reporting and alerting the public on compliance and noncompliance. Councils tend to work better at the national level, as they can more easily contribute to and influence domestic debates on fiscal policy. They would be a complement to the regional surveillance exercised by the WAEMU Commission.

FISCAL FEDERALISM AND STABILITY

A centralized fiscal risk-sharing mechanism could help smooth macroeconomic volatility. Idiosyncratic shocks are still frequent (Table 9.3) and there is limited wage and price flexibility, limited labor mobility, and constraints on the scope for countercyclical fiscal policies (for example, availability of financing). Other existing risk-sharing mechanisms are much less effective in the WAEMU, in particular when they are most needed, that is, during crises (Figure 9.2, panel 1). These mechanisms include private insurance via international capital markets (for example, through the holding of diversified portfolios of international assets or explicit insurance); saving and borrowing via international credit markets; private transfers (for example, remittances); official transfers (for example, foreign aid); and fiscal risk sharing across countries via intra-union transfers. Against this background, more efficient fiscal risk-sharing mechanisms may provide a greater insurance against shocks and increase consumption smoothing. Public saving plays a significant role in consumption smoothing during normal output fluctuations, and larger fiscal buffers would help absorb the impact of shocks. When shocks become more severe, however, a centralized fiscal mechanism could significantly increase demand smoothing in the member states.

A regional stabilization mechanism (IMF 2013) could provide an effective instrument to deal with asymmetric shocks within the region. The mechanism should: (1) be relatively simple; (2) automatic; (3) nonregressive (in the sense that the size of transfers and contribution do not vary with per-capita income); and (4) consist of temporary transfers that are a function of serially uncorrelated shocks and able to offset a large part of these shocks (Hammond and von Hagen 1998). Another issue to address would be the nature of shocks triggering transfers. In a region where a number of asymmetric shocks have been triggered by sociopolitical events, the mechanism would need to be set up carefully to focus on smoothing non-policy-related shocks and to reduce moral hazard issues. Such a mechanism would be financed by contributions that would be used to pay transfers to countries negatively hit by the shocks. While this exercise is highly stylized and should be interpreted cautiously, staff estimations show that a relatively small contribution of about ¾ percent of each WAEMU country's GDP would allow achieving an amount of income smoothing comparable with that observed in existing federal states (Figure 9.2, panel 2). A contribution of about 1–1¼ percent of GDP could insure WAEMU countries against even more severe downturns. Disbursed transfers would be proportional to the size of the shocks, to the relative size of each economy compared with the rest of the Union, and to the resources accumulated in the fund each year. If no country were affected by a negative shock, no disbursement would take place and contributions would be saved in the fund.

TABLE 9.3

Frequency of Asymmetric Shocks in the WAEMU

1990	1991	1992	1993	1994	1995	1996	1997	1998	1999	2000	2001	2002	2003	2004	2005	2006	2007	2008	2009	2010	2011	2012	Country
																							Benin
																							Burkina Faso
																							Côte d'Ivoire
																							Guinea-Bissau
																							Mali
																							Niger
																							Senegal
																							Togo

Source: Nguyen and Zdzienicka (2013).

Note: The idiosyncratic growth stocks are derived as part of the country-specific growth shocks that are not explained by WAEMU-wide growth shocks. Growth shocks (both for the WAEMU and individual countries) are computed as the residuals from a regression of the country's growth rate (respective to the WAEMU) over two lags. Red indicates negative shocks (inferior to 3.5 percent); Blue positive shocks (superior to 3.5 percent).

Figure 9.2. Shocks in the WAEMU

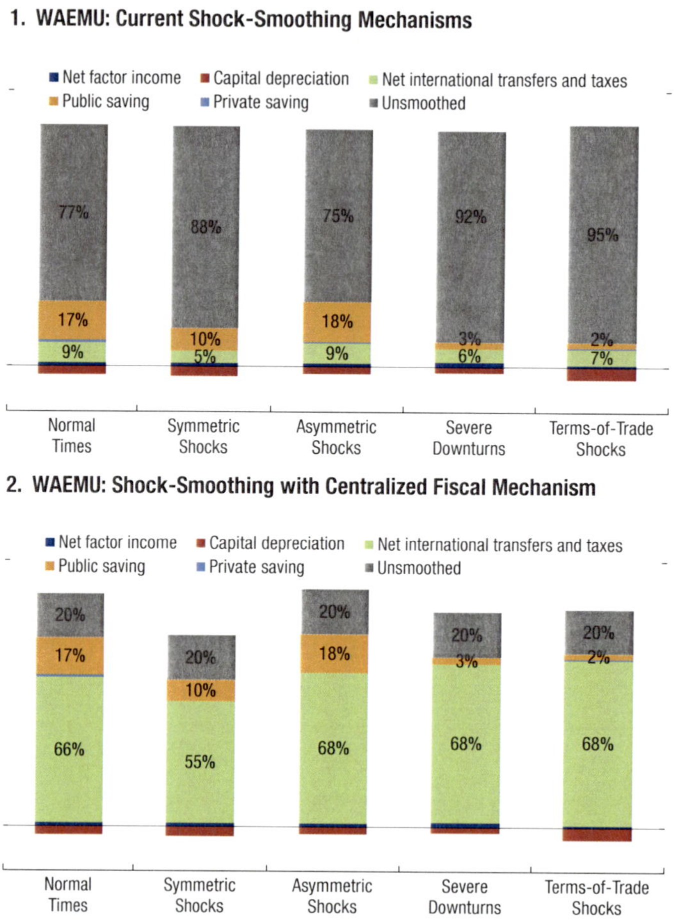

Source: Nguyen and Zdzienicka (2013).

REFERENCES

Barro, R., and D. Gordon. 1983. "Rules, Discretion and Reputation in a Model of Monetary Policy." *Journal of Monetary Economics* 12(1983): 101–21.

Drazen, A. 2000. *Political Economy in Macroeconomics*. Princeton: Princeton University Press.

Hallerberg, M., and G. Wolff. 2006. "Fiscal Institutions, Fiscal Policy and Sovereign Risk Premia." Deutsche Bundesbank Discussion Paper Series 1: Economic Studies # 35/2006.

Hammond, G., and J. von Hagen. 1998. "Regional Insurance Against Asymmetric Shocks—An Empirical Study for the EC." The Manchester School 66, 331–53.

International Monetary Fund (IMF). 2010. *From Stimulus to Consolidation—Revenue and Expenditure Policies in Advanced and Emerging Economies.* Washington: International Monetary Fund. Available from: http://www.imf.org/external/np/pp/eng/2010/043010a.pdf

———. 2013. "West African Monetary Union (WAEMU)" IMF Country Report #13/92, International Monetary Fund, Washington.

Mauro, P. 2011. *Chipping Away at the Public Debt—Sources of Failure and Keys to Success in Fiscal Adjustment.* Hoboken, New Jersey: John Wiley and Sons.

Milesi-Feretti, G. 1997. "Fiscal Rules and the Budget Process." *Giornale degli Economisti* 110, 5–40.

Nguyen, H., and A. Zdzienicka. 2013. "Risk-sharing Mechanisms in the WAEMU." Unpublished.

Spilimbergo, A., S. Symansky, and M. Schindler. 2009. "Fiscal Multipliers." IMF Staff Position Note, SPN/09/11, International Monetary Fund, Washington.

CHAPTER 10

Fiscal Discipline: Rules and Markets

ERMAL HITAJ

Are fiscal rules and market discipline effective in ensuring fiscal sustainability in the West African Economic and Monetary Union (WAEMU)? Achieving fiscal discipline in a monetary union without a central fiscal authority, while crucial for its stability, is challenging institutionally and practically. While sovereign interest rates are broadly responsive to governments' fiscal behavior, further development of the regional financial market is needed for an improvement of the effectiveness of market discipline in the WAEMU. In addition, fiscal aspects of the WAEMU's regional surveillance framework could be reconsidered to improve both design and enforceability.

FISCAL DISCIPLINE AND RULES

Achieving fiscal discipline in a monetary union without a central fiscal authority, while crucial for its stability, is challenging institutionally and practically. A monetary union is likely to increase economic and financial interconnectedness among its members. While regional integration is in itself a welcome development, it also brings new risks. One of them is that debt sustainability issues in one country could have a higher impact on the other members. Close financial linkages, such as large holdings of government debt by banks in other countries of the union, can indeed be a powerful channel of transmission of a fiscal crisis in one country to the rest of the union, with implications for the stability of the latter, as has been seen in the euro area. While ensuring fiscal sustainability in all the countries may be vital for the survival of a monetary union, some of the union's members may actually have incentives to overborrow in the absence of a credible commitment that no country will be bailed out by the others should it face an unsustainable debt burden. Countries with weaker fiscal situations may indeed benefit from the credibility of those with stronger public finances, and face lower interest rates than they would otherwise face.

Fiscal discipline can in principle be supported by rules and financial markets. Fiscal rules can be useful in anchoring expectations and providing macroeconomic stability (Morris, Ongena, and Schuknecht 2006), and have been viewed as a central pillar of the policy coordination framework that aims at ensuring the stability of a monetary union. Designing such rules is a delicate exercise. They need to help preserve fiscal discipline while leaving scope for countercyclical policies, since fiscal policy is the main tool to cope with asymmetric shocks in a monetary union. Market discipline can also help if a number of conditions are met, including free movement of capital, a credible no-bailout commitment, no monetization of the debt, and sensitivity of sovereign interest rates to fiscal behavior (Alexander and Anker 1997).

THE ROLE OF THE REGIONAL MARKET

The regional government debt market has become an important source of financing for a number of WAEMU countries (Table 10.1). The elimination of the Central Bank of West African States' (BCEAO) statutory advances to governments in 2003 served as a catalyst for the government securities market, which was sustained by excess liquidity in the banking system (Sy 2010). A few countries have accounted for the bulk of the issuances, which consist mostly of Treasury bills with

TABLE 10.1

WAEMU: Treasury Bills Issuance

	2001	2002	2003	2004	2005	2006	2007	2008	2009	2010	2011
						(CFAF billions)					
Benin	0.0	0.0	0.0	0.0	23.4	45.6	0.0	40.1	119.7	119.8	237.7
Côte d'Ivoire	0.0	0.0	16.3	15.7	47.5	0.0	164.8	103.0	538.3	1245.9	2278.8
Mali	12.0	0.0	15.2	21.0	114.9	44.1	53.1	30.5	54.1	99.5	119.6
Senegal	42.9	0.0	23.0	45.3	35.5	50.8	67.2	63.2	82.0	94.7	238.8
Burkina Faso	0.0	51.9	30.9	41.5	43.3	50.9	46.9	61.0	34.3	43.6	160.8
Niger	0.0	0.0	0.0	0.0	30.0	23.3	50.0	35.0	0.0	35.0	64.5
Guinee	0.0	0.0	0.0	0.0	6.0	6.7	0.0	0.0	0.0	0.0	0.0
Togo	0.0	0.0	0.0	0.0	0.0	0.0	0.0	10.0	15.0	30.0	60.0
WAEMU	54.9	51.9	85.4	123.5	300.5	221.4	382.0	342.7	843.5	1668.5	3160.2

Source: BCEAO (www.bceao.int).

BOX 10.1. Estimating the Disciplining Effect of the Regional Debt Market

The objective of this inquiry is to assess the relationship between interest rates requested by investors on the regional market and the fiscal behavior of sovereigns. The dataset used covers all WAEMU countries over 1997–2011. All data used in the estimations are annual. The dependent variable is the average short-term annual interest rate a country is charged by the market.

The estimates in Table 10.2 are obtained through the Arellano-Bond estimation technique, which accommodates a dynamic equation specification while controlling for time-invariant country characteristics. The variables used are:

1. *Fiscal variables*—The overall fiscal balance as a share of GDP and the general government's debt-to-GDP ratio. One would expect higher deficit and debt ratios to lead to higher interest rates, as they both increase the probability of default and therefore the credit risk premium. The debt variable used here is domestic debt, which to a large extent is composed of debt issued in the WAEMU market. External debt remains mostly owed to donors, and in the past decade has been relieved in all WAEMU countries, while regional market debt continued to be serviced.
2. *The level of excess bank reserves in the region*—With banks being the main investors, a higher level of excess reserves is likely to lead to lower interest rates.
3. *The WAEMU overall fiscal balance-to-GDP ratio*—This variable gives a sense of how much demand there is in the market for bank excess reserves. One would expect a higher WAEMU fiscal deficit to lead to higher interest rates. This variable is calculated separately for each country, excluding the country's own fiscal balance to avoid multicollinearity.
4. *The inflation rate*—A standard variable in explaining nominal interest rates.
5. *A composite index provided by International Country Risk Guide*—This measures political risk, which has been significant in a number of WAEMU countries.

a maturity of less than a year (Diouf and Boutin-Dufresne 2012). Furthermore, foreign participation in the WAEMU government securities market remains marginal, and trade in the secondary market remains limited.

While the regional market responds to fiscal variables, borrowing costs seem to be driven mostly by the relative supply and demand for excess bank reserves. An increase in domestic debt has a positive and significant impact on the interest rate, suggesting that the regional market does discriminate across sovereigns based on their fiscal behavior. However, the magnitude of the effects of the WAEMU-level excess reserves and overall fiscal balance indicates that availability of and demand for bank reserves in the regional market are the main determinants of borrowing costs. This suggests a currently limited role of WAEMU financial markets in enforcing fiscal discipline. These results are in line with those from Sy (2010), who finds that supply and demand conditions are the most important determinants of the yield curve in the WAEMU. They likely reflect the limited development of the financial system, which means, in particular, that banks have limited investment opportunities for their excess reserves, and the quasi-absence of other investors (Box 10.1).

THE ROLE OF THE REGIONAL SURVEILLANCE FRAMEWORK

The regional macroeconomic surveillance framework in the WAEMU includes key fiscal rules. Three of the four first-order convergence criteria are of a fiscal nature: (1) the basic fiscal balance should record a surplus, (2) the overall public debt-to-GDP ratio should be less than 70 percent, and (3) governments should not accumulate arrears. Second-order criteria also include a number of fiscal targets, but they are less directly aimed at the stability of the monetary union.

All WAEMU countries now have debt ratios significantly below the convergence criterion (Table 10.2). The criterion was designed at a time when all WAEMU countries were over-indebted, with debt ratios significantly above 70 percent of GDP. With Côte d'Ivoire having reached the completion point under the Heavily Indebted Poor Countries Initiative in 2012, all

TABLE 10.2

Determinants of Interest Rates in the WAEMU

Overall Balance to GDP	−0.153***	−0.0577
	(0.001)	(0.274)
Domestic Debt to GDP	0.0944**	0.103***
	(0.013)	(0.006)
Inflation	0.0608**	−0.0201
	(0.016)	(0.487)
Excess Reserves	−0.787***	−1.290***
	(0.000)	(0.000)
WAEMU Overall Balance to GDP	−0.498***	−0.228*
	(0.000)	(0.099)
Political Risk Rating		0.0502***
		(0.000)
Log Interest Rates	0.736***	0.528***
	(0.000)	(0.000)
Observations	52	47

Source: IMF staff estimations.
Note: *p*-values in parentheses, * $p < 0.10$, ** $p < 0.05$, *** $p < 0.01$.

WAEMU countries have now benefited from substantial debt relief and have debt ratios significantly below 70 percent of GDP. This major structural break raises the issue of whether the existing ceiling remains appropriate.

Previously, the basic fiscal balance criterion had rarely been met, raising issues about its relevance and credibility. Most countries repeatedly missed the target between 2001 and 2012 (Table 10.3 and Figure 10.1). This begs the question of whether policies were inadequate (in light of the repeated breaches) or if the criterion itself needs to be reconsidered.

If a country cannot come up with corrective measures or they are poorly executed, it is liable to sanctions, which can include publication of a statement on the country's economic situation, withdrawal of the Union's assistance, recommendation to the BCEAO to review its intervention policy toward the country, and finally, suspension of financial support from the Union. It is not clear how much time a country is given to take the correcting measures and whether, if adjustment fails, the process reverts to the very beginning, or to the last fulfilled step. Furthermore, the acceptable adjustment and the monetary value of the sanctions are not specified; in fact, financial sanctions have never been implemented. The ambiguity of the corrective mechanism is compounded by the leeway provided by Article 71 of the WAEMU Treaty which states that, if a member country is experiencing economic distress or is susceptible to such distress because of exceptional circumstances, the (unanimous) WAEMU Council can exempt it from the obligation to meet part or all of the convergence criteria.

SURVEILLANCE FRAMEWORK AND MARKET DISCIPLINE

The WAEMU financial market, while having developed substantially in the last decade, is still relatively shallow. Deepening the regional market would increase market discipline. This would likely result in imperfect pricing of sovereign borrowing. Market monitoring may also be hampered by banks' limited capacities to assess fiscal sustainability. Further market development, and the associated increasing reliance of governments on this kind of financing, can be expected to increase market discipline. Improving information quality and availability, which can then be used by market participants for pricing purposes, would also help. Banks, on their side, may need to improve their analytical capabilities. Finally, the supervision authorities could consider intro-

TABLE 10.3

WAEMU: First-Order Convergence Criteria, 2001–12

	2001	2002	2003	2004	2005	2006	2007	2008	2009	2010	2011	2012
Basic fiscal balance/GDP (> = 0 percent)[1]												
Benin	−3.0	−2.8	−0.1	−0.5	−1.4	0.1	1.5	−1.1	−1.5	1.5	−0.2	0.4
Burkina Faso	−2.5	−3.7	−2.9	−3.2	−3.5	−4.5	−5.8	−4.9	−1.9	0.4	1.2	−1.5
Côte d'Ivoire	1.1	−0.4	−1.7	−1.3	−1.6	−1.6	−0.6	−1.6	−1.0	−1.6	−4.0	−3.8
Guinea-Bissau	−6.9	−5.8	−7.0	−12.0	−7.2	−6.2	−7.7	−6.7	3.2	1.0	0.0	−1.4
Mali	−1.7	−1.3	−0.3	−0.7	−1.2	−0.4	−1.2	−1.2	0.4	0.2	−1.1	−1.1
Niger	−3.7	−1.9	−2.1	−2.2	−1.5	1.1	−0.2	1.9	−2.8	−1.0	−1.4	−0.4
Senegal	−1.2	1.2	0.2	−0.5	−1.2	−4.7	−2.6	−2.4	−2.1	−1.8	−4.0	−3.7
Togo	1.5	0.3	2.7	1.4	−2.0	−2.8	−2.7	−0.7	−1.4	1.3	−1.7	−3.8
WAEMU	−0.8	−0.9	−1.1	−1.3	−1.8	−2.1	−1.6	−1.8	−1.3	−0.6	−2.2	−2.4
Number of countries violating	*6*	*6*	*6*	*7*	*8*	*6*	*7*	*7*	*6*	*3*	*6*	*7*
Total debt/GDP (= < 70 percent)												
Benin	54.0	47.9	36.6	33.8	37.3	11.6	21.9	25.7	28.1	30.2	30.3	32.4
Burkina Faso	0.0	0.0	0.0	0.0	0.0	0.0	23.2	22.1	27.2	27.2	28.0	30.9
Côte d'Ivoire	175.2	150.7	133.6	120.4	107.2	107.1	75.6	75.3	66.5	66.4	71.2	49.5
Guinea-Bissau	208.3	230.7	217.3	195.6	179.3	176.9	187.5	157.6	163.8	49.0	44.2	46.9
Mali	88.7	56.1	51.6	48.4	48.3	19.9	21.0	20.8	22.9	32.8	30.1	31.4
Niger	85.2	88.9	69.9	58.8	52.3	17.2	25.1	21.0	27.8	24.3	23.1	27.1
Senegal	77.3	80.3	69.2	68.0	57.3	37.2	23.5	23.9	34.2	35.7	40.0	45.0
Togo	108.0	93.4	92.4	82.5	72.6	82.5	112.9	84.0	75.9	48.5	46.3	45.6
WAEMU	110.1	96.4	82.9	75.3	67.0	54.9	48.4	42.8	45.4	43.5	43.7	39.7
Number of countries violating	*6*	*5*	*3*	*3*	*3*	*3*	*3*	*3*	*2*	*0*	*1*	*0*
Memorandum item												
Overall fiscal balance (incl. grants)												
Benin	−4.8	−5.1	−1.7	−1.2	−2.3	−0.3	0.2	−1.7	−4.3	−1.6	−1.8	−0.7
Burkina Faso	−3.9	−4.9	−3.0	−4.5	−5.0	16.6	−5.7	−4.4	−4.8	−4.5	−2.5	−3.6
Côte d'Ivoire	0.9	−1.1	−2.1	−1.7	−1.7	−1.8	−0.8	−0.6	−1.6	−2.3	−4.3	−4.3
Guinea-Bissau	−5.4	−3.6	−1.0	−4.6	−4.9	−2.3	−2.7	1.7	2.7	−2.5	−2.8	−1.9
Mali	−3.2	−3.8	−1.3	−2.6	−3.1	31.3	−3.2	−2.2	−4.2	−2.7	−4.1	−2.1
Niger	−3.5	−3.0	−2.8	−3.6	−2.0	40.3	−1.0	1.5	−5.4	−2.5	−2.8	−3.9
Senegal	−2.4	0.0	−1.3	−3.1	−3.0	−5.7	−3.7	−4.6	−4.8	−5.2	−6.7	−5.9
Togo	−0.1	−0.4	2.4	1.0	−2.4	−2.8	−1.9	−0.9	−2.8	−1.6	−2.9	−6.3
WAEMU	−1.6	−2.1	−1.7	−2.4	−2.7	6.9	−2.2	−1.9	−3.5	−3.1	−4.0	−3.9

Sources: Country authorities and IMF staff estimations.

[1]Total fiscal revenues, excluding grants, minus total expenditures excluding foreign-financed investment expenditure. From 2009, total fiscal revenues plus budget support grants plus counterpart of Heavily Indebted Poor countries/Multilateral Debt Relief Initiative (HIPC/MDRI)-related spending for both current and capital spending less current expenditure and capital expenditure financed by own resources.

Figure 10.1. WAEMU Fiscal Balance

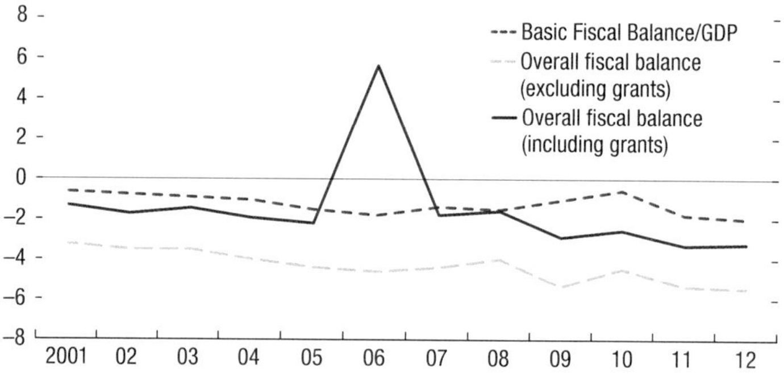

Sources: Country authorities and IMF staff estimations.

ducing a nonzero risk weight for government paper in the financial institutions' capital adequacy calculations.

The ceiling for the public debt ratio could be lowered. The current convergence criteria of 70 percent of nominal debt-to-GDP ratio should be viewed as a ceiling, not a desirable level. This ceiling was set at a time when debt ratios were much higher and has not been revised thereafter. Research conducted by World Bank and IMF staff in the context of the debt sustainability framework suggests that a ceiling of 70 percent of GDP may be higher than desirable from the perspective of limiting the risk of debt distress. It could be lowered to around 50 percent, which is the level suggested by World Bank and IMF staff for countries with low or medium quality of policies and institutions (that is, countries with a Country Policy and Institutional Assessment index lower than 3.75). Whatever its level, the ceiling should be seen as a debt level to avoid reaching, not as an optimal level.

The fiscal balance criterion design has been reconsidered to align it with the main objective of preserving fiscal sustainability. The exclusion of the foreign-financed capital expenditure definition used in the WAEMU raised two issues. First, it excluded a substantial source of debt accumulation, which in the past was a major contributor to overindebtedness. Second, it discriminated among sources of financing, to the detriment of regional financing at a time when it might actually be desirable to develop the regional market. An overall deficit target adopted now as the WAEMU convergence criterion would allow better control over debt accumulation and would not create distortions. If the authorities were to move in this direction, the next issue to address would be how to set the ceiling for the overall deficit to both ensure debt sustainability and allow for countercyclical policy responses. A solution considered in the euro area has been to set a target for the structural (cyclically adjusted) balance. However, such an approach may be more challenging to implement in the WAEMU, due to the absence of clear business cycles, as well as data quality and availability issues. A possible alternative approach would be to use the deficit level as a reference for the ceiling, which would stabilize the debt ratio in the steady state. For instance, assuming that nominal GDP grows by 7 percent at the steady state (5 percent for real growth and 2 percent for inflation, which is the BCEAO's objective), a deficit of 3.5 percent stabilizes the debt ratio at 50 percent. The ceiling could be set slightly below this level, while allowing it to exceed it temporarily (and by a limited amount) under exceptional circumstances.

Finally, the monitoring and enforcement mechanism may need to be strengthened. The WAEMU Commission encounters difficulties collecting the information it needs to do effective regional surveillance. For example, data on fiscal arrears do not seem easily available. Timeliness of information may also be an issue. Improving the availability, quality, and timeliness of information is critical if the regional institutions are to exercise meaningful surveillance. Another issue is enforcement. While the design of the Excess Deficit Procedure (EDP) could perhaps be improved, the more fundamental issue is the readiness of member states to subject themselves to strong oversight and possible sanctions from their peers. This is obviously a highly political issue, and perhaps not an urgent one, but it will need to be addressed in the medium term. A first step should be increased transparency and dissemination of regional and national fiscal outcomes.

REFERENCES

Alexander, V., and Anker, P. 1997. "Fiscal Discipline and the Question of Convergence of National Interest Rates in the European Union." *Open Economies Review* 8 (4): 335–52.

Diouf, M. A., and F. Boutin-Dufresne. 2012. "Financing Growth in the WAEMU Through the Regional Securities Market: Past Successes and Current Challenges." IMF Working Paper 12/249, International Monetary Fund, Washington.

Hitaj, E., and Y. K. Onder. 2013. "Fiscal Discipline in WAEMU: Rules, Institutions, and Markets." IMF Working Paper 13/216, International Monetary Fund, Washington.

Morris, R., H. Ongena, and L. Schuknecht. 2006. "The Reform and Implementation of the Stability and Growth Pact." Occasional Paper Series, European Central Bank, Frankfurt.

Sy, Amadou N. R. 2010. "Government Securities Markets in the West African Economic and Monetary Union: A Review." *African Development Review* 22 (2): 292–302.

CHAPTER 11

Public Investment and Fiscal Rules[1]

SÉBASTIEN DESSUS, JOSE L. DIAZ-SANCHEZ, AND ARISTOMENE VAROUDAKIS

Public investment in the West African Economic and Monetary Union (WAEMU) has been procyclical. Evidence from a panel of low-income and lower middle-income countries suggests that, contrary to other countries, public investment in the WAEMU contracts more in "bad times" than it increases in "good times" and appears to have become procyclical since the introduction of the fiscal convergence criteria in 1994. The fiscal deficit has been largely uncorrelated to GDP growth in the WAEMU because of the procyclicality of public investment, while in other low-income countries, the fiscal balance appears to have been mildly countercyclical. The procyclicality of public expenditure and the high asymmetry of shocks that affect WAEMU countries justify exploring options for greater countercyclicality of rules-based fiscal frameworks and for risk sharing. In the WAEMU, fiscal rules can become important anchors of medium-term fiscal policy over the cycle so as to preserve fiscal discipline at the aggregate level. Some flexibility to fiscal convergence criteria could help mitigate the procyclicality of public expenditures, including of public investment. A countercyclical fiscal rule would allow for some positive correlation, with smaller deficits (larger surpluses) in booms and larger deficits (smaller surpluses) in contractions. At the same time, because shocks affecting WAEMU countries are highly asymmetric, there is room for establishing fiscal federalism arrangements or for adopting a form of risk sharing (or group insurance) to mitigate the incidence of these shocks. Risk-sharing mechanisms would aim to allocate larger financial resources to the Union members exposed to negative shocks. As countries facing difficulties seem compelled to drastically cut back investment in bad times, such mechanisms would also help preserve investment levels in the WAEMU.

FISCAL RULES IN A MONETARY UNION

The debt crisis in the euro area revealed new challenges for monetary unions. Countries entering a monetary union relinquish national monetary and exchange rate policies for the benefit of greater integration associated with the union. If countries in the union are subject to large asymmetric shocks, and there are no transfers through a federal budget, national fiscal policy would be the only instrument left to cushion these shocks. Yet, despite the need for fiscal flexibility, existing monetary unions observe strict fiscal rules that typically limit the leeway of national fiscal policies to respond to shocks. Concerns about debt externalities of national fiscal policies and possibly weak incentives for fiscal restraint provide a common rationale for fiscal rules in monetary unions (De Grauwe 1992).

A precondition for market-driven discipline in monetary unions is that a no-bailout clause can be properly enforced among the members, regardless of their systemic importance or of concerns regarding financial spillovers from debt default. In the absence of effective enforcement, market interest rates will not reflect the default risk of monetary union members. Because market discipline is likely to fail, fiscal rules seem necessary to deflect debt externalities and strengthen possibly weak incentives for fiscal restraint. Externalities may arise if national fiscal policies lead to

[1]Previously published in *Journal of International Development*, Wiley Online Library (wileyonlinelibrary.com) DOI: 10.1002/jid.3047.

unsustainable levels of public debt, putting pressure on the central bank to monetize part of this debt. Externalities may also arise through the financial sector, as a debt crisis in a fiscally distressed member may spill over to banks of other members that may hold the distressed debt. Incentives for fiscal discipline may weaken when a country joins a monetary union because the interest rate on its debt declines as the risk premium of exchange rate devaluation vanishes. A factor that plays in the opposite direction of strengthening fiscal discipline is that monetary union members surrender the option of financing budget deficits through money creation and thus face a harder budget constraint compared with countries that have monetary autonomy.

However, fiscal rules may also reduce the quality of fiscal policy because they disregard the composition of fiscal adjustment necessary for compliance (Blanchard and Giavazzi 2004). The need to comply with fiscal rules may result in easy cuts in capital spending. These can have two main effects: First, they may amplify volatility through procyclical cuts in expenditure and, in particular, public investment. Second, they may have a potentially negative impact on long-term growth if the level of public investment, or its quality, are negatively affected. Thus, among the most important challenges for monetary unions is to improve their capacity to ensure fiscal convergence, while also developing efficient mechanisms to mitigate asymmetric shocks, which do not affect all members at the same time.

Fiscal convergence rules in the WAEMU impose strict limits on the budget deficit. Current rules include a balanced basic budget deficit defined as domestic revenue minus domestically financed expenditure, a public debt ceiling at 70 percent of GDP, and the nonaccumulation of public expenditure arrears. The rules have not been systematically enforced in the past, especially concerning the basic fiscal balance. Even so, they still leave only limited room for countercyclical response in countries affected by asymmetric shocks. Countercyclical response through national budgets is bound by foreign financing, originating from outside the WAEMU, of any additional spending, or of the budget deficit resulting from an adverse revenue shock. Moreover, a large part of current public expenditures are nondiscretionary (wages, transfers, debt service) and thus difficult to cut in the short run. One can therefore anticipate that an unexpected change in revenue, or current expenditure, resulting from a shock, will be to a large extent cushioned by changes in discretionary public investment. Furthermore, unlike the relative ease in cutting investment expenditures in bad times, rapidly converting unexpected revenues into new projects is often difficult, reflecting, for example, bottlenecks in project selection or in procurement. It is therefore possible that volatility of public investment may well affect its average level too. For example, finding by Celasun and Walliser (2008) on a sample of 13 developing countries (including four WAEMU countries) over the period 1992–2007 suggest that aid volatility is detrimental to public investment in physical and human capital. While unexpected shortfalls entail direct cuts in investment, unexpected windfalls do not lead to higher investments of a symmetric order of magnitude.

We extend previous empirical work on procyclical fiscal policies in sub-Saharan Africa by Thornton (2008); Lledo, Yackovlev and Gadene (2011); and Guillaumont-Jeanneney and Tapsoba (2011) who found that total public expenditure is more procyclical in WAEMU than it is in other African countries. The cyclical patterns of public investment and current public expenditure are examined separately, comparing the WAEMU to a large sample of low-income countries and lower middle-income countries in sub-Saharan Africa and in other developing regions. The patterns estimated over 1995–2012 are compared with earlier patterns in 1981–94 to gain insight on the possible impact of the fiscal convergence criteria adopted in 1994, after the devaluation of the CFA franc. We also examine how these patterns differ in recessions and booms of economic activity. The findings justify exploring options for greater countercyclicality of rules-based fiscal frameworks and options for risk-sharing mechanisms with a view to reducing the procyclicality of public investment. Risk-sharing mechanisms could include a move toward fiscal federalism through greater centralization of national budgets, the design of group insurance schemes, or both.

GROWTH, INVESTMENT, AND SHOCKS

According to the World Bank's classification, of 67 low-income and lower middle-income countries (including the eight WAEMU members) over the period 1995–2012, the WAEMU can be compared to two other country groups. The first group is comprised of 28 other sub-Saharan African low-income and lower middle-income countries (excluding the WAEMU). The second group is comprised of 31 other low-income and lower middle-income countries in the rest of the world (see Annex Table 11.1.1 for group definitions). As Table 11.1 shows, at 3.6 percent on (unweighted) average, annual real GDP growth in the WAEMU ranks well below comparator groups. Growth volatility in the WAEMU, as measured by the coefficient of variation of annual GDP growth, has been higher than in other low-income and lower middle-income countries, but lower than in other sub-Saharan African comparator countries. Public investment in proportion to GDP has also been low in the WAEMU. At 6 percent of GDP on average, it ranks well below the percentage seen in the other two country groups. Reflecting weak public investment, unsurprisingly perhaps, the WAEMU lags behind the rest of sub-Saharan Africa as a whole on almost all infrastructure indicators, with the most notable gaps in paved-road density, mainline density, and generation capacity (IMF 2010). Such infrastructure gaps could be partly responsible for WAEMU's "missing growth".[2]

Turning to the degree of synchronization of shocks, as Table 11.2 shows, over 1995–2012, the average correlation of each WAEMU member country's annual GDP growth with the unweighted average annual GDP growth of other WAEMU members was 0.117. Burkina Faso and Togo had the highest GDP growth correlation (0.56 and 0.47, respectively) with average GDP growth of other WAEMU members, while all others had no significant correlations with the rest of the WAEMU members. The low correlations of real GDP growth among WAEMU members contrast with the much higher correlations of GDP growth observed in monetary unions among advanced economies where economic integration is much higher. For example, the average real income growth correlation among 48 U.S. states over 1960–90 was 0.72, while the average real GDP growth correlation among 15 euro area members over 1961–96 was 0.56 (Fatas 1998). The terms of trade changes as a more direct measure of exogenous shocks points to a similar conclusion (Table 11.2, last column). The average correlation of individual WAEMU members' terms of trade changes with the rest of the WAEMU is 0.21, with only Benin, Burkina Faso, and Mali exhibiting relatively high positive correlations with the rest of WAEMU members.

TABLE 11.1

GDP Growth and Public Investment, 1995–2012 (in percent)

	WAEMU (8 countries)	Other SSA LIC and LMIC (28 countries)	Other LIC and LMIC (31 countries)
GDP growth per year			
Average	3.56	4.12	4.34
Standard deviation	4.32	6.58	4.15
Standard deviation/average	1.21	1.60	0.96
Public investment/GDP			
Average	6.02	7.85	7.15
Standard deviation	2.64	6.20	9.48
Standard deviation/average	0.44	0.79	1.32

Source: Authors' calculations based on data from *World Economic Outlook*.
Note: LIC = low-income countries; LMIC = lower middle-income countries; SSA = sub-Saharan Africa; WAEMU = West African Economic and Monetary Union.

[2]Infrastructure gaps may cost sub-Saharan Africa up to 2 percent per year of foregone GDP growth (Calderon 2009).

TABLE 11.2

Asymmetric Shocks in the WAEMU, 1995–2012

	GDP Growth (in percent)		Comparison with Other WAEMU Members	
	Average	Standard Deviation	Correlation of GDP Growth	Correlation of Terms of Trade Changes
Benin	4.1	1.0	0.031	0.440
Burkina Faso	5.9	2.0	0.556	0.551
Côte d'Ivoire	1.7	3.6	0.157	–0.120
Guinea-Bissau	1.1	8.9	–0.257	–0.204
Mali	4.2	3.7	0.193	0.556
Niger	4.9	4.6	–0.169	–0.023
Senegal	3.9	1.7	–0.044	0.307
Togo	2.4	2.7	0.469	0.172
Average	3.5	3.5	0.117	0.210

Source: Authors calculations based on data from *World Economic Outlook.*

PROCYCLICALITY OF FISCAL POLICY

Evidence suggests that, contrary to high-income countries where fiscal policy is mostly uncorrelated with the business cycle, in developing countries, fiscal policy is largely procyclical. That is, it turns expansionary in good times and contractionary in bad times (Talvi and Vegh 2005). The procyclicality of fiscal policy is often explained by the loss of international capital market access during bad times, which, in the absence of fiscal space through accumulated savings, makes it expensive, if not impossible, to finance expansionary policies during downturns (Aizenman, Gavin, and Hausmann, 2000; Gavin and Perotti,1997).

Another explanation of the procyclicality of fiscal policy, suggested by Talvi and Vegh (2005), emphasizes the large variations in tax bases in developing countries during the cycle. Reflecting large revenue swings, countercyclical fiscal policy would cause large budget surpluses in good times, exacerbating pressure on policymakers from various constituencies to spend the accumulated savings. To deflect such pressures and avoid wasteful use of resources, it is possible that policymakers would be tempted to avoid large surpluses by imparting procyclicality to fiscal policy.

The procyclicality of fiscal policy has been also documented in African countries. Government consumption has been found to be procyclical, the more so when dependence on foreign aid is high (Thornton 2008). Procyclicality of total public expenditure has been also found by Lledo, Yackovlev, and Gadene (2011), but with a mitigating impact of foreign aid and debt relief.

Whether fiscal rules exacerbate procyclicality of fiscal policy is largely an empirical matter. The outcome will depend on the design of rules and the incentives they create for policymakers. Strict fiscal rules that target the overall fiscal balance on an annual basis may, arguably, amplify procyclicality, as shocks would trigger immediate expenditure and tax adjustments to meet the fiscal targets. By contrast, fiscal rules targeting the structural deficit or the deficit over the cycle could mitigate procyclicality. Importantly, fiscal rules could mitigate procyclicality if they changed the incentives of policymakers toward creating fiscal space in good times for countercyclical response in bad times. There is evidence that policy incentives do change over time: experience with credit rationing during bad times, especially after the East Asian crisis in the late 1990s, prompted many developing countries to self-insure by building buffers of savings during good times. This made it possible for several emerging economies to respond countercyclically to the 2008–09 global financial crisis, including, to some extent, in Africa (Krumm and Kularatne 2013).

In what follows, we analyze the procyclicality in the WAEMU of the two components of public expenditure (public investment and current expenditure), but also of the fiscal balance. To

TABLE 11.3

The Procyclicality of Fiscal Policy (1995–2012)

Dependent Variable	(1) DLNKFIG	(2) DLNKCURX	(3) DEF/NGDP
W*DLNKGDP	7.213**	−0.0386	−0.0152
	(2.072)	(−0.0382)	(−0.0185)
(1-W)*DLNKGDP	1.409	1.225	0.590***
	(0.502)	(1.522)	(2.643)
AC dummy	4.609	0.459	0.0034
	(1.126)	(1.535)	(0.0301)
Observations	1,086	1,108	1,147
Number of countries	67	78	78
Hansen J test:			
Statistic	2.958	4.609	6.03
Chi-sq (6), *p*-value	0.8140	0.5949	0.4199

Source: Authors' calculations based on IMF IFS database.

Note: D and LN denote the first difference operator and the natural logarithm operator, respectively. DEF = fiscal balance; KCURX = current real public expenditure (total expenditure excluding public investment); KFIG = real public investment; KGDP = real GDP; NGDP = nominal GDP; W = dummy variable for WAEMU countries. AC is a dummy with value 1 for armed conflict episodes in a given year and 0 otherwise. Robust *z*-statistics (to both arbitrary heteroskedasticity and arbitrary autocorrelation) are in parentheses. ***, **,* indicate significance at 1%, 5%, and 10% confidence levels, respectively.

this end, we regress these variables on the annual GDP growth rate for WAEMU countries, but also for a large sample of other low-income and lower middle-income countries.[3]

A positive relationship between government expenditures and GDP growth could reflect not only a procyclical behavior of fiscal variables but also an increase in infrastructure and/or social services demand resulting from a higher level of income. To account for this possible simultaneity between GDP growth and the fiscal variables, a generalized method of moments estimator was used with standard errors robust for both heteroskedasticity and autocorrelation. Lags of the independent variable (the real GDP growth) are used as instruments, together with an additional instrument constructed as the product of world GDP growth and each country's ratio of exports to GDP. The overidentifying restrictions are tested through the Hansen J test, which provides a test of the general validity of the instruments used. Regression coefficients for the WAEMU countries are estimated separately from the other countries of the sample. Results for the period 1995–2012 are reported in Table 11.3.

The results confirm the validity of the overidentifying restrictions and thus of the instruments used. Public investment has been procyclical in WAEMU over the estimation period, as the estimated elasticity to real GDP growth is positive at a 95 percent confidence level. By contrast, there is no significant procyclicality of public investment in other low-income and lower middle-income countries (Table 11.3, column 1). The results for current public expenditure show an acyclical behavior of this fiscal policy variable for the two groups of countries (Table 11.3, column 2). Procyclical public expenditure is thus associated with public investment, rather than with current expenditure, in the WAEMU. This supports the perception that public investment, more than current expenditure, is a major shock absorber, or residual fiscal variable. As to the fiscal balance, there is evidence of countercyclicality in other low-income and lower middle-income countries, as the fiscal deficit (surplus) decreases (increases) when growth is stronger (Table 11.3, column 3). By contrast, in the WAEMU, the fiscal balance is acyclical. The absence of countercyclicality of fiscal deficits in the WAEMU may reflect the large compensating changes in public

[3]Data are taken from the *World Economic Outlook* and the IMF's IFS database. We include country and time-specific effects. The specification also includes a dummy for the years of armed conflict. We use the UCDP/PRIO data on armed conflict first presented in Gleditsch and others (2002) and updated in Themnér and Wallensteen (2014).

TABLE 11.4

The Procyclicality of Fiscal Policy (1981–94)

Dependent Variable	(1) DLNKFIG	(2) DLNKCURX	(3) DEF/NGDP
W*DLNKGDP	0.230	2.587	−0.450*
	(0.111)	(1.162)	(−1.810)
(1-W)*DLNKGDP	0.946	1.616**	0.209
	(0.385)	(2.140)	(0.751)
AC dummy	0.261	0.272	−0.0664
	(0.490)	(1.082)	(−0.664)
Observations	432	207	229
Number of countries	48	32	34
Hansen J test:			
Statistic	6.117	3.029	11.521
Chi-sq (6), *p*-value	0.4102	0.8052	0.0735

Source: Authors' calculations based on IMF IFS database.
Note: D and LN denote the first difference operator and the natural logarithm operator, respectively. KFIG = real public investment; KCURX = current real public expenditure (total expenditure excluding public investment); DEF = fiscal balance; NGDP = nominal GDP; KGDP = real GDP; W = dummy variable for WAEMU countries. We convert nominal variables into real variables using the GDP deflator. AC is a dummy with value 1 for armed conflict episodes in a given year and 0 otherwise. Robust *z*-statistics are in parentheses. **,* indicate significance at 5% and 10% confidence levels, respectively. The method of estimation is GMM with standard errors and statistics robust to both arbitrary heteroskedasticity and arbitrary autocorrelation. Instruments include: 1, 2, 3, and 4 lags of the two independent variables and the ratio of exports to GDP for each country multiplied by the world GDP growth. Accordingly, there are six overidentifying restrictions, equal to the total number of instruments minus the number of regressors. Each regression includes country fixed effects and time fixed effects. The null hypothesis of the Hansen J test (overidentification test) is that all moment conditions are valid; that is, the instruments used are not correlated with the residuals.

investment when fiscal revenues are affected by shocks. In bad (good) times, when fiscal revenues shrink (expand), a contraction (increase) of public investment offsets the impact of the shock on the budget, resulting in only small changes in the fiscal deficit in proportion to GDP.

Estimating the same set of regressions over the period 1981–94, preceding the introduction of the fiscal convergence criteria in the WAEMU, provides evidence on the possible impact of this fiscal framework on the cyclical patterns of public investment and current expenditures. As Table 11.4 shows, public investment exhibited a similar pattern of procyclicality in other low-income and lower middle-income countries in 1981–94 (Table 11.4, column 1). However, in the WAEMU, contrary to the more recent period (1995–2012), there is no evidence of procyclicality of public investment over the 1981–94 period. Current public expenditures in WAEMU were also found acyclical in both the 1981–94 and 1995–2012 periods (Table 11.4, column 2). This confirms the perception that since the introduction of the fiscal convergence framework, public investment, more than current expenditure, has responded procyclically in the face of shocks that affected the budget in WAEMU countries.

The procyclical changes in fiscal policy in developing countries have often been found to be asymmetric in good and bad times. For example, Gavin and Perotti (1997) found that fiscal balances in Latin America were more procyclical in bad times, when negative deviations of GDP growth from average were large. In the WAEMU, Guillaumont-Jeanneney and Tapsoba (2011) found total public expenditure to be more procyclical in recessions than in good times. In our larger sample, this issue is studied by examining whether the elasticity of public investment to GDP is different when countries face negative and positive shocks. Public investment was found to be procyclical in the WAEMU over the recent period (1995–2012). For each country, periods of negative shocks are identified as years with below-average real GDP growth (and periods of positive shocks as years with above-average real GDP growth). Regressions of real public investment growth on real GDP growth are estimated separately on periods of negative and positive shocks, while distinguishing the coefficients for WAEMU and non-WAEMU countries (Table 11.5).

In WAEMU, the elasticity of public investment to GDP is not significant in good times (Table 11.5, column 1). By contrast, in bad times, the elasticity of public investment to GDP is

TABLE 11.5

Procyclicality of Public Expenditure in "Good" and "Bad" Times (1995–2012)

Dependent Variable	GDP Growth > Average (1) DLNKFIG	GDP Growth < Average (2) DLNKFIG
W*DLNKGDP	8.166	9.423*
	(1.328)	(1.814)
(1-W)*DLNKGDP	4.655	4.513
	(1.374)	(1.156)
AC dummy	−0.949	−0.538
	(−0.689)	(−0.216)
Observations	592	493
Number of countries	66	66
Hansen J test:		
Statistic	9.752	4.329
Chi-sq (6), *p*-value	0.1355	0.6322

Source: Authors' calculations based on IMF IFS database.

Note: D and LN denote the first difference operator and the natural logarithm operator, respectively. KFIG = real public investment; KGDP = real GDP; W = dummy variable for WAEMU countries. We convert nominal GDP into real GDP using the GDP deflator. AC is a dummy with value 1 for armed conflict episodes in a given year and 0 otherwise. Robust *z*-statistics are in parentheses. **,* indicate significance at 5% and 10% confidence levels, respectively. The method of estimation is GMM with standard errors and statistics robust to both arbitrary heteroskedasticity and arbitrary autocorrelation. Instruments include: 1, 2, 3, and 4 lags of the two independent variables and the ratio of exports to GDP for each country multiplied by the world GDP growth. Accordingly, there are six overidentifying restrictions, equal to the total number of instruments minus the number of regressors. Each regression includes country fixed effects and time fixed effects. The null hypothesis of the Hansen J test (overidentification test) is that all moment conditions are valid, that is, the instruments used are not correlated with the residuals.

significant at a 90 percent confidence level (Table 11.5, column 2). Public investment seems thus to respond asymmetrically to growth shocks. That is, it contracts more in recessions than it expands in booms. In non-WAEMU countries, we do not find evidence of an asymmetric response of public investment to growth shocks

The asymmetric pattern in the response of public investment in bad and good times observed in the WAEMU suggests that shocks may affect the level of public investment, in addition to increasing its volatility. The overall public investment level will be lower with negative and positive shocks of equal variance than without shocks. This phenomenon could contribute to explaining why WAEMU countries record lower average public investment levels than do other low-income and lower middle-income countries, as documented in Table 11.1. Negative shocks in the WAEMU over 1995–2012 (in 58 instances out of 136; or, for 42 percent of observations in the sample) were, on average, equivalent to a 2.8 percentage point drop in the GDP growth rate. Positive shocks (78 observations) averaged 2.1 percentage points of GDP. With negative GDP shocks larger, on average, than positive shocks, and occurring with almost similar frequency as positive shocks, the asymmetric response of public investment in bad and good times could partly explain the lower level of public investment observed in WAEMU compared with non-WAEMU countries.

COUNTERCYCLICAL FISCAL RULES

Rules that target the overall budget balance and (binding) public debt impart procyclicality to fiscal policy, as expenditures and/or taxes have to be adjusted to be in compliance. At the same time, such rules may not lead to sufficient restraint in good times, as strong cyclical tax revenues may help meet targets concerning the overall budget balance. Procyclical rules would thus risk making the fiscal stance overexpansionary while failing to realize savings for bad times. Moreover, the existing WAEMU fiscal convergence framework that requires balancing the annual budget of domestically financed expenditure does not guarantee debt sustainability, as it excludes expenditures financed through the accumulation of foreign debt. A fiscal convergence rule accounting for all sources of financing would be a better safeguard for debt sustainability (IMF 2013).

Excluding foreign-financed expenditure from the definition of the basic budget balance has not succeeded in protecting public investment from volatility, as total public investment has become procyclical since 1994.

There are various options for amending fiscal rules to allow some cyclical flexibility.[4] At least four different options can be considered for setting the budget balance target:

1. Overall budget balance with ad hoc adjustments
2. Cyclically adjusted (structural) budget balance
3. Overall budget balance over the cycle
4. A "golden rule" with exclusion of the capital budget from the target

These options have advantages and disadvantages. When fiscal rules target overall budget balance, some degree of cyclical flexibility is possible on an ad hoc basis through changes in the numerical value of the budget balance target to accommodate shocks. Adjustments made to fiscal rules during the global financial crisis provide examples of such attempts to accommodate cyclical shocks (see Schaechter and others 2012). Latin American countries—especially Peru, Colombia, and Panama—offer recent examples of rules-based fiscal policies that target overall budget balance, as well as of changes designed to accommodate the incidence of external shocks (Berganza 2012).

The main risk of ad hoc adjustments is that it could come at the expense of the credibility of rules-based fiscal policy. A cyclically adjusted or structural budget balance target would allow flexibility to respond to output shocks. One drawback of structural budget balance rules is that output gaps and tax elasticities to income are difficult to estimate with sufficient reliability, especially for developing countries. A variant of the structural budget balance rule would require the government to achieve budget balance on average over the cycle—or any level of overall deficit or surplus deemed consistent with debt sustainability. A possible drawback could be a requirement for procyclical tightening toward the end of the cycle if fiscal policy were too loose in the earlier phases (IMF 2009).

Another drawback is that the rule requires accurate timing of the cycle and stable national accounts data to preserve the credibility of the fiscal policy framework. The so-called "golden rule" excludes capital expenditure from the targeted budget balance. Protecting this category of expenditure can be justified on the grounds that public investment contributes to long-term growth. The downside is that this approach reduces the comprehensiveness of the budget balance target and, in turn, weakens its link with the objective of debt sustainability. It also implicitly assumes that all capital expenditure is productive, while at the same time excluding current expenditures (especially in human development) that may also raise productivity growth. In any case, gradual adjustment to deviations from fiscal targets would also be warranted. The Swiss and German fiscal rules are noteworthy examples of gradual adjustment mechanisms to deviations from fiscal rule targets (Beljean and Geier 2013). Both rules allow for countercyclical flexibility by targeting the cyclically adjusted budget balance and use a notional control account to correct deviations from fiscal targets.

Targeting the structural fiscal balance may be difficult in the WAEMU zone. Flexibility could be introduced through a framework targeting the overall budget balance over the cycle, inclusive of foreign-financed expenditures. Creating a correction mechanism based on "notional control accounts" would create incentives for WAEMU countries to exercise fiscal restraint in good times in order to accumulate credits in these accounts. These savings could be used as fiscal space in bad times to offset the impact of adverse shocks. The rule could require corrective action to be

[4]When considering flexibility, it is important to distinguish temporary from permanent (or persistent) shocks. While temporary shocks can be accommodated to the extent that there is fiscal space for countercyclical response, adjustment to permanent shocks is inevitable. Such adjustment has to happen through some combination of price, labor, and capital movements. Fiscal policy can only delay, often unproductively, the necessary adjustment to permanent shocks.

exercised once accumulated deficits have reached a certain limit in proportion to GDP. It should be noted, however, that in the case of resource-rich countries where a large fraction of fiscal revenues comes from primary commodity exports, focusing on the overall balance over the cycle may not suffice. For short-term stabilization purposes, the fiscal framework would need to be supplemented by a focus on the nonresource primary fiscal balance, targeted over the cycle, as three WAEMU countries (Côte d'Ivoire, Mali, Niger) are natural resource producers, with Togo being a prospective resource exporter

FISCAL FEDERALISM AND RISK SHARING

Cushioning the impact of asymmetric shocks on monetary union members typically calls for fiscal federalism, in the form of some centralization of national budgets at the level of the union. A centralized budget works as a shock absorber, by allowing countries hit by negative shocks to receive larger transfers from, and/or pay less tax to, the federal budget. This is equivalent to an interregional transfer within the union from countries affected by positive shocks. These countries pay more tax to the central budget—thus financing transfers to those countries hit by negative shocks—or, alternatively, receive fewer transfers from the central budget. Interregional transfers can be complementary to intertemporal transfers achieved through some degree of national budget flexibility. This is because relying only on decentralized national budgets to offset shocks reduces the degrees of freedom of future national fiscal policy, as the debt issued to counter the shocks will need to be serviced in the future.

There is space for pooling resources in the WAEMU, but large-scale fiscal federalism through budget centralization might be premature. Pooling resources to finance regionally important expenditure programs—especially in infrastructure, to facilitate trade and regional integration— might produce economies of scale, as well as provide a step toward fiscal federalism. This would also shield part of the national public investment budgets from the procyclicality that they currently suffer. On the revenue side, a guiding principle for intergovernmental taxation is that local governments should tax less mobile tax bases, such as consumption or real estate, while corporate and personal income taxes should be centralized (Cottarelli 2012). It remains questionable whether significant centralization of corporate or personal income tax revenues is feasible in the WAEMU given the narrow fiscal bases and the weakness of tax mobilization mechanisms in most of its member countries.

The risk sharing implicit in fiscal federalism could also be achieved through group insurance in the form of a solidarity fiscal fund. Such a fund could perform transfers to adversely hit monetary union members. In its simplest form, a solidarity fund would be financed by contributions from all members. Adversely hit members would be entitled to withdrawals from the fund. This would enable them to cover revenue shortfalls or other insured fiscal risks. The more asymmetric the shocks that affect union members, the greater the gains from pooling resources or from contributing to a group insurance scheme, such as a solidarity fund. This would compare positively to a policy of self-insurance, which would be equivalent to using only national resources (or budgets) to offset the shocks. Intuitively, as all members are not affected at the same time by the asymmetric shocks, the pooled resources necessary to cushion shocks affecting union members at any time would be lower than the sum of resources that individual members would need to put aside to cushion shocks under self-insurance. Hence, for the same level of risk coverage, the contributions of individual union members to a solidarity fund would be lower than the amounts that member states would have to set aside under self-insurance schemes.

A solidarity fiscal fund would collect contributions from all WAEMU member states during good times, with the objective of redistributing resources to member states when they face idiosyncratic shocks. As with all insurance schemes, this would raise the issue of moral hazard. It would also require verification that idiosyncratic shocks affecting the budget are exogenous and not policy-induced by systematic slippages or manipulation of the budget. In addition, such an approach would need incentives to ensure that fiscal insurance does not dilute efforts to maintain fiscal discipline through adequate revenue mobilization and spending controls. To address these concerns, the fund could feasibly cover fiscal revenue shortfalls attributable to measurable shocks up to a certain amount or up to a proportion of the shock. One option would be to cover a certain proportion of shortfalls in revenue that derive from terms of trade shocks (Dos Reis 2004). Moreover, a risk-sharing mechanism could be designed with the aim of strengthening compliance incentives with a rules-based fiscal framework. An option would be to condition a member country's access to the fund on its compliance with a countercyclical fiscal rule, if such a rule were to be applicable to the monetary union.

POLICY IMPLICATIONS

Evidence suggests that in the WAEMU, public investment is procyclical and highly elastic to shocks, especially in bad times. Protecting public investment against shocks would help accelerate growth as infrastructure is comparatively weak in WAEMU. Some policy options for protecting public investment and mitigating the incidence of asymmetric shocks were discussed. These range from injecting more countercyclical flexibility into WAEMU's rules-based fiscal framework, to designing fiscal federalism and risk-sharing arrangements through solidarity funds. These options could be explored technically in more detail, from an implementation and coordination perspective. Ways and means to make foreign assistance more countercyclical could also be usefully explored. Despite being currently excluded from the fiscal convergence criteria, the results suggest that foreign-financed investment in the WAEMU did not contribute enough to mitigate the procyclicality of public investment. A better understanding of why this is so is warranted.

The weak response of public investment in good times raises the question of why WAEMU governments find it difficult to increase capital budget execution despite efforts in public financial management and public procurement reforms. Judging by the World Bank's Country Policy and Institutional Assessment indicators, as well as by the evidence available through Public Expenditure and Financial Accountability assessments, these efforts have resulted in significant improvements to public financial management and procurement institutions, as well as legal frameworks, policies, and systems. However, progress appears to have been uneven—stronger on upstream budget processes (budget preparation and classification) than on downstream ones (procurement, budget and contract execution, financial reporting, oversight). Change has been more evident in central finance agencies than in line ministries and at lower levels of government, and generally more focused on the de jure than on the de facto dimensions of public financial management and procurement. These reforms have arguably improved aggregate fiscal discipline compared with the situation that prevailed in the 1990s. The extent to which they have translated into a more strategic allocation of resources (to investment in particular) and, crucially, into more efficient and effective public spending remains less clear. Progress in public investment management will be critical for any risk-sharing mechanism to deliver intended results. Improving project selection, appraisal, procurement, budgeting, implementation, and ex-post evaluation will strongly contribute to reducing the negative impact of shocks.

In a monetary union, fiscal rules are important anchors of medium-term fiscal policy over the cycle so as to preserve fiscal discipline at the aggregate level. However, injecting some flexibility to existing fiscal convergence criteria could help mitigate the procyclicality of public expenditure, especially that of public investment. Because of the procyclicality of public investment, the fiscal deficit has been largely uncorrelated to GDP growth in the WAEMU while in other low-income countries the fiscal balance appears to have been mildly countercyclical. A countercyclical fiscal rule would allow for some positive correlation, with smaller deficits (larger surpluses) in booms and larger deficits (smaller surpluses) in contractions.

At the same time, because shocks affecting WAEMU countries are highly asymmetric, there is room for establishing fiscal federalism arrangements or for adopting a form of risk sharing (or group insurance) to mitigate the incidence of these shocks. Risk-sharing mechanisms would aim to allocate larger financial resources to the Union members exposed to negative shocks. As countries facing difficulties seem compelled to drastically cut back investment in bad times, such mechanisms would also help raise average public investment rates in the WAEMU.

ANNEX 11.1

ANNEX TABLE 11.1.1

Groups of Countries

WAEMU	Sub-Saharan African Countries	Lower Income and Lower Middle-Income Countries
Benin	Burundi	Afghanistan
Burkina Faso	Cameroon	Armenia
Côte d'Ivoire	Cape Verde	Bangladesh
Guinea-Bissau	Central African Republic	Bhutan
Mali	Chad	Bolivia
Niger	Comoros	Cambodia
Senegal	Democratic Republic of the Congo	Djibouti
Togo	Republic of Congo	Egypt
	Eritrea	El Salvador
	Ethiopia	Georgia
	The Gambia	Guatemala
	Ghana	Guyana
	Guinea	Honduras
	Kenya	India
	Lesotho	Indonesia
	Madagascar	Moldova
	Malawi	Mongolia
	Mauritania	Morocco
	Mozambique	Myanmar
	Nigeria	Nepal
	Rwanda	Nicaragua
	São Tomé and Príncipe	Pakistan
	Sierra Leone	Paraguay
	Sudan	Philippines
	Swaziland	Sri Lanka
	Tanzania	Syrian Arab Republic
	Uganda	Tajikistan
	Zambia	Ukraine
		Uzbekistan
		Vietnam
		Yemen, Republic of

Source: World Bank Classification (http://data.worldbank.org)

Note: For regressions explaining the current expenditure and the fiscal balance variables, the available data allowed us to increase the sample by 11 additional countries. We added Haiti, Kiribati, Kosovo, Kyrgyz Republic, Lao PDR, Liberia, Micronesia, Samoa, Solomon Islands, Timor-Leste, and Vanuatu to the sample. Bhutan and Mauritania were dropped since no data for these variables were available.

REFERENCES

Aizenman, J., M. Gavin, and R. Hausmann. 2000. "Optimal Tax and Debt Policy with Endogenously Imperfect Creditworthiness." *Journal of International Trade and Economic Development* 9 (4): 367–95.

Beljean, T., and A. Geier. 2013. "The Swiss Debt Brake—Has It Been a Success?" *Swiss Journal of Economics and Statistics* 149: 115–35.

Berganza, J-C. 2012. "Fiscal Rules in Latin America: A Survey." Occasional Paper No 1208, Banco de España, Madrid.

Blanchard, O., and F. Giavazzi. 2004. "Improving the SGP Through a Proper Accounting of Public Investment." CEPR Discussion Paper No 4220, Centre for Economic Policy Research, London.

Calderon, C. 2009. "Infrastructure and Growth in Africa." Policy Research Working Paper 4914, The World Bank, Washington.

Celasun, O., and J. Walliser. 2008. "Predictability of Aid: Do Fickle Donors Undermine Aid Effectiveness?" *Economic Policy* (23): 545–94.

Cottarelli, C. 2012. "Fiscal Federations: Lessons for the Design of a European Fiscal Union." European Central Bank-IMF Conference, Frankfurt, December.

De Grauwe, P. 1992. *The Economics of Monetary Integration.* Oxford: Oxford University Press.

Dos Reis, L. 2004. "Fiscal Insurance against Exogenous Shocks in the CFA-Franc Zone." September. G24 secretariat, Washington, D.C.

Fatas, A. 1998. "Redistribution vs. Insurance: Does EMU Need a Fiscal Federation?" *Economic Policy* 13 (26): 164–203.

Gavin, M., and R. Perotti. 1997. "Fiscal Policy and Private Saving in Latin America in Good Times and Bad." In *Promoting Savings in Latin America*, edited by R. Hausmann and H. Reisen. Paris: Inter-American Development Bank and Organisation for Economic Co-operation and Development, 149–66.

Gleditsch, N. P., P. Wallensteen, M. Eriksson, M. Sollenberg, and H. Strand. 2002. "Armed Conflict 1946–2001: A New Dataset." *Journal of Peace Research* 39 (5): 615–37.

Guillaumont-Jeanneney, S., and S. J-A. Tapsoba. 2011. "Pro Cyclicité de la Politique Budgétaire et Surveillance Multilatérale dans l'Union Economique et Monétaire Ouest Africaine." *African Development Review* 23 (2): 172–89.

International Monetary Fund (IMF). 2009. "Fiscal Rules-Anchoring Expectations for Sustainable Public Finances." Fiscal Affairs Department, December, International Monetary Fund, Washington.

———. 2010. "Sub-Saharan Africa: Resilience and Risks." *Regional Economic Outlook*, Washington, October.

———. 2013. "West African Economic and Monetary Union: Staff Report on Common Policies for Member Countries." March, Washington.

Krumm, K., and C. Kularatne. 2013. "Fiscal Policy Lessons in Sub-Saharan Africa from the 2008–09 Global Crisis." In *Is Fiscal Policy the Answer?*, edited by B. Morenon-Dodson. Washington: World Bank.

Lledo, V. D., I. Yackovlev, and L. Gadene. 2011. "A Tale of Cyclicality, Aid Flows and Debt: Government Spending in Sub-Saharan Africa." *Journal of African Economies* 20 (5): 823–49.

Schaechter, A., T. Kinda, N. Budinaan, and A. Weber. 2012. "Fiscal Rules in Response to the Crisis—Toward the Next Generation Rules." Working Paper 12/187, International Monetary Fund, Washington.

Talvi, E., and C. A. Vegh. 2005. "Tax Base Variability and Procyclical Policy in Developing Countries." *Journal of Development Economics* 78: 156–90.

Themnér, L., and P. Wallensteen. 2014. "Armed Conflict." *Journal of Peace Research* 51 (4): 1–13.

Thornton, J. 2008. "Explaining Procyclical Fiscal Policy in African Countries." *Journal of African Economies* 17 (3): 451–64.

CHAPTER 12

Fiscal Space and Investment Scaling Up

CHRISTINE DIETERICH, KARIM BARHOUMI, QIANG CUI, SERGIO SOLA, AND ALEXANDER RAABE

West African Economic and Monetary Union (WAEMU) countries face an important common challenge of creating sufficient fiscal space to finance ambitious growth, development, and poverty-reduction programs in individual countries. Such additional fiscal space can be created by either enhancing tax revenue or improving the efficiency of spending. While WAEMU countries are broadly in line with comparator countries in total tax collection, WAEMU's tax revenue relies heavily on trade taxes, which will inevitably be reduced with impending trade liberalization. Also, high reliance on trade taxes makes the WAEMU's revenue base vulnerable to the fluctuation of international prices. Panel regression and stochastic frontier analysis suggest substantial room to improve domestic tax collection in the WAEMU by 0.8 to 2 percent of GDP. The effort should be country-specific with each government focusing on its underperforming tax category. On the expenditure side, WAEMU countries have significant scope to improve efficiency of their spending on education and health. If all WAEMU countries achieve the spending efficiency of the top performer among them, the fiscal savings on average can add 1 to 3 percent of GDP annually to the available fiscal space of the region.

THE NEED FOR SCALING UP

WAEMU countries need to mobilize substantial financial resources to address the infrastructure gap, which has been widely identified as a growth bottleneck. Many studies find that inadequate infrastructure impedes growth (for example, Commission for Africa 2005 and Foster and Briceño-Garmendia 2009). Infrastructure development was estimated to have contributed about 1 percentage point to per-capita growth in West Africa in 2001–05 (for example, Calderon 2009, Figure 12.1). For Benin, Domínguez-Torres and Foster (2011) estimate that infrastructure contributed 1.6 percentage points to per-capita growth; while in Senegal, Torres, Briceño-Garmendia, and Dominguez (2011) find the contribution was about 1 percent point. Also, raising the two countries' infrastructure endowment to that of Africa's middle-income countries could boost annual growth by 3.2 and 2.7 percentage points, respectively. Recent reports also confirmed a continued infrastructure bottleneck in other WAEMU countries (for example, IMF 2013a, b, c).

To generate the financing for the scaling up of public investment while preserving macroeconomic stability, WAEMU countries have to use their fiscal space efficiently. While WAEMU countries' external debt levels declined owing to the heavily indebted poor countries/multilateral debt relief initiative, leaving some scope for external borrowing, the availability of financing at attractive terms is limited. Also, some countries' total government debt has increased considerably since those countries received the debt relief, which suggests that caution is warranted in additional borrowing. Therefore, it is essential for the sustainable financing of scaling up infrastructure investment that the two major channels for creating fiscal space be used. These channels are increasing tax revenue and increasing the efficiency of spending.

Figure 12.1. Per-Capita Growth and Changes in Selected Growth Fundamentals 2001–02

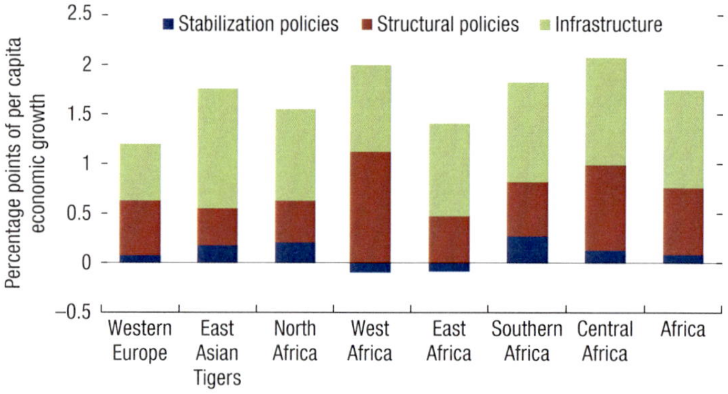

Source: Calderón 2009.
Note: East Asian Tigers = Hong Kong, Singapore, South Korea, and Taiwan.

RAISING TAX REVENUE

Improving tax collection remains the main channel for enlarging the fiscal space. This has been well recognized in the WAEMU, which has a convergence criterion of 20 percent for the tax-to-GDP ratio, even though several member countries have not been in compliance with this criterion for years.

The WAEMU's relatively high indirect tax rates have not resulted in higher tax collection. The higher indirect tax rates in the WAEMU compared with those in sub-Saharan Africa and low-income country averages,[1] especially for goods and services taxes and trade taxes, have not translated into higher revenues. Roughly, the tax-to-GDP ratio has been below the sub-Saharan Africa average throughout the observation period (2000–11), and just broadly in line with the low-income country averages (Figure 12.4). Looking at the trend over time, the WAEMU's tax-to-GDP ratio improved from 11.7 percent of GDP in 2000 to 14.7 percent of GDP in 2011, driven by a broad trend in all member countries except Côte d'Ivoire, where results were affected by internal conflicts. However, the size of improvements varied considerably among the countries. For instance, Benin's total tax revenue increased by 2.1 percentage points, while Togo's total tax revenue rose by 6.6 percentage points.

Looking at the performance tax by tax, the improvement in the WAEMU's tax ratio is driven by higher collection from income tax and goods and services taxes, while trade revenues are broadly flat due to limited trade liberalization. For example:

- *Trade taxes*—In contrast with sub-Saharan African and low-income countries, where weighted average tariff rates declined, reflecting trade liberalization over the last decade, the WAEMU's tariff rates dropped only marginally and the tax-to-GDP ratio has remained broadly stable over time (Figure 12.2). In the comparator groups, sub-Saharan Africa's drop in trade tax revenues reflects the rate decline, while it seems that low-income countries were able to offset the rate decline by efficiency measures that allowed these countries to broadly preserve the trade tax-to-GDP ratio (Figure 12.3 and 12.5).

[1]Excludes upper middle-income countries of South Africa, Botswana, Nigeria, Angola, and Namibia. The low-income countries refer to the World Bank definition of countries with a per-capita GNI of $1,025 or less in 2012.

Figure 12.2. Total and External Government Debt in the WAEMU

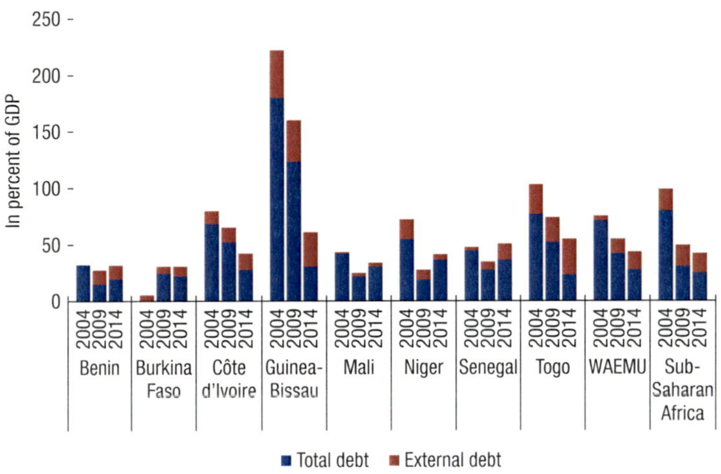

Source: IMF staff estimates.

Figure 12.3. Tax Rate in the WAEMU

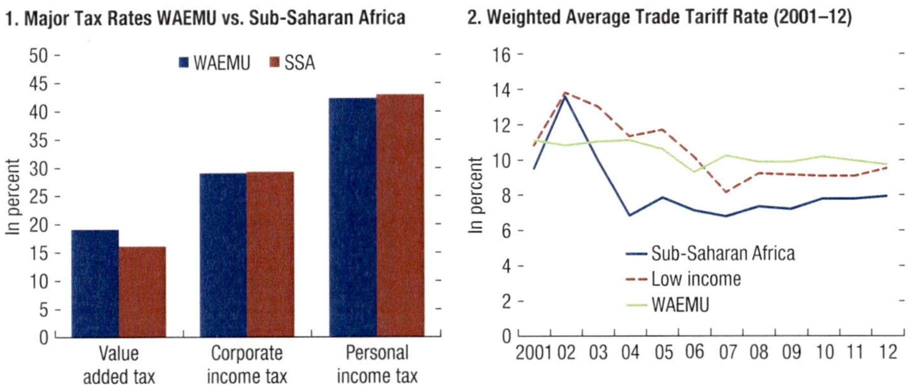

Sources: IMF Fiscal Affairs Department database; and IMF staff calculations.
Note: Data refer to 2010–13 averages. SSA = Sub-Saharan Africa; WAEMU = West African Economic and Monetary Union.

- *Income taxes*—The WAEMU increased the tax-to-GDP ratio from close to 3 to close to 4 percent of GDP, but it remained below the ratios for low-income countries and sub-Saharan Africa (Figure 12.6).
- *Goods and services taxes*—The francophone tradition of relying more on direct than on indirect taxation is reflected in the comparably higher rates. This translates into a higher level of tax revenues than is the case in comparator countries by around 0.6 to 0.8 percent of GDP. Also, the improvement in the WAEMU countries over the observation period was most pronounced in this tax category (Figure 12.4 and 12.7).

WAEMU countries show considerable variation in the drivers for revenue collection by tax categories. For example, in Togo, income tax revenue declined from 2.9 percent to 2.5 percent of GDP, but goods and service tax revenue rose sharply from 2 percent to 9.2 percent of GDP. In

Figure 12.4. Total Tax Revenue (Percent of GDP)

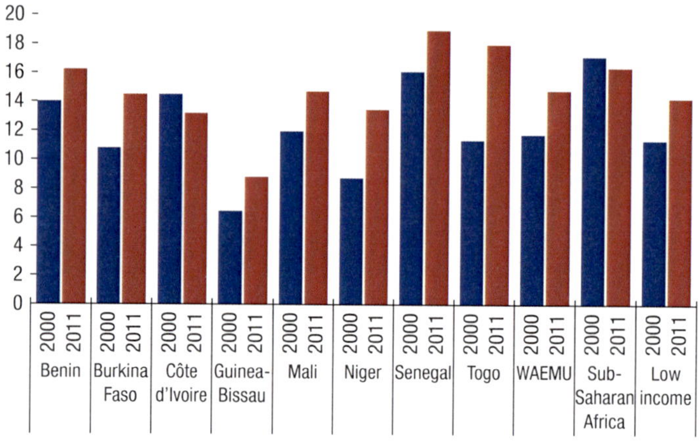

Sources: IMF Fiscal Affairs Department database; and IMF staff calculations.

Figure 12.5. Trade Tax Revenue (Percent of GDP)

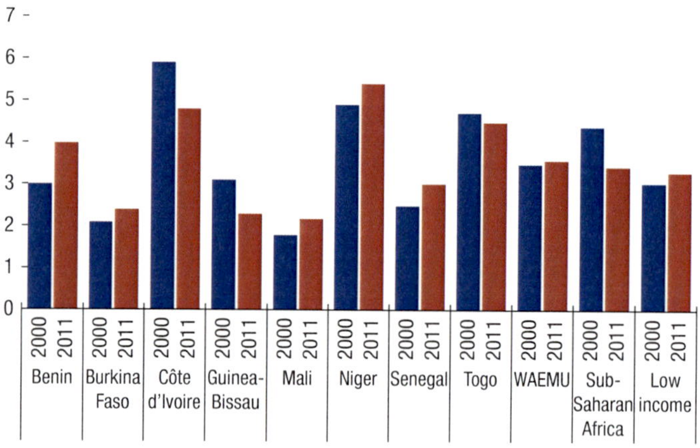

Sources: IMF Fiscal Affairs Department database; and IMF staff calculations.

Benin, the revenue gain was driven by higher trade tax revenue, while goods and services tax revenue declined. In Côte d'Ivoire, however, the decline in tax revenue was mainly driven by falling trade tax revenues.

Panel regressions were used to analyze the tax potential of WAEMU countries based on determinants identified in the literature. Drawing on the existing literature on determining tax potential (for example, Gupta 2007; Davoodi and Grigorian 2007; and Pessino and Fenochietto 2010), the following variables were considered as the determinants to estimate the tax potential, which was defined as the maximum level of tax revenue that a country can achieve given its macroeconomic fundamentals: GDP per capita, consumption, gross fixed capital formation, inflation, import and export as a share of GDP, share of agriculture in GDP, share of the urban population,

Figure 12.6. Income Tax Revenue (Percent of GDP)

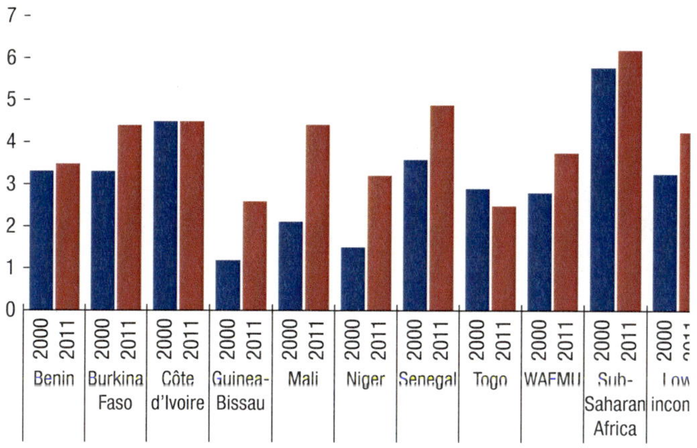

Sources: IMF Fiscal Affairs Department database; and IMF staff calculations.

Figure 12.7. Goods and Services Tax Revenue (Percent of GDP)

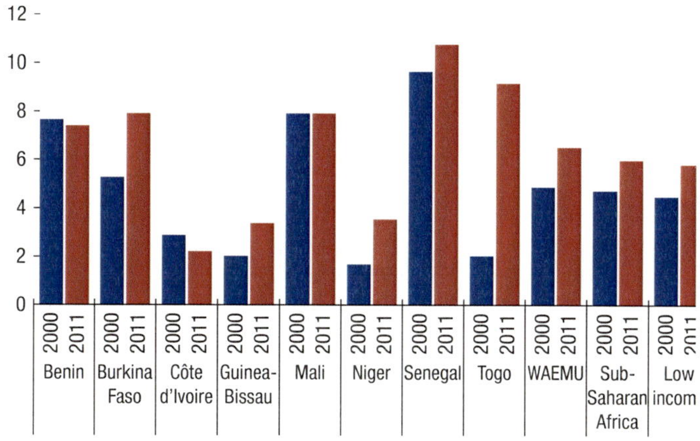

Sources: IMF Fiscal Affairs Department database; and IMF staff calculations.

natural resource rents, and broad money as a share of GDP (Annex Table 12.1.1). Obtaining the tax potential allows for calculating the tax gap, which is the percentage deviation of actual revenue from potential revenue.[2] The regression analysis is not only conducted for total tax revenue, it is also conducted for revenue in the subcategories of goods and services, trade, and income (see Annex Table 12.1.2 through Annex Table 12.1.4).

Our analysis suggests that WAEMU countries are ahead of comparator countries in their total tax collection, but have room to improve in the collection of income taxes. In 2011, total tax

[2]A positive gap signals that tax revenue collection is above potential. A negative gap implies that tax revenue collection falls short of the potential.

collection in the WAEMU exceeded the potential revenue by around 6 percent and 12 percent when compared with low-income countries and sub-Saharan African countries, respectively (Figure 12.8, panel 1). This compares favorably with 2000 when the WAEMU's total tax collection was below potential by around 4 percent compared with both low-income and sub-Saharan African countries. The following factors explain this trend:

- *Goods and services taxes*—The relative improvement between 2000 and 2011 was mainly driven by a more positive goods and services tax gap (Figure 12.8, panel 2). However, it should be taken into consideration that higher tax rates in the WAEMU explain at least part of this positive tax potential.
- *Trade taxes*—Despite the higher weighted average tariff, our tax potential analysis indicates only a moderately positive tax gap in 2011. However, improvements of the trade tax revenue compared 2000 range from below to slightly above potential (Figure 12.8, panel 3) for both benchmark groups.
- *Income taxes*—Revenue performance as measured by the tax gap deteriorated from around −1½ percent to around −5½ percent compared with the gap in sub-Saharan African countries (Figure 12.8, panel 4), and closed only slightly from around −3½ percent to around −2 percent with respect to the low-income country benchmark.

This signals a need for the WAEMU to improve income tax collection compared with the peer groups.

Our analysis on the country level shows deviations from the overall WAEMU trend for the tax gap. During the observation period, six of the eight WAEMU members augmented tax collection efforts compared with what was done in sub-Saharan African and low-income countries (Figure. 12.8, panel 1). As for income tax revenue collection efforts, only Mali, Niger, and Senegal experienced an increase in comparison with the benchmarks (Figure 12.8, panel 3). The goods and services tax gap widened in the case of Benin, Burkina Faso, Côte d'Ivoire, Guinea-Bissau, Mali, and Senegal compared with at least one benchmark group (Figure 12.8, panel 3). Among these countries, the trade tax revenue gap closed significantly or turned positive for Benin, Burkina Faso, Niger, and Senegal, meaning that the overall improvement for these countries was mostly driven by an improved trade tax collection relative to the benchmarks.[3] In sum, the diverse developments within the WAEMU group suggest the need for country-specific policies to improve revenue collection in the identified tax categories. These policies should leave room for amelioration as suggested by the empirical analysis.

Similar results were obtained with stochastic frontier analysis. Following Pessino and Fenochietto (2010), the stochastic frontier analysis estimation (Annex 12.2) applies a time-varying parameter of technical inefficiency in tax collection to the different tax categories already discussed in the panel regression analysis. The results confirm the findings using panel regressions, but with some modifications (Figure 12.9). Namely, regardless of the reference group of countries (sub-Saharan African and low-income countries) used in the estimation, the WAEMU performed relatively well in terms of tax collection. This result, however, seems to be mostly driven by trade taxes. When looking at goods and services and income taxes, WAEMU countries seem to be less efficient compared with sub-Saharan African countries and all low-income countries. The main division in this finding is the assessment of the Value Added Tax performance, which was positive in the panel regression approach and negative in the stochastic frontier analysis. In contrast, the findings were broadly consistent for income tax and trade taxes, even though the stochastic frontier analysis gave a more positive assessment of the trade tax performance than did the panel regression model.

[3]Regarding the determinants of trade tax potential, we used different models, such as incorporating a proxy for the openness or using import/GDP as well as export/GDP separately.

Figure 12.8. WAEMU Tax Revenue Gaps

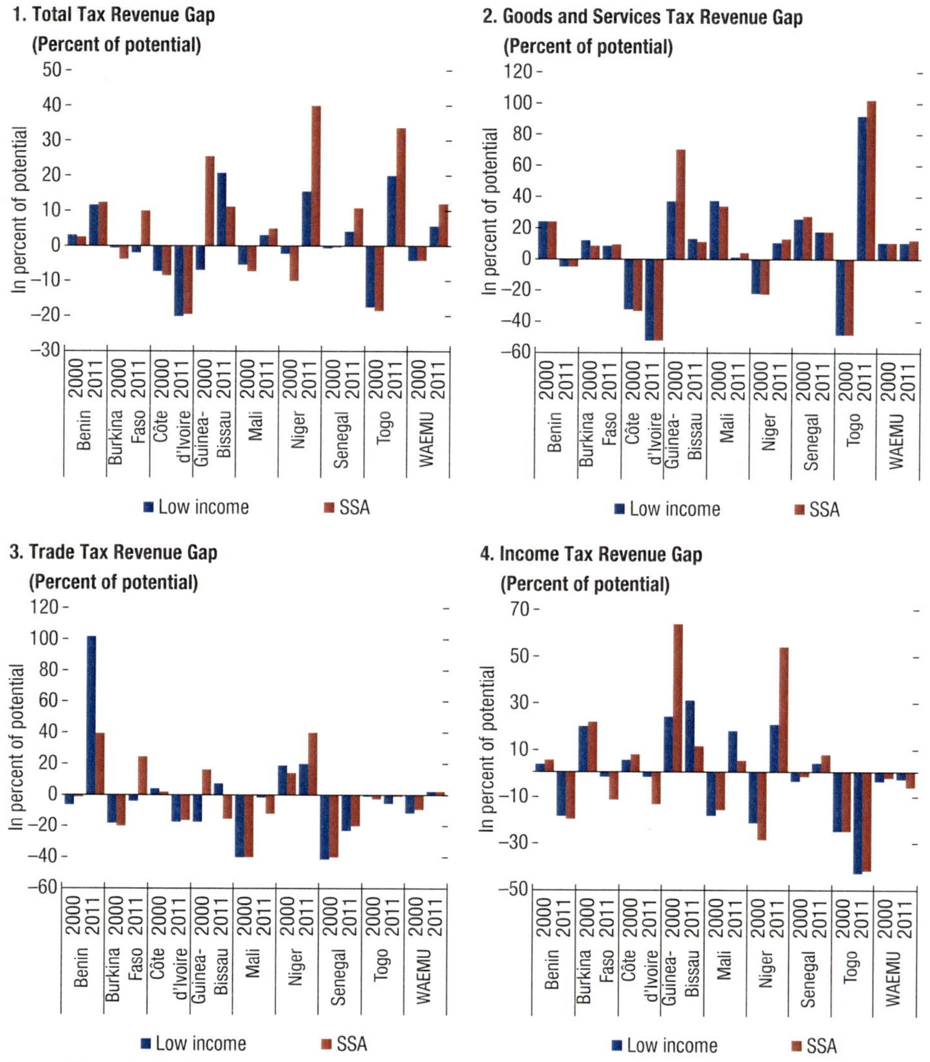

Source: IMF staff estimates.
Note: All panels estimate the potential WAEMU tax in two groups: Sub-Saharan Africa and low-income countries. More precisely, each bar refers to the WAEMU tax gap in Sub-Saharan Africa as well as low-income countries.

Overall, the WAEMU's good performance on tax revenues relies significantly on trade taxes. This situation reflects, in part, the region's heritage, as import duties have traditionally constituted the main source of tax revenue there, and, in part, the slow pace of trade liberalization. WAEMU countries have recently initiated reforms toward trade liberalization, most notably, the introduction of a common external tariff for all Economic Community of West African States countries in January 2015. While the implementation will be gradual, it is important for the WAEMU to enhance its domestic tax revenue base, in particular, income tax revenues, where both analytical approaches indicate room for improvement by around 0.8 to 2 percent of GDP.

Figure 12.9. Tax Collection Efficiency in the WAEMU by Category

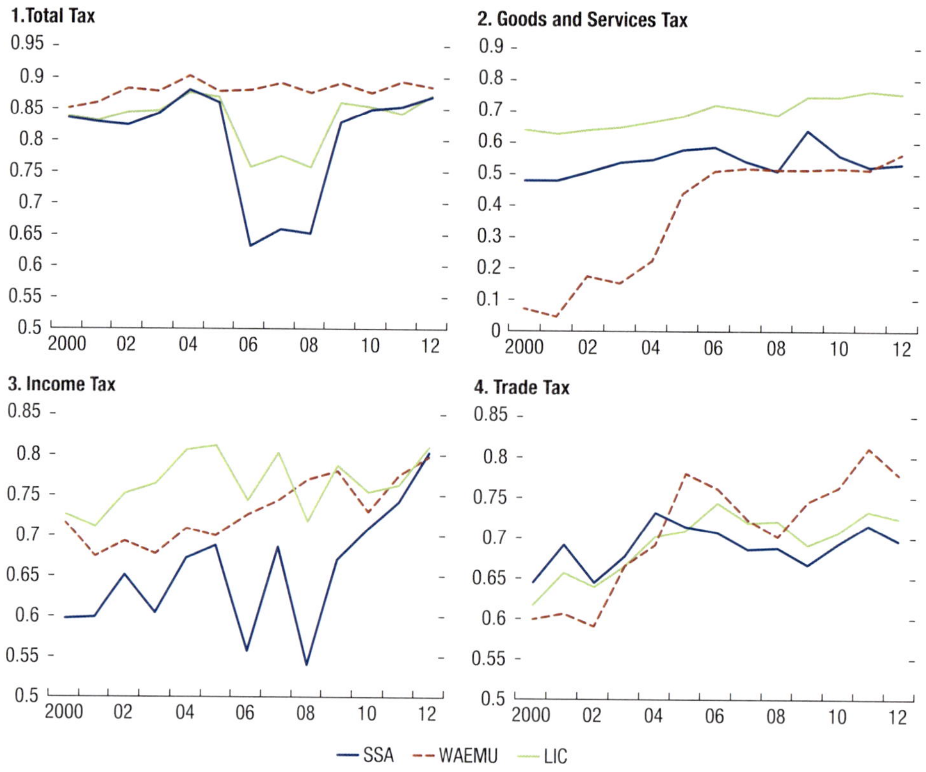

Source: IMF staff estimates.
Note: LIC = low-income countries; SSA = Sub-Saharan Africa; WAEMU = West African Economic and Monetary Union.

IMPROVING SPENDING EFFICIENCY

Is there scope for creating fiscal space by improving the efficiency of public spending? Our analysis focused on the technical efficiency of translating public spending into the corresponding results by comparing Benin's input-output performance in public spending to those of other sub-Saharan African countries with similar levels of development. In addition, to reflect WAEMU countries' aspirations to accelerate growth, specific comparisons with the fast-growing non-resource rich sub-Saharan African countries were provided.[4] Quantitative assessments were conducted through a nonparametric data envelopment analysis (DEA).[5] While public spending covers many sectors, only the education and health sectors were analyzed because these are sectors in which public spending plays a major role, and consistent cross-country data are readily available. Furthermore, based on data for 2008–12, we estimated the potential budgetary savings from higher efficiency in education and health to better inform policy discussions.

The DEA methodology provides a parsimonious model at the aggregate level to assess the efficiency of public spending based on cross-country comparison of the input-output

[4]These are countries with top growth performance in sub-Saharan Africa, as discussed in IMF (2013d): Ethiopia, Mozambique, Rwanda, Tanzania, and Uganda.

[5]The DEA method has been used in a recent analysis on the efficiency of public spending in Iceland and in cross-country studies, such as Belhocine (2013) and Grigoli and Kapsoli (2013).

relationships. It uses a nonparametric approach to identify an "efficiency frontier" from the input-output relationships across the countries that share the same technology (see Herrera and Pang 2005 and Grigoli and Kapsoli 2013 for details). Each country's efficiency is then compared with this frontier in the corresponding range of spending to obtain an efficiency score of between 0 and 100 percent, and variable returns to scales are taken into account in the estimation given the observed patterns of the data. In this analysis, data for 46 low-income and lower, middle-income sub-Saharan countries in 2003–12 were used in defining the efficiency frontier. However, data used in estimating potential savings were limited to those from WAEMU countries[6] in 2008–12 to further strengthen the cross-country comparability to arrive at the most realistic estimates.

Education sector indicators in WAEMU countries have improved significantly in recent years, largely supported by higher spending. Between 2003-07 and 2008–12, average education spending increased from 4 percent to 4.4 percent of GDP in WAEMU countries. The increased spending also supported better result indicators, such as an increase of about 14 percentage points in primary school enrollment rates and an increase of about 11 percentage points in adult literacy. But the relative magnitude of the increase in result indicators was less than that of the spending increase. For example, education spending in peer countries remains stable, but achieved a similar increase (11 percentage points) in enrollments and a much higher increase (18 percentage points) in the adult literacy rate—which better reflects the quality of the education. This suggests lower efficiency in WAEMU countries in achieving quality education results, as compared with the fast-growing sub-Saharan African countries.

The quantitative DEA analysis confirms that WAEMU countries rank low in the efficiency of education spending compared with the peers. Despite progress in improving education indicators, WAEMU countries lag behind the peer countries in the technical efficiency of their education spending. This is illustrated by the fact that all WAEMU countries are below the efficiency frontier achieved by the most efficient countries in translating education spending into the result indicators in two periods: 2003–07 and 2008–12 (Figure 12.10). For example, at an average public education spending close to 5 percent of GDP in 2008–12, Benin stays well within the efficiency frontier (Figure 12.10, panel 1) and lags behind peer countries (for example, Liberia, Rwanda, and Togo) that are located to the northwest of Benin in the scatter plot chart. This means that these countries achieved a higher adult literacy rate at a lower per-capita spending[7] than did Benin. Another example is Togo, which is closer to the frontier than is Benin, but achieved much lower adult literacy as compared with Uganda, which had the same level of spending. Based on the distance to the efficiency frontier, potential fiscal saving in achieving the same results can be estimated for WAEMU countries. To achieve realistic estimates, the calculation is limited to WAEMU countries that possess similar institutions and development status. Using this method, on average, WAEMU countries could save between 1 and 2 percent of GDP by improving their spending efficiency to the highest level in the Union (Table 12.2).

Health spending in WAEMU countries has increased significantly while the result indicators improved. Between 2003–07 and 2008–10,[8] average health spending in the WAEMU increased from about 2.3 to 2.7 percent of GDP. The results indicators also improved, including an increase in life expectancy of two years and a reduction of the child mortality rate by about 3 percentage points. Figure 12.11 shows that while WAEMU countries are also below the efficiency frontier in general, a few countries moved closer to the frontier in 2008–10 (for example, Burkina Faso,

[6]Data may not be available for all WAEMU countries, and this limits the coverage of the efficiency and saving estimates.

[7]Similar analysis using education spending as a share of GDP and the corresponding result indicators yields consistent results.

[8]Due to data constraints, the latest period is limited to 2008–10.

Figure 12.10. Efficiency of Education Spending: WAEMU and Peer Groups

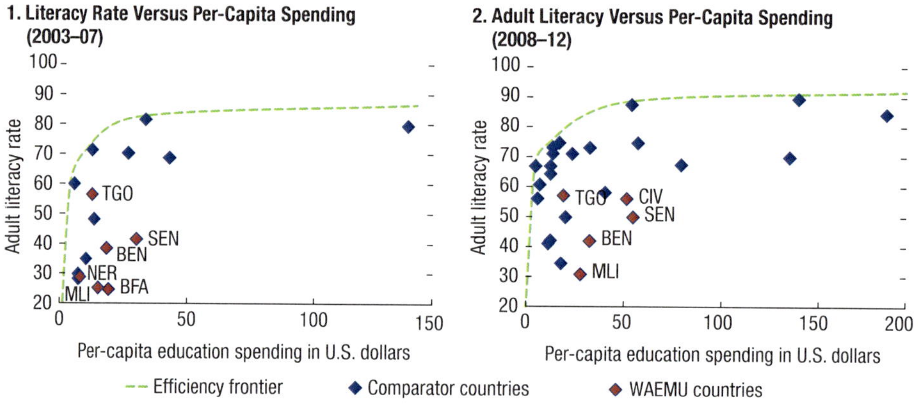

Sources: World Development Indicators; IMF Fiscal Affairs Department database; and IMF staff estimates.

TABLE 12.1

Education Spending and Result Indicators

	Education Spending in Percent of GDP		Primary Enrollment Rates (Percent)		Adult Literacy Rate (Percent)	
	2003–07	2008–12	2003–07	2008–12	2003–07	2008–12
Benin	3.7	4.7	106	124.2	38.5	42.4
Burkina Faso	4.5	3.6	55.4	76.4	24.7	na
Mali	4.2	4.3	70.8	79.8	25.1	31.1
Niger	3.3	4.2	48.6	66	28.7	na
Senegal	4.3	5.4	81.9	86.7	41.9	49.7
Togo	3.7	4.1	117.8	135.3	56.9	57.1
Ethiopia	5.5	4.9	79.2	102.9	34.9	na
Mozambique	4.9	na	102.2	na	48.2	na
Rwanda	4.3	4.5	133.8	142.6	na	71.1
Tanzania	na	6.5	na	103.3	na	73.2
Uganda	5	3.1	126.7	120.4	71.4	73.2
WAEMU mean	4	4.4	74.9	88.9	35.4	46
Peer country mean	4.9	4.8	90.7	101.5	41.5	59.2

Sources: World Development Indicators; IMF Fiscal Affairs Department database; and IMF staff calculations.
Note: Data are not available for all countries.

Mali, Senegal), where result indicators improved faster, relative to the change in public health spending (Table 12.3).

The DEA analysis confirmed the efficiency of health spending was higher than in education, but there is still a scope for potential savings. In applying the DEA to the health sector, both public and private spending needs to be included. While basic education is generally considered a public good that should be fully supported by public spending, the health sector requires significant private spending beyond public spending to achieve the corresponding results, and thus, the DEA analysis included both sources of spending. Following the same method applied to education spending, WAEMU countries' efficiency score ranges from 43 percent (Guinea-Bissau) to 100 percent (Senegal) in the baseline estimate. As a result, the estimated potential savings of increased efficiency of spending on health are about 0.4 to 0.8 percent of GDP on average (Table 12.4).

TABLE 12.2

Efficiency Scores in Education Spending and Estimated Potential Savings[1,2]

	Baseline Score	Potential Saving (Percent GDP)	Scores in Alternative Estimates	Potential Saving (Percent GDP)
Benin	35%	2.2	42–90%	0.4–2
Burkina Faso	16%	2	na	na
Mali	15%	2.6	37–57%	1.3–1.9
Niger	21%	2.3	na	na
Senegal	8%	3.8	29–32%	2.8–2.9
Togo	100%	0	100%	0%
WAEMU average		2.2		1.1–1.7

Note: Given the pattern of fixed cost and decreasing return to scale exhibited in the cross-country data and discussed in the literature, this is estimated as (*Xi*-*X*min)*(1-*Ei*), where *X* refers to spending in percent of GDP and *Ei* refers to the relative efficiency score for country *i*. This estimate represents potential savings while achieving the same level of result indicators.

[1]To estimate potential savings in spending, input efficiency scores were calculated first and then converted to relative scores based on highest scores among WAEMU countries.

[2]To enhance robustness, three input-output specifications were used: the baseline score was based on adult literacy and per-capita spending; alternative one was based on primary enrollment rates and per-capita spending; and alternative two was based on joint literacy and primary enrollment rates and per-capita spending. These specifications produced consistent rankings. The baseline specification has the best country coverage, while the other two cover less than half of the WAEMU countries.

Figure 12.11. Efficiency of Health Spending: The WAEMU and Peer Groups

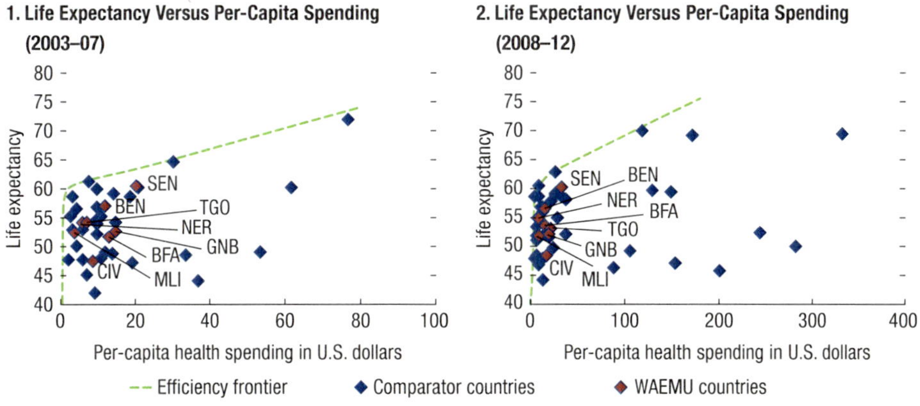

Sources: World Development Indicators; IMF Fiscal Affairs Department database; and IMF staff estimates.
Note: Three-letter International Organization for Standarization abbreviations used for country names.

Improving the efficiency of public education and health spending can contribute not only to fiscal space, but also to more inclusive growth in WAEMU countries. Our analysis found that WAEMU countries have significant scope to improve the efficiency of their spending in education and health. If all WAEMU countries could achieve the highest efficiency already reached by the top country in the union, the fiscal savings are estimated to be about 1 to 3 percent of GDP. Therefore, complementary to improved tax efforts, enhancing the efficiency of spending could provide a significant contribution to WAEMU countries' fiscal space to support the scaling up of infrastructure investments. Furthermore, education and health services are essential to enhance the well-being of WAEMU citizens and to enhance human capital and build a more productive labor force, and thus improving spending efficiency could also support more inclusive growth.

TABLE 12.3

Health Spending and Result Indicators

	Public Health Spending (Percent GDP)		Private Health Spending (Percent GDP)		Life Expectancy (in years)		Child Survival Rates (per 1,000)[1]	
	2003–07	2008–10	2003–07	2008–10	2003–07	2008–10	2003–07	2008–10
Benin	2.3	2.3	2.4	2.1	57	59	880	903
Burkina Faso	3.7	4	3	3.4	53	55	841	884
Côte d'Ivoire	1	1.5	3.5	4.7	47	49	869	886
Guinea-Bissau	1.2	1.8	4.5	4.7	52	53	844	863
Mali	3.1	3	3.4	3.7	52	54	826	862
Niger	2.5	2.7	2.5	2.5	54	57	826	872
Senegal	2.7	3.3	2.9	2.5	61	63	900	932
Togo	1.9	3.3	4.3	4	54	55	888	899
Ethiopia	2.6	2.5	1.9	2.1	57	61	890	923
Mozambique	3.9	2.9	2.4	3.2	48	49	869	899
Rwanda	4	5.4	3.7	4.7	55	62	892	935
Tanzania	2.6	3.2	2.1	3.2	54	59	909	938
Uganda	2.1	2.1	6.6	7.1	53	57	891	921
WAEMU mean	2.3	2.7	3.3	3.5	53.8	55.6	859.3	887.6
Peer country mean	3	3.2	3.3	4.1	53.4	57.6	890.2	923.2

Sources: World Development Indicators; IMF Fiscal Affairs Department database; and IMF staff estimates.
[1]This indicator is derived by 1,000 minus the under-5 child mortality rate so that the rate is expected to be positively associated with health spending.

TABLE 12.4

Efficiency Scores In Health Spending and Estimated Potential Savings[1, 2, 3]

	Baseline Score	Potential Savings (Percent GDP)	Scores in Alternative Estimates	Potential Saving (Percent GDP)
Benin	68%	0.4	54–70%	0.4–0.6
Burkina Faso	84%	0.5	36–89%	0.3–1.9
Côte d'Ivoire	65%	0.2	84–100%	0–0.1
Guinea-Bissau	43%	0.5	83–100%	0–0.1
Mali	89%	0.2	41–98%	0.1–1.2
Niger	46%	0.9	90–99%	0–0.2
Senegal	100%	0	49–50%	1.2
Togo	73%	0.6	58–73%	0.6–1
WAEMU average		0.4		0.8

[1]To estimate potential savings in spending, input efficiency scores were calculated first and then converted to relative scores based on highest scored among WAEMU countries.
[2]To enhance robustness, three input-output specifications were used: the baseline score was based on per-capita private and public spending and child survival rate; alternative one was based on per-capita public spending and child survival rate; and alternative two was based on public and private spending in percent of GDP and child survival rate. Data coverage across three specifications is similar.
[3]Similar to education spending, this is estimated as $(X_i\text{-}X\min)*(1\text{-}E_i)$, where X refers to spending in percent of GDP and E_i refers to the relative efficiency score for country i. This refers to potential savings while achieving the same level of result indicators. This estimate represents potential savings while achieving the same level of result indicators.

ANNEX 12.1. REGRESSION RESULTS BY TAX CATEGORY

ANNEX TABLE 12.1.1

Determinants of Total Tax Potential

Total Tax Revenue (Percent of GDP)	LICs	SSA
GDP per capita	5.133***	2.637
	[1.571]	[1.879]
Inflation, consumer prices (annual percent)	0.001	0.002
	[0.013]	[0.013]
Imports (percent of GDP)	0.126**	−0.09
	[0.060]	[0.089]
Exports (percent of GDP)	−0.019	0.128
	[0.058]	[0.102]
Agriculture (percent of GDP)	−0.087*	−0.166**
	[0.046]	[0.062]
Consumption (percent of GDP)	−0.009	0.105
	[0.052]	[0.093]
Gross fixed capital formation (percent of GDP)	−0.028	0.077
	[0.050]	[0.090]
Urban population (percent of total)	0.126	0.109
	[0.081]	[0.138]
Total natural resources rents (percent of GDP)	0.02	−0.015
	[0.021]	[0.043]
*M*2 (percent of GDP)	0.006	−0.001
	[0.039]	[0.027]
Constant	−27.967*	−14.466
	[13.758]	[17.255]
Observations	571	707
Number of *id*	33	38
R-squared	0.445	0.113
*R*2	0.435	0.101

Source: IMF staff estimations.
Note: *M* = broad money as a share of GDP; *id* = number of countries used on the regression; *R*-squared = coefficient of determination; *R*2 = adjusted coefficient of determination.
Robust standard errors in brackets.
*** $p < 0.01$, ** $p < 0.05$, * $p < 0.1$

ANNEX TABLE 12.1.2

Determinants of Trade Tax Potential

Trade Tax Revenue (Percent of GDP)	LICs	SSA
GDP per capita	−0.25	−1.545
	[0.739]	[1.375]
Inflation, consumer prices (annual percent)	−0.005***	−0.004
	[0.001]	[0.003]
Imports (percent of GDP)	0.050***	−0.034
	[0.012]	[0.045]
Exports (percent of GDP)	0.009	0.021
	[0.018]	[0.040]
Urban population (percent of total)	−0.036	−0.012
	[0.088]	[0.204]
Total natural resources rents (percent of GDP)	0.019	−0.008
	[0.014]	[0.034]
Trend	−0.04	−0.009
	[0.049]	[0.115]
Constant	4.878	17.929*
	[5.736]	[9.827]
Observations	590	716
Number of *id*	33	38
R-squared	0.204	0.036
*R*2	0.194	0.0261

Source: IMF staff estimations.
Note: *M* = broad money as a share of GDP; *id* = number of countries used on the regression; *R*-squared = coefficient of determination; *R*2 = adjusted coefficient of determination.
Robust standard errors in brackets.
*** $p < 0.01$, ** $p < 0.05$, * $p < 0.1$

ANNEX TABLE 12.1.3

Determinants of Income Tax

Income Tax Revenue (Percent of GDP)	LICs	SSA
GDP per capita	1.964***	2.370***
	[0.592]	[0.626]
Agriculture (percent of GDP)	−0.015	−0.035*
	[0.020]	[0.020]
Consumption (percent of GDP)	0.027***	0.025*
	[0.007]	[0.013]
Gross fixed capital formation (percent of GDP)	0.024**	0.01
	[0.010]	[0.013]
Urban population (percent of total)	0.045	0.091**
	[0.026]	[0.035]
Total natural resources rents (percent of GDP)	0.023**	0.006
	[0.010]	[0.014]
*M*2 (percent of GDP)	0.019***	0.023**
	[0.007]	[0.009]
Public wage bill (percent of GDP)	0.196***	−0.000***
	[0.042]	[0.000]
Constant	−15.962***	−19.051***
	[4.419]	[5.101]
Observations	461	629
Number of *id*	25	35
R-squared	0.462	0.201
*R*2	0.452	0.191

Source: IMF staff estimations.
Note: *M* = broad money as a share of GDP; *id* = number of countries used on the regression; *R*-squared = coefficient of determination; *R*2 = adjusted coefficient of determination.
Robust standard errors in brackets.
*** $p < 0.01$, ** $p < 0.05$, * $p < 0.1$

ANNEX TABLE 12.1.4

Determinants of Goods and Services Tax

Goods and Services Tax Revenue (Percent of GDP)	LICs	SSA
GDP per capita	3.956***	4.415***
	[1.370]	[1.270]
Inflation, consumer prices (annual percent)	0.006	0.006
	[0.008]	[0.006]
Agriculture (percent of GDP)	0.004	−0.026
	[0.037]	[0.036]
Gov. consumption (percent of GDP)	0.014	0.023
	[0.069]	[0.046]
Household consumption (percent of GDP)	−0.038	0.042
	[0.054]	[0.037]
Gross fixed capital formation (percent of GDP)	−0.042	0.003
	[0.054]	[0.034]
Urban population (percent of total)	0.157**	0.129*
	[0.072]	[0.064]
*M*2 (percent of GDP)	0.013	0.023
	[0.016]	[0.019]
Imports (percent of GDP)	0.081	0.021
	[0.060]	[0.036]
Exports (percent of GDP)	−0.043	0.021
	[0.063]	[0.035]
Constant	−26.563**	−37.550***
	[11.500]	[9.178]
Observations	571	698
Number of *id*	33	38
R-squared	0.349	0.397
*R*2	0.338	0.388

Source: IMF staff estimations.
Note: *M* = broad money as a share of GDP; *id* = number of countries used on the regression; *R*-squared = coefficient of determination; *R*2 = adjusted coefficient of determination.
Robust standard errors in brackets.
*** $p < 0.01$, ** $p < 0.05$, * $p < 0.1$

ANNEX 12.2. STOCHASTIC FRONTIER ANALYSIS

The stochastic frontier model of Pessino and Fenochietto (2010) can be represented as follows:

$$y_{it} = \alpha_i + \beta X_{it} + \varepsilon_{it}$$

$$\varepsilon_{it} = \mathrm{v}_{it} - u_{it}$$

$$\mathrm{v}_{it} \sim N\left(0, \sigma^2\right)$$

$$u_{it} - F^+\left(\delta, \sigma_u^2\right)$$

Where a represents a set of country specific intercepts, X is the vector that represents variables affecting tax revenue. The error term ε is a composite error term made of the standard component v and of a component u, which is distributed following a probability density function that is positively definite. The element u is the time varying element, which represents the degree of inefficiency: higher values correspond to higher inefficiencies. Similarly to the panel regression, four different models are estimates, each for one type of tax revenue. Starting from a general model for the estimation of the determinants of tax revenue to GDP, the model is then modified slightly to exclude variables that are not supposed to determine the behavior of some of the sub-categories of revenue.

REFERENCES

Belhocine, Nazim. 2013. "Assessing Efficiency of Public Spending on Health and Education in Iceland. In *Iceland: Selected Issues*. International Monetary Fund, Washington.

Calderón, César. 2009. "Infrastructure and Growth in Africa." Policy Research Working Paper 4914, World Bank, Washington.

Commission for Africa. 2005. *Our Common Interest: Report of the Commission for Africa*. London: Commission for Africa.

Davoodi, H., and Grigorian, D. 2007. "Tax Potential vs. Tax Effort: A Cross-Country Analysis of Armenia's Stubbornly Low Tax Collection." Working Paper 07/106, International Monetary Fund, Washington.

Domínguez-Torres, Carolina, and Vivien Foster. 2011. *Benin's Infrastructure: A Continental Perspective*. Policy Research Working Paper 5689, World Bank, Washington

Foster, Vivien, and Cecilia Briceño-Garmendia, eds. 2009. *Africa's Infrastructure: A Time for Transformation*. Paris and Washington: Agence Française de Développement and World Bank. http://www.infrastructureafrica.org.

Grigoli, Francesco, and Javier Kapsoli. 2013. "Waste Not, Want Not: The Efficiency of Health Expenditure in Emerging and Developing Economies." Working Paper 13/187, International Monetary Fund, Washington.

Gupta, Abhijit Sen. 2007. "Determinants of Tax Revenue Efforts in Developing Countries." Working Paper 07/184, International Monetary Fund, Washington.

Herrera, Santiago, and Gaobo Pang. 2005. "Efficiency of Public Spending in Developing Countries: An Efficiency Frontier Approach." Policy Research Working Paper No. 3645.

International Monetary Fund (IMF). 2013a. "Benin: 2012 Article IV Consultation and Fourth Review under the Extended Credit Facility Arrangement." Staff Report Côte d'Ivoire, Washington.

———. 2013b. "Côte d'Ivoire: 2013 Article IV Consultation and Fourth Review Under The Extended Credit Facility Arrangement." Washington.

———. 2013c. "Mali: 2012 Article IV Consultation, Request for Disbursement Under the Rapid Credit Facility and Cancellation of the Extended Credit Facility Arrangement." Staff Report, Washington.

———. 2013d. *Regional Economic Outlook: Sub-Saharan Africa*. Washington.

Pessino, Carola, and Ricardo Fenochietto. 2010. "Determining Countries' Tax Effort." *Hacienda Pública Española / Revista de Economía Pública* 195 (4/2010): 65–87.

Torres, Clemencia, Cecilia M. Briceño-Garmendia, and Carolina Dominguez. 2011. *Senegal's Infrastructure: A Continental Perspective*. Policy Research Working Paper 5817, World Bank, Washington.

CHAPTER 13

Tax Coordination and Tax Competition[1]

MARIO MANSOUR AND GRÉGOIRE ROTA-GRAZIOSI

The process of tax coordination in the West African Economic and Monetary Union (WAEMU) is one of the most advanced in the world—de jure at least—but remains in many areas ineffective de facto. The framework has, to some extent, succeeded in converging tax systems, particularly statutory tax rates, and may have contributed to improving revenue mobilization. Important lessons can be drawn from the WAEMU experience, especially in terms of whether coordination should take the form of harmonization through a top-down approach, or a softer approach of sharing best practice and limiting certain types of harmful tax competition.

TAX COORDINATION FRAMEWORK

The WAEMU is one of few regions in the developing world where member countries have had over a decade of tax coordination/harmonization experience in domestic taxation. Today, over 80 percent of member countries' tax (including tariff) revenues are derived from taxes that are subject to regional directives or regulations. This economic integration was in no small part due to the fiscal problems of the late 1980s and early 1990s, and the subsequent devaluation of the CFA Franc in 1994. Following this devaluation, member states signed the WAEMU Treaty on January 10, 1994, in Dakar; by August 1 of that year, they had all ratified it. The formation of the customs union with a common external tariff (CET) was completed by 2000; directives on value-added tax (VAT) and excises were introduced in 1998; and, by 2009, the region completed a set of directives on capital income taxation.

The evolution of the legal framework for tax coordination in the WAEMU has reflected a clear objective of ensuring that national policies (particularly trade and tax policies) do not distort the functioning of the internal market, and a number of broad and potentially conflicting objectives of harmonizing tax legislations and converging fiscal outcomes (levels and structures of tax revenues). These objectives are covered by Article 4 of the WAEMU Treaty.[2] From a tax coordination perspective, Paragraph e of Article 4 is the clearest, and most relevant. It calls for the harmonization of member states' tax legislation to the extent that it is necessary for the good functioning of the common market.[3] The use of the word "harmonization" conveys the idea that tax rates and bases should be equalized. Although this may have been the intention of policymakers in the early years of the WAEMU Treaty, the current framework is a mix of partial harmonization and

[1] Previously published in *Tax Notes International*, 2014, Vol. 74, No. 2, pp.183–204.

[2] The 1994 Treaty was modified in January 2003. The modifications clarified a number of areas, in particular: the roles and responsibilities of the institutions of the Union (the Commission; the Court of Justice and the Court of Audit; the meetings of Heads of State and the Council of Ministers); the financing of the Union; the free mobility of individuals; and the participation of other African states to the activities of the Union. These modifications do not directly affect the objectives of the Union, as stated in Article 4 of the 1994 Treaty. References to the WAEMU Treaty, unless otherwise specified, are to the modified Treaty of 2003.

[3] Again, this seems to be broader in its implications for tax coordination than the narrower Article 113 of the Treaty on the Functioning of the EU.

coordination. In recent years, member countries have pushed for more flexibility in setting their tax bases and rates, especially in the area of indirect taxation.

The other paragraphs of Article 4 allow for various, and possibly conflicting, interpretations of the role of tax coordination. For example, Paragraph a states that one objective of the Treaty is to reinforce the economic competitiveness of member countries, but does not clarify whether this objective is to make the region competitive vis-à-vis the rest of the world (ROW), or to give each member state latitude in providing its own tax incentives—which implies some degree of competition among them as well as with the ROW. The former case is compatible with coordinating the taxation of capital within the region; the second may not be. This lack of clarity is probably the main reason behind the failure to harmonize investment codes (ICs); member states tend to see the competition game as one played as much among them as with the ROW.[4] An initiative to agree on a regional IC has been ongoing for over a decade, but has not yielded any tangible results. As will be explained later, the tax content of ICs in WAEMU greatly weakens the coordination of capital income taxation. Another example is Paragraph d, which calls for the implementation of common policies in a number of economic sectors, including mining, even though there is little trade among member countries in minerals. Paragraph d is partly at the origin of the 2001 regional mining regulation, which contains tax provisions for mining activities.

After the adoption of the CET in the late 1990s, one would have expected coordination of capital income taxes to take priority, since capital tax competition in a customs union with fiscal borders is more mutually damaging than consumption tax competition. But this was not the case. It took a decade after the introduction of the VAT and excise tax directives in the late 1990s to partially harmonize the corporate tax base and introduce a range of tax rates; moreover, the provision of tax incentives through ICs and other sectoral laws has yet to be resolved. This sequencing of tax coordination in the WAEMU raises a number of difficult political economy issues, including the lack of commitment on behalf of member states to coordinate their tax policies effectively.

In order to better appreciate the intricacies of the tax coordination framework, the descriptive analysis of its various parts is separated in two sections: coordination of tariffs and indirect taxes (namely the VAT and excises), and coordination of direct taxes (capital income taxation, which includes the taxation of business profits, portfolio income, and the multilateral tax treaty (MTT)).

COORDINATION OF TARIFFS AND INDIRECT TAXES

Customs tariffs.[5] In 1996, member states put in place a transitional trade regime for most intra-community trade in anticipation of agreement on a CET.[6] The regime lifted quantitative restrictions (on extra- and intraregional trade), instituted common rules of origin, and reduced both internal and external tariffs significantly. In 1997, a CET with four rates was agreed:[7] 0 percent on essential or so-called "social goods," 5 percent on primary goods, 10 percent on capital and intermediate goods, and 20 percent on final consumption goods.[8] The top rate became effective

[4] National investment codes are the most common tool of providing tax incentives in sub-Saharan Africa. Their use has significantly increased since the early 1980s. See, for example, M. Keen and M. Mansour, "Revenue Mobilization in Sub-Saharan Africa: Challenges from Globalization II—Corporate Taxation," *Development Policy Review*, 2010, 28(5), pp. 573–96.

[5] The discussion abstracts from the recent adoption of the ECOWAS CET, which has implications for WAEMU states, particularly in relation to their trade liberalization objectives, as it increases the top rate from 20 to 35 percent on certain categories of imports.

[6] Act 04/1996.

[7] Regulation 02/1997/CM/UEMOA.

[8] This is according to the broad economic classification of the tariff; the classification at the HS 10-digit level is less clear-cut.

Figure 13.1. WAEMU Trade in Goods: 1990, 2000, and 2010

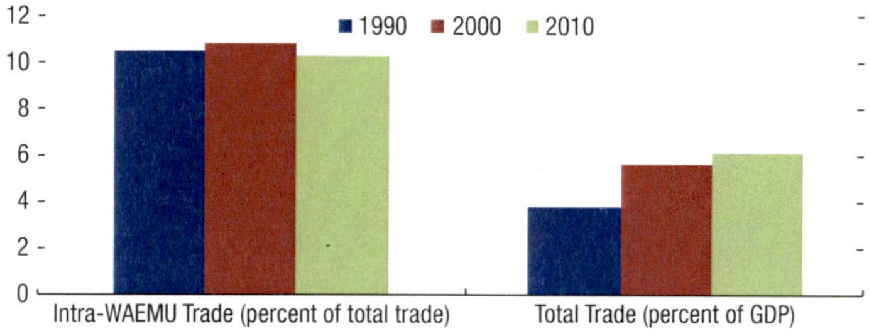

Source: Direction of Trade Statistics, IMF.

January 1, 2000—it was set at 30 percent during July 1 to December 31, 1998, and 25 percent during 1999. A 10-digit tariff classification was drafted in 1998,[9] based on the Economic Community of West African States (ECOWAS) classification; it was later changed to the 2002 Harmonized System (HS) classification of the World Customs Organization (WCO) in 2002, and to the 2007 HS classification in 2008.

Shortly after the HS classification was agreed, the Council of Ministers issued regulations detailing the procedure and conditions by which member states can request derogations from the application of the CET, that is, safeguard measures.[10] Requests for such measures must be made by a member state to the Commission, and justified on the basis of exceptional difficulties that the member state faces or could face in one or more economic sectors as a result of the application of the CET. After study of the request, the Commission gives an opinion within 30 days, valid originally for six months, and renewable.[11]

Even though the Council of Ministers can dispute the decision of the Commission, Regulation 14/1998 gave, for the first time since the WAEMU Treaty was signed in 1994, operational authority to the Commission by asking for its technical opinion on requests for safeguard measures. This was further enhanced with regulation 04/1999/CM/UEMOA, which gave the Commission authority to establish "reference values" for imports—that is, minimum values specified for a list of goods where the Commission, after consulting with member states, had reasons to believe that importers aggressively underreport values.

The speed with which the customs union and the CET were formed is remarkable, and can be partly explained by the fact that the monetary union already existed. However, in terms of impact on intracommunity trade, progress is hard to detect, and is certainly far less than policymakers had expected. The share of intracommunity trade (relative to total WAEMU trade) has not increased since the early 1990s (Figure 13.1), but trade patterns have changed. In particular, exports from Senegal and Togo to the rest of the community have increased, at the expense of those from Côte d'Ivoire, as have imports from the rest of the community to Burkina Faso and Guinea-Bissau. Egoume and Nayo (2011)[12] attribute these shifts in trade patterns largely to two factors: the relative size of Côte d'Ivoire and the high intra-WAEMU transportation costs relative to international costs. These two factors tended to reinforce one another during the Ivoirian crisis.

[9] Regulation 05/1998/CM/UEMOA.

[10] Regulation 14/1998/CM/UEMOA, which applies Article 86 of the WAEMU treaty on safeguard measures.

[11] Regulation 14/1998 does not specify whether the request for extension is time bound; in principle, safeguard measures should be time-bound under WTO rules.

[12] P. Egoume and A. Nayo, "Feeling the Elephant's Weight: The Impact of Côte d'Ivoire's Crisis on WAEMU Trade," 2011, Working Paper 11/80 (Washington: International Monetary Fund).

Total trade in relation to GDP has, however, increased significantly, from less than 4 percent in 1990 to 6 percent in 2010. Moreover, most of this increase took place before the customs union was completed in 2000, and can be attributed to the devaluation of the CFA franc.

But some problems of the customs union are much deeper, and relate to trade policy and its implementation, rather than to exogenous factors.[13] Physical borders and control of intra-community trade remain to a large extent as they were before the establishment of the CET.[14] More importantly, tariff revenue accrues to the country of final destination, which remains ultimately responsible for collecting its own revenue from the application of the CET. This provides opportunities for member states to protect their markets and for customs officials to seek rent through the enforcement of the CET. For example, Goretti and Weisfeld (2008)[15] cite administrative delays, roadblocks, and racketeering. Coupled with poor transportation and other trade support services, of which quality and cost may vary significantly across member states, these factors have undermined progress in increasing intracommunity trade.[16]

Value-added tax. The VAT directive was introduced in 1998. Its main purpose was to (1) harmonize the rules relating to the base and constrain the rates to an interval, (2) regulate the treatment of intra-WAEMU trade when fiscal borders are abolished, and (3) provide a source of financing to the Union. Member states could not agree on (2) and (3) in 1998, and therefore postponed drafting of the necessary rules until fiscal borders were removed. One primary objective of the VAT directive was to assist countries in compensating the revenue loss induced by the reduction of tariff rates with a more efficient tax than cascading sales taxes—which predated the VATs in several WAEMU countries. The experience of Benin, which after enacting a single-rate VAT with limited exemptions in 1991 saw its VAT revenue increase from less than 2 percent of GDP in 1990 to 5 percent in 1994,[17] played an important role in the design of the 1998 directive. The directive's main features are:

- A registration threshold between CFAF 30 and 50 million for the supply of goods, and 15 to 25 million for the supply of services.
- A single positive tax rate that member states can set between 15 and 20 percent.
- Common rules for the calculation of the tax base (that is, taxable transactions).
- A list of mandatory exemptions, including: health services and medications;[18] education services, books, newspapers, magazines, and other periodicals; banking, insurance and re-insurance services if they are subject to a specific tax; social tranches for household con-

[13] Despite a CET, national customs have some discretion in the value assessment of imports. Several WAEMU states have preshipment inspection programs, which consist in delegating part of the value assessment to a private firm. Often, these programs do not provide the right incentives for customs agencies to modernize. For more on this see V. Dequiedt, A. M. Geourjon, and G. Rota-Grasiozi, "Les programmes de vérification des importations (PVI) à la lumière de la théorie de l'agence," *Afrique Contemporaine*, 2009/2, 230, pp. 151–66.

[14] For a brief overview of the WAEMU CET and problems related to its application by member states, see A. M. Geourjon and M. Mansour, *Les défis de la coordination des politiques tarifaires et fiscales en UEMOA/CEDEAO*, Policy brief 61 (Clermont-Ferrand : FERDI), March 2013.

[15] M. Goretti and H. Weisfeld, "Trade in the WAEMU: Developments and Reform Opportunities," 2008, Working Paper 08/68 (Washington: International Monetary Fund).

[16] See also *The Improved Road Transport Governance Initiative*, which surveys the number of controls on six major corridors in the WAEMU (www.watradehub.com, accessed on September 13, 2012): Abidjan-Ouagadougou; Bamako-Abidjan; Bamako-Ouagadougou (via Hérémakono); Bamako-Ouagadougou (via Koury); Bamako-Dakar; Lomé-Ouagadougou. The 18th survey shows that on some corridors, especially from Senegal and Abidjan ports to Bamako and Ouagadougou (both inland cities), the number of controls frequently exceeds two per 100 km, and is rarely below 1.5.

[17] For a more detailed discussion of the history of VATs in some WAEMU states, see L. Ebrill, M. Keen, J. P. Bodin, and V. Summers, *The Modern VAT*, Washington: International Monetary Fund, 2001; in particular chapters 5 and 7.

[18] Exempt medications are listed in the annex to directive 06/2002/CM/UEMOA; they include a broad category of prescription and nonprescription drugs, prosthetics, and medical and dentistry equipment.

sumption of water and electricity; raw (unaltered) foods; real estate (both residential and commercial) if it is subject to registration fees or other specific taxes; and residential rent.

- Exports are also exempt from VAT; but VAT registrants can claim a credit/refund for VAT on inputs into exported supplies only if such supplies were taxable in the domestic market.[19]
- Member states can tax agricultural supplies or treat them as out of scope of VAT.[20]
- VAT on inputs is generally deductible from VAT on taxable outputs, except for: meals and entertainment expenses, motor vehicles (except for leasing companies), and fuel expenses. Importantly, member states can extend these exclusions to other inputs; the directive does not impose any limits on such exclusions.
- Excess VAT credits are generally refundable, except for certain retail supplies (goods that are resold unaltered.)

The food and energy price crisis of 2006–08 led to pressure to narrow the base of VAT to respond to social unrests in the region. In 2009, the WAEMU Council of Ministers approved directive 02/2009/CM/UEMOA, which accomplished this narrowing in three ways. First, the upper bound of the registration threshold was increased to CFAF 100 million for goods, and 50 million for services. Second, a lower positive VAT rate—which countries can set between 5 and 10 percent—is now permitted for a limited list of items.[21] Third, natural gas for domestic use was added to the list of exempt items.

Another change to the VAT directive was made in the directive on the taxation of portfolio income, introduced in 2010 (02/2010/CM/UEMOA). This directive deemed as exports all services related to financial markets in the WAEMU, including: financial advisory services; title issuance; funds transfers; and all accounting services related to such activities.

These changes, together with original design weaknesses (exemptions and limitations to credit/refunds), make the VAT directive distant from a modern VAT.[22] Despite the relatively good revenue performance of VATs in member states,[23] their negative impact on investment is a recurrent complaint from investors.

Excise taxes. The excise tax directive was also introduced in 1998.[24] It mandated ad valorem taxation of alcoholic beverages and tobacco products, and permitted the taxation of a list of other goods. Table 13.1 provides the list of excisable items along with minimum and maximum rates. Article 3 of the directive defines the scope and timing of taxation: excises should apply to imports and domestic production, at the time of the first sale or when goods are made available for consumption.

---

[19]This is different from zero-rating, where the VAT is neutral on the price of an exported supply irrespective of its domestic treatment.

[20]This means that suppliers cannot register for VAT even if their turnover exceeds the registration threshold. And, in case of mixed supplies, they do not have to report agricultural supplies on their tax returns. Out of scope is similar to exemptions in terms of its impact on prices and revenues since input VAT is not deductible from output VAT. The agricultural sector represents around one-third of the GDP of WAEMU member states.

[21]These are bottled and powdered milk, sugar, all types of pasta, flour, rice, wheat, and other grains; chicks; agricultural equipment (including rental and maintenance services); food for livestock and poultry; computers; solar energy equipment; and tourism-related services, including restaurants.

[22]Efficiency and revenue productivity were major objectives of reforming indirect tax systems away from cascading sales taxes. See, for example, an account of experiences, including in some WAEMU members, provided in chapter 6 of Ebrill, Keen, Bodin, and Summers (2001), *supra* note 27. Chapter 18 of the same book had already raised the potential efficiency consequences of widespread exemptions.

[23]In 2010, VAT revenue productivity, the yield of one point of the VAT rate expressed in percentage of GDP, was 0.2 in Côte d'Ivoire; around 0.3 in Burkina Faso, Mali, and Niger; 0.35 in Togo; and around 0.4 in Benin and Senegal. The low rate in Côte d'Ivoire is partly due to its high export share in GDP (oil, cocoa, and coffee).

[24]Directive 03/1998/CM/UEMOA.

TABLE 13.1

Rates under the WAEMU Directive on Excise Taxes (Percent)

	Minimum	Maximum
	(Percent)	
Mandatory taxation		
Alcoholic beverages[1]	15	50
Tobacco products[2]	15	45
Nonalcoholic beverages (except water)	0	20
Optional taxation (countries can choose six items)[3]		
Coffee	1	12
Cola	10	30
Wheat flour	1	5
Oil and other edible fats	1	15
Tea	1	12
Arms and ammunitions	15	40
Perfumes and other cosmetics	5	15
Plastic bags[4]	5	10
Marble[4]	5	10
Gold bullion[4]	3	15
Precious stones[4]	3	15
Passenger vehicles[4,5]	5	10

Source: WAEMU directives 03/1998/CM/UEMOA and 03/2009/CM/UEMOA.
[1] Minimum and maximum were increased in 2009 from 10 to 15 and 45 to 50, respectively.
[2] Minimum and maximum were increased in 2009 from 10 to 15 and 40 to 45, respectively.
[3] In addition to the mandatory list.
[4] Item added to the optional excise list in 2009.
[5] Applies only to vehicles with engines exceeding certain capacity.

The directive is unclear about how exports should be treated: whether they are taxable, in which case the excise becomes a production tax; or whether they are free of the excise, in which case the excise acts as a destination-based consumption tax, much like the VAT. Three amendments were made to the directive in 2009:[25] minimum and maximum rates on alcohol and tobacco were increased by 5 percentage points; five items were added to the optional list; and member states were limited to excise only six items from the optional list.

Some of the items on the optional list suggest that the excise tax framework serves a trade policy objective. These include: coffee, cola, wheat flour, oil and other edible fats, tea, marble, gold, and precious stones. Given the production of these items by some WAEMU states, the excise could play the role of an export tax (coffee, cola, gold bullion, marble, which are mainly exported).[26] Or, it could favor consumption of local production over imports (flour, edible oils)—given that the excise is ad valorem, its absolute value on domestically produced goods is lower than that on imported substitutes that command higher prices; moreover, imports bear a tariff which is included in the base for calculating the excise.

The main argument in favor of coordinating the setting of excise taxes in a common market is to minimize intracommunity cross-border shopping—both legal and illegal. Cross-border shopping and, more importantly, smuggling from countries outside of the community, pose difficult policy and enforcement issues; the WAEMU is surrounded by large countries with very porous borders—neighboring Mauritania, Nigeria, and Ghana are particularly problematic—, some of which apply relatively low excise taxes.[27] This could explain why minimum rates in the WAEMU excise directive were set at a low level.

[25] Directive 03/2009/CM/UEMOA.

[26] Recall that the directive does not mandate that excise taxes on exports be refunded.

[27] For example: in Nigeria, a country rich in natural resources, excise rates on alcoholic beverages and tobacco are 20 percent; until recently, Mauritania, which borders Senegal, did not impose any excises on tobacco.

A separate directive issued in 2001 covers excises on petroleum products.[28] It mandated a specific excise (per liter or kilo) but did not impose any constraint on the tax rate: it set the lower bound at zero percent, and imposed no upper bound. However, it prohibited subsidies (either directly or indirectly through differential taxation of petroleum products), and mandated that by the end of 2006 member states should impose the same tax rate on gasoline and diesel, and that the rate differential among other products should not exceed CFAF 100. In 2007, directive 01/2007/CM/UEMOA was introduced extending the deadline for implementing these rules to December 2008. The petroleum excise directive also prevents member states from imposing any other specific taxes on petroleum products—except for the tariff and the VAT.

The petroleum excise directive did not address directly tax coordination issues, like those on alcohol and tobacco. Its main purpose was first and foremost the elimination of subsidies, which weighed heavily on member states' fiscal performance, and the consolidation of a plethora of specific taxes—which were typically earmarked—into a single excise paid into the government's general fund. Despite the absence of direct subsidies, the pricing formulas applied for petroleum products (except in Niger) involve implicit subsidies, which may represent a significant part of public spending, and which are poorly targeted to support the poorest.[29]

COORDINATION OF DIRECT TAXES

The coordination of direct taxes can be usefully separated in three parts: taxes on business profits (which it referred to as the corporate income tax (CIT)); taxes on portfolio income (for example, interest, dividends, and capital gains); and the multilateral tax treaty (MTT) for preventing double taxation among member states. There are of course linkages between these parts.

Corporate income tax. The coordination of the CIT is one of the most interesting since, in some respect, the WAEMU went beyond the EU model. Two 2008 directives cover CIT coordination: directive 01/2008/CM/UEMOA defines a common corporate tax base;[30] and directive 08/2008/CM/UEMOA specifies the range for a single rate—25 to 30 percent. The first directive defines a standard CIT base where all business expenses undertaken for the purpose of earning taxable profits are deductible; the following elements are worth noting:

- A number of expenses can be capped, including: overhead expenses, wage expenses, royalties and technical services, taxes, and contributions to nonprofit organizations. Financing costs are deductible to the extent that the interest rate does not exceed the Central Bank's (BCEAO) interest rate plus three percentage points; but there is no limit, however, on how much companies can borrow from related parties. The objective of caps is to deny unreasonable deductions; note, however, that the directive does not define or describe situations of this nature or the meaning of "unreasonable."
- A general transfer pricing rule states that pricing of intracompany goods and services where one party does not reside in the member state should be at arm's-length—otherwise, it is not entirely deductible; but it leaves it to member states to define how to put this in practice.
- Penalties and fines of any nature are not deductible from the CIT base.

---

[28] Directive 06/2001/CM/UEMOA.

[29] The International Monetary Fund estimated in 2011 that this expenditure has reached on average 3.2 percent of GDP during the oil price shock in 2008.

[30] Article 1 notes that the directive applies to "industrial and commercial" profits. In a classic schedular system, this generally excludes profits from professional and artisanal activities, and agricultural activities, even if the profit is earned by a corporation. But Article 3 clarifies that irrespective of the source or type of income, the directive concerns income taxes that a member state applies to the profit of a moral person. This suggests that the directive establishes a true CIT separate from other schedular taxes.

- Loss carry forward is allowed for a minimum of three years.
- Depreciation is generally straight-line; declining-balance depreciation is allowed, with rates fixed as multiples of the straight-line rates. Accelerated depreciation (in the first year of use and subject to a maximum of twice the standard straight-line depreciation rate) is allowed only for new equipments used in the following sectors: manufacturing, maintenance services, hotels, transportation, telecommunication, and agriculture.
- Specific provisions are allowed. Banks and other financial institutions can deduct their provisions for prudential purposes.[31]

Member states should exempt from the tax base the following income sources: capital gains on business assets if the taxpayer intends, within three years, to reinvest the total proceeds from selling the assets in a WAEMU member state; and intercorporate dividends to the extent that the holding company has a controlling interest (defined as at least 10 percent of the shares) in the payer company, and that both companies are WAEMU residents—in all other cases, at least 40 percent of intercorporate dividends should be taxable.

A holding company regime was introduced in 2011 exempting from CIT the profits of such companies, their dividend distributions (from tax at the individual level), and capital gains realized on the sale of their shares.[32] The regime is targeted to venture capital companies.

Finally, a mining regulation was introduced in 2003. It provides that firms are subject to the general tax laws of member states, and to a royalty, whose base and rates will be determined later by application rules.[33] The regulation also provided for stability of the tax regime—presumably, both for taxes imposed at the national level and the royalty that was to be fixed regionally—during the life of the investment; the stability is asymmetric, ensuring against increases in taxes but allowing taxpayers to benefit from reductions. In terms of tax incentives, the regulation provided for the exemption of virtually all taxes and fees during the exploration phase. The main incentives provided during the production phase are accelerated depreciation, and a three-year tax holiday from profit and payroll taxes; the modalities for the coverage and calculation of accelerated depreciation have not been issued.

The CIT directive provides flexibility for countries to compete through the statutory tax rate as well as the tax base. The most important elements of tax base competition include: flexibility in setting tax depreciation rules; and flexibility in designing transfer pricing and thin capitalization rules,[34] which can be particularly important to foreign investors. But the most important source of tax competition among WAEMU countries remain the derogatory regimes provided in nontax legislations, such as ICs, Free Zone Codes, and other sectoral codes, which are explicitly permitted under Article 8 of the CIT tax base directive. There are two possible explanations why the directive allowed this: (1) politically, a weak directive may have been viewed as a better outcome than no directive at all; (2) since the coordination framework was to be extended to cover all sectoral laws, member states may have postponed the resolution of this issue. Although both explanations are possible, it seems unlikely today that member states will agree on a common framework for the provision of tax incentives in sectoral laws. Thus, the directive may have had the unintended effect of encouraging further the fragmentation of the tax policy framework

[31] This is the subject of a separate directive (05/2008/CM/UEMOA), which states that banks' provisioning is to follow the prudential rules of the BCEAO (Banque Centrale des États de l'Afrique de l'Ouest).

[32] Directive 02/2011/CM/UEMOA. To qualify, a holding must hold at least 50 percent of its assets in shares of nonlisted companies.

[33] Since these application rules have not been issued, we will not discuss any further the mining regulation.

[34] The directive does not prescribe a specific thin capitalization rule. Arguably though, countries can enact such rules under the general restriction on deductible expenses.

TABLE 13.2

WAEMU: Directive on Taxation of Investment Income

	Rates (Percent)	Notes
Dividends		
General	10 to 15	Member states can opt to make this a final tax; taxpayers do not have to add dividends to their income for purposes of the general income tax.[1]
Distributed by companies listed on a WAEMU stock exchange	2 to 7	Companies must be certified by the CREPMF. No consultation with national tax authorities is needed.
Interest		
General	6	
Maturity >= 5 years	0 to 6	If debt is used to invest in sectors key to economic development.
Government issued with maturity between 5 and 10 years	3	Government includes both central and local, and any government entity.
Government issued with maturity exceeding 10 years	0	Government includes both central and local, and any government entity.
Capital gains		
On disposition of equity securities	0 to 7	
On disposition of debt securities	0 to 5	

Source: Directive 02/2010/CM/UEMOA.

[1] Some WAEMU countries still apply a schedular tax system whereby different types of income are subject individually to a schedular (single rate) tax, and globally (with other incomes) to a progressive tax.

by endorsing a long-standing practice in member states.[35] This, in turn, has repercussions for the effectiveness of tax administration, which in such cases has to be exercised by multiple government agencies.

Taxes on portfolio income. Directive 02/2010/CM/UEMOA specifies the types and tax rate intervals that member countries should apply to various portfolio incomes; Table 13.2 provides a summary.

Income distributed by passive investment funds approved by the Conseil Régional de l'Epargne Publique et des Marchés Financiers (CREPMF) is exempt from tax.[36] The directive also specifies that the tax is final when withheld at source in the state where the investment is made—the residence country cannot apply any residual taxation on such income. This is at odds with the MTT.

The rate structure given in Table 13.2 is paradoxical. While one objective of the WAEMU Treaty, and the various directives, is to promote private investment in the region, dividends are taxed at higher rates than interest, and interest income on corporate bonds is taxed at higher rates than interest income on government bonds.

Multilateral tax treaty. The multilateral tax treaty (MTT) was adopted by regulation 08/2008/CM/UEMOA; application rules were issued in 2010 (005/COM/2010/UEMOA).[37] It distributes the taxing rights of WAEMU states in respect of intracommunity investment. The MTT covers taxes on income and inheritance, and registration fees and stamp duties, including those

[35] Senegal, a country where this practice has flourished over the years, consolidated most tax incentives provided in various nontax laws into its general tax code, except those contained in a 2007 law creating a special economic zone. The implications of this for the provision of tax preferences are, however, unclear: presumably, the general tax code has no more precedence over other codes than it did before this consolidation. The consolidation is, however, an innovation in the region, and it will be interesting to watch whether it will instill more transparency and less discretion in the conduct of tax policy.

[36] The CREPMF is a WAEMU body created in 1996 and tasked with regulating the issuance of public (listed or not) financial securities in the WAEMU.

[37] A thorough discussion of the MTT and its application rules is outside the scope of this paper. We limit ourselves to issues of consistency with other directives, especially regarding the distribution of taxing rights among member states.

TABLE 13.3

Main Features of WAEMU Multilateral Tax Treaty

Tax Type	Definition of Tax Base	Treatment under the Multilateral Tax Treaty
Tax on business income	Profits defined by the residence state, or the source state in case of a permanent establishment, or other fixed place of business.	Taxation by the residence state; source state has the right to tax profits of a permanent establishment.
Tax on rental income from real (immobile) assets	Rent and similar payments defined by the source state (where the assets are located).	Taxation by the source state.
Tax on income from sea and air transportations	Profits from these activities as defined by the residence state.	Taxation by the residence state (where the headquarters of the enterprise are located), or the state of effective place of management.
Tax on pension income	Pension income defined by the residence state.	Taxation by the residence state.
Tax on dividends, interest, and royalties	Income defined in the MTT, and includes any income deemed as dividends by the state where the payer company resides.	Withholding tax by the source state (max of 10% on dividends and 15% on interest and royalties); residual taxation by the residence state of the beneficiary.
Capital gains on real (immobile) property	Capital gains on real property as defined by the source state (where property is located).	Taxation by the source state; residence state has the right to tax in certain situations, where income is passive.
Inheritance tax	All types of inheritance at death, including business participation and assets, as defined by the state where such assets are located. Liabilities inherited are netted out.	Generally by the state where the assets or goods inherited are located.
Registration fees	Defined by state where property is located or document is issued. Fees can be specific or ad valorem (% of transaction value).	Taxation by state where real property is located. For all other legal documents, state where documents are presented to the authorities has a right to tax, with a credit for fees paid in the state where the document was issued.
Stamp duties	Defined by state where transaction takes place.	Taxed by state where transaction takes place.

Source: Regulation 08/2008/CM/UEMOA.

collected by the central governments on behalf of subcentral governments. Table 13.3 describes the main features of the MTT. The distribution of taxing rights under the MTT is generally as follows:

- Income from a business or a profession is taxed on a residence basis, except in the case of a permanent establishment (PE) deriving business income in a member state, in which case the income is taxed only to the extent it is attributable to the PE. Capital gains realized from selling business property are considered business income.
- Portfolio income (that is, interest, dividends, royalties, and capital gains from movable property) is taxed by both the residence and source states; the MTT limits the latter's taxing rights by capping the withholding tax rate it can impose on income of nonresidents (15 percent on interest and royalties; 10 percent on dividends), except for capital gains, which remains taxable at the schedular tax rate of the source country.
- Nonrecurrent taxes on real property (mainly registration fees and stamp duties) and capital gains tax on real property are due in the state where the property is located.

In the case of taxation by both residence and source states, the residence state should relieve the taxpayer from double taxation primarily by providing a tax credit for taxes paid to the source state; the tax credit should not exceed the residence country's tax on the same income.

The MTT also covers issues of information exchange and mutual assistance in tax collection; it has a nondiscrimination clause and provides for a dispute resolution mechanism.

One of the main differences between the MTT and model tax conventions of the OECD and the UN is that it covers a number of nonrecurrent taxes on immovable property. This is appropriate given the importance of these taxes in the region, but unlikely to have any meaningful impact since the MTT simply affirms current country practice, without any restrictions on tax rates or rules for the calculation of the tax base.

The residence principle in the MTT is inconsistent with the directive on the taxation of portfolio income discussed earlier, which makes final withholding taxes on such income by the source country; that is, the residence country cannot levy additional taxes. It is not clear which takes precedence, but the two have different consequences on tax interaction between member states. For example, the standard tax competition model suggests that under source-based taxation, tax competition for mobile capital will drive tax rates to zero—and portfolio income is by far the most mobile form of income. If the source principle were to hold, tax competition among member states can be expected to drive rates to the minimum allowed by the directive

APPLICATION OF THE FRAMEWORK IN MEMBER STATES

In general, member countries seem to follow the most visible parameters of the WAEMU directives: tax rates. Other aspects, however, are more difficult to apprehend; these include: rules regarding the calculation of certain tax bases; exemptions, especially from the VAT; and tax regimes in sectoral or special laws.

Indirect taxes. The *value-added tax* was introduced by WAEMU member states well before the 1998 directive: 1960 in Côte d'Ivoire, 1980 in Senegal, 1986 in Niger, 1991 in Benin and Mali, 1993 in Burkina Faso, and 1995 in Togo. Guinea-Bissau is also working on the VAT. Originally, some of these VATs had multiple rates, and some did not apply to all stages of the production-consumption chain. By the time the WAEMU directive had been introduced, all WAEMU VATs had moved closer to a modern VAT: a single positive rate (18 percent, except Côte d'Ivoire which experimented with 20 percent for a short period in the early 2000s); exemptions limited to a list of final consumption items and hard-to-tax transactions,[38] such as financial intermediation; and a registration threshold between CFAF 15 and CFAF 50 million. The directive was drafted in such a way to allow a member state's VATs to fall within its parameters, including most of the exemptions.

This situation, however, did not last too long. In the early and mid-2000s, a number of member states broadened their VAT exemptions in two ways: some consumption goods and services were added (for example, public transport; partially processed food items, such as frozen meat, poultry and fish; certain energy products, such as gas; and computer equipment, including software and printing machines); and some states started exempting inputs used in the production of exempt goods (for example, building equipment used in certain sectors, such as construction; various types of pesticides, insecticides, and animal feeds used in farming).[39]

Moreover, some member states argued that lower positive rates should be allowed by the directive in order to compete with North African countries in the tourism sector, and to alleviate the impact of the VAT on the price of certain processed food items that are basic necessities for

[38] Although the list of exemptions was short, it included items that are relatively important from a revenue perspective, such as basic food and housing.

[39] The WAEMU experience in this regard, especially in the agriculture sector, is an example of the so-called exemption-creep phenomenon whereby an exempt good (or service) creates pressures to exempt the inputs used to produce it, yielding, *in fine*, a zero tax rate on the good.

TABLE 13.4

Excise Tax Rates in WAEMU States, 2012 (Percent)

	Nonalcoholic Beverages	Alcoholic Beverages		Tobacco[2]
		Beer	Other[1]	
Benin	5	15	35, 40	40
Burkina Faso	10	25	27.5	22
Côte d'Ivoire	12	13	25, 30, 35, 45	23, 33, 35[3]
Mali	10	45	45	15, 20, 25
Niger	12, 15[4]	25	45	40
Senegal	2.75	40[5]	40[5]	20, 45
Togo	2	15	35	40
WAEMU Directive				
Minimum	0	15	15	15
Maximum	20	50	50	45

Sources: Tax laws of member states.
[1] Multiple rates apply according to alcohol content; the higher the content, the higher the rate.
[2] Multiple rates apply according to price categories, with lowest rate imposed on cheap cigarettes.
[3] An additional tax of 2.5 to 10 percent applies according to the price category.
[4] Rates are respectively for fruit juices and mineral water.
[5] Additional specific taxes apply.

low-income households (for example, powdered milk). The changes to the 1998 VAT directive in 2009 were largely a response to these concerns. This "accommodating behavior" is symptomatic of tax coordination in the WAEMU in general, and is not limited to the VAT case.

Member states have not yet moved to align their VATs with the 2009 directive. For example, some still exempt certain items (not mandated by the directive) instead of applying the new lower VAT rate allowed for a limited list; and many exempt certain intermediate and capital inputs used in the production of exempt supplies to mimic a lower VAT rate, or lessen the administrative burden of dealing with refunds.

It is difficult to estimate the impact of these changes on VAT revenue; member states do not usually undertake a thorough evaluation of the revenue loss attributed to policy changes, and microdata is scarce or inexistent.[40] It is somewhat reassuring, however, that between 2005 and 2010 the average VAT revenue-to-GDP ratio varied within a narrow range—5.5 to 6 percent.

On *excise taxes*, member countries generally observe the rates imposed by the directive as well as the list of items excised. This is no surprise since the excise directive poses virtually no constraints on tax rates (minimum rates are very low or zero, as is the case of petroleum products), and the extension of the list of excisable items in 2009 brought some countries back into conformity with the directive. Table 13.4 shows the rates that apply on tobacco, and alcoholic and nonalcoholic drinks. In addition to these, most countries apply excises on a number of other items allowed under the directive. The available information shows that rates are generally near the minimum mandated by the directive, suggesting that the consequences to either revenue or distortions to the common market are minimal. There are, however, a few exceptions, including cars and gold bullions; both are important in terms of values and hence would be expected to contribute significantly to revenue.

There are two main practices at the country level that diverge from the directive: (1) additional excise taxes on the same list of items allowed by the directive; (2) and rules for calculating the excise tax base. An example of the first is the application by Senegal of additional specific excises on tobacco, which may also increase the overall excise rate (ad valorem plus specific) above the maximum allowed by the directive. However, the most common form of additional excises is

[40] There is a growing concern among policy advisors to developing countries that these capacity limitations in tax policy analysis frequently lead to poor policy outcomes.

earmarked taxes on petroleum products; almost all countries have them, although they tend to be imposed at very low rates.

The second practice is more common, and is often used to provide through the excise an additional layer of protection to domestic production, over and above the CET. In principle, the directive mandates valuation of goods for purposes of the excise at the CIF (cost, insurance and freight) value for imports, and at the ex-factory price for domestic production—including the tariff and other indirect levies, but excluding the VAT. Rules for calculating the CIF value are the same as those for purposes of the CET, and so in principle are harmonized.[41] However, the excise directive does not define the "ex-factory" price in the case of domestic production; it does not specify, for example, that the price should be arm's-length. This can result in effective rates being lower than the statutory rate, and undermine the minimum positive rates that are compulsory for certain items (tobacco and alcohol). For taxpayers (producers and consumers), the benefit is obvious: paying less tax. For governments, the benefit resides mainly in the ability to compete beyond what is allowed by the directive using the base rather than the rate.

Direct taxes. In the area of the *corporate income tax*, the common accounting heritage of WAEMU states explains much of the convergence of their national tax laws in relation to the determination of taxable profits. Directive 01/2008/CM/UEMOA, defining the base of the CIT, endorses this heritage while recognizing the need to modernize the CIT by taxing all incomes earned by corporations at a single rate. But since most WAEMU states still rely on schedular income taxes, corporations can deduct from their business profits rental and portfolio incomes that are taxed at their respective schedules—for example, Mali and Côte d'Ivoire. These countries are therefore not consistent with directive 01/2008/CM/UEMOA. Burkina Faso and Senegal are no table exceptions; they introduced in 2010 and 2012, respectively, a CIT applicable to all corporate income, irrespective of its type.

All member states have reduced their rates on corporate profits to the 25–30 percent interval allowed under directive 08/2008/CM/UEMOA (Table 13.5). Countries that have a schedular tax apply the new rate only to commercial and industrial profits, but not to other incomes earned by corporations.

There are other sources of divergence between state's laws and the CIT directives. For example, in some countries, the tax rate varies according to economic activity: Niger and Benin apply 40 and 45 percent respectively on corporate profits from upstream petroleum activities; Guinea-Bissau taxes domestic sales of minerals at a lower rate than exports. Also, all countries have a minimum tax that is typically proportional to turnover, and subject to a minimum fixed amount (Table 13.5). This tax, which is not envisaged in the directive (and hence arguably illegal when applied to corporations) represents in some cases a nonnegligible part of CIT revenue, and could be very distortionary.

On the *portfolio income tax*, the directive seems to have been written to include most current practices in member states. It therefore reflects the diverse treatment of portfolio income within and across countries. This diversity is mostly present in the treatment of interest income, where rates vary according to the issuer (government vs. private entities), and maturity (short- vs. long-term). For example, in Senegal, rates vary between 6 and 20 percent.

By trying to accommodate country practices, the directive raises a number of issues, not least is the potential to worsen distortions to capital income taxation rather than reduce them, and weaken revenue mobilization rather than strengthen it.[42] The main reason for this is that the rate gap in the taxation of various capital income sources will increase for some countries. For example, Benin, which imposes a 3 percent tax rate on all government bonds, is now in violation

[41]Some countries change CIF values through administrative practices that are inconsistent with the CET and its rules.
[42]Taxes on portfolio income rarely account for more than 3 percent of total tax revenue in WAEMU states.

TABLE 13.5

Tax Rates on Profits and Minimum Taxes in WAEMU States, 2011

	Tax Rate (Percent)		
	Individual	Corporate	Minimum Tax
Benin	25	30	0.75% of TO or CFA 200 K
Industry		25	
Upstream petroleum		35 to 45	
Burkina Faso	27.5	27.5	0.5% of TO or CFA 500 K
Mining		17.5	
Côte d'Ivoire[1]	20	25	0.5% of TO
Banks and insurance			0.15% of TO; max of CFA 60 M
Energy, water, upstream petroleum			0.1% of TO
Guinea-Bissau	25	25	0.5% of TO
Minerals, domestic sales		22	
Minerals, exports		30 to 45	
Mali	30	30	0.75% of TO or CFA 610.8 K
Niger	30	30	0.1% of TO
Senegal[2]	25	25	CFA 0.5 M if TO < CFA 250 M CFA 0.75 M if 250 M < TO < 500 M CFA 1 M if TO > 500 M
Togo		30	CFA 50 K if TO > 5 M … CFA 200 M if TO > 30 B
Industry		27	

Sources: Tax laws of member states.
Note: TO = turnover; K = thousands; M = millions; B = billions.
[1]The minimum is 2 percent for persons subject to the simplified profit tax, and 5 percent for noncommercial profits.
[2]Senegal increased its rate to 30 percent in January 2013.

of the directive, which calls for a rate differential of 3 percentage points according to whether the bond has a maturity between five and 10 years (in which case the tax rate is 3 percent), or a maturity exceeding 10 years (in which case the tax rate is 0 percent). Similarly, Senegal imposes at 6 percent all bonds with maturity of five years or more.

Finally, in the area of *special tax regimes*, nontax laws, and primarily investment codes (ICs), have been used in WAEMU states to circumvent the constraints imposed by regional tax directives. This behavior is sometimes allowed by the same directives that are supposed to harmonize or coordinate national tax policies. Special tax regimes raise the issue of credibility of tax coordination and the role of regional institutions, in particular the WAEMU Commission and the Court of Justice.

There are no directives or regulations at the regional level dealing with the provision of special tax regimes in member states.[43] Generally, each directive provides for exemptions or rate reductions that are either compulsory or optional. An example is the VAT directive, under which member states must exempt a list of items from their VATs, and may apply a reduced rate between 5 and 10 percent on a limited list of items. Another example is the directive on portfolio income, under which member countries must exempt or apply a reduced rate on income from certain holdings. Yet another example is the list of exemptions from the CIT defined in Article 9 of the CIT base directive (01/2008/CM/UEMOA). These incentives can provide a tax advantage to WAEMU states relative to the ROW, but they do not provide any advantage to one member state relative to another.

[43]The WAEMU Commission issued a directive on free zones in 2008 (14/2008/CM/UEMOA) that contained no special tax provisions. Free zone laws at the national level may contain important preferential regimes; for example, Senegal provides income tax holidays up to 50 years in its 2007 free zone law.

One exception is Article 8 of the directive defining the CIT base. It states that countries cannot provide tax reductions other than those in Article 9 of the directive, except those provided in ICs or other sectoral laws, such as mining and petroleum, tourism, and so on. In other words, Article 8 seems to endorse the special tax regimes provided in existent non-tax laws at the time of the introduction of the CIT base directive. Since it does not state that any future changes to these laws would be consistent with the directive, it may have been written with the purpose of a compromise: including then-existent country CIT incentives, but disallowing any future changes.

The question whether the directive intended simply to grandfather existing incentives, disallowing any future changes, remains open. Today, all WAEMU states provide special tax regimes that depart from the tax treatment under their general tax laws, and some are more recent than the CIT directive. In addition to those in non-tax laws, these regimes can be discretionary—provided by presidential or ministerial decrees, and generally without parliament's consent. Often, they involve a contractual agreement or written understanding between the state and the taxpayer. Whether grounded in a law or a contractual agreement, these regimes usually refer to existing tax laws as a starting point, modifying them to arrive at a certain tax package.

Table 13.6 summarizes the main types of tax incentives provided under existing ICs—note that three are more recent than the CIT directive: Benin, Burkina Faso, and Guinea-Bissau. Some commonalities can be observed:

- Most ICs exclude the retail sector, and some other service sectors, from eligibility for tax incentives. Countries thus view manufacturing activities as more worthy of tax subsidies than the service sector.
- Mining and petroleum activities are also excluded in countries where such activities are important. One possible reason for this is institutional: the upstream energy sector in WAEMU is typically under the responsibility of an independent ministry, separate from that in charge of the economy. Tax rules for the sector, including tax incentives, are often drafted in the sectoral law, borrowing where necessary from the tax laws.
- The standard tax incentive takes invariably the form of a temporary exemption or reduction from various taxes during the two phases of an investment: (1) during the development phase, exemptions are given from indirect taxes—mainly tariff and VAT; (2) during the operation phase, exemptions or reductions are given from taxes on profits, patents (a fixed or proportional-to-turnover tax),[44] minimum taxes, and employer's payroll taxes. The incentives during the operation phase are perhaps the only area of ICs where differences across member states may occur, and hence may create a tax distortion across countries. For example, the tax holiday period in many states depends on the amount invested—the greater the amount the longer the holiday. This can be seen as reflecting the relative negotiating powers of investors and governments, and can be a source of tax competition among member states. This relation is supported empirically by Klemm and Van Parys (2012),[45] who find that tax exemptions result in part from strategic interactions between member states. Van Parys and James (2010) establish empirically that this tax competition behavior is not very effective in attracting foreign investment.[46]

[44] *Patentes* are usually set and collected by central governments on behalf of local governments, and are an important element of local government finances. Central governments rarely compensate local governments for the revenue loss from these exemptions.

[45] A. Klemm and S. Van Parys, "Empirical Evidence on the Effects of Tax Incentives." *International Tax and Public Finance*, 2012, 19, pp. 393–423.

[46] S. Van Parys, Stefan, and S. James, "The Effectiveness of Tax Incentives in Attracting Investment: Panel Data Evidence from the CFA Franc Zone." *International Tax and Public Finance*, 2010, 17, pp. 400–29.

TABLE 13.6

Summary of Tax Incentives Provided by WAEMU's States' Investment Codes

Country and Date of Enactment	Excluded Activities	Tax Incentives Provided: Development Phase	Tax Incentives Provided: Operation Phase	Length of Holiday During Operation Phase (Years)
Benin August 11, 2008	Retail, reconditioning activities, and polluting activities.	Exemption from registration fees, tariff, and VAT.	Exemption from CIT, patent, and exit tax.	5 to 9: Depends on amount invested and location.
Burkina Faso January 29, 2010	Retail, mining, banking, telecoms.[1]	Tariff reduced to 5 percent, exemption from VAT.	Longer loss carry-forward period; exemption from employer payroll taxes, patent; investment tax credit; and holiday period extended by 3 years for investment in rural areas.	5 to 7: Depends on amount invested.
Côte d'Ivoire June 7, 2012	Retail and financial services.		Exemption from CIT and patents; reduction of social contributions and customs duties on equipment to 50 percent.	5 to 15: Depends on activities.
Guinea-Bissau December 31, 2009	Mining, petroleum, forestry.	Tariff (Guinea-Bissau does not have a VAT).	Exemption from CIT and employer payroll tax; annual reduction of CIT to 90 percent, 80 percent, 60 percent, 40 percent, and 20 percent thereafter.	2
Mali August 19, 2005	Retail, mining, and petroleum.	Exemption from tariff (if no local substitute) and VAT.	Exemption from CIT and patent.	5 to 8: Depends on amount invested.
Niger July 12, 2001	Retail, mining, and petroleum.	Exemption from tariff (if no local substitute) and VAT.	Exemption from CIT, minimum tax, patent, and "contribution fonciere."	5
Senegal February 6, 2004	Retail.	Exemption from tariff (if no local substitute) and VAT.	Investment allowance of 50 percent; exemption from employer payroll tax.	5 to 8: Depends on invested amount and whether firm is new or established.
Togo October 31, 1989	Retail.	Exemption from tariff.	Exemption from CIT and minimum tax; employer payroll tax rate reduced to 2 percent.	Not specified.

Sources: Investment codes of member states.
Note: CIT = corporate income tax
[1] Excludes activities for which a government agreement was signed with the investor.

A positive aspect of ICs, at least in principle, is to substitute rules for total discretion, hence improving transparency and governance in the provision of tax incentives. The idea is that tax incentives would still be provided upon request and subject to review and approval by committees (typically at the ministerial level), but the rules would be laid out clearly in the IC. In practice, however, experience suggests that this has not worked as well as expected. Two reasons can be given for this. First, the eligibility rules are lengthy and complex, allowing review committees to exercise discretion in the choice of eligible investment. Second, these rules are based on investors' intentions, not actions; they can almost always be met, especially by medium and large sophisticated investors. Moreover, governments seem to have lacked credibility in reversing their decisions once the investment is sunken, but not all conditions are met (for example, minimum local value-added, minimum monetary amount invested, project development period, and so on). This raises doubt about the usefulness of such complex eligibility criteria relative to providing incentives automatically as part of filing a tax return and subject to general audit rules (for example, an investment tax credit). This may seem counterintuitive since enforcing the rules should, in principle, strengthen government credibility, not weaken it; the explanation perhaps lies in the opaque nature and governance of the process of administering ICs.

In summary, the differences in ICs among member states are essentially limited to the length of income tax holidays during the operation phase of an investment. They are not large enough to have any significant impact on companies' choice of country location within the WAEMU region.

EXPERIENCE WITH REVENUE MOBILIZATION

Tax coordination has brought about some convergence of national tax policies, but many distortions to the internal market have not been eliminated. Moreover, any progress in furthering integration in the current coordination framework seems highly unlikely. This section deals with the second most important objective of tax coordination as stated in the WAEMU treaty: mobilizing domestic tax revenue. In this regard, tax coordination is seen as key to increasing tax revenue to the Convergence Pact level of 17 percent of GDP, and beyond in the long run. A closely related objective is the tax transition (*transition fiscale*), which was spelled out in a 2006 decision;[47] it seeks to shift the tax revenue structure of member states from taxes on international trade to domestic taxes. This shift implies a reduction in tariff rates in the long run, and this is indeed the intention of the Economic Partnership Agreements (EPAs) with the EU. But the recent ECOWAS CET goes against this objective by increasing the tariff on some categories of imports.

Has tax coordination helped in increasing the revenue performance of WAEMU states particularly since the start of the WAEMU Treaty in 1994 and the implementation of the CET in 2000?

The database used in this section, described in Mansour (2014),[48] covers 41 sub-Saharan countries over the period 1980–2010. It distinguishes between tariffs and domestic revenues, with the latter split between indirect tax revenues (essentially VAT and excises), CIT revenue, personal income tax revenue, other direct tax revenues, and other tax revenues. This representation of

[47] See Decision 10/2006/CM/UEMOA, Decision 34/2009/CM/UEMOA, and Decision 35/2009/CM/UEMOA. Decision 10/2006 reaffirmed the objective of intracommunity free trade, and called for the removal of nontariff barriers and all tariff measures inconsistent with the CET, the VAT and excise tax directives; it also called for the removal of all measures that create distortions to intracommunity trade and capital mobility (that is, special tax regimes); and it signaled the need to harmonize direct taxes, which was accomplished a few years later with the introduction of the directives on capital income taxation, and the MTT.

[48] M. Mansour (2014).

Figure 13.2. Structure of Tax Revenues in WAEMU - 1980–2010 (Percent of GDP)

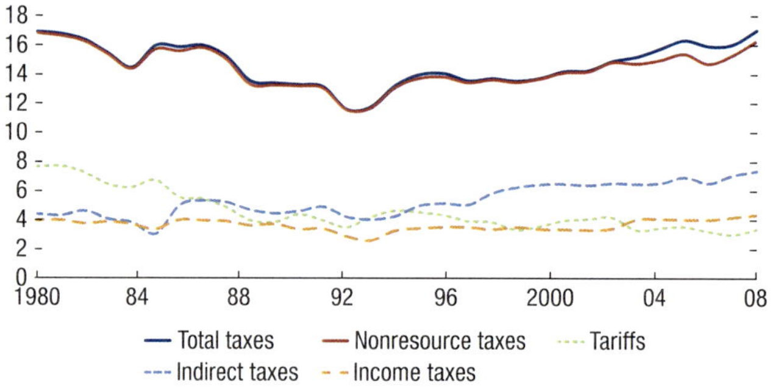

Source: Mansour (2014).

revenues allows for the study of the various tax sources that are subject to regional coordination. Importantly, a distinction is made between revenues from extractive industries and the rest, with the former comprising resource royalties, CIT from companies undertaking upstream activities, and in some cases the government's share of production sharing agreements on such activities.

Figure 13.2 depicts the composition of tax revenue in WAEMU. The drastic deterioration of the overall tax-to-GDP ratio in the 1980s and early 1990s was followed by some improvement in the second half of the 1990s, and a steep increase in the first half of the 2000s. Econometric analysis lends support to the hypothesis that tariff and tax coordination may have improved revenue mobilization; a Chow test suggests that there is a structural break in the tax-to-GDP ratio in 2000, the year the CET was fully phased in and less than two years after the VAT and excise directives.[49]

In terms of changes to the revenue structure, Figure 13.2 shows the now familiar impact of trade liberalization on tariff revenue,[50] which in WAEMU caused a loss of about 4 percentage points of GDP, most of which occurred in the 1980s. These were recouped by indirect taxes, mainly the VAT, starting only in the early 1990s. The CET, which was completed in 2000, may have therefore helped to stabilize the revenue from this source by limiting tariff competition among member countries. Also interesting is the fact that the increase in indirect tax revenues since 1998 (date of introduction of the VAT and excise directives) is modest (about two percentage points of GDP).

The evolution of income taxes is unimpressive, with their yield stable around 4 percent of GDP over the period. A closer look at the corporate tax, however, reveals some interesting developments (Figure 13.3). After losing half of its yield in the 1980s and early 1990s, the CIT recovered quickly in the mid-1990s, and has remained relatively stable since, around 1.4 percent of GDP (excluding the contribution of upstream mining and oil and gas activities). Figure 13.3 also shows the relative importance of Côte d'Ivoire to the regional CIT revenue, where the contributions of agricultural exports such as cocoa and coffee are significant.

[49] The econometric analysis, not reported here, consists in applying the Chow test to the following regression (variables in log form): $T_{it} = \propto_{it} + \beta X_{it} + \varepsilon_{it}$ where $i = 1,\ldots,n$ denotes the country, $t = 1,\ldots,T$ time, α and β are unknown parameters, X is a vector of independent variables (which include GDP, trade openness, urbanization, and so on), and ε_{it} is a random error.

[50] See International Monetary Fund, *Revenue Mobilization in Developing Countries*, Washington: International Monetary Fund, 2001; T. Baunsgaard and M. Keen, "Tax Revenue and (or?) Trade Liberalization," *Journal of Public Economics*, 2010, 94(9-10), pp. 563–77 on developing countries in general; and Keen and Mansour (2010), on sub-Saharan Africa.

Figure 13.3. Corporate Tax Rates and Revenues in The WAEMU, 1980–2010

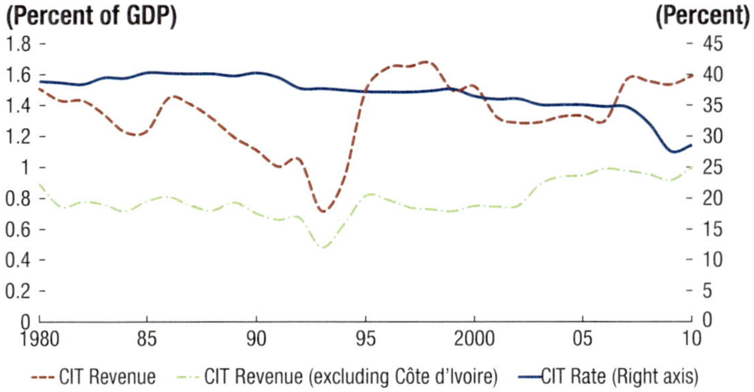

Source: Mansour (2014).
Note: CIT = Corporate income tax revenue excludes the contribution of upstream oil and gas and mining.

Development in the CIT rate shows a slow decline over 1990–2005, and then a steep one that coincided with the introduction of the CIT rate and base directives in 2008. It is interesting that the CIT interval prescribed by the rate directive imposed a minimum rate of 25 percent, 10 points below the rates practiced by WAEMU countries in 2008. It is possible that one of the main aims of the directive was to preempt some countries from lowering their rate below 25 percent. But the imposition of a maximum of 30 percent forced some countries, where the CIT acts as a rent tax on upstream resource activities, to compensate for the revenue loss with more distortionary taxes—for example, Mali reduced its CIT rate from 35 to 30 percent to abide by the CIT rate directive, and introduced instead an export tax of 3 percent on gold production (which essentially acts as additional royalty).

Although there is no clear indication that CIT rate reductions in WAEMU since the early 1990s contributed, on average, to a revenue loss, the recent decline in rates suggests that the future of the CIT as a revenue source in the nonresource sector is uncertain. Downward pressure on the CIT rate is likely to continue in sub-Saharan Africa, and unless the tax base is broadened by scaling back tax incentives, revenue will ultimately suffer. The recent speed at which sub-Saharan Africa countries have reduced their CIT rates suggests that this outcome may not be too distant a possibility. In 2005, only five sub-Saharan Africa countries had a standard CIT rate lower than 30 percent; the number increased to 13 in 2010, and 15 in 2012; all WAEMU countries now have a CIT rate between 25 and 30 percent.

At the country level experience varies significantly among WAEMU states, and suggests that both the structure and the level of tax revenues have not progressed significantly toward the objectives set by the WAEMU Treaty (Figure 13.4). This is not surprising given the flexibility in base setting provided by the various directives, ongoing tax competition through special tax regimes, and the differences in the evolution of the composition of GDP across member states.

In terms of tax levels, Burkina Faso, Guinea-Bissau, and Togo are well below the convergence criteria of 17 percent of GDP; their revenue effort improved only marginally since 2000. Mali and Niger have mobilized significant revenue since 1995, but mostly from the mining sector. The revenue increase in Niger is especially impressive over 2005–10, a period of significant increase in commodity prices. Benin has capitalized on its strategic geographical location with respect to

Figure 13.4. Structure of Tax Revenues in WAEMU States, 1980–2010 (Percent of GDP)

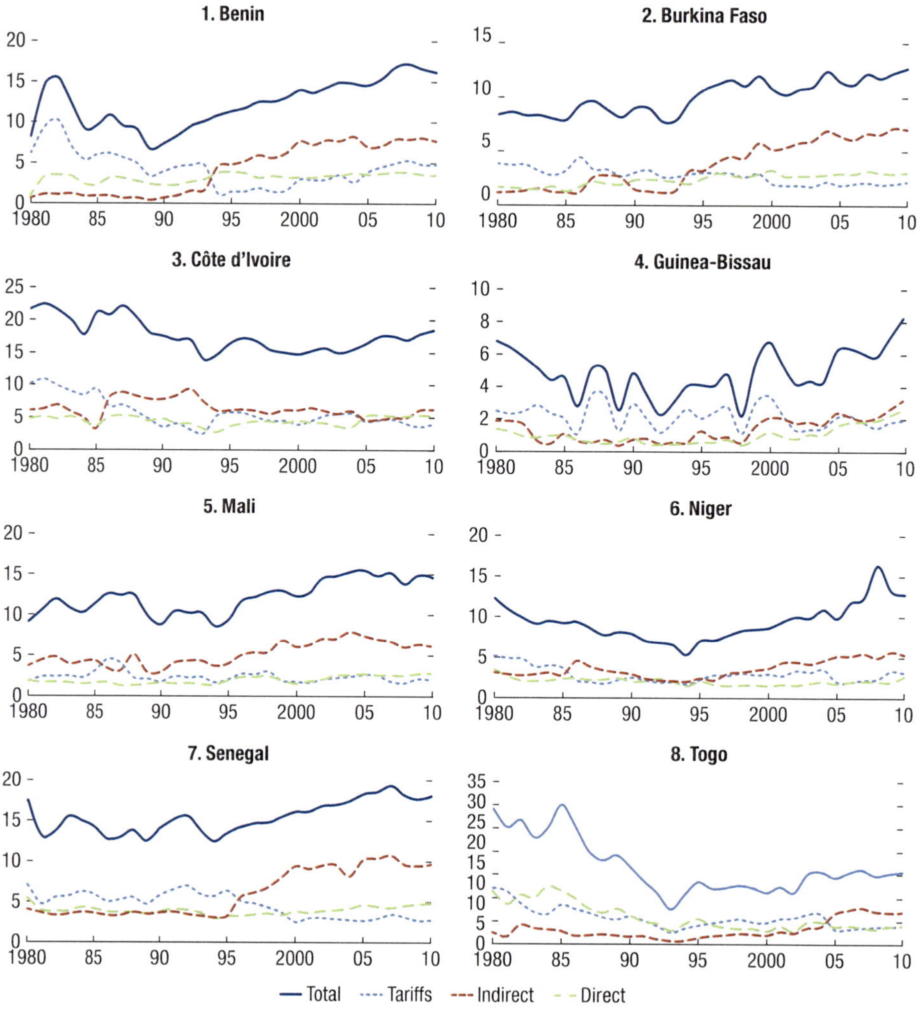

Source: Mansour (2014).

Nigeria to improve its tariff revenue through reexports. It is the only country where this source of revenue increased significantly since 1995 in tandem with an increase in VAT revenue; in other countries, VAT revenue has substituted for tariff revenue. Senegal's revenue performance is impressive and almost entirely linked to the VAT and excises, which account for over 50 percent of tax revenue. Senegal, and to a lesser extent Burkina Faso, seem to have progressed best in transiting from tariff to domestic tax revenue.

Based on a structural break test in 2000 in total nonresource tax revenue, trade and tax coordination in WAEMU may have helped to improve revenue mobilization. An important and related question is the revenue performance in WAEMU relative to other trading groups in sub-Saharan Africa that do not coordinate to the same extent their tariff and tax policies. Figure 13.5 shows the

Figure 13.5. Change in Tax Revenues in Selected Sub-Saharan Africa Groups, 2000 and 2010
(Percentage points of GDP)

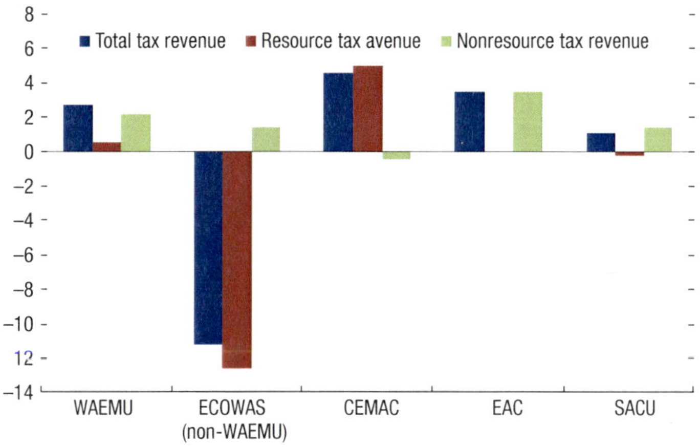

Source: Mansour (2014).
Note: CEMAC = Economic Community of Central African States; EAC = East African Community; ECOWAS = Economic Community of West African States; SACU = Southern African Customs Union; WAEMU = West African Economic and Monetary Union.

change in the (nonresource) tax-to-GDP ratio for five such groups between 2000 and 2010.[51] WAEMU has performed better than the Southern African Customs Union (SACU) and Central African Economic and Monetary Community (CEMAC), but not as well as the East African Community (EAC). This lends some support to the hypothesis that WAEMU states did relatively well since they started tariff and tax coordination. The WAEMU also compares favorably to the other selected regions in terms of current tax-to-GDP levels; only the SACU outperforms it.

LESSONS LEARNED

The speed with which the WAEMU has built a tariff and tax coordination framework is remarkable. The region succeeded in forming a customs union and coordinating the setting of main domestic taxes through a partial harmonization approach. From the experience of the WAEMU, important lessons can be drawn for other regions that are contemplating the coordination of their tax policies. Some of these lessons are general in nature, and relate to the process of economic integration and tax coordination; others are more specific and apply to certain areas of tax coordination, in particular the CIT and the related topic of investment tax incentives.

The first important lesson is that political leaders in the WAEMU have probably underestimated the difficulties and challenges of tariff and tax coordination. This is most obviously clear in the gaps that exist between the objectives of economic integration as set out in the WAEMU Treaty of 1994, and the effectiveness of the tax directives and regulations that were produced in order to meet these objectives.

[51]These groups coordinate their trade policies to various extents, but less than WAEMU, and they do not coordinate their domestic tax policies—with the exception of CEMAC, which has VAT and excise directives similar in design to those in WAEMU. Therefore, they constitute good comparators.

Second, policymakers did not take sufficiently into account the implementation and enforcement implications at the regional level, particularly the need for effective surveillance. This partly explains the gaps between de jure and de facto coordination.

Third, the credibility of the coordination framework depends in large part on the credibility of its regional institutions. It is ironic that, having borrowed extensively from the EU model of economic integration and tax coordination, the WAEMU has yet to provide its regional institutions with the necessary resources to undertake effective surveillance. The fact that neither the WAEMU Commission nor member states have called upon the regional Court of Justice in cases of noncompliance with the tax directives, has undermined the credibility of the coordination framework and its institutions. One result of this has been that the WAEMU Commission recently changed some of its directives to allow noncompliant countries to become compliant, for example, VAT and excise directives. This accommodating approach is likely to further erode the coordination framework and the credibility of the Commission.

Fourth, the tax coordination framework may have had the unintended effect of contributing to the fragmentation of policymaking at the national level by providing countries with the incentive to enact special tax regimes outside their tax laws. This is particularly the case of investment incentives, where the framework allows unfettered tax competition as long as it is done outside countries' main tax laws. This, in turn, has made tax systems opaque, increased their complexity, and contributed to a culture of "tax negotiation."

Fifth, and on a more positive note, the coordination framework has allowed some convergence of countries' tax systems (notably statutory tax rates), which in turn may have contributed to the positive revenue performance observed in WAEMU member states. This is particularly the case of VAT and excises on tobacco products and alcoholic beverages. However, the future of the CIT (other than on resource activities) is uncertain in the region, as there is little evidence that the 2008 CIT directives have had any impact on corporate tax competition.

In conclusion, the future of the tax coordination framework in WAEMU is uncertain. Although it must evolve to respond to the objectives of economic integration, the current approach of coordination has shown its limits in certain areas. Two options may be envisaged. The first would deepen harmonization through stronger political commitment, and authority and resources to regional institutions to effectively monitor compliance and impose sanctions. This option is consistent with the objectives of the 1994 Treaty but its conditions are very hard to achieve, particularly political commitment. The second option would take the lack of commitment as given, and put more emphasis on a negative approach to tax coordination.[52] For instance, instead of trying to establish a common investment code, the WAEMU Commission could establish a list of taxes that may not be reduced or exempted at the national level. Beyond these two approaches, a more flexible way to coordinate would be based on soft laws, such as best practices, information sharing, and on self-enforcing commitments. It is less ambitious in legal terms, but it may improve the effectiveness of tax coordination by preserving the objectives of integration while providing countries with more flexibility in setting their national tax policies.

The WAEMU tariff and tax coordination framework is likely to evolve with a mixed approach combining partial or full harmonization, negative coordination, and sharing of information and best practices. The difficulty resides in identifying at various milestones of the integration process, which approach works best and for what tax—a task where improvement in the leadership and analytical competencies of the WAEMU Commission can make an important contribution to the integration process.

---

[52] Positive and negative integration is a conventional dichotomy in the integration literature. The first refers to the definition of common policies among countries, which determine conditions under which markets operate, while the second corresponds to the elimination of some national restrictions, which affect market competition See, for example, G. Majone, *Dilemmas of European Integration by Stealth*, Oxford: Oxford University Press, 2005.

ANNEX 13.1

Tax Revenues in Selected SSA Groups—2000 and 2010 (Percentage of GDP)

	2000			2010		
	Total Tax Revenue	Resource Tax Revenue	Non-Resource Tax Revenue	Total Tax Revenue	Resource Tax Revenue	Non-Resource Tax Revenue
WAEMU	**13.6**	**0.2**	**13.4**	**16.3**	**0.7**	**15.6**
Benin	14.1	0.0	14.1	16.3	0.0	16.3
Burkina Faso	10.8	0.0	10.8	12.7	0.0	12.7
Côte d'Ivoire	14.7	0.2	14.5	18.4	1.1	17.4
Guinea-Bissau	6.8	0.0	6.8	8.3	0.0	8.3
Mali	12.3	0.8	11.5	14.8	2.5	12.4
Niger	8.7	0.0	8.7	12.8	0.5	12.3
Senegal	16.1	0.0	16.1	18.1	0.0	18.1
Togo	11.3	0.2	11.1	15.7	0.0	15.7
ECOWAS (non WAEMU)	**31.3**	**24.8**	**6.5**	**20.0**	**12.1**	**7.9**
Cape Verde	18.2	0.0	18.2	19.1	0.0	19.1
Gambia	11.2	0.0	11.2	12.0	0.0	12.0
Ghana	11.0	0.0	11.0	13.2	0.0	13.2
Guinea	9.9	2.7	7.3	14.9	3.9	11.0
Liberia	n.a.	n.a.	n.a.	n.a.	n.a.	n.a.
Nigeria	36.7	31.2	5.5	21.4	14.5	6.8
Sierra Leone	10.8	0.0	10.8	11.7	0.0	11.7
CEMAC	**20.6**	**11.3**	**9.2**	**25.0**	**16.3**	**8.8**
Cameroon	15.7	4.9	10.8	16.0	4.5	11.5
Central African Republic	8.2	0.0	8.2	8.4	0.3	8.1
Chad	6.9	0.0	6.9	25.7	16.0	9.7
Congo, Republic of	26.2	20.3	5.9	37.1	29.6	7.5
Equatorial Guinea	18.3	15.1	3.3	28.7	26.9	1.8
Gabon	33.2	22.6	10.7	27.6	15.2	12.3
EAC	**12.3**	**0.0**	**12.3**	**15.7**	**0.0**	**15.7**
Burundi	18.3	0.0	18.3	18.0	0.0	18.0
Kenya	16.2	0.0	16.2	18.3	0.0	18.3
Rwanda	9.7	0.0	9.7	12.0	0.0	12.0
Tanzania	9.1	0.0	9.1	15.8	0.0	15.8
Uganda	9.9	0.0	9.9	11.8	0.0	11.8
SACU	**21.8**	**1.2**	**20.6**	**22.9**	**0.9**	**21.9**
Botswana	34.6	23.3	11.3	27.2	9.0	18.2
Lesotho	34.1	0.0	34.1	36.8	0.0	36.8
Namibia	28.7	1.5	27.2	26.5	1.3	25.1
South Africa	21.0	0.3	20.7	22.5	0.6	21.9
Swaziland	22.5	0.0	22.5	24.4	0.0	24.4

Source: Mansour (2014), *supra* note 5.
Note: Weighted averages are shown in bold. "n.a." means not available.

REFERENCES

Egoume, P. and A. Nayo. 2011. "Feeling the Elephant's Weight: The Impact of Côte d'Ivoire's Crisis on WAEMU Trade." Working Paper 11/80, International Monetary Fund, Washington.

Goretti, M. and H. Weisfeld. 2008. "Trade in the WAEMU: Developments and Reform Opportunities." Working Paper 08/68, International Monetary Fund, Washington.

Klemm, A. and S. Van Parys. 2012."Empirical Evidence on the Effects of Tax Incentives." *International Tax and Public Finance,* 19: 393–423.

Mansour, M. 2014. "A Tax Revenue Dataset for Sub-Sahara Africa: 1980–2010." FERDI Working Paper I19, Foundation of Studies and Research on International Development, Clermond-Ferrand, France.

Van Parys, S., and S. James. 2010. "The Effectiveness of Tax Incentives in Attracting Investment: Panel Data evidence from the CFA Franc Zone." *International Tax and Public Finance,* 17: 400–29.

CHAPTER 14

Regional Sovereign Debt Market

WAMU Securities Agency

The West African Economic and Monetary Union (WAEMU) zone is undertaking an ambitious program to develop the regional market for government securities as a means to mobilize additional financing for development. In the past decade, the sovereign debt issuances increased rapidly. However, the development of the sovereign debt market has been held back by the absence of the infrastructure for the secondary market, market fragmentation of both issuance procedures and issued instruments, lack of a structured issuance policy, and other problems. To address these issues, the regional authorities established the WAMU Securities Agency with the mandate to assist member countries with resource mobilization needed to finance growth at manageable cost and consistent with debt sustainability. The Agency has undertaken a number of important initiatives—coordinated issuance calendar, organized securities auctions, provided market oversight and distributed market information through internationally recognized platforms, prepared market guides, and provided training to market participants. These efforts allowed for reinvigorating the market and making it more transparent and accessible for potential investors. While the regional sovereign debt market still remains at an early stage of development, substantial further reforms are planned for the near future.

CREATION OF THE REGIONAL SOVEREIGN DEBT MARKET

The need to reform monetary policy was the original motive for creating the financial market.

The need to reform monetary policy led the High Authorities of the Union in 1999 to put an end to direct lending to member states of the Union by the Central Bank of West African States (BCEAO). To replace that form of financing for covering countries' budgetary deficits and cash shortfalls, the Union undertook an ambitious program to create and develop a subregional financial market, for government securities in particular, and that market has since grown swiftly.

The Central Bank initially suspended recourse by member States to direct lending from the BCEAO in 1999, and in April 2010, upon entry into force of the institutional reform of the WAEMU and the BCEAO, they eliminated that facility outright. That reform thus established the regional financial market as one of the alternative sources for financing the needs of member States.

SOVEREIGN DEBT MARKET IN 2001–13

From 2001–13 the market grew rapidly. However, it has faced a number of obstacles.

Between 2001 and 2013, the volume of issuances of public securities on the regional financial market rose from CFAF 54.9 billion to 2,274.3 billion, distributed as follows:

- 1,411.4 billion in Treasury bills awarded by auction.
- 455.8 billion in Treasury bonds awarded by auction.
- 407.1 billion in public offerings (*Appels Publics à l'Epargne*, APE)

Figure 14.1. Issuance of Government Securities, 2001–13 (CFA billions)

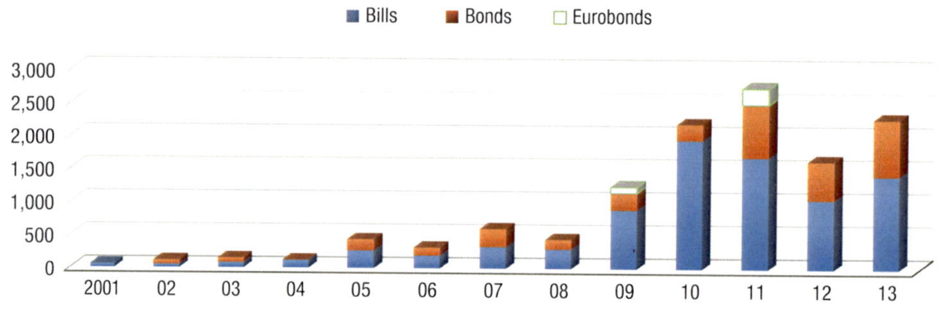

From 2001–13, issuances of sovereign securities were dominated by short-term securities. Treasury bills were issued at maturities ranging from three months to two years, and Treasury bonds at maturities beyond two years (see Figure 14.1).

However, this booming performance of the regional financial market quickly ran into a number of challenges that have hobbled its development. Those challenges relate primarily to the following factors.

Lessons Learned

After more than a decade of operations, the competent authorities of the Union have identified a series of obstacles to the proper functioning of the regional financial market.

This assessment of the functioning of the regional market was designed to allow the market to respond to the steadily growing financing needs of the Union's member economies, with respect to investment promotion policies, particularly in the social and infrastructure sectors.

The obstacles to proper functioning of the market also have to do with deep-ranging structural questions as well as with the operational organization of issuances.

a) The sovereign debt market is still primarily a "buy and hold" market.

It is apparent to the Community authorities that the lack of a dynamic secondary market constitutes an obstacle to the development of the financial market. Thus, the measures planned in the market reform are intended to increase the liquidity of the securities issued by boosting the secondary market for government securities.

b) The high degree of fragmentation of the market is harmful to its liquidity.

As government securities are issued by auction or by syndication, the Central Depository of the securities as well as the clearing system are divergent. The first [auctioned] group are handled through the BCEAO, while the second group are traded on the Regional Securities Exchange (*Bourse Régionale des Valeurs Mobilières*, BRVM). To this situation must be added the multiplicity of issuance instruments which, in addition to T-bills and bonds, include the "Sukuk" [Sharia-compliant instruments].

c) There is a lack of standardization among the securities issued.

The plethora of characteristics specific to the different issuances of the Union (interest payment due dates, modalities for amortizing principal, variable grace periods) makes it difficult to standardize securities, in contrast to the "in fine" [bullet] maturities system that is found in most developed markets. This situation also tends to make the instruments more complex, while adversely affecting their liquidity.

d) Development of the financial market has been held back by the lack of a structured issuance policy.

The issuance strategies followed have not allowed member states to maintain a presence at all points along the yield curve, or even to establish a coherent "benchmark" for constructing a yield curve.

e) A number of other weaknesses have been identified in the market.

These are:

- The need to coordinate the various calendars of the national treasuries for issuances on the regional market.
- Expanding the base of investors, which consists primarily of banking institutions in the Union.
- The application of different tax treatment from one member State to the next, a factor that does nothing to promote capital market integration.
- The need on the part of market players for better information.
- The relative lack of expertise on the part of market players, both issuers and investors.
- The need to promote government securities.

It is apparent, then, that growing resort by member States of the Union to the regional financial market will demand institutional strengthening of the issuing environment.

WAMU SECURITIES AGENCY

The governor of the BCEAO created the WAMU Securities Agency (Agence UMOA-Titres) on March 15, 2013, following a decision of the WAEMU Council of Ministers (Box 14.1).

BOX 14.1. Wamu Securities Agency

Principal mandates

The Agency provides assistance to the national treasuries in preparing government issuance strategies, coordinating their issuance program, strengthening the capacities of the national treasuries, promoting government securities among national, regional and international investors, and managing the auctioning of issuances. It is responsible for organizing issuances at auction on the regional financial market, and it assists States in placing instruments on other capital market segments. This is the case with public offerings [French *APE*, in this translation "POs"] and issuances on the international market.

Organization and financing

The Agency's organization chart comprises three bodies: the Steering Council [*Conseil d'Orientation*], which administers the Agency, supported by the Supervisory Board [*Conseil de Surveillance*] and an executive body constituted by Management.

The Steering Council is chaired by the Governor of the BCEAO or his representative, and includes the General Directors of the Treasuries of Member States of WAMU and the President of the West African Development Bank (WADB). Among its other responsibilities, it approves the strategy for mobilizing resources for the member States on the capital market, and it defines the operational means and modalities of the Agence UMOA-Titres.

The Supervisory Board is composed of the Secretary General of the Regional Council for Public Savings and Financial Markets (CREPMF) and two other members appointed by the Governor. Its primary duty is to oversee the regularity of the management of the Agence UMOA-Titres and to support and assist the Director in running the Agency.

The Director, assisted by a deputy director and an advisor, is in charge of implementing the decisions of the Steering Council, as well as the organization and management of the Agency's activities.

Financing for the Agency is derived primarily from the commissions it charges on the auctions of government securities.

In light of the assessment of the state of the regional financial market, the Council of Ministers of the Union, at its meeting of May 10, 2012, authorized the BCEAO to create a Community Agency to assist member States in mobilizing resources on the capital markets. On the basis of that decision, and with due regard to the relevant provisions of the WAEMU treaty and the charter of the BCEAO, on March 15, 2013 the governor of the Central Bank created the "*Agence UMOA-Titres*" as the regional Agency to support the issuance and management of public debt instruments.

As such, the Agency is responsible for carrying out reforms to improve the functioning of the market and to foster its development.

The Agence UMOA-Titres has the mandate to assist member States in making use of the capital markets to mobilize the resources needed to finance growth in those countries, at manageable cost and in a manner consistent with the requirements of debt sustainability.

The Agency is a market institution and its organization reflects this intention, in terms both of personnel recruitment and of its approach to financing.

SOVEREIGN DEBT MARKET REFORMS

Following its creation in March 2013, the Agency began activities in September of that year. The year 2014 thus constituted the Agency's first full year of operations.

In the wake of the exhaustive assessment of the regional financial market conducted by the Union authorities, the Agence UMOA-Titres is now responsible for taking steps, under the direction of the Steering Council, and within the framework of a coherent medium-term strategy, to gradually overcome the main obstacles to the development of the market.

During 2014 and 2015 it continued to carry out its tasks, which have related primarily to implementing reforms to strengthen the issuing environment and the operational organization of government securities auctions.

The initiatives taken by the Agency are discussed below:

a) Preparation of issuance calendars for the government securities of the Union

In consultation with the national treasuries and on the basis of budgets and cash management plans prepared by the member states, the Agency drew up annual programs for the issuance of government securities for the years 2014 and 2015. These programs, validated by the Agency's Steering Council, were distributed to domestic and international investors and to the general public. Investors have found these calendars to be a useful forecasting tool for their cash management.

Based on the lessons drawn from implementation of the issuance calendar in 2014, the Steering Council has put in place new modalities for carrying out the issuance program in 2015. This reform has optimized interventions by states of the Union on the financial market in 2015, and has offered investors greater visibility as to the operations.

b) Organization of auctions

Since its creation, the Agency has gradually taken in hand the practical organization of auctions, from the programming stage to carrying out the operations of raising funds on the financial market. With the introduction of the SAGETIL-UMOA [application], the Agency is able to play its full role in operations involving the issuance of sovereign securities through auction, offering validation and advice at all stages of the process.

The Agency's responsibilities in this context relate in particular to preparing calls for tender, pre-issue notes, and the results of issuances, which are drafted prior to and following each transaction and sent to the issuers.

c) Oversight and market intelligence

The Agency supervises the market on behalf of the national treasuries. Prior to each issuance, a pre-issue note is prepared, informing the issuer about the status of the market and the future outlook, with a view to preparing the management of the issuance concerned and the taking of decisions downstream.

Upon conclusion of the issuance, a summary report is prepared and distributed to all sovereign issuers.

d) Referencing government securities on the Reuters and Bloomberg information platforms

As part of its effort to expand the investor base and to promote government securities to local and international institutional investors, the Agency has finalized the referencing of government securities on the Reuters and Bloomberg information platforms.

At the present time, all securities in circulation are referenced on these platforms. The same is true for the issuances organized by the Agency, which are now announced via these channels, and the outcomes of these operations are also published.

Similarly, each member State of the Union, as well as the Agency, now has a presentation page, bringing together all the operations that concern it.

e) Encoding of WAMU government securities

The government securities issued at auction in the Union are encoded within the issuing institution by means of a system known as the Regional Identification Number (*Numéro d'Identification Régional*, NIR).

In a move to standardize the different compartments of the subregional market and allow the identification of securities issued through auction at the international level, the Agency has established a partnership with the regional Central Deposit and Settlement Organization (*Dépositaire Central /Banque de Règlement*, DR/BR) in order to give itself the means to codify (using the ISIN code) all securities in circulation as well as the entire stock of securities issued by auction.

Implementation of this reform should enhance investor awareness of the subregional market and facilitate the entry of international investors in the Union.

f) Development of a Guide to Good Market Practices concerning the issuance of public securities in the Union

The Agency has worked in collaboration with Afritac West to prepare a "Guide to Good Market Practices in Issuing Public Securities in the Union," defining the main guidelines to be observed in government interventions in regional and international financial markets. It is intended to serve as a reference document for issuers, by spelling out best practices to be observed, from the preparation of issuance operations until their conclusion, as well as in managing the issuer-investor relationship.

The Guide constitutes a code of good conduct, and its guidelines will be implemented progressively by member States of the Union.

g) Primary Dealers system (Spécialistes en Valeurs du Trésor, SVT)

This is the term used to designate credit institutions and Intermediation and Management Companies (*Sociétés de Gestion et d'Intermédiation*, SGI) licensed to act as privileged partners of one or more treasuries of member States of the Union in the context of operations dealing with public debt instruments, in particular participation in issuances and in the placement of public securities.

The steps involved in making the Primary Dealers System operational are well under way, and the BCEAO has initiated the selection process. It should be completed shortly, and will help to strengthen the market by consolidating the investor base and making the secondary market more dynamic.

h) Training activities

The Agence UMOA-Titres hosts training and information seminars for national treasury staff and investors. It has already held a regional seminar on "Preparation of a public securities issuance program in the WAMU zone." Seminars on the subject of assimilation have also been organized for market players.

i) Promoting securities: "road-shows" within the Union and at the international level

In cooperation with the national treasuries, the Agency has been organizing road-shows in the capitals of member states, as of the second half of 2014, in response to the growing needs of issuers, on one hand, and also to keep investors better informed.

Thus, in each of these financial centers, meetings have been organized with the leading institutional investors—banks, insurance companies, and fund administrators—now active on the public securities market.

In addition, the Agency has participated in a number of international events to promote the WAMU public securities market. It has been in regular attendance at international conferences and meetings focused on African financial markets, and has assumed a lead role in publicizing the sovereign debt of member states of the WAMU zone.

j) Launch of a website for the Agency: "www.umoatitres.org"

To improve the availability of information on sovereign issuers in the zone, the Agency has launched an Internet site—www.umoatitres.org—devoted to the issuance of public securities in the Union. That site posts notices of tender for issue auctions and the results of those auctions, as well as useful information on the regional financial market.

All these activities on the part of the Agency during 2014 and 2015, under the direction of its Steering Council, have helped, at least to a limited extent, to rationalize the environment for the issuance of public securities in the Union.

MARKET PERFORMANCE

The record of public securities issuances in the Union is a reflection of the growth strategy defined by its member States. It can be attributed, in part, to the promotion of public investments.

Table 14.1 reveals the thrust of economic policies that have had an impact on the issuance of public securities in the Union, particularly since 2013.

The acceleration in economic growth, based in part on the promotion of public investments, has led to a relative deterioration of government deficits, which are covered in part by resort to the regional and international capital markets (Eurobond issues).

The resulting issuances of public securities are presented in Table 14.2.

The determination of member States of the Union to promote public investments has had an impact on the choice of issuance maturities, which have become longer over time, as shown in Figure 14.2.

Figure 14.3 shows the lengthening of issuance maturities, reflecting in part the financing needs of public investments.

Containing the costs of issuances remains a major objective of national treasuries and of the Agence UMOA-Titres.

The rates on issues registered on the auction market during the first half of 2015 began to show a downward trend for all issuers, taken individually and for all their interventions since the beginning of the year.

TABLE 14.1

Selected Macroeconomic Indicators (Percent)

	2010	2011	2012	2013	2014	2015
Stock of market debt (excl EB)/GDP	5.42	6.91	7.28	8.41	10.59	13.16
Stock of market debt (inc EB)/GDP	5.67	9.45	9.36	10.35	12.39	15.00
Credit to the economy/GDP	19	20.7	21	22.9	24.4	25.2
Budget deficit including grants/GDP	-3.27	-3.91	-2.89	-3.07	-3.13	-3.95
Public investment rate	6.9	7.1	7.4	9	9.3	10.2
Total investment rate	21.2	18.8	22.3	25.7	24.7	26
Real growth rate of GDP	4.3	0.8	6.8	5.9	6.5	6.7

Source: BCEAO.
Note: EB = Eurobonds.

TABLE 14.2

Issuances of Public Securities in the Union

		2013	2014	2015
Treasury Bill Issues		1,411	1,467	1,127
Treasury bond issues	Regional money market	455.80	1,048.98	1,636.50
	Regional financial market (POs)	407.10	555.67	540.46
	International market	—	620.00	584.84
Total		2,274.34	3,691.36	3,889.13

Figure 14.2. Issuances of Public Securities, 2013–15
(In billions of CFA)

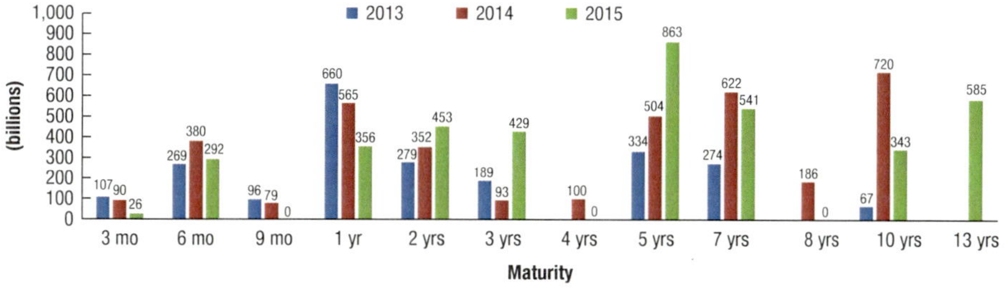

Figure 14.3. Average Weighted Term to Maturity
(In years)

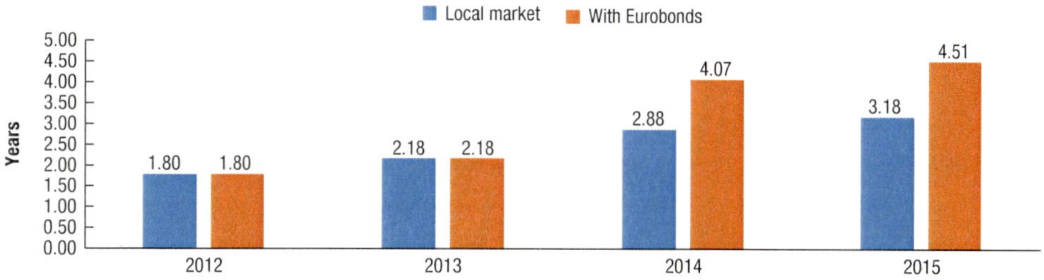

ANNEX TABLE 14.1

Issuance of Public Securities (by maturity)

	3 mos	6 mo	9 mo	1 yr	2 yrs	3 yrs	4 yrs	5 yrs	7 yrs	8 yrs	10 yrs	13 yrs	Total
Benin													
2013				247.10									247.10
2014				201.99	110.71				56.72				369.41
2015*				55.00	66.00	71.58		165.00	242.00				599.58
Burkina													
2013	91.35								121.60				212.95
2014	90.41	104.14						41.68					236.23
2015*	26.25	185.70						96.72					308.68
Côte d'Ivoire													
2013		59.26	40.63	153.06	195.84	120.88		141.43	152.20				863.30
2014				68.48	115.69	27.20		170.69	445.94	185.83	474.92		1488.75
2015*				43.10	102.81			150.00	266.99		243.27	584.84	1391.01
Guinea-Bissau													
2013					10.00								10.00
2014				15.00									15.00
2015*				11.00	15.00								26.00
Mali													
2013		108.58	55.51	74.75									238.83
2014		206.00	43.95	121.00	40.00			44.11					455.06
2015*				78.50	124.30	143.00		148.50					494.30
Niger													
2013	15.71	76.15						25.00					116.86
2014		69.80		41.00				93.30					204.10
2015*		73.50		40.00		25.00		94.80					233.30
Senegal													
2013				73.84	73.31	67.68		101.72			66.94		383.49
2014				22.41	85.54	65.90	100.00	37.17	119.00		245.00		675.00
2015*				32.00	82.17	159.18		115.46	32.26		100.20		521.27
Togo													
2013		25.00		111.35				65.46					201.81
2014			35.00	95.60				117.21					247.81
2015*		33.00		96.00	63.00	30.00		93.00					315.00
WAMU													
2013	107.06	268.99	96.14	660.10	279.15	188.56	0.00	333.61	273.80	0.00	66.94	0.00	2274.34
2014	90.41	379.94	78.95	565.47	351.94	93.10	100.00	504.15	621.65	185.83	719.92	0.00	3691.36
2015*	26.25	292.20	0.00	355.60	453.28	428.76	0.00	863.48	541.26	0.00	343.47	584.84	3889.14

* Estimates

PART 4

Regional Monetary Policy

PREFACE

The West African Economic and Monetary Union (WAEMU) is a currency union with a fixed exchange rate and limited capital mobility and, therefore, an independent monetary policy in the short term. The Central Bank of West African States (BCEAO) conducts the single monetary policy with the main goal of preserving price stability and supporting economic growth. However, the effectiveness of the WAEMU's monetary policy remains low, with a weak reaction of market interest rates and inflation to BCEAO's policy actions.

The institutional framework for monetary policy has been recently revamped. The new framework includes changes to the BCEAO's decision-making bodies, revisions to the objectives of monetary policy, and a larger set of operational tools. The main decision makers now include the governor; the Monetary Policy Committee (MPC); the board of directors; the audit committee; and the national credit councils, with one council in each member state of the WAEMU. The MPC is responsible for setting monetary policy in the WAEMU. It is headed by the governor and meets four times a year for ordinary sessions. In addition, ad hoc sessions may be called. The MPC is also responsible for defining the instruments used to achieve the policy objectives. The BCEAO regularly publishes communiqués on the meetings of the MPC and quarterly a detailed report on monetary policy. To strengthen financial supervision, a Financial Stability Committee, headed by the governor and comprising mainly regulators (banking commission, social security regulator, insurance regulator, and the regional council for savings and financial markets) has also been put in place.

Price stability is the main objective of monetary policy. Price stability is defined as an annual average inflation rate of 2 percent plus or minus 1 percentage point and set over a 24-month horizon. This rate is set as the operational indicator. A number of secondary objectives of monetary policy are mentioned in the WAEMU documents. The BCEAO Statute (Article 8) also mentions support of sound and sustainable growth as a secondary objective of its monetary policy. Under the WAEMU Treaty (Article 62), monetary policy should also support integration in the economic union, "without prejudice to objectives assigned to it." In addition, the Statute of the BCEAO specifies an intermediate target of monetary policy (Article 76). For three consecutive months, the ratio of the average foreign assets of the BCEAO to its sight liabilities (banknotes in circulation and deposits of banks, governments, and other organizations) should exceed 20 percent. In the opposite case, the MPC must take an appropriate action to restore the ratio.

In the institutional setup with a fixed exchange rate, is there scope and need for monetary policy in the WAEMU? Chapter 15, Monetary Policy in a Currency Union, seeks to answer this question. Although at first glance, the answer would appear to be "no," as the WAEMU is a currency union with a fixed peg to the euro. However, the limited de facto capital mobility provides some scope for monetary policy. Institutional and other characteristics jointly needed for an independent monetary policy under a fixed exchange rate regime are present. The BCEAO can control regional interest rates, which diverge substantially from the euro area rates, as capital mobility is limited. Moreover, the BCEAO has substantial weight in the banking system and therefore can exercise sufficient influence on monetary conditions in the area. The BCEAO has the needed instruments (interest rates and reserve requirements) for achieving the goals of its monetary policy. In the absence of the exchange rate channel, all other channels of monetary policy transmission (through the volume of credit, interest rates, asset prices, and expectations) can, in principle, be more active. However, shallow financial markets and interest rate rigidities impede the transmission of monetary policy signals and the link from the BCEAO's policy actions to market interest rates and inflation remains extremely weak, and can affect both only marginally. To improve monetary policy implementation, the BCEAO should also continue developing deep and functioning interbank, secondary debt, stock, and other financial markets. Improving the transmission of BCEAO policy actions to inflation by reducing price and interest rate rigidities, in particular by introducing more flexibility of deposit rates, is also important.

The transmission of the BCEAO's single monetary policy to individual WAEMU countries has remained limited, despite some recent progress in regional financial development. Chapter 16, Country Effects of a Single Monetary Policy, assesses the effectiveness of the transmission mechanism of the BCEAO's monetary policy for individual members of the WAEMU. The impact of a single monetary policy, although limited for the region as a whole, may be significant for individual countries with more developed financial markets and/or different product market structures and institutions. The hypothesis of an asymmetric transmission of the single monetary policy actions to individual countries can be tested empirically. In particular, the impact of the policy interest rate changes on each WAEMU country's deposit and lending rates and inflation can be tested. BCEAO policy rate changes have no impact on deposit rates. The main channel of transmission of the single monetary policy to individual countries is through the link between the BCEAO's single policy rate and the lending rates in individual countries; this link is relatively strong in Benin, Burkina Faso, Guinea-Bissau, Mali Senegal, and Togo and very weak in Côte d'Ivoire and Niger. The link to core inflation is observed only in some countries. However, the link to overall inflation, which is the ultimate goal of monetary policy, can be reliably traced only in Benin, Senegal, and Togo. In this context, further developing financial markets, increasing financial intermediation, and fostering competition in the banking sector are crucial to improving the effectiveness of the single monetary policy for individual WAEMU countries.

Liquidity injections by the BCEAO to commercial banks have increased recently and a substantial part has been used to fund purchases of government securities. Chapter 17, Liquidity Injections and Risks, documents that the liquidity position of the commercial banking system vis-à-vis the BCEAO has recently swung from a structural liquidity surplus to a deficit. The underlying causes are likely to include a combination of widening fiscal and external imbalance, and carry-trade activity by some banks. These developments, in turn, pose risks to fiscal and financial stability, financial development, and monetary policy effectiveness. WAEMU authorities should nevertheless monitor closely these trends in liquidity and consider whether any preemptive policy action might be appropriate, in order to prevent such risks from crystallizing. Possible measures include reducing fiscal deficits of individual WAEMU countries, which would reduce commercial banks' demands for funding from the central bank to finance them; discouraging carry-trade activity by commercial banks; mitigating market distortions through changes in prudential regulation; relaxing regulatory barriers to entry for financial institutions other than domestic banks; and issuing a greater share of public debt externally.

The implementation of the BCEAO's monetary policy with a view to achieving the objective of price stability requires a better understanding of the degree of sensitivity of the inflation rate to changes in the economic and financial environment. Chapter 18, Monetary Policy and Inflation, explored the impact of a change in the key interest rates of the BCEAO, as well as other economic, monetary, and financial aggregates, on inflation in the WAEMU. Specifically, the effects of interest rates, the money supply, imported inflation from the euro area, domestic credit, the fiscal deficit, and the output gap on inflation are evaluated. Econometric models suggest that most monetary and financial variables have an impact on the inflation rate. Monetary and financial variables have an influence on inflation. Their impact on the evolution of prices is evident over the short and long term. In particular, the impact of the BCEAO marginal lending rate and money market rate on inflation is significant, irrespective of the time horizon. As for the impact of domestic credit, it is just as significant as that of the BCEAO's key rates and the money supply. The impact of domestic credit on inflation appears to be stronger than that of interest rates. Furthermore, the output gap, which has been negative, has had an overall moderating effect on inflation over the recent period. The impact observed over the long term is related to the fact that the transmission of interest rate fluctuations to inflation depends to a large extent on how they are reflected in borrowing rates and in demand among economic agents. Finally, the fiscal deficit (or public spending), as well as imported inflation, have considerable effects on the dynamics of inflation in the WAEMU. The impact of imported inflation has been generally stronger than that of the marginal lending rate.

CHAPTER 15

Monetary Policy in a Currency Union

ALEXEI KIREYEV

Is there scope and need for monetary policy in the West African Economic and Monetary Union (WAEMU)? At first glance the answer would appear to be "no," as the WAEMU is a currency union with a fixed peg to the euro. However, the limited de facto capital mobility provides some scope for monetary policy. The institutional and other characteristics jointly needed for an independent monetary policy under a fixed exchange rate regime are present. The Central Bank of West African States (BCEAO) can control regional interest rates, which diverge substantially from the euro area rates, as capital mobility is limited. Moreover, the BCEAO has substantial weight in the banking system and therefore can exercise sufficient influence on monetary conditions in the area. The BCEAO has the needed instruments (interest rates and reserve requirements) for achieving the goals of its monetary policy. In the absence of the exchange rate channel, all other channels of monetary policy transmission (through the volume of credit, interest rates, asset prices, and expectations) can, in principle be more active. However, shallow financial markets and interest rate rigidities impede the transmission of monetary policy signals and the link from the BCEAO's policy actions to market interest rates and inflation remains extremely weak and can affect both only marginally. To improve monetary policy implementation, the BCEAO should also continue developing deep and functioning interbank, secondary debt, stock, and other financial markets. Improving the transmission of BCEAO policy actions to inflation by reducing price and interest rate rigidities, in particular by introducing more flexibility of deposit rates, is also important.

The goal of this chapter is to explore the preconditions needed for the BCEAO to have an impact on domestic demand and price conditions in the WAEMU. On theoretical grounds, under the constraints of a fixed exchange rate regime and capital controls, several preconditions should be met. First, the BCEAO should have an adequate monetary policy framework and functioning monetary policy instruments. Second, there should be a clear transmission between these instruments and market interest rates. This precondition requires that the BCEAO should be able to influence regional market rates and that they are not determined by exogenous forces, given the peg to the euro. Finally, there should be a clear link between BCEAO policy actions and inflation.

A priori, based on theoretical considerations, in a fixed exchange rate arrangement any central bank should have some scope for an independent monetary policy, if capital mobility is restricted. This follows directly from the so called "trilemma" in international macroeconomics, suggesting that countries cannot simultaneously enjoy full capital mobility, fixed exchange rates, and monetary autonomy (Obstfeld, Shambaugh, and Taylor 2005 and 2008; Montiel 2009). Recently, Klein and Shambaugh (2013) confirmed that extensive capital controls enable a country to have monetary autonomy, as suggested by the trilemma. Partial capital controls, however, do not generally enable a country to have greater monetary control than is the case with open capital accounts, unless they are quite extensive. According to Rey (2013), the global financial cycle has transformed the trilemma into a dilemma. Now, independent monetary policies are possible if and only if the capital account is managed directly or indirectly, irrespective of the exchange rate regime.

MONETARY POLICY FRAMEWORK

The BCEAO prepares an annual macroeconomic framework to inform decisions on monetary policy. The framework includes projections for the real, fiscal, monetary, and external sectors. The level of credit to the economy is aligned with the nominal growth and is adjusted by changing the money supply using the assumption on velocity. The macroeconomic framework is used to inform decisions of the Monetary Policy Committee (MPC) and helps identify key challenges that may face the region in the upcoming year, in particular regarding inflation and growth.

The BCEAO is working on an improved model for inflation forecasting. The model is intended for forecasting inflation by components, such as underlying inflation (total inflation excluding energy and fresh agricultural products), petroleum products, solid fuels, electricity, and others. The projection horizons are 3, 12, and 24 months. Projections for the current year are made public on the BCEAO website. One of the purposes of the model is to identify the component of inflation controllable by monetary policy instruments. Preliminary results indicate that inflation in the zone is largely determined by import prices (because a substantial part of the Consumer Price Index basket is imported), local supply-side shocks (droughts and conflicts), public expenditure (mainly salary and other current expenditure increases), and, to a lesser extent, excess money supply.

The WAEMU region maintains a fixed exchange rate regime but defense of the exchange rate is not currently a binding constraint. The unlimited support and the convertibility guarantees provided to the CFA by the French Treasury reduce the need to build up reserves and therefore allow the BCEAO to change its balance sheet to achieve the goals of economic policy. The operations account with the French Treasury functions as a current account for the zone. All purchases or sales of foreign currencies or euros against CFA francs are settled through a debit or credit to the operations account. The stock of reserves cannot be less than 20 percent of the base money. This should drive corrective measures. In practice, the BCEAO's official reserves have always exceeded this threshold substantially and have been about 100 percent of the base money in recent years. In principle, the operations account can turn negative in the case of balance of payments difficulties, but this has never happened. In such a case, the French Treasury would provide foreign reserve advances to the BCEAO account in its overdraft option.[1]

According to traditional metrics, the BCEAO's official reserves have been adequate for defending the peg. They amounted to CFAF 6,942 billion (about US$12 billion) at the end of 2015. Reserves coverage remained adequate at 4.3 months of next-year imports, 40 percent of broad money, and about 80 percent of short-term liabilities. An alternative method to assess adequacy takes into account the cost of holding reserves, and their benefits in terms of mitigating the impact of macroeconomic volatility. According to this approach, the optimal reserve coverage in the WAEMU varies between 5 and 10 months of imports, depending on the interest rate differential with the rest of the world. This approach, however, does not take into account the access to reserves guaranteed by the French Treasury under the franc zone arrangement.

CAPITAL MOBILITY

The WAEMU region maintains capital controls on most capital transactions with nonresidents. In all WAEMU countries, the mechanisms of capital controls are comparable and administered jointly by the national ministry of finance and the BCEAO. Although the rules differ slightly from country to country, in general, prior approval by the ministry of finance is required for virtually

[1] Although convertibility is guaranteed by the French Treasury, it does not mean that this guarantee is without any limits. For instance, large imbalances in the region ultimately led to a devaluation of the CFA franc in 1994.

all *outward capital transfers*, except for the amortization of debts and repayment of short-term loans. In particular, the authorization by the ministry of finance is required for the following capital flows from residents to nonresidents: (1) all direct investment abroad by residents, including investment through foreign companies under direct or indirect control of residents; (2) purchases of foreign securities; (3) purchases of money market instruments; (4) granting of guarantees and sureties; (5) financial credits and loans; (6) reinvestment of liquidation proceeds; and (7) gifts, endowments, and other transfer of assets (AREAER, 2014). In addition, outward transfers necessary to service credit facilities to nonresidents require an exchange authorization, subject to approval by the BCEAO.

Although the regulation of *inward capital transfers* is more liberal, and many are subject to declaration just for statistical purposes, substantial restrictions exist. For example, authorized foreign exchange dealers must surrender to the BCEAO in exchange for CFA francs all assets denominated in euros and other currencies held in their establishments; securities and mutual funds issued outside the WAEMU by nonresidents may not be listed on a regional securities exchange; prior authorization by the Regional Council on Public Savings and Financial Markets is required for issue by nonresidents of securities, real assets, and money market instruments; sales of corporate securities to nonresidents resulting in foreign control of domestic establishments require declaration to the national ministry of finance.

The use of the CFA franc outside the WAEMU is not allowed. The CFA franc cannot be used as payment for current international transactions or as capital with countries outside the WAEMU. Swaps of CFA francs for foreign currencies are prohibited. Registered intermediaries must refrain from carrying out any transactions involving forward selling of CFA francs in their relations with nonresidents. Travelers can export CFA franc banknotes, and the BCEAO does not repurchase exported banknotes. In addition, the exchange of BCEAO banknotes between authorized intermediaries and their correspondents outside the WAEMU is prohibited. The export of BCEAO banknotes between licensed intermediary banks and their correspondent banks outside the WAEMU is strictly prohibited. The exchange system is free of restrictions on payments and transfers for current international transactions.

In the case of the WAEMU, limited capital mobility and different credit risks are also reflected in a substantial and persistent differential between the policy rates in the euro area and in the WAEMU. Until recently, the changes of the BCEAO policy rate have broadly followed the trend—but have not reflected the level—of the European Central Bank (ECB) policy rates. Since 2009, the BCEAO maximum lending rate has been historically higher than the ECB marginal lending facility rate by 250 basis points (Table 15.1). The gap between the BCEAO's minimum bid rate and the ECB's deposit facility rate has been even larger, at 300 basis points for the minimum policy rate, reflecting aggressive interest rate cuts by the ECB to forestall the impact of the financial crisis. The gap between both minimum and maximum policy rates declined in 2013 to 250 basis points as the BCEAO cut its policy rates three times during the year. In 2014, the differential increased again to over 300 basis points. This persistent divergence of policy rates may have reflected differences in macroeconomic priorities. While the ECB was concerned mainly with providing additional stimulus to the economy to address the crisis in the euro area, there was no visible crisis in the WAEMU area, and the BCEAO focused primarily on handling second-round inflationary pressures from import prices and domestic supply shocks.

MONETARY CONTROL

Three approaches have been suggested in the literature for checking monetary policy independence under the fixed exchange rate regime. The first approach, suggested by Shortland and Stasavage (2004) and Veyrune (2007), implies checking for cointegration between reserve money

TABLE 15.1

BCEAO and ECB Policy Rates

	Ceiling Policy Rate			Central Policy Rate			Floor Policy Rate		
	ECB	BCEAO	Differential	ECB	BCEAO	Differential	ECB	BCEAO	Differential
	Marginal lending facility rate	Marginal lending rate		Main refinancing operations rate (fixed rate)	n.a.	n.a.	Deposit facility rate	Minimum bid rate	
2006	4.50	4.25	−0.25	3.50	n.a.	n.a.	2.50	3.25	0.75
2007	5.00	4.25	−0.75	4.00	n.a.	n.a.	3.00	3.25	0.25
2008	3.00	4.75	1.75	2.50	n.a.	n.a.	2.00	3.75	1.75
2009	1.75	4.25	2.50	1.00	n.a.	n.a.	0.25	3.25	3.00
2010	1.75	4.25	2.50	1.00	n.a.	n.a.	0.25	3.25	3.00
2011	1.75	4.25	2.50	1.00	n.a.	n.a.	0.25	3.25	3.00
2012	1.50	4.00	2.50	0.75	n.a.	n.a.	0.00	3.00	3.00
2013	1.00	3.50	2.50	0.50	n.a.	n.a.	0.00	2.50	2.50
2014	1.00	3.50	2.50	1.50	n.a.	n.a.	1.00	2.50	1.50

Sources: Central Bank of West African States (BCEAO); and European Central Bank (ECB).

ECB

Marginal lending facility rate is the rate charged for the overnight provision of liquidity. It normally provides a ceiling for the overnight market interest rate.

Main refinancing operations rate (fixed rate) is the rate set for regular liquidity-providing reverse transactions with a weekly frequency and a maturity of one week.

Deposit facility rate is the rate paid for overnight deposits with national central banks. It normally provides a floor for the overnight market interest rate.

BCEAO

Minimum bid rate (taux minimum de soumission, Taux minimum des appeles d'offres), is the minimum policy rate at which commercial banks can submit their bids for liquidity at weekly or monthly liquidity auctions conducted by the BCEAO.

Taux du guichet de prêt marginal is the maximum policy rate at which banks can borrow liquidity at the BCEAO outside auctions for one or seven days against an appropriate collateral.

and net foreign assets of the central bank. The second approach is based on assessing the deviation of inflation, as the main target of monetary policy, in the country of interest from the country of the peg. Finally, the third approach views monetary independence as the ability of countries to set their own nominal interest rates and implies testing the sensitivity of the local interest rate to the foreign rate.

The first approach is based on the assumption that, with a fixed exchange rate, central banks cannot control money supply because they have to buy and sell foreign exchange to maintain the peg. Therefore, their balance sheets and the changes in reserve money may largely reflect the movements of net foreign assets, without leaving space for monetary policy, unless such movements are fully sterilized. In the case of the WAEMU, if the BCEAO is indeed successful in controlling its reserve money, irrespective of the fixed exchange rate arrangement, then there should be no correlation between its reserve money and net foreign assets. If changes in reserve money correlate with the changes in net foreign assets, the BCEAO most likely cannot control the net foreign assets counterpart of reserve money and therefore has no scope for an independent monetary policy. On the contrary, if changes in reserve money do not correlate with changes in net foreign assets, this may mean the BCEAO has scope for an active monetary policy aimed at changing its reserve money by influencing its key counterparts. The problem with this approach is that changes in net domestic assets may also lead to changes in reserve money. The results of this approach should hold only if the impact of net domestic assets on reserve money is controllable by the national governments and the BCEAO, which may be the case, as net domestic assets largely depend on the change in the net government position vis-à-vis the banking system and credits extended by the BCEAO to the commercial banks in the area. Therefore, in principle, the BCEAO, in close cooperation with the government, can control its net domestic assets and the impact of its changes on reserve money.

The second approach to assessing monetary independence would consist of looking at the deviation of regional inflation in the WAEMU from inflation in the euro area. The efficiency of an active monetary policy could be then assessed by the degree of deviations between regional inflation and the inflation in the euro area. Because of exogenous price shocks affecting WAEMU countries, the WAEMU-euro area inflation differential may have justified an interest rate differential between the euro area and WAEMU rates. However, in the WAEMU context, large inflation differentials may not signal directly the absence of monetary control because inflation in the WAEMU is highly sensitive to WAEMU-specific shocks.

In this chapter, the third approach is used to check directly the impact of changes in the interest rates in the euro area on the interest rates in the WAEMU area (Annex 15.1). If the rates in the euro area and the WAEMU are each nonstationary and individually integrated, but a certain linear combination of them has a lower order of integration, then they could be considered cointegrated. Assuming changes in WAEMU rates depend mainly on changes in the rates in the euro area, in this case the BCEAO would not be able to conduct an independent monetary policy. In the opposite case, if no cointegration is found between the two rates, the BCEAO may have some scope for monetary policy. These results should be interpreted with caution. The existence of a cointegration relationship does not imply that changes in euro rates are directly translated to WAEMU rates. Cointegration would simply mean that the interest rates tend to move together in the long term.

Marginal lending facility rates, as reported by the ECB and the BCEAO, are used for the estimation. The data used are average monthly marginal lending facility rates (called money market rates in the WAEMU) for 2008–13 (through October) for the ECB and the BCEAO. The BCEAO published weekly, monthly, and quarterly marginal lending rates. The choice of the average monthly rate was based on the fact that it represents a weighted average rate for liquidity injections at both weekly and monthly liquidity auctions. Alternatively, interbank rates could have been used but in the case of the WAEMU, these rates are not representative of the financial system, as the interbank market is very limited. Although other researchers used mainly OLS regressions of the domestic interest rate on a foreign interest, this chapter applies a more sophisticated cointegration framework that allows testing simultaneously for a potential short-term and long-term impact of ECB marginal lending facility rates on corresponding BCEAO rates.

In the WAEMU, econometric testing finds no cointegration between ECB and BCEAO rates. A multivariate test for stationarity of each variable strongly suggests that both BCEAO and ECB rates are not stationary and that the search for a cointegration is legitimate. The cointegration rank is zero, which may be interpreted as evidence of no cointegration vectors between the two rates (Annex Table 15.1.1). The trace statistic with a degree of freedom adjustment is well below the 95 percent critical value. The estimated adjustment coefficient in the BCEAO regression is negative and in the ECB is positive, but both are not statistically significant. This suggests their linear combination cannot potentially converge to the steady state suggesting lack of a cointegration vector.

Therefore, the BCEAO has all of the institutional characteristics jointly needed for an independent monetary policy, at least in the short term: (1) a monetary policy framework with price stability as a primary target; (2) capital controls, mainly on outflows; and (3) the ability to set nominal interest rates in the region that are not sensitive to changes in the euro area rates.

Does the BCEAO have adequate monetary policy instruments and can it effectively control them? In principle, the BCEAO has at its disposal two main monetary policy instruments: interest rates and reserve requirements. Both are set by discretionary decisions of the MPC in pursuit of the goals of the BCEAO's monetary policy. Since 2009, it has changed the policy rates five times (four of which came after 2012) and amended the reserve requirements three times.

INTEREST RATES

The BCEAO sets discretionarily two policy rates and targets the level of the interbank rate as an operational indicator for its monetary policy (Box 15.1).

The BCEAO targets the interbank interest rate as its operational target. In the past few years, the BCEAO has broadly succeeded in keeping the interbank rate within the corridor between the two policy rates. The one-week interbank rate has largely stayed within the targeted interval, with the exception of a period of high volatility in mid-2012 and again in mid-2014, although its behavior remains very erratic (Figure 15.1). Such behavior of the interbank rate may show that the interbank market is very narrow, segmented between a few relatively large international banks and many small local banks, and banks with abundant liquidity seem unwilling to lend to other relatively weaker banks. Moreover, the interbank rate is set mainly in transactions between banks of the same groups. Therefore, smaller banks, which do not belong to such groups, largely do not have access to liquidity on the interbank market.

BOX 15.1. BCEAO: Policy and Market Interest Rates

Policy Interest Rates

- The minimum bid rate (*taux minimum de soumission*) is the minimum rate at which commercial banks can submit their bids for liquidity at weekly or monthly liquidity auctions conducted by the BCEAO. It is the main policy rate.
- The maximum lending rate (*taux du guichet de prêt marginal*) is the maximum policy rate at which banks can borrow liquidity from the BCEAO outside auctions for one or seven days against appropriate collateral. It is currently set at 100 basis points above the minimum bid rate.

Market Interest Rates. Other rates depend on market conditions. The money market rate—the marginal rate of liquidity injections (*taux marginal*)—is set by multiple rate auctions for the BCEAO's liquidity injections. Historically, the BCEAO's marginal rate of liquidity injections has always been close to the minimum bid rate, largely making the BCEAO a price maker at liquidity auctions. The interbank rate (*taux interbancaire*) is set in the interbank market. For statistical purposes, the BCEAO calculates an average weighted rate (*taux moyen pondéré*) and a reference rate (*taux de référence contreparties éligibles*) for the collateral used in each auction.

Figure 15.1. WAEMU: Policy and Market Interest Rates
(Percent)

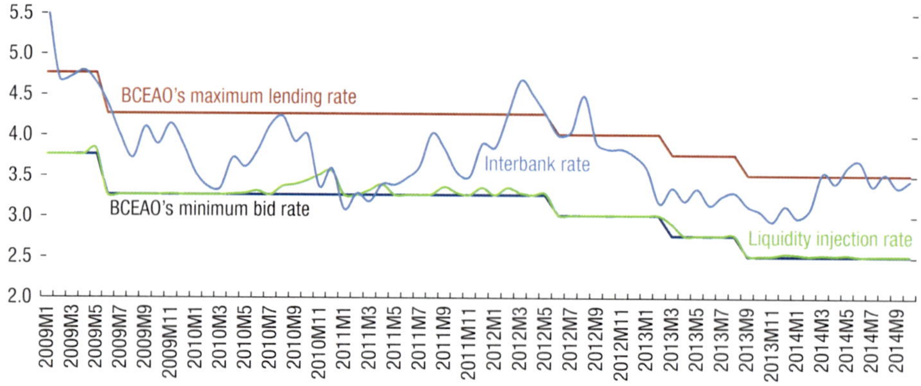

Source: Central Bank of West African States.
Note: BCEAO = Central Bank of West African States; WAEMU = West African Economic and Monetary Union.

To steer the interbank rate within the corridor, the BCEAO uses liquidity injections operations. Short-term (one-week) liquidity injections are made mainly by a weekly tender (*guichet hebdomadaire des appels d'offres*). The amounts injected at each auction largely depend on the change in the interbank rate required to keep it within the corridor and forecasts of cash requirements by banks. The BCEAO offers liquidity at the marginal liquidity injection rate, which generally has been close to the minimum bid rate, currently set at 2.5 percent. Although historically the marginal liquidity injection rate diverged from the minimum bid rate, in particular at end-2010, later the gap between the minimum bid rate and the marginal rate narrowed sharply to almost zero. Long-term (1–12 month) liquidity injections are performed by a monthly tender (*guichet des appels d'offres à un mois*). Through this window, the BCEAO offers liquidity at auctions at variable or fixed interest rates. Monthly amounts offered at weekly liquidity auctions in 2014 amounted to about CFA 5,000 billion compared with CFA 750 billion injected at monthly auctions.

LIQUIDITY INJECTIONS

In the past several years, the WAEMU region has been characterized by structural liquidity surpluses. In 2002–14, commercial banks held, on average, half of their reserves in excess reserves with the BCEAO (Figure 15.2).

In spite of excess liquidity, the BCEAO has injected additional liquidity. In addition to steering the interest rate, an important reason for these injections was that the BCEAO had to step in for a narrow and highly segmented interbank market and help weaker banks to get liquidity, which they could not obtain from the interbank market. As a result, the level of reserves in the banking system stayed broadly unchanged. Moreover, their composition remained also broadly unchanged, with roughly half attributable to required reserves and half to excess reserves (Table 15.2).

However, the sources of financing of banks' reserves have changed. In the past, accumulation of net foreign assets was a main factor behind the fluctuations of banks' excess reserves. But since mid-2011, banks' own reserves (that is, reserves net of BCEAO interventions), have been declining, reflecting a decline of net foreign assets, driven by a growing current account deficit and nonrepatriation of export proceeds by some exporters (Figure 15.3). The coverage ratio of banks' required reserves by their own reserves fell from 1.4 to –0.7 between 2011 and 2014. Banks found themselves in a structural liquidity deficit. The BCEAO had to step up injections and

Figure 15.2. WAEMU: Required and Excess Reserves (CFA billions)

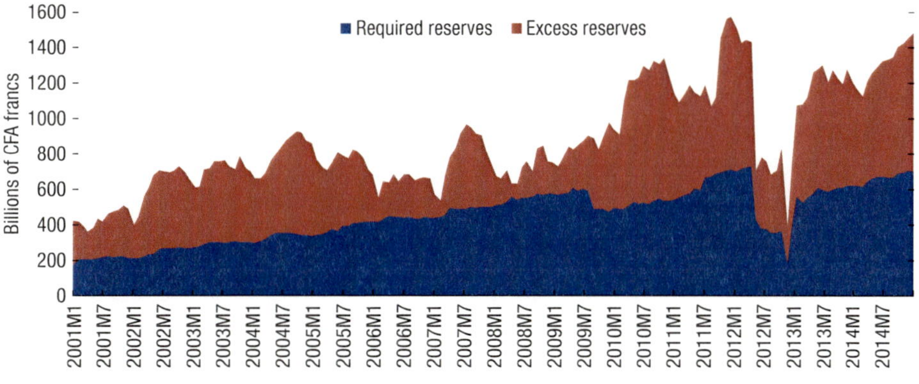

Source: Central Bank of West African States.

TABLE 15.2

Banks' Reserves: Composition and Sources of Financing (Percent)

	Required and excess reserves											
	Dec-11	Jun-12	Sep-12	Dec-12	Mar-13	Jun-13	Sep-13	Dec-13	Mar-14	Jun-14	Sep-14	Dec-14
Composition of reserves	100	100	100	100	100	100	100	100	100	100	100	100
Required reserves	51	42	44	49	48	47	49	55	52	49	49	47
Excess reserves	49	58	56	51	52	53	51	45	48	51	51	53
Sources of reserves	100	100	100	100	100	100	100	100	100	100	100	100
BCEAO refinancing	41	66	73	89	83	88	92	134	131	145	140	134
Banks' own reserves	59	34	27	11	17	12	8	−34	−31	−45	−40	−34
Own reserves/required reserves	1.1	0.8	0.6	0.2	0.4	0.2	0.2	−0.6	−0.6	−0.9	−0.8	−0.7
BCEAO refinancing/ excess reserves	0.8	1.1	1.3	1.7	1.6	1.7	1.8	3.0	2.7	2.9	2.7	2.5

Source: IMF staff calculations based on Central Bank of West African States information.
Note: Bank reserves = Banks' own reserves + BCEAO injections.

Figure 15.3. Evolution of Banks' Own Reserves (CFA billions)

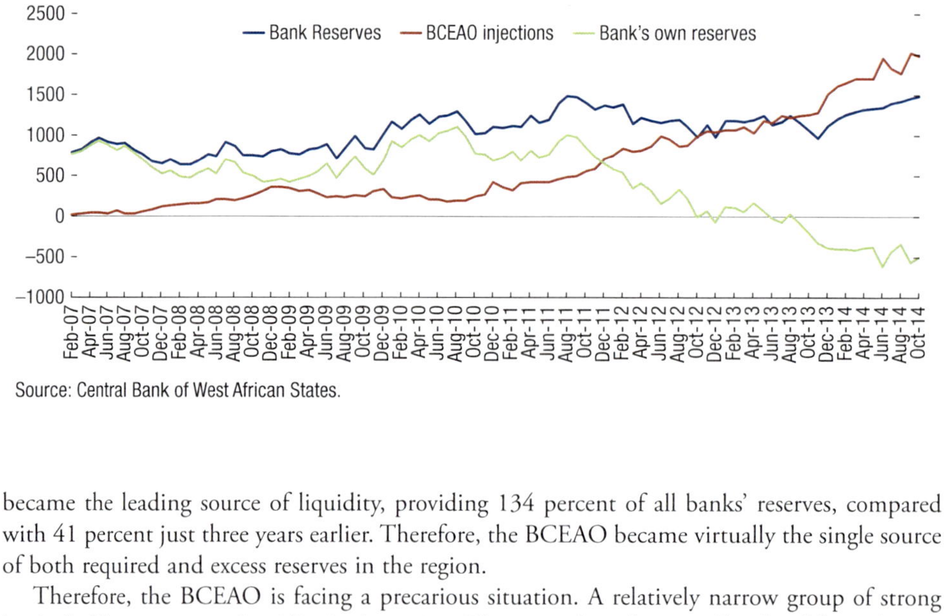

Source: Central Bank of West African States.

became the leading source of liquidity, providing 134 percent of all banks' reserves, compared with 41 percent just three years earlier. Therefore, the BCEAO became virtually the single source of both required and excess reserves in the region.

Therefore, the BCEAO is facing a precarious situation. A relatively narrow group of strong banks holds most excess liquidity in the region. This excess liquidity is well isolated from the rest of the banking system, as stronger banks cannot use it at all to buy government securities because most of them have already reached their internal statutory ceilings on country-specific exposures imposed by their headquarters. These banks do not lend to the private sector either, as outside seasonal financing of agricultural campaigns there are not feasible projects meriting financing in the region. Finally, they do not lend to weaker banks through the interbank market either, as strong banks simply do not trust them. At the same time, the majority of banks in this fragmented banking system have so little liquidity that they are not capable of meeting the reserve requirement ratio.

Therefore, excess liquidity seems to be isolated in a few banks and does not spill over into the rest of the banking system. This precarious situation creates a de facto structural liquidity deficit and should, in principle, help the BCEAO in conducting monetary policy. Therefore, the BCEAO has an active tool for monetary policy in the form of liquidity injections and can, in principle, influence the interest rate level in the region. However, this interest rate does not fully reflect liquidity conditions, as the interbank market is very shallow and consists of several relatively weak banks trading with each other, with stronger banks not participating at all. Moreover, in addition to managing the interest rate, the BCEAO has to use these injections to provide liquidity to banks facing structural liquidity needs, mainly to preserve the integrity of the financial system. Such injections allow weaker banks to engage in the carry trade by acquiring government paper and remain afloat profiting from the interest rate differential.

Massive liquidity injections by the BCEAO have adverse implications for the development of the interbank market. With a segmented banking system across individual WAEMU countries and inside each country between large national and small local banks, continued BCEAO injections used to replenish reserves create strong disincentives for weaker individual banks to actively seek liquidity in the market, ultimately delaying further development of a functioning interbank market.

The increased provision of liquidity to commercial banks and their rising exposure to governments may also pose risks to financial stability. In particular, it exposes banks to sovereign risks and potential maturity and liquidity mismatches should the BCEAO be required to tighten monetary policy in the future. The rising share of credit to sovereigns financed by central bank liquidity provision also stifles financial market development.

There may be an alternative view of the sharp increase of BCEAO's refinancing operations. This increase can be seen as temporary and necessitated by the nascent stage of development of the interbank market. With the development of the interbank market, the need for central bank refinancing will abate.

In sum, interest rates are the BCEAO's single most active monetary policy instrument. Liquidity injections have played an important role in steering the interbank rate, signaling to market participants the BCEAO's clear intention to conduct a more active monetary policy and influence financial conditions in the area. Such injections have also sent an important signal of the BCEAO's ability to step in temporarily for an inactive interbank market and address liquidity shortages in certain parts of the segmented financial system to preserve its stability. At the same time, the BCEAO's role in the financial system has become substantial, which poses prudential risks and may delay market development.

RESERVE REQUIREMENTS

The BCEAO sets reserve requirements and uses them mainly as a monetary policy instrument, and also as a tool of prudential regulation. The reserve requirement ratio is calculated as a share of banks' deposits, short-term credit, and gross external assets. For many years, the required reserve ratios were differentiated by country to address country-specific problems, primarily differences in liquidity conditions among individual countries (Table 15.3). The highest ratios applied to commercial banks in Benin, Burkina Faso, Mali, Niger, and Senegal. Guinea-Bissau, Togo, and Côte d'Ivoire had the lowest required reserve ratio. Because the differentiated reserve requirements led to a number of distortions, the BCEAO gradually reduced the differences in the required coefficients among the WAEMU countries and ultimately unified the reserve requirement at 5 percent for all banks in the region in 2012.

Reserve requirements have had an impact on excess reserves in the regions. Based on historical trends, there has been an obvious correlation between the reserve requirement ratio and the level of excess reserves (Figure 15.4). For example, in 2002–05, the BCEAO increased, in steps, the average reserve requirement, which was associated with a decline in excess reserves. The cuts in the reserve requirement ratio in 2009 and 2012 were associated with increased excess reserves. In 2005–09, however, when the reserve requirements did not change, the trend in excess reserves was not clear, with sharp swings in both directions.

TABLE 15.3

Reserve Requirements Ratio (Percent)

	11/16/2000–04/15/2002	04/15/2002–03/15/2004	03/16/2004–06/15/2005	05/16/2005–05/15/2009	06/16/2009–05/16/2010	05/16/2010–12/16/2010	12/16/2010–03/15/2012	After 03/15/2012
Benin	9.00	9.00	13.00	15.00	9.00	7.00	7.00	5.00
Burkina Faso	3.00	3.00	3.00	7.00	7.00	7.00	7.00	5.00
Côte d'Ivoire	5.00	5.00	5.00	5.00	5.00	5.00	7.00	5.00
Guinea-Bissau	3.00	3.00	3.00	3.00	3.00	5.00	7.00	5.00
Mali	3.00	9.00	9.00	9.00	7.00	7.00	7.00	5.00
Niger	5.00	5.00	5.00	9.00	7.00	7.00	7.00	5.00
Senegal	9.00	9.00	9.00	9.00	7.00	7.00	7.00	5.00
Togo	3.00	3.00	3.00	3.00	3.00	5.00	7.00	5.00
Average	5.00	5.75	6.25	7.50	6.00	6.25	7.00	5.00

Source: Central Bank of West African States.

Figure 15.4. Reserve Requirements and Excess Reserves

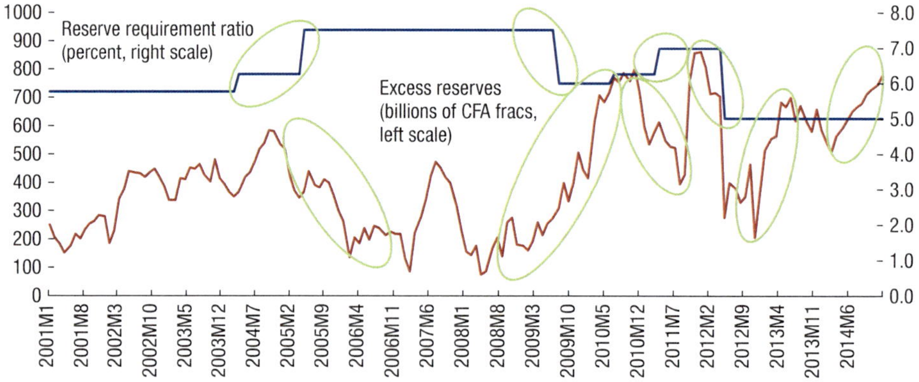

Sources: Central Bank of West African States; and IMF staff calculations.

Therefore, reserve requirements can be viewed as a supplementary monetary policy instrument available to the BCEAO. Obviously, as many other factors affect excess reserves in addition to the reserve requirement ratio, this visible negative correlation between the required reserve ration and excess reserves suggests that potentially reserve requirements also can be used as instruments of monetary policy, in particular to create and, if needed, to enlarge a structural liquidity shortage needed for effective conduct of monetary policy.

MONETARY POLICY TRANSMISSION MECHANISM

Is there a functioning transmission mechanism between BCEAO's instruments and market interest rates? The monetary transmission mechanism describes how changes in monetary policy instruments impact inflation, output, and employment. In a pursuit of broad macroeconomic objectives, the BCEAO sets policy rates or changes the reserve requirements to control a certain financial market variable, which serves as an intermediate target (the money market rate, the interbank interest rate, or the level of reserves in the banking system). The value of this intermediate target is linked through a feedback rule to the ultimate target, which in the WAEMU, is the level of inflation and growth.

The monetary transmission mechanism in the WAEMU can be presented in a stylized way as seen in Figure 15.5. However, not all channels of monetary policy transmission are active.

The *credit channel* allows the BCEAO to affect the volume of banks' lending and influence market interest rates indirectly. Through this channel, the BCEAO changes the volume of funds available for lending, which adjusts their costs for potential borrowers. Cuts in the policy rate, liquidity injection, or reduction in reserve requirements increase banks' free liquidity, which

Figure 15.5. Transmission Mechanism of Monetary Policy

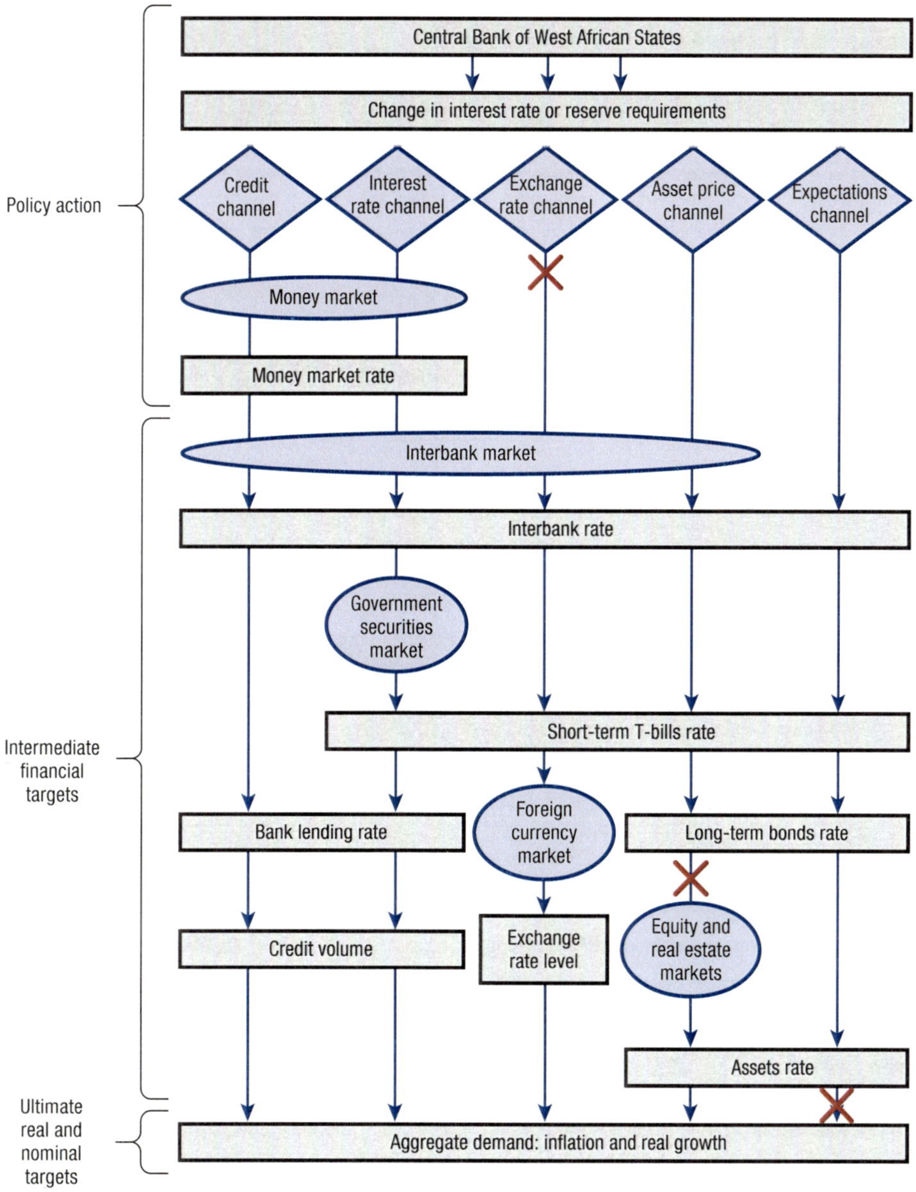

Source: Author's presentation.

allows them to increase the volume of loans and reduce the lending rate. In parallel, the lower lending rates would attract potential borrowers, increasing demand for credit. With higher credit, borrowers would increase their investment or consumption expenditure with a direct impact either on real growth, inflation, or both.

The *interest rate channel* consists of the BCEAO directly influencing interbank rates. Cutting the policy rate reduces the marginal rate of liquidity injection at which the BCEAO provides liquidity to regional banks at their demand. With the liquidity available at lower cost from the BCEAO, banks are induced to reduce the rates on the interbank market at which they trade liquidity with each other. The overall lower cost of funds allows banks to reduce their lending rates, not only to the private sector but also to governments, therefore driving down the cost of government borrowing. The impact on the volume of credit and nominal demand for credit is broad, as in the credit channel.

The *exchange rate channel* is applicable only under a flexible exchange rate regime. Cuts in the policy rate usually lead to a nominal depreciation of the local currency as deposits in local currency become less attractive. Depreciation makes domestic goods cheaper in foreign currencies and stimulates net exports. Expenditure switches in favor of domestically produced goods. Export demand increases and stimulates growth. This channel for the transmission of the monetary policy is not applicable in the WAEMU because of the fixed exchange rate arrangement.

The *asset channel* should allow the BCEAO to influence stock prices and real estate prices, which exert wealth effects on private investment and consumption. Regarding stock prices, a cut in interest rates tends to raise stock prices and reduce the cost of capital, expanding investment and growth. Such policy also has balance sheet effects, as higher stock prices increase the net worth of firms and households and lead to higher lending, higher investment and consumption expenditure, and, ultimately, higher growth. Regarding real estate prices, an expansionary monetary policy reduces the cost of housing financing, leading to higher real estate prices, and higher individual wealth, consumption, and expenditure.

Finally, the impact of monetary policy through the *expectations channel* is most uncertain because it depends on the public's perception of monetary policy signals. In principle, the BCEAO's changes in monetary policy stance can affect expectations of the general public in the region regarding inflation, employment, and growth. For example, a cut in the policy rate may be viewed as a signal that the economy is going to expand in the future, boosting confidence to consume and invest. On the other hand, cuts in policy rates may also be viewed by the public as evidence that the economy is weaker than previously expected, thus forcing the central bank to take policy measures, and therefore lowering confidence and ultimately consumption and investment.

FINANCIAL MARKETS AND MONETARY POLICY

For monetary policy to be efficient, financial markets should be fully operational to serve as a conduit of monetary policy signals. Four financial markets (Figure 15.5) should be capable of efficiently redistributing liquidity and transmitting policy signals from the BCEAO to the real economy. These are the money market (between the BCEAO and commercial banks), the interbank market (among commercial banks), the government securities (public debt) market (mainly between the banking sector and governments), and the equity and real estate (assets) market (among private agents and banks). Unfortunately, none of these is sufficiently developed in the WAEMU.

The *money market* is critical for an appropriate functioning of the credit and interest rate channels of monetary policy. In the WAEMU, this market is relatively large but is essentially limited to the BCEAO's liquidity injections. Using the two available windows, the BCEAO regularly auctions liquidity and sets the marginal rate of liquidity injections. On a monthly basis, the BCEAO calculates an average weighted rate of the money market and communicates this rate to all banks in the region. The banks usually use this rate as the base for setting their deposit rates. There are no other highly liquid instruments with short maturities available for trading. Moreover, only weak local banks, which represent a small part of the banking system, usually bid for the BCEAO's liquidity injections. Therefore, the average money market interest rate set in this market cannot be viewed as fully representative of the market conditions in the regional banking system as a whole and cannot be seen as a basis for a representative short-term reference interest rate. With the absence of such a rate, the expectation channel lacks the reference point and would not be fully functional either.

The *interbank market* is also needed for the credit, interest rate, and asset price channels to function. In the WAEMU, this market is very small and interbank loans do not exceed 2 percent of total loans. While loan maturity has increased in recent years and a yield curve has emerged, the interbank market does not yet have a major role in the reallocation of liquidity. The banking system remains segmented, and weaker banks that need liquidity cannot get it from larger banks that have abundant liquidity but cannot lend it out because of their internal restrictions, risk management procedures, and absence of collateral.

The regional *government securities market* is needed to make the interest rate channel more active. In the WAEMU, this market is limited to the primary market for mainly short-term government paper. Governments issue most of their debt to banks through auctions organized by the BCEAO in T-bills with short average maturities. There is no significant secondary market for government debt. Debt securities have also been issued by private companies and governments on the regional stock exchange. With the capitalization at about 2 percent of GDP at end-2014, debt securities do not represent a significant source of financing for the private sector. There is no significant secondary market for both government and private paper. Without a secondary debt market for debt and given a very weak transmission through the bank lending channel, the BCEAO cannot fully influence the short-term interest rates on government T-bills and, thus, the cost of government borrowing.

Finally, the regional *equity and real estate market* is needed for the asset prices channel of monetary transmission to work properly. In the WAEMU, this market is also very shallow. With less than 40 listed companies, equity market capitalization is only about 10 percent of GDP. Most activities consist of bond issuances by governments, while private stock trading is very secondary. The market is dominated by investors from Côte d'Ivoire and there are very few foreign investors. With the BCEAO's very limited impact on interest rate policy for short-term Treasury bill rates, this impact does not translate into the long-term rates on government bonds. And, with the shallow equity market, this impact does not visibly affect most asset prices. Therefore, the assets channel of monetary transmission cannot fully function either.

Therefore, the limited depth of financial markets reduces the effectiveness of the BCEAO's instruments of monetary policy. Among all available channels of transmission, only the credit channel seems relatively active, with a visible impact on the volume of credit, mainly to governments, through liquidity injection. The interest rate channel has some marginal impact on interbank and lending rates in individual countries. Shallow financial markets obstruct the transmission of monetary policy signals. Only the money market is relatively active, but still very limited in scope and depth.

IMPACT ON INFLATION

Finally, is there a link between BCEAO policy actions to inflation? Earlier estimates suggest that the impact has been limited. According to the BCEAO's estimates (BCEAO 2012b), an increase of 1 percentage point of the BCEAO's policy rate has no impact on inflation in the short term but may lead to a reduction in inflation of 0.05 percent after a 14-month lag. An increase in broad money by 1 percentage point may lead to an increase in inflation by 0.07–0.12 percent in the short term and by 0.16–0.21 percent in the long term. Among the components of money supply, only credit to the economy has an impact on inflation, with a lag of 16–24 months. The

BCEAO estimates that an annual increase in credit to the economy up to 20 percent has no inflationary impact and translates mainly into real growth. Any credit increase above this benchmark usually leads to an increase in the component of inflation linked to the monetary factor. An increase in the policy rate has a very marginal impact on growth, with an elasticity of –0.12 (BCEAO 2012a). Other estimates (Kolerus and Zdzienicka 2013) suggest that an increase in the BCEAO policy rate of 1 percent reduces growth of credit to the private sector by about 4 percent and the inflation rate by 0.05 percentage point in the long run. The BCEAO also estimates that cuts to the policy rate translate into a decrease in banks' lending rates with a lag of two months (BCEAO 2013b).

Our estimations are based on a distributed lag model. It links key variables in the monetary transmission chain as $Y_t = \alpha_0 + \beta_{r+1} X_{t-r} + \varepsilon_t$, where Y_t is the dependent variable of interest regressed on an independent variable X_t and r of its lags. The independent variable X_t is sequentially represented by the BCEAO policy rate, the marginal rate of liquidity injections, and the interbank rate, under the assumption that these three common interest rates are directly linked to the BCEAO's monetary policy actions, and then by the deposit and lending rates of each individual WAEMU country. The dependent variable Y_t is sequentially represented by the marginal rate of liquidity injections, by the deposit and lending rates, and by the core and overall inflation in the region. Separate estimates are performed for each possible transmission link.

Our estimation strategy aims at establishing dynamic causal effects from changes in the BCEAO's policy rates on all other interest rates and inflation. The strategy consists of three steps: (1) run an ordinary least squares regression on the effects of unit changes in each X_t on Y_t and get the contemporaneous (zero period) dynamic multiplier or impact effect; (2) if the impact coefficient is significant and has the right sign, augment the model by adding 12 lags of the independent variable; (3) choose the appropriate lag structure by an autometric model reduction (Ericcson 2011). The estimation period is February 2007–September 2013 on monthly data (80 observations). The selected estimation period reflects the most active recent period of the BCEAO's monetary policy, when it started managing liquidity more actively by introducing liquidity injections in February 2007 and discontinued the discount rate (*taux d'escompte*), which was used mainly for penalty calculations. At the same time, the BCEAO established the marginal lending window with a corresponding maximum lending rate, which replaced the repo rate (*taux de pension*), and the minimum bid rate at liquidity auctions.

The BCEAO's changes in policy rates have been associated with some changes in interest rates in the region, other than the deposit rate (Table 15.4). For example, there seems to be a statistically significant impact of changes in BCEAO policy rates on the money market rate and the interbank rate, at the average lending rate and average inflation in the region. However, the impact of money market rates has been probably the most pronounced, as both estimates, with and without lags, give approximately the same results: An increase by 1 percentage point in the BCEAO policy rates is associated with about a 1.4 percentage point increase in the money market rate and a 1.9 percentage point increase in the interbank rate, a 0.7 percentage point increase in the lending rate, 0.03 percentage point decline in core inflation, and a 0.05 percentage point decline in overall inflation. The impact is either contemporaneous or with one lag because coefficients on both lags are significant and close in magnitude. There is, however, no significant impact on the average deposit rate, and even the sign of the coefficient is wrong.

Although there may be some impact from the BCEAO's policy actions on regional interest rates and inflation, this impact is very marginal. The main reason is that the strength of transmission from the BCEAO's policy rates to the intermediate targets (the interbank rate) and from the intermediate target to the ultimate targets (inflation and GDP) is different. The transmission between the policy and the interbank rates is already relatively weak because of shallow financial markets, and it usually breaks at the points marked by an "X" on Figure 15.5. But the overall

TABLE 15.4

The Impact from Policy Rate Changes on Market Interest Rates and Inflation

	Lags	Coefficient	*T*-value	Sign
Policy Interest Rate On				
Money market rate	0	1.35	12.3	
	0	0.70	2.78	
	1	0.97	3.49	
Interbank rate	0	1.91	8.11	
	0	1.89	9.66	
Average deposit rate	0	−0.22	−3.35	wrong
	3	−0.24	−3.45	wrong
Average lending rate	0	0.69	4.79	
	1	0.72	5.53	
	11	0.67	3.88	
Average core inflation	0	−0.03	−1.95	
	12	−0.04	−3.50	
Average inflation	0	−0.05	−3.95	
	1	−0.05	−2.77	
Money Market Rate On				
Interbank rate	0	1.36	11.2	
	0	1.00	5.61	
	2	0.48	2.65	
Average deposit rate	0	−0.14	−3.52	wrong
	1	−0.15	−3.56	wrong
Average lending rate	0	0.25	2.56	
	6	0.44	4.35	
Average core inflation	12	−0.02	−2.29	
Average inflation	0	−0.02	−3.07	
	12	−0.03	−2.52	
Interbank Rate On				
Average deposit rate	0	−0.12	−5.33	wrong
	1	−0.13	−5.85	wrong
Average lending rate	0	0.06	1.01	
	10	0.17	2.04	
Average core inflation	12	−0.02	−2.68	
Average inflation	0	−0.01	−1.55	
	12	−0.01	−2.59	
Average Deposit Rate On				
Average lending rate	0	−0.10	−0.35	wrong
Average core inflation	5	0.04	2.72	wrong
Average inflation	5	0.04	2.35	wrong
Average Lending Rate On				
Average core inflation	0	−0.02	−2.43	
Average inflation	0	−0.03	−3.95	
	0	−0.02	−2.32	
	3	−0.03	−3.16	

Source: IMF staff estimates.
Note: The number of zero lags appears twice, as the model was estimated in two specifications, the first with no lags (first zero) and, second, if the coefficient is significant, again with up to 12 lags. In the cases of the money market rate and the interbank rate, the model with lags, the zero lag (second zero), and some other lag were significant. Only statistically significant coefficients are shown in the table.

transmission mechanism seems to be even weaker because of substantial problems in the transmission between the interbank rate and the ultimate target. The main underlying reasons may lie (1) in the segment's interbank market where intragroup rates differ substantially from the rates set between small independent banks, and (2) in largely rigid deposit rates, which do not respond at all to the changes in the policy rate and where even the signs of coefficients are wrong. This leads to the low efficiency of both the BCEAO's monetary policy instruments and the weaknesses of the transmission mechanism.

The BCEAO has the capacity for monetary policy in the short-to-medium term. The institutional characteristics jointly needed for an independent monetary policy under a fixed exchange rate regime (a monetary policy framework, capital controls, and the capacity to manage regional interest rates) are present. In addition, the BCEAO has substantial weight in the banking system because its balance sheet represents about a third of the consolidated balance sheet of the banking system. The BCEAO, therefore, can exercise sufficient influence on monetary conditions in the area.

The BCEAO's ability to conduct active monetary policy remains constrained. While both monetary policy instruments (interest rates and reserve requirements) are available and can be used simultaneously, their efficiency is very limited in the presence of excess liquidity, which the BCEAO has to maintain to help weaker banks. While all channels of monetary policy transmission (through the volume of credit, interest rates, the exchange rate, asset prices, and expectations) can, in principle, be active, none of them can fully transmit policy signals, which are blocked shallow financial markets. Finally, while there is a link from the BCEAO's policy actions to market interest rates and inflation, it remains extremely weak and can affect both only marginally. The main underlying problem in the transmission mechanism may be the segmented interbank market and rigid deposit rates.

Important structural changes are needed before the BCEAO can reap the full benefits of its potential for an active monetary policy. These include (1) creating a true structural liquidity deficit by gradually disengaging the BCEAO from the market and adequately calibrating the liquidity injections to market conditions based on improved liquidity projections; (2) developing a deep and functioning interbank market by introducing adequate infrastructure and collateral procedures, and instilling mutual confidence in market participants; this market will allow banks to exchange liquidity and will reduce the need for BCEAO liquidity injections; creating a functioning secondary debt market and deepening the equity market; (3) allowing a gradual emergence of an interbank reference rate and an interest rate curve by developing an institutional framework and supporting infrastructure, adapting regulations to encourage banks to trade liquidity between them, and gradually reducing the injections of liquidity through auctions (a once-a-week interbank rate would be an appropriate reference interest rate); and (4) understanding better the impediments hampering the transmission of BCEAO policy actions to inflation and how to remove them.

The BCEAO is undertaking important reforms to improve the effectiveness of its monetary policy. Authorities are continuously upgrading their model for inflation and liquidity projections. To improve the transmission mechanism of monetary policy, the BCEAO has launched an electronic platform to computerize liquidity injections and absorptions, auctioning of government securities, and monitoring of banks' compliance with the established reserve requirements. Also, the WAEMU Securities Agency was created to help governments mobilize resources on the capital markets needed to finance their economic development policies, provide assistance to national treasuries, and coordinate their activities. In addition, a regulatory framework for primary dealers and markets was adopted. The authorities have embarked on a set of projects to upgrade their regulations to international standards and strengthen prudential supervision. A deposit insurance fund has been established. A number of other important initiatives are also underway.

ANNEX 15.1 EMPIRICS OF MONETARY CONTROL

Fitting a simple error-correction model may help clarify the relationship between BCEAO and ECB money market rates. Based largely on Ericsson (2011), the methodology suggests that if ECB rates and BCEAO rates are each I(1), that is, nonstationary and individually integrated, but if a certain linear combination of them has a lower order of integration such as I(0), then ECB rates and BCEAO rates could be considered cointegrated. Therefore, changes in ECB rates would translate directly into changes in BCEAO rates. If changes in BCEAO rates depend only on the changes in ECB rates, the BCEAO cannot conduct an independent monetary policy. In the opposite case, if no cointegration is found, the BCEAO may have some scope for monetary policy.

The estimated model is:

$$\Delta BCEAO_t = \alpha\Delta ECB_t + \beta(BCEAO_{t-1} - \gamma ECB_{t-1}) + \varepsilon_t$$

where $\alpha\Delta ECB_t$ can be interpreted as an immediate impact of the change in ECB rates on the change in BCEAO rates and, therefore, α as a short-run elasticity; $\beta(BCEAO_{t-1} - \gamma ECB_{t-1})$ can be viewed as a disequilibrium effect, with $BCEAO_{t-1} - \gamma ECB_{t-1}$ as an error-correction term, β as a feedback coefficient, and γ as a long-run elasticity. With short-term rates and long-term elasticities built into the model, testing for cointegration between BCEAO rates and ECB rates would reveal the time-dependent properties of the model, because the impact of ECB rates on BCEAO rates may differ, depending on the time horizon. The cointegration framework tests two hypotheses: (1) In the short term, there may be some scope for an independent monetary policy; in this case $\alpha = 0$, and BCEAO rates and ECB rates are not cointegrated; (2) In the long term, there may still be a scope for an independent monetary policy; in this case, $\gamma = 0$ and BCEAO and ECB rates are not cointegrated. However, the opposite may also be true; in this case, $\gamma \neq 0$, and BCEAO rates and ECB rates are cointegrated.

The test for cointegration between BCEAO rates and ECB rates is performed in four steps: (1) visual analysis of data plots in level, logs, and first differences to assess their time-varying properties and comovements; (2) evaluation of the order of integration of each variable by an augmented Dickey-Fuller test; only nonstationary variables integrated of order 1 and above can be cointegrated; (3) estimation of the cointegration vector by the Johansen procedure; and (4) testing the restrictions on the long-term and short-term elasticities.

The data plot suggests several important statistical properties of BCEAO rates and ECB rates. Both series are trending downward and most likely are not mean stationary. It is difficult to establish whether they follow the same pattern, other than in late 2008 to mid-2009 when both decreased substantially as both central banks cut their policy rates in response to the financial crisis. The distance between two series changes insignificantly and even switches the sign in late 2008, as ECB money market rates, which exceeded BCEAO rates, suddenly become substantially lower than those of the BCEAO (Annex Figure 15.1.1).

Plotting the same data in first differences the same series may be stationary, suggesting an I(1) process. Reserve money is more volatile than net foreign assets, in particular after 2003 (Annex Figure 15.1.2).

A more formal test for the order of integration confirms that both series are integrated of order 1. The augmented Dickey-Fuller (1981) statistics and the tested leg length are selected by the Akaike information criterion on a model with a maximum of six lags, with an intercept and no trend or seasonal component (Annex Table 15.1.1). The tests are presented for the levels of both variables (LBCEAO and LECB), their first differences (DLBCEAO and DLECB), and second differences (DDLBCEAO and DDLECB), all in logs. The null hypothesis presence of a unit root is not rejected at the 1 percent critical level for levels of both variables but is strongly

Annex Figure 15.1.1. Evolution of BCEAO and ECB Money Market Rates, 2007–13

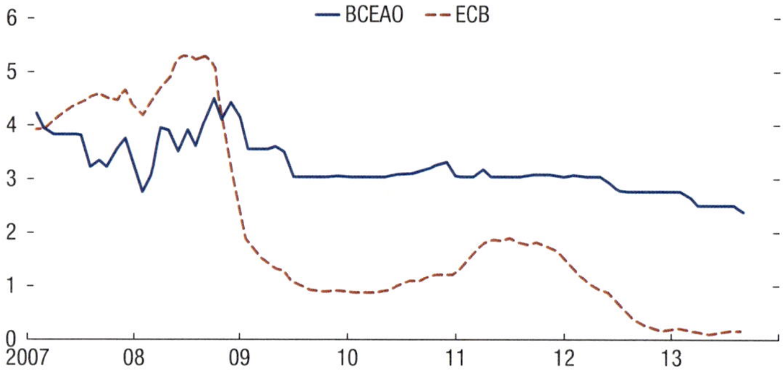

Sources: Central Bank of West African States; and European Central Bank.

Annex Figure 15.1.2. BCEAO and ECB Money Market Rates in First Differences (logs)

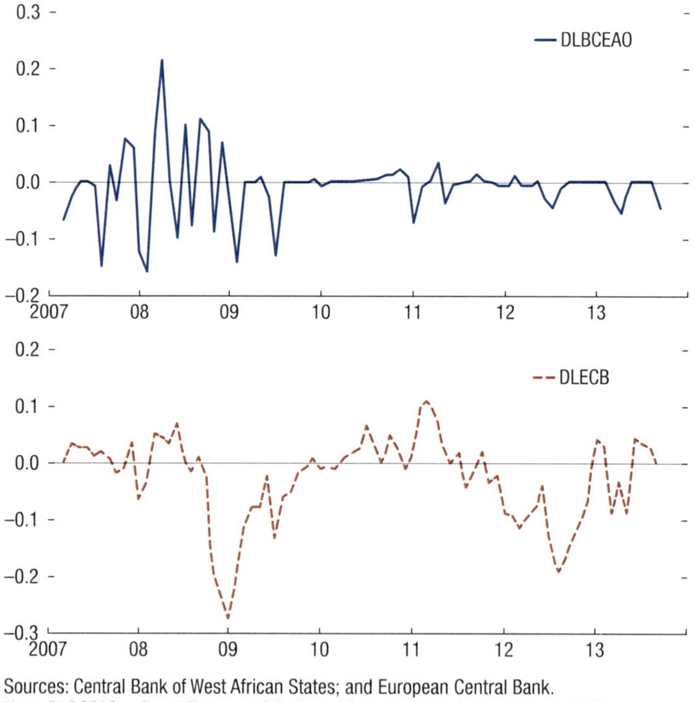

Sources: Central Bank of West African States; and European Central Bank.
Note: DLBCEAO = first difference of the log of Banque Centrale des Etats de l'Afrique de l'Ouest (BCEAO) money market rate; fSLECB = first difference of the log of European Central Bank (ECB) money market rate.

rejected for the first differences of BCEAO rates and second differences of ECB rates. Therefore, BCEAO and ECB money market rates in levels do not seem to be stationary, and ECB rates may not even be stationary in first differences. Both series should be differenced at least once or more to achieve stationarity. Therefore, both series can be treated as at least I(1), and their cointegration analysis in levels is possible.

ANNEX TABLE 15.1.1

AFD Statistics for BCEAO and ECB Money Market Rates, Monthly 02/1997–09/2013 (T = 80)

Variable	Null hypothesis	Selected lag length	t_{ADF}	Estimated root	σ	AIC
LBCEAO	I(1)	5	−1.08	−0.05	0.0386	−6.407
DLBCEAO	I(2)	4	−3.578**	−1.00	0.0387	−6.418
DDLBCEAO	I(3)	4	−8.798**	−4.24	0.0413	−6.284
LECB	I(1)	1	−2.005	−0.02	0.0497	−5.959
DLECB	I(2)	0	−2.863	−0.24	0.0509	−5.927
DDLECB	I(3)	0	−8.309**	−1.05	0.0540	−5.807

Source: Author's estimates.
Note: ADF = augmented Dickey-Fuller test; AIC = European Central Bank, Akaike information criterion; BCEAO = Banque Centrale des Etats de l'Afrique de l'Ouest; D = first difference; L = log.

ANNEX TABLE 15.1.2

Cointegration Analysis of BCEAO and ECB Money Market Rates (Logs, with 12 Lags and Unrestricted Intercept, 2008[2] – 2013[9])

$$\Delta BCEAO_t = \alpha \Delta ECB_t + \beta(BCEAO_{t-1} - \gamma ECB_{t-1}) + \varepsilon_t$$

rank of π	$r = 0$	$r \leq 1$	$r \leq 2$
Log-Likelihood log(λ_τ)	249.58	256.64	256.72
Eigenvalue λ_τ	–	0.1875	0.0023
		Null Hypothesis	
Trace Statistic λ_{max}	14.12	0.16	0.1
95% Critical Value	47.21	29.68	15.41
Variable		Eigenvectors	
BCEAO	1.00	−29.50	
ECB	−0.19	1.00	
Variable		Adjustment coefficients	
BCEAO	−0.4862	0.00023	
ECB	0.01489	0.00097	
	Statistics for testing the significance of a given variable in β′x		
	BCEAO	ECB	
$X^2(1)$	−3.6692**	32.450**	
	Multivariate statistics for testing stationarity		
	BCEAO	ECB	
$X^2(2)$	10.619**	1.2308	

Source: Author's estimates.
Note: BCEAO = Central Bank of West African States; ECB = European Central Bank.

Testing for cointegration using the Johansen procedure suggests no cointegration between ECB and BCEAO rates. The multivariate test for stationarity of each variable using a wider information set than the regular ADF test, and taking into account the potential for cointegration, strongly suggests that both BCEAO and ECB series are not stationary and that the search for a cointegration between them is legitimate. All eigenvalues are small and statistically are not different from zero (Annex Table 15.1.2). The eigenvalue statistic λ_τ accepts the null hypothesis of no cointegration and assigns it the cointegration rank of $r = 0$. This may be interpreted as evidence of no cointegration vectors between ECB and BCEAO money market rates. The trace statistic λ^a_{max} with a degrees of freedom adjustment is well below the 95 percent critical value. The normalized eigenvector β' in a common notation presented in the table with the opposite signs can be normally written as $BCEAO = 0.19ECB$ if the cointegration relationship is present. The estimated adjustment coefficient for the BCEAO equation, which shows how much of its past disequilibrium affects the current disequilibrium, is –0.049 and negative. This suggests the linear combination of variables may potentially converge to the steady state. The estimated coefficient on the ECB rate is 0.01, very small and positive, suggesting their possible divergence from the steady state. Moreover, both coefficients are not significant for the potential cointegration vector.

The ECM model may still contain useful information about the long- and short-term elasticities of responses to changes in the ECB on BCEAO rates. The restrictions on parameters $\alpha = 0$ and $\gamma \neq 0$ can be tested in their autoregressive distributed lag presentation of the ECM. From $\Delta BCEAO_t = \alpha \Delta ECB_t + \beta(BCEAO_{t-1} - \gamma ECB_{t-1}) + \epsilon_t$ it follows that $BCEAO_t - BCEAO_{t-1} = \alpha(ECB_t - ECB_{t-1}) + \beta(BCEAO_{t-1} - \gamma ECB_{t-1}) + \epsilon_t$. Removing the lagged term $BCEAO_t = \alpha_0 ECB_t - \alpha_1 ECB_{t-1} + \alpha_1 BCEAO_{t-1} + \epsilon_t$, where $\alpha = \alpha_0$; $\beta = \alpha_2 - 1$ and $\gamma = -\dfrac{\alpha_0 + \alpha_1}{\alpha_2 - 1}$.

Testing amounts to exclusion restrictions on parameters in the autoregressive distributed lag equation. The estimated autoregressive distributed lag equation is $BCEAO_t = \underbrace{0.0572}_{(0.691)} ECB_t - \underbrace{0.0582}_{(-0.066)} ECB_{t-1} + \underbrace{0.6592}_{(7.571)} BCEAO_{t-1}$. The restriction $\alpha_0 = 0$ has test statistics $\chi^1(1) = 0.47748$ [0.4896] and the null hypothesis that $\alpha = 0$ in the ECM equation is not rejected. From $\gamma = -\dfrac{\alpha_0 + \alpha_1}{\alpha_2 - 1} = -\dfrac{0.0572 - 0.582}{0.6592 - 1} = -0.029$, which is clearly very close to zero. Therefore, it seems that the fact that in the ECM equation $\alpha = 0$ supports the hypothesis that in the short term there may be some scope for an independent monetary policy because changes in the ECB money market rates do not affect BCEAO rates contemporaneously. Because $\gamma = 0$, there may be some scope for an independent monetary policy even in the long term, because changes in the ECB money market rates still do not affect BCEAO rates, even after a lag.

REFERENCES

Annual Report on Exchange Arrangements and Exchange Restrictions (AREAER), 2014, IMF.

Central Bank of West African States (BCEAO). 2013a. *Perspectives économiques des Etats de l'Union en 2013*. www.bceao.int, BCEAO, Dakar.

———. 2013b. *Rapport sur les Conditions de Banque dans l'UEMOA en 2012*. www.bceao.int, BCEAO, Dakar.

———.2012a. "Synthèse des Etudes Relatives aux Mécanismes de Transmissions de la Politique Monétaire: Cas de l'UEMOA." Mimeo. BCEAO, Dakar.

———.2012b. "Analyse des Liens Entre L'inflation et D'autres Variables Economiques, Monétaires et Financières." Document de travail, le 7 mai 2012. Available at www.bceao.int, BCEAO, Dakar.

Ericsson, N. 2011. "Empirical Modeling of Economic Time Series." IMF Course Lecture Notes, International. Monetary Fund, Washington.

Klein, M., and J. Shambaugh. 2013. "Rounding the Corners of the Policy Trilemma: Sources of Monetary Policy Autonomy." NBER Working Paper No. 1946, National Bureau of Economic Research, Cambridge, Massachusetts.

Kolerus, C., and A. Zdzienicka. 2013. "Smoothing Shocks in the WAEMU." Unpublished, International Monetary Fund, Washington.

Montiel, P. 2009. *International Macroeconomics*. Wiley-Blackwell: Chichester, United Kingdom and Malden, Massachusetts.

Obstfeld, M., J. C. Shambaugh, and A. M. Taylor. 2005. "The Trilemma in History: Tradeoffs among Exchange Rates, Monetary Policies, and Capital Mobility." *The Review of Economics and Statistics* 87 (3): 423–38.

———. 2008. "Financial Stability, The Trilemma, and International Reserves." NBER Working Paper 14217, National Bureau of Economic Research, Cambridge, Massachusetts.

Rey, H. 2013. "Dilemma not Trilemma: The Global Financial Cycle and Monetary Policy Independence." CEPR Discussion Paper. Center for Economic Policy Research, London.

Shortland, A., and D. Stasavage. 2004. "What Determines the Monetary Policy in the Franc Zone? Estimating a Reaction Function for the BCEAO." *Journal of African Economies* 13 (4): 518–35.

Veyrune, R. 2007. "Fixed Exchange Rates and the Autonomy of Monetary Policy: The Franc Zone Case." Working Paper 07/34, International Monetary Fund, Washington.

CHAPTER 16

Country Effects of a Single Monetary Policy

ALEXEI KIREYEV

The transmission to individual West African Economic and Monetary Union (WAEMU) countries of the Central Bank of West African States' (BCEAO's) single monetary policy has remained, on average, limited and asymmetric, despite some recent progress in regional financial development. The impact of a single monetary policy can be limited for the region as a whole but may be significant for individual countries with more developed financial markets and/or different product market structure and institutions. The hypothesis of an asymmetric transmission of the single monetary policy actions to individual countries can be tested empirically, in particular, the impact of the policy interest rate changes on each WAEMU country's deposit and lending rates and inflation. BCEAO policy rate changes have no impact on deposit rates. The main channel of transmission of the single monetary policy to individual countries is through the link between the BCEAO's single policy rate and the lending rates in individual countries; this link is relatively strong in Benin, Burkina Faso, Guinea-Bissau, Mali, Senegal, and Togo and very weak in Côte d'Ivoire and Niger. The link to core inflation is observed only in some countries. However, the link to overall inflation, which is the ultimate goal of monetary policy, can be reliably traced only in Benin, Senegal, and Togo. In this context, further developing financial markets, increasing financial intermediation, and fostering competition in the banking sector are crucial to improving the effectiveness of the single monetary policy for individual WAEMU countries.

INTEREST RATES AND INFLATION

Setting interest rates is the main monetary policy instrument of the BCEAO, and price stability is the main objective of its monetary policy. The rates are set by discretionary decisions of the Monetary Policy Committee in pursuit of the goals of the BCEAO's monetary policy. In the past, the BCEAO has used this instrument sparingly, although more actively in the recently past. Price stability is defined as an annual average inflation rate of 2 percent plus or minus 1 percentage point and set over a 24-month horizon. This rate is set as the operational indicator.[1]

In the WAEMU region, economic agents face a number of common interest rates. The common interest rates are set for the region as a whole and include two BCEAO policy rates (*taux directeures*), the money market rate (*taux du marché monetaire*), and the interbank rate (*taux interbancaire*) (Figure 16.1, panel 1). The BCEAO policy sets two policy rates—the minimum bid rate for liquidity injections (*taux minimum de soumission*) and the maximum lending rate (*taux de guichet de prêt marginal).* The two rates are usually set at 100 basis points from each other, so only the maximum lending rate is included in Figure 16.1, panel 1. The money market rate (*taux du marché monetaire*) is set at liquidity auctions between the BCEAO and commercial banks. The BCEAO also calculates three money market rates: the weekly liquidity injection rate (*taux marginal des appels d'offres hebdomadaires*), the average monthly money market rate (*taux*

[1]In addition to the interest rates, the BCEAO has a second instrument of monetary policy—reserve requirements—and a complementary goal of contributing to growth in the WAEMU region, which are not discussed here.

Figure 16.1. WAEMU: Regional Interest Rates and Inflation

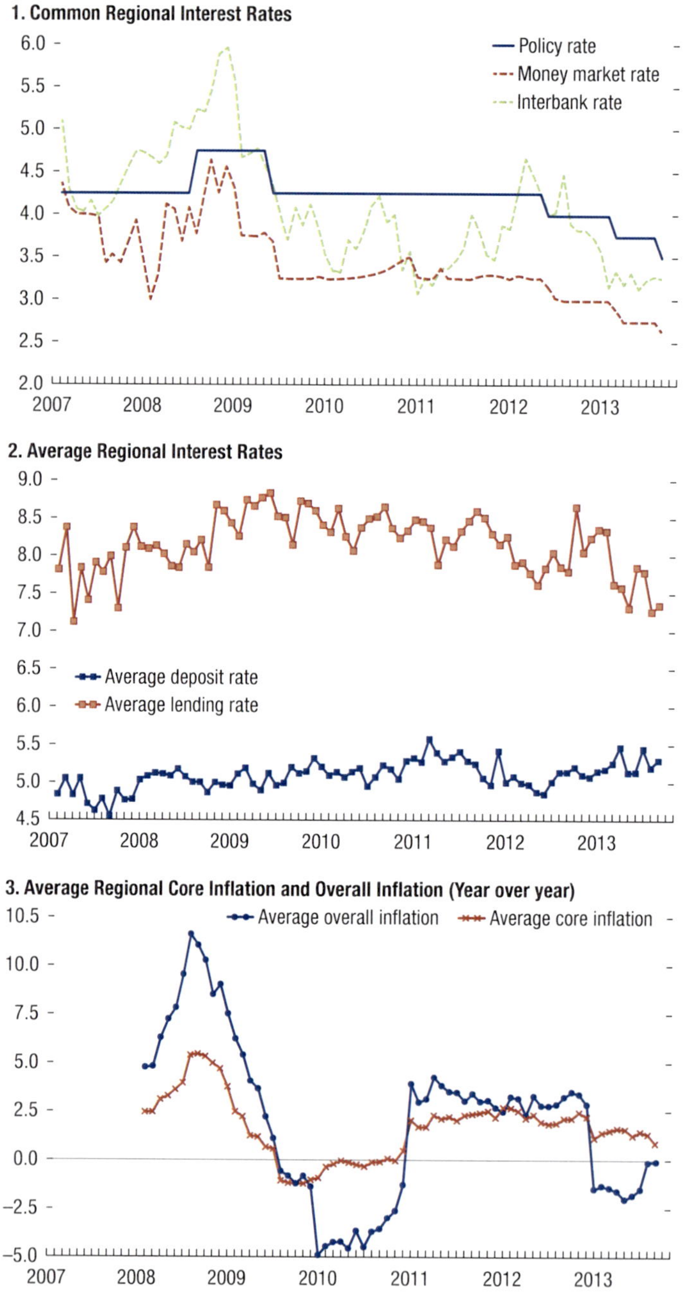

Source: Central Bank of West African States.

moyen mensuelle du marché monetaire, TMM), and the average-weighted monthly money market rate (*taux moyen panderé du marché monetaire, TMP*). Finally, the interbank rate (*taux interbancaire*) emerges at liquidity trading between commercial banks on the interbank market. The average interbank interest rate for the region is the intermediate objective of the BCEAO's monetary policy.

For analytical purposes, the BCEAO also calculates an average deposit rate and the average lending rate for the region as a whole. In the recent past, both rates have moved only marginally, with the deposit rates in the 4.5–5.5 percent range and the lending rates in the 7.5–8.5 percent corridor. While the deposit rate has remained broadly unchanged in the past few years, the average lending rate has declined from its peak level in 2009 (Figure 16.1, panel 2). The average weighted deposit and lending rates were 5.3 and 7.7 percent, respectively, in 2013 through September.

Because controlling inflation is the ultimate goal of monetary policy, the BCEAO also calculates an average inflation rate for the region. The core inflation rate excludes food and fuel prices and has been less volatile than has overall inflation, which reflects substantial spikes during droughts, and food and fuel price hikes. On a year-over-year basis, core inflation has remained in the range of 2–3 percent in the recent past, while overall inflation has fluctuated widely (Figure 16.1, panel 3).

All other interest rates in the WAEMU region are country specific. These include deposit rates (*taux créditeur*) and lending rates (*taux débiteur*). These rates differ substantially among WAEMU countries (Figure 16.2). Only Côte d'Ivoire and Senegal had lending rates lower than the average for the region. In all other countries in the region, the lending rates exceeded the average for the WAEMU, with Benin, Guinea-Bissau, and Niger having the highest lending rates in the region. In all WAEMU countries, the gap between the deposit and lending rates remains substantial, at about 3 percentage points on average in 2009–13. In recent years, the gap has declined only in Benin, Senegal, and Togo.

Inflation rates in the WAEMU also differ substantially by country (Figure 16.3). In 2008–13, 12-month overall inflation in Benin, Burkina Faso, Mali, and Togo was substantially higher than the average for the region, with Benin and Togo recording the highest average inflation rate of 3.9 percent during this period. In other countries, the overall inflation rate was substantially lower, in particular in Senegal, where it averaged only 1.8 percent. The same is true for core inflation, when the most volatile food and fuel prices are excluded from calculations. The highest core inflation (2.6 percent) was recorded in Togo and the lowest in Niger (0.4 percent).

The variability of both country-specific interest rates and inflation has been limited. The low variation in market interest rates can be explained in part by insignificant variability of the BCEAO's policy rates, because the standard deviation from the mean of both policy rates has been very low, at about 0.2 in 2008–13 (Figure 16.4, panel 1). The money market and the interbank rates had larger dispersion around the mean. Substantial differences exist at the country level, with more important fluctuation in lending rates in Benin, Guinea-Bissau, and Niger than in other countries (Figure 16.4, panel 2). At the same time, country-specific variations in inflation are much larger in magnitude than those of interest rates, with an average standard deviation of about 4 in the past five years (Figure 16.4, panel 3). The largest volatility in both overall and core inflation was observed, again, in Guinea-Bissau and Niger, two of the three countries with the highest variability in lending rates.

The BCEAO's regional monetary policy should affect regional inflation through individual countries. Changes in single regional rates (policy, money market, interbank) should ultimately have an impact on country-specific deposit and lending rates. In turn, changes in these rates may influence the inflation rate in each country. Interest rates and inflation rates are substantially different among individual countries, possibly suggesting the BCEAO's monetary policy actions have different impacts on individual countries.

Figure 16.2. Country-Specific Interest Rates (Percent)

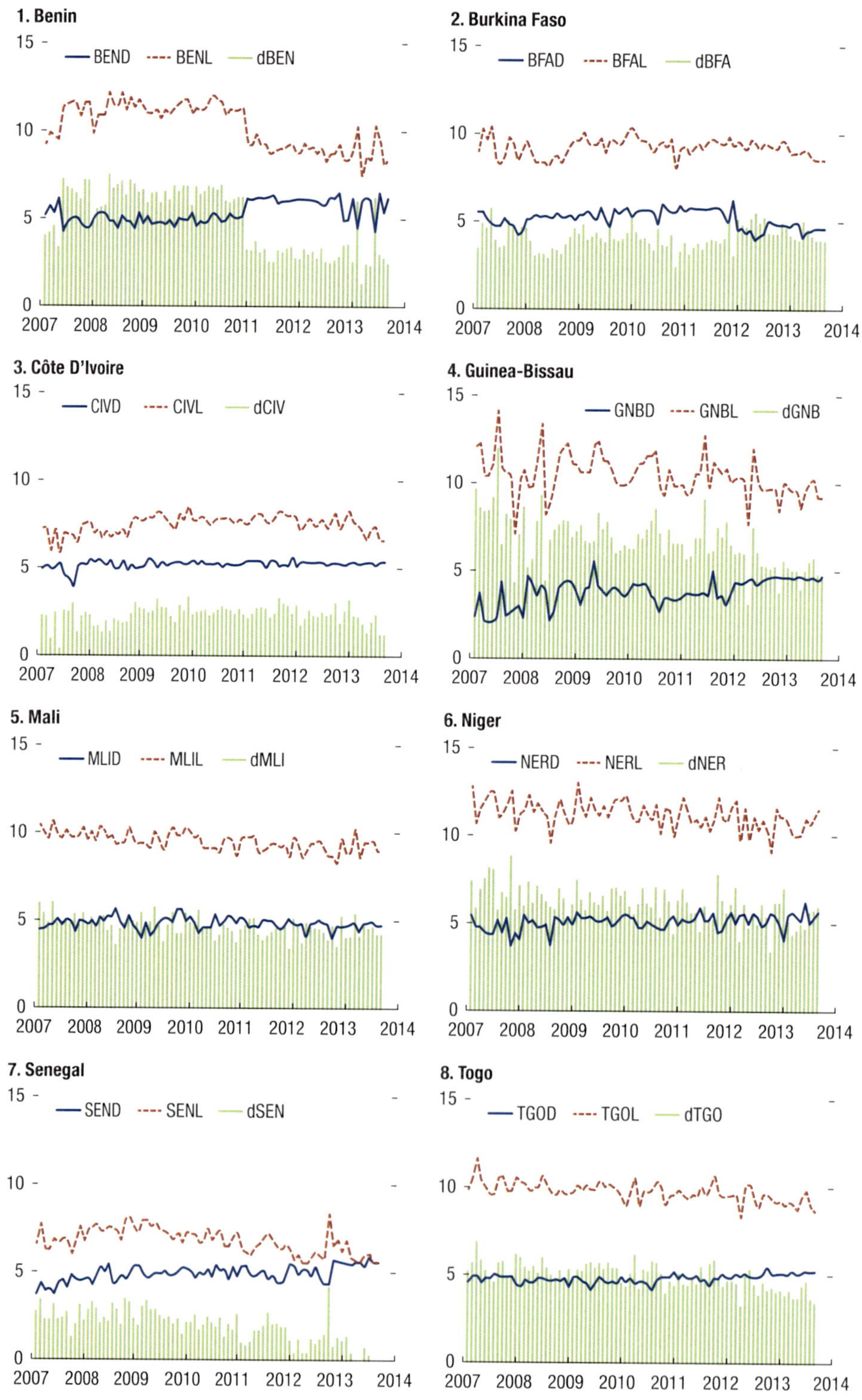

Source: Central Bank of West African States
Note: D = deposit rates; L = lending rates; d = differential. Three-letter International Organization for Standardization abbreviations used for country names.

Figure 16.3. Country-Specific Inflation Rates (12-month changes, percent)

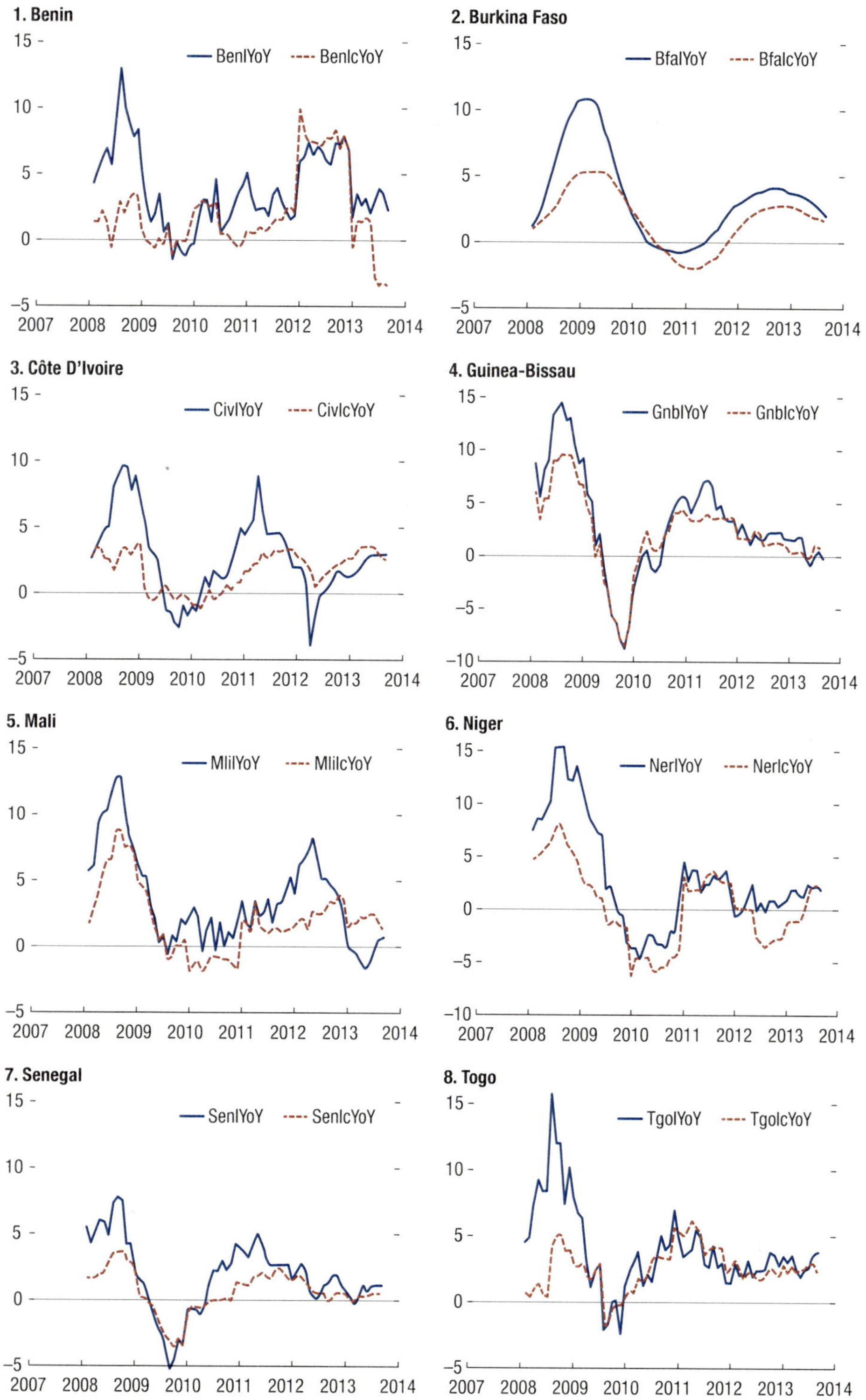

Source: Central Bank of West African States

Note: IYoY = overall inflation; IcYoY = core inflation. Three-letter International Organization for Standardization abbreviations used for country names.

Figure 16.4. Standard Deviation of Interest Rates and Inflation, 2008–13

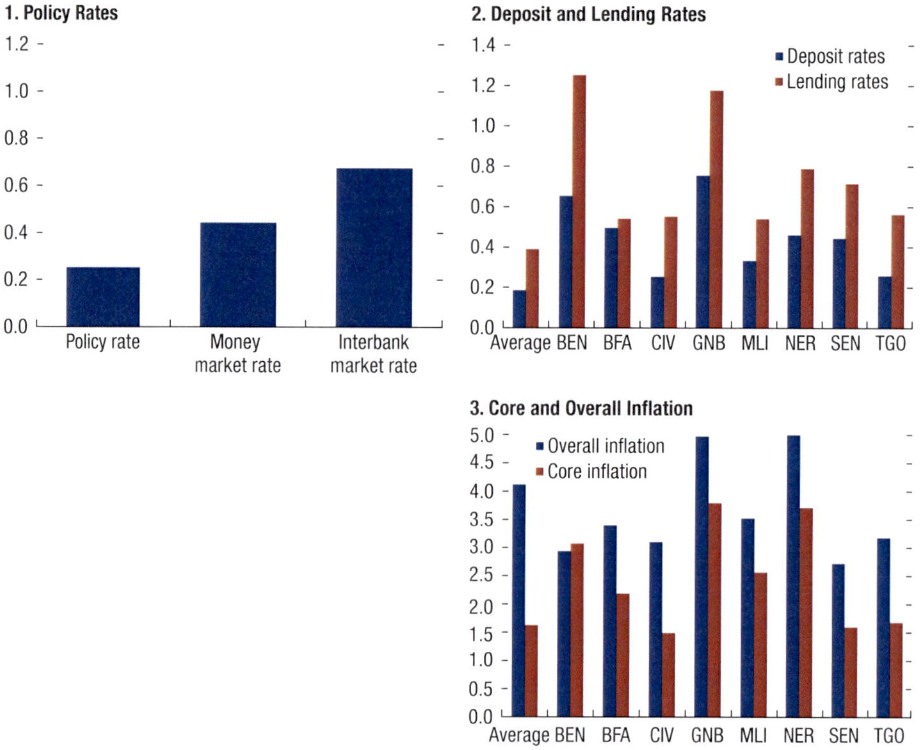

Source: IMF staff calculations.
Note: BEN = Benin; BFA = Burkina Faso; CIV = Côte d'Ivoire; GNB = Guinea-Bissau; MLI = Mali; Ner = Niger; SEN = Senegal; TGO = Togo.

THE INTEREST RATE CHANNEL

The monetary transmission mechanism in the WAEMU can be presented in a simplified way as follows. In pursuit of broad macroeconomic objectives, the BCEAO sets two policy rates, aiming to control a certain financial market variable that serves as an intermediate target for its monetary policy, such as the money market rate or the one-week interbank interest rate. The value of this intermediate target then should be, in principle, linked through a feedback rule to banks' deposit and lending rates, and to the ultimate target, which in the WAEMU is the level of inflation.

In principle, in the WAEMU not all channels of monetary policy transmission should be active. Earlier research (Kireyev 2014) suggests that among possible channels of transmission (through volume of credit, interest rates, exchange rate, asset prices, and expectations) the credit and interest rate channels (sometimes presented as the combined bank lending channel) are somewhat active. The exchange rate channel is not functioning because of the fixed exchange rate regime, while the shallow financial system in the WAEMU constrains other channels. Of four key financial markets, only the money market is relatively developed. However, it still is not representative of the whole banking system. The interbank, debt, and equity markets are very small and lack the needed depth for the transmission of monetary policy signals. Therefore, this chapter focuses only on the interest rate channel.

The interest rate channel consists of the BCEAO influencing the lending and deposit rates in the regional banking system. In pursuit of broad macroeconomic objectives, the BCEAO sets policy rates to control interbank rates. This aggregate serves as an intermediate target whose value is linked through a feedback rule to the ultimate target, which in the WAEMU is the level of inflation. Cutting the policy rate would reduce the marginal rate of liquidity injection at which the BCEAO provides liquidity to regional banks at their demand. With liquidity available at lower cost from the BCEAO, banks would be induced to reduce the rates on the interbank market at which they trade liquidity with each other. The overall lower cost of funds would allow banks to reduce their lending rates, not only to the private sector but also to governments, therefore driving down yields on government Treasury bills and costs of government borrowing. Changes in lending rates should also have an impact on the volume of credit and nominal demand for credit.

The transmission of the monetary policy to individual countries through the interest rate channel can be presented in a stylized way (Figure 16.5). The BCEAO sets discretionary policy rates. Because the rates have been set within 100 basis points of each other, for the purposes of this analysis they can be treated as a single policy rate. Policy rates have an impact on all other rates in the region—single (money market, interbank) and country-specific (deposit, lending)—and through them, on inflation in each WAEMU country. Once the change in the policy rate is reflected in the single money market rate, the latter also affects all other rates in the region, other than the deposit rate, and inflation. Once the interbank rates internalize changes in the policy and money market rates, they, in turn, affect all other country-specific rates and inflation. Changes in single regional rates should in principle have an impact on the deposit rate because deposits, along with the interbank market, are the main sources of funds for banks. Thereafter, changes in country-specific deposit rates should also have an impact on lending rates. Finally, changes in lending rates should affect inflation.

Figure 16.5. Transmission of Monetary Policy: The Interest Rate Channel

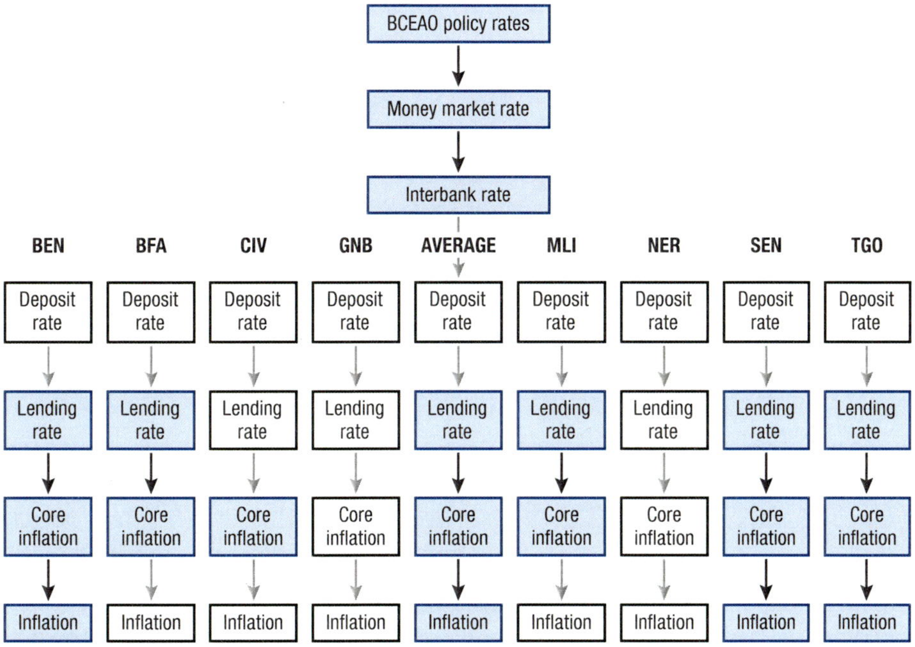

Source: Author's presentation.
Note: BCEAO = Central Bank of West African States; BEN = Benin; BFA = Burkina Faso; CIV = Côte d'Ivoire; GNB = Guinea-Bissau; MLI = Mali; NER = Niger; SEN = Senegal; TGO = Togo.

As a result, the transmission mechanism of the BCEAO's monetary policy has two intermediate components. These are a set of single regional interest rates and a set of country-specific rates, each of which should in principle have an impact on inflation. Although only sequential linkages are shown, each next interest rate may influence all other rates, as shown in Figure 16.5. Given potential multiplicity and the overlapping nature of transmission channels, the impact of the monetary policy action on market interest rates or inflation may occur with a lag. This suggests that an estimation of dynamic multipliers, which would allow establishing the cumulative effect of unit changes in each independent variable X_t on the dependent variable Y_t over r lags. The interpretation of the coefficients in a distributed lag model as causal dynamics effects assumes the independent variable is exogenous. If the policy rate or its lagged values are correlated with the error term, the conditional mean of the error term will depend on the independent variable or its lags. In this case, the independent variable is not exogenous.

The BCEAO's policy rates have to be treated as exogenous in the monetary transmission model. Although the BCEAO sets the policy rate at its discretion, it does not set it at random, but rather endogenously. That is, the BCEAO determines the policy rate based on its assessment of the current and future state of the regional economy and its financial conditions, in particular, that of the current and expected future inflation rates. Therefore, the policy rate is most likely endogenous to the model. The problem is that the causal dynamic effect of a change in the policy rate can be consistently estimated using a distributed lag model only if the policy rate is exogenous. This means the conditional mean of the error term in the regression of inflation on the policy rate does not depend on the current and past values of the policy rate, or even better, is strictly exogenous. That is, it does not depend on the past, present, and expected future value of the policy rate either.

Earlier research has shown that the overall transmission of monetary policy signals in the region has been very weak. According to estimates (Kolerus and Zdzienicka 2013), the bank lending channel seems the most effective channel of transmission, because an increase of 1 percentage point in the BCEAO's policy rate reduces private credit growth by about 3 percentage points one quarter later and by 4 percentage points (cumulative) after one year. According to BCEAO estimates, an increase of the policy rate by 1 percentage point raises the interbank rate by 0.61 percent in the short term and 1.55 percent in the long term. In turn, a 1 point increase of the interbank rate translates into an increase of the lending rate by 0.1 percent (BCEAO 2012b). Finally, a 1 percentage point increase in the lending rate leads to a 0.05 percent increase in inflation in the long term.

MODEL SPECIFICATION

Our estimations are based on a distributed lag model. They link key variables in the monetary transmission chain

$$Y_t = \alpha_0 + \alpha_{r+1} X_{t-r} + \varepsilon_t$$

where Y_t is the dependent variable of interest regressed on an independent variable X_t and r of its lags. Separate estimates are performed for each possible transmission link. The independent variable X_t is sequentially represented by the BCEAO policy rate, the marginal rate of liquidity injections, and the interbank rate under the assumption that these three common interest rates are directly linked to the BCEAO's monetary policy actions, and then by the deposit and lending rates of each individual WAEMU country. The dependent variable Y_t is sequentially represented by the marginal rate of liquidity injections, by the deposit and lending rates, and the core and overall inflation of each individual country.

The estimation strategy aims at establishing dynamic causal effects from changes in the BCEAO's policy rates on all other interest rates and inflation. The strategy consists of three steps: (1) run an ordinary least squares regression on the effects of unit changes in each X_t on Y_t and get the contemporaneous (zero period) dynamic multiplier or impact effect; (2) if the impact coefficient is significant and has the right sign, augment the model by adding 12 lags of the independent variable; (3) choose the appropriate lag structure by an autometric model reduction. Given the problem of collinearity in the independent variable, select the lag structure that does not change with the changes in the specification.

The data were received directly from the BCEAO. The estimation period is February 2007–September 2013 on monthly data (80 observations). The selected estimation period reflects the most active recent period of the BCEAO's monetary policy when it started managing liquidity more actively by introducing liquidity injections in February 2007 and discontinued the discount rate (*taux d'escompte*), which was used mainly for penalty calculations At the same time, the BCEAO established the marginal lending window with a corresponding maximum lending rate, which replaced the repo rate (*taux de pension*), and the minimum bid rate at liquidity auctions. During the estimation period, the BCEAO has changed its policy rate only six times, four of which were in 2012–13, giving very little variability in the key independent variable.

Insignificant variability in certain interest rates in the WAEMU leads to collinearity in repressors and hinders econometric estimations of the transmission mechanism. If two or more independent variables in a multiple regression model are highly correlated, one can be linearly predicted from the others with a nontrivial degree of accuracy. In this situation the coefficient estimates may change erratically in response to small changes in the model or the data. Multicollinearity does not reduce the predictive power or reliability of the model as a whole, at least within the sample data. It affects only calculations regarding individual independent variables. That is, a multiple regression model with correlated independent variables can indicate how well all independent variables together predict the dependent variable, but it may not give valid results about any individual independent variable, or about which independent variables are redundant with respect to others. One option to handle the problem of multicollinearity is to leave the model as is, despite multicollinearity. This option was chosen in this chapter. The presence of multicollinearity doesn't affect the efficacy of extrapolating the fitted model to new data provided that the independent variables follow the same pattern of multicollinearity in the new data as in the data on which the regression model is based.

ESTIMATION RESULTS

The BCEAO's changes in policy rates have been associated with changes in all single and average interest rates in the region, other than the deposit rate (Table 16.1). For example, there seems to be a statistically significant impact of changes in BCEAO policy rates on the money market rate and the interbank rate, at the average lending rate and average inflation (Table 16.1). However, the impact of money market rates has been probably the most pronounced as both estimates, with and without lags, give approximately the same results: an increase by 1 percentage point in the BCEAO policy rates is associated with about a 1.4 percentage point increase in the money market rate, a 1.9 percent increase in the interbank rate, a 0.7 percent increase in the lending rate, a 0.03 percent decline in core inflation, and a 0.05 percent decline in overall inflation. The impact is either contemporaneous or with one lag, because coefficients on both lags are significant and close in magnitude. There is, however, no significant impact on the average deposit rate, and even the sign of the coefficient is wrong.

Other single interest rates can be viewed as a secondary source of the monetary policy signal. If the money market rate is treated as the main source for the impulse in the monetary transmission mechanism, the picture is broadly similar, but the coefficients are smaller. A 1 percentage

TABLE 16.1

Policy Rate Impact on the Single and Average Interest Rates

	Lags	Coefficient	*T*-value	Sign
BCEAO Policy Rate On				
Money market rate	0	1.35	12.30	
	0	0.70	2.78	
	1	0.97	3.49	
Interbank rate	0	1.91	8.11	
	0	1.89	9.66	
Average deposit rate	0	−0.22	−3.35	Wrong
	3	−0.24	−3.45	Wrong
Average lending rate	0	0.69	4.79	
	1	0.72	5.53	
	11	0.67	3.88	
Average core inflation	0	−0.03	−1.95	
	12	−0.04	−3.50	
Average inflation	0	−0.05	−3.95	
	1	−0.05	−2.77	
Money Market Rate On				
Interbank rate	0	1.36	11.20	
	0	1.00	5.61	
	2	0.48	2.65	
Average deposit rate	0	−0.14	−3.52	Wrong
	1	−0.15	−3.56	Wrong
Average lending rate	0	0.25	2.56	
	6	0.44	4.35	
Average core inflation	12	−0.02	−2.29	
Average inflation	0	−0.02	−3.07	
	12	−0.03	−2.52	
Interbank Rate On				
Average deposit rate	0	−0.12	−5.33	Wrong
	1	−0.13	−5.85	Wrong
Average lending rate	0	0.06	1.01	
	10	0.17	2.04	
Average core inflation	12	−0.02	−2.68	
Average inflation	0	−0.01	−1.55	
	12	−0.01	−2.59	
Average Deposit Rate On				
Average lending rate	0	−0.10	−0.35	Wrong
Average core inflation	5	0.04	2.72	Wrong
Average inflation	5	0.04	2.35	Wrong
Average Lending Rate On				
Average core inflation	0	−0.02	−2.43	
Average inflation	0	−0.03	−3.95	
	0	−0.02	−2.32	
	3	−0.03	−3.16	

Source: IMF staff estimates.

point increase in the money market rate leads to an increase in the interbank rate by about 1.4 percentage points, an increase in the average lending rate by 0.3 percentage point, and a decline in core and overall inflation by 0.02 percent. The interbank rate plays an even smaller role in monetary transmission, as it seems to affect only the lending rate with an insignificant impact on inflation. The average deposit rates do not seem to play any role in the transmission process. Finally, the impact of the lending rates changes as inflation appears to be less significant and more delayed (up to three months) in time.

Country-specific estimates are broadly in line with common effects, but some significant differences exist across countries (Table 16.2). The link between the policy and the money market, on the one hand, and the lending rate, on the other, is also the main channel of monetary

TABLE 16.2

Country-Specific Effects of a Single Monetary Policy

	BCEAO Policy Rate				Money Market Rate				Interbank Rate			
	Lags	Coefficient	*T*-value	Sign	Lags	Coefficient	*T*-value	Sign	Lags	Coefficient	*T*-value	Sign
BEN												
Deposit rate	None	None	None		0	−0.62	−3.92	Wrong	3	−0.32	−1.91	Wrong
					10	−0.75	−4.66	Wrong	12	−0.47	−5.12	Wrong
Lending rate	0	2.65	2.23		1	1.42	6.54		0	0.96	6.50	
					12	1.54	7.39		12	1.51	10.30	
					12	−0.05	−3.03					
Core inflation	0	−0.10	−6.93		0	−0.06	−6.13		0	−0.02	−3.22	
Inflation	0	−0.08	−1.89		0	−0.17	−7.62		None	None	None	
					5	0.04	2.36	Wrong				
BFA												
Deposit rate	1	0.62	3.43		0	2.01	7.27		12	0.21	2.07	
	10	0.61	3.43		5	−0.89	−3.19	Wrong				
					11	0.49	2.77					
Lending rate	2	0.66	3.59		2	0.71	2.95		0	0.36	3.00	
	12	1.50	8.30		6	−0.56	−2.14	Wrong				
					11	0.62	3.38					
Core inflation	0	−0.05	−6.12		0	−0.04	−7.59		0	−0.02	−6.06	
					0	−0.03	−4.28		0	−0.02	−2.44	
					11	−0.02	−2.28					
Inflation	1	0.17	2.77	Wrong	2	0.09	2.87	Wrong	0	0.08	6.80	Wrong
	6	0.33	4.48	Wrong	4	0.12	3.33	Wrong	6	0.06	3.23	Wrong
					11	0.18	6.88	Wrong	8	0.04	2.18	Wrong
									11	0.07	4.95	Wrong
CIV												
Deposit rate	None	None	None		None	None	None		3	1.04	2.28	
									6	−1.06	−2.18	Wrong
									12	0.62	2.76	
Lending rate	None	None	None		None	None	None		3	1.48	2.01	
									6	−1.70	−2.10	Wrong
									12	1.00	2.80	

(continued)

TABLE 16.2 (*continued*)

Country-Specific Effects of a Single Monetary Policy

	BCEAO Policy Rate				Money Market Rate				Interbank Rate			
	Lags	Coefficient	*T*-value	Sign	Lags	Coefficient	*T*-value	Sign	Lags	Coefficient	*T*-value	Sign
Core inflation	0	−0.07	−9.13		0	−0.04	−7.22		0	−0.02	−6.06	
	0	−0.06	−4.14						0	−0.02	−2.44	
	12	−0.03	−2.15									
Inflation	0	−0.08	−4.66		1	−0.04	−4.78		0	−0.01	−3.18	
	10	−0.09	−4.62		7	0.02	2.01	Wrong	12	−0.03	−7.77	
					10	−0.03	−3.42					
					12	−0.05	−5.57					
GNB												
Deposit rate	0	−0.22	−0.61	Wrong	0	−0.61	−2.63	Wrong	None	None	None	
					5	0.67	2.79					
Lending rate	1	2.44	82.4		0	1.22	2.87		None	None	None	
					3	−1.82	−3.02	Wrong				
					4	1.71	2.95					
Core inflation	0	−0.04	−3.39		0	−0.02	−2.29					
	7	−0.08	−5.37		10	−0.03	−4.04					
	12	−0.05	−3.1		12	−0.04	−4.82		12	−0.03	−6.58	
Inflation	2	−0.05	−2.09		10	−0.04	−2.93		12	−0.05	−3.94	
	12	−0.10	−3.93		12	−0.05	−4.49					
MLI												
Deposit rate	9	0.53	2.15		5	−0.33	−2.44	Wrong	None	None	None	
					11	0.39	3.00					
Lending rate	1	0.87	4.14		0	0.42	2.48		None	None	None	
	12	1.31	6.29		11	0.80	4.52					
Core inflation	0	−0.05	−5.79		0	−0.03	−4.66		0	−0.01	−2.65	
	2	−0.05	−2.28		12	−0.02	−2.06		1	−0.05	−5.56	
									12	−0.04	−3.33	
Inflation	None	None	None		0	−0.06	−4.30		0	−0.02	−2.53	
NER												
Deposit rate	0	−1.56	−3.44	Wrong	None	None	None		None	None	None	
	1	1.61	3.48									
Lending rate	1	1.32	4.16		9	0.88	3.67		12	0.39	2.80	
	12	1.27	4.03									

Core inflation	0	0.05	5.81	Wrong	0	0.03	6.62	Wrong	0	0.02	6.57	
	0	0.05	3.27	Wrong	0	0.03	5.17	Wrong	0	0.02	5.72	
	7	0.04	2.74	Wrong	8	0.02	4.46	Wrong	8	0.01	4.45	
	12	−0.05	−2.82									
Inflation	9	0.06	2.17	Wrong	0	−0.06	−4.30		0	−0.02	−2.53	
	12	−0.06	−2.37						3	−0.01	−2.04	
									12	−0.03	−4.74	
SEN												
Deposit rate	None	None	None		None	None	None		8	0.19	1.92	
Lending rate	0	1.60	4.38		0	0.84	4.09		0	0.42	3.42	
	10	0.88	2.09						8	0.37	2.81	
									12	0.31	2.34	
Core inflation	0	−0.01	−2.4									
	0	−0.02	−4.49		10	−0.01	−2.58					
	12	−0.03	−4.34		12	−0.01	−2.36		12	−0.01	−3.69	
Inflation	3	−0.07	−5.32		4	−0.02	−2.51		12	−0.03	−7.52	
	12	−0.07	−5.05		12	−0.04	−6.33					
TGO												
Deposit rate	2	−0.43	−2.93	Wrong	0	−0.19	−2.36	Wrong	0	−0.11	−2.32	Wrong
	9	−0.33	−2.02	Wrong	1	−0.17	−2.37	Wrong	3	0.15	2.47	
					12	−0.27	−3.74	Wrong	11	−0.21	−4.93	Wrong
Lending rate	7	0.70	2.22		0	0.38	2.75		0	0.23	2.53	
					10	0.62	4.42		2	0.27	2.79	
									8	−0.48	−2.14	Wrong
									9	0.51	2.37	
Core inflation	0	−0.11	−7.44		0	−0.07	−7.37		0	−0.04	−5.79	
	0	−0.10	−7.30		0	−0.03	−3.61					
	11	−0.08	−4.21		2	−0.02	−2.63					
					10	−0.03	−3.15					
					12	−0.05	−5.84		12	−0.04	−2.80	
Inflation	0	−0.05	−3.95		0	−0.10	−7.49		0	−0.04	−5.68	
	1	−0.11	−5.04		0	−0.03	−2.88		12	−0.05	−2.97	
	10	−0.08	−3.46		2	−0.04	−3.36					
					7	0.03	2.57	Wrong				
					10	−0.05	−4.55					
					12	−0.06	−6.08					

Source: IMF staff estimates.
Note: Three-letter International Organization for Standardization abbreviations used for country names.

transmission at the individual country level. While this link is relatively strong in Benin, Burkina Faso, Guinea-Bissau, Senegal, Mali, and Togo, it seems almost nonexistent in Côte d'Ivoire and Niger. Some differences exist also in the impact and pace of monetary transmission. For instance, in Benin and Senegal, lending rates react quickly to changes in policy, money market, and interbank rates, while the impact is more delayed in Burkina Faso and Togo. Deposit rates seem to be affected by changes in policy rates only in Mali, but not by money market rates. The impact of policy and money market rates on core inflation is more pronounced than it is on overall inflation, and it is statistically significant in all WAEMU countries other than Niger. But once core inflation is distorted by food and fuel prices, the impact becomes very asymmetric, with no significant impact in Burkina Faso, Côte d'Ivoire, Guinea-Bissau, Mali, and Niger, unlike in Benin, Senegal, and Togo.

A more detailed analysis of the impact on individual countries reveals diverging trends (Table 16.2). In Benin, lending rates seem to react strongly to changes in the BCEAO policy rate and money market rates, but not to interbank rates. The lag of the impact is unclear in money market rates. The coefficients are close in magnitude with no lags and at the 12th lag, which may suggest strong collinearity in the independent variable. The coefficient for the impact on inflation is significant and has the right sign, and it is relatively large compared with that of other countries. In Burkina Faso, only lending rates seem to react to the changes in the single policy rate and the interbank rate, but these do not react to the money market rate. The lags most likely do not exceed one to two months, as the coefficients are comparable in magnitude. Monetary policy has no impact on inflation, as all coefficients have the wrong sign. Côte d'Ivoire seems to be the WAEMU country where the single monetary policy has the least impact because almost all coefficients are insignificant. Neither deposit nor lending rates react to the changes in any of the single rates. There is some impact on local inflation, most likely directly from policy rates. This may be partially explained by the fact that the country underwent a deep political crisis during the estimation period, possibly distorting the transmission mechanism and having a negative impact on data quality. In Guinea-Bissau, there seemed to be some impact of single policy rate and money market rates on lending rates and—very marginally—on inflation, both core and overall. All other coefficients have signs opposite to what would be predicted by economic theory.

The impact on other countries is different. In Mali, only lending rates react to changes in policy rates and money market rates, although with a significant lag. The impact on core inflation is very small, and it does not pass through to overall inflation. In Niger, lending rates seem to react to monetary policy signals, but the lag structure remains unclear, as similar coefficients emerged on both the first and the twelfth lags. There is no impact on core inflation, because the coefficients have the wrong sign, or on overall inflation because lagged coefficients cancel each other. In Senegal, monetary transmission is probably the strongest among all WAEMU countries, as both lending rates and inflation seem to react strongly to changes in all three single rates. Lending rates and core inflation seem to react instantaneously, but overall inflation is affected only with a lag of about a quarter. Finally, in Togo, lending rates react to changes in policy and money market rates, but most likely with substantial lags. Inflation is also responsive, although the lag structure is not clear.

A large part of deposit rates is not market determined. Over 60 percent of deposits in the region consist of current accounts of enterprises and individuals, which pay virtually zero interest rates. Both sight and saving deposits are remunerated by banks at market rates but there is very little variability in these rates, as the large base of current accounts allows banks to keep deposits rated broadly stable, irrespective of monetary conditions. This probably explains the lack of transmission of monetary policy signals to deposit rates.

Heterogeneity in monetary transmission could be generally explained by countries' different financial sector development. Overall, the more competitive and developed the financial sector, the more efficient the single monetary policy is for a country. Earlier research found substantial cross-country asymmetries in the transmission of a single monetary policy and explained them by differences in financial structure, labor market rigidities, and industry mix in individual countries (Georgiadis 2012). Generally, the asymmetry can be explained by a country's structural characteristics and policies, although countries with more developed financial systems and flexible exchange rates experience stronger transmission of monetary policy signals (Saborowski and Weber 2013). Monetary transmission is usually stronger if a financial system is dominated by small and medium-size banks with less liquidity and lower capital because large commercial banks are more capable of isolating their lending activities from changes in monetary policy conditions. Small banks are best placed to refinance the real economy, in particular small and medium-sized firms, which are the biggest generators of employment in the economy (De Santis and Surico 2013).

Research on the WAEMU suggests that the strength of country-specific transmission depends on the country's level of financial development and competition in the banking sector (Weber and Kireyev, 2014). Level of financial development was found highly relevant for the transmission of monetary policy rates to inflation. In response to a one standard deviation increase in the monetary policy rate, the lending rate increased significantly if the economy had a higher level of financial development in terms of the credit-to-GDP ratio within the WAEMU. This in turn contributed to a significant reduction in the inflation rate by about 1 percentage point. However, at low levels of financial development, no impact was found from monetary tightening of the lending rate or the inflation rate. Monetary tightening was associated with lower inflation if the banking sector was not very concentrated and the level of competition was relatively high, whereas in countries with a highly concentrated banking sector, monetary policy actions had no effect on inflation. These results are consistent with previous findings that monetary policy is most effective in Benin, Senegal, and Togo, which are the three WAEMU countries with the highest financial depth and competition in the banking sector.

The transmission of monetary policy signals is asymmetric and is more pronounced for some WAEMU countries than others. Preliminary results suggest that policy rates have an impact on other interest rates, whose size and significance vary across countries. They also have a significant, if small, impact on inflation. Preliminary results are that:

1. BCEAO policy rates have the largest impact on other single and country-specific rates in the region, with the notable exception of the deposit rate; the impact of the single money market rate is also significant, most likely because this rate closely follows the policy rate.
2. Single regional rates have some impact on the average core and overall inflation in the region, but this impact is very small.
3. The main channel of transmission of the single monetary policy to individual countries is through the link between the BCEAO's single policy rate and the lending rates in individual countries; this link is relatively strong in Benin, Burkina Faso, Guinea-Bissau, Mali Senegal, and Togo, and almost nonexistent in Côte d'Ivoire and Niger.
4. Even with the relatively clear impact on lending rates, the link to core inflation is observed only in some countries; however, the link to overall inflation, which is the ultimate goal of monetary policy, can be reliably traced only in Benin, Senegal, and Togo. The channels of country-specific effects of the single monetary policy are shown by shaded areas in Figure 16.2.

The characteristics of the financial sector seem to explain the heterogeneity in monetary transmission across countries. The effectiveness of monetary policy increases with the level of financial development and the degree of competition in the financial sector. This could explain why, for instance, monetary policy seems to be more effective in Benin, Senegal, and Togo, whose financial depth is higher.

The transmission of monetary policy can be improved by further developing financial markets. More developed financial markets would also allow banks to trade liquidity more actively, limiting the need for liquidity injections by the BCEAO, and allowing for the emergence of an interbank rate that would provide highly valuable information for the conduct of monetary policy. The low level of financial market development is an impediment for monetary policy effectiveness in the WAEMU.

REFERENCES

Central Bank of West African States (BCEAO). 2012a. Synthèse des Etudes Relatives aux Mécanismes de Transmissions de la Politique Monétaire: Cas de l'UEMOA. Unpublished. Central Bank of West African States, Dakar.

———. 2012b. Analyse des liens entre L'inflation et D'autres Variables Economiques, Monétaires et Financières. Document de Travail, le 7 Mai 2012. Available at www.bceao.int. Central Bank of West African States, Dakar.

De Santis, R., and P. Surico. 2013. "Bank Lending and Monetary Transmission in the Euro Area." Working Paper Series No. 1568, European Central Bank, Frankfurt.

Georgiadis, Georgios. 2012. "Towards an Explanation of Cross-country Asymmetries in Monetary Transmission." Discussion Papers 07/2012, Deutsche Bundesbank, Research Centre, Frankfurt.

Kireyev, A. 2014. "Monetary Policy Under a Fixed Exchange Rate Arrangement: The Case of the WAEMU." Working Paper (forthcoming), International Monetary Fund, Washington.

Kolerus, C., and A. Zdzienicka. 2013. "Smoothing Shocks in the WAEMU." Unpublished. International Monetary Fund, Washington.

Mishra, P., P. Montiel, and A. Spilimbergo. 2012."Monetary Transmission in Low-Income Countries: Effectiveness and Policy Implications." *IMF Economic Review* 60 (2): 270–302.

Saborowski, C., and S. Weber. 2013. "Assessing the Determinants of Interest Rate Transmission Through Conditional Impulse Response Functions." Working Paper 13/23, International Monetary Fund, Washington.

Weber, S., and A. Kireyev. 2014. "Monetray Policy Transmission in WAEMU Countries." Country Report No.14/84, International Monetary Fund, Washington. Avaible at http://www.imf.org/external/pubs/ft/scr/2014/cr1484.pdf.

CHAPTER 17

Liquidity Injections and Risks

JOHN HOOLEY

In 2013, the liquidity position of the commercial banking system vis-à-vis the Central Bank of West African States (BCEAO) swung from a structural liquidity surplus to a deficit. This reflected a sharp increase in commercial banks' borrowing from the BCEAO, which was used to fund purchases of government securities. The underlying causes likely included a combination of widening fiscal and external imbalances, and carry-trade activity by some banks. These developments, in turn, pose risks to fiscal and financial stability, financial development, and monetary policy effectiveness. West African Economic and Monetary Union(WAEMU) authorities should nevertheless monitor closely these trends in liquidity and consider whether any preemptive policy action might be appropriate, in order to prevent such risks from crystallizing. Possible measures include: reducing fiscal deficits of individual WAEMU countries, which would reduce commercial banks' demands for funding from the central bank to finance them; discouraging carry-trade activity by commercial banks; mitigating market distortions through changes in prudential regulation; relaxing regulatory barriers to entry for financial institutions other than domestic banks; and issuing a greater share of public debt externally.

SURGE IN LIQUIDITY INJECTIONS

From 2011, commercial banks in the WAEMU increased sharply their use of BCEAO liquidity and, as a result, moved from a structural liquidity surplus to a deficit (Figure 17.1, panel 1). Between the end of 2011 and the end of November 2014, outstanding central bank credit provided by the BCEAO to commercial banks increased from CFAF 630 billion to CFAF 1,980 billion. During the same period, banks' own reserves held at the BCEAO fell from CFAF 890 billion to CFAF –500 billion, leading to a decline in the coverage ratio (own reserves to required reserves) from 0.8 to –0.7. As a result, in 2013 the liquidity position of the banking system vis-à-vis the central bank swung from surplus into deficit. A liquidity deficit in the banking system is in principle desirable, as it potentially affords the BCEAO greater traction over the transmission of monetary policy.

Purchases of government securities were the main counterpart to the increase in borrowing from the central bank (Figure 17.1, panel 3). Commercial banks expanded their holdings of government securities from 17.7 percent to 22.0 percent of total assets between 2011 and 2014—a magnitude similar to the increase in their stock of outstanding borrowing from the BCEAO (from 4.3 percent to 9.0 percent of total assets). Over the same period, the level of banks' excess reserves remained broadly constant (Figure 17.1, panel 2), suggesting that banks may have increased their recourse to central bank credit, not for liquidity management purposes, but to fund higher levels of lending to the government. Consistent with this, individual bank-level data from 2014 (Figure 17.1, panel 4) also show that higher levels of borrowing from the BCEAO tend to be associated with larger holdings of government securities.

Around half of the WAEMU banking system currently draws on BCEAO liquidity. Individual bank-level data suggest that 46 out of a total of 106 banks that submitted data for stress-testing purposes at the end of the second quarter of 2014 had outstanding borrowings from the BCEAO. The biggest users of BCEAO liquidity were based in Benin, followed by Senegal, Côte d'Ivoire, and Burkina Faso.

Figure 17.1. WAEMU Developments in Commercial Banks' Balance Sheets

In 2013, commercial banks moved from a liquidity surplus to a deficit increasing their use of central bank liquidity, while running down their own reserves.

1. Source of Commercial Bank Reserves
(In billions of CFA francs)

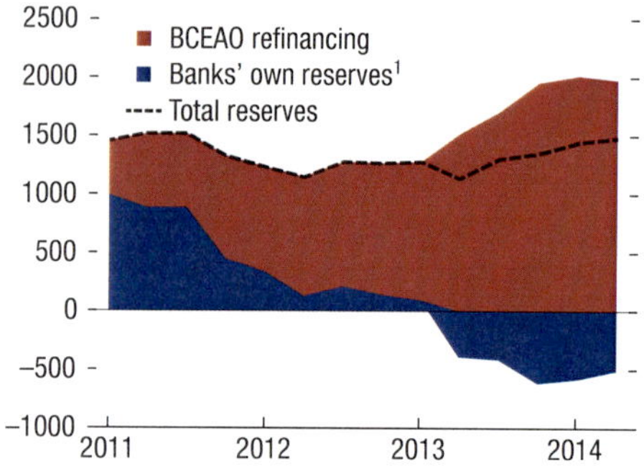

Source: Central Bank of West African States (BCEAO).
[1] Defined as total reserves less BCEAO refinancing.

Higher levels of borrowing from the central bank do not seem to have been motivated by banks' desire to bolster liquidity.

2. Commercial Banks' Excess Reserves

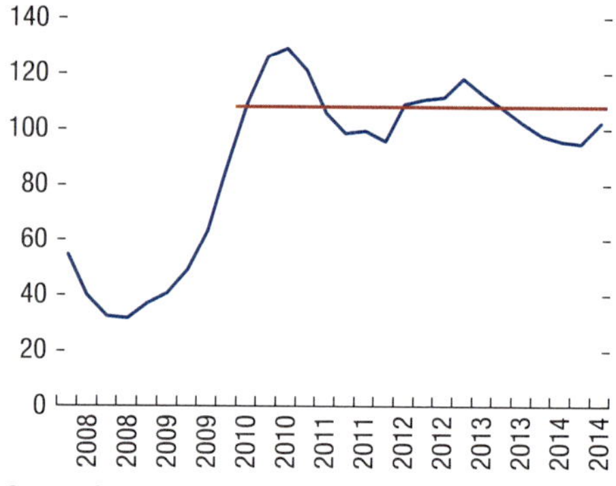

Source: Central Bank of West African States (BCEAO).

Banks appear to have used BCEAO funds to invest in government securities. This is evident both over time...

3. Commercial Banks: Outstanding Borrowings from the BCEAO and Holdings of Government Securities

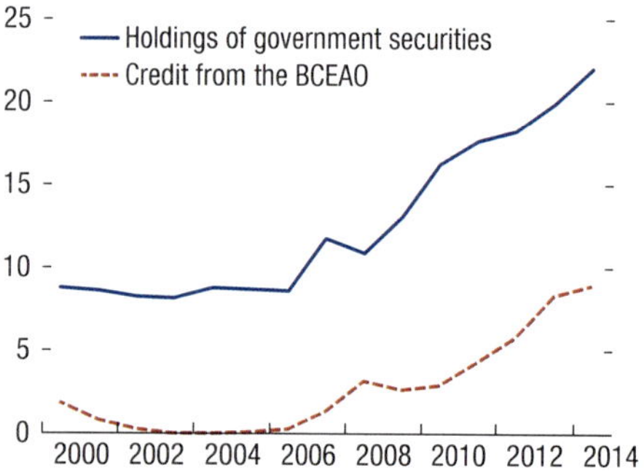

Source: Central Bank of West African States (BCEAO).

...and in the cross section of individual banks.

4. Government Securities Holdings and Borrowings from the BCEAO (2014:Q2)

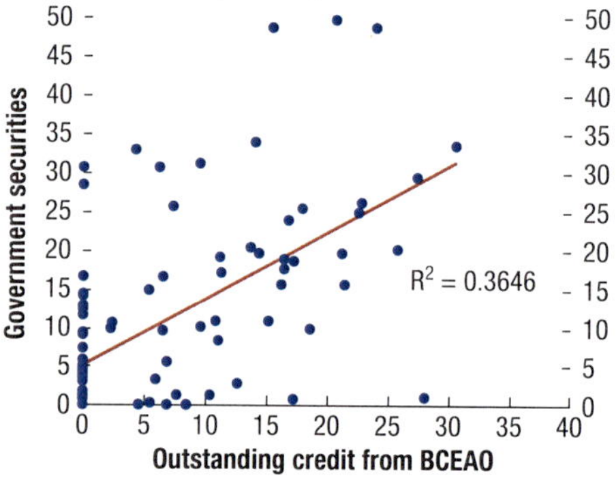

Source: Central Bank of West African States (BCEAO).

The level of central bank liquidity provision to commercial banks is unusually high in the WAEMU compared with other African countries...

5. Commercial Bank Liabilities to the Central Bank
(Percent of commercial bank assets)

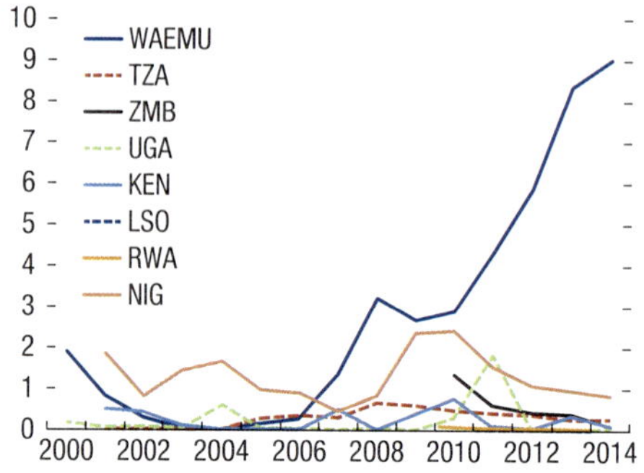

Source: National authorities.
Note: Three-letter International Organization for Standardization abbreviations used for country names.

...while the level of commercial banks' holding of government securities in the WAEMU is more similar to that of other countries, although the recent sharp increase is not.

6. Commercial Bank Claims on Government
(Percent of commercial bank assets)

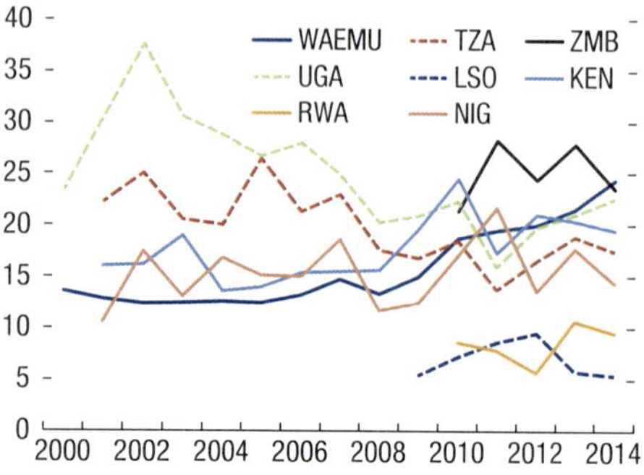

Source: National authorities.
Note: Three-letter International Organization for Standardization abbreviations used for country names.

Figure 17.2. WAEMU: Fiscal and External Imbalances

Fiscal and external balances deteriorated between 2011 and 2014...

1. Fiscal and External Balances (Percent of GDP)

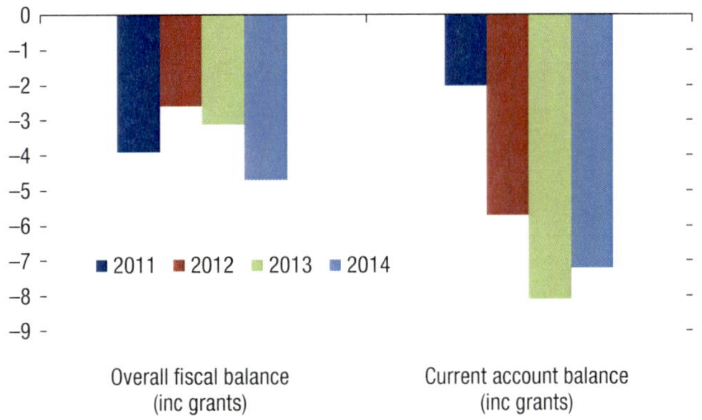

...while the share of government debt held by the domestic banking sector increased.

2. Holdings of WAEMU Public Debt (Percent of total debt)

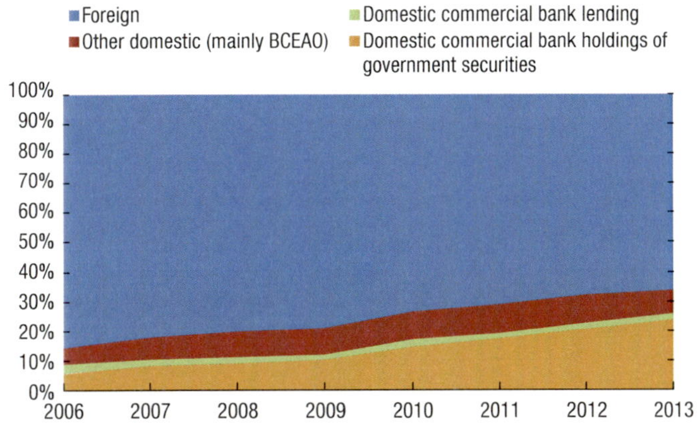

Sources: National authorities; and IMF staff calculations.

Cross-country comparison suggests that the level of central bank liquidity provision to commercial banks is unusually high in the WAEMU. In 2014, credit from the BCEAO represented around 9 percent of commercial bank assets in the WAEMU, compared with less than 1 percent in other African comparator countries (Figure 17.1, panel 5). And while the level of WAEMU commercial banks' holdings of government securities is more similar to that of other countries (at around 20 percent of assets), the sharp increase in such holdings is not (Figure 17.1, panel 6).

POSSIBLE CAUSES

The underlying driver of these developments was likely a combination of widening fiscal and external imbalances and carry-trade activity by banks.

In 2014, the overall fiscal deficit in the WAEMU increased to 4.7 percent of GDP, a historic high (Figure 17.2, panel 1). Much of this extra borrowing was necessarily financed by the

Figure 17.3. WAEMU Interest Rates
(In percent)

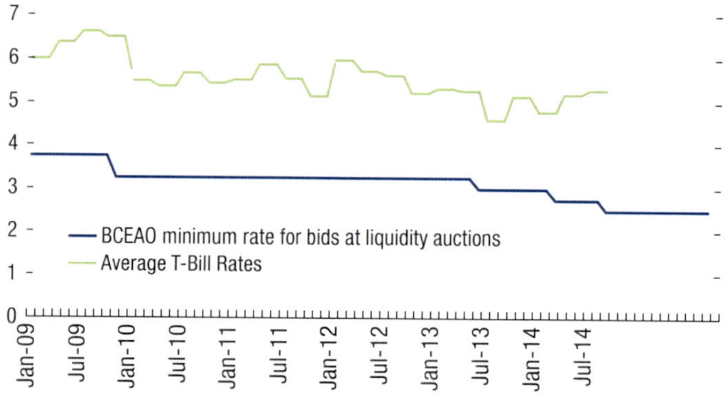

Source: Central Bank of West African States (BCEAO).

domestic commercial banks, given the lack of nonbank domestic investors and the limits on external borrowing for WAEMU members in order to maintain external debt sustainability following debt relief.

The fact that commercial banks appear to have financed additional lending to governments with central bank credit suggests that current levels of sovereign borrowing may be excessive, relative to the capacity of the regional market. Increased government financing constraints are also evident from data on WAEMU Treasury bill auctions, which in 2014 were undersubscribed.

Higher fiscal deficits also coincided with widening external deficits. The current account deficit in the WAEMU was 7.2 percent of GDP in 2014, compared with 2 percent in 2011. As the demand for foreign exchange among importers increased, the foreign exchange reserves of commercial banks declined, leading to deterioration in the banks' liquidity position. The BCEAO was then obliged to provide the shortfall in liquidity in order to meet its operational target of maintaining short-term money market rates close to the policy rates.

Market contacts suggested that some banks may have taken advantage of cheap short-term funding from the BCEAO in order to purchase longer-term and higher-yielding government securities. Given a large spread between the BCEAO minimum bid rate and Treasury bills (2.5 percent and about 5 percent, respectively, at the end of 2014), this strategy could potentially generate significant profits for banks (Figure 17.3).

RISKS TO STABILITY

The elevated and increasing level of central bank liquidity provision to commercial banks poses several potential macrofinancial risks, including to fiscal and financial stability, financial development, and the effectiveness of macroeconomic policy.

First, government borrowing that is indirectly financed by short-term BCEAO credit poses liquidity risks for governments and banks. If WAEMU governments become too dependent on BCEAO liquidity injections to the banking system in order to finance their deficits, a tightening of the monetary stance could create a financing gap. At the same time, a monetary tightening could leave banks unable to finance their holdings of longer-term government securities. If banks are unable to sell these securities due to the lack of a liquid secondary market, this could pose risks to financial stability.

Figure 17.4. WAEMU Interbank Market Activity by Maturity (Change: 2014 over 2013, in billions of CFA francs and percent)

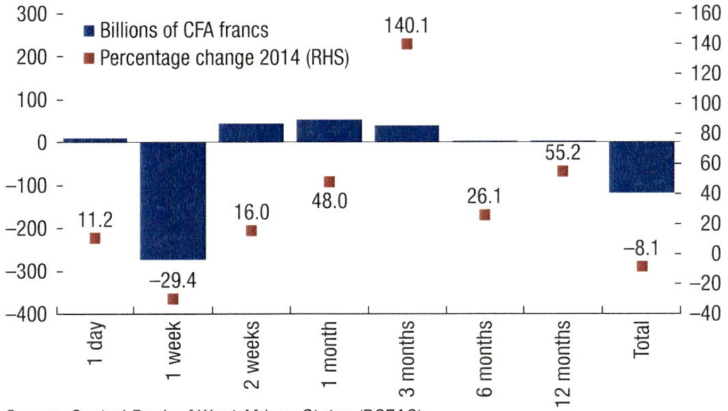

Source: Central Bank of West African States (BCEAO)

Second, a high concentration of government debt held by the domestic banking system creates potentially risky sovereign-bank feedback loops. In 2013, 26 percent of government debt was held by the domestic banking sector, compared with 17 percent in 2010. A high concentration of government debt held by domestic banks creates a direct feedback loop between fiscal and bank stability. Banks in the WAEMU are protected from market risk by holding government securities to maturity—and due to the lack of a well-functioning secondary market. Nevertheless, a sovereign default by one or more WAEMU members could still pose risks to bank solvency, given that banks are not obliged to hold capital against their lending to governments. On the other hand, WAEMU governments may find it difficult to finance their deficits in the event of instability in the domestic banking system.

Third, the development of interbank and other financial markets may be hindered. The development of the interbank market can be stymied if banks can borrow more cheaply and easily from the central bank, rather than from other banks. Indeed, between 2013 and 2014, interbank market activity contracted by 8 percent (Figure 17.4). On the other hand, high demand for bank credit from governments risks crowding out the development of consumer and corporate credit markets. Such underdevelopment, in turn, leads the financial sector to be less efficient (with potentially harmful consequences for growth), but also less resilient, since banks rely on one sole provider of liquidity—the central bank.

Finally, monetary policy may not be optimally set and the transmission mechanism may be weakened. If the risks to fiscal and financial stability discussed previously are material, the cost of tightening monetary policy will be higher when there is increasing inflationary pressure. And to the extent that elevated levels of central bank lending to commercial banks hinders the development of the interbank market, the transmission of monetary policy will be weakened. In developed financial markets, transmission of official policy rates from the central banks' direct counterparties to the wider financial system typically occurs through the interbank market. Underdevelopment of the interbank market in the WAEMU means this important channel is not fully active.

POLICY OPTIONS

WAEMU authorities should monitor closely the provision of central bank liquidity to commercial banks and, in light of the risks discussed in previous sections, consider whether a preemptive policy response might be required. Such a response could include fiscal, monetary, prudential, and debt-management policies.

A reduction in fiscal deficits is likely to be the most effective way of bringing down the elevated level of central bank liquidity provision to commercial banks. Lower fiscal deficits would reduce commercial banks' demands for funding from the central bank to finance them. But a tighter fiscal stance would also help to improve the external deficit and, hence, ease the pressure on banks' liquidity positions that results from drawdowns of their foreign exchange holdings.

Therefore, it is crucial that the authorities implement their planned consolidation plans. According to projections, under these plans, the fiscal deficit would fall to 2.8 percent of GDP and the current account deficit (including grants) to 5.5 percent of GDP by 2019. In the absence of this planned consolidation, monetary policy would have to be tightened to reduce private sector demand to preserve external stability.

The rules governing central bank liquidity operations could be modified to discourage carry trade activity by commercial banks. Given the current benign inflation outlook, an increase in the policy rate is inappropriate at this juncture. However, the BCEAO could use more targeted policies to tighten liquidity only for those banks that have high levels of borrowing from the central bank. For example, the refinancing ratio (the maximum permitted stock of outstanding BCEAO refinancing relative to total assets, applied on an individual bank basis) could be reduced from its current level of 35 percent.

Market distortions that incentivize banks to invest in government securities could be mitigated through changes in prudential regulation. For example, the capital requirement applied to banks' holdings of government securities could be raised from its current level of zero. The tax exemption relating to interest received on holdings of government securities could also be removed.

Regulatory barriers to entry for financial institutions other than domestic banks could be relaxed. An increased market presence of nonbank financial institutions in the WAEMU—both domestic and foreign—could relieve the burden on the domestic banking system to finance government borrowing.

Finally, a greater share of public debt could be issued externally. A higher share of public debt held by foreigners would also ease the burden on the domestic banking system to finance government debt and lessen sovereign-bank feedback loops. However, any increase in external debt would need to be consistent with external debt sustainability.

BIBLIOGRAPHY

Kireyev, A. 2015. "How to Improve the Effectiveness of Monetary Policy in the West African Economic and Monetary Union." IMF Working Paper 15/99, International Monetary Fund, Washington.

Mishra, P., P. Montiel, and A. Spilimbergo. 2012. "Monetary Transmission in Low-Income Countries: Effectiveness and Policy Implications." *IMF Economic Review* 60(2): 270–302.

Saxegaard, M. 2006. "Excess Liquidity and Effectiveness of Monetary Policy: Evidence from Sub-Saharan Africa." IMF Working Paper 06/15, International Monetary Fund, Washington.

CHAPTER 18

Monetary Policy and Inflation

CENTRAL BANK OF WEST AFRICAN STATES (BCEAO)

The objective of this chapter is to determine the impact of a change in the key interest rates of the Central Bank of West African States (BCEAO), as well as other economic, monetary, and financial aggregates, on inflation in the West African Economic and Monetary Union (WAEMU). Specifically, the effects of interest rates, the money supply, imported inflation from the euro area, domestic credit, the fiscal deficit, and the output gap on inflation are evaluated. To this end, error correction models (ECMs) are used to calculate short- and long-term elasticities, while vector autoregressive (VAR) models are used to evaluate the generalized impulse response functions. The results show that most monetary and financial variables have an impact on the inflation rate. The impact of domestic credit on inflation seems to be greater than that of interest rates. Furthermore, the impact of the fiscal deficit on price trends is generally felt only over the long term. Therefore, efforts to control inflationary pressures should focus on the use of monetary policy instruments as well as on structural reforms to increase supply, which partially explains the evolution of the overall price level in the short term.

Targeting price stability

The institutional reform of the West African Economic and Monetary Union (WAEMU), which took effect on April 1, 2010, established price stability as an explicit objective for the central bank. The framework implemented by the bank with the aim of achieving this objective comprises three components: a definition of price stability as an annual variation in the Harmonized Index of Consumer Prices (IHPC) of between 1 and 3 percent; the use of the inflation forecast as the principal indicator for the implementation of monetary policy; and the adoption by the Monetary Policy Committee, on a quarterly basis, of the measures necessary to achieve this objective.

The overall aim of this paper is to determine the impact of different economic, monetary, and financial variables on inflation in economies of WAEMU. Specifically, the intent is to measure the impact of a change in the key BCEAO rates, as well as other economic and financial aggregates, on inflation. In this process, owing to the diverse factors that could affect the inflation forecasts, it would be important to look at all of the variables that could influence changes in the overall price level. Monetary and credit aggregates, the economic outlook, and measurements of the output gaps are of interest, in particular for inflation rates over the medium term. Over the short term, factors such as the exchange rate, prices for major commodities such as petroleum products, administered prices, and profit margins would seem to be more significant a priori (Assenmacher-Wesche and Gerlach 2007).

In empirical terms, a number of studies have been performed within the BCEAO since 1996, with the aim of achieving a better understanding of the implementation of monetary policy. These empirical studies have made it possible to identify the determining factors in price dynamics within the Union. They have addressed issues such as imported inflation (Dembo Toé 2010; Doe and Diallo 1997), interest rates (Nubukpo 2003; Diop and Adoby 1997), the money supply (Dembo Toé and Hounkpatin 2007), domestic output (Nubukpo 2003), food production (Diallo 2003), public spending (Doe and Diallo 1997), and the nominal effective exchange rate (Dembo Toé 2010).

Most of these studies use relatively similar methodologies. They usually construct and estimate econometric models of the VAR or ECM type. Specifically, Diop and Adoby (1997) deal with the determination of "simple ratios for measuring the impact of monetary policy on prices" and it contains calculations of elasticity coefficients that allow measuring the impact of monetary policy on prices. Based on monthly data, they estimate a model derived from the balance in the money market. This model has as explanatory variables the money supply (M2) and the interest rate from money market auctions. The results obtained revealed differences in the effects of variations in the money supply and the interest rate on prices within the Union's member countries. An increase of 1 percentage point in the money supply over the long term resulted in a rise in the consumer price index of 0.43 percentage point in Benin, 0.28 percentage point in Burkina Faso, 0.45 percentage point in Côte d'Ivoire, and 0.41 percentage point in Mali. The influence of the money supply on prices appeared to be minor in Niger, Senegal, and Togo. The authors explain the absence of a relationship in certain countries, Senegal in particular, by the fact that a strictly administered price regime was in place during the period of the study. An increase of 1 percentage point in the interest rate over the long term caused a drop in prices by 0.30 percentage point in Benin, 0.18 percentage point in Burkina Faso, 0.41 percentage point in Niger, and 0.36 percentage point in Senegal. In Côte d'Ivoire, Mali, and Togo, the interest rate did not have a significant influence on inflation.

Empirical studies performed in other African countries reveal the impact of money supply and the output gap on inflation. Barnichon and Peiris (2008) use the following as explanatory variables for inflation in countries in sub-Saharan Africa: the output gap, money (the real money gap, that is, the difference between the money supply and demand), and rainfall. The results of their study produce elasticities of 0.28 for the output gap, 0.34 for money, and –0.13 for rainfall. The elasticity of the output gap is 0.42 for the countries outside the CFA zone and 0.32 for countries in the sample within the CFA zone (Cameroon, Côte d'Ivoire, Mali, Niger, Senegal). The elasticity of money is also higher in the countries outside the CFA zone (0.37) than in countries within the CFA zone (0.15). Ocran (2007), in an inflation model for Ghana, obtains a money supply elasticity of 0.42. Kovanen (2011), however, shows that money explains only a small part of the evolution of prices in Ghana and obtained an elasticity of the output gap with respect to inflation of 0.91.

A number of studies also point to the role of inflation inertia in the majority of countries in sub-Saharan Africa and the limited ability to explain the evolution of inflation by changes in the money supply. For the WAEMU, Dembo Toé and Hounkpatin (2007) show that the current level of inflation depends heavily on lagged price changes. Thus, 82.6 percent of the forecast error of the IHPC in the WAEMU is due to its own innovations (residuals), 3.8 percent is due to those in the nominal effective exchange rate, 8.8 percent is due to the evolution of imported inflation, and 4.8 percent to variation in the money supply.

Adebiyi (2007) obtains similar results for Ghana and Nigeria. Over a four-year horizon, 72 percent of the forecast error for inflation in Nigeria and 93 percent of the forecast error in Ghana is due to its own innovations (residuals), while 27 percent in Nigeria and 6 percent in Ghana is due to fluctuations in the money supply. Furthermore, the elasticity of the inertial component of inflation is estimated to be 0.54 for countries in sub-Saharan Africa (Barnichon and Peiris 2008). The present study expands upon the approach taken by Diop and Adoby (1997) by taking other economic and financial variables into account in the modeling, on the one hand, and by considering more recent statistical data, on the other hand.

A number of studies conducted for WAEMU member countries have looked at the influence of different economic and financial variables, in addition to the money supply and the interest rate, on inflation. These variables include, in particular, lagged inflation, imported inflation, oil prices, the evolution of liquidity, and variables related to pressures on the commodity markets and food production. The study by Cecchiti, Chu, and Steindel (2000) defines three main categories of variables used to predict inflation. These are, first, the prices for raw materials (oil prices, gold prices, price indices for a set of commodities, and so on). A steady rise in prices for these products would result in an increase in inflation. Second, financial indicators (the exchange rate, monetary aggregates, the difference between long-term and short-term interest rates) would affect the inflation rate. A decline in the exchange rate or a rapid increase in monetary aggregates could signal a rise in inflation. Finally, indicators of the state of the real economy (capacity utilization rate, unemployment rate, and the like) could serve as variables for predicting inflation. A steady rise in the capacity utilization rate or a drop in the unemployment rate beyond a certain threshold would result in inflationary pressures.

Inflation dynamics

During the period January 2001 to December 2014, the year-over-year average inflation rate was 3.6 percent. If 2008 is excluded—a year marked by a sharp rise in prices for foodstuffs—the average inflation rate was 2.8 percent (Figure 18.1).

Figure 18.2 shows a similar profile for the evolution of inflation in the WAEMU and trends in overall liquidity. A lag between the fluctuations in the money supply and the changes in prices is visible.

Figure 18.1. Evolution of Year-Over-Year Inflation in WAEMU (Percent)

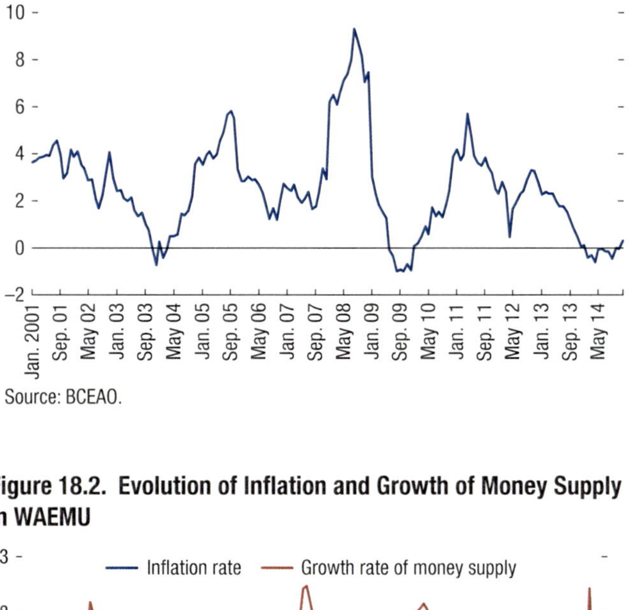

Source: BCEAO.

Figure 18.2. Evolution of Inflation and Growth of Money Supply in WAEMU

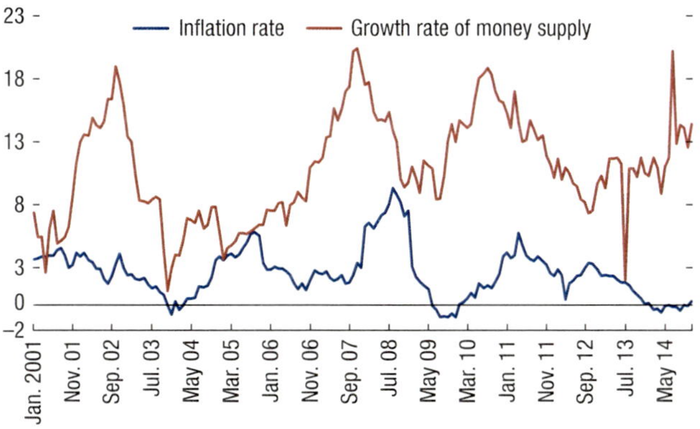

Source: BCEAO.

Figure 18.3. Comparative Trends in the Inflation Rate in the WAEMU and the BCEAO Key Rate (Year-over-Year)

Source: BCEAO.

The BCEAO's marginal lending rate was modified a number of times during the period January 1997 to December 2014 (Figure 18.3). These changes are generally consistent with the evolution of inflation. Indeed, most of the reductions in the marginal lending rate occurred within the context of a slowdown in inflation, while increases in the rate took place during periods of an acceleration of inflation. Nevertheless, it should be noted that these rates remained fixed during certain episodes of inflationary pressures in the Union, in particular in 2001, 2005, and 2011.

Methodology

The specification of the relationship between inflation and the different variables is based on the theoretical and empirical foundations of the determinants of inflation. In theoretical terms, the changes related to monetary policy instruments, primarily the key lending rates and control over the money supply, can affect the overall price level. According to Mishkin and others (2010), monetary policy influences the level of economic activity through four channels—interest rates, bank lending, asset prices, and exchange rates—as well as expectations. In their study of the monetary policy being pursued by the BCEAO, Ary Tanimoune and Tenou (2010) found that the two main channels used in the WAEMU economies appear to be interest rates and lending. In this connection, the present study includes variables related to these channels, including the maximum marginal lending rate, the money market rate, the bank borrowing rate, and lending to the economy by banks.

Furthermore, with the aim of identifying other variables that could interact with the overall price level, two main theoretical models were considered—the traditional monetarist model and a model derived from the new Phillips curve. According to the monetarist approach, growth in the money supply, its lagged and current values, are the key variables affecting inflation. In addition to these variables, changes in food and energy prices (supply shocks), as well as an increase in budget spending, could affect overall price levels. The new formulation of the Phillips curve is based on the Keynesian school of thought. This theoretical approach identifies three main determinants of inflation, namely, the output gap, which represents the difference between actual output and potential output; expected inflation, lagged inflation, or both; and supply shocks. It should be mentioned that other models could be used to identify explanatory factors related to the overall price level (Mehra 1988). The choice of models takes into account empirical studies performed for WAEMU countries, as well as economic shocks, such as the currency devaluation of 1994 and the sharp rise in food prices in 2008.

To measure the link between inflation and the different variables, error correction and VAR models were used. The ECM models allowed for a determination of the short- and long-term elasticities among several variables. The VAR models were used to analyze the impact of each of the variables on the others. Finally, the impact of a shock on the variables and the reaction times of each variable following the shock on other variables were evaluated based on the impulse response functions of the VAR models.

In practical terms, an analysis of the stationarity properties of the variables showed that the variables are not stationary. They do have a first order of integration and there is a cointegrating relationship among them. Therefore, several versions of the ECM (equation 18.1) following the specification of Davidson and Hendry (1978) were estimated:

$$\begin{aligned} Dlog(IHPC_t) = a + \beta_1 Dlog(X_t) + \beta_2 Dlog(M2_t) + \beta_3 log(IHPC_{t-1}) \\ + \beta_4 log(X_{t-1}) + \beta_5 log(M2_{t-1}) + \varepsilon_t \end{aligned} \quad (18.1)$$

in which $IHPC_t$ represents the inflation rates for year t, $M2_t$ is the money supply at time t, and X_t is a set of explanatory variable or variables of the selected models; t is the index for the year, α is the constant, ε_t are the error terms,

The β_1 and β_2 parameters are coefficients that describe the short-term dynamics, while β_4 and β_5 are the long-term coefficients. The β_3 parameter is the error correction coefficient. For the ECM to be valid, this coefficient needs to be negative, statistically significant, and have an absolute value of less than 1. All data series are derived from the BCEAO database. The study was performed on the basis of monthly and annual data, depending on the models used. The monthly data cover the period from January 2001 to December 2014. Given the absence of intra-annual data on GDP, annual data from 2001 to 2014 were used to estimate the elasticities of the output gap.

IHPC refers to the Harmonized Index of Consumer Prices in WAEMU countries, which has been calculated by the national statistics offices according to a harmonized methodology since 1997. The selection of the gross IHPC, rather than the underlying inflation indicator is due both to a desire not to deviate from the measurement used in the definition of target inflation, and to a desire to have benchmarks similar to those of other relevant studies that deal primarily with the gross IHPC.

The following dependent variables are subsumed for the estimated equations.

CRED refers to domestic credit

IHPC_ZEURO is the Harmonized Index of Consumer Prices in the euro area. It is a proxy for imported inflation in the equations based on monthly data.

The output gap (*GAPUEMOA*) represents the gap between the real level of GDP and its potential level. Two quite different paths can be taken to define potential GDP: the statistical approach, which consists of extracting *a posteriori* the trend, deterministic or stochastic, of a GDP series; and the economic approach, which attempts to determine the maximum level of activity compatible with price stability. In this study, the output gap is measured by the difference between the logarithm of actual output (real GDP) and the logarithm of potential output (Y*). Potential output is determined by the Hodrick-Prescott (HP) filter H-P filter (see Diop 2000 for details).

TGPM is the maximum marginal lending rate of the BCEAO. The central bank's key lending rate is the minimum auction rate for one week. This rate was established in August 2008. The marginal lending rate (repo rate) is also a key rate of the BCEAO. It is equal to the minimum auction rate plus 100 basis points. Thus, the variations in these two key rates are technically synchronous. The marginal lending rate is used here primarily because of its availability throughout the entire period covered by the study.

TMM is the money market rate, while *TDEBITEUR* represents the bank borrowing rate.

DEP is the ratio of the government spending to the real GDP of the Union.

DEFICIT refers to the ratio of deficits to the real GDP of the Union.

The dummy variables *DUM94* and *DUM08* capture the respective effects of the shocks of 1994 and 2008.

The expected signs of variables are the following:

A decline in the key rates (–) allows banks to obtain refinancing at a lower cost. Banks can thus pass on the reduction in refinancing costs to the borrowing rates that they offer to households and businesses, which encourages activity, but this can also place upward pressure on demand and on prices. Conversely, a rise in key rates tends to boost borrowing rates, which could curb activity and could lead to a drop in prices.

The money supply should have a positive impact on inflation over the short and long terms. In fact, an increase in overall liquidity, in particular through domestic credit, leads to an increase in total demand, which results in additional inflation, all else equal. The same is true for the other monetary variables (currency in circulation, narrow money, base money).

The sign of the output gap (*GAPUEMOA*) should be positive. Theoretically, during peaks in the economic cycle, the output gap is positive: output is temporarily higher than its equilibrium level and enterprises can achieve this level of output only by incurring higher costs, in particular salary costs, which are reflected in prices. In this case, there is an increase in inflation. Conversely, during economic downturns, the gap is negative and inflation drops.

Imported inflation (*IHPC_ZEURO*) can also be responsible for cost inflation. Owing to globalization and the fact that a number of firms import a significant proportion of their raw materials or semifinished products, companies may be forced to raise the prices of their products to deal with a decline in the exchange rate, a rise in raw materials prices in the international market, or an external shock.

The fiscal deficit ratio (*DEFICIT*) is expected to have a positive effect on the overall price level. The effect of fiscal policy on prices in countries in the Union can be explained by the nature of public spending and the method used for financing fiscal deficits.

For credit (*CRED*), an increase in this lending could cause a rise in the overall price level in connection with the pressure that an easing of credit terms could put on the economy as a whole.

An increase in government spending (DEP) could induce an upward pressure on the overall price level. Thus, a positive sign would be expected.

Finally, economic shocks related to devaluation and to a steep rise in food prices could have a positive impact on inflation in the countries in the Union. Thus, the dummy variables (*DUM94* and *DUM08*) should have positive signs.

Policies and inflation

The results of the estimates presented in Table 18.1 show the influence of monetary, financial, and economic variables on the dynamics of the IHPC. In an effort to avoid the risks of multicolinearity among the explanatory variables and to show the impact of each of them on the IHPC, they have been included gradually in the different regressions (see models 1 through 7 in Table 18.1). The econometric tests showed that the variables with a monthly frequency all have a first order of integration (I(1)), with the exception of the money market rate (*TMM*) and the fiscal deficit ratio (*DEFICIT*) for the annual data (see Annex 18.1, Annex Table 18.1.1). The variables in models 1 through 6 are all cointegrated, however, with the exception of those in model 7.

The adjustment coefficient, which appeared to be negative, significant (in models 1 through 6), and less than 1 in absolute terms, validates the ECM. This coefficient represents the speed at which any imbalance between the desired and actual levels of the IHPC is absorbed in the month following any shock. Consequently, the influence of the maximum marginal lending rate (*TGPM*), the

TABLE 18.1

Error Correction Models of the Link between Inflation and Different Variables in the WAEMU*

Explanatory Variables	Model 1	Model 2	Model 3	Model 4	Model 5	Model 6	Model 7
DLOG(TGPM)	−0.0104*** (−8.9)						
DLOG(TMM)		−0.4016*** (−4.4)					
DLOG(TDEBITEUR)			−0.152** (−2.64)				
DLOG(M2)					0.0199** (2.5)		
DLOG(IHPC_ZEURO)						0.1086*** -2.2	
DLOG(CRED)				0.5432*** -13.89			
D(DEFICIT)		0.0087* -1.94	0.0066*** (5.1)				
LOG(IHPC(−1))	−0.0167*** (−7.1)	−0.4560*** (−5.28)	−0.0503*** (−4.78)	−0.1359*** (−9.1)	−0.0976*** (−9.6)	−0.1469** (−6.8)	
LOG(TGPM(−1))	−0.0752*** (−4.8)						
LOG(TMM(−1))		−0.2860*** (−4.92)					
LOG(TDEBITEUR(−1))			−0.1121*** (−5.40)				
LOG(M2(−1))					0.0229*** (8.3)		
LOG(IHPC_ZEURO(−1))						0.1815*** -6.3	
LOG(CRED(−1))				0.3278*** (9.01)			

(continued)

TABLE 18.1 (continued)

Error Correction Models of the Link between Inflation and Different Variables in the WAEMU*

Explanatory Variables	Model 1	Model 2	Model 3	Model 4	Model 5	Model 6	Model 7
DEFICIT(−1)		0.0105***	0.0067***				
		(2.34)	(4.23)				
LOG(GAPUEMOA)							0.1376***
							−8.06
LOG(DEP)							0.5718***
							(7.15)
DUM94				0.2018***			0.1095***
				(32.5)			(4.62)
DUM08	0.0030**				0.0092***	0.0043***	
	(2.5)				(8.8)	(10.2)	
Constant	0.1265***	2.5130***	−0.0167	0.2187	0.0803***	−0.1099***	−4.5898***
	(7.1)	(5.23)	(−0.29)	−1.1	−5.8	(−4.0)	(−3.85)
R^2	0.718	0.838	0.87	0.818	0.678	0.837	0.907
Prob(F-Stat)	0	0.011	0.001	0	0	0	0
S.E.	0.001	0.019	0.006	0.004	0.002	0.001	0.074
DW	2.571	2.849	2.686	2.501	2.098	2.374	1.81

* Note: The values between (...) represent the Student's t values. Models 1, 4, 5, and 6 are estimated on the basis of monthly data and models 2, 3, and 7 are based on annual data. (***) significant at the 1% level; (**) significant at the 5% level; (*) significant at the 10% level.

The results of the Eviews program are provided in the Annex and the results of the robustness tests are available.

money market rate (*TMM*), the borrowing rate (*TDEBITEUR*), the money supply (*M2*), domestic credit (*CRED*), imported inflation (*IHPC_ZEURO*), and the fiscal deficit ratio (*DEFICIT*) on the Harmonized Index of Consumer Prices in the WAEMU is sufficiently captured by the short- and long-term dynamics. Furthermore, the tests indicate a lack of a cointegration relationship between the output gap (*GAPUEMOA*) and the Harmonized Index of Consumer Prices (*IHPC*). In other words, long-term dynamics should be sufficient to explain the influence of a percentage variation in the gap between actual output and potential output on inflation in the WAEMU (model 7, Table 18.1).

The estimates show that the models are generally statistically significant with coefficients that present the expected signs. In addition, 67.8 percent and 90.7 percent of the fluctuations in the IHPC in the WAEMU can be explained by the short-term and long-term variables used, respectively. Furthermore, the coefficients of all of the explanatory variables are statistically significant at the 5 percent level over the short and long terms. Following a robust estimate of heteroscedasticity, the tests performed on the residuals showed that they are normally distributed, and that they are not autocorrelated but homoscedastic. In addition, the Ramsey test (RESET) was used to confirm that the models are properly specified.

Interest rates and inflation. The estimates indicate a negative and significant relationship between changes in the marginal lending rate and changes in inflation in the WAEMU over the short and long terms (Model 1). An increase of 1 percent in the marginal lending rate would result in a drop in prices in the Union by 0.01 percent and 0.08 percent over the short and long terms, respectively. In addition, the impulse response function (Annex Figure 18.1.1) of the VAR model shows that a shock to the BCEAO key rate, specifically the marginal lending rate, would result in a drop in inflation, which would stabilize after about 14 months. The impact of the marginal lending rate and the money market rate on inflation is transmitted primarily through bank borrowing rates. In fact, it is expected that an increase in the central bank's key rates would result in a rise in bank borrowing rates and ultimately in a decline in the demand for credit and in lower prices.

On the whole, changes in the main interest rates have an impact on inflation in the WAEMU. Thus, by modifying the key rates, the central bank can influence the future level of inflation in the WAEMU. In this connection, the impact of interest rates on price trends is clearly evident over the short and long terms. At the same time, the impact is relatively weak compared with that of domestic credit and the bank borrowing rate, and particularly compared with the level of domestic output and imported inflation. An increase of 25 basis points in the BCEAO's marginal lending rate would lead to a reduction in inflation of just 0.26 percentage point over the short term and by 0.19 percentage point over the long term. On this basis, actions aimed at countering inflationary pressures should be aimed both at the use of monetary policy instruments and at structural reforms to increase supply.

Money supply, domestic credit, and inflation. Changes in the money supply (M2) and in domestic credit have a significant impact on inflation in the WAEMU over both the short term and the long term (models 4 and 5). An increase in the money supply of 1 percentage point would result in additional inflation of 0.02 percentage point over the short term and 0.023 percentage point over the long term. These results are in line with those obtained by Barnichon and Peiris (2008) for countries in the CFA zone. The impulse from a monetary shock would result in a positive inflationary reaction that would dissipate after 14 months. The elasticity of inflation with respect to the money supply in the Union also appears to be weaker than that estimated for countries outside the CFA zone, in particular Ghana and Nigeria. Furthermore, growth in domestic credit of 1 percent would result in an increase in inflation of 0.54 percentage point over the short term and 0.33 percentage point over the long term. This finding is consistent with the results obtained by Héricourt and Matei (2007) for central and eastern European countries. The impact of domestic credit on inflation in the WAEMU is greater than the impact of the BCEAO's key rates.

On the whole, changes in the money supply and in domestic credit have an influence on the dynamics of inflation in the WAEMU. The impact, however, is relatively weaker than that observed in other countries in sub-Saharan Africa. The low level of elasticity of inflation in relation to the money supply is a reflection of the prudent monetary policy stance in the WAEMU, which is characterized by the monitoring of injections of liquidity and moderate changes in base money. Indeed, the monetary policy implemented by the BCEAO has ensured that changes in the money supply are in line with changes in GDP, so as not to contribute to inflation in the Union.

The output gap and inflation. The impact of the output gap on inflation is estimated on the basis of annual data owing to the absence of quarterly GDP data over an extended period. The growth rate in potential output dropped from about 4 percent in 1972 to 1.5 percent on average in the 1980s. It fell following the devaluation in 1994 and remained at about 0.3 percent between 1995 and 2014 (Figure 18.4). The output gap calculated by the percentage variation in the difference between actual output and potential output has been consistently negative throughout the past 10 years. This situation reflects actual output that falls short of the economy's potential. Figure 18.5 also shows an essentially positive relationship between the output gap and the inflation rate. An inverse relationship between the trends in inflation and the output gap has been observed during several periods, however, including 2002, 2004, 2006–07, 2009, and 2011, most of which were marked by droughts, when the theoretical relationship between the output gap and inflation does not hold up.

In the WAEMU countries, changes in GDP do, in fact, depend primarily on the performance of the primary sector (agricultural production). Thus, a substantial decline in agricultural

Figure 18.4. Actual Output and Potential Output in the WAEMU
(as a percentage)

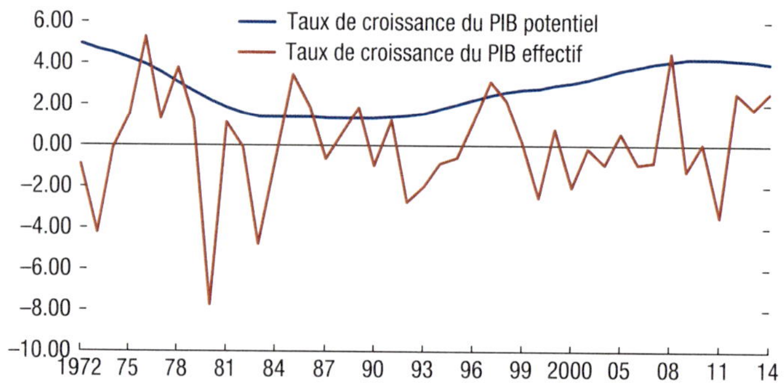

Figure 18.5. Inflation and the Output Gap in the WAEMU
(as a percentage)

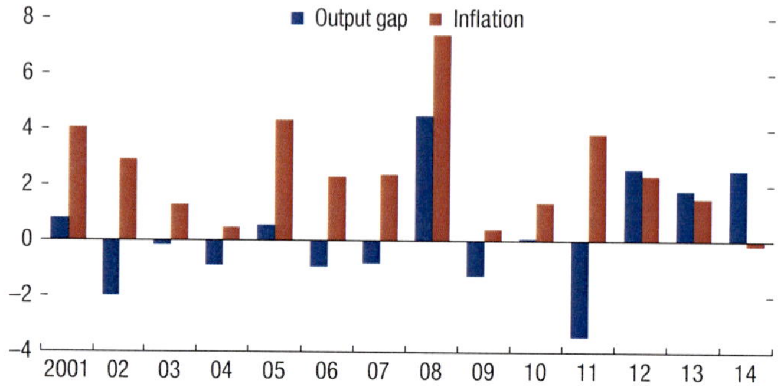

production linked to a period of drought is reflected in a drop in actual output, a contraction of the output gap, and a rise in inflation. Likewise, a positive output gap is not often the result of an overheated economy, but rather strong agricultural production. A dummy variable has been introduced to neutralize some of the phenomena described above (*DUM08*).

The estimation of an ECM indicates the absence of a relationship between inflation and the production gap over the short term. Over the long term, an increase in the output gap by 1 percentage point would result in a rise in the inflation rate by 0.57 percentage point (model 7, Table 18.1). This elasticity of 0.14 is lower than the figure of 0.3 obtained by Barnichon and Peiris (2008) for countries in sub-Saharan Africa, the figure of 0.4 estimated by Diop (2000) for WAEMU member countries, and the indicator of 0.91 for Ghana (Kovanen 2011). This result is related to the stability of the inflation rate observed in the WAEMU zone.

The fiscal deficit and inflation. The estimations indicate that the fiscal deficit (and public spending, accordingly) in relation to GDP has a positive and significant impact on inflation in the WAEMU over both the short term and the long term. In fact, an increase of 1 percent in the fiscal deficit would result in a rise in inflation of between 0.67 percentage point and 0.87 percentage point over the short term and between 0.66 percentage point and 1.05 percentage point over the long term (models 2 and 3). In addition, an increase in the ratio of public spending to GDP would mean an increase in the inflation rate of 0.14 percentage point.

Domestic inflation and inflation imported from the euro area. The results show a positive link between inflation in the WAEMU and inflation imported from the euro area. Thus, a 1 percent decline in inflation in the euro area would result in a decline in inflation in the WAEMU by 0.11 percentage point over the short term and by 0.18 percentage point over the long term. Indeed, a rise in imported inflation causes an upturn in domestic inflation through imports of goods. These imported products represented on average about 32 percent in 2005–13) of goods and services in the consumer basket in the WAEMU. Furthermore, a significant number of local goods consumed by households have considerable import content. In view of this, the evolution of prices in the Union's main trading partners in the euro area has an impact on domestic inflation. This finding is in line with the results obtained by Doe and Diallo (1997), who find that imported inflation, from France in particular, is the principal factor affecting the evolution of prices in the WAEMU over both the short term and the long term. The impulse response function indicates that domestic inflation reacts positively to a positive imported inflation shock, with a return to its long-term equilibrium after 15 months.

Certain transitory shocks, in particular the currency devaluation of 1994 (*DUM94*) and the shock to food prices (*DUM08*), significantly affected the dynamics of the inflation rate in the WAEMU.

Table 18.2 summarizes the elasticities determined using various equations based on the different models.

TABLE 18.2

Elasticities of Inflation with Respect to Different Variables

Variable	Direction and Amount of Variation in the Variable	Elasticities (as %) Short Term	Long Term	Maximum Time Period
Marginal lending rate	1% increase	−0.01	−0.05	15 months
Money market rate	1% increase	−0.4	−0.29	15 months
Borrowing rate	1% increase	−0.15	−0.11	
Money supply (M2)	1% increase	0.12	0.21	14 months
Domestic credit	1% increase	0.54	0.33	14 months
Imported inflation (IHPC_ZEuro)	1% increase	0.11	0.18	15 months
Output gap	1% increase	–	0.14	–
Fiscal deficit/GDP	1% increase	0.67 to 0.87	0.66 to 1.05	

ANNEX 18.1

ANNEX TABLE 18.1

Unit Root Test

	Level				First Difference				
	ADF ca	ADF th	TREND	Constant	ADF ca	ADF th	TREND	Constant	CONCLUSION
LOG (IHPC)	-2.1	-2.95	yes	yes	-3.51	-2.95	no	yes	I(1)
LOG (IPC_ZEURO)	-3.43	-3.48	yes	yes	-5.58	-2.91	no	yes	I(1)
LOG (M2)	-3.29	-3.55	yes	yes	-3.62	-2.95	no	yes	I(1)
LOG (CRE)	-2.05	-2.95	no	yes	-3.05	-2.91	no	yes	I(1)
LOG (TGPM)	-1.5	-2.9	no	no	-4.9	-1.9	no	no	I(1)
LOG(TMM)	-3.84	-3.55	yes	yes	–	–	–	–	I(0)
LOG (TDEBITEUR)	-3.34	-3.55	yes	yes	-4.37	-3.55	no	no	I(1)
LOG (GAPUEMOA)	-2.92	-3.95	no	no	-6.16	-4.95	no	no	I(1)
LOG (DEFICIT)	-4.95	-3.55	yes	yes					I(0)
LOG(DEP)	-1.92	3.95	yes	no	-10.03	-3.55	no	no	I(1)

(*) I(0) at the 5% level; ADF ca: calculated value of the augmented Dickey-Fuller (ADF) statistic; ADF th: critical theoretical value of the ADF statistic.

Figure 18.A1. Response of Inflation to a Shock to the Marginal Lending Rate, the Money Market Rate, the Money Supply, and Domestic Credit

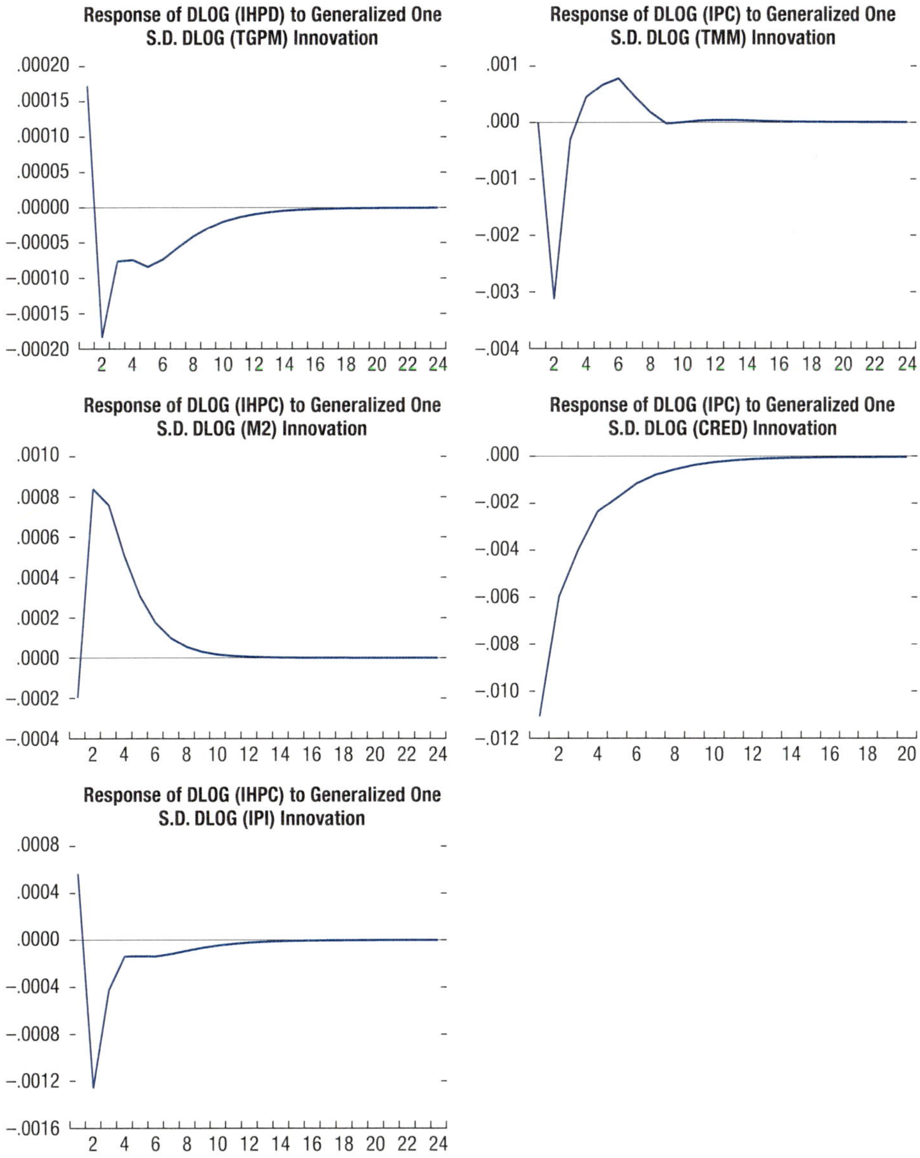

Source: BCEAO estimates.

REFERENCES

Adebiyi, M. A. 2007. *Inflation Targeting: Can We Establish a Stable and Predictable Relationship between Inflation and Monetary Policy Instruments in Nigeria and Ghana?* University of Lagos, Nigeria.

Ary Tanimoune, N. et Tenou K. 2010. « La politique monétaire dans l'UEMOA : le canal strict du crédit », présenté au cinquième Colloque BCEAO – Universités et Centres de recherche sur le thème : Quel secteur bancaire pour le financement des économies de l'UEMOA? Dakar, les 25 et 26 mai 2010.

Assenmacher-Wesche, K., and S. Gerlach. 2007. "Understanding the Link between Money Growth and Inflation in the Euro Area." In *The Travails of the Eurozone: Economic Policies, Economic Development*, edited by David Cobham, 10–29. Basingstoke, United Kingdom: Palgrave Macmillan.

Barnichon, R., and S. J. Peiris. 2008. "Sources of Inflation in Sub-Saharan Africa." *Journal of African Economies* 17 (5): 729–46.

Cechetti, G., Rita S. Chu, and C. Steindel. 2000. "The Unreliability of Inflation Indicators." *Current Issues in Economics and Finance* 6 (4). Federal Reserve Bank of New York. Published in French as "Comment prévoir l'inflation." *Problèmes Economiques*, No. 2683, October 2000.

Davidson, J. E. H., and D. F. Hendry. 1978. "Econometric Modeling of the Aggregate Time-Series Relationship between Consumers' Expenditure and Income in the United Kingdom." *Economic Journal* 88 (352): 661–92.

Dembo Toé, M. 2010. *Modèles de prévision de l'inflation dans les pays de l'UEMOA* [Models for Inflation Forecasting in WAEMU Countries] (in French). Document d'Etude et de Recherche, DER/10/03, BCEAO, décembre 2010 BCEAO.

———, and M. Hounkpatin. 2007. Lien entre la masse monétaire et l'inflation dans les pays de l'UEMOA [Link between the money supply and inflation in WAEMU countries] (in French). Document d'Etude et de Recherche, DER/07/02, BCEAO.

Doe, L. et Diallo, M. L. 1997, «Déterminants empiriques de l'inflation dans les pays de l'UEMOA», BCEAO, Etudes et Recherches, Notes d'Information et Statistiques (476), décembre 1997.

Diallo, M. L. A. 2003. L'impact de l'offre locale des produits vivriers sur les prix dans l'UEMOA [The impact of the local supply of foodstuffs on prices in the WAEMU] (in French). Document d'Etude et de Recherche, DER/03/01, BCEAO.

Diop, P. L. 2000. *Estimation de la production potentielle dans les pays de l'UEMOA* [Estimation of Potential Output in WAEMU Countries] (in French). BCEAO.

Diop, P. L. et Adoby, C. 1997. « Ratios simples de mesure de l'impact de la politique monétaire sur les prix », Document d'Etude et de Recherche, DRS/SR/97/01, BCEAO, Juin 1997.

Héricourt, J. and Matei, I. 2007. « Transmission de la politique monétaire dans les Pays d'Europe Centrale et Orientale: que savons-nous vraiment ? », Économie et Prévision, Programme National Persée, vol. 180 (4): 221–38.

Kovanen, A. 2011. "Does Money Matter for Inflation in Ghana?" IMF Working Paper 11/274, International Monetary Fund, Washington.

Mehra, Y. P. (1988), "The Forecast Performance of Alternative Models of Inflation." *Economic Review*, September/October 1988.

Mishkin, F., Bordes, C., Hautcoeur, P-C., Lacoue-Labarthe, D. et X. Ragot (2010) : « Monnaie, banque et marchés financiers », 9ème édition, Pearson.

Nubukpo, K. 2001. L'impact de la variation des taux d'intérêt directeurs de la BCEAO sur l'inflation et la croissance dans l'UMOA [The impact of a variation in key interest rates of the BCEAO on inflation and growth in the WAMU] (in French). Document d'Etude et de Recherche, DER/01/07, BCEAO.

———. 2003. « Dépenses publiques et croissance des économies de l'UEMOA », CIRAD, Monpellier (France). pp. 1–28.

Ocran, M. K. 2007. "A Modelling of Ghana's Inflation Experience: 1960–2003." AERC Research Paper 169, African Economic Research Consortium, Nairobi, Kenya.

PART V

Financial Development and Stability

PREFACE

The West African Economic and Monetary Union (WAEMU) aims at enhancing financial sector stability and development, and spearheading financial deepening and integration in the region. WAEMU authorities are working on enforcing the existing prudential standards required from banks and raising them to standards observed in other African countries and the rest of the world. Ongoing efforts to strengthen bank supervision and raise prudential standards go in the right overall direction. Holding of banking groups originating in the WAEMU are subject to regulation and consolidated supervision. Efforts to enhance crisis management and resolution frameworks have just started. A roadmap to Basel II/III is being implemented, with complete implementation anticipated by 2017–18.

Nevertheless, financial inclusion remains low. While it is increasing in the WAEMU, it lags behind that observed in the sub-Saharan African benchmark countries—Ghana, Kenya, Lesotho, Rwanda, Tanzania, Uganda, and Zambia. Financial inclusion in the WAEMU lags even further behind that seen in the Asian benchmark countries—Bangladesh, Cambodia, India, Laos, Nepal, and Vietnam. Only 6 percent of the WAEMU population has deposits in commercial banks, or about half the share found in African benchmark countries. Outstanding deposits with commercial banks amount to 30 percent of GDP, at par with African benchmark countries, but less than half the amount observed in Asian benchmark countries. The share of the population with access to microfinance institutions, about 10 percent, is about twice the share with access to the banking sector, but the outstanding credit of microfinance institutions amounts to only about 2 percent of GDP. Only 20 percent of firms have access to bank credit. On average, WAEMU countries rank in 125th place among 189 countries on access to credit. Compliance with key prudential ratios remains weak, and many prudential limits are lax.

The WAEMU's financial sector comprises:

- *The banking sector*—The banking sector includes 106 banks and 13 financial institutions, which together hold more than 90 percent of the financial system's assets. Five banks account for about 50 percent of banking assets. The ownership structure of the sector is changing fast, with the rapid rise of foreign-owned (pan-African) banks.
- *Microfinance institutions*—There are 759 registered microfinance institutions in the WAEMU, 61 of which are classified as large institutions with assets or deposits above CFAF 2 billion and are supervised by the Banking Commission. These account for 90 percent of the microfinance sector's assets.
- *Financial markets*—The regional stock market is based in Abidjan and has about 40 quoted companies and a capitalization of about12 percent of the WAEMU GDP. The debt market consists mostly of government paper and is about 10 percent of the WAEMU GDP. There is no significant secondary debt market, including for government paper.

Development of the financial sector can contribute to growth acceleration and broader inclusiveness of become an impediment for both. Chapter 19, Financial System Structure, reveals that the WAEMU's financial system is dominated by the banking sector, but is evolving rapidly with the emergence of new transnational banking groups and microfinance institutions. The regional securities and equity market is a marginal source of funding, except for governments. The interbank market remains shallow. The banking system in the region is highly heterogeneous. While most banks are adequately capitalized and profitable, pockets of vulnerability, including public banks, were identified. Compliance with prudential norms remains low for a number of ratios, suggesting a degree of regulatory forbearance, and some of these norms are not in line with international standards. Stress tests and financial soundness indicators show that concentration of lending and asset quality pose significant risks. The rising sovereign-bank linkage requires close monitoring.

The development of the WAEMU's financial sector largely lags behind that of most other comparator countries, including in sub-Saharan African countries. Chapter 20, Financial Development: Level, Depth, and Access, assesses the level of financial sector development in the WAEMU with respect to its depth, breadth, and access to financial services. This is compared with WAEMU countries themselves, with sub-Saharan African averages, and with individual countries. For each country and each key financial sector indicator, a structural benchmark is estimated, based on the country's economic and structural characteristics. The eight financial sectors of the WAEMU are assessed according to their depth, breadth, and access to financial services. Comparisons are also made with selected countries outside the WAEMU, namely Ghana and Kenya, as well as with the average and median for sub-Saharan Africa. Ghana is a natural comparator for many WAEMU countries, given its characteristics and geographic proximity. Kenya is an example of a sub-Saharan African economy with a rapidly developing financial sector. The mean and median for sub-Saharan Africa (including South Africa) reflect the development of the rest of the continent. To get a better sense of the progress needed to achieve a higher level of financial development, the WAEMU's financial depth can be evaluated relative to a group of high growth non-oil-exporter countries. Policy and institutional asymmetries between two groups of countries usually explain the gap in performance.

Insufficient development of the financing sector leads to low financial inclusion. Chapter 21, Financial Inclusion, looks at participation in the financial system and the sharing of benefits that arise from having access to financial services. WAEMU countries largely lag behind benchmark countries in several dimensions of financial inclusion. Access to finance is low, especially for the most vulnerable parts of the population, and the financial sector appears to only modestly contribute to the population's ability to deal with shocks as well as firms' investment programs. Private sector credit-to-GDP ratios, however, appear broadly in line with WAEMU countries' fundamentals. Public policies, such as investments in infrastructure and the social sectors, could help close these gaps. From firms' perspectives, policies to reduce participation costs in the financial sector and to lower collateral requirements could increase firms' access to financing, and thus significantly boost GDP.

Further development and inclusion require financial stability, which is critical for the proper functioning of the financial system. Chapter 22, Financial Sector Stability, looks in detail at the WAEMU's regulatory and supervisory framework, and finds that strengthening is necessary to address existing and new risks. The emergence of regional banking groups requires the development of supervision on a consolidated basis and strengthening of cooperation with banking supervisors in countries where these groups operate. The increasing exposure of banks to sovereigns is also a risk that needs to be recognized, including through a nonzero weight on government paper in capital adequacy calculations. Microprudential regulation should be revised to bring certain prudential standards closer to international best practices, for example on risk concentration, classification of claims and provisioning, while taking into account the regional context. The move to Basel II will would help address many of these issues. The WAEMU's financial crisis prevention and management framework needs strengthening. Crisis prevention requires greater transparency, including through the regular and timely compilation and publication of financial soundness indicators for all member countries. Regular stress tests would be a welcome step toward the introduction of an early warning system. There is also substantial scope for improving the bank resolution framework, which would reduce the budgetary cost of government intervention. Swift action in this area, including by giving broader powers to the supervisor and by collaborating closely with other supervisors in the case of cross-border groups, is necessary.

Mobile banking represents a unique opportunity to increase financial inclusiveness at a relatively low cost and to accelerate the development of the financial system. Chapter 23, Mobile Banking, discusses constraints to mobile banking in the WAEMU. With relatively high mobile phone penetration and a large market for cross-border payments in the WAEMU, the potential for growth in this area is high. This was evidenced by comparing the stance of mobile payments in WAEMU countries to those in other countries, such as Kenya and Tanzania. Transaction costs, issues of network interoperability, and legal and regulatory barriers may represent substantial constraints to development of the mobile market in the WAEMU. An overview of oversight issues on mobile payments uncovers the key pillars necessary to safeguard stability: minimum market entry requirements, financial integrity controls, funds safeguards, and payment stability.

CHAPTER 19

Financial System Structure

PATRICK IMAM AND CHRISTINA KOLERUS

The financial system in the West African Economic and Monetary Union (WAEMU) is dominated by the banking sector, but is evolving rapidly with the emergence of new transnational banking groups and microfinance institutions. The regional securities and equity market is a marginal source of funding, except for governments. The interbank market remains shallow. The banking system in the region is highly heterogeneous. While most banks are adequately capitalized and profitable, pockets of vulnerability, including public banks, were identified. Compliance with prudential norms remains low for a number of ratios, suggesting a degree of regulatory forbearance, and some of these norms are not in line with international standards. Stress tests and financial soundness indicators show that concentration of lending and asset quality pose significant risks. The rising sovereign-bank linkage requires close monitoring.

OVERVIEW

The financial system in the WAEMU remains largely bank-based. The banking sector comprises 107 banks and 13 financial institutions, which together hold more than 90 percent of the financial system's assets (Table 19.1). Five banks account for about 50 percent of banking assets (see Figure 19.1). The ownership structure of the sector is changing fast, with the rapid rise of foreign-owned (pan-African) banks. This contributes to higher competition but also rising heterogeneity in the banking system, with large and profitable cross-country groups competing with often weaker country-based (and sometimes government-owned) banks. Nonbank financial institutions are developing quickly, notably insurance companies, but remain overall small.

Microfinance institutions (MFIs) represent a small but rising share of the financial system and contribute strongly to improving access to finance by lower-income households and small- and medium-sized enterprises.[1] The WAEMU has 759 registered MFIs. Some 61 entities are classified as large institutions with assets or deposits above CFAF 2 billion and are supervised by the Banking Commission. These entities account for 90 percent of the MFI sector's assets. Although significantly smaller than the banking system—MFIs' total loans amount to about 8 percent of total bank credit—more people, particularly in rural areas, have accounts at MFIs than at banks, which helps raise overall access to the financial system from 5 to about 15 percent of the population. In countries such as Benin, Senegal, and Togo, MFIs have helped lift the overall access ratio to more than 20 percent of the population. Most MFIs are operated as credit unions ("Mutuelles") or by civil society organizations, and have a social mandate such as lending to farmers in remote regions. Overall, the sector is profitable but many of the smaller networks are loss-making and rely heavily on donor financing.

Regional financial markets remain a marginal source of funding except for governments. The regional stock market, based in Abidjan, has about 40 quoted companies. Its capitalization is

[1] Access to finance refers to the possibility that individuals or enterprises can access financial services, including credit, deposit, payment, insurance, and other risk-management services.

TABLE 19.1

Structure of the WAEMU Financial System

	Number of		Total Assets		Deposits Outstanding	Loans Outstanding
	Institutions as of end-2011	Branches as of end-2011	Billions of CFA francs	Percent of GDP	Amount (billions FCFA)	Amount (billions FCFA)
Private depository institutions						
Banks	107	1,853	19,725	53.8	11,173	8,465
Microfinance institutions[1]	880	3,179			517	501
Nondepository financial institutions	14	NA			NA	NA
Public financial institutions	NA	NA			NA	NA
Total financial system (excluding BCEAO)						

Sources: Authorities and IMF staff estimates.
[1] Data for end-2010.

small (about 12 percent of the WAEMU GDP). Companies listed are mostly in the financial and industrial sectors; Sonatel (a Senegalese telecom company) and Ecobank (a regional bank, headquartered in Togo) are the two largest companies, accounting for close to 50 percent of market capitalization. The debt market consists mostly of government paper and is also small (about 10 percent of the WAEMU GDP). There is no significant secondary debt market, including for government paper.

THE BANKING SECTOR

The banking sector has expanded in recent years. Bank credit to the economy has increased substantially in most countries since the mid-2000s (Figure 19.1). The number of bank branches and bank accounts also has increased significantly in recent years. Credit is largely short term, and goes mostly to the manufacturing and service sectors (particularly trade, hotels, and restaurants). Clients vary substantially across banks, with some dealing mostly with bigger firms (including subsidiaries of multinationals, in the case of foreign-owned banks) and others are more focused on domestic retail clients. In some countries, increased competition from MFIs and new business strategies from entrants have led to diversification of the banks' traditional customer base and higher competition. Most banks are significantly exposed to government securities and more generally to the public sectors.

An important recent development has been the emergence in the WAEMU of cross-border (pan-African) banking groups. This has often occurred through the purchase of domestic banks, in particular by Moroccan and Nigerian groups seeking to expand out of their home markets. Twenty large groups, accounting for most of the banking system, are involved in cross-border activities within the WAEMU (Figure 19.1). These groups, which are mostly incorporated as subsidiaries, are funded through local deposits. This funding model, coupled with their domestic orientation, explains why the direct impact of the global crisis was rather mild on these banks. European banks have remained engaged in the region, while pan-African banking groups have taken the opportunity to expand.

However, banking in the WAEMU is still conducted within national borders. Cross-border flows to households or corporations within the region are largely in the form of syndicated loans involving a sister bank located in the country of the client; in the recent period, Côte d'Ivoire and Senegal were net recipients of these flows, while most other countries were net exporters. The flows are still relatively small. Limited integration is also attested by large differences in lending and deposit rates for households and enterprises across countries. Limited banking integration reflects a number of factors, such as still-limited economic integration, but also the importance

Figure 19.1. WAEMU: Evolution of the Banking Sector

Outstanding credit by the banking system has grown steadily in all WAEMU countries...

1. Outstanding Credit, 2000–11 (CFAF million)

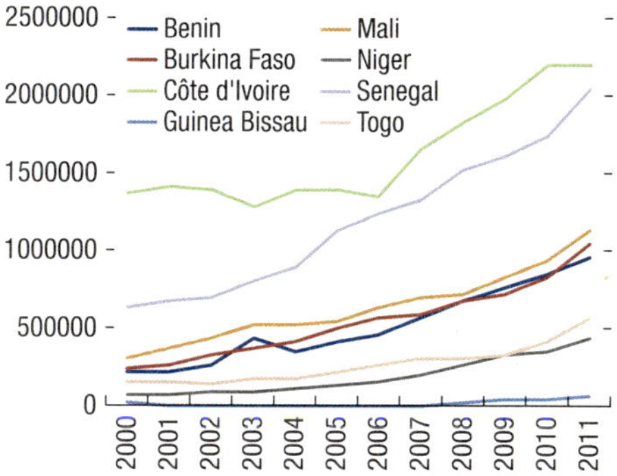

...with the largest share allocated to retail and wholesale trade.

2. Sectoral Distribution of Credit

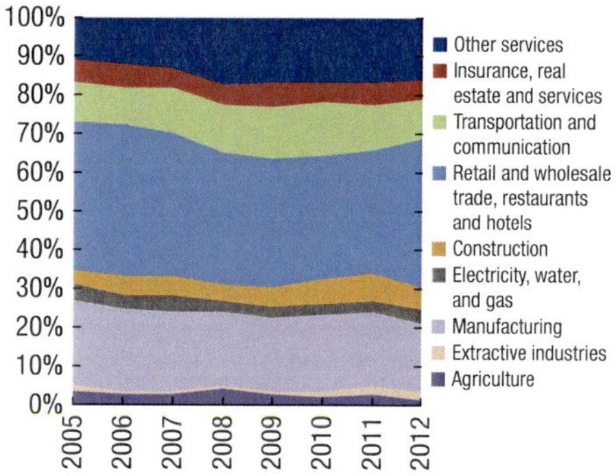

Interregional cross-border banking liabilities, however, remained small, with lending flows mainly to Senegal and Côte d'Ivoire...

3. Intraregional Net Lending, 2011

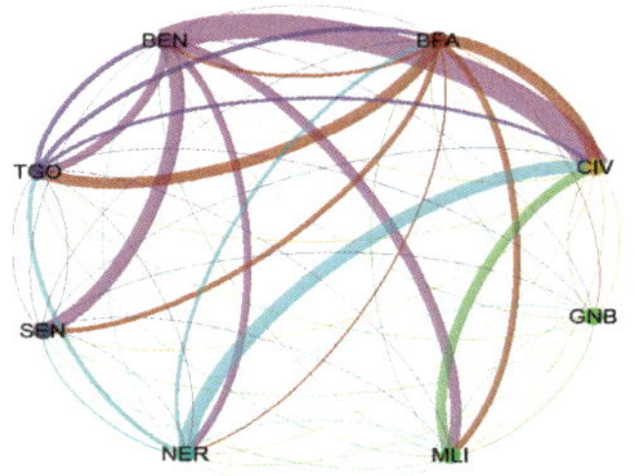

Note: The links indicate net lending flows originating from the country with the same-color nod. Three-letter International Organization for Standardization abbreviations used for country names.

...and limited convergence of cross-country lending rates implying limited integration.

4. Lending Rates by Country, 2006–10

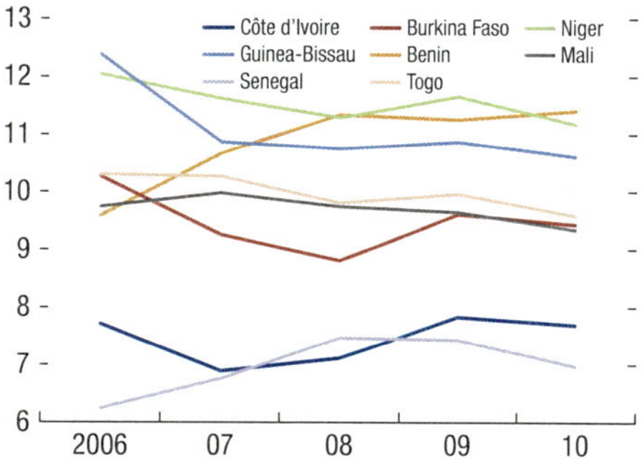

Banking groups have evolved in the region and are expanding rapidly.

5. Main Banking Groups in the WAEMU

Group	Presence in countries	Market share (%)	Number of agencies	Number of accounts
Ecobank	8	15.3	225	1,131,339
Société Généràl	4	11.2	129	524,584
Bank of Africa Group	6	10.1	145	573,827
Attijariwafa Bank	4	8.7	210	571,078
BNP Paribas	7	7	176	362,658
ABI (Ex-AFG)	4	6.2	81	442,144
United Bank for Africa	4	3.3	59	212,941
BSIC	7	2.4	73	68,649
Total		63.9	1,098	3,887,220

Côte d'Ivoire remains the largest market in terms of bank assets, closely followed by Senegal.

6. Distribution of Bank Assets by Country, 2011

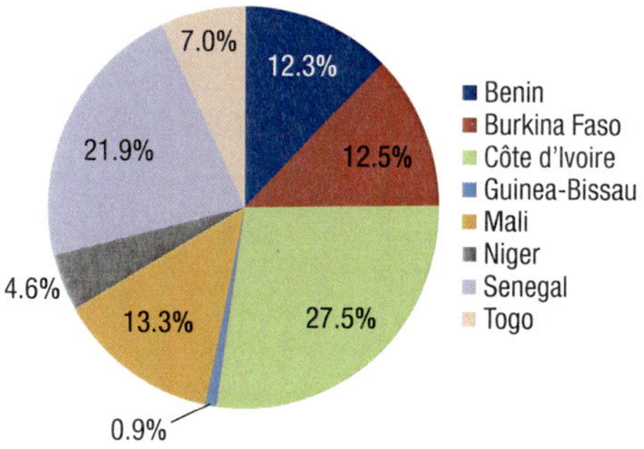

Sources: Banking Commission of the West African Economic and Monetary Union; Central Bank of West African States; and IMF staff calculations of local knowledge for lending activities. The main cross-border financial flows in the WAEMU involve bank purchases of government paper.

On average, the banking system is liquid and well capitalized, although the situation varies substantially across banks and countries (Box 19.1, Figure 19.2, and Table 19.2). As mentioned, banks are very heterogeneous with regard to business models, size, geographical coverage, profitability, and vulnerabilities. Aggregate information hides this diversity and therefore needs to be complemented by a more granular approach. The analysis of financial soundness indicators (which are highly aggregated, available with long lags, and backward looking) and the results of the stress tests (which rely on bank-by-bank data) confirm the need for a dual approach. Both lending concentration, which is high in all countries of the region, and quality of assets, as reflected in high gross nonperforming loans, represent the main risks. Lack of data regrettably did not allow us to assess risks related to the exposure of banks to WAEMU sovereigns, but this exposure is clearly increasing, raising new (possibly systemic) risks. The broader exposure of banks to the public sectors (that is, through public enterprises) is even more substantial. The emergence

BOX 19.1. Banking System Soundness: Findings from the Stress Tests

In collaboration with WAEMU authorities, stress tests were performed on the banking systems of seven of the eight WAEMU countries. Data for Guinea-Bissau were not available. The stress tests were based on data from the end of 2011; for two countries, granular data were only available for the end of 2010. The stress tests covered all banks—public, private, and foreign owned—and tested for market risk, credit risk, and interest-rate risk. Stress tests were not performed for exchange-rate risks, given the credible peg to the euro, or for sovereign risks because of insufficient data. The lack of recent and comprehensive data is an important limitation to the use of stress tests for crisis prevention purposes. The tests performed did not incorporate macroeconomic feedbacks and other second-round effects, and assumed no policy response. The stress tests calibrated a series of large but plausible shocks, which comprised sectoral risks, including default by the largest individual borrower, interest rate spikes of 500 basis points as well as liquidity shocks—deposit runs with losses of 5 percent of deposits per day for 10 days.

The results illustrated some of the known strengths and vulnerabilities of the system.

- *Limited interest-rate risk*—As the asset side of banks' portfolios are typically short-term in nature (reducing maturity mismatches) and bonds are typically held until maturity, banks in most countries are resistant to large changes in interest rates.
- *Limited liquidity risk*—With large liquidity buffers in most banks, only smaller ones face liquidity risks.
- *Severe sectoral/company concentration*—The lack of economic diversification and the large informal sector lead banks to concentrate lending on only a few sectors and corporations. In the WAEMU, the 50 largest companies account for 1/3 of total bank credit. This is a major vulnerability for banks, and the risk can be systemic if banks are substantially exposed to the same large borrower (like ICS in Senegal a few years ago).
- *Weak asset quality*—While varying across banks, the generally weak quality of assets is reflected in large nonperforming loan ratios (even after accounting for provisioning). Local accounting rules take longer to write off nonperforming loans compared with rules in most jurisdictions, with some of these nonperforming loans likely to be old and potentially reflecting difficulties in exercising guarantees through the judicial system. Data on nonperforming loan flows were not available to assess recent trends.

Other vulnerabilities, known but not explored in the stress tests, include:

- *Political instability*—This risk is high in the region, as shown by the crises in Côte d'Ivoire, Mali, and Guinea-Bissau in the past two to three years.
- *Weather-related risks*—Given the still important role of the agricultural sector in the WAEMU economy, climate hazards (for example, floods and droughts) subject the system to large, exogenous shocks.
- *Sovereign-bank relationship*—WAEMU banks hold over 70 percent of public debt issued by eight WAEMU sovereign countries, and cross-border holdings are sometimes large. In the case of Côte d'Ivoire in late 2010 (when the crisis started), more than half of the debt was held by residents of other WAEMU countries, generally banks. A default on this debt could have created a systemic bank crisis in the region.

Figure 19.2. WAEMU: Financial Soundness

Although the banking sector appears well capitalized overall, banks in Côte d'Ivoire are significantly undercapitalized on average.

1. Capital Adequacy Ratio, June 2012

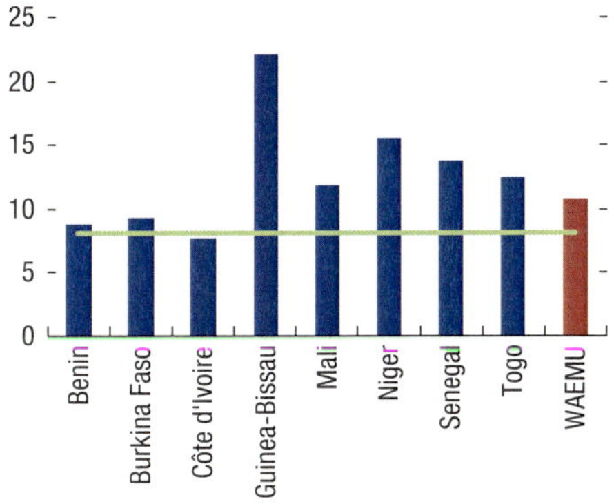

Nonperforming loans are high albeit trending downwards for some countries...

2. Nonperforming Loans, 2005–12
(Percent of total loans)

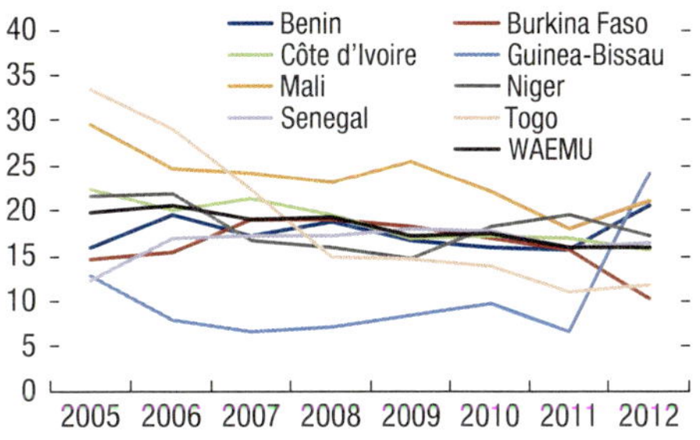

... and progress in compliance with prudential regulation has been limited.

3. Prudential Regulations
(Percent of banks complying)

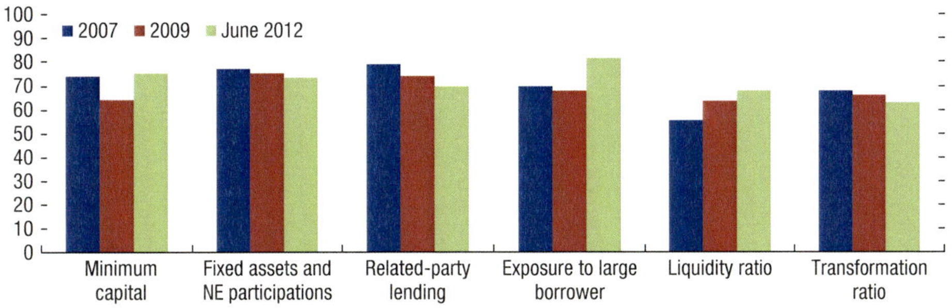

4. Respect of Prudential Norms by Country, end-June 2012

	Solvency Ratios		Other Prudential Ratios				
Number of Banks per country	Capital ratio	Fixed assets and NE participations	Exposure to large borrower	Concentration risk	Related-Party Lending	Transformation ratio > 50%	Liquidity ratio
Benin (12)	10	9	5	10	9	5	7
Burkina (12)	9	10	6	10	11	10	7
Côte d'Ivoire (23)	13	16	12	16	16	11	18
Guinea-Bissau (4)	3	3	3	3	3	2	1
Mali (13)	12	11	9	12	10	7	5
Niger (10)	7	8	8	8	8	5	3
Senegal (19)	16	18	14	18	16	8	10
Togo (12)	9	8	10	9	9	4	6
WAEMU (105)	79	86	65	87	82	52	57

Sources: Central Bank of West African States; IMF, African Department database; and IMF, Regional Economic Outlook database.

TABLE 19.2

WAEMU: Financial Soundness Indicators 2010–14 (Percent, unless otherwise indicated)

	2005 Dec.	2006 Dec.	2007 Dec.	2008 Dec.	2009 Dec.	2010 Dec.	2011 Dec.	2012 Dec.	2013 June	2013 Dec.	2014 June
Solvency Ratios											
Regulatory capital to risk weighted assets	9	8	7	10	10	11.1	10.7	10.7	10.7	10.1	9.3
Tier I capital to risk-weighted assets	9	8	6	9	10	10.6	10.1	9.9	10.0	9.3	8.3
Provisions to risk-weighted assets	15	14	13	12	11	12.1	10.4	10.5	11.0	10.5	10.4
Capital to total assets	6	5	4	6	6	6.4	6.5	6.3	6.2	5.6	5.1
Composition and Quality of Assets											
Total loans to total assets	63	62	59	59	58	55.3	55.2	55.0	55.1	55.9	55.7
Concentration: loans to 5 largest borrowers to capital[1]	89	74	92	81	43	43.2	34.4	106.9	99.5	97.8	130.1
Sectoral distribution of loans											
Agriculture	4	3	3	4	3	2.0	2.9	2.6	2.3	2.9	2.4
Extractive industries	1	1	1	1	1	2.0	2.2	1.6	1.7	1.8	2.1
Manufacturing	22	21	20	18	18	18.9	18.8	18.2	17.1	17.0	17.2
Electricity, water and gas	4	3	4	3	3	3.4	3.2	3.2	3.6	3.7	4.6
Construction	4	5	5	4	5	6.1	6.7	6.7	7.7	7.8	7.7
Retail and wholesale trade, restaurants and hotels	38	39	37	33	33	31.9	32.3	34.7	33.5	33.5	32.7
Transportation and communication	10	10	12	12	13	13.6	11.2	10.1	11.5	11.2	10.9
Insurance, real estate and services	6	6	5	5	6	5.2	5.5	6.1	5.9	6.0	6.7
Other services	11	12	13	17	17	17.0	17.1	16.8	16.7	16.2	15.6
Gross nonperforming loans to total loans	20	21	19	19	17	17.6	15.9	16.0	17.0	15.4	15.7
Provisioning rate	67	66	66	68	61	63.7	64.2	63.4	60.7	61.0	59.3
Net nonperforming loans to total loans	8	8	7	7	7	7.2	6.3	6.5	7.4	6.6	7.1
Net nonperforming loans to capital	83	91	91	69	69	62.0	54.1	56.5	66.2	66.6	76.7
Earnings and Profitability											
Average cost of borrowed funds	2	2	2	3	3	2.9	2.4	2.4	. . .	2.8	
Average interest rate on loans	10	9	10	11	10	10.9	9.7	9.8	. . .	10.7	
Average interest margin[1]	8	7	8	8	8	8.0	7.3	7.3	. . .	7.9	
After-tax return on average assets (ROA)						1.1	1.2	0.9	. . .	1.2	
After-tax return on average equity (ROE)	5	5	5	2	15	12.6	13.7	10.1	. . .	14.6	
Noninterest expenses/net banking income	58	61	63	61	64	64.8	61.6	61.0	. . .	60.2	
Salaries and wages/net banking income	27	28	28	27	27	27.1	26.4	25.7	. . .	26.2	
Liquidity											
Liquid assets to total assets	42	41	38	37	34	33.3	33.6	32.5	31.9	32.2	31.2
Liquid assets to total deposits	55	54	51	50	46	45.1	46.1	45.8	44.7	47.1	45.3
Total loans to total deposits	84	82	79	82	78	84.0	84.3	86.2	86.1	90.0	89.2
Total deposits to total liabilities	76	75	75	73	73	74.1	72.9	71.1	71.3	68.5	68.9
Sight deposits to total liabilities[2]	38	38	38	37	36	36.7	37.8	36.5	36.8	35.5	35.6
Term deposits to total liabilities	38	37	36	36	37	37.5	35.1	34.6	34.5	33.0	33.3

Source: Central Bank of West African States.

[1] Excluding tax on bank operations.

[2] Including saving accounts.

of cross-border banking groups also brings new risks; for instance, cross-border banks may propagate foreign shocks into the domestic economy. Another potential risk arises when large banking groups have similar portfolios making them susceptible to similar shocks. In this case, while the diversification of the banking portfolio reduces the probability of an idiosyncratic failure, it increases the probability of a systemic crisis. Some of these banking groups are large enough to be considered domestic systemically important financial institutions.

Compliance with prudential norms remains low for a number of ratios. As shown in Figure 19.1, compliance varies across countries and across ratios. Also, there are banks in all countries breaching the capital adequacy ratio (lack of granular data did not permit us to scale the compliance of prudential ratio by banks' assets). Compliance has improved recently, but this reflected changes made to two ratios (the transformation ratio, which was lowered from 75 to 50 percent; and the ratio on portfolio structure, which was abolished). Progress over the last few years has been limited, which suggests a degree of regulatory forbearance. In addition, some of these norms are not in line with international standards. Low compliance is particularly problematic for ratios that are less demanding than are international standards, such as the one on risk division. As discussed in the last section, there are other important issues to address with regard to the supervision of regional groups and the crisis prevention and resolution frameworks.

MICROFINANCE

Following a rapid expansion, the microfinance sector is consolidating in many countries. The quick expansion of microfinance networks in the early 2000s was welcome from the perspective of access to finance. For example, in Benin, authorized MFIs serve 1.5 million customers in a total active population of 4.5 million. However, the quick expansion led to a proliferation of often small and unprofitable MFIs, which have partially operated out of the authorities' control. Consolidation is ongoing in most countries both through mergers and acquisitions among MFIs and at the initiative of the authorities. Some countries are well advanced in the consolidation process—more than 100 institutions have been closed in Senegal—while others are still registering existing networks. A survey conducted in Benin in 2011, for example, revealed that 721 MFIs were operating then in the country, but only 226 were licensed (IMF 2012). Overall, the number of branches or points of service in the WAEMU has remained broadly constant since 2004. Outstanding credit, however, has increased significantly in most countries (see Figure 19.3). Microfinance is particularly developed in Senegal (Imam and Kolerus 2013).

The authorities have started to address governance and profitability problems of the sector. The MFI sector is profitable overall, but the situation varies greatly depending on the size of the institutions, with the largest being the most profitable. Nonperforming loans are on an increasing trend and governance problems are frequent due to a lack of accountability. A regulatory reform initiated in 2008–09 has led to a reorganization of supervisory responsibilities, with the larger institutions holding assets and/or deposits of more than CFAF 2 billion now supervised by the WAEMU Banking Commission. Smaller institutions remain supervised by national authorities, typically ministries of finance, and countries have started to build up their capacities in this area. Many MFIs report access to refinancing as a major issue, given their relatively high transformation ratio, as well as short-term resources (cash deposits), and an increasing demand for longer-term financing. Larger MFIs are able to get refinancing from banks, and these loans have recently become eligible for refinancing at the BCEAO. However, smaller MFIs cannot avail themselves of this option. The BCEAO is also considering how to include MFIs in the payment system, as the current MFI license does not allow for money transfer. Mobile banking is just starting in the WAEMU.

Figure 19.3. WAEMU: Microfinance

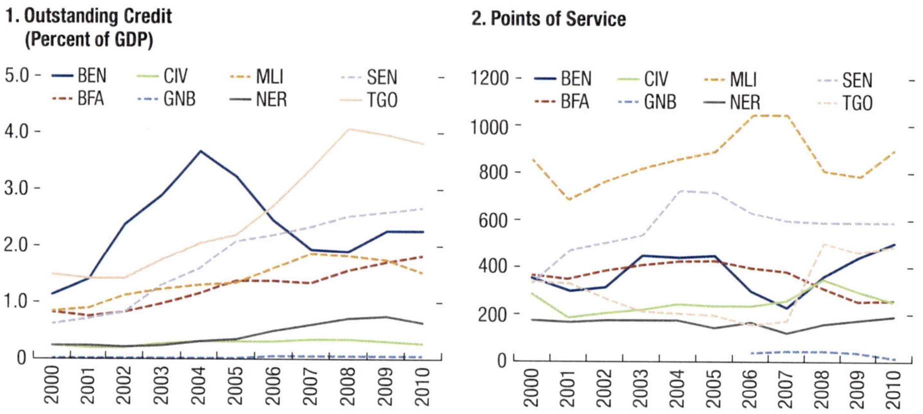

Source: BCEAO.
Note: Three-letter International Organization for Standardization abbreviations used for country names. WAEMU = West African Economic and Monetary Union.

REGIONAL MARKETS

Despite signs of development, interbank market activity remains limited. Interbank loans have amounted to less than 2 percent of total bank loans in the past five years. Loan maturity has tended to increase in recent years and the slope of the implicit, yet imperfect, yield curve has become positive; it was virtually flat a decade ago. Moreover, the interbank rate has remained broadly within the policy rate corridor since 2009 (Figure 19.4). However, the interbank market does not yet perform a major role in the reallocation of liquidity. Despite excess reserves at the banking system level, the BCEAO still needs to inject massive amounts of liquidity to a large number of banks that cannot get this liquidity from the market. This phenomenon is another illustration that the banking system is highly heterogeneous and segmented. In the absence of collateralized operations, highly liquid banks—in general, though not exclusively, the subsidiaries of large foreign banks, which also happen to be the more profitable ones—are reluctant to lend to others. As a result, most interbank loans take place within banking groups to avoid any counterparty risk. Because access to the BCEAO's standing facility for liquidity provision is not yet fully electronic and therefore entails significant transaction costs, some operations on the interbank market still take place at rates greater than the higher policy rate of the BCEAO. These operations may also reflect implicit profit transfers between banks belonging to the same group.

The regional debt market has developed rapidly in the past years, mostly for government paper (Figure 19.5). Securities can be issued by private companies and governments on the regional stock exchange, the Bourse Régionale des Valeurs Mobiliéres (referred to as BRVM, its French acronym). The BRVM has 46 bond lines, of which 28 are from private issuers and the rest from four sovereign countries of the WAEMU. Government bond issues represented 75 percent of all issuance by syndication in 2011, with Côte d'Ivoire and Senegal the most active issuers. The average interest rate on sovereign bonds was at 6.7 percent in 2011 (average duration: 5.5 years), while the average interest rate on listed bonds issued by private corporations was 6.8 percent (at similar duration). Interest rates, however, do not provide a full account of differences in the cost

Figure 19.4. WAEMU: Interbank Market

The amount of outstanding credit has increased from 2007 onwards...

1. Oustanding Credit
(Millions of CFA francs)

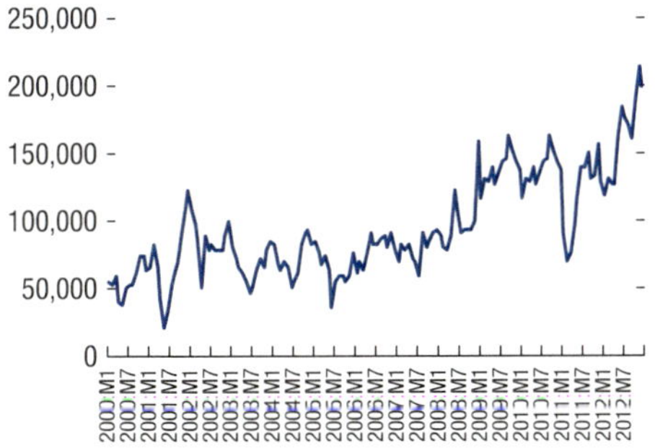

...while the share of credit on the interbank market to total bank credit has remained broadly constant at low levels.

2. Share of Interbank Credit to Total Bank Credit
(Percent, end of period)

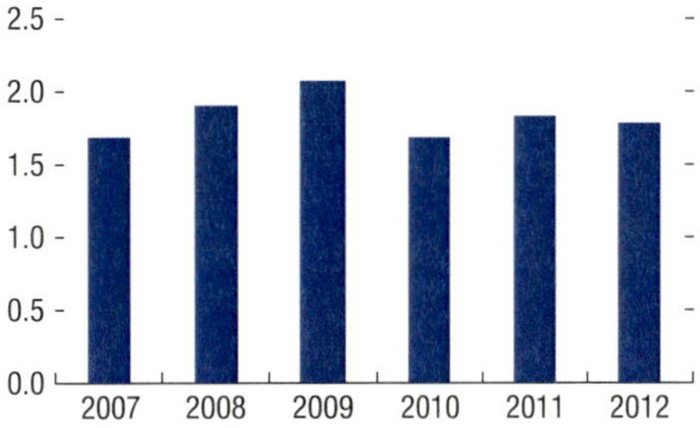

Note: 2012 refers to end September

One-day contracts have been replaced with one-week contracts...

3. Loan Size by Duration
(Millions of CFA francs)

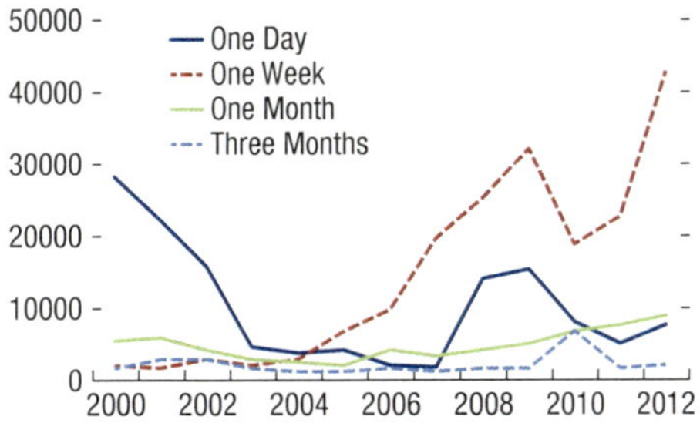

...and interest rates increasingly reflect term structure.

4. Interest Rate by Duration
(Percent, weekly average)

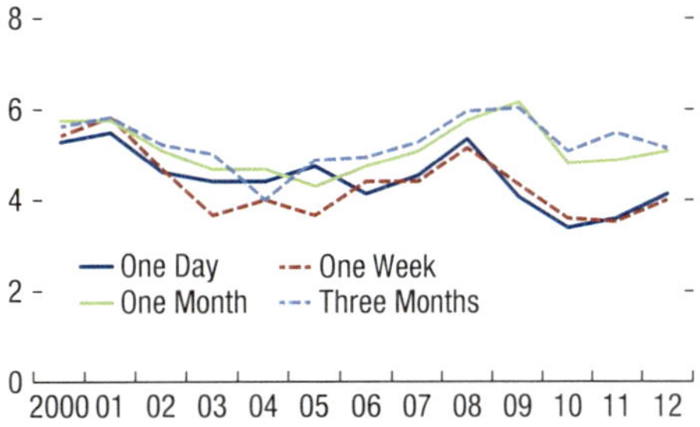

The interbank rate has broadly remained within the policy rate corridor.

5. Policy Rate Corridor and Interbank Rate

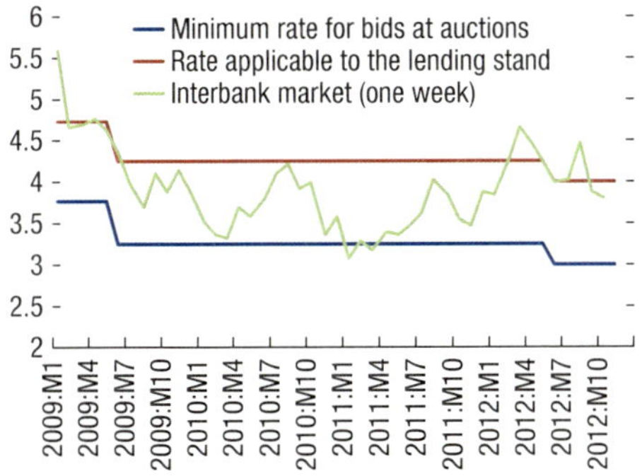

Sources: Central Bank of West African States (BCEAO); and IMF staff calculations.

However, the interbank market does not sufficiently absorb and reallocate liquidity in the system and banks increase borrowing from the BCEAO.

6. Excess Reserves and BCEAO Refinancing
(Billions of CFA francs)

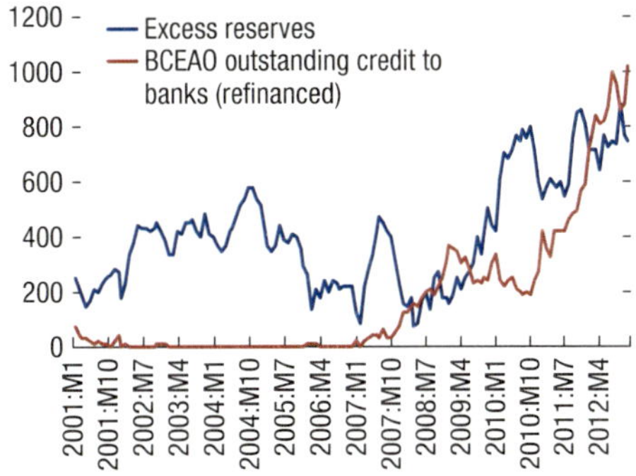

Note: Exess reserves are defined as the difference between required reserves and actual reserves at the BCEAO.

Figure 19.5. WAEMU: Debt Markets

The stock of longer term debt is on the rise...

1. Treasury Bill and Bond Issuances by Auction, 2010–12 (In billions of CFA francs)

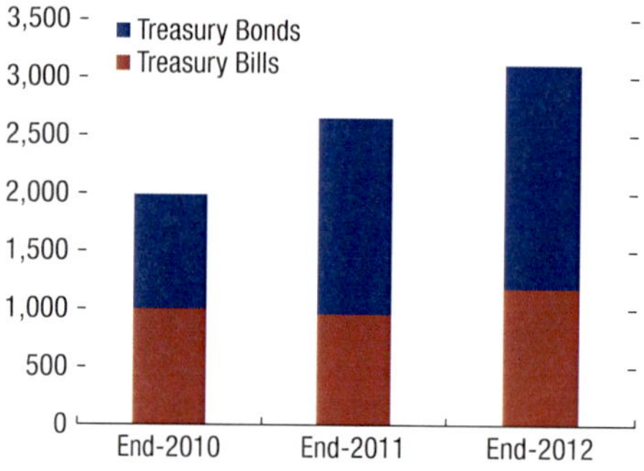

...with the average cost of borrowing on the decline.

2. Interest Rates by Maturity, 2009–12

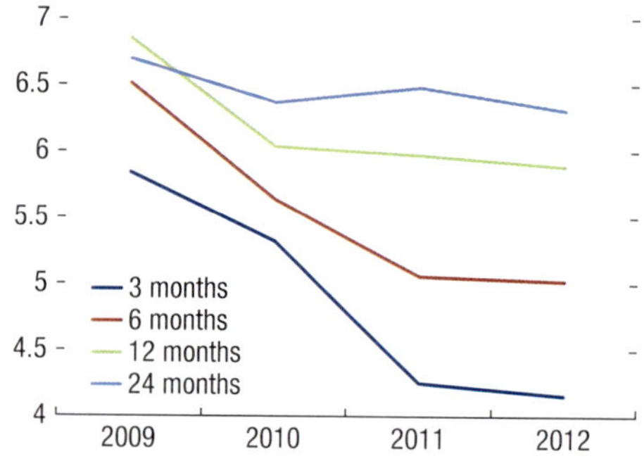

Côte d'Ivoire dominates the few issuances by syndication...

3. Sovereign Issuances by Syndication, 2003–11

Country	Interest Rate (in percent)	Amount (FCFA billions)	Duration (years)	Year of subscription
Senegal	5.50	45.0	5	2005
Togo	6.50	36.3	5	2006
Côte d'Ivoire	6.00	51.7	3	2007
Senegal	5.50	55.2	5	2008
Côte d'Ivoire	6.25	61.2	4	2009
Côte d'Ivoire	6.95	107.3	5	2009
Côte d'Ivoire	6.25	64.8	3	2010
Senegal	6.75	76.8	5	2011
Côte d'Ivoire	7.00	22.9	7	2011
Togo	6.50	60.0	5	2011
Côte d'Ivoire	6.50	160.2	5	2011
Average	6.34	67.4	4.7	

...but corporate issuances risk being crowded out by sovereign activity.

4. Debt Issuances by Syndication, 2003–11 (In billions of CFA francs)

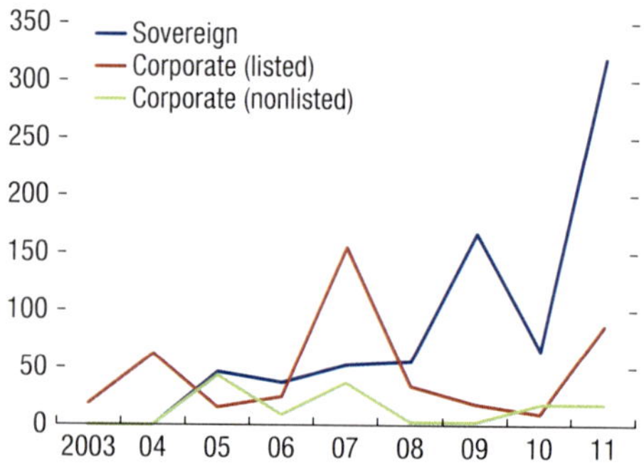

Exposure of the banking sector to sovereign debt is significant...

5. Government & BCEAO Securities in Bank Balance Sheets, 2011 (Share of total bank assets)

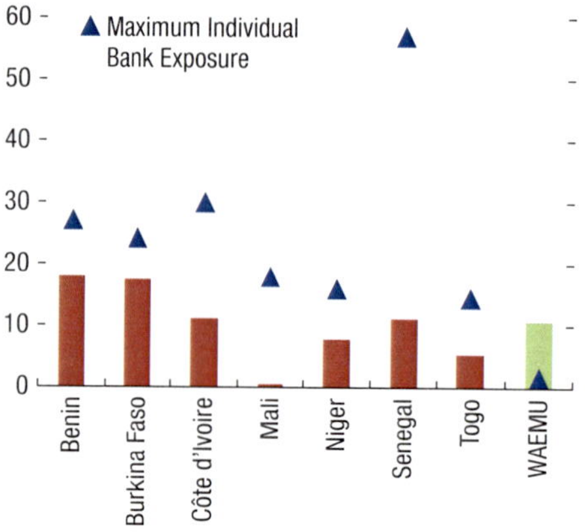

...and extends across borders, with banks from Benin and Senegal financing Ivorian debt.

6. Cross-border Sovereign-Banking Nexus

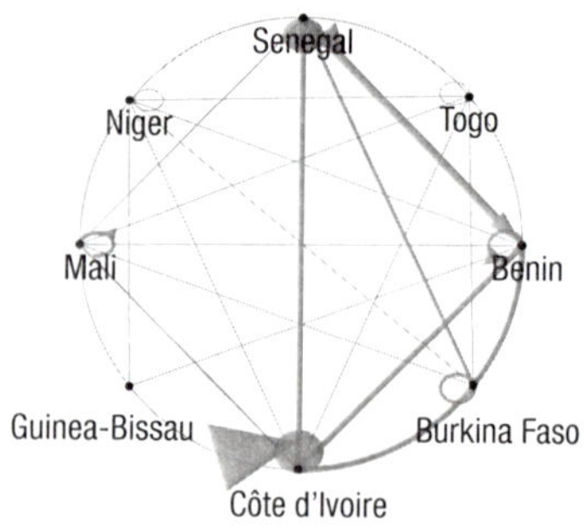

Sources: Bourse Regionale des Valeurs Mobilieres; Central Bank of West African States; and IMF staff calculations.

Note: Dots represent the sovereign, and links to dots are purchases of banks from other countries.

of financing between the public and private sector. Private sector issuance required until recently a 100 percent guarantee by a certified institution (for example, the West African Development Bank), which added the equivalent of 1 to 2 percentage points to issuance costs. Overall, the BRVM debt market remains small. Its total capitalization stood at about 2.4 percent of GDP at the end of 2014. It is not a significant source of financing for the private sector and there is no significant secondary market.

Most government debt, however, is still issued to banks through auctions organized by the BCEAO. This segment has been very dynamic in recent years and outstanding government debt issued on this market is about 10 times larger than that issued at the BRVM. Debt issued this way is mostly in the form of Treasury bills. It has a relatively short average maturity and can be used for refinancing at the BCEAO. There is no significant secondary market for this type of government debt.

The regional equity market remains shallow (Figure 19.6). Launched in 1998, the BRVM started off with 36 listed companies carried over from the previous stock exchange in Abidjan. The number of companies listed has remained broadly stable, with 37 in early 2013, as new listings broadly offset the number of companies taken off the list. Market capitalization increased from 4.3 percent of GDP in 2002 to 13.2 percent of GDP end 2014. Foreign investors are allowed in, and their stakes in Sonatel and ETI (Ecobank) are reportedly fairly large. The average market return in 2011 was 8.6 percent in local currency, and 27 companies paid dividends. BRVM is supervised by the Regional Council for Public Savings and Financial Markets.

SYSTEMIC RISK AND SURVEILLANCE

Systemic risk is defined as any threat of disruption to financial services that is caused by an impairment of all or part of the financial system and that has the potential to have serious negative consequences for the real economy. It is a form of negative externality that occurs when a bank failure, market seizure, or breakdown of the infrastructure can have serious adverse implications for market participants. Systemic risk can be decomposed into time-series and cross-sectional risk. In the time-series dimension, the buildup of risk over time interacts with the macroeconomic cycle. Financial institutions and borrowers may take on excessive amounts of leverage in the upswing of an economic cycle only to become overly risk averse in a downswing. This amplifies the boom and bust cycle in the supply of credit and liquidity—and by extension in asset prices—that can be damaging to the real economy. In the cross-sectional dimension, the growing size and complexity of the financial system is raising interconnectedness and common exposures, which may increase contagion when problems arise. As a result, the failure of one institution—particularly one of significant size or with strong interconnections—can threaten the system as a whole.

As discussed in Imam and Kolerus (2013), time-series systemic risk might be limited at this juncture in the WAEMU, though some cross-section risks are present. No sector seems highly leveraged in Senegal. Banks tend to finance mostly prime borrowers with short-term credit such as trade finance, implying that risks to the financial system, besides from exogenous shocks, are likely to be low, except for concentration risk. Capital inflows and outflows are limited. Many of these features likely apply to other WAEMU countries.

However, some systemic linkages are evolving rapidly and could change this assessment in the near future. These include:

- *Cross-sector linkages*—Those that exist between the financial and nonfinancial sectors. These are on the rise as banks are increasingly lending to sovereigns through the regional market.

Figure 19.6. WAEMU: The BRVM–Stock Market

While trending upward, both BRVM indices experienced downturns during the global financial crisis and the 2011 Ivorian crisis.

1. Stock Market Indices, 1998–2012

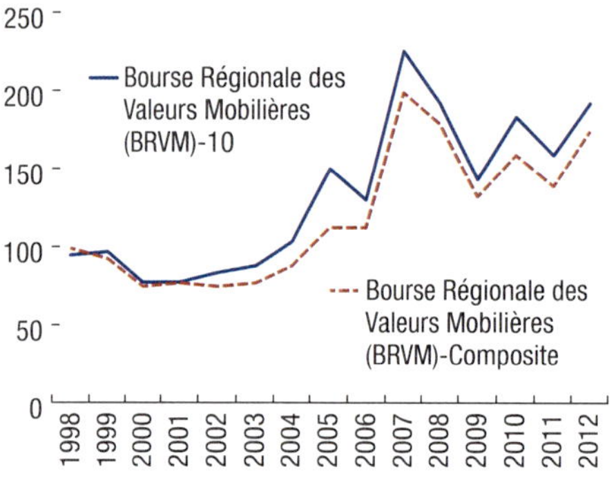

Note: Indices = 100 on September 16, 1998

From 1998 to 2012, 11 companies entered the market, mainly in finance and telecommunications...

2. New Listings

Corporations	Admission to BRVM	Sector
SONATEL	Oct-98	Telecommunication
SIVOA	Apr-99	Industry
PALM CI	Oct-99	Agriculture
SERVAIR Abidjan	Mar-00	Distribution
NEI	Apr-00	Industry
BOA-Benin	Nov-00	Finance
BOA-Niger	Dec-03	Finance
ETI	Sep-06	Finance
ONATEL	Apr-09	Telecommunication
BOA-Cote d'Ivoire	Apr-10	Finance
BOA-Burkina Faso	Dec-10	Finance

Source: BRVM

...which leaves capitalization dominated by companies from finance and industry titles, closely followed by agriculture.

3. Capitalization by Sector, February 2013

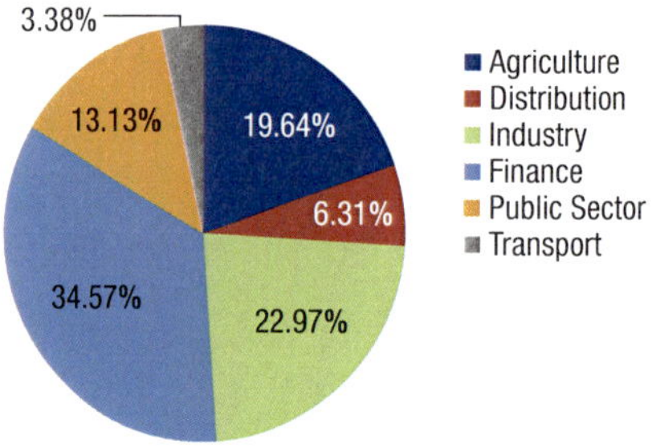

The big majority of investors' accounts is located in Côte d'Ivoire.

4. Accounts by Country, 2011

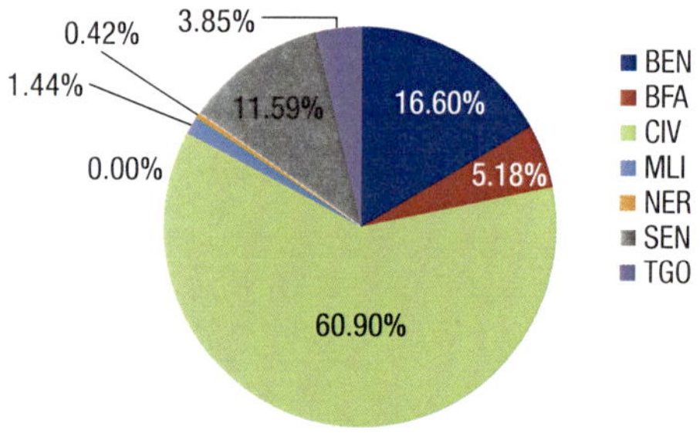

Note: Three-letter International Organization for Standardization abbreviations used for country names.

Capitalization has increased again in 2012...

5. Market Capitalization
(Billions of CFA francs)

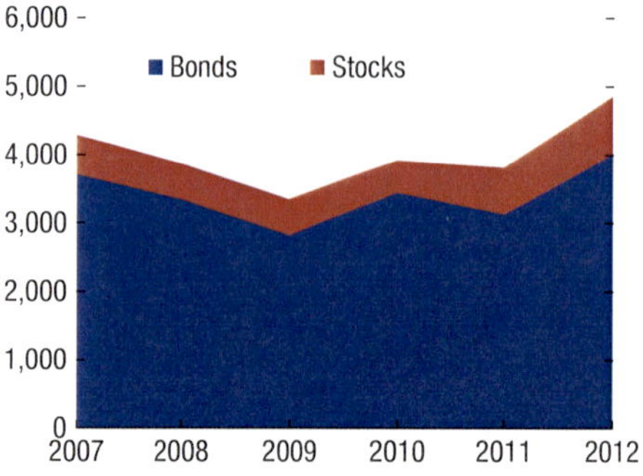

2012 total is official, stocks and bonds are estimates.

...but activity is concentrated on bond issuances, mostly by governments.

6. Funds Raised on the Market
(Billions of CFA francs)

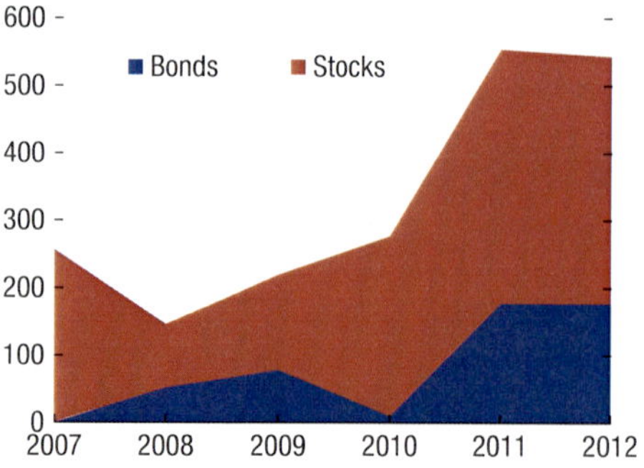

Sources: Bourse Régionale des Valeurs Mobilières (BRVM), Conseil Régional de l'Epargne Publique et des Marchés Financiers (CREPMF).

- *Cross-border linkages*—Those between the financial system of the WAEMU and the world economy, but also those within the WAEMU. These are intensifying as large WAEMU banks and foreign banks, especially from Morocco and Nigeria, seek opportunities within the WAEMU and the region.
- *Cross-institution linkages*—Those that exist between bank and nonbank financial institutions. The Senegal pilot showed the increasing linkages among banks and insurance companies and MFIs, whether through equity ownership, debt holdings, or deposits.

Financial stability in the WAEMU also faces particular challenges. In a heterogeneous monetary union, business cycle synchronization is limited, as is the case in the WAEMU (see Chapter 5, Shocks to Growth). In such circumstances, monetary policy may not necessarily act as a stabilizing force to all the national financial systems, as a focus on average regional inflation might imply that monetary policy is too accommodative in some parts of the Union that have high inflation levels and too tight in others that have low inflation levels. Limited financial development also means that the scope for countercyclical fiscal policy is reduced, as it may be difficult to issue large amounts of government paper in a shallow market during a downturn, although such policy should play a critical role in absorbing asymmetric shocks (and even symmetric ones given the limited effectiveness of monetary policy). With limited shock-absorption mechanisms, a robust financial crisis prevention and resolution framework is even more critical.

As indicated in Imam and Kolerus (2013), there is in principle a clear division of labor between national and regional authorities on the supervision of the financial system. The banking sector and MFIs with more than CFAF 2 billion in deposits or loans are supervised by the WAEMU Banking Commission. Smaller MFIs are supervised by national authorities. The regional financial market is under the supervision of the Regional Council for Public Savings and Financial Markets. Ministries of Finance, together with the regional regulator, supervise the insurance sector. Finally, the Financial Stability Committee is responsible for macroprudential supervision and for guaranteeing the stability of the overall financial system at the regional level. As banking licenses are provided by the BCEAO—after a qualified opinion is issued by the WAEMU Banking Commission—following request from the national governments, there is an understanding that banks and subsidaries that are in trouble will have to be supported by the governments of the countries in which they are located, and not of the country of the parent company.

REFERENCES

Imam, Patrick, and Christina Kolerus. 2013. "Senegal: Financial Depth and Macrostability." African Departmental Paper, International Monetary Fund, Washington.

International Monetary Fund. 2012. "Benin Article IV: Financial Sector Review." Washington: International Monetary Fund.

CHAPTER 20

Financial Development: Level, Depth, and Access

CALIXTE AHOKPOSSI, PATRICK IMAM, KAREEM ISMAIL, SUDIPTO KARMAKAR, CHRISTINA KOLERUS, AND MESMIN KOULET-VICKOT

The level of the financial sector development in the West African Economic and Monetary Union (WAEMU) can be assessed with respect to its depth, breadth, and access to financial services by comparing the level within WAEMU countries to sub-Saharan Africa averages and to individual comparator countries. For each country and each key financial sector indicator, we have estimated a structural benchmark based on the country's economic and structural characteristics. Comparisons were also made with selected countries outside the WAEMU, namely Ghana and Kenya, as well as with the average and median for sub-Saharan Africa. Ghana is a natural comparator for many WAEMU countries given its characteristics and geographic proximity. Kenya is an example of a sub-Saharan African economy with a rapidly developing financial sector. The mean and median for sub-Saharan Africa (including South Africa) reflect the development of the rest of the continent. To get better sense of the progress needed to achieve a higher level of financial development, the WAEMU's financial depth can be evaluated relative to a group of high-growth, non-oil-exporter countries. Policy and institutional asymmetries between two groups of countries usually explain the gap in performance.

STRUCTURAL CHARACTERISTICS

The WAEMU's banking systems have significantly deepened in all WAEMU countries in recent years and most of them meet or exceed the main statistical benchmarks for depth. Togo, Senegal, and Benin have the deepest banking systems in the region (in absolute terms, not relative to benchmarks), while Guinea-Bissau and Niger have the shallowest ones. Depth of nonbank financial sectors is very heterogeneous across WAEMU countries. The equity market is clearly underdeveloped relative to structural characteristics. Figure 20.1 provides more detail by country and over time.

Structural benchmarks were calculated for WAEMU countries using a large dataset of countries. Each financial indicator was regressed on a set of structural characteristics, such as GDP per capita and its square, population size and density, the age-dependency ratio, country-specific dummies, and year fixed effects. The structural benchmarks were calculated based on Beck and others (2008), Feyen and Kibuuka (2012), and FinStats from the World Bank. A negative difference between the observed value and the benchmark suggests scope for policy action, while a positive difference could reflect successful reforms. A positive difference, however, should not be construed as absence of scope for further development. The benchmarks are not optimal levels, but rather an indication of where countries with similar characteristics stand with regard to financial development. The analysis was carried out using data from 1995 onward, where available, and the tool was developed by the World Bank for this purpose.

Breadth of the banking sector—assessed through the range of products, markets, and providers—is generally limited in the WAEMU. Competition in the banking system, proxied by the asset concentration of the three largest banks, appears relatively low in all countries and seems to have decreased in recent years. Credit to the public sector relative to GDP has increased

Figure 20.1. WAEMU: Selected Indicators on Financial Sector Depth

Despite large heterogeneity, all countries outperformed the median statistical benchmark for credit to GDP in 2011...

1. Private Credit to GDP
(Percent of GDP)

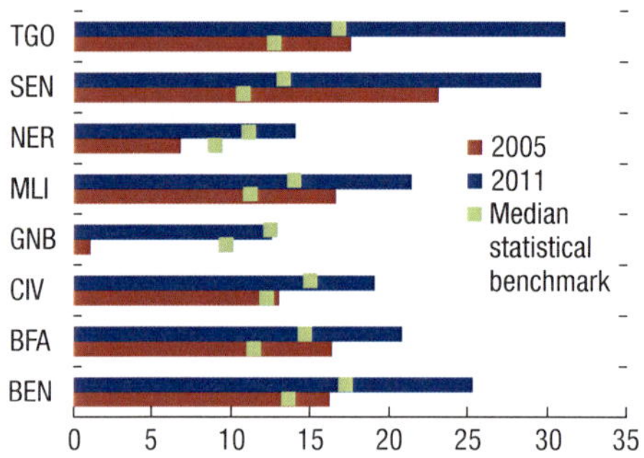

....and all but Niger outperformed for the deposit-to-GDP benchmark.

2. Domestic Bank Deposits to GDP
(Percent of GDP)

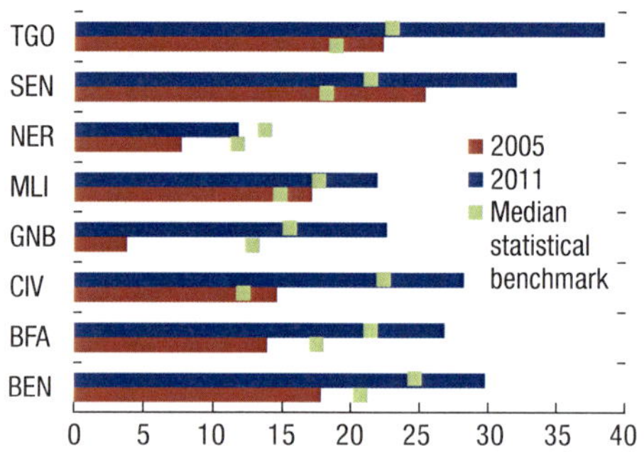

Bank intermediation is below the benchmark in Côte d'Ivoire and Guinea-Bissau.

3. Private Credit to Deposits
(Percent of deposits)

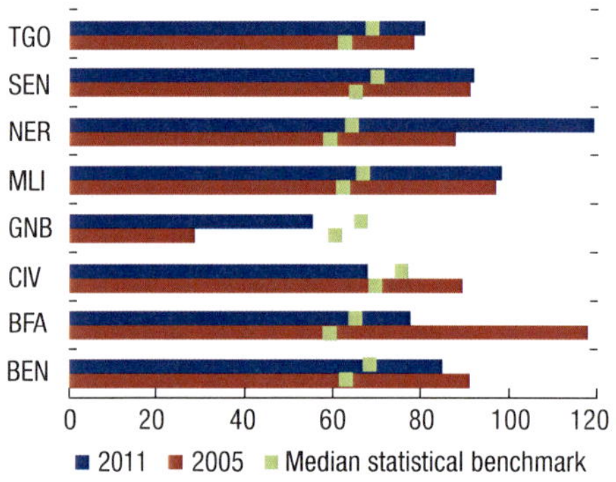

The Ivorian insurance sector is significantly more developed than its peers and the statistical benchmark.

4. Insurance Company Assets to GDP
(Percent of GDP)

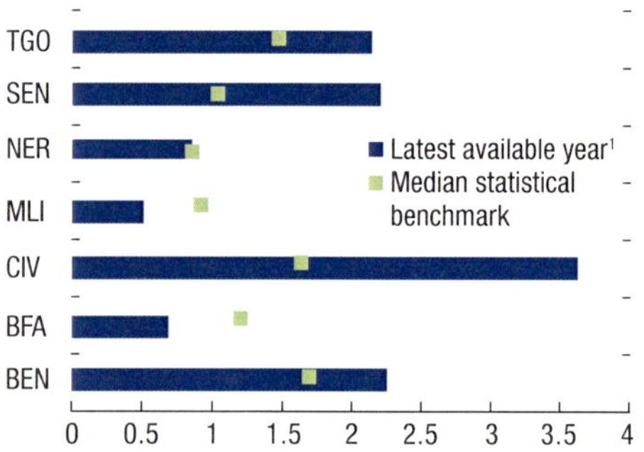

Stock market performance is substantially below the turnover benchmark...

5. Stock Market Turnover Ratio
(Percent)

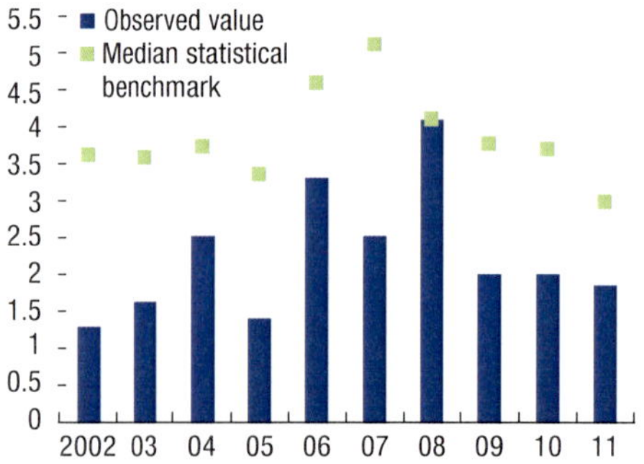

... as well as the market capitalization benchmark.

6. Stock Market Capitalization
(Percent of GDP)

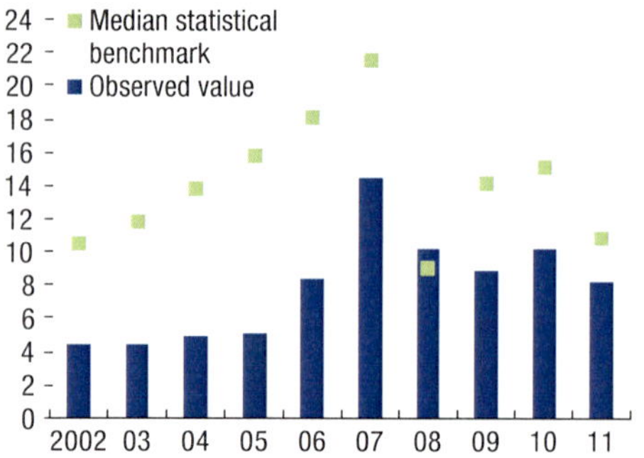

Sources: FinStats database; and IMF staff calculations.
Note: Three-letter International Organization for Standardization abbreviations used for country names.
[1]Latest available year was 2010 for Benin; 2009 for Burkina Faso, Côte d'Ivoire, Mali, Niger, and Togo; 2008 for Senegal. Guinea-Bissau was omitted due to missing data.

substantially, a trend that is usually not interpreted positively in terms of breadth, but which reflects in the WAEMU the end of central bank advances to governments and the development of the regional market. Life insurance is more developed than is indicated by the benchmarks, suggesting diversification of the range of financial products. The number of companies whose stock is listed on the regional stock exchange, called the Bourse Régionale des Valeurs Mobiliéres (BRVM), is very low compared with the benchmark. In addition, active trading is limited to a few of these countries. Figure 20.2 provides more detail by country and over time.

Access to finance has increased substantially in all countries and is in line with or exceeds structural benchmarks in most of them. Both banks and microfinance institutions contributed to this development, with microfinance institutions playing an important role in Benin, Togo, and Senegal. Figure 20.3 provides more detail by country and over time.

Figure 20.2. WAEMU: Comparing the WAEMU with Selected Benchmark Countries

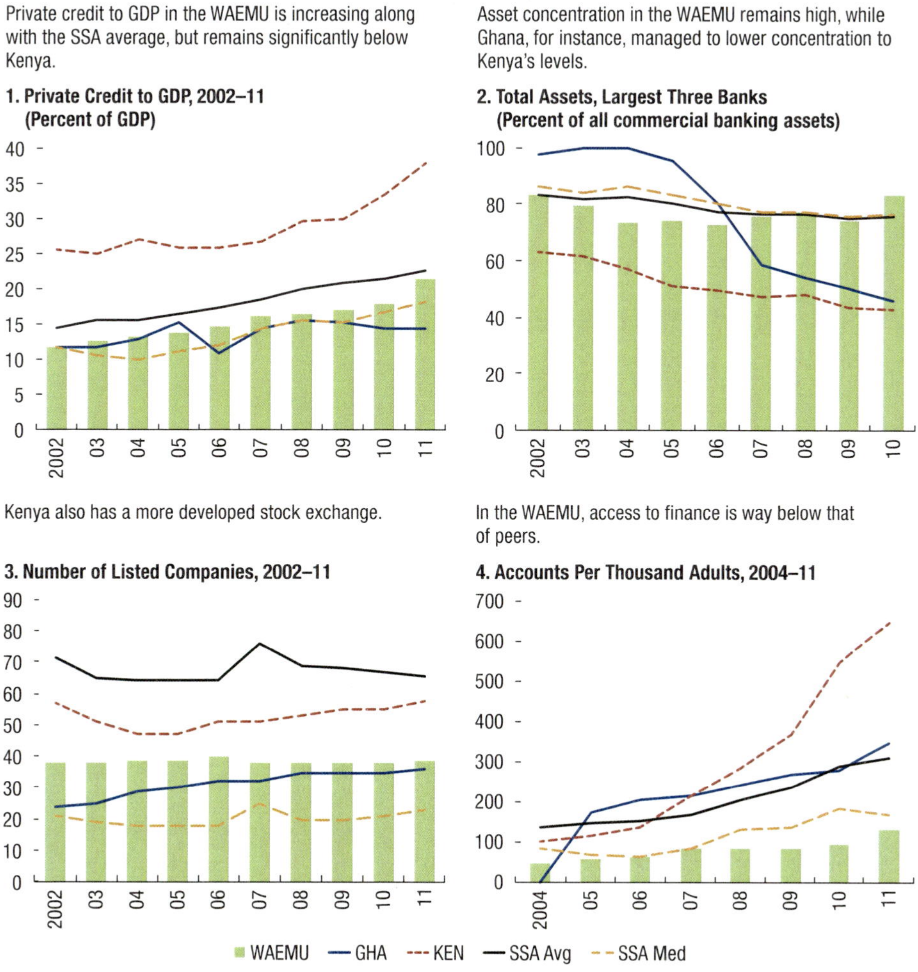

Sources: Central Bank of West African States; FinStats database; and IMF staff calculations.
Note: Simple average for all WAEMU countries. Three-letter International Organization for Standardization abbreviations used for country names. SSA = Sub-Saharan Africa; WAEMU = West African Economic and Monetary Union.

Figure 20.3. Selected Indicators on Breadth and Access in the WAEMU

Asset concentration of banks has increased in recent years and is higher than the statistical benchmark for all countries except Mali.

1. Total Assets of Three Largest Banks (Percent of all commercial banking assets)

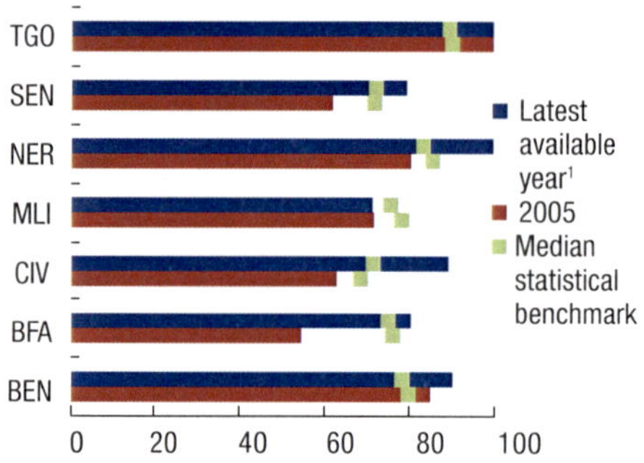

[1]Latest available year was 2011 for Burkina Faso; Côte d'Ivoire, Senegal, and Togo; 2010 for Benin, Mali, and Niger. Guinea-Bissau omitted due to missing data.

Credit to the public sector has quadrupled in some countries from 2005–11, largely exceeding the statistical benchmark.

2. Credit to Government and State-Owned Enterprises (Percent of GDP)

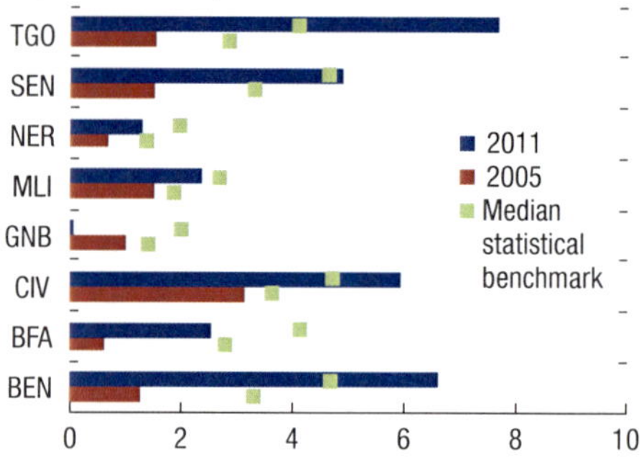

In 2010, diversification into life insurance exceeded structural benchmarks in all countries.

3. Insurance Premiums (Life), 2010 (Percent of GDP)

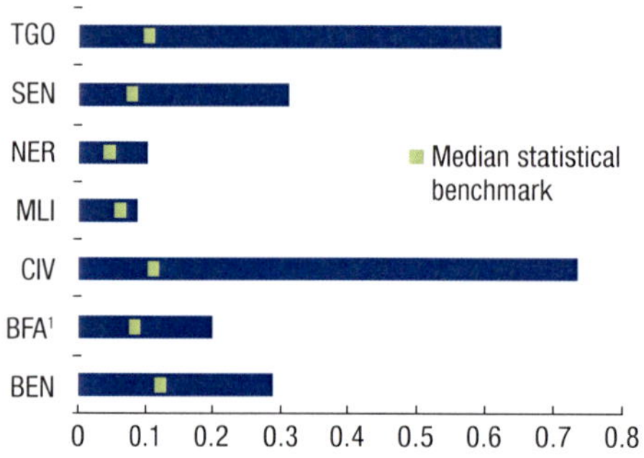

2009 data is used for Burkina Faso.
Guinea-Bissau omitted due to missing data.

Access to financial services such as bank accounts was in line with, or exceeded, the benchmarks in most countries in 2011...

4. Accounts Per 1,000 Adults

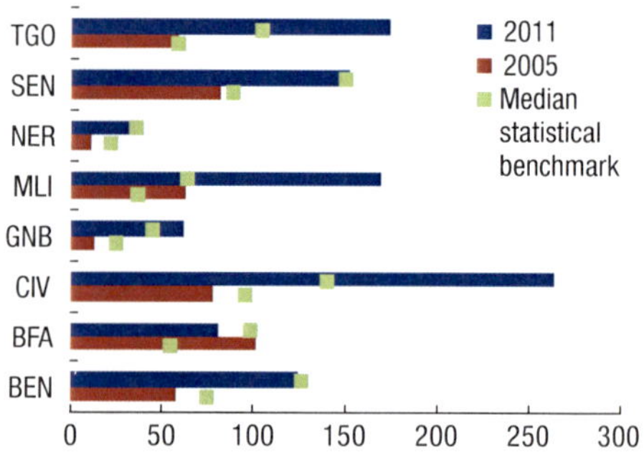

...with a similar outcome with respect to the number of bank branches.

5. Branches Per 100,000 Adults

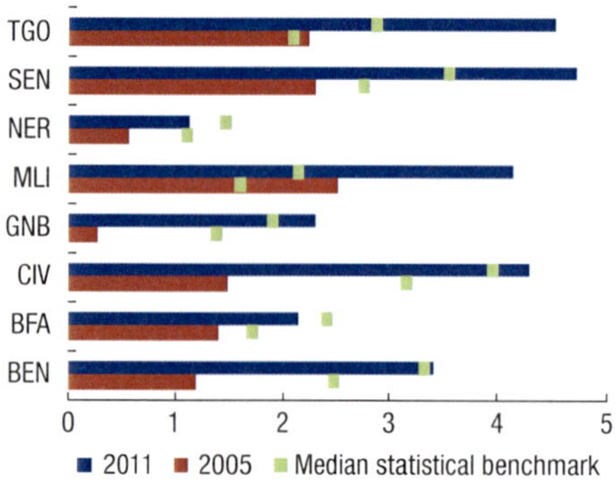

The number of accounts has also increased significantly for microfinance institutions.

6. Number of Accounts at Microfinance Institutions

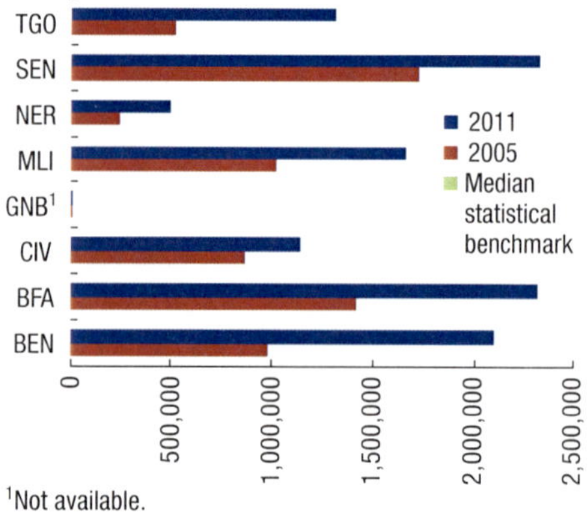

[1]Not available.
Number of Accounts is not included in FinStat, hence there is no statistical benchmark.

Sources: Central Bank of West African States; FinStats database; and IMF staff estimates.
Note: Three-letter International Organization for Standardization abbreviations used for country names.

While statistical benchmarking shows that the WAEMU is not lagging in terms of financial sector depth and access, direct comparison with selected peer countries suggests substantial scope for further development. An agenda for further research would be to understand what drives differences with comparator countries, and in particular whether certain reforms could be replicated in the WAEMU to further develop the financial system.

- *Depth*—Private credit to GDP in the WAEMU is on average comparable to the sub-Saharan African average. It is larger than in Ghana, but significantly lower than in Kenya; in the latter, the increase has also been faster than in the WAEMU.
- *Breadth*—While Ghana has managed to reduce significantly asset concentration in the banking system and has reached a level comparable to Kenya's, concentration remains high in the WAEMU. The stock market is also broader in Kenya.
- *Access*—Access is an area where the WAEMU is lagging behind all comparator countries. Kenya and, to a lesser extent, Ghana have made impressive progress in this area in recent years.

STYLIZED FACTS

In the literature, financial depth is generally measured by either the ratio of liquid liabilities to GDP or the ratio of private credit to GDP. Although these two measures are correlated, they have different focuses. The liabilities side measure captures the degree of mobilization of monetary resources as a share of GDP, while the credit measure focuses on the extent to which banks finance economic activity. Figures 20.4, 20.5, and 20.6 compare the WAEMU with the control group along these two basic indicators of financial depth, as well as two measures of efficiency. It appears that the WAEMU is lagging relative to the control group. In the WAEMU, the ratio of private sector credit to GDP increased marginally from 12 percent to 17 percent between 1997–2009, while it accelerated from 17 percent to 37 percent of GDP in the control group (Figure 20.4). The ratio of broad money to GDP, a measure of the degree of monetization, followed a similar profile. Broad money relative to GDP grew from 31 percent to 52 percent in the benchmark countries, while rising from 20 percent to 29 percent in the WAEMU over the period (Figure 20.5).

The banking system in the WAEMU is not only shallower compared with the benchmark countries, but it is also less profitable. Return on assets, weighted by bank assets, remained constant at around 1.3 percent in the WAEMU, half of the level found in HGNOEs (Figure 20.6). The contrast is also striking for return on equity (Figure 20.6).

In explaining the differences in financial depth across countries, the empirical literature (Demirgüç-Kunt 2006) distinguishes between structural factors and policy factors. *Structural factors* are country-specific characteristics that cannot be altered by policies in the short term. These include the overall level of economic development and other characteristics such as population size and density and age dependency. The overall level of development, measured by per-capita income, can affect financial depth by elevating demand for financial services and higher supply of savings. Countries with larger populations and higher population density can have deeper financial penetration and lower cost of financial intermediation from economies of scale. The share of nonworking young and old populations (age dependency) affects savings and lending patterns. *Policy factors* are those that may impact the banking environment. These include macroeconomic policies (such as inflation, fiscal balance, and debt), institutional policies (regulatory and supervisory frameworks, accounting and disclosures practices, credit information, and contract enforcement), and other financial sector reforms that may liberalize credit markets or enhance market compeititon.

Figure 20.4. Credit to the Private Sector (Percent of GDP)

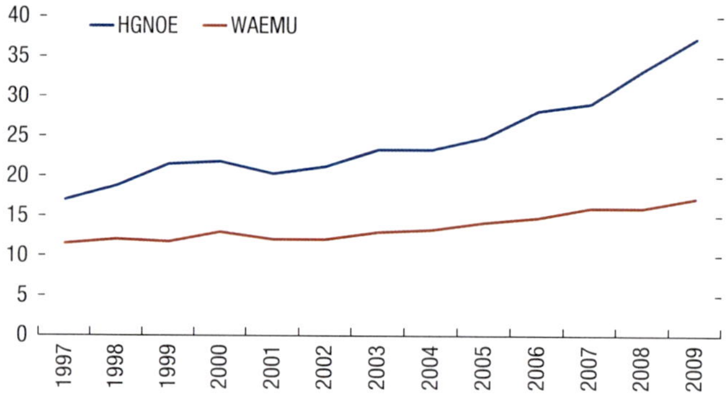

Source: Bankscope database.
Note: HGNOE = high-growth, non-oil-exporter countries; and WAEMU = West African Economic and Monetary Union.

Figure 20.5. Broad Money (Percent of GDP)

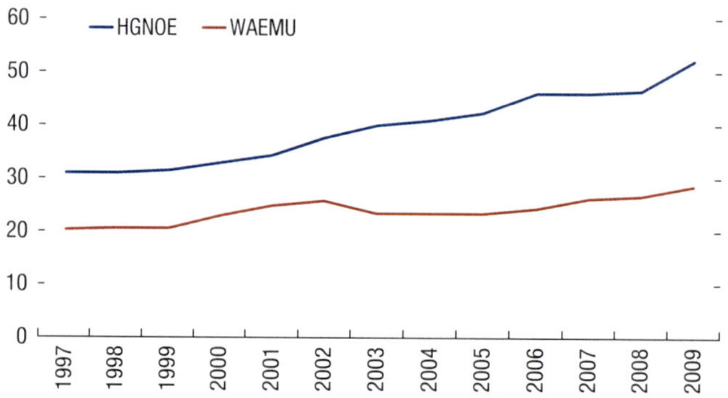

Source: Bankscope database.
Note: HGNOE = high-growth, non-oil-exporter countries; and WAEMU = West African Economic and Military Union.

There is evidence in the literature that both structural factors and macroeconomic policies can have an impact on financial deepening. Levine (2003) and Claessens and Feijen (2006) show the importance of overall economic development, measured by per capita income. On macroeconomic policies, Detragiache, Gupta, and Tressel (2005) find a negative impact of inflation on financial depth, while Boyd, Levine, and Smith (2001) highlight the nonlinear relationship between inflation and financial development.

Looking beyond macroeconomic performance, there is also evidence that contract enforcement, credit infrastructure, and market liberalization play an important role. Using bank-level cross-sectional data, Demetriades and Fielding (2012) investigated the determinants of individual banks' loans in the WAEMU, and found that banks are reluctant to lend because the infrastructure to screen and monitor borrowers is not developed. Governance in all its aspects (government effectiveness, control of corruption, and rule of law) also plays a role. Detragiache, Gupta, and Tressel (2005) found that contract enforcement and property rights matter in financial development. Sacerdoti (2005) explains the low ratio of credit to private sector to GDP by a deficiency in

Figure 20.6. Return on Assets and Return on Equity

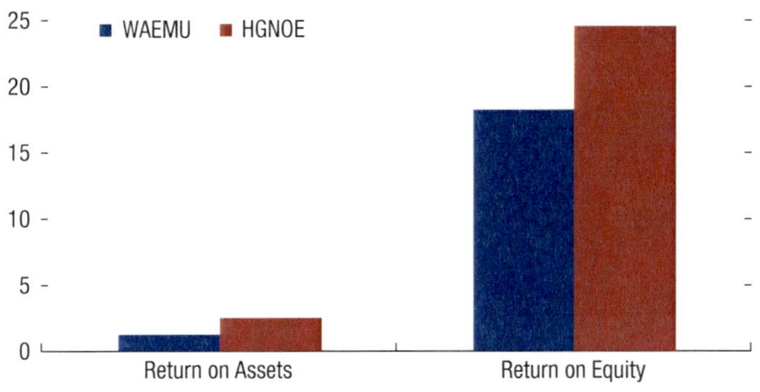

Source: Bankscope database.
Note: HGNOE = high-growth, non-oil-exporter countries; and WAEMU = West African Economic and Military Union.

the supporting institutional framework. Ghura, Kpodar, and Singh (2009) explain low financial depth in the CFA franc zone countries through the weaker legal, contractual, and institutional environment in the region compared with sub-Saharan Africa. Using the financial liberalization index constructed by McDonald and Schumacher (2007) that captures some aspects of financial reforms (credit controls, interest rate controls, informal financial sector), Ghura, Kpodar, and Singh (2009) found that this aggregate index is related to greater depth in financial development.

TWO APPROACHES TO ASSESSING

Where does the WAEMU stand relative to some selected economies in terms of its financial depth, and which factors may help explain this performance? The benchmark group of this case study is comprised of some frontier sub-Sarahan African countries—the high-growth, non-oil-exporter countries.[1] Our analysis focuses on a group of African countries with shared monetary and financial policies, and compares it with a group of high-performing countries in sub-Saharan Africa. We use two complementary empirical approaches to compare the two groups of countries: first, a regression analysis to identify the factors that explain the difference in financial depth between the WAEMU and the control group; and second, a case study based on the financial benchmark methodology developed by the World Bank (Beck and others 2008; Feyen and Kibuuka 2012). The results are consistent with the literature: stronger rule of law, infrastructure, and credit information collection and dissemination have a strong impact on financial depth.

FINANCIAL DEPTH DETERMINANTS

The difference between financial depth in the WAEMU and in the comparator group can be assessed empirically. The measure of financial sector depth is credit to the private sector as a share of GDP, which reflects the extent of financial intermediation in sub-Saharan Africa and the inter-

[1] High-growth, non-oil-exporter countries are the countries with an average per capita growth rate of at least 3 percent during 1995–2009. Eight frontier sub-Saharan African countries fall into this category: Botswana, Cape Verde, Ethiopia, Mauritius, Mozambique, Rwanda, Tanzania, and Uganda (IMF 2010).

linkage between economic activity and the financial system better than do other liabilities-based measures. The period is sufficiently long to capture the lagged impact of policy reforms on improving the financial environment. The analysis is based on a panel of 16 countries (eight countries from the WAEMU, and eight high-growth, non-oil-exporter countries) over the period 1997–2009 at annual frequency. The panel analysis allows us to track the WAEMU countries over a relatively long time horizon and compare them with other peer economies.

Credit to the private sector as a share of GDP is estimated using the following model:

$$S_{c,t} = \alpha_1 + \sum_j \beta_j X_{c,t}{}^j + \sum_m \beta_m Y_{c,t}{}^m + d_t + \upsilon_{i,t} \tag{1}$$

where the vector $X_{c,t}$ contains macroeconomic variables specific to country c at time t. $Y_{c,t}$ contains country-specific institutional and policy variables. d_t is a vector of dummy variables that takes a value 1 if the country belongs to the WAEMU region and zero otherwise.

The macroeconomic indicators include the log of GDP per capita and the log of inflation. Per capita GDP measures the overall level of economic development and is expected to positively affect credit to the private sector. As income rises, demand for financial services increases and that might lead to better penetration. Also with higher incomes, there might be greater savings, which means the banks will have more resources to lend from. Low inflation is considered a sign of macroeconomic stability, which promotes financial intermediation. Thus, the expected coefficient sign for inflation is negative.

Policy and institutional variables include indices on rule of law, political stability, credit coverage, Internet coverage among adults, and the quality of contract enforcement. The rule of law represents a measure of the extent to which banks have faith in contract enforcement, police, and courts, and the likelihood of crime and violence. A strong rule of law is expected to create an environment conducive to bank lending. Property rights capture the dimension of rule of law related to the strength of collateral entitlements and enforcement, which helps banks extend collateralized credit. Political stability, measured here by the perceptions of the likelihood that the government will be destabilized or overthrown by unconstitutional or violent means (Worldwide Governance Indicators), is another factor that we consider in explaining financial penetration. When the political environment is stable, there is less uncertainty, and banks are more willing to lend. The quality of contract enforcement, measured by the number of days required to enforce a contract, is also an important determinant of bank lending. The longer it takes to enforce a contract, the costlier the borrowers' default for banks, the smaller the amount of credit disbursed by banks. Credit coverage captures the quality of credit information. Credible credit bureaus encourage the expansion of credit as they enable, on the one hand, lenders to better screen borrowers, assess and manage risks, and on the other hand, borrowers to gain access to finance. Internet coverage is used as a proxy for infrastructure development, which reduces the cost of bank penetration and helps improve banks' geographical coverage. Good Internet coverage indicates a solid telecommunication infrastructure, which is critical to and for bank transactions and transfers.

Tables 20.1 and 20.2, respectively, show some descriptive statistics and correlations. Table 20.3 shows the definition and sources of the variables used in the analysis. Credit to the private sector relative to GDP is most correlated with infrastructure, rule of law, and GDP per capita. Various measures of the quality of legal environment (rule of law, property rights, and political stability) are highly correlated with each other, suggesting that they may be measuring similar attributes of the credit environment.

To further the analysis, we use a two-step Feasible Generalized Least Squares to estimate the model previously explained. The estimation approach allows us not only to address issues of heteroscedasticity, but also to estimate the impact of time-invariant variables such as the

TABLE 20.1

Descriptive Statistics, 1997–2009

Variable	Observations	Mean	Std. Dev.	Min	Max
Credit to private/GDP	168	0.16	0.15	0.01	0.85
WAEMU_dummy	208	0.50	0.50	0.00	1.00
Inflation	206	0.05	0.04	–0.09	0.16
GDP per capita	208	6.28	1.03	4.73	8.94
Rule of law	160	–0.44	0.66	–1.90	1.05
Political stability	160	–0.26	0.88	–2.28	1.13
Internet per hundred	207	2.55	4.36	0.00	25.00
Credit coverage	67	2.76	4.84	0.00	21.80
Property	160	38.41	16.51	10.00	75.00

Sources: World Development Indicators (World Bank); World Governance Indicators (World Bank), Heritage Foundation Database.
Note: Max = maximum; Min = minimum; Std. Dev. = standard deviation; WAEMU = West African Economic and Monetary Union.

TABLE 20.2

Correlation Matrix

		1	2	3	4	5	6	7	8	9
Credit to private/GDP	1	1.00								
WAEMU_dummy	2	–0.26	1.00							
Inflation	3	0.08	–0.47	1.00						
GDP per capita	4	0.76	–0.26	0.12	1.00					
Rule of law	5	0.72	–0.45	0.09	0.74	1.00				
Political stability	6	0.52	–0.10	–0.05	0.58	0.76	1.00			
Internet per hundred	7	0.86	–0.26	0.11	0.64	0.56	0.39	1.00		
Credit coverage	8	0.61	0.03	–0.34	0.44	0.33	0.37	0.65	1.00	
Property	9	0.65	–0.38	0.03	0.77	0.86	0.58	0.53	0.38	1.00

Source: Authors' calculations.

WAEMU dummy, while controlling for country-specific effects. Several model specifications have been estimated and the results are presented in Table 20.4.

The WAEMU dummy is negative and significant even after controlling for macroeconomic variables (Table 20.4, column 1), thereby providing evidence that financial deepening is indeed weaker in the WAEMU than it is in high-growth, non-oil-exporter countries in sub-Saharan Africa. The sign and significance of the WAEMU variable are, however, not stable when policy and institutional factors are accounted for.

As expected, macroeconomic variables are important determinants of credit to the private sector relative to GDP. The impact of inflation is negative and significant in most specifications of the model. Per-capita GDP is positively associated with the financial depth in all specifications.

Looking at institutional/policy variables, we find that political stability, availability of information on borrowers, strength of legal framework, and quality of infrastructure are associated with deeper financial markets (Table 20.4, columns 2–6). The introduction of some of these variables substantially weakens the control variable for WAEMU countries, suggesting that they may explain away most of the differences in financial depth between the WAEMU and the non-oil-exporter countries.

Both rule of law and property rights capture the quality of the legal environment and are highly correlated (Table 20.2). They both are significantly associated with financial depth (Table 20.4, columns 2 and 6). However, the introduction of rule of law in the regression weakens the WAEMU control variable, which becomes insignificant. In other words, once rule of law is accounted for, the difference between the WAEMU group and the non-oil-exporter countries becomes statistically insignificant. This result is in line with the literature that finds that a stronger legal framework promotes financial development because depositors can provide longer-term

TABLE 20.3

Definition of Variables

Variable	Definition	Source
Credit to private/GDP	Credit to the private sector as percentage of GDP	International Financial Statistics
WAEMU_dummy	Take value 1 if the country belongs to the WAEMU	International Financial Statistics
Inflation	Inflation rate	
GDP per capita	Gross domestic product per capita	International Financial Statistics
Rule of law	Rule of law captures perceptions of the extent to which agents have confidence in and abide by the rules of society, and in particular the quality of contract enforcement, property rights, the police, and the courts, as well as the likelihood of crime and violence. Estimate gives the country's score on the aggregate indicator, in units of a standard normal. Distribution, that is, ranging from approximately −2.5 to 2.5	Worldwide Governance Indicators (World Bank)
Political stability	Political stability and absence of violence/terrorism captures perceptions of the likelihood that the government will be destabilized or overthrown by unconstitutional or violent means, including politically motivated violence and terrorism. Estimate gives the country's score on the aggregate indicator, in units of a standard normal distribution, that is, ranging from approximately −2.5 to 2.5.	Worldwide Governance Indicators (World Bank)
Internet per hundred	Internet users are people with access to the worldwide network (number per hundred people).	Worldwide Governance Indicators (World Bank)
Credit coverage	Public credit registry coverage reports the number of individuals and firms listed in a public credit registry with current information on repayment history, unpaid debts, or credit outstanding. The number is expressed as a percentage of adult population.	Worldwide Governance Indicators (World Bank)
Property	An index measuring the ability of individuals to accumulate private property, secured by clear laws that are fully enforced by the state.	Heritage Foundation Database

Source: Authors' presentation.

TABLE 20.4

Financial Development in the WAEMU and HGNOE in SSA, 1997–2009

VARIABLES	(1)	(2)	(3)	(4)	(5)	(6)	(7)	(8)
WAEMU_dummy	−0.028	−0.003	−0.029	−0.010	0.013	−0.023	0.012	0.075
	0.005***	0.007	0.007***	0.006	0.014	0.006***	0.012	0.021***
Inflation	−0.171	−0.180	−0.273	−0.126	−0.063	−0.164	−0.156	−0.094
	0.067***	0.075***	0.076	0.072*	0.132	0.068***	0.097	0.106
GDP per capita	0.114	0.083	0.089	0.056	0.074	0.099	0.044	0.059
	0.003***	0.003***	0.004***	0.006***	0.011***	0.004***	0.008***	0.012***
Rule of law		0.078					0.045	0.077
		0.006***					0.020***	0.020***
Political stability			0.033				0.009	−0.008
			0.003***				0.009	0.009
Internet per hundred				0.020			0.018	0.015
				0.002***			0.002***	0.003***
Credit coverage					0.010			0.003
					0.004			0.002
Property						0.001	0.001	−0.003
						0.000***	0.001	0.001***
Constant	−0.519	−0.300	−0.349	−0.217	−0.337	−0.479	−0.151	−0.166
	0.021***	0.024***	0.027	0.030***	0.067***	0.023	0.054***	0.056***
Observations	167	132	132	167	52	138	122	51
Number of countries	17	17	17	17	15	17	17	14
Chi square (Wald Test)	1231.91	1638.05	727.28	489.96	116.77	1267.99	588.84	204.56

Source: Authors' calculations.
Note: SSA = Sub-Saharan Africa; HGNOE = high-growth, non-oil-exporter countries; WAEMU = West African Economic and Monetary Union.

savings and banks can extend more credit, as they have a greater chance at recovering nonperforming assets through courts.

The results also indicate that political stability matters for financial depth (Table 20.4, column 3). In a politically stable environment, banks have more confidence to lend because there is less uncertainty and a greater chance of recovering their outlays. While political stability matters, it does not explain away the differences between the WAEMU and the non-oil-exporter countries, as the WAEMU control variable remains significant.

Quality of infrastructure, as measured by Internet coverage, positively affects financial depth (Table 20.4, column 4). It also explains away the difference in financial depth between the WAEMU and non-oil-exporter countries. Better infrastructure allows financial institutions to reach borrowers at a lower cost, thereby encouraging more lending.

Information on borrowers as measured by credit coverage is another important factor that is positively associated with financial depth (Table 20.4, column 5). The introduction of credit coverage in the regression also explains away the difference between the WAEMU and non-oil-exporter countries. If banks have more information on their customers, they will screen them better and will engage in greater lending, as they will be less exposed to defaults. Small and medium-sized enterprises and other entrepreneurs with good quality projects and good track records will have access to credit and be able to undertake profitable investment projects.

Overall, the results show that the difference in financial depth between the WAEMU and non-oil-exporter countries is explained by the quality of the legal environment, infrastructure, and information available on borrowers. When rule of law, property rights, and political stability are simultaneously introduced in the model, only rule of law is significant (Table 20.4, column 7), indicating that there is some overlap in the dimension of the institutional environment measured by these variables.

FINANCIAL POSSIBILITIES FRONTIER

The concept of financial benchmarking is predicated on the idea that there are structural factors that determine the level of financial development a country can attain. Some factors are conducive to financial sector development (for example, income levels) and others inhibit it (for example, low density of population, which makes infrastructure deployment costly relative to the population served and minimizes the benefit of economies of scale in banking). The benchmarking allows for cross-country comparisons to see how a specific country is doing relative to other countries with similar structural characteristics and at similar stages of development. The benchmarking approach assumes that once appropriate controls are introduced, the process of financial development is broadly comparable across countries and stages of development. Financial sector development is affected by three types of factors: economic development, other structural characteristics, and the policy environment.

$$X_t = \alpha Y_t + \beta P_t + \gamma Z_t + \varepsilon_t \tag{1}$$

where X is an indicator of financial sector development, Y is an indicator of economic development, P represents the policy environment, Z is a vector of structural characteristics, and ε is a residual.

Economic development is captured by income per capita. Demand for financial services increases as income grows. On the supply side, richer countries have better infrastructures and higher competition, which lower the price of financial services. Income per capita is endogenous, but financial sector development affects income per capita with a delay. The reason is that changes in the policy environment affect the financial sector first, and the financial sector in turn then affects economic growth. Therefore, we can write:

$$Y_t = \alpha' P_t + \beta' P_{t-1} + \gamma' Z_t + \varepsilon'_t \tag{2}$$

The policy environment does not change radically overnight. Good policies today are generally linked to the good policies of yesterday but also to today's innovations.

$$P_t = \alpha'' P_{t-1} + \upsilon_t \tag{3}$$

The structural variables included in the benchmarking analysis are a set of factors that are considered as external to policy, at least in the short term. These factors include: population, age dependency, a time factor, and special circumstances. Countries with larger populations and higher population density can have deeper and lower cost of providing financial services, thanks to economies of scale. The share of nonworking young and old populations (age dependency) affects saving and lending patterns. Over time, all financial systems tend to improve, albeit at different speed, because of global factors that "lift all boats." To account for this, a time trend is included in the regression. Many special factors affect financial sector development. In oil exporting countries, for instance, income per capita can be out of proportion with the financial and overall economic development of the country. In contrast, offshore financial centers have a financial sector that is disproportionately larger than the overall economy.

When one runs a regression of financial development on economic development and structural factors only, policy innovations are captured by the residual. To see this, one can substitute equations (2) and (3) into (1), and get the following reduced form expression:

$$X_t = \left(\alpha + \frac{\beta\alpha''}{\alpha'\alpha'' + \beta'}\right) Y_t + \left(\gamma - \frac{\beta\alpha''\gamma'}{\alpha'\alpha'' + \beta'}\right) Z_t + \left(\varepsilon_t - \frac{\alpha''}{\alpha'\alpha'' + \beta'}\varepsilon'_t + \frac{\beta\beta'}{\alpha'\alpha'' + \beta'}\upsilon_t\right) \tag{4}$$

The policy innovation factor is now in the residual. When the benchmark is constructed using the economic and structural variables (*Y* and *Z*), the distance between the benchmark and the actual level of financial development is assumed to reflect the country's policy environment. Countries with better policies (higher *u*) would tend to have more developed financial sectors compared with countries with worse policies.

FinStats estimates equation (4) via quantile regressions, using data from 177 countries. It then compares a given country to its own potential (benchmark) or to its comparator countries. In the first approach, the country's benchmark is calculated using its economic and structural variables in equation (4). In the second approach, comparator countries are chosen based on their similarity with the reference country on two dimensions: GDP per capita and populations. The comparator countries are those with the smallest distance to the reference country, where distance is calculated as follows:

$$\Delta_{ij} = W_{gdppc} \mid \mathrm{PR}(gdp_i) - PR(gdppc_j) \mid + (1 - W_{gdppc}) \mid PR(POP_i) - PR(POP_j) \mid$$

where *PR* is the percentile rank of the country. FinStats uses the expected 25th and 75th percentiles (see Annex 1).

The results in Annex 1 show that most WAEMU countries are lagging relative to their potential. A closer analysis of the biggest and most financially advanced economy in the WAEMU (Côte d'Ivoire) against a comparable country in the control group (Mozambique) indicates that strength of contract enforcement and credit information constitute the main difference between Côte d'Ivoire and Mozambique over the later part of the observed period. Mozambique's

Annex 1. Benchmarking WAEMU Countries Against Their Potential

1. Benin: Private Credit
(Percent of GDP)

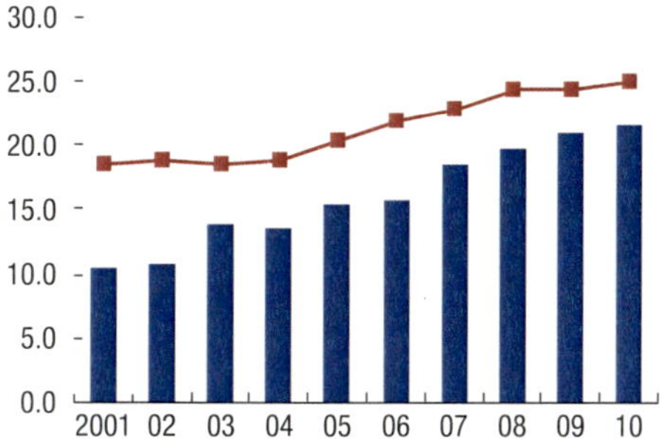

2. Burkina Faso: Private Credit
(Percent of GDP)

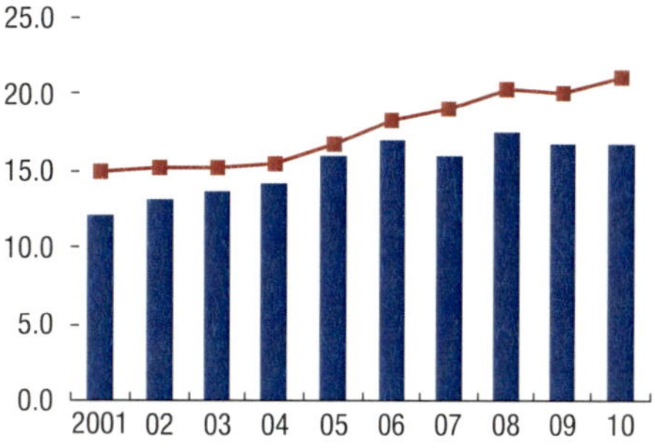

3. Mali: Private Credit
(Percent of GDP)

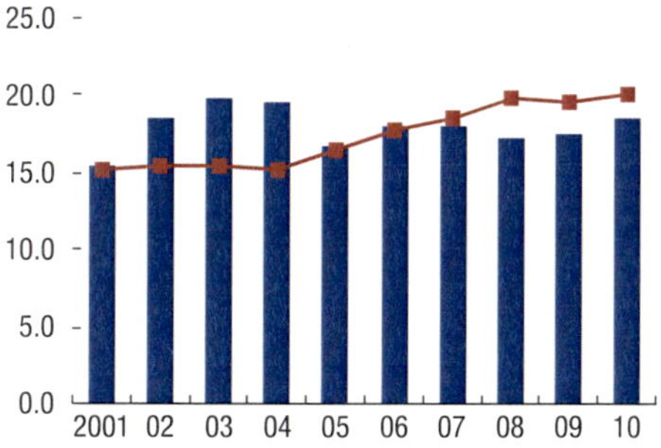

4. Niger: Private Credit
(Percent of GDP)

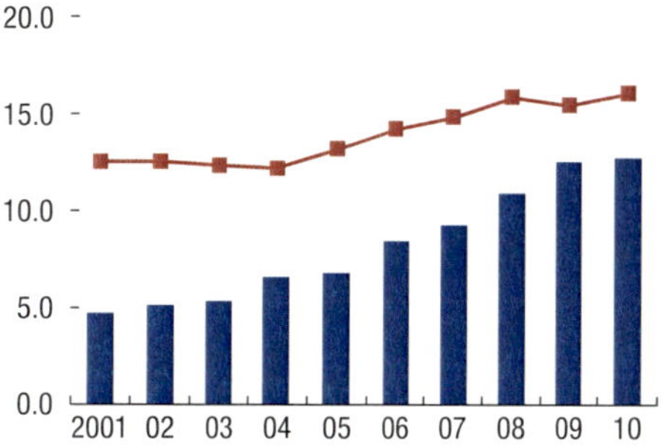

5. Senegal: Private Credit
(Percent of GDP)

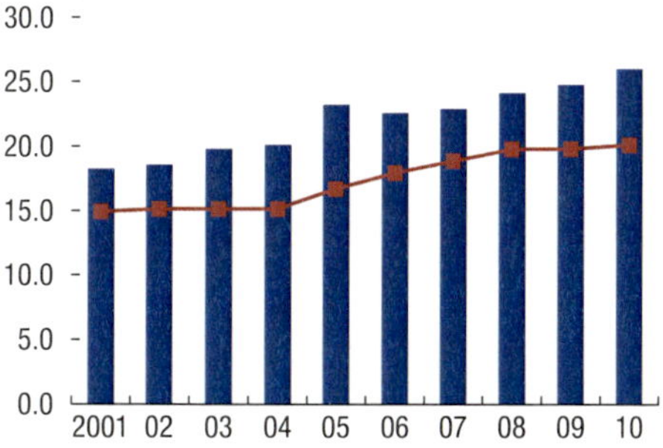

6. Togo: Private Credit
(Percent of GDP)

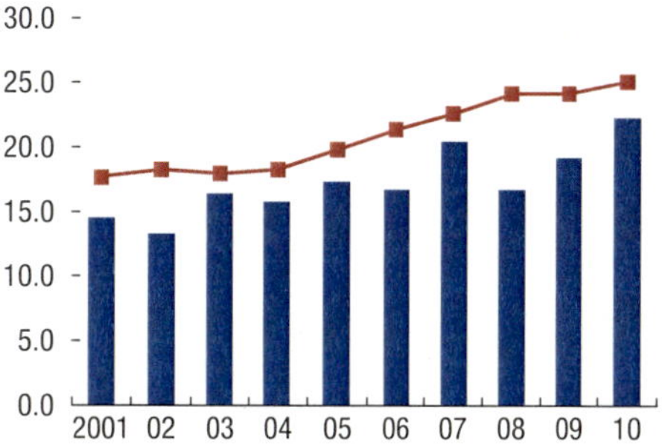

7. Côte d'Ivoire: Private Credit Relative to Mozambique
(Percent of GDP)

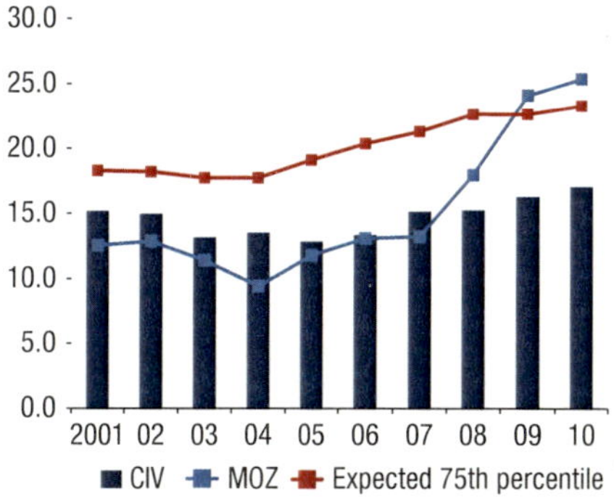

Source: Author's calculations.

government took forceful actions in strengthening contract enforcement, with establishment of a specialized commercial court and the introduction of performance measures. As a result, the time taken to resolve a dispute fell by 72 percent (Doing Business 2008). Furthermore, a new legal framework for credit registries has been enacted in Mozambique, which resulted in expanding the scope and accessibility of credit information. Several other reforms undertaken by Mozambique's authorities over this period helped increase the flow of credit (FSAP 2009). These include: (1) transitioning from an overall compliance-supervisory regime to risk-based supervision; (2) enhancing the financial infrastructure by significantly improving the national payments system; and (3) new legislation on microfinance.

REFERENCES

Beck, T., E. Feyen, Alain Ize, and F. Moizeszowicz. 2008. "Benchmarking Financial Development." Policy Research Working Paper, World Bank, Washington.

Boyd, J. H., R. Levine, and B. D. Smith. 2001. "The Impact of Inflation on Financial Sector Performance." *Journal of Monetary Economics* 47 (2): 221–48.

Claessens, S., and E. Feijen. 2006. "Finance and Hunger: Empirical Evidence of the Agricultural Productivity Channel." Policy Research Working Paper Series 4080, World Bank, Washington.

Demetriades, P., and D. Fielding. 2012. "Information, Institutions, and Banking Sector Development in West Africa." *Economic Inquiry* 50: (3).

Demirgüç-Kunt, A. 2006. "Finance and Economic Development: Policy Choices for Developing Countries." Policy Research Working Paper Series 3955, World Bank, Washington.

Detragiache, E., P. Gupta, and T. Tressel. 2005. "Finance in Lower Income Countries: An Empirical Exploration." Working Paper WP/05/167, International Monetary Fund, Washington.

Feyen, E., and K. Kibuuka. (2012). "FinStats 2012: A Ready-to-Use Tool to Benchmark Financial Sectors Across Countries and Time." Unpublished, World Bank.

Ghura, D., K. Kpodar, and R. J. Singh. 2009. "Financial Deepening in the CFA Franc Zone: The Role of Institutions." Working Paper WP/09/113, International Monetary Fund, Washington.

International Monetary Fund (IMF). 2010. "Sub-Saharan Africa: Resilience and Risks." In *Regional Economic Outlook,* October.

Levine, R. 2003. "More on Finance and Growth: More Finance, More Growth?" *Federal Reserve Bank of St. Louis Review* 85 (4): 31–46.

McDonald, C., and L. Schumacher. 2007. "Financial Deepening in Sub-Saharan Africa: Empirical Evidence on the Role of Creditor Rights Protection and Information Sharing." Working Paper WP/07/203, International Monetary Fund, Washington.

Sacerdoti, E. 2005. "Access to Bank Credit in Sub-Saharan Africa." Working Paper WP/05/166, International Monetary Fund, Washington.

CHAPTER 21

Financial Inclusion

Monique Newiak and Rachid Awad[1]

West African Economic and Monetary Union (WAEMU) countries lag behind benchmark countries in several dimensions of financial inclusion: access to finance is low, especially for the most vulnerable parts of the population, and the financial sector appears to only modestly contribute to the population's ability to deal with shocks as well as firms' investment programs. Private sector credit-to-GDP ratios, however, appear broadly in line with WAEMU countries' fundamentals. Public policies, such as investments in infrastructure and the social sectors, could help closing these gaps. From the perspective of firms, policies to reduce participation costs in the financial sector and to lower collateral requirements could increase firms' access to financing, and thus significantly boost GDP.

BENCHMARKING FINANCIAL ACCESS

Financial access in the WAEMU remains comparatively low. Figure 21.1 compares different indicators of financial access in the WAEMU against a group of fast-growing regional and Asian benchmark countries.[2] It shows that:

- WAEMU countries, on average, lag behind benchmark groups in the provision of basic financial infrastructure such as the density of ATMs and the number of bank branches.
- The relative amount of deposit and loans at commercial banks is broadly in line with African benchmark groups, but significantly lower than those in Asian benchmark countries; the number of people with deposits at commercial banks is relatively low.
- The shortcomings in financial access are also revealed by enterprise surveys in each WAEMU country, with more than half of respondents identifying access to finance as a major constraint for their businesses.

While modest in general, financial access appears to be lowest for the most vulnerable parts of the population (Figure 21.2). Young adults and the population at the bottom of the income distribution (bottom 40 percent) are the groups with the lowest relative number of bank accounts (less than 5 percent of the respective part of the population), but the population living in rural areas, those with less education, and women are also less often in the possession of a financial account than is the average WAEMU inhabitant. In general, accounts are most often used for business purposes or to receive payments such as wages or remittances.

The main modes to access finance and make deposits are similar to those in benchmark countries, but several payment methods are less pronounced in the WAEMU (Figure 21.3). As in

[1]With valuable contributions from Filiz Unsal (IMF), Era Dabla-Norris (IMF), and Eva Van Leemput (University of Notre Dame). The findings should not be reported as representing the views of the IMF. The section "Identifying the Most Binding Constraints to Firms' Financial Inclusion" is part of a research project on macroeconomic policy in low-income countries, supported by United Kingdom's Department of International Development. The findings should not be reported as representing the views of this department.

[2]African benchmark countries include: Ghana, Kenya, Lesotho, Rwanda, Tanzania, Uganda, and Zambia. Asian benchmark countries include: Bangladesh, Cambodia, India, Laos, Nepal, and Vietnam. Sub-Saharan Africa is provided as a comparator in many cases as well.

Figure 21.1. Financial Access

The penetration of ATM remains comparatively low in the WAEMU on average, and...

1. Number of ATMs, 2013
(Per thousand square kilometers and 100,000 adults)

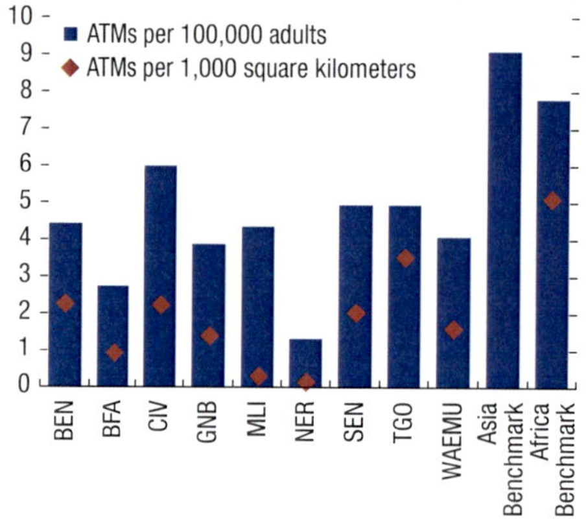

Source: IMF, Financial Access Survey.
Note: Three-letter International Organization for Standardization abbreviations used for country names.

...the number of branches remains comparatively low even for the WAEMU country with the highest branch density.

2. Commercial Bank Branches
(Per 100,000 adults)

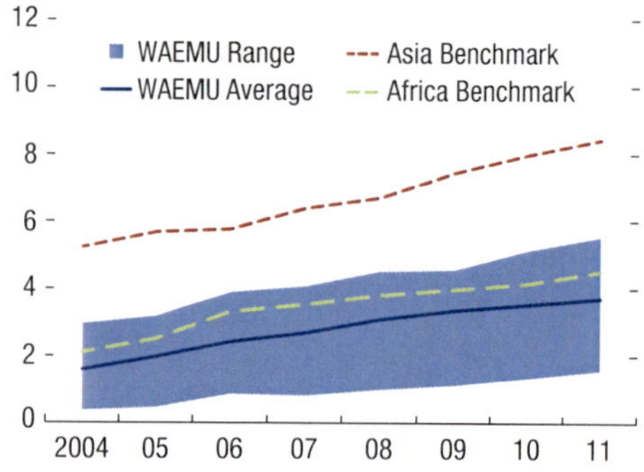

Source: IMF, Financial Access Survey.

Though far exceeded by Asian benchmarks, deposit ratios are on average in line with sub-Saharan Africa benchmark countries...

3. Outstanding Deposits with Commercial Banks
(Percent of GDP)

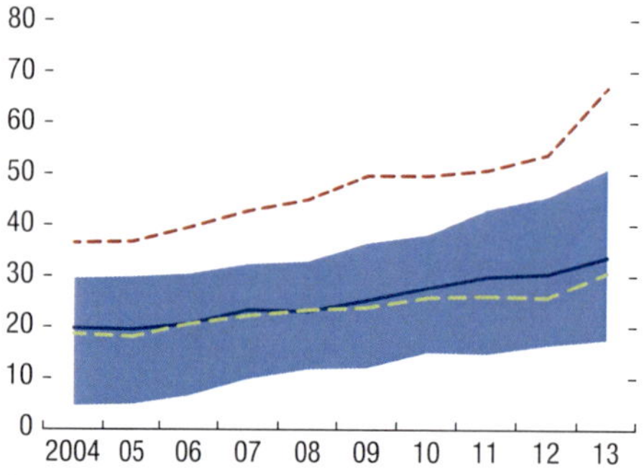

Source: IMF, Financial Access Survey.

...and loans are somewhat higher that for the average sub-Saharan Africa benchmark country.

4. Outstanding Loans from Commercial Banks
(Percent of GDP)

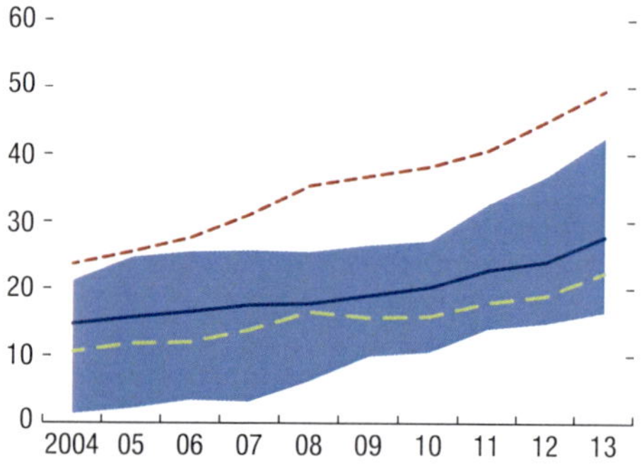

Source: IMF, Financial Access Survey.

The share of the population with deposits at commercial banks has increased, but remains relatively low.

5. Depositors with Commercial Banks
(Per thousand adults)

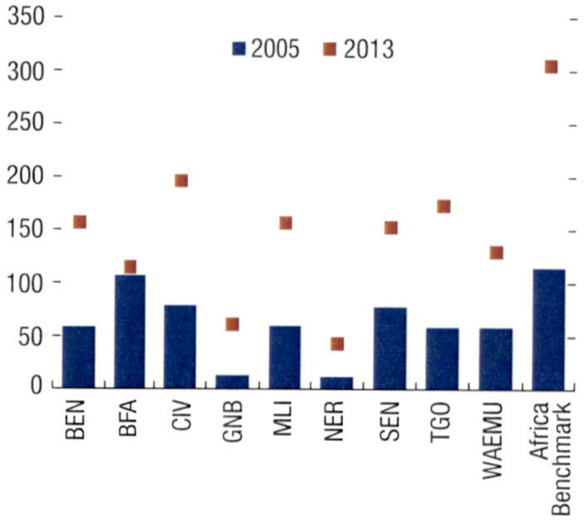

Source: IMF, Financial Access Survey.
Note: Three-letter International Organization for Standardization abbreviations used for country names. WAEMU = West African Economic and Monetary Union.

Most firms consider access to finance as a major constraint.

6. Percent of Firms Identifying Access to Finance as Major Constraint (In percent of respondents)

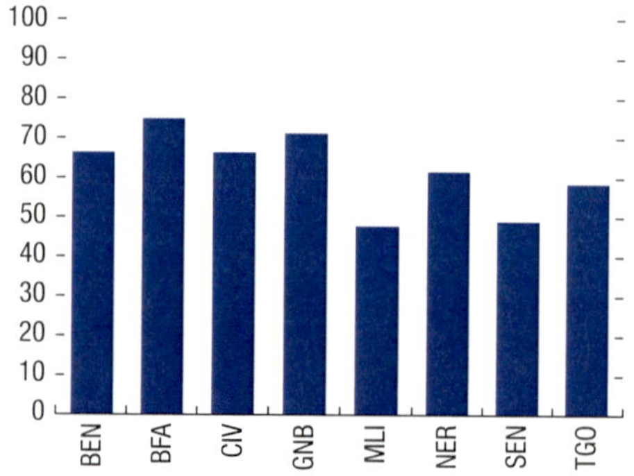

Source: World Bank, Enterprise Survey.
Note: Three-letter International Organization for Standardization abbreviations used for country names.

Figure 21.2. Demographic Characteristics of Financial Access

Gaps in financial access compared with benchmarks are largest for young adults and lower-income groups.

1. Account Used to Receive Government Payments
(In percent of respective group)

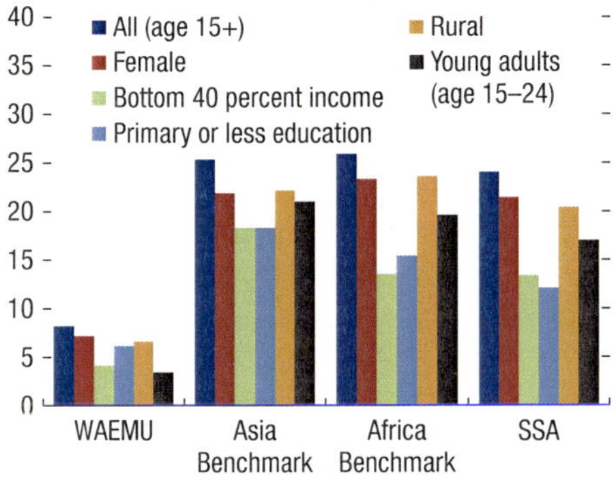

Accounts are mainly used for business purposes.

2. Account Used for Business Purposes
(In percent of respective group)

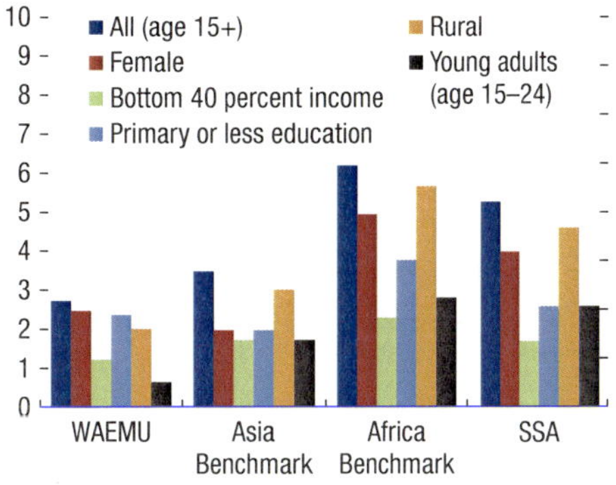

Accounts are also used to receive government payments…

3. Account Used to Receive Government Payments
(In percent of respective group)

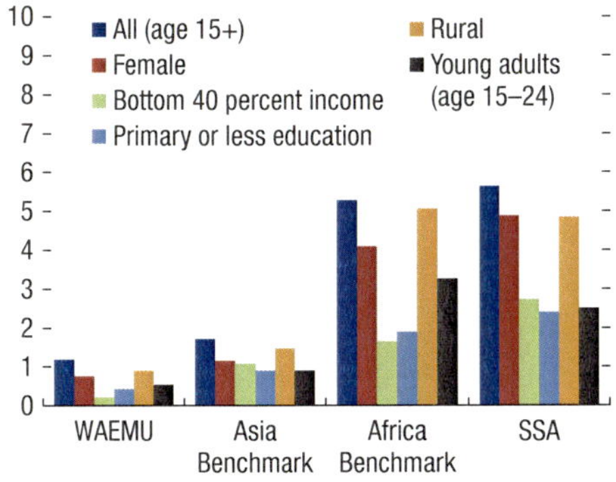

…to receive remittances…

4. Account Used to Receive Remittances
(In percent of respective group)

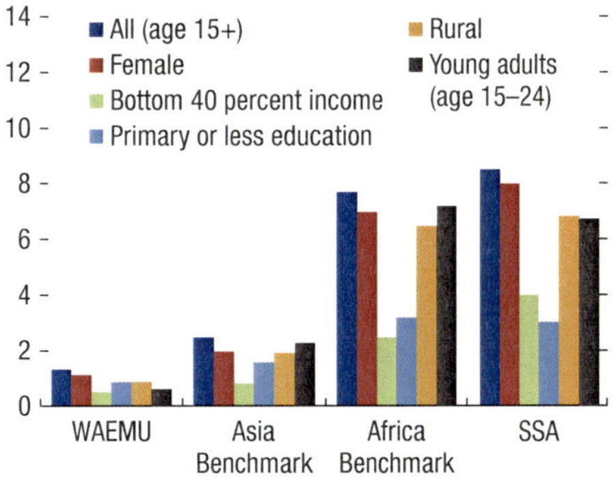

…deposit wages, or…

5. Account Used to Receive Wages
(In percent of respective group)

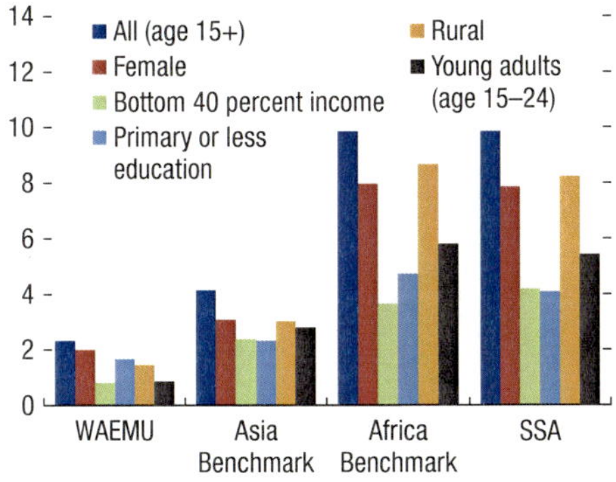

…to send remittances, with some upside potential.

6. Account Used to Send Remittances
(In percent of respective group)

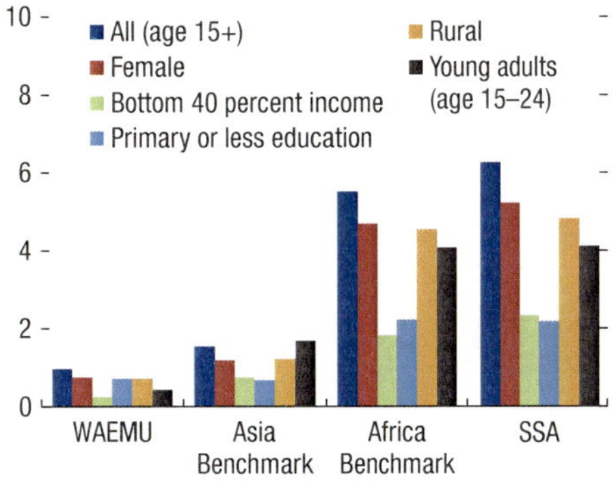

Source: Findex, 2011.
Note: Three-letter International Organization for Standardization abbreviations used for country names.
SSA = Sub-Saharan Africa; WAEMU = West African Economic and Monetary Union.

Figure 21.3. Deposit and Payment Modes

The frequency of use of a bank agent to make deposits is comparable to African peers…

1. Bank Agent Is the Main Mode of Deposit
(In percent with an account, age 15+)

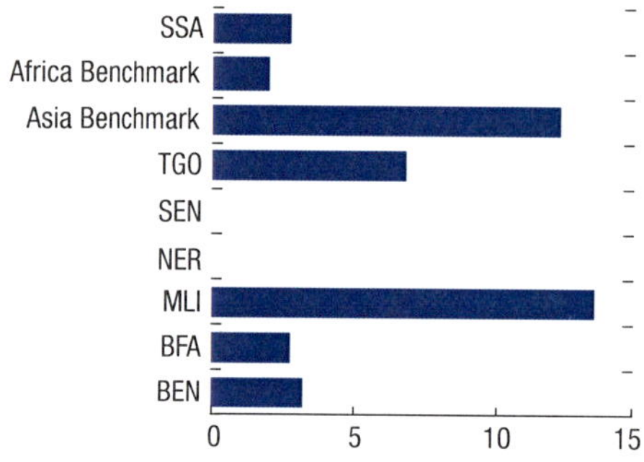

…and the use of a bank teller for deposits is dominant for both WAEMU and comparator groups.

2. Bank Agent Is the Main Mode of Deposit
(In percent with an account, age 15+)

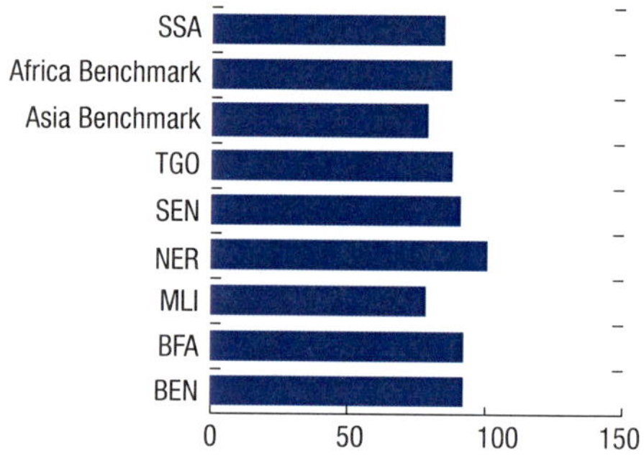

Mali is closest in its use of checks to benchmark groups.

3. Checks Used to Make Payment
(In percent with an account, age 15+)

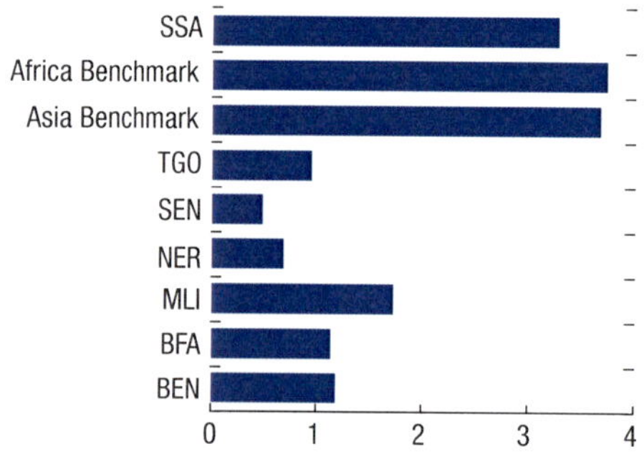

Electronic payments are rare.

4. Electronic Payment Used to Make Payment
(In percent with an account, age 15+)

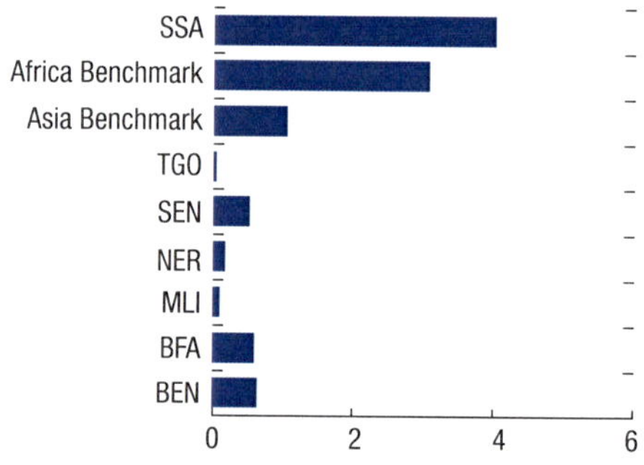

Less than 1 percent of the population has access to a credit card in the WAEMU.

5. Possession of Credit Card
(In percent with an account, age 15+)

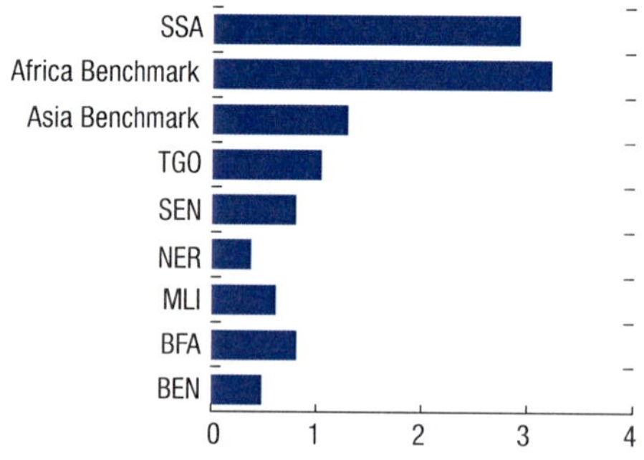

Access to debit cards is somewhat higher, but still significantly below that of peers.

6. Possession of Debit Card
(In percent with an account, age 15+)

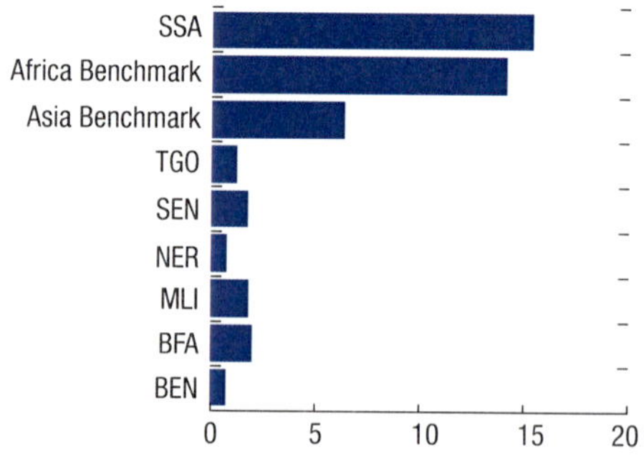

Source: Findex 2011.
Note: Three-letter International Organization for Standardization abbreviations used for country names. SSA = Sub-Saharan Africa.

benchmark countries, the use of a bank teller is the main way to make a deposit. Checks and electronic payments, however, are much less developed modes of payments in WAEMU countries than they are in the comparator groups, and a much smaller share of the WAEMU's population is in possession of a credit or debit card.

The use of loans and the purposes of saving point to relatively weak social protection and only a modest contribution of the financial sector in shock mitigation (Figure 21.4). While the share of the population with outstanding loans for educational fees is comparable to that in benchmark countries, the share of indebted people due to health issues or other emergencies is relatively high in the WAEMU. The population appears relatively less covered by health insurance and, with the exception of Mali, by agricultural insurance. Fewer people (are able to) save for potential emergencies. While pointing to absolute and relative weaknesses in social protection, these indicators also suggest that the financial sector provides insufficient help to the population to insure against or deal with shocks.

The banking sector's contribution to firms' investment programs also appears limited (Figure 21.5). Enterprise surveys indicate that, while most firms possess a bank account, less than 30 percent of firms access a loan or a line of credit in most WAEMU countries. The majority of loans require collateral. The value of such collateral, on average, exceeds the value of the loan, indicating problems with liquidation of the collateral. Loans from banks constitute only a small fraction of firms' investment financing, while internal funds appear to be the main source of financing investments.

PRIVATE SECTOR CREDIT GAPS

Private sector credit-to-GDP ratios are broadly in line with the benchmark for the WAEMU on average, but there are variations across countries (Figure 21.6). Following the methodology in Al Hussainy and others (2011) and Barajas and others (2013), we estimated a benchmark ratio of private sector credit to GDP based on a number of structural factors in a panel of over 120 emerging and developing countries for the period 1986–2013. We regressed the ratio of private sector credit to GDP on: (1) the log of GDP per capita and its square, (2) the log of the population to proxy for market size, (3) the log of population density to proxy for the ease of service provision, (4) the log of the age dependency ratio to account for demographic trends and the related savings behavior, and (5) an oil-exporters dummy and time dummies to control for global factors. The fitted values from these regressions serve as the private sector-to-GDP benchmark. While generally following the dynamics of the benchmarks well, actual credit to GDP has been lower than the benchmark in 2013 in four countries (Benin, Burkina Faso, Côte d'Ivoire, Guinea-Bissau), higher in three (Mali, Niger, Togo), and broadly consistent with the benchmark in Senegal.

A number of policies could help countries to increase private sector credit relative to the benchmark (Figure 21.7, Table 21.1). In the next step, a regression of the financial gap (actual private sector credit to GDP minus its benchmark) on macroeconomic, institutional, and policy variables helps identifying the drivers of the deviations from the benchmark for 2004–13. Table 21.1 highlights the factors that help increase private sector credit relative to the benchmark, while Figure 21.7 depicts the change in the private sector credit to GDP relative to the benchmark if these underlying factors are changed by one standard deviation. Factors that relate positively to private sector credit to GDP include trade openness and foreign direct investment inflows on the external side, lower inflation and higher social and educational spending on the macroeconomic (policy) side, and better infrastructure and institutions (in this exercise, the International Country Risk Guide index, ICRG).

Figure 21.4. Use of Loans

The share of the population with loans for health or emergencies is comparatively high in the WAEMU…

1. Outstanding Loans for Health or Emergencies (In percent, population age 15+)

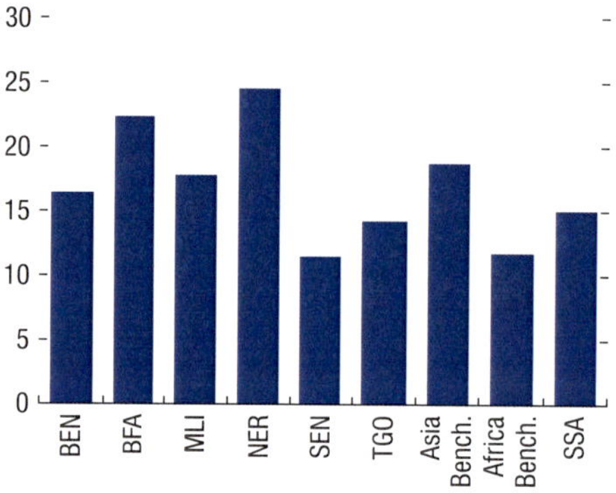

…while outstanding loans for education are in line with comparator groups.

2. Outstanding Loans for School Fees (In percent, population age 15+)

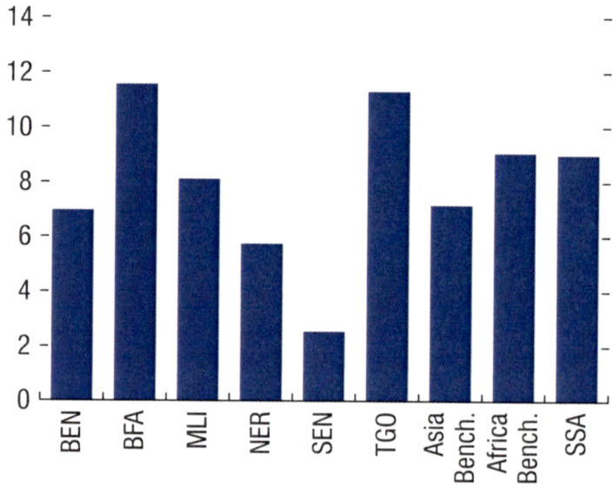

Coverage by health insurance is low…

3. Personally Paid for Health Insurance (In percent, population age 15+)

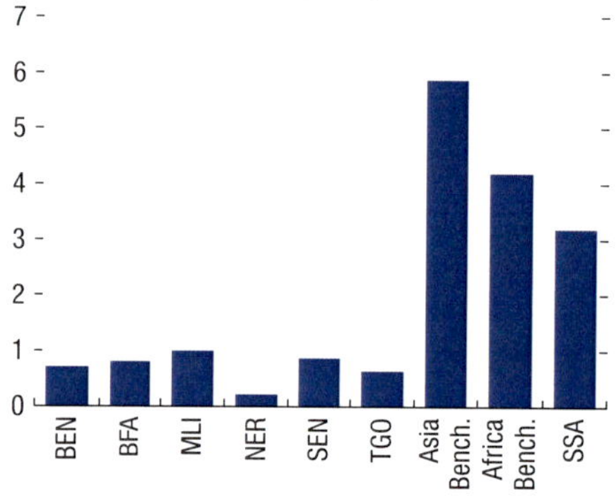

…and insurance against agricultural shocks is less prevalent on average than in benchmark countries.

4. Bought Agricultural Insurance (In percent, population age 15+)

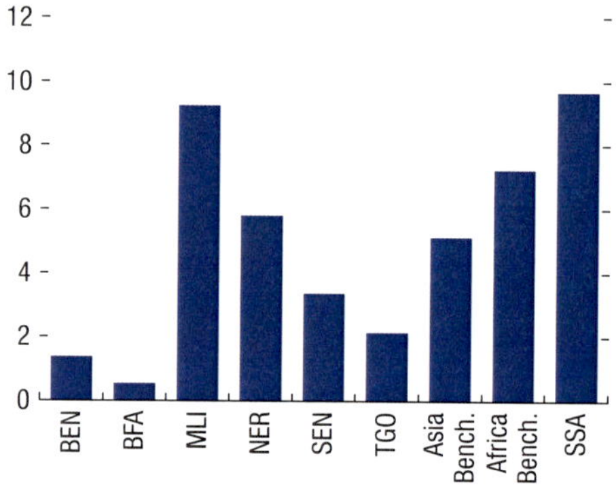

A large part of the population saves for future expenditures, …

5. Saved for Future Expenses in the Past Year (In percent, population age 15+)

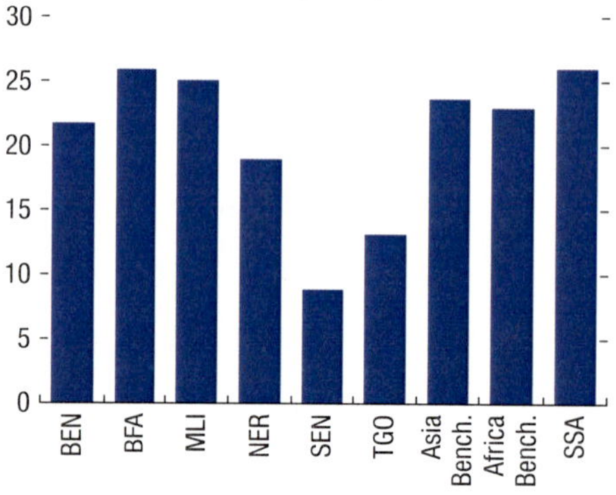

…in particular those that could be related to an emergency.

6. Saved for Emergencies in the Past Year (In percent, population age 15+)

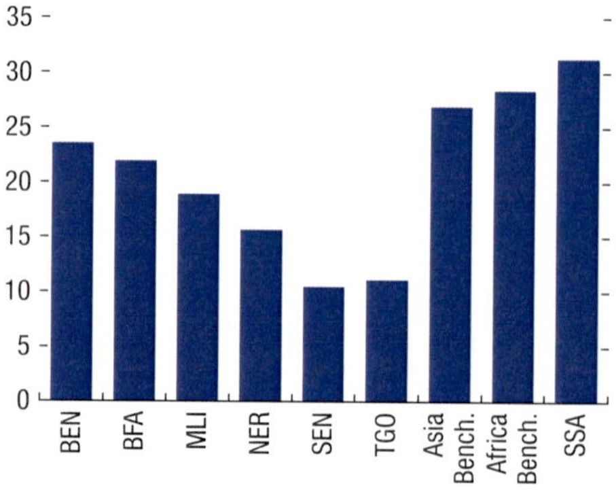

Source: Findex, 2011.
Note: Three-letter International Organization for Standardization abbreviations used for country names. SSA = Sub-Saharan Africa.

Figure 21.5. Firms

While most firms have an account at a bank, access to credit is low, ...

1. Firms with Accounts or Credit
(In percent of firms)

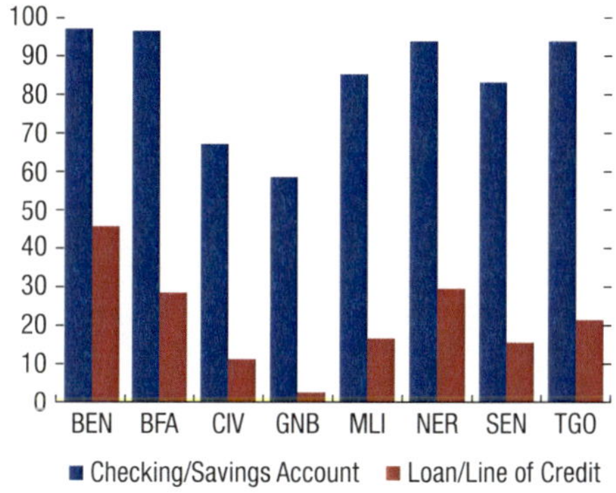

...and in most WAEMU countries, almost all loans require collateral.

2. Loans Requiring Collateral
(In percent of loans)

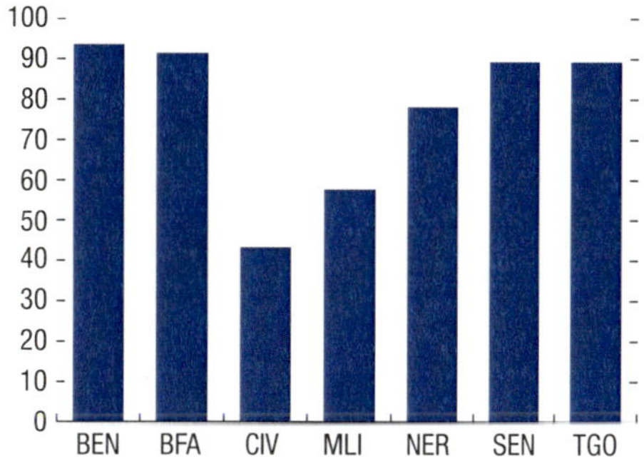

The value of the collateral often significantly exceeds the value of the loan.

3. Value of Collateral Needed
(In percent of loan amount)

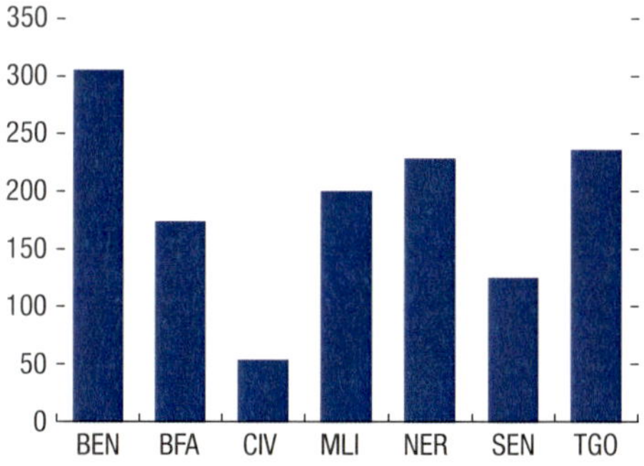

Less than half of the firms rely on banks to finance investment or their working capital.

4. Firms Using Banks to Finance Investment and Working Capital
(In percent of firms)

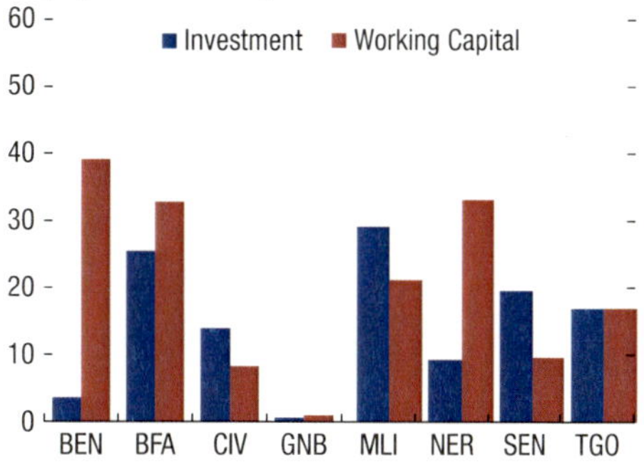

Most investment financing is generated through internal sources, ...

5. Sources to Finance Investment
(In percent of investment amount)

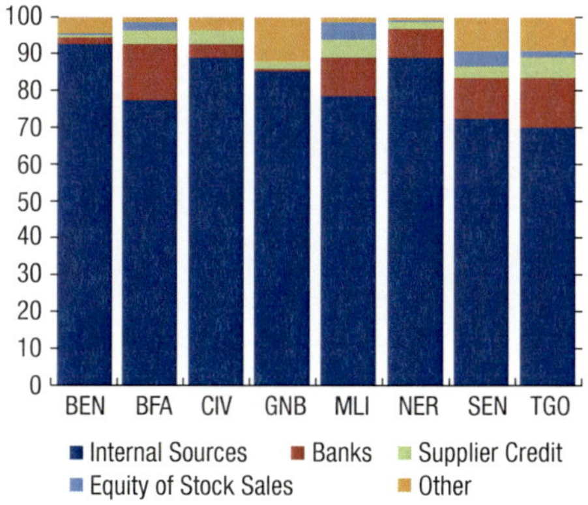

...while the amount of financing contributed through banks is relatively small.

6. Sources to Working Capital
(In percent of working capital)

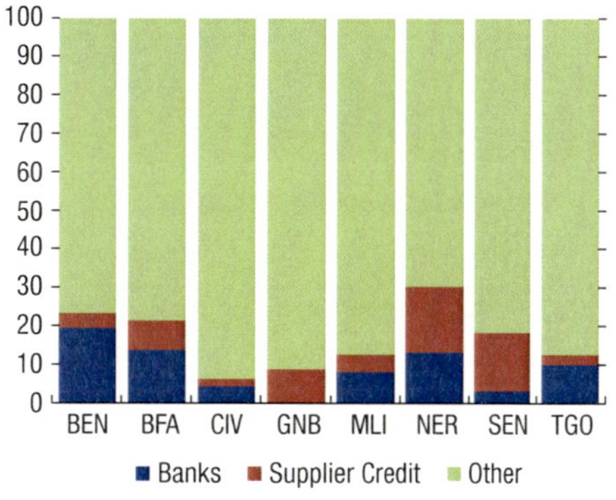

Source: World Bank, Enterprise Surveys.
Note: Three-letter International Organization for Standardization abbreviations used for country names.

Figure 21.6. Credit to the Private Sector (Share of GDP)

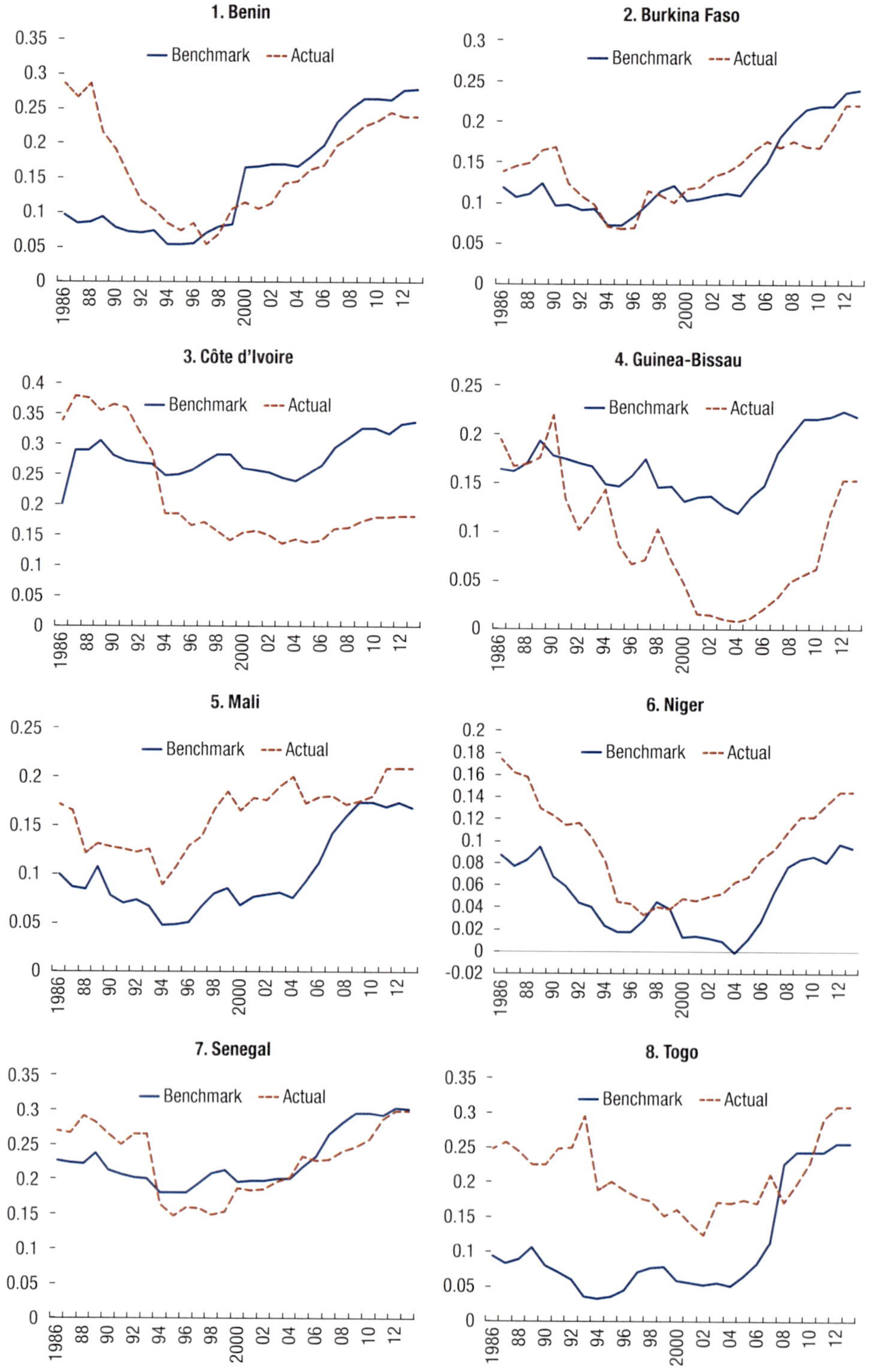

Source: World Economic Outlook database.

Figure 21.7. Drivers of the Financial Gap

Effects Increase in Selected Variables on Financial Gap
(One WAEMU Standard Deviation Increase, in Percent of GDP)

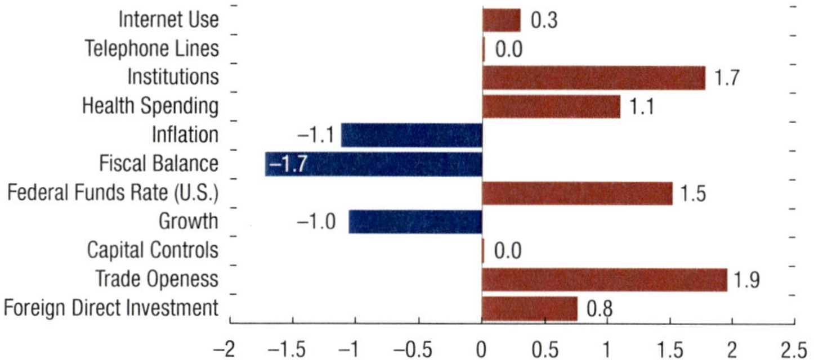

TABLE 21.1

Determinants of Financial Inclusiveness Gaps, 2004–2013

	(1)	(2)	(3)	(4)	(5)
Economic Environment					
Growth	–0.004***				–0.004***
	(–3.08)				(–3.04)
U.S. Federal Funds Rate[1]	0.003				0.008**
	(0.69)				(2.17)
External Stance					
FDI/GDP		0.002***			0.002***
		(2.92)			(3.17)
Trade Openess		0.209***			0.217***
		(3.49)			(3.40)
Capital Controls		0.076***			0.115***
		(3.96)			(5.73)
Policies					
Fiscal Balance (cycl. adjusted)/GDP			–0.185**		–0.247**
			(–2.16)		(–2.52)
Inflation			–0.004***		–0.003***
			(–5.50)		(–4.48)
FX Regime			0.007		
			(1.15)		
Health Spending/GDP			1.575***		1.202***
			(3.61)		(2.57)
Institutions and Infrastructure					
Institutions (ICRG)				0.295***	0.234***
				(4.38)	(3.14)
Telephone Lines				0.000***	0.000***
				(11.44)	–11.74
Internet Use				0.001**	0.001*
				(2.01)	(1.75)
Credit Information Depth				–0.002	
				(–0.69)	
Constant	0.019*	–0.119***	–0.033	–0.183***	–0.308***
	(1.76)	(–5.03)	(–1.17)	(–5.74)	(–7.38)
Number of observations	1055	1055	1055	1055	1055
R-squared	0.01	0.04	0.04	0.09	0.18

Source: Authors' calculations.

Note: Robust *t*-statistics in parentheses; significance levels at 10 percent (*), 5 percent (**), and 1 percent (***) levels, respectively. FDI = foreign direct investment; FX = foreign exchange regime; ICRG = International Country Risk Guide rating; cycl = cyclically adjusted.

[1] Proxy for external environment.

CONSTRAINTS TO FINANCIAL INCLUSION[3]

A microfounded general equilibrium model helps identify the most binding constraints to financial inclusion from the perspective of firms. In this section, the microfounded general equilibrium model by Dabla-Norris and others (2014) is calibrated to quantify the most binding constraints to financial inclusion and, as a consequence, growth, productivity, and a more equal income distribution. Agents in the model differ from each other in wealth and talent and can choose to become entrepreneurs or supply labor for wages. They face three financial frictions:

- Participation costs ψ, which limit access to credit, in particular for smaller and poorer entrepreneurs
- Intermediation costs χ, due to asymmetric information between banks and borrowers, which result in deposit-lending spreads
- Imperfect enforceability of contracts, which results in collateral requirements and thus smaller collateral leverage ratios λ

To determine the values of the parameters ψ, χ, and λ, as well as other parameters for the calibration, a range of macroeconomic and financial indicators were fed into the model (Table 21.2).

The results point to participation costs and high collateral requirements as the main borrowing constraints on average in the WAEMU. Based on calibration, Figures 21.8, 21.9, and 21.10 depict the effects of relaxing individually each of the three financial constraints on the number of firms accessing credit, GDP, productivity, income inequality, interest rate spreads, and the nonperforming loan ratio. They suggest that, while both lower participation costs and lower collateral requirements could yield significant GDP gains, they have differentiated effects on other variables, in particular:

- *Increasing financial access (Figure 21.8)*—Lowering participation costs (such as transaction costs), institutional impediments, and bureaucratic hurdles could increase the fraction of firms with credit substantially. With more access to credit, which leads to higher investments, GDP increases significantly. From the WAEMU's current position, lower participation costs could also decrease income inequality as measured by the Gini coefficient, because previously constrained (less wealthy) entrepreneurs overproportionately benefit from the change when they enter the market. Overall productivity may decline for the same reason.
- *Lowering collateral constraints (Figure 21.10)*—Policies that could help decrease collateral requirements, such as the introduction of collateral registries, could also yield large GDP gains and increase productivity through gains in efficiency. The latter effect differs from the impact of policies, which increase financial access described previously, as it overproportionately benefits more talented entrepreneurs. While relaxing the collateral constraints allows all firms to borrow more, less talented businesses do not scale up their businesses by the same magnitudes, as their maximum business scale is sooner achieved. As a consequence, the policy may lead to an increase in income inequality.

TABLE 21.2

Target Moments

Savings (percent of GDP)	14.5
Collateral (percent of loan value)	170
Firms with Credit (percent of firms)	20
Nonperforming Loans (percent of loans)	17
Interest Rate Spread	7.4

Source: Authors' estimates.

[3]We thank Eva Van Leemput for calibration of the model by Dabla-Norris and others (2014) for this section.

Figure 21.8. Lowering Participation Costs
(From left to right, dot indicates initial position)

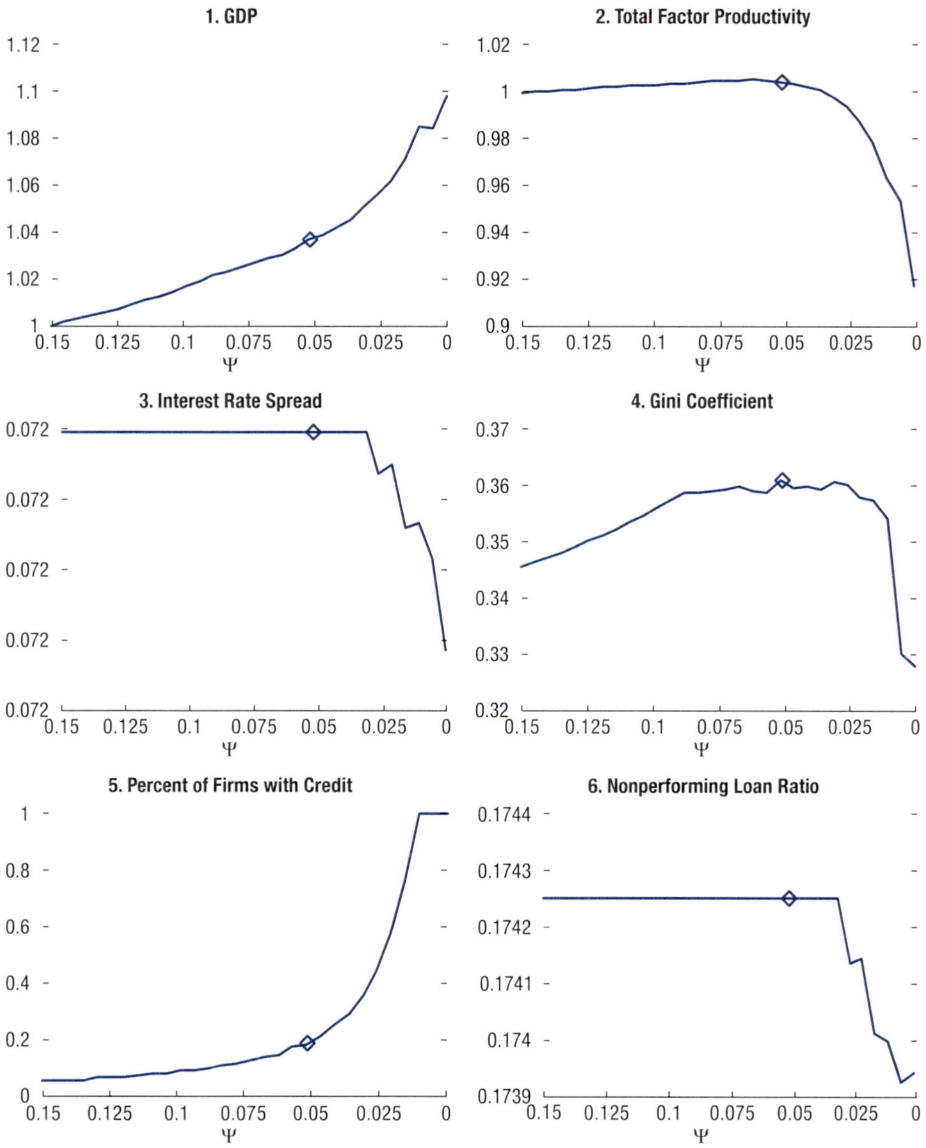

Source: Author's estimate.

Figure 21.9. Lowering the Cost of Intermediation
(From left to right, dot indicates initial position)

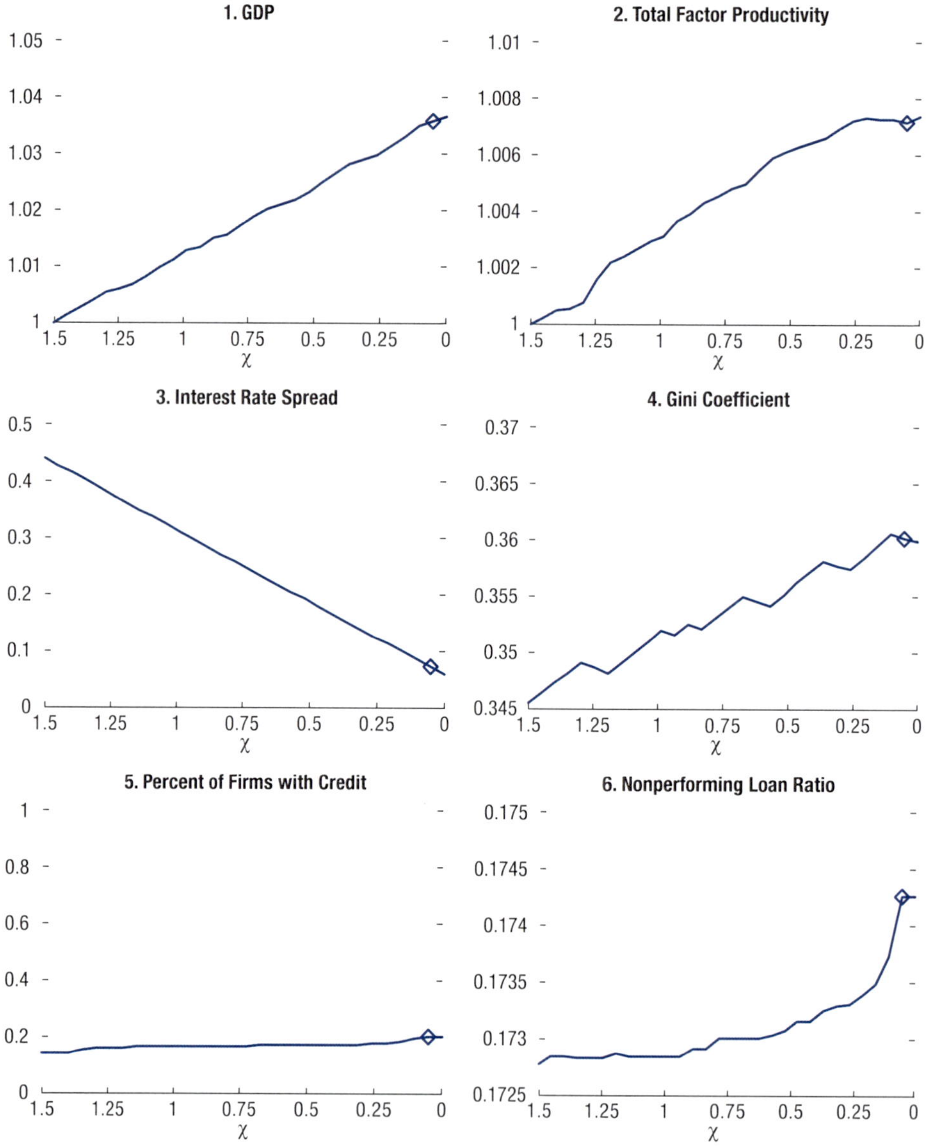

Source: Authors' estimates.

Figure 21.10. Lowering Collateral Constraints (From left to right, dot indicates initial position)

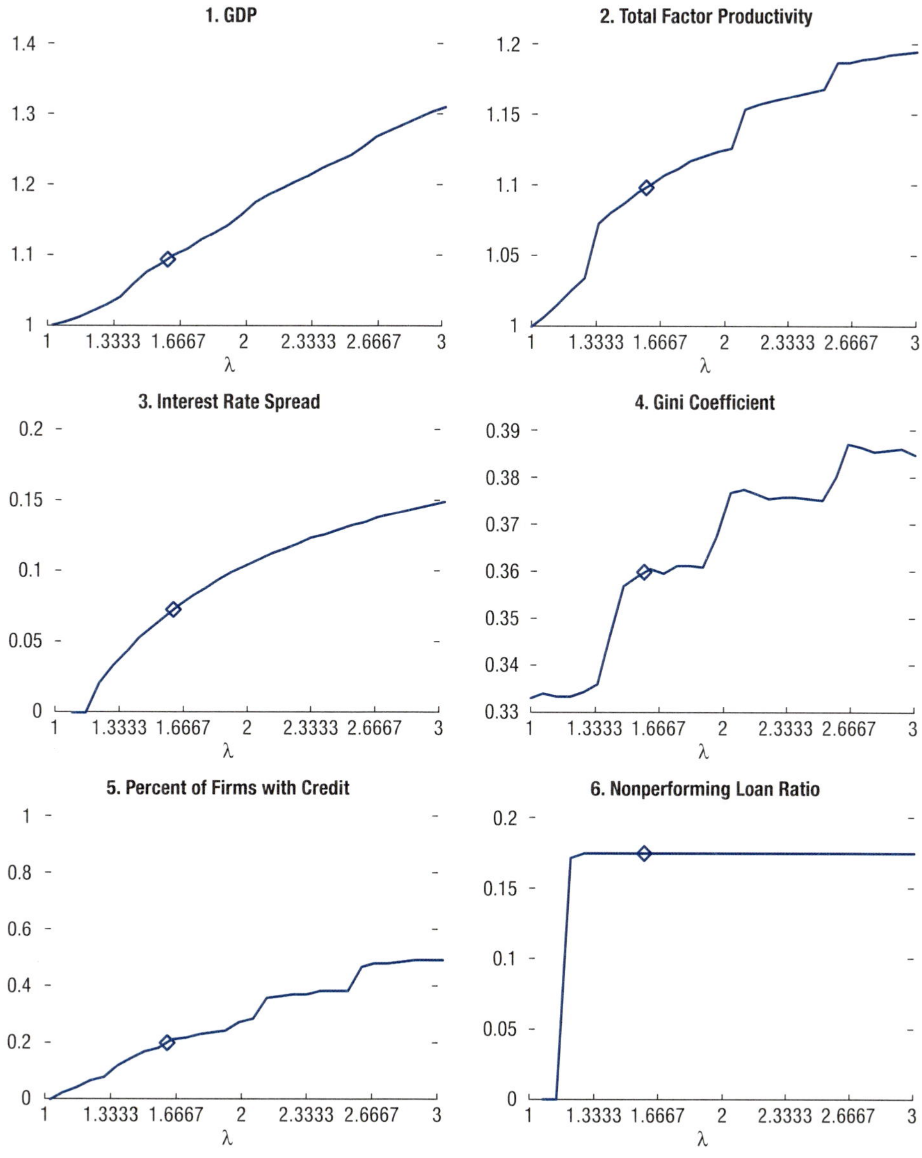

Source: Authors' estimates.

REFERENCES

Al Hussainy, Ed, Andrea Coppola, Erik Feyen, Alain Ize, Katie Kibbuka, and Haocong Ren. 2011. "A Ready-to-Use Tool to Benchmark Financial Sectors Across Countries and Over Time." FinStats 2011, World Bank, Washington.

Barajas, Adolfo, Thorsten Beck, Era Dabla-Norris, and Seyed Reza Yousefi. 2013. "Too Cold, Too Hot, or Just Right? Assessing Financial Sector Development Across the Globe." Working Paper WP/13/81, International Monetary Fund, Washington.

Dabla-Norris, Era, Yan Ji, Robert Townsend, and Filiz Unsal. 2014. "Identifying Constraints to Financial Inclusion and Their Impact on GDP and Inequality: A Structural Framework for Policy." Working Paper, International Monetary Fund, Washington.

CHAPTER 22

Financial Sector Stability

PATRICK IMAM AND CHRISTINA KOLERUS

Financial stability is critical for the proper functioning of the financial system and is critical for growth. In the West African Economic and Monetary Union (WAEMU), a significant strengthening of the regulatory and supervisory framework is necessary to address existing and new risks. The emergence of regional banking groups requires the development of supervision on a consolidated basis and the strengthening of cooperation with banking supervisors in countries where these groups operate. The increasing exposure of banks to sovereigns is also a risk that needs to be recognized, including through a nonzero weight on government paper in capital adequacy calculations. Microprudential regulation should be revised to bring certain prudential standards closer to international best practices, for example on risk concentration, classification of claims, and provisioning, while taking into account the regional context. The move to Basel II would help address many of these issues. The WAEMU's financial crisis prevention and management framework needs strengthening. Crisis prevention requires greater transparency, including through the regular and timely compilation and publication of financial soundness indicators for all member countries. Regular stress tests would be a welcome step toward the introduction of an early warning system. There is also substantial scope for improving the bank resolution framework, which would reduce the budgetary cost of government intervention. Swift action in this area, including by giving broader powers to the supervisor and close collaboration with other supervisors in the case of cross-border groups, is necessary.

OBSTACLES TO FINANCIAL DEVELOPMENT

Strong financial crisis prevention and management frameworks are critical in a region like the WAEMU (see Wagner 2010). WAEMU countries are affected by frequent and often asymmetric shocks. As shock absorption mechanisms are limited, economic agents face substantial macroeconomic volatility that can test the stability of the financial sector (see Kolerus and Zdzienicka 2013). Other issues, such as asymmetric information and weak judicial and business environments, impose extra risks for financial institutions. Such a context requires a strong microprudential framework, adapted to the risky environment, and strong bank supervision to enforce it and detect problems early. These should be completed by adequate macroprudential surveillance to address systemic risks.

The obstacles have been well identified by the authorities and described in detail in the pilot studies on Senegal (Imam and Kolerus 2013) and Benin (IMF 2012). They include: imperfect information on borrowers, due to limited availability of audited company statements and absence of credit bureaus, leading to adverse selection and moral hazard issues, and ultimately to credit rationing; weak business and judicial environments, including the absence of formalized property rights in large parts of the countries, which increases the difficulty of using land as collateral in lending; a tax regime that is not favorable to financial activities; and insufficient financial skills and expertise. The responsibility for addressing many of these obstacles rests with the national authorities (for example, improving judicial systems). The rest of this section will focus on obstacles for which the responsibility rests to a large extent with the regional authorities.

The Central Bank of West African States (BCEAO) and staff agree that the development of key regional markets, such as the interbank market and the secondary government debt market, is a priority. The BCEAO expects major reforms in this area to be launched by mid-2013. These reforms include the introduction of collateralized operations (repos) to address the reluctance of liquid banks to lend to illiquid ones; the rollout of an electronic platform to auction and trade liquidity and government paper (application Trésor); and the introduction of primary dealers, which should accelerate the development of the secondary government debt market. A regional debt agency (Agence UMOA-Titres) has been launched with the main mission of advising national treasuries on debt management, improving issuance coordination, and contributing to the development of the government debt market. It is expected to facilitate liquidity management. Broadening the investor base in the government debt market is highly desirable; governments will face lower rollover risks and interest rates and might be able to extend maturities.

Policies aimed at the development of the government debt market may have hampered development of the private debt market and led to mispricing of risks—two issues that will need to be addressed. Distortions include tax advantages for sovereign paper, zero-risk weighting for government bonds, and eligibility for refinancing at the BCEAO. Now that the (primary) government debt market has taken off, a more balanced approach may need to be considered. At a minimum, governments should avoid providing new incentives/distortions in favor of government paper. A more level playing field with regard to taxation and riskiness would be desirable.

Recent reforms are expected to contribute to financial market development. The Conférence Interafricaine de la Prévoyance Sociale recently introduced a set of measures to (1) improve the quality of financial information, (2) develop skills and awareness toward equity finance of economic actors, and (3) lower the high entry costs to the equity market. More specifically the measures cover:

- *Introduction of ratings*—Before 2012, corporations that wanted to issue bonds on the regional market were required to provide a 100 percent guarantee to investors. Those guarantees added about 1 to 2 percentage points to interest rate costs. The reforms abolish the guarantee requirement if the company is rated investment grade or higher. For companies with lower ratings, the guarantee requirement remains, but may be less than 100 percent. Currently, all private issuances are from companies that are rated lower than (local) investment grade. There are, however, a number of companies in the WAEMU that are rated above investment grade. These companies currently use their ratings to improve their credit conditions vis-à-vis banks rather than issuing on the securities market. As the problems with rating agencies during the subprime crisis have illustrated, ratings are no panacea, but they can help in other circumstances (in particular, to reduce information asymmetries); they have yet to be fully accepted in the region, as companies are reluctant to disclose information and data.
- *Enabling mortgage refinancing and securitization operations*—Two financial agents have been granted securitization licenses. The WAEMU member states are currently reviewing options in this area.
- *More competitive pricing*—Commissions and fees on equity issuance, which were previously at very high levels even in international comparison, have been significantly reduced to improve access to the market and attract new clients.
- *Introduction of a new electronic data management system*—This includes a surveillance mechanism of the secondary market.
- *Promoting innovative forms of banking*—This includes mobile banking (and products) that are adapted to the local environment.

Further reforms to improve market infrastructure and access are to be implemented in 2013–14, such as the shift to continuous trading and the introduction of a market for small and medium-sized enterprises with lower fees and less stringent rules (for example, on accounting records). The supply of financial assets can also be increased if governments list public companies and ensure that the 20 percent floating requirement—at least 20 percent of the company's stock must be listed—be strictly enforced. In addition, the Bourse Régionale des Valeurs Mobiliéres is in talks with the stock exchange of Ghana and Nigeria for closer cooperation.

Information quality and dissemination are critical for the development of financial activities. From this perspective, ongoing work on the establishment of credit and guarantee bureaus is welcome and should be accelerated. Staff noted that the willingness of having a regional approach to this issue, while understandable, should not lead to excessive delays. Efforts at all levels to improve data quality, coverage, and timeliness should continue. The data should be widely shared at the national and regional levels between the authorities and with the public. Also, market abuse regulations—such as those that regulate against insider information—currently under discussion should be introduced as soon as possible.

Close coordination between the national and regional levels is required to ensure that the regional policy framework is sufficiently responsive to new needs. As indicated in Imam and Kolerus (2013), the Senegal report, these new needs are likely to emerge first at the national level. When a country is at the forefront of financial sector reform, the need to develop or amend the policy framework at the regional level may slow financial development in that country. While there are positive externalities for other countries from a regional approach, the time needed for developing it should be limited to a minimum.

MICROPRUDENTIAL REGULATION

Compliance with microprudential norms needs to increase through strengthened supervision. The persistence of a situation of partial compliance suggests enforcement weaknesses and poses a reputational risk to the Banking Commission. Part of the problem is insufficient resources, which, for instance, do not allow the Banking Commission to meet its objective of an on-site inspection for each bank every two years. The recent increase in staff resources should contribute to improving the situation, although it may not be sufficient. The Banking Commission will also need to have the power to impose sufficiently elevated pecuniary penalties that would deter inappropriate behavior of banks. The supervision of state-owned banks will also need to be reviewed and strengthened to eliminate any (even apparent) political interference. Finally, it is critical to improve reporting, including for supervision purposes.

A number of regulatory standards and practices will need to be introduced or brought closer over time to best international practice. More specifically, the following areas need to be covered:

- *Concentration risk*—The current ratio sets a limit to single-risk exposure at 75 percent of capital, rather than the international norm of 25 percent. Stress tests clearly show that concentration risk is the main threat to the banking system. The 75 percent limit needs to be brought down progressively to international norms.
- *Nonperforming loan classification and provision*—While international norms classify a loan as nonperforming after 90 days of nonpayment, a looser definition of 180 days is used in the WAEMU. This suggests that the nonperforming loan situation could be even worse than implied by the current high ratios. Provisioning requirements may also need to be tightened, as currently no provisioning is needed for two years for nonperforming loans when the initial credits were provided with guarantees. The authorities may want to take advantage of the planned changes in bank accounting and transition to International Financial Reporting Standards (IFRS) standards to change these rules.
- *Sovereign risk weighting in capital requirements*—The recent crises in Côte d'Ivoire, Guinea-Bissau, and Mali clearly show that sovereign debt cannot be seen as riskless in the region.

- *Broadening application of capital requirements*—This would allow for the inclusion of other risk categories besides counterparty risks, such as market risks (even though still limited at this juncture) and operational risks, which seem to be relatively high in the WAEMU (see also Demirgüç-Kunt et al. 2008).
- *Timeliness and transparency of information*—The quality and timeliness of data collected for analytical and prudential purposes need to improve, and must be disseminated to the markets.
- *Ensuring an adequate regulatory perimeter*—It will be important that the regulatory net be cast wide enough so that borrowers and lenders do not shift their activities to markets that are unregulated or insufficiently regulated. Pyramid schemes, such as those discussed in the Benin pilot (IMF 2012), could thereby be more easily prevented.

The authorities intend to address many of these issues in the context of the transition to Basel II. They expect to launch this multiyear project shortly and expressed interest in technical assistance from the IMF in this area. Progress was made in reforming two prudential norms that were of questionable effectiveness. With regard to the concentration risk, a concern is that it reflects the fact that the formal sector remains relatively narrow. Lowering the risk-division ratio should therefore be done gradually, and in a way that does not affect the provision of financing to key economic sectors.

Risk will need to be monitored on a consolidated basis to capture the full spectrum of activities undertaken by large, complex financial groups. The Banking Commission currently has limited capacity to conduct prudential oversight of complex and rapidly expanding pan-African banking groups. Consolidated supervision is also hampered by the Banking Commission lacking powers to supervise financial holding companies. These shortcomings must be addressed forcefully. The authorities are aware of these issues, which have also been identified recently by the FSC. A study on how to move toward consolidated supervision is being prepared.

Adequate supervision of cross-border groups also requires a strengthening of collaboration with other supervisors. There are currently a few cross-border cooperation agreements (for example, with France, Guinea, and Morocco), with several ones being worked out. Such agreements are welcome. However, the effectiveness of such agreements is not assured in a crisis context, as illustrated in other regions during the international financial crisis. Improved collaboration with foreign supervisors would require: (1) signing cooperation protocols with the full range of foreign supervisors of parent banks and subsidiaries of lending institutions located in the Union (at present only half a dozen protocols have been drawn up and signed); (2) setting up a schedule of regular meetings with foreign supervisors structured according to types of risks; (3) instituting a regular sharing of information between supervisors, in particular regarding the assessment and monitoring of risks and internal auditing within corporate entities; and (4) in collaboration with foreign supervisors, clarifying the actual responsibilities of parent companies in recapitalizing their branches and subsidiaries, especially when problems arise. The authorities could therefore consider: (1) taking the lead in proposing and organizing supervisory colleges for each of the pan-African banking groups; (2) coordinating with the Nigeria supervisory authorities the formation of college groups for Ecobank and the United Bank for Africa; and (3) heading a review of the legal obstacles that may hinder the sharing of information across different supervisory bodies. At the WAEMU level, the existing college of supervisors is essentially a working group that can share information and promote harmonization, but not a supervisory college with the mandate, power, organization, and capacity to monitor and inspect the activities of each banking group headquartered in the region.

MACROPRUDENTIAL REGULATION

An important lesson from the global financial crisis is the need to supplement microprudential policies with macroprudential ones. Taken together, these policies help enhance the shock absorbers in the financial system in terms of capital and liquidity, place constraints on overall leverage

TABLE 22.1

Macroprudential and Microprudential Policies

	Macroprudential	Microprudential
Proximate Objective	Limit financial system-wide distress	Limit distress of individual institutions (solvency risk)
Ultimate Objective	Minimize output costs	Consumer (investor/depositor) protection
Model of Risk	(In part) endogenous	Exogenous
Interconnectedness and Substitutability	Important	Irrelevant
Calibration of Prudential Controls	In terms of system-wide distress; top-down	In terms of solvency risk; bottom-up

Source: International Monetary Fund 2010.

and extend the regulatory perimeter to all systemically important institutions, markets, and instruments (Table 22.1).

Macroprudential surveillance is recent in the WAEMU and needs to be strengthened in the following areas:

- *Early warning systems*—The BCEAO has initiated work on this issue, but is facing a number of data and methodological issues. Financial data are scarce and their informational content might be limited because of the shallowness of markets. In addition, the past might be a poor guide for estimating an early warning system, as a number of banking/financial crises in the region may have been caused by (exogenous) shocks difficult to foresee (for example, political crisis, governance issues).
- *Coverage*—Sectoral balance sheets (household, corporate, financial institutions, and public sectors) are often critical for financial stability analysis but are not readily available in the WAEMU. This gap could be partially filled through the use of targeted surveys of firms, households, and corporations. Cross-border linkages also need to be monitored more closely and analyzed. Financial network risk analysis could be used for the map of risks in the financial sector that the authorities are currently designing. Finally, coverage of other nonbank financial institutions, such as insurance companies and pension funds, will need to expand.
- *Disaggregation of information*—The use of aggregated data can sometimes mask pockets of vulnerabilities. For that reason, financial stability analysis should also rely on disaggregated data to estimate the distribution of risks across sectors. For example, analyzing the breakdown of borrowing by industry and region can be informative. Analysis of disaggregated data on banks can also be critical given the heterogeneity of the banking system, and could be used actively by the Banking Commission to develop risk-based supervision.
- *More active use of stress testing*—The regional authorities have decided to develop their capacity in this area. Once they have become familiar with basic stress testing and improved the quality and timeliness of data, they could explore ways to refine the exercise, including by incorporating macroeconomic variables and developing a range of plausible scenarios.
- *Publication of information*—The recently established Financial Stability Council (FSC) could consider producing and publishing a financial stability report to communicate and convey to economic agents the risks and challenges faced by the financial system. Consideration could be given to making disaggregated data publicly available.

The range of macroprudential instruments will need to be expanded (see Hansen 2012). Reserve requirements are presently the only instrument available to the authorities. Reserves requirements have been harmonized and, therefore, cannot be used to address asymmetric shocks. The authorities will therefore need, at some point, to consider broadening their toolkit with other instruments. Given the limited correlation between macroeconomic variables and financial ones—business cycles in WAEMU countries are often driven by weather-related or political shocks that cannot be forecasted—introducing instruments to address these risks (such as countercyclical capital requirements) would not necessarily be effective at this juncture. In staff's view, while macroprudential policies could play a very useful role in a heterogeneous region, more urgent tasks for the authorities include: (1) developing a monitoring system, which is a prerequisite; and (2) improving microprudential regulation and supervision.

CRISIS MANAGEMENT

In a financial crisis, emergency liquidity assistance may need to be provided to illiquid but solvent institutions. Emergency liquidity assistance is distinguished from the normal provision of liquidity to individual institutions under the central bank's standing facilities. While standing facilities are available on demand and the rules of access are clear *ex ante*, emergency liquidity assistance is typically available only in exceptional circumstances at the discretion of the central bank, with adequate but unconventional collateral.

The BCEAO currently does not have an explicit mandate to provide emergency liquidity assistance. The ambiguity arising from this situation may be a double-edged sword. While the absence of a mandate protects, in principle, the BCEAO's balance sheet, historical evidence suggests that it is hard for a central bank to avoid getting involved in a systemic liquidity crisis. Once this happens, the risk to the central bank's balance sheet might actually be much more difficult to contain. To avoid such a situation, it would be desirable for the BCEAO and the national governments to discuss *ex ante* how the BCEAO could get involved in the provision of emergency liquidity assistance and how it would be indemnified by the governments for this activity should losses arise.

Where a financial institution's problems extend beyond short-term liquidity and are more deep seated, recourse to recovery or resolution strategies is needed in which regulators and management work together to address the underlying problems, and so, maintain the firm as a "going concern." If this fails, a resolution strategy to close the firm in a structured and orderly way should be developed. The objective in each case will be to minimize the impact on the rest of the financial system, and by doing so, help sustain the provision of essential services to the economy. In both cases, the cost to the budget will also be an important consideration.

The Banking Commission needs to improve detection of early problems and to rely more on prompt and forceful corrective action. An effective supervisory framework requires that problems are detected early on and that this is followed by early intervention in the form of prompt corrective action to restore an institution's health. As discussed earlier, the authorities need to use financial and prudential information from institutions much more proactively so as to be able to anticipate better problems and move to risk-based supervision; this will also require better reporting. Their track record suggests that problems have been permitted to persist longer than is desirable. Many banks in the WAEMU have indeed been insolvent for long periods without the situation being resolved. These "zombie banks" have incentives to gamble for resurrection and can have an adverse impact on other banks. More forceful action would therefore be desirable in the future, including with a view to reducing intervention costs. Absent a robust and effective resolution regime, the WAEMU authorities have little choice but to bail out such banks at great public expense—which perpetuates moral hazard.

In case a bank cannot be recovered, it must be closed down, but the WAEMU resolution regime lacks key attributes recommended by the Financial Stability Board (Table 22.2). Adopting some of the Financial Stability Board recommendations would require strengthening the powers of the regulator. For instance, the Banking Commission, acting within a well-defined framework

TABLE 22.2

The Financial Stability Board's Recommendations for Effective Resolution Regimes: Where Does the WAEMU Stand?

Key Attributes for Resolution Regimes	Ensure continuity of systematically important financial services, and payment, clearing and settlement functions	Protect, where applicable and in coordination with the relevant insurance schemes and arrangements such depositors, insurance policy holders and investors as are covered by such schemes and arrangements, and ensure the rapid return of segregated client assets	Allocate losses to firm owners (shareholders) and unsecured and uninsured creditors in a manner that respects the hierarchy of claims	Not rely on public solvency support and not create an expectation that such support will be available
WAEMU Status	Not clear	Not adopted	Adopted	Not adopted
Key Attributes for Resolution Regimes	Avoid unnecessary destruction of value, and therefore seek to minimize the overall costs of resolution in home and host jurisdictions and, where consistent with the other objectives, losses for creditors	Provide for speed and transparency as much predictability as possible through legal and procedural clarity and advanced planning for orderly resolution	Provide a mandate in law for cooperation, information exchange and coordination domestically and with relevant foreign resolution authorities before and during a resolution	Ensure that nonviable firms can exit the market in an orderly way
WAEMU Status	Not adopted	Not adopted	Not adopted	Not clear
Key Attributes for Resolution Regimes		Stabilization options that achieve continuity of systematically important functions by way of a sale or transfer of the shares in the firm or of all or parts of the firm's business to a third party, either directly or through a bridge institution, and/or an officially mandated creditor-financed recapitalization of the entity that continues providing the critical functions	Liquidation options that provide for the orderly closure and wind-down of all or parts of the firm's business in a manner that protects insured depositors, insurance policy holders, and other retail customers	
	Not clear	Not adopted	Not applicable	

Source: Financial Stability Board 2013.

that protects the rights of depositors and creditors, would be able without undue delay to order the transfer of assets and liabilities, undertake mergers, and decide on changes in shareholders.

Some of the difficulties in resolving banks could reflect coordination failures between the regional and national authorities. The resolution of a bank involves the Banking Commission, which makes the decision, and the concerned national government, which needs to approve that decision. In case of a disagreement, the government can appeal to the WAEMU Council of Ministers to reverse the decision. Before-the-event burden-sharing arrangements could be designed to overcome some of the issues of delaying bank resolution. The authorities should also pursue explicit support from parent companies with respect to their branches or subsidiaries when a request for a banking license is examined, with a view to obtaining substantial resources for intervention from shareholders should the need arise. As public banks in some of the countries have often been a source of problems, privatization may also be worth considering.

To avoid moral hazard problems, a systematic investigation of the responsibilities of directors, shareholders, and auditors involved in a bankruptcy should be conducted. This should be particularly the case in instances in which public funds were engaged. Conclusions should be drawn from investigations with regard to the suitability of the concerned stakeholders for future jobs in the financial sector. Inappropriate behavior should be prosecuted to the full extent of the law.

Well-designed financial safety nets are critical to an effective crisis management system. Their mere existence may go a long way to stabilizing financial systems in times of stress. Deposit insurance systems are an important part of financial safety nets, particularly to address smaller (idiosyncratic) banking crises if not systemic ones. Credible systems are those that have appropriate coverage, timely payouts, and adequate funding.

The authorities are working on a deposit insurance system and on an insurance fund to guarantee all payments made through the real-time gross settlement system. They are still considering some aspects of coverage, payouts, and funding but expect the system to be launched in the near future. It would cover deposits with banks and microfinance institutions. IMF staff suggested that the authorities consider giving a role to the deposit insurance system in bank recovery, as is the case in a number of countries. This might allow reducing the final cost, as recovery is often less expensive than liquidation.

Finally, the authorities are working on a Financial Stability Fund, whose main goal would be to avoid possible debt payment incidents by sovereigns facing liquidity problems. Work is still ongoing on a number of key issues, such as financing of the Financial Stability Fund and terms of its financing. IMF staff flagged a number of issues to be considered, such as the identification of the nature of shocks (that is, temporary vs. permanent, which is, for instance, particularly difficult to assess in the case of political instability), how to address moral hazard (Is there a role of conditionality? Should financing be provided on market or concessional terms?), and the seniority of Financial Stability Fund financing, which could raise issues if a restructuring is eventually needed.

REFERENCES

Demirgüç-Kunt, Asli, Thorsten Beck, and Patrick Honohan. 2008. *Finance for All?: Policies and Pitfalls in Expanding Access.* Washington: The World Bank.

Hansen, Lars Peter. 2012. "Challenges in Identifying and Measuring Systemic Risk." National Bureau of Economic Research, Cambridge, Massachusetts. http://www.nber.org/papers/w18505

Imam, Patrick, and Christina Kolerus. 2013. "Senegal: Financial Depth and Macrostability." *African departmental paper.* Washington, D.C.: International Monetary Fund.

International Monetary Fund. 2012. "Benin Article IV: Financial Sector Review" (Washington, IMF).

Kolerus, Christina, and Aleksandra Zdzienicka. 2013. "Smoothing Shocks in the WAEMU." International Monetary Fund, Washington. Unpublished.

Wagner, W. 2010. "Diversification at Financial Institutions and Systemic Crises." *Journal of Financial Intermediation* 19: 96–111.

CHAPTER 23

Mobile Banking

RACHID AWAD AND MONIQUE NEWIAK[1]

Mobile banking systems present a unique opportunity to increase financial inclusiveness at a relatively low cost and have been largely successful in other sub-Saharan African countries. But there are substantial constraints to mobile banking in the West African Economic and Monetary Union (WAEMU). With relatively high mobile phone penetration and a large market for cross-border payments in the WAEMU, the potential for growth in this area is high, as evidenced by comparing the stance of mobile payments in the WAEMU to countries such as Kenya and Tanzania. Transaction costs, issues of network interoperability, and legal and regulatory barriers may represent substantial constraints to development of the mobile market in the WAEMU. An overview of oversight issues on mobile payments uncovers the key pillars necessary to safeguard stability: minimum market entry requirements, financial integrity controls, funds safeguards, and payment stability.

MOBILE PAYMENTS

As conventional financial infrastructure is still limited, but mobile phone penetration is high, mobile payments could boost financial inclusion in the WAEMU (Figure 23.1, panel 1). Financial access in the WAEMU remains low. Only about 10 percent of the population has deposits at a commercial bank and less than one-third of firms access credit and payment methods such as checks (Musuku et al. 2011).The use of credit and debit cards and electronic payments in general are much less developed relative to benchmark countries. However, while direct contact with financial infrastructure remains low, in particular for the most vulnerable parts of the populations, mobile phone penetration has increased rapidly in the WAEMU over the last decade. In some WAEMU countries, it even exceeds mobile phone penetration in countries that have pioneered mobile payments, such as Kenya and Tanzania. The development of mobile financial services could thus serve as a means to increase financial inclusiveness.

The market for mobile payments in the WAEMU appears large, in particular for cross-border payments, and has increasingly attracted operators in the last few years (Figure 23.1, panel 2; and Figure 23.2). In addition to a large unbanked population, the magnitude of remittances in the region suggests a substantial market for cross-border mobile payments. Providers appear to have responded to the large demand in the region, as the number of mobile payment operators has more than doubled since 2010, with most of the providers now operating in Côte d'Ivoire and Senegal.

A series of initiatives have been taken by the Central Bank of Western African States (BCEAO) to promote the mobile payment sector in the last decade. (Pénicaud and Katakam 2014). In order to promote the use of noncash payment instruments, the BCEAO enacted an e-money law in 2006 requiring financial institutions to make full use of electronic money. In 2012, to unlock the mobile money market, it embarked on an extensive assessment process that includes: (1) visiting other countries in which mobile payment services are more successful, such as Kenya and the

[1]This chapter draws heavily on the recommendations provided in Khiaonarong (2014).

Figure 23.1. The WAEMU's Market for Mobile Payments

1. Mobile Cellular Subscriptions (Per 100 people)

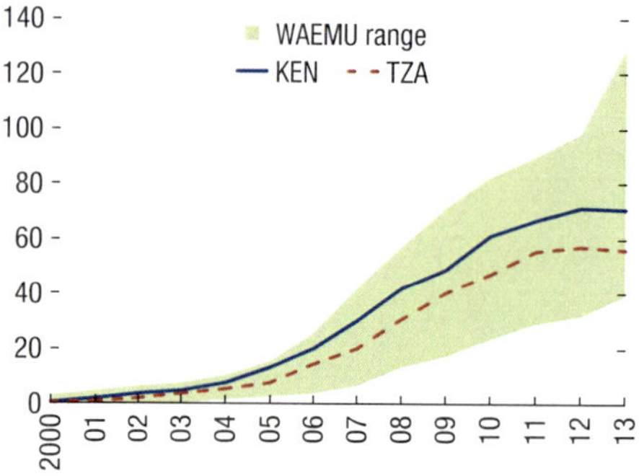

Source: World Development Indicators 2014.

2. Personal Remittances Received, 2012 or Latest (In millions of U.S. dollars)

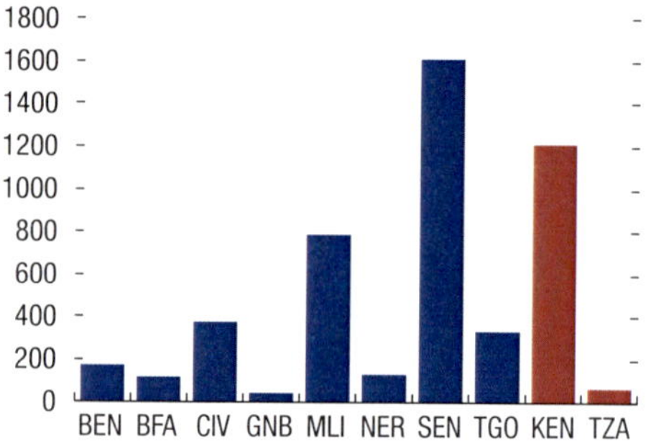

Source: World Development Indicators.
Note: Three-letter International Organization for Standardization abbreviations used for country names. WAEMU = West African Economic and Monetary Union.

Figure 23.2. Mobile Payment Providers in the WAEMU

The number of mobile payment operators has increased in the past few years...

1. Number of Providers Launching Mobile Services since 2008 (Cumulated launches since 2008)

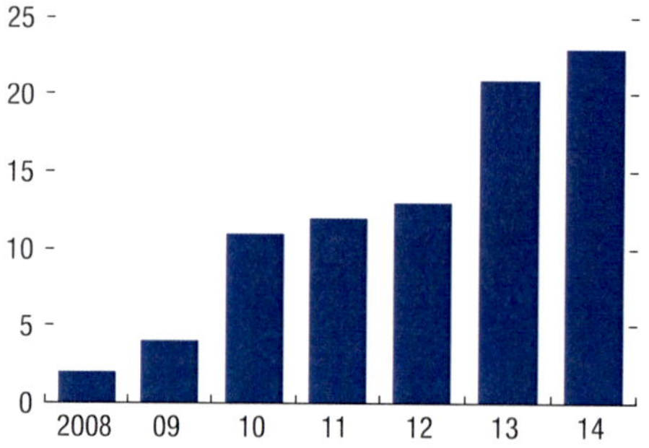

...with most operators located in Senegal and Côte d'Ivoire.

2. Number of Providers per WAEMU Country, 2014

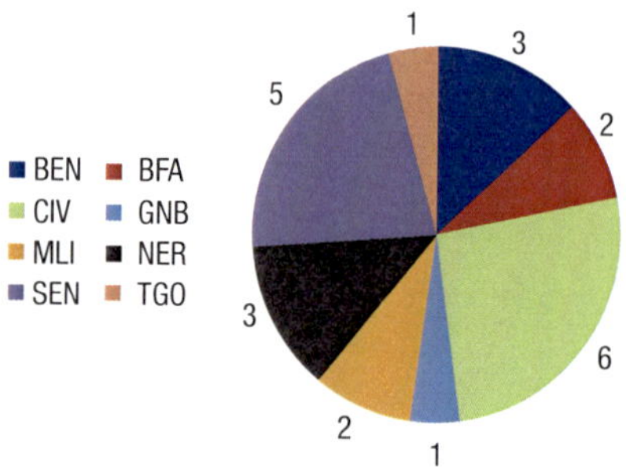

Source: Groupe Speciale Mobile Association (GSMA) 2014.
Note: Three-letter International Organization for Standardization abbreviations used for country names. WAEMU = West African Economic and Monetary Union.

Philippines, to draw lessons from their approaches; (2) hosting a regional consultation conference to explore how to develop further mobile money across the WAEMU, such as streamlining the licensing process, avoiding increases in minimum capital requirements, allowing greater simplification of account openings, and developing financial education programs for the wider public; and (3) undertaking a study to gain a more informed understanding of how citizens use formal, semiformal, and informal financial services.

The volume of mobile payments has grown recently but remains lower than the volume in benchmark countries, especially for the most vulnerable parts of the population. Mobile payments have expanded rapidly over the last years. In the period between December 2013 and

September 2014, the number of existing accounts increased by 35 percent, to 17 million. In the same period, the number of transactions increased by more than 40 percent, to almost 179 million and a transaction value of FCFA 2,445 billion (about 5 percent of 2014 GDP). However, the use of informal channels of cash-based money transfers remains dominant, and the provision of mobile financial services has been far lower than it has been in benchmark countries such as Tanzania and Kenya. The latest available indicators suggest that mobile payments have been less frequently accessed by the more vulnerable parts of the population, such as the bottom 40 percent of the income population, the population living in rural areas, and females (Figure 23.3).

IMPEDIMENTS TO MOBILE PAYMENTS

The following factors may be impeding the success of the mobile payments sector in the WAEMU:

- *Cost* (Figure 23.4)—The relatively high cost of using electronic payment services, especially for smaller transactions, appears to make mobile payment services unattractive for the population at the lower end of the income distribution. In particular, Figure 23.4 highlights for selected operators in the WAEMU, that the cost of making an in-network transfer are particularly high relative to the transaction amount for smaller transaction (up to $10). These costs may be related to the high cost incurred by mobile service providers investing in networks and access points.
- *Intermediation* (Figure 23.5)—The current regulatory framework for providing payment services in the WAEMU requires some form of intermediation by banks. This may be limiting room for innovation and making it difficult for new players to compete with banks. It may also be contributing to the increasing costs of mobile payment services due to the fees associated with bank intermediation. In contrast, Kenya and other countries that witnessed a rapid growth in the use of mobile payment services have adopted nonbank-led models in line with their levels of national economic and financial sector development. These countries have also been partnering up with an on-average larger group of banks and remittance partners.
- *Number of services and interoperability* (Figure 23.6)—Most providers in the WAEMU offer basic transfer and bill-payment services. Other services, however, are still less developed than they are in benchmark countries. While the potential for cross-border transaction is high, it is not explored by most providers. Such services would require interoperability among different service networks, a feature that appears to be still relatively weak in the WAEMU, owing to regulatory constraints, among other things (Musuku et al. 2011). For example, payment system providers are licensed on a national basis, making it difficult to expand into other WAEMU countries. Newer services, such as mobile loan disbursements and microinsurance, are not yet developed in the WAEMU (African Development Bank Group 2013).

OVERSIGHT OF MOBILE PAYMENTS

Mobile payment services promote financial inclusion, but they carry a number of risks that may be mitigated by an oversight framework with the following components:

- *Minimum entry requirement into the sector*—Entry requirements, such as minimum capital requirements for nonbank mobile service providers, will help reduce the potential for abuse of mobile services. Such protection is particularly important given that mobile payment services are mostly addressed to the most vulnerable parts of the population.

Figure 23.3. Mobile Banking across Demographic Groups, 2011

Mobile payments are less common in the WAEMU than in other parts of sub-Saharan Africa.

1. Mobile Phone Used to Pay Bills/Receive Money, 2011
(In percent of population, age 15+)

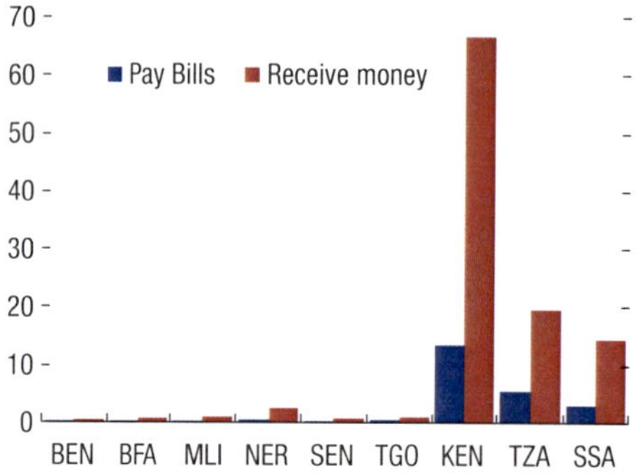

Mobile services are more often used by men than women.

2. Mobile Phones Used to Pay Bills, 2011
(In percent of respective population group)

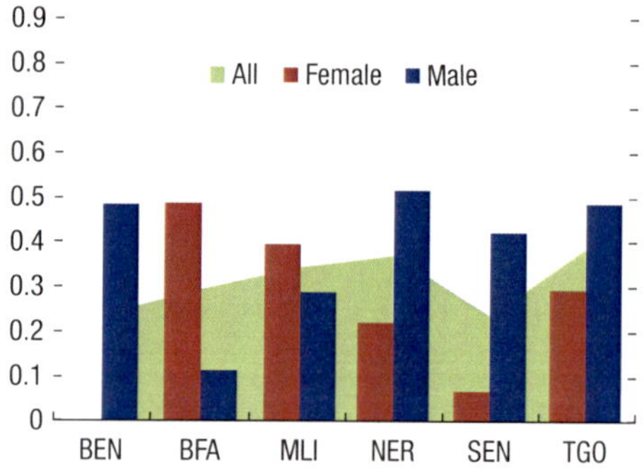

The use of mobile phones to receive money varies across the region.

3. Mobile Phones Used to Receive Money, 2011
(In percent of respective population group)

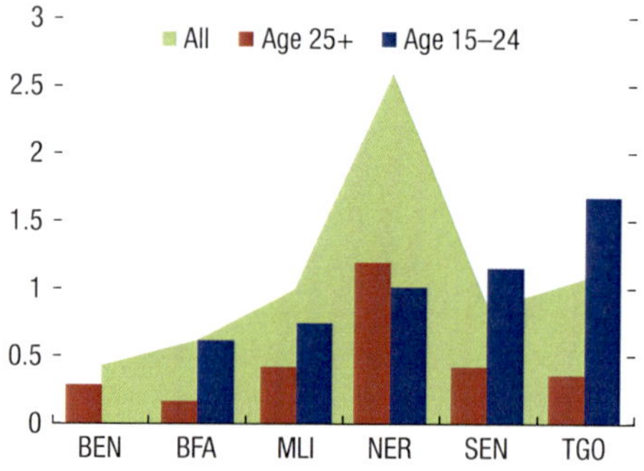

The use of mobile payments is underdeveloped in rural areas, …

4. Mobile Phones Used to Receive Money, 2011
(In percent of respective population group)

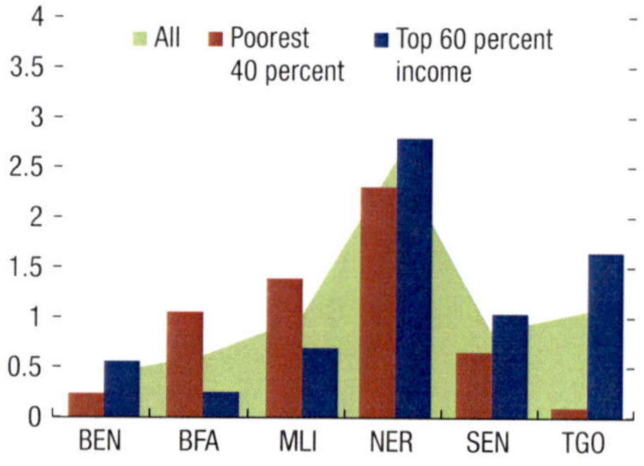

… in lower educational groups, …

5. Mobile Phones Used to Pay Bills, 2011
(In percent of respective population group)

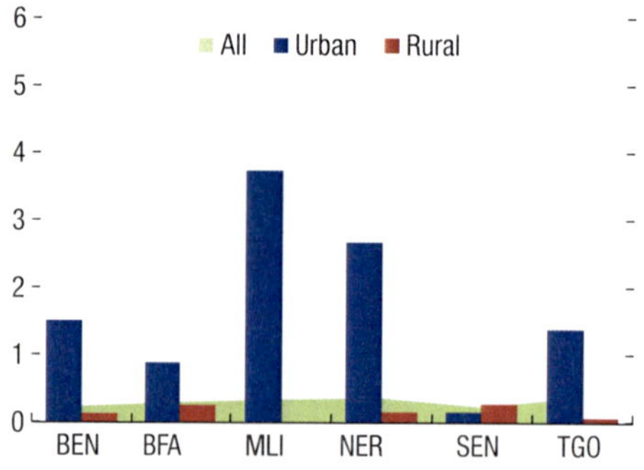

… and among the poorest parts of the population.

6. Mobile Phones Used to Pay Bills, 2011
(In percent of respective population group)

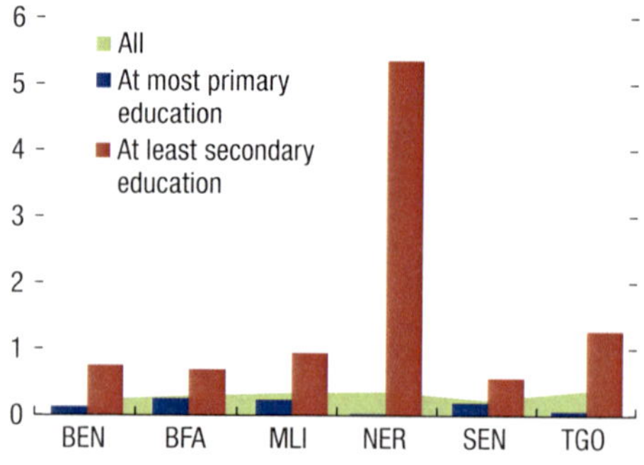

Source: Findex.
Note: Three-letter International Organization for Standardization abbreviations used for country names.

Figure 23.4. Transaction Cost for Selected Providers

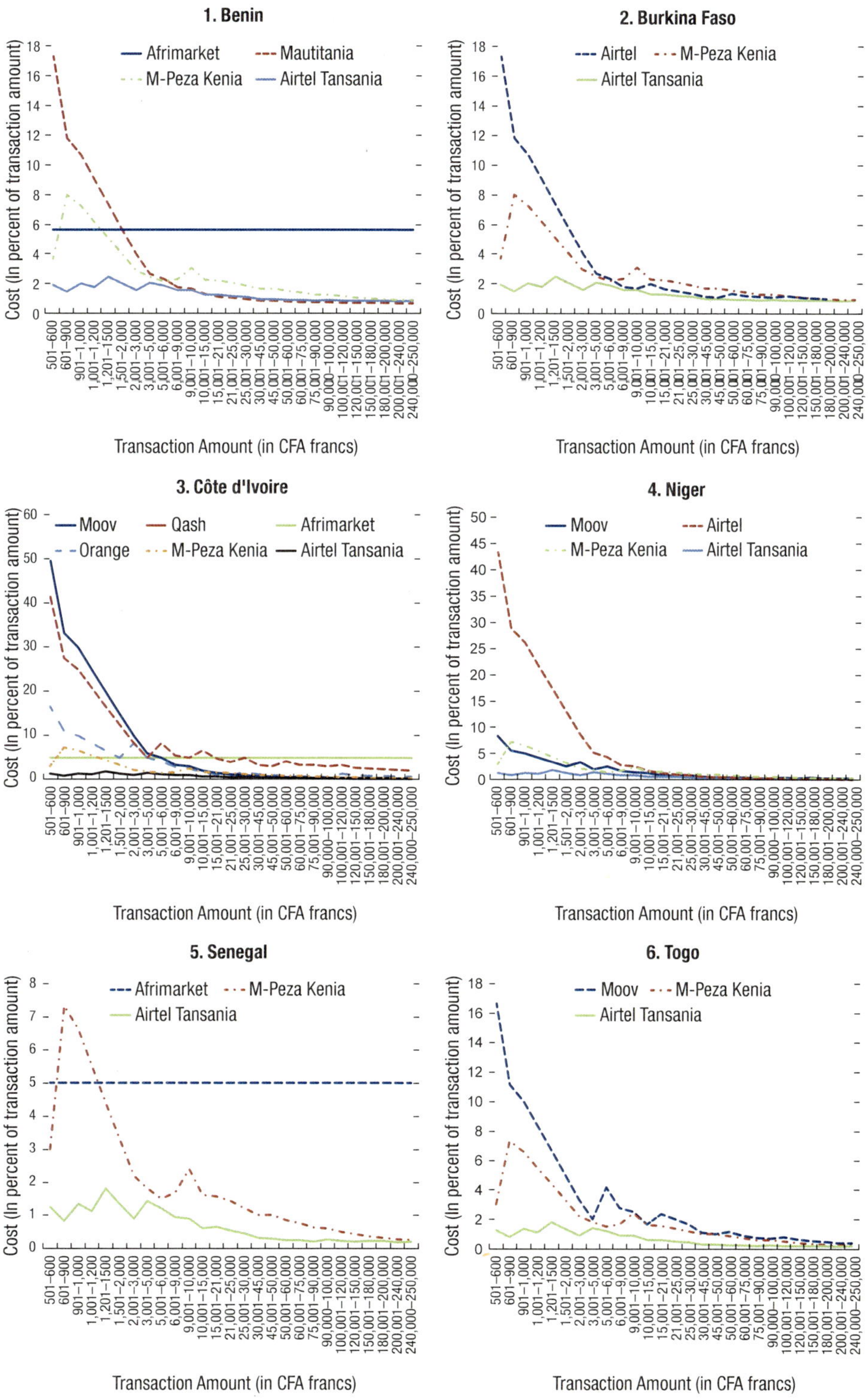

Figure 23.5. Number of Bank and Remittances Partners (Absolute number per country, 2014)

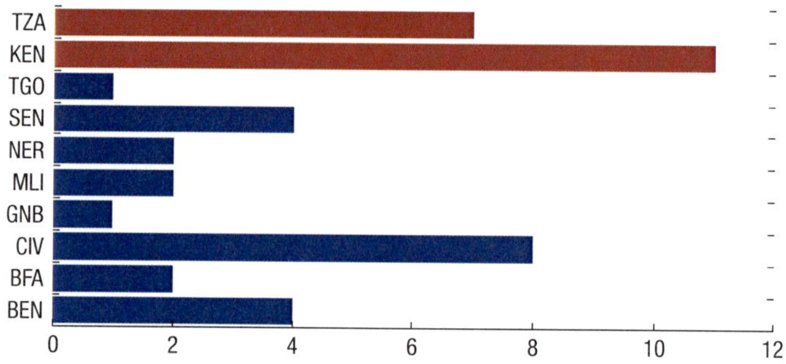

Sources: Groupe Speciale Mobile Association (GSMA; Mobile Money for the Unbanked (MMU) Deployment tracker.
Note: Three-letter International Organization for Standardization abbreviations used for country names.

- *Financial integrity controls*—Mobile payments may increase the complexity of payments and give rise to money laundering and financing of terrorism risks. Therefore, these services should be subject to adequate controls and checks by the supervisory authorities. Their providers should be assessed and supervised based on their cooperation with detecting and reporting suspicious activities.
- *Fund safeguarding*—As mobile payment services address mostly people at the lower end of the income distribution, they should include some form of guarantee or insurance to cover funds in case of failure of the mobile financial service provider. Such guarantees can be in the form of coverage by insurance companies or the inclusion of these services within the scope of deposit insurance schemes applicable in some countries.
- *Operational resiliency*—Mobile payment services may run substantial operational risks, particularly when functioning under poor or limited infrastructure. Therefore, mobile payment providers' business continuity plans should be regularly tested for viability and effectiveness.
- *Payment system stability*—The high number of transactions connected with mobile payments may create settlement risk, which might translate into both liquidity and credit risks that potentially affect financial stability. Therefore, mobile payment services, particularly those performed by nonbanks, should be subject to a very robust clearance and settlement system leveraging on the system used for bank transactions.

Subject to a strong oversight framework, the development of mobile financial services in the WAEMU should be promoted further. Mobile payment services have been picking up in the WAEMU, but there is potential for a further expansion. Policies should be targeted at reducing cost, in particular for small transaction amounts. Policies that favor the expansion of interoperability between networks could further open the market for cross-border payments. To safeguard stability, such development of mobile payment services should go hand in hand with measures to strengthen the oversight framework.

Figure 23.6. Mobile Service Provided in the WAEMU, Kenya, and Tanzania

		P2P Transfer (Domestic)	Bill Payment	Other Bulk Payment	Airtime Top Up	Merchant Payment	International Remittances	Link to Other Banking Products	Mobile Microinsurance	Loan Disbursement or Repayment
BEN	Afrimarket					X	X			
	Flooz	X	X		X	X		X		
	MTN Mobile Money	X	X	X	X	X	X			
BFA	Airtel Money	X	X	X	X					
	Inovapay	X	X	X	X	X	X		X	
CIV	Afrimarket Côte d'Ivoire					X	X			
	Celpaid Côte d'Ivoire	X	X	X	X					
	Flooz	X		X	X	X				
	MTN Mobile Money	X	X	X	X	X	X			
	Orange Money	X	X	X	X	X		X		
	Qash Mobile Banking	X	X		X		X			
GNB	MTN Mobile Money	X	X		X	X				
MLI	MobiCash									
	Orange Money	X	X		X	X	X			
NER	Airtel Money	X	X	X	X	X				
	Flous	X	X		X	X		X		
	Orange Money	X	X		X	X				
SEN	Afrimarket Senegal					X	X			
	Orange Money	X	X	X	X	X				
	Tigo Cash	X			X					
	W@ri	X			X					
	Yoban'tel	X	X	X			X			
TGO	Flooz	X	X		X	X				
KEN	Agrilife		X	X						
	Airtel Money	X	X	X	X	X		X		X
	M-PESA	X	X	X	X	X	X	X		X
	Orange Money	X	X	X	X			X		
	Tangaza Pesa Mobile Money Transfer	X	X	X	X					X
	Yucash	X	X		X					
TZA	Airtel Money	X	X	X	X					
	ezyPesa	X			X	X				
	Tgo Pesa	X	X	X	X		X			
	Vodacom M-pesa	X	X	X	X	X	X		X	

Source: Groupe Speciale Mobile Association 2014; Mobile Money for the Unbanked Deployment tracker.
Note: Three-letter International Organization for Standardization abbreviations used for country names.
P2P = peer to peer.

REFERENCES

African Development Bank Group. 2013. "Financial Inclusion and Integration through Mobile Payments and Transfer." African Development Bank, Tunis.

Khiaonarong, Tanai. 2014. "Oversight Issues in Mobile Payments." Working Paper WP/14/123, International Monetary Fund, Washington.

Musuku, T.B., M. C. Malaguti, A. McEwan Mason, and C. Pereira. 2011. "Lowering the Cost of Payments and Money Transfers in UEMOA." Africa Trade Policy Notes, Note #23, The World Bank Group, Washington

Pénicaud, C., and A. Katakam. 2014. "State of the Industry 2013: Mobile Financial Services for the Unbanked." Groupe Speciale Mobile Association Association, London.

PART VI

Competitiveness and Integration

PREFACE

In the West African Economic and Monetary Union (WAEMU), trade integration followed monetary integration and it remains less developed. Regional trade is limited, as there are little complementarities in the economic structures of WAEMU countries. The international competitiveness of their goods is relatively low, with insufficient diversification, limited investment, and a poor business climate weighing heavily on exports. Reforms have helped to improve the business environment in some countries, but not much has happened at the regional level. Therefore, there is a need to reinforce the regional growth agenda through concrete and coordinated actions to improve competitiveness, accelerate regional integration, increase trade, attract foreign investment, and reduce income disparities.

The WAEMU region maintains a fixed exchange rate regime. The regional currency, the CFA franc, is officially pegged to the euro at a fixed rate of CFAF 655.957 per euro. Exchange rates for other currencies are derived from the rate for the currency concerned vis-à-vis the euro. The WAEMU aims at establishing a common market and a common trade policy. The region has introduced full mobility of goods, labor, and capital but in practice mobility remains low. WAEMU countries formed a customs union with the Economic Community of West African States (ECOWAS) by adopting a common external tariff, which became effective in 2015. All WAEMU members are members of ECOWAS, which also includes Cape Verde, Gambia, Ghana, Guinea, Liberia, Nigeria, and Sierra Leone. As part of the Economic Partnership Agreement, ECOWAS is negotiating a free-trade zone with the European Union.

The WAEMU's competitiveness remains relatively low compared with that of most other countries. The current account deficit is relatively high and driven by continued investment efforts. In the medium term, it should gradually decline and be matched by sufficient financial inflows, assuming governments' consolidation plans are implemented and oil prices are favorable. The real effective exchange rate of the CFA franc appears to be broadly in line with fundamentals, based on different methodologies that give qualitatively similar assessments. However, international reserve coverage should increase to provide stronger buffers against immediate short-term risks. Structural nonprice competitiveness and investment efficiency remain low and improvements will be essential to ensure that planned large investment programs translate into growth and export gains, as well as increased private inflows into the region.

Regional trade among WAEMU countries is limited and has substantial potential to become an engine for growth and improved competitiveness. Chapter 24, Regional Trade Network, looks at the unrealized potential of regional trade from the network prospective. The regional trade network is dominated by three countries (Côte d'Ivoire, Senegal, Mali) and four flows (from Côte d'Ivoire to Burkina Faso and Mali, from Senegal to Mali, and from Togo to Benin). The basic structure of trade interconnectedness in the WAEMU remains broadly unchanged, although regional trade has become tighter, on average, with increased bilateral flows and more focus by individual countries on regional trade. The power structure in the region has shifted, with Côte d'Ivoire emerging as the only key trading partner and Senegal remaining mainly an intermediary.

There is a large core (Côte d'Ivoire-Senegal-Mali) and a small periphery (Guinea-Bissau-Niger) in regional trade. All WAEMU countries participating in regional trade experience a network effect. This effect explicitly takes into account the fact that a country is connected to other countries in the region and assesses the value of these connections. The difference between the nominal GDP and the network value of a country can be positive, neutral, or negative, depending on the value of its connections to other countries in the region. Côte d'Ivoire, Senegal, and Mali can be the main origins of shocks for the rest of the WAEMU economies, including the core and the periphery. Côte d'Ivoire and Senegal are simultaneously playing the gate-keeping role, and can be factors for either the propagation or absorption of shocks that originate elsewhere in the network.

The WAEMU has taken an important step toward enhancing its regional market by replacing its common external tariff with the ECOWAS common external tariff. Chapter 25, Macroeconomic Implications of Tariff Changes, assesses the impact of the ECOWAS's common external tariff, which became effective in 2015 for WAEMU countries. The new tariff will have an impact on trade levels, government revenue, and growth. It is likely to increase WAEMU imports from other ECOWAS countries but reduce imports from the rest of the world. The tariff's impact on government revenue will vary widely by country, ranging from a loss in most countries by up to 2½ percent of current revenue to an increase in a few countries by up to 3 percent. Finally, an increase in relative import prices induced by an increase in the average tariff rate could yield a negative effect on GDP.

Foreign investment in the WAEMU remains limited and contributes only marginally to growth. Chapter 26, Foreign Investment in Government Debt, looks at the reasons why even the least risky investment instrument attracts very little attention from nonresident investors, unlike what occurs in neighboring Ghana and Nigeria. Possible reasons for this situation include unattractive nominal interest rates in the region, the relatively small size of the market, the lack of a secondary market, cumbersome exchange controls and regulations, fragmentation of the regional market, insufficient communication on issuances, language issues, insufficient political stability, and a poor investment climate. To make the regional market more attractive to foreign investors, sound macroeconomic policies and a solid financial sector are prerequisites. Beyond this, communication with nonresidents should be improved, with WAEMU Securities Agency playing a key role; development of WAEMU financial markets, including the secondary market for government securities, should be accelerated; the size of the market should be increased by eliminating segmentation of the sovereign bond market; taxation should be harmonized; and double taxation should be avoided.

WAEMU experience shows that economic integration may have a significant impact on poverty reduction. Chapter 27, Integration and Poverty Reduction, addresses this issue. WAEMU experience suggests that to improve the poverty reduction impact of economic integration, community policies should target sectors where regional policy's comparative advantage is the strongest. It is therefore a political priority to strengthen regional public goods supply, particularly for regional transportation and energy networks, but also for regional financial information networks. Particular attention must be given to the distributive effects of economic integration. The effect of integration policies on living and poverty standards within the WAEMU is different across sectors. A number of regional policies spontaneously contribute to gap reductions between member countries, including agricultural market integration, epidemics reduction programs, and financial service access development. Inversely, trade integration, transportation network development, and skilled labor mobility can lead to a concentration of benefits in the initially richest countries. An increased momentum for intra-community transfers must accompany a strengthened integration in order to compensate for its distributive effects.

CHAPTER 24

Regional Trade Network

ALEXEI KIREYEV

Regional trade among West African Economic and Monetary Union (WAEMU) countries is not exploited to its full potential as an engine for growth. Regional trade is dominated by three countries (Côte d'Ivoire, Senegal, Mali), and four flows (from Côte d'Ivoire to Burkina Faso and Mali, from Senegal to Mali, and from Togo to Benin). The basic structure of trade interconnectedness in the WAEMU has remained broadly unchanged in the past decade, although regional trade has become tighter on average, with increased bilateral flows and more focus by individual countries on regional markets. The power structure in the region has shifted as Côte d'Ivoire emerged as the only key trading partner and Senegal remained mainly an intermediary. There is a large core (Côte d'Ivoire, Senegal, Mali) and a small periphery (Guinea-Bissau, Niger) in the regional trade. All WAEMU countries participating in regional trade experience a network effect. The network effect explicitly takes into account the fact that a country is connected to other countries in the region and assesses the value of these connections. The difference between the nominal GDP and the network value of a country can be positive, neutral, or negative, depending on the value of its connections to other countries in the region. Côte d'Ivoire, Senegal, and Mali can be the main origin of shocks for the rest of the WAEMU economies, including the core and the periphery, and to each other, as they belong to the same cluster. Côte d'Ivoire and Senegal are simultaneously playing a gate-keeping role and can be factors for either the propagation or absorption of shocks originating elsewhere in the network.

NETWORK PROPERTIES OF REGIONAL TRADE

The WAEMU is developing regional trade along several lines. According to the WAEMU treaty, the goal of regional trade is to strengthen the competitiveness of financial and economic activities of the member states in the framework of an open, competitive, and harmonized legal environment; ensure the convergence of economic performance and policies of member states; create a common market based on free movements of persons, goods, services, and capital; create a common external tariff and a common commercial policy; coordinate national sectoral policies by setting and implementing joint actions and possibly common policies, particularly in human development, planning, transport, telecommunications, the environment, agriculture, energy, industry, and mining; and, finally, to harmonize the legal systems of member states, and in particular, the tax systems. Progress has been achieved in all these areas, but the overall level of regional trade remains low.

Any regional trade can be presented in a network form (Easley and Kleinberg 2010; Jackson 2008; Newman 2010; Borgatti et al. 2013). The data on intraregional trade were aggregated into adjacency matrices, a mathematical representation of a weighted graph that helps identify the nodes (countries) and links (trade flows) among them (see Acemoglu et al. 2013; Duenas and Fagiolo 2013; Kubelec and Sa 2012 for similar treatment). The individual country nodes were scaled by the share of each country in the total intraunion trade flow, and the respective trade flows between countries were also scaled by their values. The network represents a directed, weighted, incomplete, and asymmetric graph. It is directed, as links explicitly denote a flow from

Figure 24.1. WAEMU: Regional Trade Network

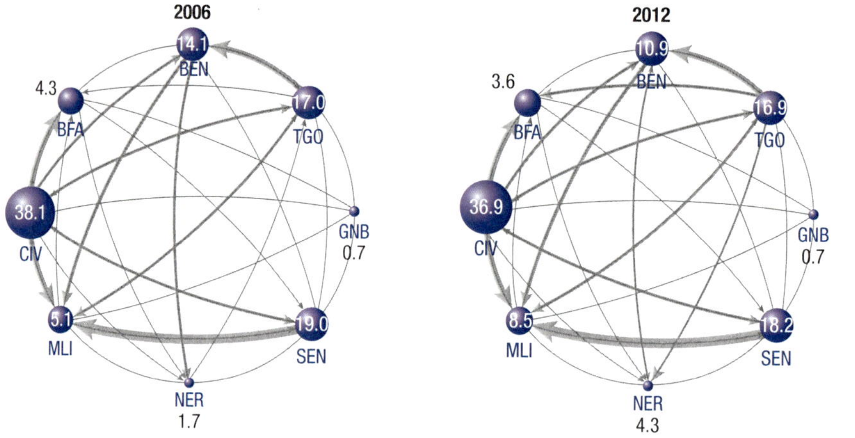

Sources: Central Bank of West African States (BCEAO); and IMF staff calculations.
Note: The nodes are proportional to the share of countries in the intra-WAEMU exports and the links are proportional to the volume of their exports. BEN = Benin; BFA = Burkina Faso; CIV = Côte d'Ivoire; GNB = Guinea-Bissau; MLI = Mali; NER = Niger; SEN = Senegal; TGO = Togo.

one country to another; weighted, as they reflect some value relative to other links; incomplete, as not all countries are connected among themselves in each network; and asymmetric, as the number of out-links differ from the number of in-links for most nodes.

An initial visual inspection of the graphs may reveal important patterns of regional trade. For example, in the case of the WAEMU in 2006–12, there were few changes in the relative role of individual countries in intraregional trade (Figure 24.1). Côte d'Ivoire remained the dominating regional economy, with its share in trade at about 38 percent. The only visible movement in terms of the shares of individual countries in intrazone trade is an increase in the role of Mali and a corresponding decline of the share of Burkina Faso, which is reflected in the changes of the relative sizes of their nodes. In terms of flows, the largest flows also remain broadly unchanged and include exports from Côte d'Ivoire to Burkina Faso and Mali, from Senegal to Mali, and from Togo to Benin. Only exports from Côte d'Ivoire to Burkina Faso and Mali and from Senegal to Mali increased in relative terms, which can be inferred from the width of the corresponding arrows. At the same time, of the 56 maximum pairs of directed links (exports or imports) in the trade network, only 50 were present in both 2006 and 2012 suggesting that at least 10 percent of possible trade flows remain absent altogether. There is no trade between Guinea-Bissau and Benin, Niger, and Togo, and it is tiny with all WAEMU countries, other than Senegal, as the links among these countries are not shown in Figure 24.1. Other insignificant trade flows include exports from Niger to Senegal, Mali to Benin and Togo, and from Niger to Côte d'Ivoire. Overall, in recent years the basic structure of trade interconnectedness has remained broadly unchanged.

Cohesion properties assess tightness of regional trade statically for each year along different dimensions (Table 24.1). Given that the network has only eight nodes, most of the metric related to cohesion should be relatively high. For example, in 2012 in the WAEMU, the *average degree* (the average number of links to and from each country) also points at a relatively higher cohesion of the regional trade network, as each country in it has on average more than six links connecting it to other countries. The *Hirsh index*, which takes into account both a country's own links and the links from its partners to other countries, also suggests that an average WAEMU country has trade links to at least six other countries, each of which also has at least the same number of links.

TABLE 24.1

Overall Cohesion Properties

	2006	2007	2008	2009	2010	2011	2012
Avg. degree	6.375	6.625	6.5	6.25	6.375	6.5	6.375
Hirsch index	6	6	6	6	6	6	6
Density	0.911	0.946	0.929	0.946	0.911	0.929	0.911
Components	1	1	1	1	1	1	1
Component ratio	0	0	0	0	0	0	0
Connectedness	1	1	1	1	1	1	1
Fragmentation	0	0	0	0	0	0	0
Compactness	0.955	0.973	0.964	0.973	0.955	0.964	0.955
Breadth	0.045	0.027	0.036	0.027	0.045	0.036	0.045
Reciprocity	0.833	0.917	0.917	0.846	0.852	0.923	0.958
Transitivity	76.364	87.273	82.927	87.273	84.177	85.185	79.63
Closure	0.906	0.96	0.938	0.96	0.964	0.958	0.921
Avg. geodesic distance	1.089	1.054	1.071	1.054	1.089	1.071	1.089
Diameter	2	2	2	2	2	2	2
SD distance	0.285	0.225	0.258	0.225	0.285	0.258	0.285

Source: IMF staff estimates.

The *density* of the trade network, which is simply the number of existing links as a proportion of all possible links in the network, is also substantial, because more than 90 percent of possible links are present in the trade network.

Other cohesion metrics show how tightly countries are linked to each other. The trade network has a single main *component* (the maximal set of countries in which each country can reach all others by some path) and, correspondingly, the *component ratio* of zero, suggesting their strong cohesion among network members. *Connectedness* (the proportion of countries in the same component) and *fragmentation* (the number of countries that cannot reach each other at all) for the trade network are at maximum and minimum, correspondingly, broadly pointing at the high cohesiveness of the trade network. *Compactness*, which weighs the links connecting countries by their values, is close to the maximum for the trade network. The opposite is true for *breadth*, its reciprocal. *Reciprocity*, the share of reciprocal links in all pairs of countries that have any connections, suggests that in 2012 about 96 percent of flows in the trade network went in both directions.

Cohesion properties may also help identify key links in regional trade patterns. For example, high *transitivity* and *closure* (a set of nodes with no outgoing links) in the trade network may point to tighter regional trade along certain flows, but also at a potentially clumpy structure. Most triads of WAEMU countries are transitive in trade, meaning that if country A exports to country B, and country B exports to country C, in almost 80 percent of cases, country A also exports to country C. All measures based on the geodesic distance, the shortest path between any two countries, indicate that goods may flow relatively fast through the trade network, as on average, any country can reach any other country in slightly more than one step. This may suggest relatively rapid shock diffusion through the network, as the *diameter*, the length of the longest geodesic distance, is only 2 in the trade network. Moreover, these trade flows are broadly predictable because the standard deviation *distance* of the average geodesic metric is relatively stable and low. Therefore, the impact of the shock should also be relatively predictable.

The evolution of cohesion metrics may indicate the direction of evolution of regional trade integration. In the WAEMU, for example, cohesion has become on average tighter in recent years. From 2006 to 2012, average cohesion (a simple average of all calculated cohesion metrics) increased by 3 percent, suggesting higher overall tightness in the regional trade network (Figure 24.2). A substantial improvement occurred in 2007, and the average level of cohesion has

Figure 24.2. Cohesion Properties Dynamics, 2006–12

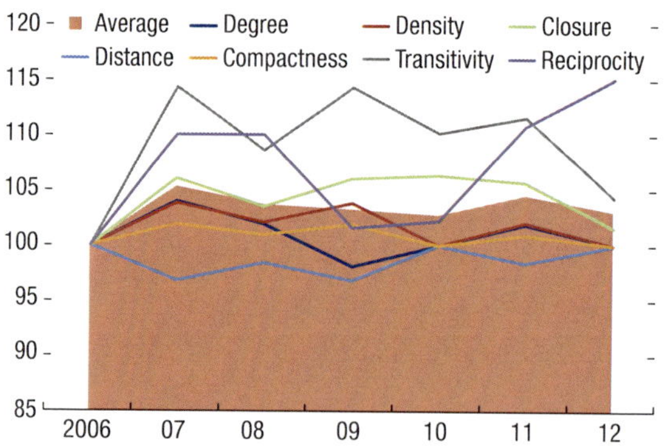

Source: IMF staff estimates.

stayed broadly unchanged since then. Of all cohesion metrics, substantial improvements in reciprocity, transitivity, and closure of bilateral flows have been driving tighter regional trade integration. The number of reciprocal flows increased by 15 percent, and the degree of transitivity increased by 4 percent, suggesting flows from one country to the other through a third country became slightly smoother on average. Also, closure of the network increased slightly, suggesting that some WAEMU countries have put more emphasis on intraregional trade. At the same time, density, compactness, reciprocity, and distance of the regional trade network remained broadly unchanged from 2006–12.

Power properties allow measuring the role of individual countries in the regional trade network. Analysis of the network power of individual countries is important, as more powerful countries may potentially have a disproportionally high impact on the rest of the network. The more links a country has to other countries, the closer it is to them (degree centrality), and because the country lies on the flow between other countries, the more power it may have (betweeness centrality). Centrally placed countries can play a major role in the transmission of economic flows through the network, thereby controlling the flows. Conversely, these countries' internal failures may disconnect the network and have material impact on the remaining countries.

Power properties of individual countries in a regional trade network can be measured by degree centrality and closeness. Countries with high *degree centrality* (that is, having more links *to* other countries [*out-degree centrality*] and *from* other countries [*in-degree centrality*], may be considered in an advantageous position in the trade network because they have more alternative export markets and ways to satisfy their import needs (Table 24.2). For example, Côte d'Ivoire, Mali, Niger, and Senegal, which export to every other country and have less out-degree variability, can be considered more stable sources of exports to their partners compared with Benin, Burkina Faso, and Togo, which export to 86 percent of other WAEMU countries, and Guinea-Bissau, which exports to only 43 percent of countries and has substantially higher out-degree variability. *Closeness centrality* is the sum of geodesic distances from one country to all others, and therefore the smaller the number, the more central the country is to the network. Côte d'Ivoire, Senegal, and Togo are clearly central for the trade network because their *farness* from other countries is the lowest. *Nearness*, a reciprocal to farness, normalizes values to the greatest nearness observed and indicates the minimum speed at which a commodity exported from one country can reach other countries through the trade network. This minimum speed may be viewed as an indicator of efficiency of the institutional framework of regional trade. For Guinea-Bissau, the speed should be about 64 to 70 percent of that of Côte d'Ivoire.

TABLE 24.2

Power Centrality Metrics, 2012

	Degree Centrality						Closeness Centrality				Betweeness Centrality				
	Out-Degree	Mean	Standard deviation	In-Degree	Mean	Standard deviation	Farness		Nearness		Beta power		Average reciprocal degree		Betweenes
							In	Out	In	Out	Out	In	Out	In	
BEN	6	0.86	0.35	6	0.86	0.35	8	8	87.5	87.5	1262	1236	6.5	6.5	0.00
BFA	6	0.86	0.35	6	0.86	0.35	8	8	87.5	87.5	1262	1236	6.5	6.5	0.00
CIV	7	1	0	7	1	0	7	7	100	100	1349	1349	7	7	2.08
GNB	3	0.43	0.50	4	0.57	0.50	10	11	70	63.636	631	824	5	5.5	0.00
MLI	7	1	0	6	0.86	0.35	8	7	87.5	100	1349	1236	7	6.5	0.75
NER	7	1	0	6	0.86	0.35	8	7	87.5	100	1349	1236	7	6.5	0.75
SEN	7	1	0	7	1	0	7	7	100	100	1349	1349	7	7	2.08
TGO	6	0.86	0.35	7	1	0	7	8	100	87.5	1262	1349	6.5	7	1.33

Source: IMF staff calculations

Note: Three-letter International Organization for Standardization abbreviations used for country names.

If a trade flow from a country has to go through some other country to reach its destination, the transit country may have additional power in the network. *Betweeness centrality* helps to measure how often a country falls along the shortest path in the flows between two other countries. Obviously, in the case of the WAEMU trade network, Côte d'Ivoire and Senegal most often are in the path between other countries. In all cases, the same countries are characterized by the highest *beta power*, which shows the total potential influence a country can have on others through direct and indirect channels weighted by their length, but not necessarily the shortest *reciprocal distances*. This suggests that the location of a country on a major flow is more important for its power than is the distance between that country and other countries in the network. Countries with high betweeness can play a gate-keeping or toll-taking role, as they have the power to stop relaying the economic flow, making other countries reroute their flows through a less efficient path. Alternatively, countries with high betweens enhance the transmission and improve efficiency of the overall network.

Power properties of regional trade networks can evolve over time. For example, in the case of the WAEMU, in 2006–12, Côte d'Ivoire, Senegal, and to some extent Togo, increased their *out-degree centrality* at a rate above the average for the WAEMU, suggesting a substantial strengthening of their power as key exporters on the regional level (Figure 24.3, panel 1). Although some other countries also increased their relative exports (Mali and Niger), the increase was substantially lower than the average and did not lead to a substantive change in their export power in the region. In terms of the *in-degree centrality*, Mali and Burkina Faso, and marginally Benin, increased imports relative to the other network members, allowing them to strengthen their relative power in the regional trade network, with most other countries falling substantially behind (Figure 24.3, panel 2). Remarkably, Guinea-Bissau's role remained broadly unchanged.

Being connected to a country that has multiple connections is more important in a trade network than is being connected to a detached country with no or few other connections. *Bonacich eigenvector centrality* allows evaluating the power of a country in a network not only by the number of connections it has, but also by the importance of its trading partners. By this metric, Côte d'Ivoire, Burkina Faso, Mali, and Senegal are clearly the most powerful traders in the WAEMU area (Figure 24.3, panel 3). In 2011, Côte d'Ivoire and Mali lost part of their trading power but Senegal and Burkina Faso gained power, most likely because of the political crisis in Côte d'Ivoire. However, all countries broadly reestablished their positions by 2012. Finally, the dynamics of *Freeman betweenness centrality* is not entirely discernible (Figure 24.3, panel 4). There was a huge increase in Senegal's betweenness in 2010, mirroring a comparable drop in Côte d'Ivoire betweenness. Although in 2012 the betweenness of Côte d'Ivoire, Senegal, Mali, and Togo was broadly the same, suggesting that these countries may play a similarly important role on signal transmission, depending on the nature of the flow.

Shape properties allow finding groups of countries with the most substantial impact on the rest of the network. Partitioning countries in a regional trade network into core and periphery is based on the density of trade interactions during each year under consideration. A network with a core-periphery structure can be seen as having two kinds of countries: core countries, which are connected to each other and to other countries, and peripheral countries, which are connected only to the core countries. As a result, countries in each year can be divided into four blocks: countries strongly connected to each other (core), countries connected only to the core countries but not to each other (periphery), core countries well connected with the periphery countries (core-periphery), and peripheral countries well connected to the core (periphery-core). For a complete block model, density of the core block should be one and density of the peripheral block should be zero.

There may be a clear core and periphery structure in a trade network. In the case of the WAEMU, in 2006–12, fitness (the overall correlation between the block structure of the WAEMU and an ideal block structure) has been unstable and has changed substantially, from

Figure 24.3. Power Properties Dynamics

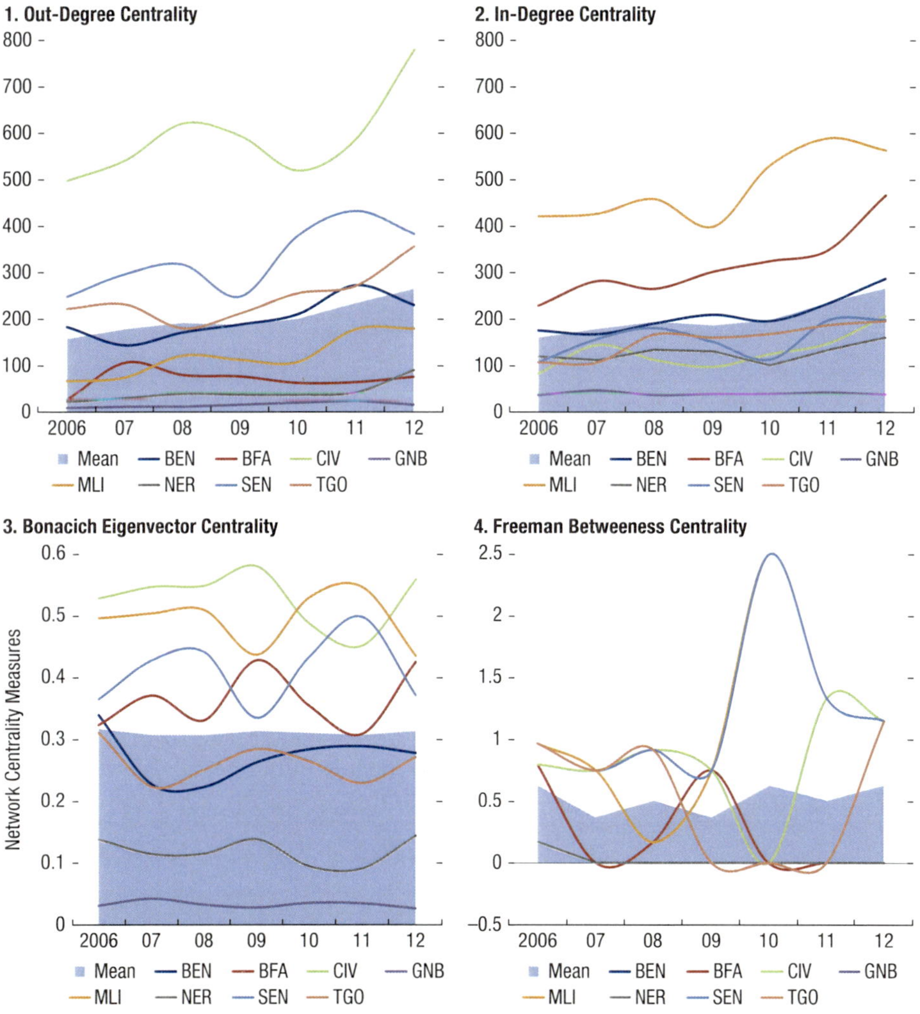

Source: IMF staff estimates.
Note: Three-letter International Organization for Standardization abbreviations used for country names.
BEN = Benin; BFA = Burkina Faso; CIV = Côte d'Ivoire; MLI = Mali; NER = Niger; SEN = Senegal; TGO = Togo.

relatively low at about 0.20, to relatively high at 0.45–0.65. This may suggest that the core-periphery structures, although present, may not be sufficiently stable and may change depending on the pattern of trade from year to year. Because the networks are directional, the core may be both symmetric and asymmetric. As seen in the density matrices in Table 24.3 (the 1 × 1 quadrant), only 2008 and 2011 have almost perfect cores with density above 90, highest fitness, which clearly single out three core countries—Côte d'Ivoire, Mali, and Senegal. In all other years, the same three countries have also been identified as part of the core (in bold), which may be seen as an indirect confirmation that these countries should be considered the core of the WAEMU network, regardless of the trade patterns in each particular year. In all other years, some other countries are also present as potential members of the core, but the overall fit and density of their interaction in these configurations is substantially lower.

TABLE 24.3

Network Core and Periphery

Year	Fitness	Core (1)	Periphery (2)	Density matrices		
2006	0.195	BEN	**GNB**		1	2
		BFA	**NER**	1	36.3	2.6
		CIV		2	13.0	0.0
		MLI				
		SEN				
		TGO				
2007	0.452	BFA	BEN		1	2
		CIV	**GNB**	1	65.0	14.3
		MLI	**NER**	2	15.0	15.9
		SEN	TGO			
2008	0.645	**CIV**	BEN		1	2
		MLI	BFA	1	92.6	13.0
		SEN	**GNB**	2	33.6	14.3
			NER			
			TGO			
2009	0.208	BEN	**GNB**		1	2
		BFA	**NER**	1	42.05	4.41
		CIV		2	14.27	0.19
		MLI				
		SEN				
		TGO				
2010	0.193	BEN	**GNB**		1	2
		BFA	**NER**	1	46.5	4.9
		CIV		2	11.7	0.1
		MLI				
		SEN				
		TGO				
2011	0.570	**CIV**	BEN		1	2
		MLI	BFA	1	98.5	18.8
		SEN	**GNB**	2	36.5	19.8
			NER			
			TGO			
2012	0.219	BEN	**GNB**		1	2
		BFA	**NER**	1	60.2	8.8
		CIV		2	16.8	0.0
		MLI				
		SEN				
		TGO				

Source: IMF staff estimates.
Note: Three-letter International Organization for Standardization abbreviations used for country names.

The periphery of a regional trade network can also be identified with substantial certainty. The lowest density of interaction (0.0–0.2) is found between Guinea-Bissau and Niger in most years (the 2×2 quadrant for each year), while it increases when some other countries are added to the network, as in 2008 and 2011. Because these two countries are identified as part of the periphery for each year, either individually or in a larger group (in bold), these may be classified firmly as the periphery of the WAEMU trading network.

The distribution of trade flows between the core and the periphery of the network is usually less evident. In the core-periphery interaction (the 1×2 quadrant), the peripheral densities are on average somewhat higher, on the order of 13–37 for each year than in the periphery-core interaction (about 14–20). This may indicate that the remaining three WAEMU countries—Benin,

Burkina Faso, and Togo—can most likely be considered part of the core-periphery group; and in 2006, 2009, 2010, and 2012, they indeed were included in the core group. Only in two cases, 2008 and 2011, can they be classified as part of the periphery-core group. In 2007, their classification is ambiguous.

DYNAMICS OF REGIONAL TRADE

Clustering of countries within a regional trade network can help uncover properties important for signal diffusion. One way to establish the clustering structure is by finding cliques, maximally complete subgraphs where every country in the clique is adjacent to every other country. This would allow identifying clusters, that is, subsets of the network in which countries are more closely and intensely tied to each other than they are to other countries in the network. As examples, the tree diagram (dendrogram) reorders WAEMU countries so they are close to other countries in similar cliques (Figure 24.4). Similarities among countries in different cliques would indicate they belong to the same cluster.

The number and composition of cliques in regional trade networks may vary. In the WAEMU, for example, the clique percolation algorithm identifies only two cliques. Notably, the dendrograms for 2007 and 2012 are identical. In 2012, two cliques can be identified: (1) Benin, Burkina Faso, Côte d'Ivoire, Mali, Niger, Senegal, and Togo; and (2), Côte d'Ivoire, Guinea-Bissau, Mali, Senegal, and Togo. The first clique includes all WAEMU countries other than Guinea-Bissau and most likely represents one cluster. Each country that belongs to both cliques has the same characteristics in the sense that each of them has trade connections to all other countries. Benin, Burkina Faso, Côte d'Ivoire, Mali, Niger, Senegal, and Togo belong to the second clique. The important characteristic of the second clique is that it includes some countries from the first clique, and not all countries in it are interconnected. For example, Benin, Burkina Faso, and Niger are connected to all others in the first clique but only to 80 percent of countries in the second clique. Guinea-Bissau, to the contrary, is connected only to 57 percent of countries in the first clique but to all countries in the second clique. In all years cliques overlap, as Côte d'Ivoire, Senegal, Togo, and Mali belong to both cliques. Because Guinea-Bissau almost always is shown as a separate branch, this may suggest that it actually does not belong to any of the cliques and should be treated individually.

Belonging to a clique may be viewed as an indication of a cluster in a regional trade network. In the specific case of the WAEMU, Côte d'Ivoire, Senegal, Mali, and Togo are clearly included in the same cluster based on similarities in their network properties. The second cluster is somewhat amorphous as it includes all WAEMU countries other than Togo and largely overlaps with the first cluster. Submitting clustering results to the hierarchical clustering procedure would allow distilling nonoverlapping clusters, if they exist as the most active countries in each cluster (Table 24.4). The levels indicate the degree of association (dissimilarity) among countries within clusters. For example, their level in the 2012 network (3.6) means that Benin, Burkina Faso, and Guinea-Bissau are each not more that 3.6 units distant from one other country in the same cluster. Belonging to a cluster makes it easy for a given country to diffuse its economic signal to other members of the same cluster but substantially more difficult to diffuse to the countries belonging to other clusters.

The hierarchical clustering procedure does not always allow establishing clearly nonoverlapping clusters. Overall, the higher the level of the cluster, the less similar the countries in the cluster are. The hierarchical clustering starts when clusters have at least one common member country, which leads to a breakdown into two nonoverlapping clusters. Again, in the case of the WAEMU, in 2006–12, according to this procedure, Côte d'Ivoire is an outlier and does not belong to any clusters. At the same time, depending on the year, the nonoverlapping clustering starts at a very high level of dissimilarity (11.8–22.1) and the composition of the clusters changes

Figure 24.4. WAEMU: Hierarchical Clustering Dendrograms

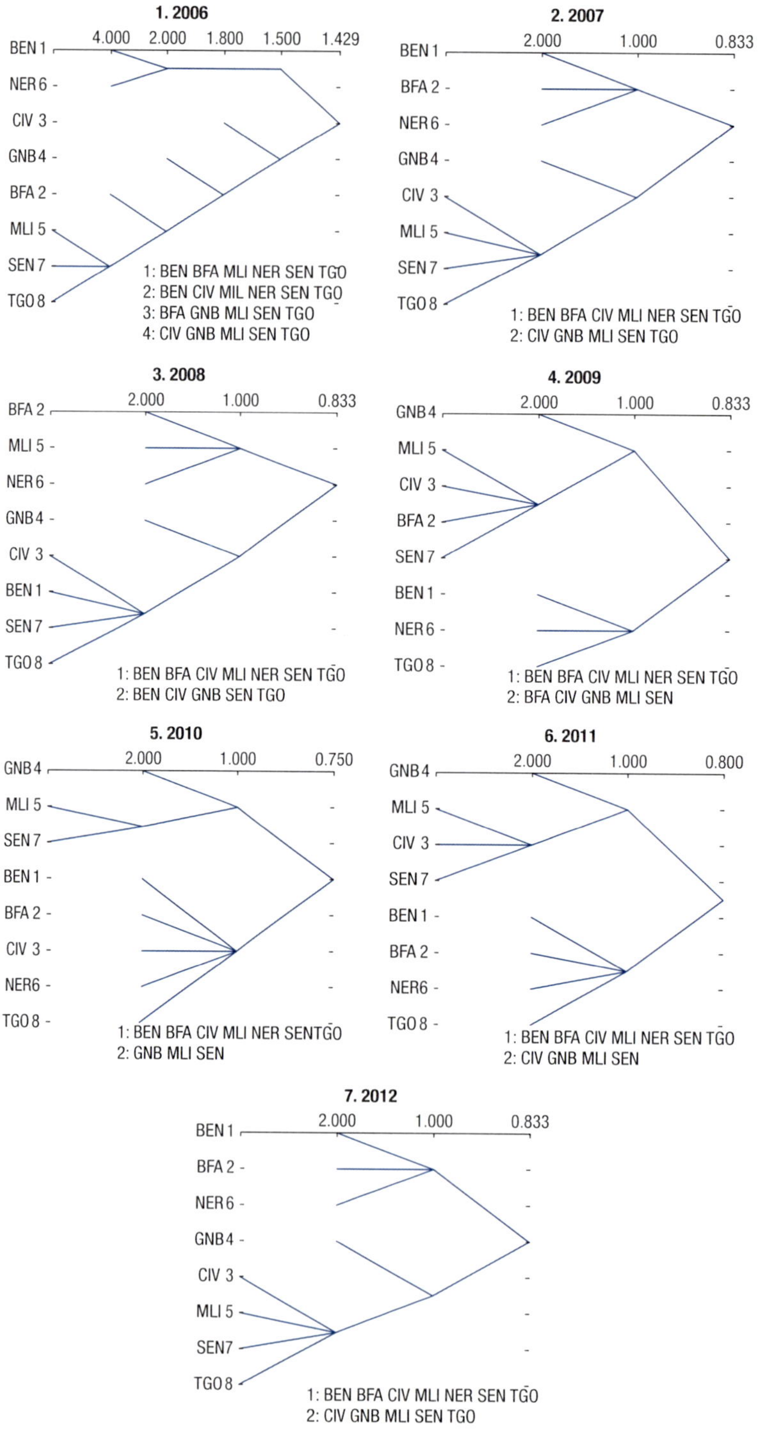

Sources: IMF staff estimates. The scale at the top gives the level at which countries are clustered.
Note: The level at which any pair of countries is aggregated is the point at which both can be reached by tracing from right to left. Countries on the left are listed in different orders for each year based on their hierarchical clustering.
Three-letter International Organization for Standardization abbreviations used for country names.
Horizontal axis in each panel represents network clustering coefficients.

TABLE 24.4

Hierarchical Network Clustering

Hierachical clustering of overlap matrix

2006	3		2		1		4		5		6		7		8
Level	CIV		BFA		BEN		GNB		MLI		NER		SEN		TGO
0	.		.		X	X	X		.		.		.		.
1.6	.		.		X	X	X		.		X	X	X		.
2.7	.		X	X	X	X	X		.		X	X	X		.
7.9	.		X	X	X	X	X		.		X	X	X		.
15.6	.		X	X	X	X	X	X	X		X	X	X		.
23.1	.		X	X	X	X	X	X	X		X	X	X	X	X
41.5	X	X	X	X	X	X	X	X	X	X	X	X	X	X	X

2009	3		5		1		2		4		6		7		8
Level	CIV		MLI		BEN		BFA		GNB		NER		SEN		TGO
0.0	.		.		.		X	X	X		.		.		.
2.8	.		.		.		X	X	X		X	X	X		.
4.9	.		.		X	X	X	X	X		X	X	X		.
11.8	.		.		X	X	X	X	X		X	X	X	X	X
20.1	.		.		X	X	X	X	X	X	X	X	X	X	X
30.1	.		X	X	X	X	X	X	X	X	X	X	X	X	X
49.4	X	X	X	X	X	X	X	X	X	X	X	X	X	X	X

2007	3		2		7		4		1		5		6		8
Level	CIV		BFA		SEN		GNB		BEN		MLI		NER		TGO
0.0	.		.		.		X	X	X						.
3.1	.		.		.		X	X	X		X	X	X		.
7.5	.		X	X	X		X	X	X		X	X	X		.
9.6	.		X	X	X		X	X	X	X	X	X	X		
22.1	.		X	X	X		X	X	X	X	X	X	X	X	X
23.9	.		X	X	X	X	X	X	X	X	X	X	X	X	X
48.9	X	X	X	X	X	X	X	X	X	X	X	X	X	X	X

2010	3		1		2		5		4		6		7		8
Level	CIV		BEN		BFA		MLI		GNB		NER		SEN		TGO
0.1			.		.		.		X	X	X		.		.
4.8			.		.		X	X	X	X	X		.		.
6.8			X	X	X		X	X	X	X	X		.		.
11.3			X	X	X		X	X	X	X	X		X	X	X
16.4			X	X	X	X	X	X	X	X	X		X	X	X
34.8	.		X	X	X	X	X	X	X	X	X	X	X	X	X
46.0	X	X	X	X	X	X	X	X	X	X	X	X	X	X	X

2008	3		1		2		7		5		4		6		8
Level	CIV		BEN		BFA		SEN		MLI		GNB		NER		TGO
0.0	.		.		.		.				X	X	X		.
2.8	.		.		.		.		X	X	X	X	X		.
4.9	.		.		X	X	X		X	X	X	X	X		.
12.1	.		.		X	X	X		X	X	X	X	X	X	X
14.4	.		X	X	X	X	X		X	X	X	X	X	X	X
27.3	.		X	X	X	X	X	X	X	X	X	X	X	X	X
52.3	X	X	X	X	X	X	X	X	X	X	X	X	X	X	X

2011	5		3		1		2		4		6		7		8
Level	MLI		CIV		BEN		BFA		GNB		NER		SEN		TGO
0.0	.		.		.		X	X	X		.		.		.
3.8	.		.		.		X	X	X	X	X		.		.
7.9	.		.		.		X	X	X	X	X		X	X	X
12.8	.		.		X	X	X	X	X	X	X		X	X	X
26.7	.		.		X	X	X	X	X	X	X	X	X	X	X
47.9	.		X	X	X	X	X	X	X	X	X	X	X	X	X
54.7	X	X	X	X	X	X	X	X	X	X	X	X	X	X	X

2012	3		1		2		4		6		7		5		8
Level	CIV		BEN		BFA		GNB		NER		SEN		MLI		TGO
0			.		X	X	X		.		.		.		.
3.6			X	X	X	X	X		.		.		.		.
6.6			X	X	X	X	X		X	X	X		.		.
15.6			X	X	X	X	X		X	X	X		X	X	X
16.5			X	X	X	X	X	X	X	X	X		X	X	X
43.5	.		X	X	X	X	X	X	X	X	X	X	X	X	X
70.4	X	X	X	X	X	X	X	X	X	X	X	X	X	X	X

Source: IMF staff estimates.

Note: X denotes membership and identifies clusters at different levels. X between columns links the closest nonoverlapping cluster. BEN = Benin; BFA = Burkina Faso; CIV = Côte d'Ivoire; GNB = Guinea-Bissau; MLI = Mali; NER = Niger; SEN = Senegal; TGO = Togo.

every year. For example, in 2012 at the 16.5 level there seem to be two nonoverlapping clusters, Benin-Burkina Faso-Guinea-Bissau-Niger-Senegal on one side, and Mali-Togo on the other. But sequential clustering suggests that based on this metric, Côte d'Ivoire, and probably Mali and Togo, should be treated as not belonging to any cluster. At the 15.6 level, there are already three possible clusters; only two are left at the 6.6 level and one at the 3.6 level, which are still indicating a very substantial degree of dissimilarity among countries. Overall, the hierarchal clustering procedure confirms that it is difficult to identify clearly nonoverlapping clusters in the WAEMU trade network and that such clusters, when they exist, dynamically are not stable.

Additional clustering metrics allow also identifying gatekeepers, that is, countries through which shocks may be transmitted from one cluster to another. Gatekeeper countries bridge across different clusters, allowing contagion to spread out. Owing to their capacity to act as transmitters, gatekeepers can potentially also amplify or mitigate shocks. The *cluster (clique) participation score* measures the extent to which a country belongs to the cluster. If the country has no direct connection to a cluster, the score is zero; cluster members have the score of one. This method allows calculating the number of times each pair of countries is included in different clusters. The *country-by-country cluster membership* shows how many clusters each pair of countries is member of. Finally, the *cluster-by-cluster comembership* shows the number of common members in different clusters. In principle, the larger the number of comembers among different clusters, the higher the capacity of the network to transmit signals among its member countries.

In the case of the WAEMU, for example, several countries can potentially play the role of gatekeepers. Based on cluster *participation scores*, only Senegal has been a clear gatekeeper for each year in the sample, as it had consistently the highest cluster participation scores, regardless of the year and the number of clusters identified (Table 24.5). Côte d'Ivoire and Mali most likely could also be seen as gatekeepers, as their cluster participation is also high, with the exception of one year for each of them. Interestingly, Guinea-Bissau is completely outside the cluster structure in the trade networks. The *country-by-country cluster membership* shows that Senegal, Côte d'Ivoire, and Mali are members of the most clusters with the scores consistently 2 and above in most years, whereas in addition to these countries only Burkina Faso and Togo may claim the role of the gatekeeper in some years. Finally, the *cluster-by-cluster comembership* shows that the WAEMU trade network has two to four common members in each cluster, depending on the year. In all cases, Senegal and Mali can be seen as gatekeepers.

TRADE ARCHITECTURE

The overall architecture of a regional trade network can finally be derived based on its properties. For example, in the WAEMU during 2006–12, the basic structure of trade interconnectedness remained broadly unchanged, with exports from Côte d'Ivoire to Burkina Faso and Mali, from Senegal to Mali, and from Togo to Benin representing the main flows, with about 10 percent of total possible links within WAEMU countries missing altogether and Guinea-Bissau being the most disconnected country in the region (Figure 24.5). The evolution of network cohesiveness suggests that regional trade has become on average tighter in recent years, with increased bilateral flows and regional closure, as countries have put somewhat more emphasis on regional trade relative to their links to other partners. The power structure in the region has shifted slightly. If in 2006 Côte d'Ivoire and Senegal were clearly the most powerful countries in the regional trade by the centrality metric, and Mali by its betweeness position, in 2012 Côte d'Ivoire emerged as the only key trading power in terms of both centrality and betweeness, with Senegal remaining central only in terms of betweenness, and Mali losing its power position.

In the overall network architecture of regional trade, there may be a core-periphery structure and overlapping clusters. In the case of the WAEMU, for example, the core-periphery structure remained broadly unchanged in 2006–12. There is a solid core consisting of Côte

TABLE 24.5

Clustering and Gatekeepers

2006

Clique Participation Score

	Cliques 1	2	3	4
BEN	1	1	0.8	0.8
BFA	1	0.83	1	0.8
CIV	0.83	1	0.8	1
GNB	0.67	0.67	1	1
MLI	1	1	1	1
NER	1	1	0.8	0.8
SEN	1	1	1	1
TGO	1	1	1	1

Country-by-Country Clique Comembership

	BEN	BFA	CIV	GNB	MLI	NER	SEN	TGO
BEN	2	1	1	0	2	2	2	2
BFA	1	2	0	1	2	1	2	2
CIV	1	0	2	1	2	1	2	2
GNB	0	1	1	2	2	0	2	2
MLI	2	2	2	2	4	2	4	4
NER	2	1	1	0	2	2	2	2
SEN	2	2	2	2	4	2	4	4
TGO	2	2	2	2	4	2	4	4

Clique-by-Clique Participation Score

	Cliques 1	2	3	4
1	6	5	4	3
2	5	6	3	4
3	4	3	5	4
4	3	4	4	5

2007

	Cliques 1	2
BEN	1	0.8
BFA	1	0.8
CIV	1	1
GNB	0.57	1
MLI	1	1
NER	1	0.8
SEN	1	1
TGO	1	1

Country-by-Country Clique Comembership

	BEN	BFA	CIV	GNB	MLI	NER	SEN	TGO
BEN	1	1	1	0	1	1	1	1
BFA	1	1	1	0	1	1	1	1
CIV	1	1	2	1	2	1	2	2
GNB	0	0	1	1	1	0	1	1
MLI	1	1	2	1	2	1	2	2
NER	1	1	1	0	1	1	1	1
SEN	1	1	2	1	2	1	2	2
TGO	1	1	2	1	2	1	2	2

Clique-by-Clique Participation Score

	Cliques 1	2
1	7	4
2	4	5

2008

Clique Participation Score

	Cliques 1	2
BEN	1	1
BFA	1	0.8
CIV	1	1
GNB	0.57	1
MLI	1	0.8
NER	1	0.8
SEN	1	1
TGO	1	1

Country-by-Country Clique Comembership

	BEN	BFA	CIV	GNB	MLI	NER	SEN	TGO
BEN	2	1	2	1	1	1	2	2
BFA	1	1	1	0	1	1	1	1
CIV	2	1	2	1	1	1	2	2
GNB	1	0	1	1	0	0	1	1
MLI	1	1	1	0	1	1	1	1
NER	1	1	1	0	1	1	1	1
SEN	2	1	2	1	1	1	2	2
TGO	2	1	2	1	1	1	2	2

Clique-by-Clique Participation Score

	Cliques 1	2
1	7	4
2	4	5

2009

	Cliques 1	2
BEN	1	0.8
BFA	1	1
CIV	1	1
GNB	0.57	1
MLI	1	1
NER	1	0.8
SEN	1	1
TGO	1	0.8

Country-by-Country Clique Comembership

	BEN	BFA	CIV	GNB	MLI	NER	SEN	TGO
BEN	1	1	1	0	1	1	1	1
BFA	1	2	2	1	2	1	2	1
CIV	1	2	2	1	2	1	2	1
GNB	0	1	1	1	1	0	1	0
MLI	1	2	2	1	2	1	2	1
NER	1	1	1	0	1	1	1	1
SEN	1	2	2	1	2	1	2	1
TGO	1	1	1	0	1	1	1	1

Clique-by-Clique Participation Score

	Cliques 1	2
1	7	4
2	4	5

(continued)

TABLE 24.5 (continued)

Clustering and Gatekeepers

2010

Clique Participation Score

	Cliques 1	2
BEN	1	0.67
BFA	1	0.67
CIV	1	0.67
GNB	0.29	1
MLI	1	1
NER	1	0.67
SEN	1	1
TGO	1	0.67

Country-by-Country Clique Comembership

	BEN	BFA	CIV	GNB	MLI	NER	SEN	TGO
BEN	1	1	1	0	1	1	1	1
BFA	1	1	1	0	1	1	1	1
CIV	1	1	1	0	1	1	1	1
GNB	0	0	0	1	1	0	1	0
MLI	1	1	1	1	2	1	2	1
NER	1	1	1	0	1	1	1	1
SEN	1	1	1	1	2	1	2	1
TGO	1	1	1	0	1	1	1	1

Clique-by-Clique Participation Score

	Cliques 1	2
1	7	2
2	2	3

2011

Clique Participation Score

	Cliques 1	2
BEN	1	0.75
BFA	1	0.75
CIV	1	1
GNB	0.43	1
MLI	1	1
NER	1	0.75
SEN	1	1
TGO	1	0.75

Country-by-Country Clique Comembership

	BEN	BFA	CIV	GNB	MLI	NER	SEN	TGO
BEN	1	1	1	0	1	1	1	1
BFA	1	1	1	0	1	1	1	1
CIV	1	1	2	1	2	1	2	1
GNB	0	0	1	1	1	0	1	0
MLI	1	1	2	1	2	1	2	1
NER	1	1	1	0	1	1	1	1
SEN	1	1	2	1	2	1	2	1
TGO	1	1	1	0	1	1	1	1

Clique-by-Clique Participation Score

	Cliques 1	2
1	7	3
2	3	4

2012

Clique Participation Score

	Cliques 1	2
BEN	1	0.8
BFA	1	0.8
CIV	1	1
GNB	0.57	1
MLI	1	1
NER	1	0.8
SEN	1	1
TGO	1	1

Country-by-Country Clique Comembership

	BEN	BFA	CIV	GNB	MLI	NER	SEN	TGO
BEN	1	1	1	0	1	1	1	1
BFA	1	1	1	0	1	1	1	1
CIV	1	1	2	1	2	1	2	2
GNB	0	0	1	1	1	0	1	1
MLI	1	1	2	1	2	1	2	2
NER	1	1	1	0	1	1	1	1
SEN	1	1	2	1	2	1	2	2
TGO	1	1	2	1	2	1	2	2

Clique-by-Clique Participation Score

	Cliques 1	2
1	7	4
2	4	5

Source: IMF staff estimates.

Note: BEN = Benin; BFA = Burkina Faso; CIV = Côte d'Ivoire; GNB = Guinea-Bissau; MLI = Mali; NER = Niger; SEN = Senegal; TGO = Togo.

d'Ivoire, Senegal, and Mali; and a small periphery including Guinea-Bissau and Niger, with Burkina Faso, Benin, and Togo holding intermediate, most likely the core-periphery, positions. The clustering structure has been unstable and has changed over the years. In 2006, there were four somewhat amorphous and statistically insignificant clusters of countries with similar characteristics in each clique. In 2012, however, the clustering structure became more pronounced. There are two overlapping clusters: Côte d'Ivoire, Mali, Senegal, and Togo, on one hand (Cluster 1), and Benin, Burkina Faso, Côte d'Ivoire, Mali, Niger, Senegal, and Togo, on the other (Cluster 2), with Guinea-Bissau in all cases being a clear outlier. A very significant cluster comembership suggests several countries can play at the same time the role of gatekeepers in shock transmission

Figure 24.5. Overall Trade Network Architecture, 2006 and 2012

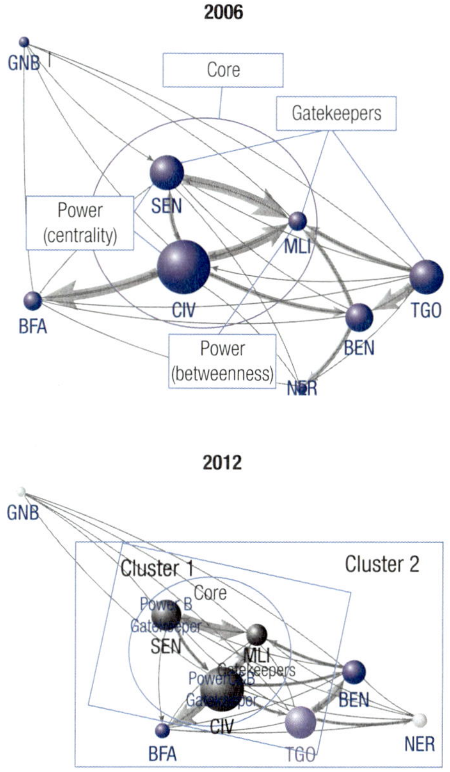

Source: IMF staff estimates.
Note: Three-letter International Organization for Standardization abbreviations used for country names. Fruchterman-Reinhold algorithm, strength of repulsive forces between vertices at 10, and 100 iterations. The nodes are proportional to the share of counties in the intra-WAEMU exports and the links are proportional to the volume of their exports.

between different clusters (at least Côte d'Ivoire, Senegal, and Mali) and therefore an economic signal may diffuse relatively easily between members of different clusters. Côte d'Ivoire and Mali (both in the core of the trade network) were affected by crises in 2011–12, which may have potentially had strong spillover effects on the peripheral countries. However, the impact on the region from these shocks was largely contained, at least through the trade channel, which can be explained by the fact that Côte d'Ivoire and Mali belong to the same cluster.

NETWORK EFFECTS

The network analysis can also shed light on signal diffusion across trading partners in a region. In the macroeconomic context, signal diffusion can be viewed as either a negative or positive economic shock to one or several countries in a region. The network architecture would allow identifying ways to enhance the impact of positive shocks and constrain the impact of negative shocks. Several elements are important for signal diffusion through the network: the economic size of the country emitting the signal, the size and direction of the economic flow between it and other countries, the size of other countries, the network properties in the transmitting and relaying countries, and the potential indirect feedback channels.

TABLE 24.6

Dependency Matrix

Exports From	Imports By BEN	BFA	CIV	GNB	MLI	NER	SEN	TGO	Nominal GDP	Network Value	Network Effect (percent)
BEN	0.9021	0.0029	0.0075	0.0021	0.0132	0.0232	0.0139	0.0312	9.19	9.30	1.2
BFA	0.0022	0.9008	0.0099	0.0003	0.0054	0.0055	0.0033	0.0026	13.41	12.58	–6.2
CIV	0.0331	0.0580	0.9041	0.0062	0.0287	0.0231	0.0536	0.0408	30.01	29.89	–0.4
GNB	0.0001	0.0001	0.0003	0.9002	0.0012	0.0001	0.0017	0.0017	1.00	0.96	–3.8
MLI	0.0051	0.0112	0.0282	0.0033	0.9017	0.0062	0.0177	0.0080	12.63	12.83	1.5
NER	0.0073	0.0017	0.0019	0.0003	0.0076	0.9004	0.0026	0.0040	8.24	7.72	–6.2
SEN	0.0051	0.0085	0.0232	0.0862	0.0376	0.0059	0.9023	0.0089	17.08	16.92	–0.9
TGO	0.0451	0.0169	0.0249	0.0015	0.0047	0.0356	0.0049	0.9028	4.76	6.12	28.6

Source: IMF staff estimates.
Note: BEN = Benin; BFA = Burkina Faso; CIV = Côte d'Ivoire; GNB = Guinea-Bissau; MLI = Mali; NER = Niger; SEN = Senegal; TGO = Togo.

Using the regional trade network, single diffusion can be modeled in a simple cascading framework (Elliott, Golub, and Jackson 2013). Starting from the trade adjacent matrix and GDP size of each country (depicted in Figure 24.1, panel 1), establishing the "network value" of each country should be the first step. This network value takes into account the network effects, that is, the indirect costs and benefits for a particular country of being connected to other countries in the region. For that, a dependency matrix A is calculated as $A = \hat{C}(I - C)^{-1}$, where C is the trade adjacency matrix expressed (by column) as shares of imports by each country from other countries, I is a unitary matrix, and $\hat{C}$ is a diagonal matrix containing the share of trade by countries in the region with the countries outside the region. In the case of the WAEMU,[1] considering that intraregional trade is about 10 percent of the total trade of WAEMU countries, the value of trade with other countries was uniformly set to 90 percent. The dependency matrix describes how much each WAEMU country depends on its exports to other WAEMU countries. For example, if Côte d'Ivoire for any reason stopped its imports from Benin, the impact on Benin would be 0.0075 (Table 24.6).

The network effect may be assumed to be proportional to the relative weight of each country in regional GDP. For example, normalizing to unity the 2012 GDP of Guinea-Bissau, the smallest WAEMU country, allows calculating the relative weight structure of the WAEMU. For example, the economies of Burkina Faso and Mali are about 13 times larger than that of Guinea-Bissau, and that of Côte d'Ivoire is about 30 times larger. The network value of a country can then be calculated directly as a product of the dependency matrix and the normalized nominal GDP. The difference between the nominal GDP and the network value of a country is akin to the difference between the accounting book value of a firm and its market value, which factors its book value and all the links—valuable, not particularly valuable, and even worthless—the firm has with other market participants.

The difference between the normalized nominal GDP and the network value of a country can then be interpreted as a network effect. The sign of the network effect is an outcome of the interplay between the relative weights of countries with larger network values with countries of smaller network values compared with the network value of a given country and a given year. On average, for all WAEMU countries the network effect in 2006–12 was positive, pointing at the benefits of regional trade for all member countries (Table 24.7).

The benefits of participation in trade networks may be distributed unevenly among countries of the region. For example, on average for 2006–12, the network effect in the WAEMU was

[1] WAEMU regional trade is used purely as a numerical illustration of the network value concept. Substantial additional analytical work is needed to infer policy conclusions from these calculations.

TABLE 24.7

Dynamic Network Effects

	Network Effect (Percent)							
	2006	2007	2008	2009	2010	2011	2012	Average
BEN	2.7	−0.2	4.5	5.2	3.1	4.5	1.2	3.0
BFA	−8.6	0.9	−1.4	−3.4	−5.3	−6.0	−6.2	−4.3
CIV	−1.9	−1.5	−1.1	−1.2	−2.8	−1.7	−0.4	−1.5
GNB	3.0	2.8	−1.4	6.3	13.8	6.1	−3.8	3.8
MLI	3.3	−0.7	0.8	0.5	−0.1	2.2	1.5	1.1
NER	−6.4	−5.1	−6.3	−7.3	−6.1	−6.6	−6.2	−6.3
SEN	−1.5	−1.7	−1.4	−1.1	1.3	−0.3	−0.9	−0.8
TGO	38.9	28.6	16.9	20.8	31.5	23.6	28.6	27.0
Average	3.7	2.9	1.3	2.5	4.4	2.7	1.7	2.7

Source: IMF staff estimates.
Note: Three-letter International Organization for Standardization abbreviations used for country names.

positive for Benin, Guinea-Bissau, Mali, and Togo, which means that these countries exported relatively more to countries with higher network values relative to their own network value than they did to countries with lower network values. As should be expected, the network effect is higher for smaller countries, as they benefit the most from trade cooperation with larger countries. As Guinea-Bissau has the lowest network value in the WAEMU, the network effect for this country is strongly positive (+4 percent), as should be expected. The effect was not as strong as for Togo (+27 percent) because Guinea-Bissau exports relatively less to countries with higher network values than Togo. The network effect is negative for Burkina Faso (−4 percent) and Niger (−6 percent), suggesting that their trade links with the rest of the WAEMU actually diminish the network value of these countries, primarily because they export relatively more to countries with network values lower than their own. Senegal and Mali have no statistically significant network effects, because they export roughly equally to countries with higher and lower network values than their own, and Côte d'Ivoire because it is the largest WAEMU country and should, in principle, experience the network effect proportional to itself.

SHOCK DIFFUSION

The network effect allows identifying the channels and sequencing of the diffusion of both positive and negative signals through the network. The cascading effect shows a possible sequencing of signal reduction as a result of a negative shock and signal amplification as a result of a positive shock. It is based on a simple algorithm for identifying simple cascade hierarchies (Elliott, Golub, and Jackson 2013). For a cascade to occur there should be an initial shock. This shock should be contagious (that is, it should be important for other countries), and the country affected by the shock should be interconnected to other countries so the shock could propagate. The model assumes that the initial signal is sufficiently strong, as the diffusion through the network starts only after a certain threshold is exceeded. For the WAEMU, three thresholds are set at 80, 90, and 95 percent of the 2012 nominal GDP for each WAEMU country, that is, the diffusion through the network starts only if the initial shock is larger than 20, 10, and 5 percent of GDP, respectively. The thresholds are calculated relative to the network value of each country (Table 24.8). For simplicity, it is assumed that the initial shock affects the nominal GDP of only one country. The cascading effect is then calibrated relative to the corresponding thresholds.

Assume first that a large country (by regional standards) experiences a negative nominal shock. In the case of the WAEMU, Côte d'Ivoire is the largest country. As a result, Côte d'Ivoire's nominal GDP declines by 10 percent in 2012, but its network value remains unchanged, as all of its

TABLE 24.8

Signal Diffusion

	Nominal GDP	Network Value	Thresholds 0.8	Thresholds 0.9	Thresholds 0.95	Cascading Effect 0.8	Cascading Effect 0.9	Cascading Effect 0.95
BEN	9.190	9.301	7.441	8.371	8.836	23.5	9.8	4.0
BFA	13.406	12.576	10.060	11.318	11.947	33.3	18.4	12.2
CIV	27.011	29.885	23.908	26.897	28.391	13.0	0.4	-4.9
GNB	1.000	0.962	0.770	0.866	0.914	29.9	15.4	9.4
MLI	12.632	12.828	10.262	11.545	12.187	23.1	9.4	3.7
NER	8.237	7.722	6.178	6.950	7.336	33.3	18.5	12.3
SEN	17.081	16.921	13.537	15.229	16.075	26.2	12.2	6.3
TGO	4.762	6.124	4.900	5.512	5.818	−2.8	−13.6	−18.2
	Nominal GDP	**Network Value**	**Thresholds 0.8**	**Thresholds 0.9**	**Thresholds 0.95**	**Cascading Effect 0.8**	**Cascading Effect 0.9**	**Cascading Effect 0.95**
BEN	9.190	7.803	6.242	7.022	7.412	47.2	30.9	24.0
BFA	13.406	9.904	7.923	8.914	9.409	69.2	50.4	42.5
CIV	30.013	27.732	22.185	24.958	26.345	35.3	20.2	13.9
GNB	1.000	1.090	0.872	0.981	1.035	14.7	2.0	-3.4
MLI	12.632	10.261	8.209	9.235	9.748	53.9	36.8	29.6
NER	8.237	6.197	4.957	5.577	5.887	66.1	47.7	39.9
SEN	15.372	16.675	13.340	15.007	15.841	15.2	2.4	-3.0
TGO	4.286	4.794	3.835	4.315	4.555	11.7	-0.7	-5.9

Source: IMF staff estimates.
Note: Three-letter International Organization for Standardization abbreviations used for country names.

trade links to other countries are at their optimal levels. As seen in Table 24.8, top panel, there are no cascading effects for Côte d'Ivoire at the 0.8 and 0.9 thresholds, and the decline at the 0.95 threshold reflects only the nominal shock to Côte d'Ivoire itself. However, signal diffusion will be relatively strong. Togo will be the first country to feel the contagion as the negative impact from reduced demand from Côte d'Ivoire for its exports will be the strongest at all threshold levels, most likely because of Togo's large trade exposure to Côte d'Ivoire relative to its economic size. Although the threshold is not breached with a larger nominal shock in Côte d'Ivoire, at the next step, Mali and Benin may also be affected because of their import exposure to Côte d'Ivoire and their economic size, which is relatively small relative to Côte d'Ivoire. Finally, Senegal will feel a negative impact, but in this case because the trade flow from Côte d'Ivoire to Senegal is significant by regional standards, although Senegal's economic size is also relatively large, which helps absorb a significant part of the shock. The assumed initial shocks are very high and the impact only on a few countries may suggest that the transmission of shocks is not strong.

Assume now that the country with the highest network value is affected by a negative nominal shock. Togo is the country with the highest network value in the WAEMU example. Suppose its nominal GDP declines by 10 percent in 2012 (Table 24.8, bottom panel). The cascade of the impulse would have an impact mainly on Togo itself, as it loses a substantial share of its own network value, and will be very strong at all thresholds. Because Togo imports a lot from other WAEMU countries relative to its size, the shock from lower import demand would reverberate to itself and not to other countries. At the second and third stages, Guinea-Bissau and Senegal also will be affected, the former as it has relatively substantial exports to Togo relative to its economic size and the latter, again, most likely because of its gatekeeper position and the high betweeness in the overall framework. The negative signal from Togo will not diffuse further to other countries.

The network architecture may help explain this pattern of signal diffusion. Overall, substantial signal diffusion should be expected in the trade network, as it is relatively cohesive and dense, and among countries within the core and belonging to same cluster. For example, signal diffusion from Côte d'Ivoire to Senegal should be more intense, as both countries are in the core and belong to the same cluster in the network architecture. In Togo, the signal most likely reaches it directly from Côte d'Ivoire and indirectly through Senegal, which is an important regional gatekeeper and the country with the largest betweenness. Guinea-Bissau, although a clear outlier in the network architecture, is not affected, most likely because its direct trade links with all three affected countries—Côte d'Ivoire (the source), Senegal (the gatekeeper), and Mali (part of the core)—are very limited. Other countries are not affected by the shock mainly because they belong to a different cluster in the WAEMU architecture, have fewer links to the gatekeeper countries, and have a fortunate combination between the value of their imports from Côte d'Ivoire and their economic size.

CONCLUSIONS

The dynamic network analysis allows identifying key topological properties of regional trade and their evolution. Based on formal network metrics, inferences can be made regarding the overall cohesiveness of trade integration, and the role of individual countries and their possible location in the core or the periphery of the network and attribution to different clusters. For example, in the case of the WAEMU, regional trade has achieved progress in recent years, although overall it has remained relatively limited. Regional trade is dominated by three countries (Côte d'Ivoire, Senegal, Mali) and four flows (from Côte d'Ivoire to Burkina Faso and Mali, from Senegal to Mali, and from Togo to Benin). From 2006–12, the basic structure of trade interconnectedness in the WAEMU remained broadly unchanged, although regional trade became on average tighter with increased bilateral flows and more focus by individual countries on regional trade. The power structure in the region shifted as Côte d'Ivoire emerged as the only key trading partner and Senegal remained mainly an intermediary. There remains a large core (Côte d'Ivoire-Senegal-Mali) and a small periphery (Guinea-Bissau-Niger) in regional trade. The shape properties of regional trade have not changed in recent years, pointing to possible imbalances in the development of regional trade, as peripheral countries continue to face difficulties in joining the core. Most likely there are two overlapping clusters, although the clustering structure has been highly unstable, suggesting continuous shifts in trade patterns. A significant cluster comembership indicates that several countries can potentially act as gatekeepers and have an important role in economic signal transmission through the region.

All countries participating in regional trade experience a network effect. The network effect explicitly takes into account the fact that a country is connected to other countries in the region and assesses the value of these connections. The difference between the nominal GDP and the network value of a country can be positive, neutral, or negative, depending on the value of its connections to other countries in the region. If a country is well connected through trade with the strongest performing countries in the region, and the economy of its main trading partner is thriving, the value of such connections for the country is clearly positive, and its network value would be higher than its GDP. In the opposite case, if a country is mainly connected to countries whose macroperformance is weaker than its own, or whose main trading partner is going through a major economic crisis, the value of such connections most likely will be negative and the network value of the country will be lower than its GDP.

Signal proliferation through a regional trade network depends on the network's shape and other properties. High signal proliferation should be expected if the network is highly cohesive; the signal originates in a powerful country in terms of its centrality or the betweenness in the network. If a negative signal originates from a country in the core of the network, its diffusion may be expected to affect both the core and the periphery, with a major impact on regional stability. If the signal originates in the periphery of the network, it will likely affect mainly peripheral countries with no major impact on the core and regional stability. To the contrary, a positive economic signal originating in the core, but not in the periphery, may pull the whole region to a higher level of affluence. For example, clusters, which are not very pertinent for the WAEMU region, may, in principle, obstruct signal diffusion, because the signal usually loses its power in the diffusion between countries belonging to different clusters. Côte d'Ivoire, Senegal, and Mali can be the main origins of shocks for the rest of the WAEMU economies, including the core and the periphery, and to each other, as they belong to the same cluster. Côte d'Ivoire and Senegal are simultaneously playing the gate-keeping role and can be factors for either the propagation or absorption of shocks originating elsewhere in the network. Informal trade not captured in this network analysis may also play a role in shock diffusion. Signal proliferation through a regional trade network can be viewed also from the prism of risk sharing through the trade channel. This technique could be used to account for the other channels of risk sharing, such as remittances, trade, tourist spending, and foreign direct investments.

The network analysis of regional trade can help identify policies that can accelerate and deepen regional trade integration. For example, in the case of the WAEMU, the following policy recommendations may be considered: (1) step up efforts in regional trade by exploring the potential of the regional market to expand its size and internal cohesiveness; (2) have central regional powers play a leadership role in promoting regional trade because the most connected countries in the region affect the network value of smaller countries; (3) rebalance regional trade substantially through more active involvement of disconnected and poorly connected countries in the trade network, allowing them to attenuate the core periphery, which inhibits deeper regional trade; (4) monitor the evolution of the unstable clustering structure of regional trade continuously to identify potential boundaries of possible shock diffusion promptly; (5) pay particular attention to the macroeconomic policies of the gatekeeper countries, as they play a critical role in augmenting positive economic signals and mitigating adverse shocks proliferating though the trade network in the union; and (6) assess the network effect for individual countries and take policy measures to eliminate or reduce the impact of negative externalities.

REFERENCES

Acemoglu D., V. Carvalho, A. Ozdaglar, and A. Tahbaz-Salehi. 2012. "The Network Origins of Aggregate Fluctuations." *Econometrica* 80 (5): 1977–2016, September.

Borgatti S., M. Everett, and J. Johnson. 2013. *Analyzing Social Networks.* Thousand Oaks, California: Sage Publications.

Borgatti, S. P., M. G. Everett, and L. C. Freeman. 2013. *Ucinet for Windows: Software for Social Network Analysis.* Harvard, Massachusetts: Analytic Technologies.

Duenas, M., and G. Fagiolo. 2013. "Global Trade Imbalances: A Network Approach." May, Scuola Superiore Sant'Anna, Pisa, Italy. Available at Social Science Research Network: http://ssrn.com/abstract=2266320

Easley, D., and J. Kleinberg. 2010. *Networks, Crowds, and Markets. Reasoning about a Highly Connected World.* New York: Cambridge University Press.

Elliott, M., B. Golub, and M. Jackson. 2013. "Financial Networks and Contagion." Available at Social Science Research Network: http://ssrn.com/abstract=2175056.

Jackson, M. 2008. *Social and Economic Networks.* Princeton: Princeton University Press.

Kubelec, C., and F. Sa. 2012. "The Geographical Composition of National External Balance Sheets: 1980–2005." *International Journal of Central Banking* (June).

Newman, M. 2010. *Networks: An Introduction.* Oxford University Press.

CHAPTER 25

Macroeconomic Implications of Tariff Changes

WILLIAM GBOHOUI, KARIM BARHOUMI, QIANG CUI, AND MONIQUE NEWIAK

The common external tariff (CET) for the Economic Community of West African States (ECOWAS), which includes all West African Economic and Monetary Union (WAEMU) countries, became effective in January 2015. The macroeconomic effects of a replacement of the WAEMU CET with the ECOWAS CET on WAEMU member states could be substantial. The new tariff could have an impact on trade levels, government revenue, and growth. It is likely to increase WAEMU imports from other ECOWAS countries but reduce imports from the rest of the world. We estimate that the tariff's impact on government revenue will vary widely by country, ranging from a loss in most countries by up to 2½ percent of current revenue to an increase in a few countries by up to 3 percent. Finally, an increase in relative import prices induced by an increase in the average tariff rate could yield a negative effect on GDP.

REGIONAL TRADE AND TARIFFS

The CET for the ECOWAS was adopted at a Heads of State Summit in October 2013 and became effective in January 2015. As a consequence of this CET, WAEMU countries, a subset of ECOWAS countries, will be subject to a new tariff structure. Currently WAEMU countries (all members of the ECOWAS), impose tariffs within the range of 0 to 20 percent on goods from all non-WAEMU countries, including ECOWAS countries, with a simple average import tariff of about 12 percent. After adopting the CET, WAEMU countries will eliminate tariffs on goods from all ECOWAS countries, but tariffs on products from non-ECOWAS members will increase. The revenue implications of this policy change could be significant, as many WAEMU countries rely heavily on import duties (Figure 25.1, panel 3).

While the literature on trade agreements in West Africa is vast, the revenue effects of implementation of the CET have not been quantified. This chapter contributes to the existing research by estimating the revenue implications of the implementation of the ECOWAS CET on WAEMU member states. First, the chapter takes stock of the current tariff structure in the WAEMU and current intra- and extra-ECOWAS trade flows. It also provides a description of the implied changes to the tariff structure with the ECOWAS CET. Second, it estimates the elasticity of import demand for individual members of the WAEMU. Third, a partial equilibrium framework is used to assess the potential trade and revenue effects of the tariff change. Finally, a panel vector auto regression (VAR) model assesses the dynamic macroeconomic effects of changes in trade tariffs in the WAEMU.

Trade between WAEMU countries and the rest of ECOWAS is rather low. The WAEMU's interregional trade as well as trade with the rest of the ECOWAS remains weak, with some variation across countries. Burkina Faso, Guinea-Bissau, and Mali are the only WAEMU countries for which intra-WAEMU imports constitute more than one-fifth of the total import value, and only Côte d'Ivoire, Niger, and Senegal import close to or more than 10 percent from non-WAEMU ECOWAS countries (Figure 25.1, panel 1). Trade balances between the WAEMU and the rest of

Figure 25.1. Stylized Facts: Trade within ECOWAS

Imports into the WAEMU from other ECOWAS countries are currently low…

1. Import by Origin, 2013
(In percent of total imports)

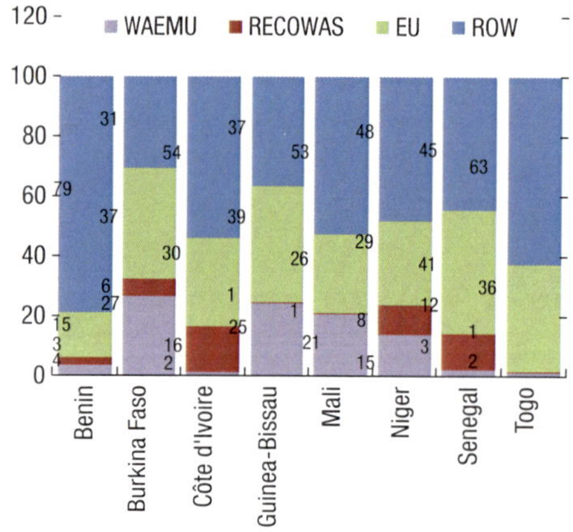

… and the WAEMU's trade balance with other ECOWAS members is insignificant.

2. Trade Balance of WAEMU Members with ECOWAS, 2013
(In percent of GDP)

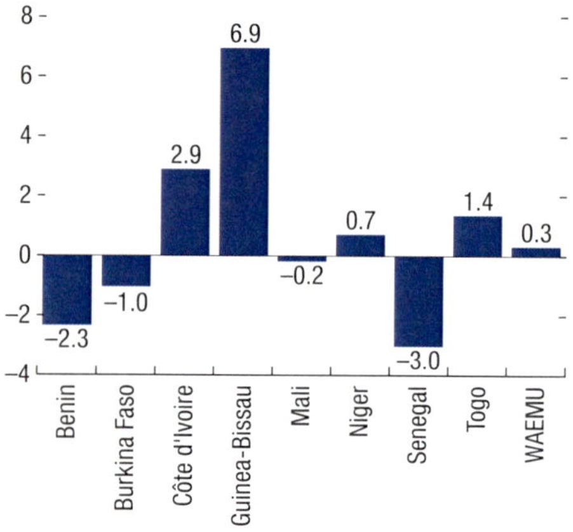

Source: Direction of Trade Statistics.

Import duties constitute a significant share of government revenue in the WAEMU, with the highest share in Benin.

3. Evolution of Import Duties
(In percent of government revenue)

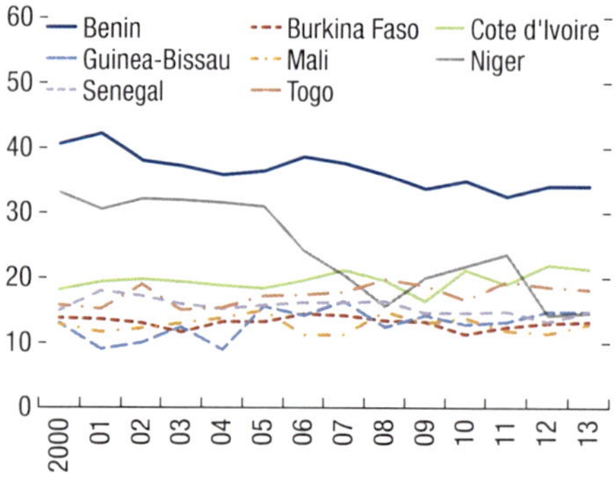

Sources: Country authorities; and IMF staff estimates.

The majority of imports are taxed within the two highest tariff bands.

4. Import Value by Tariff Band
(In percent of total imports, 2010)

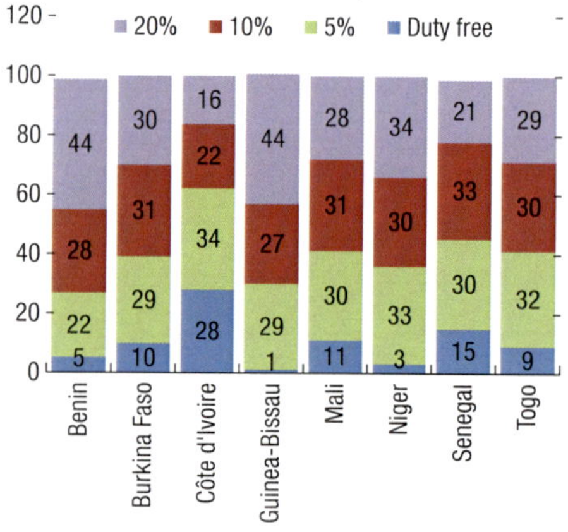

Source: WTO Tariff Analysis Online Facility.

Sources: Country authorities; Direction of Trade Statistics; World Trade Organization Tariff Analysis Online Facility; IMF staff estimates.
Note: ECOWAS = Economic Community of West African States; WAEMU = West African Economic and Monetary Union; RECOWAS = rest of ECOWAS, i.e., ECOWAS without WAEMU member states.

the ECOWAS thus remain low, with only Guinea-Bissau individually showing a trade surplus with the rest of ECOWAS of almost 7 percent of its GDP.

WAEMU countries in general rely heavily on import duties (Figure 25.1, panel 3). These duties constitute a substantial source of revenue for WAEMU countries, representing at least 8 percent of total government revenue in any WAEMU country over the period 2000–13. In 2013, import duties represented at least 13 percent of total government revenue in all WAEMU countries, with the highest share of 34 percent in Benin. With the exception of Côte d'Ivoire, more than half of imports to any WAEMU country face a tariff rate of 10 or 20 percent.

TABLE 25.1

Structure of ECOWAS and WAEMU Common External Tariff

Category	Description	WAEMU Duty Rate (In percent)	ECOWAS Duty Rate (In percent)
0	Essential social goods	0	0
1	Goods of primary necessity, raw materials, and specific inputs	5	5
2	Inputs and Intermediate goods	10	10
3	Final consumption goods	20	20
4	Specific goods for economic development	–	35
–	**Average**	**11.9**	**12.3**

Source: Roquefeuil and others (2014); and the West African Economic and Monetary Union Commission.
Note: The structure of the Economic Community of West African States common external tariff as in the version agreed upon by the region's ministers in Praia in March 2013; details on the tariff bands applied to each tariff line are shown in WAEMU Regulation 23/2002/CM/UEMOA.

The introduction of the ECOWAS CET eliminated tariffs on the WAEMU's imports from other ECOWAS countries but increased tariffs on imports from the rest of the world. The ECOWAS CET is organized in five bands. The first four bands are taken from the WAEMU CET (see Table 25.1). However, the ECOWAS CET includes a fifth tariff band of 35 percent for specific goods for economic development, which implies a customs tax increase for WAEMU countries and a reduction for non-WAEMU ECOWAS countries, such as Nigeria and Guinea.

TARIFF EFFECTS

To quantify each WAEMU member country's import responsiveness to price and tariff changes, the price elasticity of the volume of trade is estimated in a first step. To this end, an import function is postulated in which the quantity of imports depends on the price of imports, the price of other domestic consumable commodities, and domestic income. Controlling for further determinants of imports, the following relationship is estimated econometrically

$$\ln(M_t) = \beta_0 + \beta_1 \ln \frac{P_t^m}{\text{CPI}_t} + \beta_2 \ln(\text{GDP}_t) + \beta_3 \ln(\text{TAXM}_t) + \varepsilon_t,$$

in which in each year t, M_t is the import volume index, $\frac{P_t^m}{\text{CPI}_t}$ is the ratio between the import price index and Consumer Price Index, TAXM_t is the level of import duties, and GDP is the real GDP_t level (constant 2005 prices). β_0, β_1, β_2 β_3, and ε_t represent a constant, the price elasticity of import demand, the income elasticity of import demand, the elasticity of import to collected duties revenue, and the error term, respectively. The estimated import demand elasticities are presented in Tables 25.2 and 25.3.

TABLE 25.2

Price Elasticities of Imports: Individual Countries

	Benin	Côte d'Ivoire	Mali	Togo
Import price-CPI ratio	−2.43***	−0.22*	−0.87**	−0.63***
GDP	−4.00***		1.19***	
Import duties	1.11***	0.25**	0.35**	
GDP-export		1.08***		0.71**
Volume of exports		0.86***		1.12***
Constant	33.91***	−10.65**	−4.32**	−5.58**
p-value; *F* test	0	0	0	0

Source: Author's estimates.
Note: ***; **; * significant at 1, 5, and 10 percent level, respectively; Heteroskedasticity corrected by White (1980) estimator; Serial Correlation corrected by Cochrane-Orcutt (1949) estimator.

TABLE 25.3

Price Elasticity of Imports: WAEMU

	WAEMU
Import price-CPI ratio	−0.39***
Real GDP	0.73***
Import duties	0.46***
Constant	−0.79

Source: Author's estimates.
Note: ***; **; * significant at 1, 5, and 10 percent level, respectively; Panel corrected standard errors (control for heteroskedasticity/cross sectional dependence); Serial correlation corrected by Prais Wintsen (1954) estimator with panel specific AR(1) coefficient.

The price elasticity of import demand varies strongly across WAEMU countries. The results indicate that the percent decrease in import demand due to a one percent change in the import price varies from about 0.2 (in Côte d'Ivoire) to 2.4 (in Benin), with an average of about 0.4 for the WAEMU region as a whole. The high elasticity in Benin may be explained by the informal reexports of Benin to Nigeria, estimated to represent 50 percent of imports going through the Port of Cotonou (see Box 25.1).

The change in the tariff structure is expected to increase the WAEMU's imports from other ECOWAS countries, but decrease its imports from the rest of the world. The trade effects are estimated using the methodology described in Box 25.2. With the exception of Togo, for which the share of non-ECOWAS imports in total imports is very high, trade creation is estimated to be larger than trade diversion in all WAEMU countries. In other WAEMU countries, the tariff change would imply an increase in imports from non-WAEMU ECOWAS countries by approximately 6 percent, with the highest increase, of 52 percent, in Benin (Figure 25.2, panel 1). The increase in the average tariff for non-ECOWAS countries is estimated to slightly reduce WAEMU countries' imports from the rest of the world, with imports decreasing by less than 0.2 percent for most WAEMU countries, and the highest effect, of a ¾ percent decrease, expected in Benin (Figure 25.2, panel 3).

The estimated trade effects of tariff elimination should be considered as the upper bound of the potential effects. Similarly to the effects after the introduction of the WAEMU CET, trade

BOX 25.1. Revenue Impact in Benin

The estimated revenue impact related to trade liberalization is much stronger in Benin than it is in other WAEMU countries due to Benin's unique trade patterns, which are dominated by informal trade with neighboring Nigeria (Figure 25.1.1). This box provides more details on such trade and its potential revenue impact.

Benin's trade with Nigeria mainly takes the form of informal reexports to Nigeria due to trade restrictions on certain products. The proximity to Nigeria and a relatively porous border has made Benin the preferred platform for importing certain goods that Nigeria forbids either through bans or through prohibitive tariffs. These products include frozen poultry, rice, used cars, and textiles. It is estimated that about 50 percent of imports going through the Port of Cotonou are destined for Nigeria. Overall, at least 20 percent of Benin's GDP is generated through informal trade (World Bank 2014).

These reexport activities are a significant source of tax revenue for Benin. The Beninese authorities reached an agreement with the Nigerian government to not reexport certain goods, so that the only way for Beninese importers to reach the Nigerian market is to first declare imported goods for domestic consumption, pay the value-added tax, and then reexport the goods informally to Nigeria. According to Geourjeon, Chambas, and Laporte (2008), the tax revenue gain stemming from this activity could be about 2 percent of GDP or 14 percent of total tax revenue, respectively. This highlights Benin's fiscal dependence on informal reexport activities with Nigeria.

Trade liberalization in Nigeria would thus result in significant revenue losses in Benin. Based on customs data from 2009–12, the impact of a full trade liberalization scenario in Nigeria is estimated to result in a revenue loss of at least 2 percent of GDP (Sola and others 2013).

BOX 25.1. (*continued*)

Figure 25.1.1. Revenue Implications of a Full Liberalization of Nigeria's Trade Regime for Benin[1] (2011, in percent of GDP)

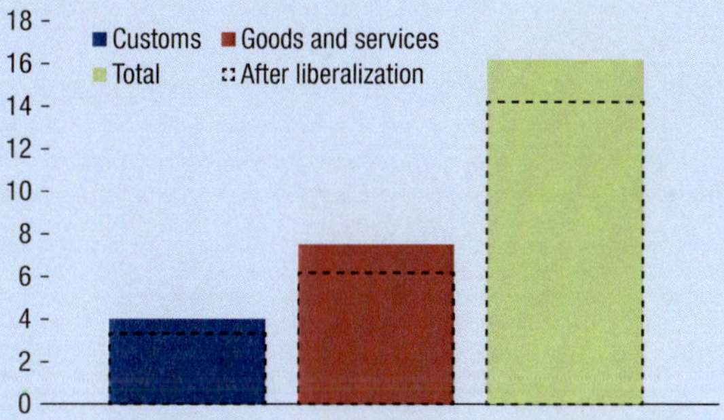

Sources: Beninese authorities; and IMF staff estimates.
[1]The tax revenue after liberalization is estimated based on the assumptions that potential losses due to full liberalization of Nigeria's trade regime are distributed as 1/3 for customs revenue and 2/3 for goods and services tax revenue

BOX 25.2. Assumptions and Analytical Framework

Assumptions (Figure 25.2.1.)—The world is divided into three blocks from which WAEMU countries import: WAEMU countries, other ECOWAS countries that are not members of the WAEMU (the rest of ECOWAS), and the rest of the world. The supply of products to the WAEMU has perfect supply elasticity (overall supply to WAEMU countries for products is infinite at a given price). In each WAEMU country, local consumers substitute imperfectly products from these regions, but all products from the three alternative sources are equally substitutable. The elimination of tariffs within the ECOWAS is *assumed to have negligible competition effects between intra-WAEMU exports to a given WAEMU country.*

Figure 25.2.1. Composition of Domestic Demand

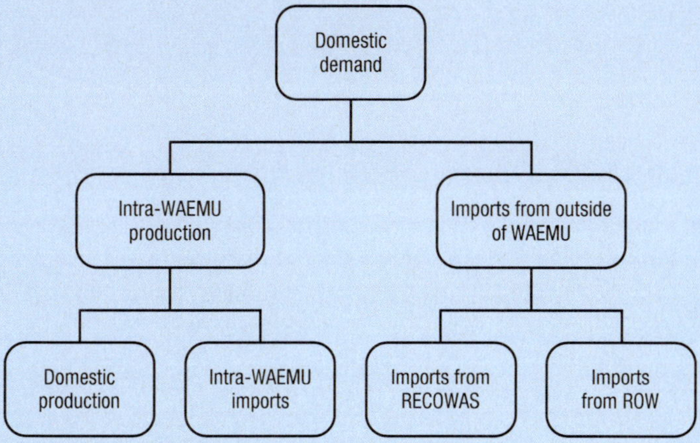

Source: Author's illustration.

BOX 25.2 (*continued*)

Trade creation—This refers to the substitution of domestic production by imports from the rest of the ECOWAS, resulting from tariff elimination. Trade creation between WAEMU country i and the rest of ECOWAS is

$$TC_{i,RECOWAS} = -M_{i,RECOWAS}\eta_i^m\left[\frac{\tau^{WAEMU}}{1+\tau^{WAEMU}}\right],$$

in which $M_{i,RECOWAS}$ *is the value of imports from RECOWAS by country i,* τ^{WAEMU} *is the WAEMU's CET average tariff and* η_i^m *is the import demand elasticity.*

Trade diversion—This is the substitution of imports from the rest of the world by imports from the rest of the ECOWAS, resulting from the elimination of tariffs between WAEMU and ECOWAS countries. It is defined by

$$TD_{i,RECOWAS} = \frac{TC_{i,RECOWAS}}{GDP_i}M_{i,ROW}.$$

Other trade effects—The ECOWAS CET against non-ECOWAS members is higher than those applied initially by the WAEMU CET to non-ECOWAS countries. The implementation of the ECOWAS CET by the WAEMU thus eliminates their tariff against other ECOWAS countries but increases their tariff against non-ECOWAS countries. It may thus lead to a trade loss within WAEMU countries and the rest of the world. This other trade effect (OTE) is the change in WAEMU country i's demand for import from non-ECOWAS country j, resulting from the increase in tariffs associated with the adoption of ECOWAS CET. The OTE can be written as

$$OTE_{i,ROW} = M_{i,ROW}\eta_i^m\left[\frac{\tau^{ECOWAS}-\tau^{WAEMU}}{1+\tau^{WAEMU}}\right],$$

where $M_{i,ROW}$ is the value of imports from the rest of the world (ROW) by the country i, τ^{ECOWAS} is the average tariff of ECOWAS's CET, τ^{WAEMU} is WAEMU's CET average tariff, and η_i^m is the import demand elasticity of country i.

The overall net trade effect can then be computed as

$$NTE_i = TC_{i,RECOWAS} + TD_{i,RECOWAS} + OTE_{i,ROW}.$$

creation may be lower because some nontariff barriers may remain in place after the implementation of the ECOWAS CET. Trade diversion may also be lower because some WAEMU imports from non-ECOWAS countries have no substitute in other ECOWAS countries, so that the decrease in imports from non-ECOWAS countries could be lower than the effect estimated in this chapter.

REVENUE IMPLICATIONS

Based on the projected trade effects, the revenue implications are estimated. The change in revenues in the WAEMU would be the combined effect of changes in tariff income from imports from non-ECOWAS countries (higher tariff versus lower import value) and tariff income from non-WAEMU ECOWAS countries (lower tariff versus higher import value):

$$\Delta R_i = \left[M_{i,ROW} - TD_i\right]\left[\tau^{ECOWAS} - \tau^{WAEMU}\right] - \left[M_{i,RECOWAS} + TD_{i,RECOWAS}\right]\tau^{WAEMU}$$

In this equation, $M_{i,ROW}$ and $M_{i,RECOWAS}$ represent the value of imports from non-ECOWAS countries and non-WAEMU ECOWAS by country i, respectively. $TD_{i,RECOWAS}$ is the trade

Figure 25.2. Trade and Revenue Implications of the Tariff Change

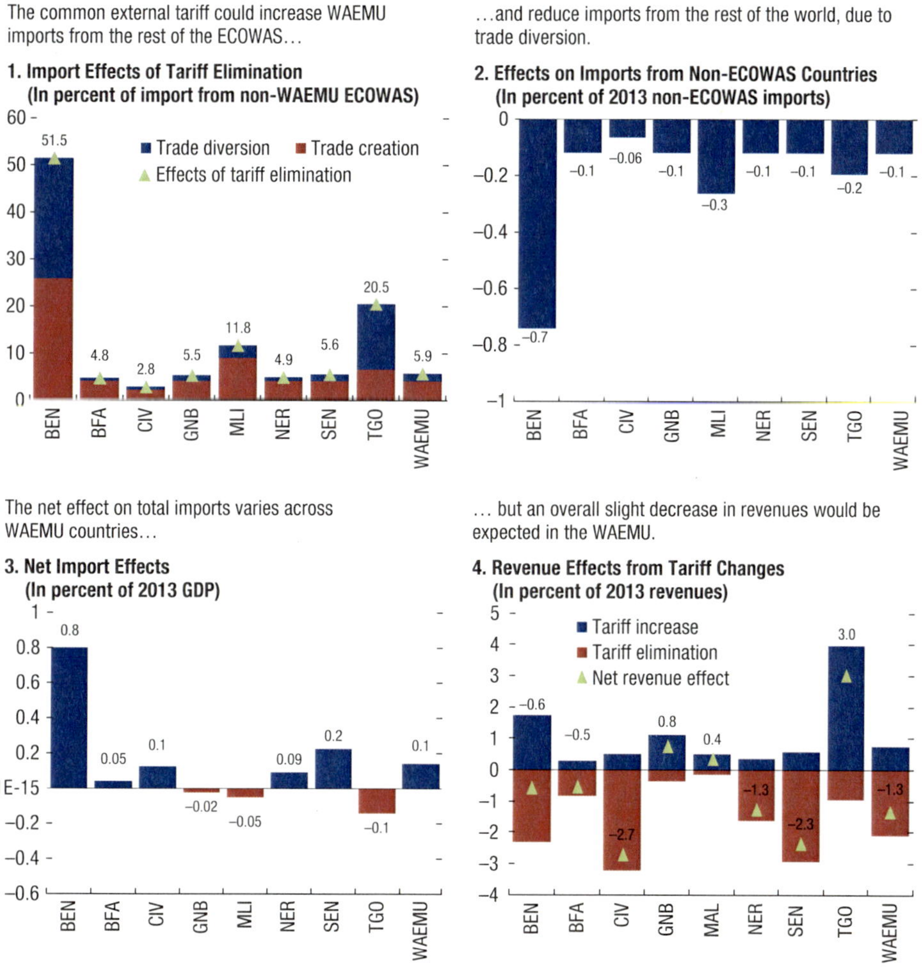

Source: Country authorities; own estimates; IMF staff estimates.
Note: BEN = Benin; BFA = Burkina Faso; CIV = Côte d'Ivoire; GNB = Guinea-Bissau; MLI = Mali; NER = Niger; SEN = Senegal; TGO = Togo; WAEMU = West African Economic and Monetary Union; ECOWAS = Economic Community of West African States.

diversion from the non-ECOWAS countries to non-WAEMU ECOWAS countries. τ^{ECOWAS} and τ^{WAEMU} are the average tariffs of the ECOWAS CET and the WAEMU's CET, respectively.

The changes in tariffs could have ambiguous effects on revenue across WAEMU countries. The elimination of tariffs on imports from other ECOWAS countries would decrease government revenue. However, the tariff increase for products from the non-ECOWAS countries could have a positive impact on revenues. Based on the assumptions in Box 25.1 and the preceding paragraph, revenues in Benin, Burkina Faso, Cote d'Ivoire, Niger, and Senegal could decrease by ½ to approximately 2½ percent from their 2013 levels (Figure 25.2, panel 4). However, consistent with current trade profiles implying a low share of imports from non-WAEMU ECOWAS countries, revenues could increase by ½ to 3 percent in Guinea-Bissau, Mali, and Togo.

Data limitations prevent accounting for informal trade in the WAEMU. The decrease in government revenue may be higher in some countries if informal trade is taken into account. For instance, this may be the case in Benin, where informal reexports to Nigeria are estimated to contribute 2 percent of GDP to fiscal revenue (Box 25.2). The implementation of the ECOWAS CET is more likely to imply a stronger fall in imports for reexports and hence the reexports, implying a loss in import duty revenue as well as value-added tax revenue. Due to trade policy restrictions, Beninese importers can only reach the Nigerian market by declaring imported goods for domestic consumption, paying the value-added tax, and reexporting informally the goods to Nigeria.

MACROECONOMIC EFFECTS

To assess the dynamic effects of changes in tariff structure on imports in the WAEMU, the traditional VAR model is combined with a panel data approach. A first order Panel VAR model is specified as

$$Y_{it} = \Gamma_0 + \Gamma_1 Y_{it-1} + e_{it},$$

in which Y_t is a four-variable vector (import duties, real GDP, relative import price, import). An impulse response function then determines the transmission channels of an exogenous change in import tariffs to imports based on a Choleski decomposition assuming the same ordering.

An increase in relative import prices induced by an increase in the average tariff rate could yield a negative effect on GDP. Table 25.4 depicts the results of the estimation of the previously mentioned model for a panel of WAEMU countries for the period between 1995 and 2013. Column 2 implies a statistically significant negative relationship between import prices and GDP. An increase in the average tariff rate, which implies an increase in import prices, would thus be expected to affect GDP negatively as well. In terms of the dynamic effects (Figure 25.3), the impulse response function shows that import prices adjust to an increase in tariff with a one-period lag, and imports simultaneously induce a decrease in imports. Current increases in relative import prices dampen economic growth within one period. Increases in GDP result in higher demand, including the demand of foreign goods and higher domestic production of importable goods later on. However, as domestic production of importable goods rises faster than domestic consumption of importable goods, lagged GDP decreases imports.

TABLE 25.4

Estimated Coefficients of Panel VAR

	Response to							
Response of	**Import duties (t−1)**		**Import Prices (t−1)**		**Import (t−1)**		**GDP (t−1)**	
Import duties (t)	−0.007	−0.12	0.051	−0.175	0.131	−0.132	−1.624	−1.104
Import Prices (t)	0.132*	−0.08	−0.046	−0.104	0.037	−0.101	0.577	−0.68
Import (t)	0.05	−0.091	0.149	−0.144	−0.085	−0.123	−2.367**	−1.014
GDP (t)	0.004	−0.018	−0.055**	−0.023	−0.003	−0.021	−0.069	−0.183

Source: Author estimations.

Note: ***; **; * significant at 1, 5, and 10 percent level, respectively, with standard errors in parentheses; First lags of dependent variables in the model are instrumented by the same lags; Stability test shows that all eigenvalues are inside the unit circle, i.e., the PVAR is stable. VAR = Vector Autoregression; PVAR = Panel VAR; t = time.

Figure 25.3. Transmission Channels of Changes in Tariff Structure to Imports[1]

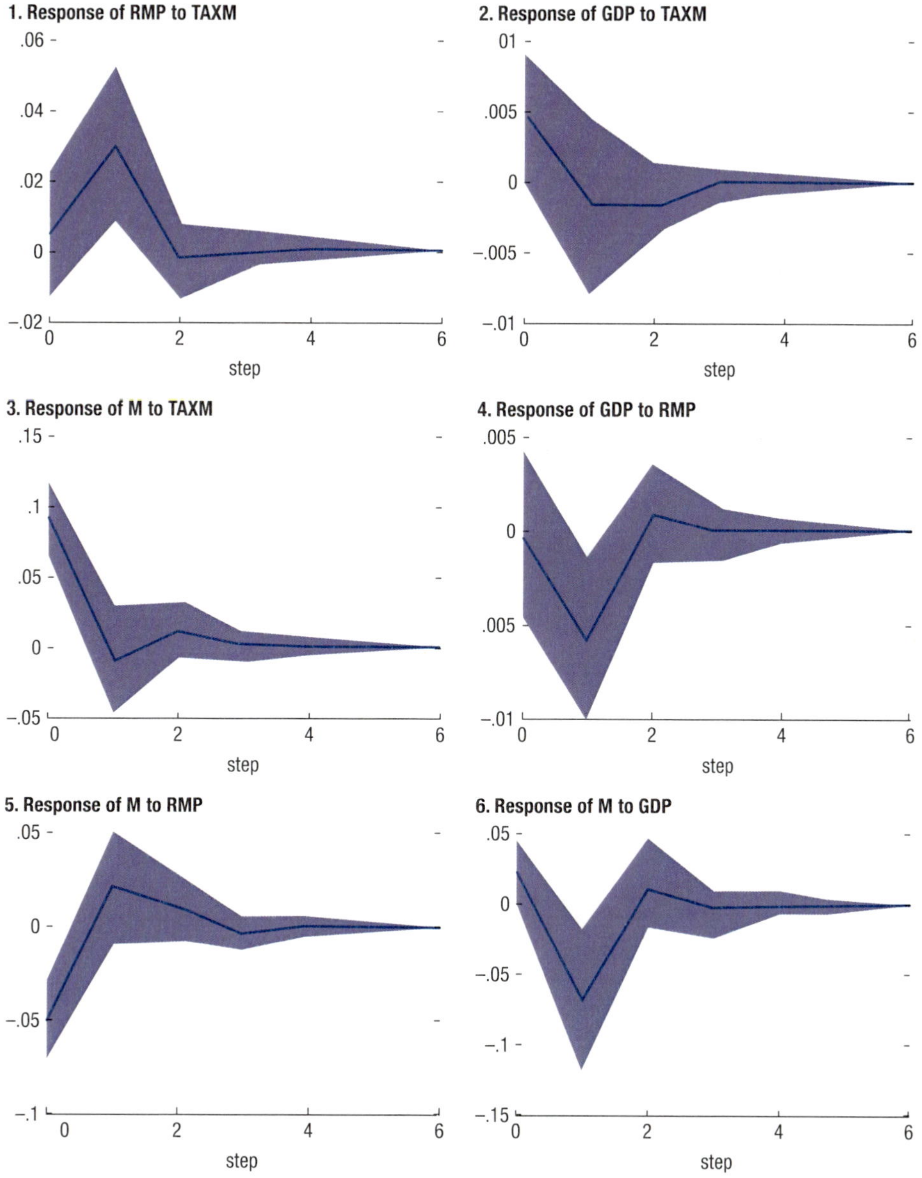

Source: Own estimations.
[1]RMF Notes: RMP = relative import price; TAXM = import duties; M = imports. IRF of response variables to one standard deviation increase in impulse variables. Confidence intervals computed using Monte Carlo Simulations.

REFERENCES

Geourjon, A. M., G. Chambas, and B. Laporte. 2008. "République du Bénin. Modernisation du Système Fiscal. Orientations et Stratégie de Réformes." September. International Monetary Fund, Washington.

Roquefeuil, Q. de, D. Plunkett, and F. Ofei. 2014. "The Impact of Closer Regional Economic Integration on Food Security in West Africa: Focus on the ECOWAS Common External Tariff." Discussion Paper No. 154. European Centre for Development Policy Management, Brussels.

Sola, S., G. Parent, J. Russell, A. Ould Boilil, and G. Barker. 2013. "République du Bénin. Bilan des Reformes et Poursuite du Renforcement de l'administration Douanière." International Monetary Fund, Fiscal Affairs Department, June.

World Bank. 2014. "Benin Diagnostic Trade Integration Study (DTIS) Update: From Rents to Competitiveness." World Bank, Washington.

CHAPTER 26

Foreign Investment in Government Debt

PATRICK IMAM

Foreign investment in the West African Economic and Monetary Union (WAEMU) remains limited. Even government debt, the least risky investment instrument, attracts very little attention from nonresident investors, unlike the attention received in neighboring Ghana and Nigeria. Possible reasons for this situation include unattractive nominal interest rates in the region, the relatively small market size, lack of a secondary market, cumbersome exchange controls and regulations, fragmentation of the regional market, insufficient communication on issuances, the language issue, insufficient political stability, and a poor investment climate. To make the regional market more attractive to foreign investors, sound macroeconomic policies and a solid financial sector are prerequisites. Beyond this, communication with nonresidents should be improved with Agence UMOA-Titres playing a key role; development of WAEMU financial markets, including the secondary market for government securities, should be accelerated; market size should be increased by eliminating segmentation of the sovereign bond market; and finally, taxation needs to be harmonized and double taxation avoided.

PARTICIPATION BY NONRESIDENTS

Appetite for sub-Saharan "frontier markets'" debt has been growing in recent years. Since the launch of the Ghana Eurobond in 2007, more and more countries in the region have borrowed overseas in foreign currency (see IMF 2013). A more recent trend has been the increase in purchases of local currency bonds. The profile of investors is also shifting, with traditional niche players increasingly joined by dedicated institutional frontier market funds and large institutional investors, mainly from the United States and the United Kingdom.

There is little evidence of significant investment by nonresidents from outside the WAEMU in the regional government debt market. This is in contrast with the situation in neighboring Ghana and Nigeria. While comprehensive information has not been compiled, available data on Senegal—one of the main issuers on this market—suggest that less than 2.5 percent of its debt issued on the WAEMU market is held by nonresidents (see Figure 26.1). This contrasts with the case in Ghana and Nigeria, where foreign ownership of government debt hovers at around 20 and 25 percent, respectively.

This situation is surprising, as the WAEMU has characteristics that should make its market attractive to foreign investors, including:

- *High growth*—At about 6 percent in 2012 and 2013, and expected to remain robust
- *Sound fundamentals*—Fiscal sustainability was restored with debt relief and maintained since through appropriate fiscal policies. Structural reforms have been implemented to improve governance and the business environment.
- *Diversification*—Debt issued in the WAEMU is less likely, for instance, to be affected by the fluctuations of key commodity prices, unlike in other sub-Saharan African countries, which are typically dependent on a single commodity.
- *Low foreign exchange risk*—The credible peg to the euro reduces the exchange rate risk.
- *Donor support*—Remains substantial and cushions the impact of external and fiscal shocks

Figure 26.1. Size of Domestic Sovereign Debt Market

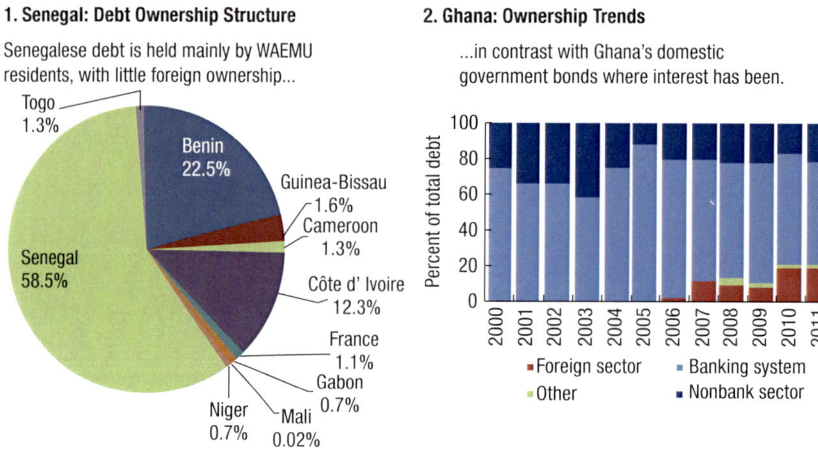

Sources: Bloomberg L.P.; Central Bank of West African States (BCEAO); IMF, African Department database.

THE VIEW OF FOREIGN INVESTORS

Market participants view the risk-adjusted nominal interest rates on the WAEMU market as unattractive. Investors in frontier markets consider both the yield on domestic debt and the exchange rate. The yields on the WAEMU market are viewed as low—when compared with the yields in other African countries (Figure 26.2)—even once the greater exchange rate stability associated with the exchange regime is taken into account. There is a perception that the regional market does not price risks adequately, a perception also underpinned by the fact that yields across sovereign issuers do not seem to reflect the range of fiscal situations. Yields may be driven down by the lack of alternative investments for domestic banks, which are the main investors on the WAEMU market. Foreign investors are also uncertain about the extent to which solidarity across WAEMU countries could play in the event of a debt crisis. This makes risk pricing more challenging.

The size of the WAEMU market is too small. The WAEMU market amounts to about 8 percent of the regional GDP. All but one WAEMU countries have issued on the market. Even for the larger issuers (Côte d'Ivoire, Senegal), the outstanding stock of debt on the WAEMU market is relatively small (Figure 26.3). By contrast, Nigeria's and Ghana's domestic debt markets are much deeper. Size is important to foreign investors, as it is generally associated with liquidity and better pricing. Small size also means that no debt issued on the WAEMU market is included in Local Currency Bond (LCB) global indices, which bond funds often use to benchmark their exposure. Nigeria was included in 2012 in the JP Morgan Government Bond-Emerging Markets Index, which triggered additional demand for its debt.

Lack of a secondary market is also an issue. Without the ability to sell bonds or bills on a secondary market (including because of the "buy-and hold" strategy of domestic investors), a foreign investor is constrained to hold these instruments until maturity (or perhaps to sell them at a deep discount). As a result, foreign investors will, at best, be interested in short-term paper. The lack of an active secondary market also makes pricing at issuance more difficult.

Exchange control regulations and practices are viewed as cumbersome in the WAEMU. In principle, there are no regulatory obstacles to capital inflows to buy government securities on the WAEMU market, or to the repatriation of proceeds. However, according to investors, observance

Figure 26.2. Interest Rates on Domestic and Foreign Bonds in Selected Countries

Yield on domestic and foreign WAEMU debt do not differ significantly.

Domestic and Foreign Treasury Issuances (Yield to maturity)

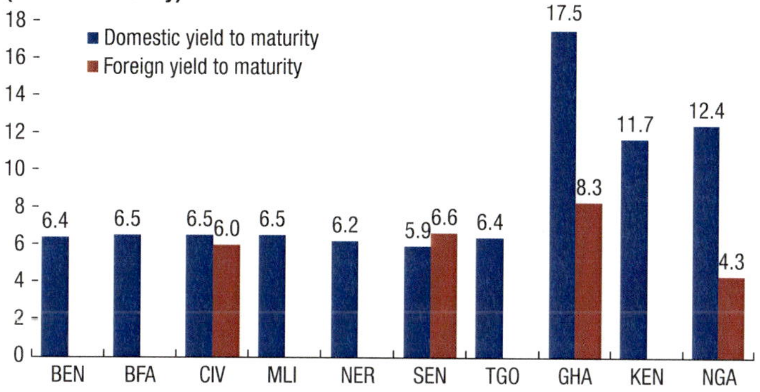

Sources: Bloomberg, L.P.; Central Bank of West African States (BCEAO); and Dealogic.
Note: Benin 2009 issuance, 7-year maturity; Burkina Faso 2012 issuance, 5-year maturity; Côte d'Ivoire Eurobond 2012 issuance, 20-year maturity; CIV 2013 domestic issuance, 7-year maturity; Guinea-Bissau has not offered long-term bonds the last few years; Mali 2010 issuance, 5-year maturity; Niger 2013 issuance, 5-year maturity; Senegal Eurobond 2011 issuance, 10-year maturity; Togo 2013 issuance, 5-year maturity; Ghana 2013 Eurobond issuance, 10-year maturity; Kenya 2013 issuance, 15-year maturity; Nigeria 2013 issuance, 5-year maturity.
BEN = Benin; BFA = Burkina-Faso; CIV = Côte d'Ivoire; MLI = Mali; NER = Niger; SEN = Senegal; TGO = Togo, GHA = Ghana; KEN = Kenya; NER = Nigeria.

of rules and regulations on capital flows requires a number of administrative steps and is very burdensome in practice, particularly on the way out. This tends to dissuade capital inflows in the first place. Another concern expressed by investors is that capital repatriation might become even more difficult in the event of a crisis. Investors' perception is that investing in Ghana or Nigeria is much easier. While Ghana uses macroprudential policies—such as foreigners only being allowed to purchase longer-term paper—and Nigeria has only a few restrictions, the policies in both countries are seen as transparent and not cumbersome.

In the wake of the euro area crisis, investors also mention issues related to currency union architecture. A country in a monetary union does not issue its currency. In the event of a loss of confidence from investors, there may therefore not be a "buyer of last resort" to restore confidence, with a liquidity problem that may turn into a solvency problem (De Grauwe 2011). In the WAEMU, direct financing of governments by the Central Bank of West African States (BCEAO) has been phased out, and there are strict rules on the amount of government paper the BCEAO can accept for bank refinancing purposes. The Financial Stability Fund is expected to play the role of a liquidity backstop for governments in the future, but it is not yet operational.

The regional market for government securities in the WAEMU is fragmented. This does not just refer to the fact that an investor has to choose between eight different sovereigns. Government paper is issued through two different channels: (1) auctions by the BCEAO on the money market, and (2) the regional stock exchange (only longer-term paper). This fragmentation reduces liquidity and raises the costs of investing.

Communication targeting foreign investors is very limited. Until the creation of Agence UMOA-Titres there was no structured communication about the WAEMU market. The only

Figure 26.3. Size of Domestic Sovereign Debt Market

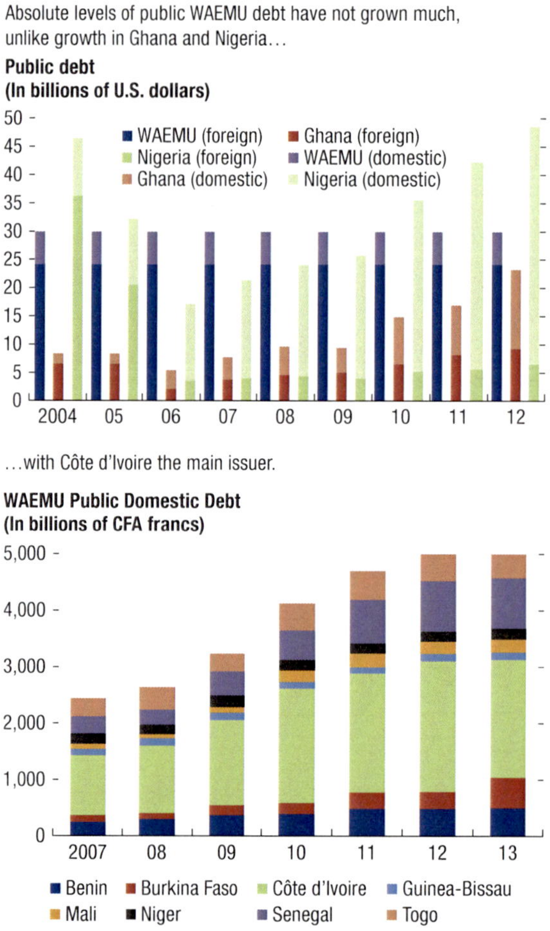

Sources: Bloomberg, L.P.; Central Bank of West African States (BCEAO); and IMF, African Department database.

roadshows were done for Eurobonds. Also, the dissemination of economic and financial information by national and regional authorities has been limited until recently, and has generally been exclusively in French. Discussions with investors clearly illustrated that they had limited knowledge or understanding of key developments or institutional arrangements in the WAEMU. A good example of this is the lack of awareness of rules and institutions supporting the exchange rate regime.

Language is another important barrier. Limited English is spoken in francophone Africa, and information and documents are mainly in French. The major international capital markets are, however, Anglophone. Language issues add to the complexity of dealing with legal traditions and institutions with which foreign investors may not be familiar. News flows emanating from francophone African countries are also lower than those from Anglophone African countries, given the dominance of English-speaking news outlets. This creates an additional information gap.

Political stability and the investment climate may be perceived as less favorable than in other frontier markets. As detailed in Chapter 4, which covers growth in the WAEMU, the region tends to have lower scores in these areas in available international surveys. Tax issues may also play a role. Within the Union, interests are subject to taxation for investors who do not reside in the issuing country, with tax rates varying from country to country. A foreign investor can only buy on the WAEMU market by opening a bank account in a WAEMU country. To optimize taxation, an investor interested in all the sovereigns would therefore need to open an account in each of the issuing countries. Double taxation (in the investor's home country) may also be an issue. Finally, financial infrastructure, rules, and practices (for example, regulations, custody, and settlements) in WAEMU countries may also lag behind those of Anglophone competitors. For instance, custodians and brokers are typically the same entity, though U.S. law requires a separation of these two activities for U.S. investors. The technological platform with real-time pricing only came into effect in 2013.

REFORM PRIORITIES

Nonresident investment in the WAEMU market should be sought and increased gradually, while addressing the related risks. Governments have a choice of financing their deficits through domestic and external funds, with different costs and benefits. Tapping external savings increases the resources available to the economy and reduces the risk of crowding out, although it should be recognized that the latter has likely been limited in the WAEMU until recently due to excess liquidity in the banking system. External savings can be tapped by issuing on international markets (for example, Eurobonds) or on the regional market. The advantage of the latter option is that it contributes to the development of the market, which in principle increases liquidity, and reduces costs and a number of risks through a diversification of the investor base. Issuing in local currency also eliminates the exchange rate risk. This type of capital inflow, however, raises other challenges for which the authorities need to prepare. Some foreign investors may be more footloose than domestic ones, and their large size can generate volatility in a small market. This complicates monetary policy, reserve management, and the preserving of financial stability. On balance, however, a gradual move to higher nonresident participation in the WAEMU market is desirable and should be accompanied by adequate safeguards.

A number of steps could be taken by the authorities to increase the attractiveness of the WAEMU market. Sound macroeconomic and financial sector policies are prerequisites, as discussed previously. Beyond this, based on the obstacles described in this chapter, the following measures could be considered:

- *Improve communication with nonresidents*—Agence UMOA-Titres will have a key role to play in this area in the short term. The BCEAO has improved its external communication in the past two years and should continue doing so, for instance by publishing English versions of key documents (such as the quarterly reports prepared for the monetary policy council). Governments should also improve the dissemination of key economic and financial information, including in English.
- *Accelerate ongoing reforms to develop the WAEMU market*—Significant foreign investment in the WAEMU market is unlikely to take place until the market reaches a larger size and there is a secondary market. The ongoing reforms in this area (and to develop the interbank market) are therefore critical. Another important reform in this area is the establishment of the financial stability fund, which could address some of the liquidity concerns raised by investors.
- *Reduce the segmentation of the sovereign bond market*—This would help increase the size of the market and therefore liquidity.

- *Harmonize taxation*—This will ensure that foreign investors see the WAEMU market as one single integrated market. Double taxation should also be avoided.

REFERENCES

De Grauwe, Paul. 2011. "Managing a Fragile Eurozone." *CESifo Forum* 12: 40–45.

International Monetary Fund (IMF). 2013. "Issuing International Sovereign Bonds: Opportunities and Challenges for Sub-Saharan Africa." In *Regional Economic Outlook*. Washington: International Monetary Fund.

CHAPTER 27

Integration and Poverty Reduction

SAMUEL GUERINEAU

West African Economic and Monetary Union (WAEMU) experience shows that economic integration may have a significant impact on poverty reduction, even if the "growth channel" is weak. On the one hand, until now, the capacity of trade, financial, and deep integration to foster growth has been rather disappointing, and this partly due to weak implementation of regional rules. On the other hand, the WAEMU benefits from a good growth-to-poverty-reduction conversion. It seems that such capacity is based on both its performances in terms of macroeconomic and monetary stability and its ability to mitigate negative impacts of political conflicts thanks to regional institutions. In addition to this long-term positive impact of common institutions, WAEMU experience suggests two lessons to improve the poverty reduction impact of economic integration. First, community policies should be targeted in sectors where the comparative advantage of regional policies is the strongest. It should therefore be a political priority to strengthen regional public goods supply, particularly for regional transportation and energy networks, but also for regional financial information networks. Second, particular attention must be given to the distributive effects of economic integration. The effect of integration policies on living and poverty standards within the WAEMU is different across sectors. A number of regional policies spontaneously contribute to gap reduction between member countries: agricultural market integration, epidemic-reduction programs, and financial service access development. Inversely, trade integration, transportation network development, and skilled labor mobility can lead to a concentration of benefits in the countries initially the richest. An increased momentum for intracommunity transfers must accompany strengthened integration in order to compensate its distributive effects. This may also decrease national incentives to delay the implementation of regional rules.

TRADE INTEGRATION AND POVERTY

Since the end of the 1990s, the WAEMU has been quite an integrated trading zone in the form of a customs union. This customs union was recently broadened to the Economic Community of West African States (ECOWAS), with the implementation of the ECOWAS common external tariff (CET) in Januray 2015,[1] with a view to also establishing a common market. As part of the Economic Partnership Agreement negotiations to set up a free-trade zone with the European Union, it was decided to favor negotiations with the ECOWAS as a customs union rather than with the WAEMU.[2] Trade integration within the WAEMU has been associated with tariff dismantling in relation to the rest of the world, and is consistent with developing countries' best practices (Geourjon and others 2013a). Nevertheless, the ECOWAS CET produces a slight increase in the average tariff rate (from 11.5% to 14.7%) and allows temporary high tariff rates on some products.

[1] A free trade area has existed since 2003 (see The ECOWAS Trade Liberalization Scheme (ETLS), ECOWAS Protocol A/P1/1/03).

[2] The trade integration diagnosis is taken from Geourjon and others (2013a).

Trade integration in the zone is constrained by implementation problems and nontariff factors. Implementation problems in the WAEMU include: (1) divergence between CET tariff rates and actual rates; (2) lack of harmonization of customs value calculation procedures; (3) extensive use of customs exemptions; and (4) use of internal customs transit system rather than a single first entry point customs clearance (free circulation). The intrazone trade still faces nontariff barriers, although limited in range. The effects of explicit trade restrictions (quantitative restrictions, import licenses, forced import channels) are quite low in the WAEMU. However member states use seasonal and temporary measures on some agricultural produce (see this chapter's section on agricultural products). Sanitary and phytosanitary and safety regulations do not represent a major impediment to regional integration, as they are of limited use and nonsystematic application due to weak administrative management capacity. The most important nontariff barriers are the lengthiness of customs procedures and nonrecognition of certificates of origin at internal borders.

The overarching objective of trade integration is to increase trade volume and diversification within the zone. The achievements seem disappointing on both dimensions. Intraregional trade is limited and declining, with a 12 percent to 10 percent total decrease between 1995 and 2010. However, intraregional trade is much higher (five times larger) than it is in the other African franc zone monetary union, the Central African Economic and Monetary Community (CEMAC). WAEMU countries' exports diversification is relatively low but tends to increase. In an analysis of the export concentration Theil index and the number of exported products (HS-6), Cadot, Carrère, and Strauss-Khan (2011) showed that concentration is strong in the WAEMU. In order to assess the export diversification of a country, it is useful to compare it to similar per capita income countries, since an increase in per capita income promotes export diversification. Senegal seems diversified (that is, more diversified than the average of similar per-capita revenue countries), whereas Côte d'Ivoire and Togo are average and other countries seem overconcentrated. Over the last decade, a concentration decrease trend has been observed. It is mainly based on intracommunity exports and the number of exported goods increase (extensive margin). New export products seem to be first tested on the more easily accessed regional market before being exported to the rest of the world.

Econometric analyses highlight a positive impact of WAEMU membership on intraregional trade. Observed trends in intraregional and global trade do not allow a reliable assessment of trade integration efficiency, as many other factors have substantially impacted trade, particularly on infrastructure quality, trade partner growth, and exchange rate fluctuations. Econometric analysis allows circumventing of this obstacle. Using a gravity model, Araujo-Bonjean, Brunelin, and Carrère (2013) showed that industrial goods intraregional trade is four times higher between WAEMU countries than if this Union had not existed. This result is consistent with previous studies (Carrère 2006). However, the existence of the Union causes a deflection of trade, as imports from third countries are lower than their expected values. In comparison, intraregional trade stimulation is not identified in the CEMAC. WAEMU is not only a customs union but also a monetary union and this may have an additional impact on intraregional trade. Adding nominal exchange rate volatility to trade contributing factors allows for a distinction of their effects. Monetary stability seems to contribute to intraregional trade increase and trade diversion mitigation. The strengthening of integration identified on industrial goods has been confirmed on agricultural products markets. Trade integration benefits are higher for originally diversified countries. Detailed analysis of trade integration impacts shows that, originally, most diversified countries (Senegal, Côte d'Ivoire, Togo) benefit from intraregional and extraregional trade creation. Inversely, in Sahelian countries and Benin, intraregional imports increase is detrimental to extraregional exports, which is indicative of trade diversion. In the WAEMU context, industrial goods trade remains limited, justifying a specific focus on agricultural products.

The trade integration process aims at stimulating growth through intraregional trade but also through global trade increase. The expected impact on extracommunity trade is medium-term.

Building a regional market larger than the national market should foster regional products competitiveness and attract foreign direct investments in exporting sectors. In the WAEMU context, regional integration was combined with trade liberalization with the rest of the world, and this should have short-term effects. Expected effects of trade integration in the WAEMU have a lot in common with those of trade liberalization. However, given the trade diversion risks, effects related to trade increase can be lessened. Inversely, the trade integration process may mitigate economic instability in creating a broader and more diversified economic space. It is therefore possible to analyze economic integration impacts on poverty, drawing from literature related to the link between trade liberalization and poverty.

The first trade liberalization transmission channel toward poverty is growth. This mechanism rests on a two-way relationship, first, between opening up to trade and growth, and second, between growth and poverty reduction. Economic liberalization can improve company productivity, and therefore growth, through several additional channels. These include access to more efficient technologies, economies of scale, and competitive pressure. In the context of regional integration, trade diversion can lower overall trade increase but this mitigation of static gains can be offset by a combination of dynamic gains and regional integration (broader market size, community policies). Quantitative studies suggest that the positive effect of opening up trade is dependent on other factors: investment, education, and political stability (Winters, McCulloch, and McKay 2004). The poverty incidence reduction allowed by this additional growth is very heterogeneous, since the poverty reduction/growth elasticity is itself heterogeneous (Ravallion and Chen 1997). The effect of liberalization on the poor also depends on its relationship with macroeconomic stability. Indeed, a risk linked to opening up trade is to produce a macroeconomic instability increase. Trade integration should mitigate this macroeconomic instability risk by creating a larger size regional market. Direct tests on the trade liberalization/poverty relation usually do not identify significant direct effects of opening up trade (Beck, Demirgüç-Kunt, and Levine 2007). Over a 30-African country panel covering the 1980–2010 period, Le Goff and Singh (2013) found a conditional effect of trade liberalization: it reduces poverty when financial, educational, and governance development levels are high.

Trade liberalization can impact poverty for a given growth level. These direct effects (not linked to growth) can be arranged in three categories, from the individual level to the most aggregated level: price channel, corporate channel, and public finances channel (Winters, McCulloch, and McKay 2004). Figure 27.1 proposes a summary of transmission channels. First, opening up trade directly affects household purchasing power in modifying the sale price of the household's production and the buying price of their consumption. Border-price transmission depends on internal transportation costs and the margin deducted by distribution channels and by the government as taxes. Porto, Depetris Chauvin, and Olarreaga (2011) showed that the competitive structure of input distribution and product marketing networks significantly impacts farmer income. In the highly concentrated context of cotton in Burkina Faso, the leader split (85 percent market share) into two separate entities would generate (according to Porto's simulation) a 12 percent increase in the average income of producers. Second, trade liberalization can significantly modify companies' profitability. Changes in companies' profitability impacts their labor needs and proposed wages. If this leads to an increase in unskilled labor, it can raise wages and contribute to poverty reduction. However, this transmission channel is limited by the small share of the manufacturing sector in low-income countries. Third, trade liberalization introduces a risk of lower government tax revenue, which can lead to cuts in social expenditure benefiting the poor. The direct effect of trade liberalization is to drastically reduce import tariffs and potential export taxes. This effect can be mitigated, even offset, by collecting value-added taxes on increased imports and the process of tax transition (Chambas 2005). Finally, for any given decrease in public revenue, budget options can, to a certain extent, protect targeted expenditure, which benefits the poor. In the case of an economic union, transfers can be arranged to the countries most affected by lower revenue.

Figure 27.1. Trade Liberalization and Regional Trade Integration Impacts on Poverty

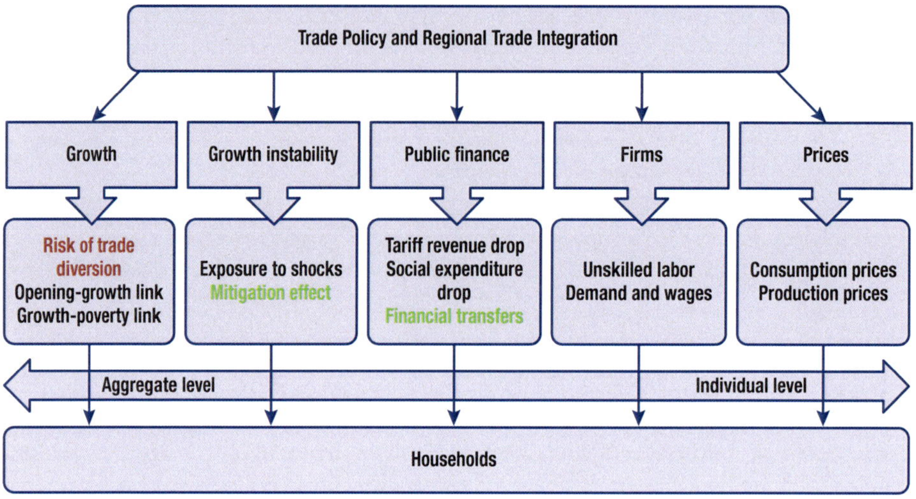

Source: Author, based on Winters, McCulloch, and McKay 2004.

In the African context, trade liberalization can be a driver of poverty reduction through its effect on growth. On the one hand, as on broader samples, studies on the liberalization/growth link on African countries sample have identified a positive impact (Mbabazi, Milner, and Morrissey 2006). On the other hand, the analysis of the growth/poverty reduction link in Western African countries shows an approximately proportional relation (poverty rate/per capita income growth elasticity is close to −1). In other words, growth gains from opening up trade contribute to significant poverty reduction. As for most developing countries, tests on the trade liberalization/poverty link in the WAEMU have not identified a direct effect of opening up trade. On a WAEMU countries sample (Kiendrebeogo 2010), the trade liberalization variable did not systematically impact poverty when the growth variable was introduced as a contributing factor. This result suggests that the main effect of opening up trade on poverty reduction is through growth.

The WAEMU is marked by a decrease of growth in the last decade and a slightly lower growth instability than are the groups to which it belongs (sub-Saharan Africa, non-oil-developing countries, low-income countries) (see Table 27.1). The magnitude of external shocks experienced by WAEMU countries (exports and agricultural production) being also smaller than that of the comparison groups (sub-saharan Africa, non-oil-developing countries, low-income countries) one cannot assert that the Union existence is the explanation for a better stability. Nevertheless, this decrease in instability over a trade liberalization period is a convincing sign of the Union's capacity (in all of its dimensions: commercial, monetary, and economic) to absorb the new risks related to opening up.

The WAEMU economic integration process was not associated with a government revenue decrease. This risk was anticipated at the WAEMU level because the treaty plans for compensation of customs revenue loss (article 58). To this aim, a community solidarity levy (Prélevement Communautaire de Solidarité, PCS) was established in 1996, corresponding to a 0.5 percent tax, raised to 1 percent in 1999, of the customs value of goods imported from third countries by Union member states. This levy is applied by each member state and paid to the WAEMU commission. The community solidarity levy is the WAEMU main own resource, but the compensation system of customs losses ended in 2005. Furthermore, community policies can be used to

TABLE 27.1

Macroeconomic Instability Evolution by Geographical Zones (1980–2009)

	Number of	Exports			Agricultural Production			GDP Growth		
	Countries	80–89	90–99	00–09	80–89	90–99	00–09	80–89	90–99	00–09
Developing countries	128	17.5	17.1	13	6.5	6.2	5.8	5.1	4.6	3.6
Non-oil-developing countries	108	17.2	16.3	12.3	6.2	6.3	5.6	4.9	4.1	3.3
LIC	63	17.8	18.8	16.2	5.1	5.6	5.2	4.3	4.4	3.6
SSA	48	18.3	17.9	16.6	6.2	6.5	5.7	4.9	5.6	3.8
Non-oil SSA	42	17.6	16.9	15.9	6.5	6.9	6.1	4.5	4.5	3.3
CEMAC	8	22	19.3	17.3	3.8	4.6	3.3	7	11.1	6.4
WAEMU	**6**	**17.8**	**14.2**	**11**	**8.5**	**5.7**	**6.2**	**4.4**	**5**	**2.5**
Non-oil FZ	9	17.1	13.6	10.7	7.9	5.5	5.9	4.6	5	2.6

Source: FERDI (*Fondation pour les études et recherches sur le développement international*); Box prepared for the 2012 Banque de France Franc Zone Report.
Note: CEMAC = Central African Central and Monetary Community; FZ = franc zone; LIC = Low income countries; SSAF = sub Saharan Africa.

support the zone's poorest countries through project funding. The establishment of real transfers comparable to European structural funds could be considered.

The public levy has increased in all WAEMU countries since the customs union was established in 2000, and in six countries out of eight, if compared with 1994. This result is naturally the product of growth performance over the period, but also of supporting policies accompanying trade reform, particularly the tax transition process. Thus, the share of customs duties in overall tax revenue in Senegal went from 39 percent in 1996 to 14 percent in 2012. Simultaneously, there was a symmetrical increase in goods and services tax revenue, notably value-added taxes. This process is relevant for all WAEMU countries, although its effect was less noticeable in a number of countries. Thanks to this tax revenue progression, social expenditure was not reduced over the period. On the contrary, the debt cancellation process for highly indebted countries (HIPC Initiative) has simultaneously freed up extra budgetary resources and directed expenses toward social sectors through the Poverty Reduction Strategy Paper.

THE ROLE OF AGRICULTURE

Agriculture is a sector where regional integration can have significant impacts on poverty. First, agricultural trade exchanges are substantial in western Africa. Second, agricultural products represent a significant part of the income and consumption of the poor. Therefore, it is useful to analyze in detail the extent of integration in this field and its effects. Agricultural market integration has been reinforced in the WAEMU by the establishment of the free-trade zone. However, as in the rest of Africa, integration has been hindered by a series of other obstacles including nontariff measures, rules governing input trade (seeds, fertilizer), high transportation costs, and food product distribution network margins (see World Bank 2012).

Agricultural products move freely within the free-trade zone. Movement is further eased by the fact that community origin certificates that must accompany products are not required for agricultural products. The establishment of the ECOWAS free-trade zone in 2003 further enlarged the single market. WAEMU countries are authorized to implement temporary protection mechanisms whenever global market price volatility is too high or whenever unfair export subsidizing practices threaten national producers. Such mitigation measures are national and cannot exceed six months, although they are renewable. They can be used to manage extracommunity import flows but their national characteristic can introduce intracommunity trade distortions.

Nontariff trade challenges remain despite the customs union. First, transportation costs remain extremely high due to transportation infrastructure weaknesses and traveling risks incurred. Recent conflicts in western Africa have increased these costs, as some routes have been closed off. Second, agricultural products are subject to a number of controls and levies between the place of production and the place of consumption. These include central government, local community, and professional trade association interventions, but they can also come from criminal organizations. The various controls, particularly at borders, remain time consuming and frequently cause the loss of perishable goods.

Despite the free-trade zone, official trade restrictions are sometimes used by national authorities. Indeed public authorities use—without any regional consultation—temporary export prohibition measures whenever there is a case of bad crops or a significant food price increase. These trade restrictions have reappeared in the past few years (during the 2007–08 food price boom) although in total contradiction of the free-trade regional agreement principles. These measures are resorted to by coastal countries more than by landlocked countries, as coastal countries benefit from natural protection with transportation costs. Furthermore, input trade restrictions have been used unpredictably for farmers. In order to better contribute to the food safety objective and improve compliance with regional agreements, mitigation measures should be defined at the regional level.

These persisting obstacles must not overshadow the achievements of the past two decades generated by the establishment of the free-trade zone, followed by the customs union, and which can be assessed by analyzing regional agricultural market integration.

Price spread analyses on agricultural markets show that regional market integration has been strengthened over the past decade. For agricultural goods subject to significant informal trade, the exchange volume evolution cannot be analyzed. The border-effects method enables this difficulty to be overcome. Its principle is to test the integration of regional markets by comparing their price evolution. The less price changes are transmitted between various countries' markets, the more substantial the "border-effect," which gives a measure of trade barriers. Araujo-Bonjean and others (2013) identify a border-effect drop on millet, sorghum, and maize markets among Benin, Burkina Faso, Mali, and Niger between 1990 and 2011. Trade barriers seem higher with countries outside the WAEMU (Ghana, Guinea, Mauritania), but the small number of analyzed markets moderates the solidity of the result.

The improvements observed in agricultural market integration may significantly impact poverty evolution. This effect operates through exchange flows and prices. Intracountry and intracommunity trade allows both deficit areas' populations to access lower food prices and surplus areas' agricultural producers to sell at a higher price. Within the WAEMU, such imbalances are significant for a number of products.The opportunity to sell one's products at a remunerative price also encourages the producer to develop his or her products' volume, which reinforces midterm food supply security. Trade liberalization also contributes to smoothing food prices over time. Trade allows the exploitation of cropping calendar diversity and production conditions. It also allows for supply shock mitigation: an exceptional harvest will be less likely to lower product price as the increase in supply will be absorbed by a broader market. To sum up, market integration mitigates price fluctuation over time, and, therefore, has a key role to play in revenue stabilization and in the building of food supply security (World Bank 2012).

However, opening up trade entails two kinds of distributive risks that must be anticipated. First, as demonstrated by recent experience, food price fluctuation in international markets can be substantial. Yet trade liberalization severely restricts a government's capacity to protect consumers from these variations. Resorting to price controls is particularly incompatible with community trade freedom. In such a context, the urban poor subjected to food price increases without benefiting from income increases are the most affected. Under these pressures, governments took emergency measures including lowering customs tariffs and value-added taxes in 2007 and 2008 (Benin, Burkina Faso, Côte d'Ivoire, Niger, Senegal, FAO 2009), which had the advantage of being effective quickly. However, such measures have a very high budgetary cost, since they apply to all consumers. Measures specifically targeting the poor seem preferable, especially the setting up of safety nets, but this demands time and a less tense social context. Second, trade liberalization has structural distributive effects that can create internal tensions. Generally, the urban poor are net agricultural produce consumers and therefore benefit from trade liberalization-related lower prices. In rural areas, two production types must be distinguished. Producers of global market export crops (for example, coffee and cotton) and producers of regional crops (for example, local cereal and livestock) producers are privileged. But producers of goods for the national market are disadvantaged, as they struggle to be competitive with imported substitutes. This effect is mitigated if the customs union maintains some kind of protection at the entry point.

However, case studies show that it is difficult to anticipate effects in a country without a specific knowledge of consumption and production structures; it seems all the more unreliable to generalize effects between countries. In the case of Morocco, Ravallion and Lokshin (2008) identified a gain for urban populations and a loss for rural populations. This result seems contradictory with the fact that poor rural households are usually net cereal consumers. However, a part of these households is a net producer, and losses experienced by these households offset net consumer household gains. Studies of this kind would be useful to assess the effect of agricultural market integration in the WAEMU.

The overarching objective of regional agricultural policy is to reduce poverty reduction and build food-supply security. Potential advantages of agricultural market integration for poverty reduction have been noted and regional strategies have been developed to show these priorities. In western Africa, in May 2002, heads of state or government gave the ECOWAS the mandate to coordinate the various components of the New Partnership for Africa's Development, including an agricultural component, the Comprehensive Africa Agriculture Development Program. A regional agricultural policy was adopted at the ECOWAS level in January 2005, with the aim of modernizing agriculture and reinforcing food sovereignty and food-supply security. The ECOWAS is built around three focus areas, the first one being centered on food-supply security and poverty reduction. This policy includes the components of the Common Agricultural Policy defined in the WAEMU context, but also the action plans of specialized regional organizations such as Permanent Interstates Committee for Drought Control in the Sahel (Comité permanent Inter-Etats de Lutte contre la Sécheresse dans le Sahel, CILSS). The importance of building food-supply security was also reiterated at the G20 summit held in Paris in 2011. Emergency food reserve creation was considered and a pilot project is being implemented under the ECOWAS with the support of the World Food Program.

MONETARY INTEGRATION AND POVERTY

The WAEMU common monetary policy combined with CFA franc pegging to the euro contributed to low inflation, of approximately 3 percent, over the past decade (Table 27.2). This inflation level is close to that of the CEMAC but is greatly below the average sub-Saharan African level. It also lower than that of the average fixed exchange rate system countries, the oil-importing countries, and other African economic unions (the Southern African Development Community and the Common Market for Eastern and Southern Africa). The WAEMU has also benefited from lower historical inflation volatility, having had no inflation episode over 8 percent since 2001 (see Part 4, Regional Monetary Policy).

Inflation usually has a negative impact on the poor, as they have few means to protect themselves from inflation costs. For an initial low-income level, a minimal real income loss can cause impoverishment dynamics, as no asset can be used to offset the shock. Empirical literature

TABLE 27.2

Average Annual Inflation Rate by Regional Groups (2001–2010)

	2001–2010	Standard Deviation	Max
Sub-Saharan Africa	9.6%	2.9	15.7
Franc Zone	3.1%	1.7	6.8
UEMOA over	2.9%	2.2	7.9
CEMAC	3.3%	1.7	5.7
SADC	10.1%	5.3	21.5
COMESA	15.2%	10.1	40
Fixed exchange rate system countries	5.6%	5.2	16.7
Floating exchange rate system countries	10.5%	2.7	16.3
Oil-exporting countries	12.7%	5.1	22.8
Oil-importing countries	8.4%	3.1	13.8

Source: IMF *Regional Economic Outlook*—Africa, 2005 and 2012.
Note: CEMA = Central African Economic and Monetary Community; COMESA = Common Market for Eastern and Southern Africa; SADC = Southern African Development Community; WAEMU = West African Economic and Monetary Union

generally shows a negative impact of inflation on the income of the poor, which is logically positive on poverty (Honohan 2003; Beck, Demirgüç-Kunt, and Levine 2007; Le Goff and Singh 2013). This effect is not systematically robust to changes in poverty measurement (incidence of poverty, intensity of poverty, bottom quintile revenue in income distribution). On a sample restricted to the WAEMU, Kiendrebeogo (2010) did not identify a negative impact of inflation on poverty. These countries had little inflation for a significant part of the study period and the results provide an indirect test of the nonlinear aspect of inflation impact. In comparison with the average effect observed on all developing countries (significantly negative), these results show the gain WAEMU countries have drawn from weak inflation over the recent period.

Gain generated by monetary stability can be reduced if the choice of extremely low inflation target induces growth costs. This is a recurring issue within the WAEMU, where the targeted inflation rate is linked to that of the European Union. In addition, inflation/growth relation analyses show such relation to be nonlinear. Inflation only undermines growth when it is greater than a ceiling, the said ceiling being dependent on each country's characteristics. For developing countries, this threshold seems to vary between 7 percent and 15 percent (Espinoza, Leon, and Prasad 2010). The cost associated with the choice of a too-low inflation target depends on the effect—positive or null—of inflation on growth below the threshold. On the basis of the previously mentioned studies, the cost of a 3 percent targeted inflation instead of 8 percent within the WAEMU would be nonexistent, low (0.1 percent of annual growth), or high (0.75 percent of annual growth). Such estimated costs correspond with the direct effect of inflation and can be reduced if inflation negatively impacts other growth-determining drivers (particularly investment). The "optimal" inflation target is then below the estimated threshold. In the WAEMU context, the inflation target level increase is, however, limited by its fixed parity with the euro.

FINANCIAL INTEGRATION AND POVERTY

Financial integration is stronger than in the rest of Africa, but disappointing as regards the institutional context. In particular, banking system integration is expected to improve, given the existence of regional rules (a single banking law and common supervision) and the development of regional banks (see Part 5, Financial Development and Stability, and Guérineau and Guillaumont Jeanneney 2013).

Financial integration is likely to bring substantial gains for financial services users by facilitating deposit access and banking credit access. It can translate into lower service prices (particularly for interest rates), mid-term and long-term lending increases, and a broader range of financial services. Indeed, financial services production is marked by the significance of fixed costs such as payment infrastructures and legal services. A bigger-sized market would allow the spread of these fixed costs, thereby lowering prices for such services (economies of scale). Therefore, financial integration fosters financial development. In turn, financial development has an impact on poverty that can be broken down, as for trade liberalization, into an indirect effects via growth, and direct effects. These direct effects occur when financial development brings specific benefits for the poor.

Financial development acts as a stimulus for economic growth through five "classical" functions: (1) exchange facilitation, (2) pooling of savings, (3) and (4) investment project selection and supervision, and (5) risk management (Beck and Honohan 2007)[3]. Studies on the relationship between financial development and growth systematically identify a positive effect between financial depth (money- or credit-to-GDP ratio) and growth (Beck and others 2011), even if financial development also incurs costs, particularly in terms of instability in the case of a financial crisis. The statistical relation between financial inclusion measures and growth seem more fragile than does the one tested with financial depth measures. Financial development seems to have a positive effect on poverty reduction, but this effect is more actively questioned than the one on growth. On one hand, financial development is likely to impact poverty by extending the poor's access to credit ("intermediation effect") (Beck, Demirgüç-Kunt, and Levine 2007), and by facilitating savings, which can be used to self-finance small investments ("capital channel effect"). On the other hand, it may increase inequalities.

The various mechanisms can be analyzed in a single framework characterized by conditional effects on the relationship between financial growth and development. Below a first financial development threshold, the poor do not have access to banking services and borrower information is very limited. In this context, standard financial development (lower interest rates and a broader range of financial services) particularly benefits the wealthy population, tends to increase inequalities, and has no effect on poverty. Nevertheless, at this stage, financial development favorable to the poor can aim at extending bank deposit access (capital channel effect) and extending credit access to the poor, thanks to microfinancing institutions. Beyond this first threshold, the poor benefit from financial service access development, which can have strong effects on poverty reduction (Rajan and Zingales 2003). However, financial development induces new risks and must therefore be associated with financial system regulation instruments (notably banking supervision). If such regulation is flawed, there is a strong financial instability risk. In this context, financial development can cause an increase in poverty, as the cost of crisis and general macroeconomic instability is extremely high for the poor (Guillaumont Jeanneney and Kpodar 2011). Figure 27.2 summarizes the impacts on poverty of monetary and financial integration and financial development.

The effects on poverty reduction of various financial development dimensions are very heterogeneous. Using a sample of developing countries, Guillaumont Jeanneney and Kpodar (2011) show that growth of the broad-money-to-GDP ratio (and more particularly savings deposits) positively impacts poverty reduction, beyond the effect obtained via financial development on growth. Lending to the economy is only efficient in reducing poverty in countries with a high banking services penetration rate. The positive effect of finance over growth in the WAEMU context has been identified for the 1996–2005 period but not for the previous period (1989–95) in Kpodar and Gbenyo (2010), which suggests that this effect is subject to other factors. Kpodar

[3]Beck and Honohan (2007) propose a complementary breakdown of financial services according to the type of financed operation: (1) market financing, including commercial credits and other short-term credits used for exchange purposes; (2) growth financing, which allows investment financing; and (3) finance for the overall population, particularly small and medium-sized enterprises and poor households. This third financial development dimension has a specific impact on poverty reduction.

Figure 27.2. Monetary and Financial Integration and Financial Development: Impacts on Poverty

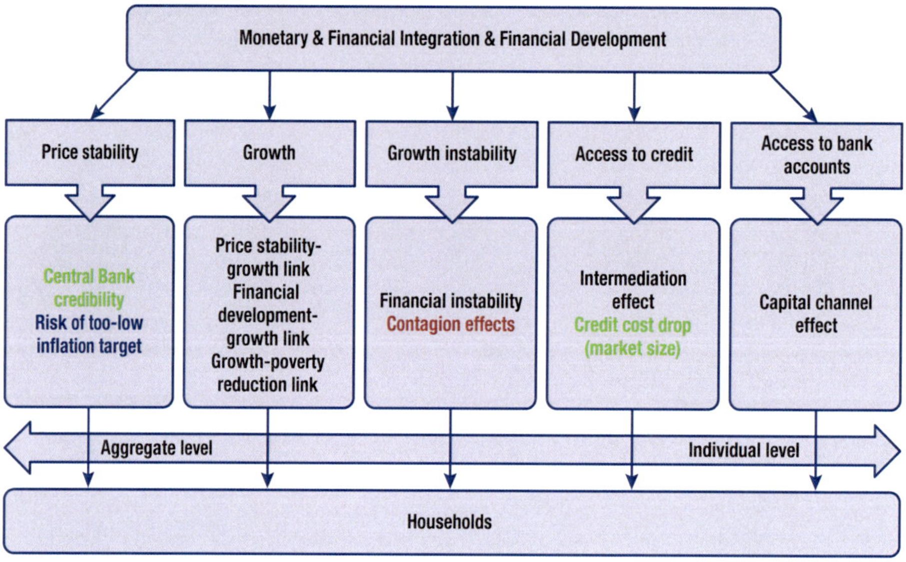

Source: Author's presentation.

and Gbenyo (2010) also show that the effect of long-term credits is much higher (approximately double). Microeconomic studies have shown that, in developing countries, credit demand is more sensitive (or elastic) to maturities lengthening than to debit interest rate lowering (Karlan and Zinman 2007).

Existing studies lead to two useful lessons on the relationship between financial development and poverty reduction within the WAEMU. First, in the current context, financial services remain barely accessible to the poor, and poverty reduction is mainly based on active financial-inclusion policies. The aim is to both extend bank deposit services and to develop the supply of microfinance services. Potential gains of such policies in terms of poverty reduction are high, particularly for the poorest and least financially developed countries. Second, the WAEMU financial system is relatively invulnerable to financial crisis risks. This low vulnerability is linked to the banking restructuration carried out in the early 1990s, to the existence of a regional banking supervision body, and to the overall macroeconomic stability of the zone. Therefore, instability-related costs are currently limited, and should remain so if regulation accompanies the regional integration building currently in progress. Overall, the WAEMU is undergoing a phase during which financial development benefits are much higher than costs, but during which the scope of benefits is reduced by low private sector credit and banking inclusion. Such benefits can be further strengthened through improved borrower information sharing, interbanking transaction security building, and more generally legal environment security building, as these are remaining weaknesses in the WAEMU.

DEEP INTEGRATION AND POVERTY

The WAEMU objective is not only to constitute a goods and capital free movement zone, but also to promote deep integration therein by setting up a common market and community policies. Deep integration–associated objectives pertain to both economic efficiency and political economy factors (Chauffour and Maur 2010). From an economic perspective, productive efficiency must be strengthened through intraregional specialization and factor mobility (common market), but also through the production of regional public goods (community policies). From a political economy standpoint, deep integration is a means toward reform implementation or previous reform preservation (policy anchoring), as well as a way to mitigate national crisis effects through community institutions. These various mechanisms can significantly impact poverty reduction in the WAEMU as well as gaps between Union member countries.

Deepening of the common market is based on the free movement of individuals, the right of establishment, and the harmonization of business law through the Organization for the Harmonization of Business Law in Africa (Plane and others 2013). Free movement is effective within the WAEMU and has been extended to the ECOWAS perimeter. It is obvious that administrative controls on commercial routes slow down transportation, but they do not question the principle of free movement. Intraregional migration flows are structurally high, particularly from Sahelian countries to coastal countries. The Côte d'Ivoire is the WAEMU's main migrant recipient. On the basis of the latest data from the Global Migrant Database, updated in 2007, the Côte d'Ivoire hosts 1.6 million WAEMU nationals, among whom 1 million are Burkinabe and 500,000 are Malians (in addition, 300,000 are Ghanaians). Other main regional migration flows are less significant (from Benin to Togo, and from Guinea to Senegal).

The right to establishment under the WAEMU 1994 treaty faces significant challenges. Under the treaty, "member state population has the right to any employment on each state territory, except in public services, has the right to set up a business, provide services and benefit from the same conditions as the national population." Subsequently, guidelines were introduced to specify the establishment conditions for doctors, physicians, architects, lawyers, and accountants. However, the implementation of such principle faces greater obstacles than the free movement of individuals. The red tape required for the establishment and the practice of various liberal professions constitutes a very high entry cost. For professions governed by a professional order (such as doctors and lawyers), the possibility of establishing in another country is, in fact, extremely limited. For professions not governed by a professional order, rules can be used to limit establishment freedom, including restricting access to a number of positions to nationals or imposing specific constraints on foreigners wishing to establish their business.

There are instruments for the harmonization of business law, but their application remains limited. All WAEMU states are members of the Organization for the Harmonization of Business Law in Africa, which has a total of 17 members. The objective of the organization is to reinforce the legal and judicial security of transactions between member countries. Its first function is to develop "uniform acts" defining common rules in company and business law, legal status of traders, debt collection, and other areas. Application of these standards is the responsibility of member states. A community body, the Common Court of Justice and Arbitration acts as a court of cassation for the member states. The results from this harmonization on regional exchange stimulation remain disappointing. An explanation lies with the limited effective power granted to the institutions and supranational decisions, as it is particularly difficult to ensure the implementation of a ruling outside of the country where it was made (exequatur procedure).

Regional service trade within the WAEMU is badly documented and appears weak. International service trade mainly focuses on transportation, communication, energy, tourism, education, professional services (those offered by accountants, legal counselors, architects, and engineers), and finance sectors (see Part 2). Service exchange development implies reinforced individual mobility, but also simplified administrative procedures. In a study on Eastern and Southern Africa, Coste, Dihel, and Grover (2013) show that the main challenges to professional service trade are the procedures to establish an activity and the rules governing the participation of nationals in investments. Inversely, electronically delivered services, making it easier to circumvent many border obstacles, have been rapidly developing. Central Bank of West African States (BCEAO) data on service trade are insufficient to identify intracommunity service trade. Overall in the WAEMU, the two main services exchanged are travel (net exports of tourism services) and transportation (net imports of freight services). In both cases, the exchanges mainly occur with countries outside the WAEMU, which suggests that intracommunity service exchanges are limited.

Service trade could significantly contribute to poverty reduction by improving the supply of services and reducing their prices. Indeed, many economic policies' efficiency and poverty-reduction capacity are dependent on education levels and financial development (for example, economic liberalization, see Le Goff and Singh 2013), which can be stimulated by regional exchanges. The increase in transportation service competition would allow a reduction in transportation costs (Raballand 2013), which weigh heavily on the prices paid to producers.

The WAEMU is leading community policies that can contribute to poverty reduction, particularly in the agricultural production, infrastructure, education, and health sectors. However, the scope remains limited. These policies are particularly justified to produce regional public goods (namely transportation or energy-producing infrastructures) and to fight against negative externalities such as contagious diseases. Community policies are financed by the WAEMU's own resources (mainly the prélevement communautaire de solidarité, PCS), funding from the West African Development Bank, and external partners. The WAEMU Commission manages the Regional Fund for Agricultural Development and the Regional Integration Aid Fund, whereas the Energy Development Fund, created in 2008, is managed by the West African Development Bank.

Physical infrastructure efficiency (transportation, energy, communication) to stimulate production and trade largely depends on regional dimensions. In transportation, the road corridor quality between coastal countries and landlocked countries is crucial for the growth of the latter. Potential gains from a regional policy on energy infrastructures are equally important. Electricity supply quality is currently extremely weak in WAEMU and disparities are very strong within the WAEMU. The electric connection delays reach 158 days in Benin, compared with only 33 days in Côte d'Ivoire; the cost of electricity represents 150 times the average annual income in Benin and only 40 times the annual income in Côte d'Ivoire. Regional electric infrastructure projects and interconnections can therefore have a significant effect on supply improvement in the most disadvantaged areas. Supply improvement reduces formal sector entry barriers for small businesses, fostering, in turn, their growth, employment development, and consequent poverty reduction. Regarding infrastructures, WAEMU projects are structured within the WAEMU Regional Economic Program and one of the objectives is poverty reduction. It is combined with the Program for Infrastructure Development in Africa, led by the African Union.

Existing health community policies can be reinforced to reduce sanitary risks, as these create poverty traps. Regional policies are particularly justified when they produce positive externalities between countries, for example a fight against epidemics, drug purchasing cost reduction, and health personnel training. The WAEMU has established a number of initiatives to fight against communicable, endemic, and childhood infectious diseases. A first instrument is the subregional epidemic monitoring system, which monitors for cholera, meningitis, and avian flu. A second project deals with the fight against malaria by supplementing national protection programs, such as insecticide-treated mosquito nets and indoor spraying, with antilarvae programs. The WAEMU has also implemented a community pharmaceutical policy based on regulation harmonization and group purchase of medicines. The overarching objective of the policy is to increase access to medication by lowering its cost and limiting drug counterfeiting. A third aspect of the community health policy deals with medical staff mobility in order to ensure better sanitary coverage in the most poorly serviced countries. Under these policies, in 2005 the WAEMU established free movement and the freedom to establishment in any member country for doctors.

These community policies play a direct part in poverty reduction, as being in good health is the main asset held by the poor. Becoming ill or injured can cause a vicious circle of impoverishment for the worker and his or her family.

Regional education policies have had limited results thus far, but their potential impact on poverty reduction is significant. Regional policies are particularly able to benefit from economies of scale (extremely specialized training costs, which are too high for national demand levels) and to foster skilled staff mobility. Under the WAEMU treaty, "common actions to rationalize and improve postsecondary education and vocational training performances" should be undertaken. The main activities deal with the establishment of community training centers of excellence, regional recognition of diplomas obtained at these institutions, and equal treatment of students from other member states. To date, these education sectors still contribute too little to development and poverty reduction objectives (UEMOA 2004). Although regional policies focus on postsecondary education and vocational training, their role in poverty reduction is substantial. Postsecondary education and vocational training are responsible for filling the qualified personnel gaps to ensure basic health (see above the paragraph on the freedom to establishment) and primary education, which, in turn, both play major parts in poverty reduction. Furthermore, postsecondary education's capacity to train qualified personnel is a major determining factor in direct investment attraction, which also contributes to growth dynamics and therefore to poverty reduction.

Regional integration is a means to mitigate the vulnerability of WAEMU countries' small economies. WAEMU countries are small in size and vulnerable to exogenous economic shocks (natural or external). Literature on drivers of developing countries' growth has shown that these features contributed to growth performance reduction. Indeed, a small-sized economy cannot benefit from economies of scale and is a barrier to competitive diversification of internal production. The frequency and scope of exogenous shocks render entrepreneur investment choices and government economic policies more uncertain (and therefore less efficient). Both of these effects result in a combined growth reduction effect.

Existing retrospective analysis based on growth equations does not reveal any growth gain for WAEMU members. In terms of growth, the past advantage of WAEMU membership can be evaluated by introducing—in a growth-explanatory equation—a dummy variable on top of usual growth factors. An estimate by Guillaumont (2013, based on a sample of 75 developing countries over the 1975–2010 period, divided into five-year periods—on average—did not reveal any significant gain linked to the WAEMU.

It is also possible to assess the growth potential associated with regional integration by simulating a perfect integration situation where the WAEMU would make up one single economy (Guillaumont 2013). The first step of this method consists of estimating a growth equation including the usual determining factors and one size indicator (logarithm of the population) and one exogenous shock indicator (export instability). The estimated equation allows, in turn, the evaluation of the expected growth rate for each country and each period. A third step consists of obtaining the potential growth rate of each country by replacing its size indicator by that of the WAEMU and its export instability indicator by that of aggregated exchanges in the Union. This exercise estimates the potential integration gain to 1.7 percent on average over the period, including 1.4 percent for economies of scale and 0.3 percent for shock mitigation. These estimates, which should be interpreted with caution, suggest that the effects of integration on poverty reduction can be strong, both through the growth channel and the macroeconomic instability mitigation effect, whose overall effect is smaller, but which strongly impacts the poor.

Benefits from WAEMU membership in terms of poverty reduction depend on both the growth surplus and the capacity to transform this growth in poverty reduction. To assess the

Figure 27.3. Growth/Poverty Reduction Relation in and Outside the Franc Zone (1994–2010)

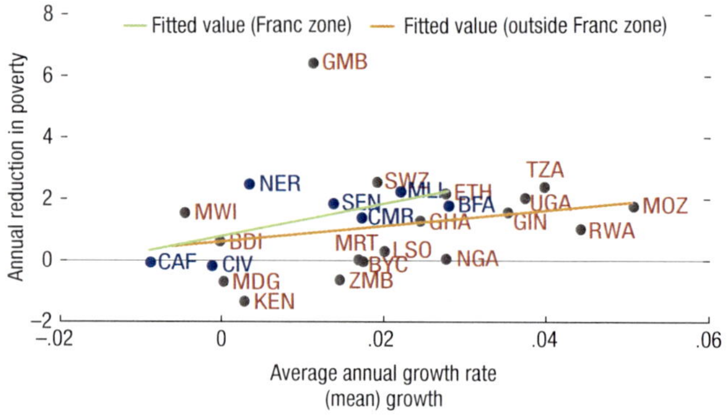

Source: Guillaumont (2013).
Note: Three-letter International Organization for Standardization abbreviations used for country names.

combined effects of trade, financial, and economic integration on poverty reduction, it is possible to compare the growth/poverty relationship among country groups. Such a comparison was carried out between African franc zone countries and the rest of sub-Saharan Africa by Guillaumont (2013) (Figure 27.3). The relation between the average annual economic growth rate and average annual poverty reduction over the same period seems stronger in the franc zone, since the slope of the adjustment line for franc zone countries is larger. To the extent that this difference does not seem to be attributed to an impact of original poverty levels, the author suggested it could be due to the lower franc zone inflation.

Deep regional integration requires delegating part of the national sovereignty to the regional level, which can protect economic policies from national constraints. First, delegating a number of decisions to the regional level allows the implementation of reforms, which may be halted by national private interests (Chauffour and Maur 2010). It can also help to preserve previous reform results in case of changes in the national political context caused by an increase in reform exit costs. In the case of the WAEMU, regional tariff consistency seems to be a benefit from the regional dimension of negotiation. Finally, the presence of community institutions generates a pole of stability in case of national political crisis.

It seems that WAEMU countries were less affected by the consequences of conflicts than were other African countries over the past decades. This also constitutes a protection for poor populations. Up until the 1990s, WAEMU countries (and CEMAC countries) experienced fewer armed conflicts than did the rest of Africa. However, this past decade saw the cancelling of this advantage as the number of conflicts increased in Côte d'Ivoire and Mali, whereas there has been a decreasing trend in the rest of the continent. Yet, strikingly, Côte d'Ivoire and other Franc zone countries (such as Chad) have experienced critical conflict periods without it translating the kind of economic collapse often observed elsewhere in such cases of internal conflict. It is likely that low inflation, currency convertibility, and the continuity brought by regional institutions have had a mitigating effect on the economic and social impact of conflicts. To summarize, conflicts seem to have had a less negative impact on growth in the Franc zone than in the rest of Africa. Given the enhanced impact of economic crises and hyperinflation on the poor, this crisis-mitigating effect makes for a substantial gain of regional integration. Figure 27.4 presents a summary of deep integration impacts on poverty.

Figure 27.4. Deep Integration Impacts on Poverty

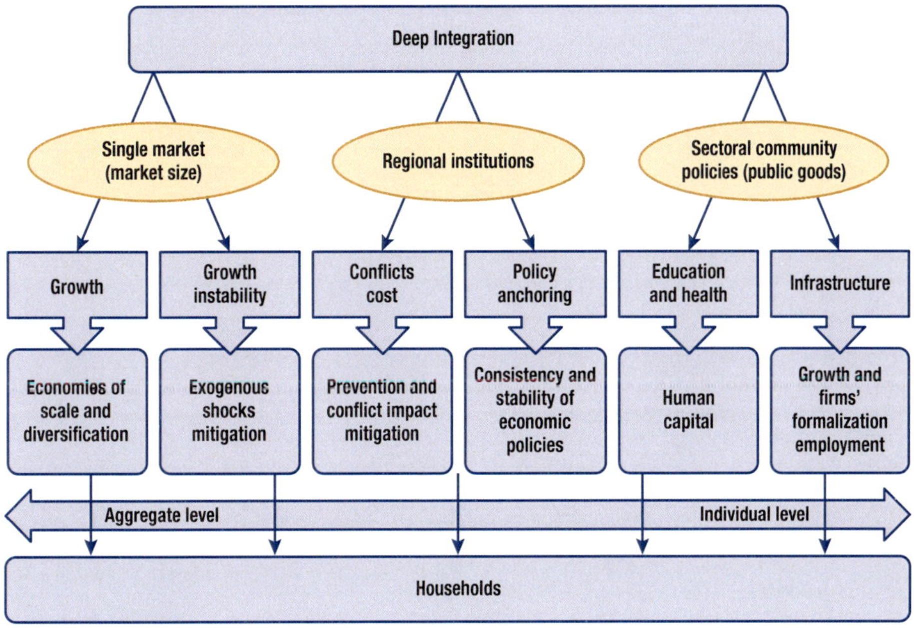

Source: Author illustration.

REFERENCES

Araujo-Bonjean, C., S. Brunelin, and C. Carrère. 2013. "Chapitre 6: Impact de l'intégration sur le commerce," in Geourjon, Guérineau, Guillaumont, and Guillaumont Jeannney (eds.), Intégration régionale pour le développement en Zone franc, Economica: Paris.

Beck, T., S. M. Maimbo, I. Faye, and T. Triki. 2011. "Financing Africa: Through the Crisis and Beyond." Washington: World Bank.

Beck, T., A. Demirgüç-Kunt, and R. Levine. 2007. "Finance, Inequality, and the Poor." *Journal of Economic Growth*, 12 (1): 27–49.

Beck, T., and P. Honohan. 2007. "Making Finance Work in Africa." Washington: World Bank.

Cadot, O., C. Carrère, and V. Strauss-Khan. 2011. "Export Diversification: What's behind the Hump?" *Review of Economics and Statistics* 93 (2): 590–605.

Carrère, C. 2006. "Revisiting the Effects of Regional Trading Agreements on Trade Flows with Proper Specification of the Gravity Model." *European Economic Review* 50 (2): 223–47.

Chambas, G. 2005. *Afrique au sud du Sahara: Mobiliser les Ressources Fiscales pour le Développement*. Economica: Paris.

Chauffour, J. P., and J. C. Maur. 2010. "Beyond Market Access: The New Normal of Preferential Trade Agreements." Policy Research Working Paper WPS5454, World Bank, Washington.

Coste, A., N. Dihel, and A. Grover. 2013. "Professional Services in Eastern and Southern Africa." Learning event, Raising the Profile of Trade in Africa, World Bank, Addis-Ababa, June 5.

Espinoza, R., H. Leon, and A. Prasad. 2010. "Estimating the Inflation-Growth Nexus—A Smooth Transition Model." Working Paper WP/10/76, International Monetary Fund, Washington.

Food and Alimentation Organization. 2009. "Country Responses to Food Security Crisis: Nature and Preliminary Implications of the Policies Pursued, Initiative on Soaring Food Prices." FAO, Rome.

Geourjon, Guérineau, Guillaumont, and Guillaumont Jeannney (eds.). 2013. Intégration régionale pour le développement en Zone franc, Economica: Paris.

Geourjon, A. M., O. Cadot, G. Chambas, and B. Laporte. 2013. « Chapitre 2: Intégration commerciale et harmonisation fiscale », in Geourjon, Guérineau, Guillaumont and Guillaumont Jeannney (eds), 2013.

Guérineau, S., and S. Guillaumont Jeanneney. 2013. « Chapitre 1: Intégration monétaire et financière » in Geourjon, Guérineau, Guillaumont, and Guillaumont Jeannney (eds.), Intégration régionale pour le dévelopment en Zone France, Ecomica, Paris.
Guillaumont Jeanneney, S., and K. Kpodar. 2011. "Financial Development and Poverty Reduction: Can There be a Benefit without a Cost?" *The Journal of Development Studies* 47 (1): 143–63.
Guillaumont, P. 2013. "Chapitre 7: Impact de l'intégration sur la croissance » in Geourjon, Guérineau, Guillaumont and Guillaumont Jeannney (eds), Intégration régionale pour le développement en Zone franc, Economica: Paris.
Honohan, P. 2003. "Financial Development, Growth, and Poverty: How Close Are the Links?" WB Working Paper Series No. 3203. The World Bank, Washington.
International Monetary Fund (IMF). 2005 and 2012. *Regional Economic Outlook—Africa.* Washington.
Karlan, D., and J. Zinman. 2007. "Credit Elasticities in Less-Developed Economies: Implications for Microcredit." Working Paper, 110, Center for Global Development, Washington.
Kiendrebeogo, Y. 2010. « Développement Financier et Pauvreté dans l'UEMOA », Université Bordeaux IV-Larefi, Working Paper.
Kpodar, R., and K. Gbenyo. 2010. "Short- Versus Long-Term Credit and Economic Performance: Evidence from the WAEMU." Working Paper WP/10/115, International Monetary Fund, Washington.
Le Goff, M., and R. J. Singh. 2013. "Does Trade Reduce Poverty? A View from Africa." Policy Research Working Paper, No. 6327, World Bank, Washington.
Mbabazi, J., C. Milner, and O. Morrissey. 2006. "Trade Openness, Trade Costs and Growth: Why Sub-Saharan Africa Performs Poorly." *Credit Paper* No. 06/08, CREDIT-U, Nottingham University, Nottingham.
Plane, P., (d') R. Aiglepierre, C. Araujo-Bonjean, M. Audibert, S. Brunelin, and J. Mathonnat. 2013. "Chapitre 4: Approfondissement du marché commun et politiques régionales sectorielles" Intégration régionale pour le développement en Zone franc, Economica: Paris.
Porto, G., N. Depetris Chauvin, and M. Olarreaga. 2011. *Supply Chains in Export Agriculture, Competition, and Poverty in Sub-Saharan Africa.* Washington: The World Bank.
Raballand, G. 2013. "The Forgotten Factor: Why Trucking Services Matter for Reducing Transports is Sub-Saharan Africa." Raising the Profile of Trade in Services in Africa, World Bank, Addis-Ababa, June 5th.
Rajan, R. G., and L. Zingales. 2003. "The Great Reversals: The Politics of Financial Development in the 20th Century." *Journal of Financial Economics* 69 (1): 5–50.
Ravallion, M., and S. Chen. 1997. "What Can New Survey Data Tell Us about Recent Changes in Distribution and Poverty?" *World Bank Economic Review* 11 (2): 357–82, May.
———, and M. Lokshin. 2008. "Winners and Losers from Trade Reform in Morocco." In *The Impact of Macroeconomic Policies on Poverty and Income Distribution: Micro-Macro Evaluation Techniques and Tools,* edited by F. Bourguigon, M. Bussolo, and L. A. Pereira. Washington: The World Bank.
UEMOA. 2004. Etude sur l'enseignement supérieur dans les pays de l'UEMOA.
Winters, A., N. McCulloch, and A. McKay. 2004. "Trade Liberalisation and Poverty: The Evidence So Far." *Journal of Economic Literature* 42: 72–115, March.
World Bank. 2012. *Africa Can Help Feed Africa: Removing Barriers to Regional Trade in Food Staples.* Washington: The World Bank.

Index

Note: Page numbers followed by *b* indicate box, *f* figure, and *t* table.